Implementing the Precautionary Principle

Approaches from the Nordic Countries, EU and USA

Edited by Nicolas de Sadeleer
EU Marie Curie Chair on Risk and Precaution, Oslo University

London • Sterling, VA

First published by Earthscan in the UK and USA in 2007

ISBN: 1–84407–312–2   hardback
         978–1-84407–312–2   hardback

Typesetting by Saxon Graphics Ltd, Derby
Printed and bound in the UK by Cromwell Press, Trowbridge
Cover design by Andrew Corbett

For a full list of publications please contact:

Earthscan
8–12 Camden High Street
London, NW1 0JH, UK
Tel: +44 (0)20 7387 8558
Fax: +44 (0)20 7387 8998
Email: earthinfo@earthscan.co.uk
Web: **www.earthscan.co.uk**

22883 Quicksilver Drive, Sterling, VA 20166–2012, USA

Earthscan is an imprint of James and James (Science Publishers) Ltd and publishes in association
with the International Institute for Environment and Development

A catalogue record for this book is available from the British Library

Library of Congress Cataloging-in-Publication Data
Implementing the precautionary principle : approaches from the Nordic countries,
EU and USA / edited by Nicolas de Sadeleer.
      p. cm.
   Includes index.
   ISBN–13: 978-1-84407-312-2 (hardback)
   ISBN–10: 1-84407-312-2 (hardback)
  1. Environmental law–European Union countries. 2.   Environmental risk
assessment–Law and legislation–European Union countries. 3.   Environmental
law–Scandinavia. 4.   Environmental risk assessment–Law and legislation–
Scandinavia   I.   Sadeleer, Nicolas de.
   KJC6242.I485 2006
   344.2404'6–dc22   2006016205

The paper used for the text pages of this book is FSC certified. FSC (the Forest
Stewardship Council) is an international network to promote responsible
management of the world's forests.

Mixed Sources
Product group from well-managed
forests and other controlled sources
www.fsc.org Cert no. TT-COC-2082
© 1996 Forest Stewardship Council

FSC

Printed on totally chlorine-free paper

Contents

List of Contributors

Helle Tegner Anker, LLM, PhD, is Professor of Law at the Royal Veterinary and Agricultural University, Copenhagen, Denmark. She specializes in planning law, nature conservation law, water law and other environmental law issues at the European Union (EU) as well as national level. Helle Anker is coordinator of the Nordic Environmental Law Network (NELN). She graduated from Aarhus University, Denmark.

Nicholas A. Ashford is Professor of Technology and Policy at the Massachusetts Institute of Technology (MIT), where he directs the Technology and Law Programme and teaches courses. He has written two textbooks, both currently in the process of publication: one on environmental law, policy and economics and one on technology, globalization and sustainable development. Professor Ashford holds both a PhD in chemistry and a Law Degree from the University of Chicago, where he also received graduate education in economics. He also holds adjunct faculty positions at the Harvard and Boston University Schools of Public Health. In addition, he teaches two intensive courses (on sustainable development and on EU and international environmental law) at Cambridge University, UK.

Ellen Margrethe Basse is a Doctor of Law (*dr. juris*) and Professor in Environmental Law at the University of Aarhus, Denmark. She has received a Juris Doctor (H.C.) from Uppsala University. She has published several books and articles on environmental law, administrative law and jurisprudence. She is a former Professor of Procedural Law, Associate Professor of Administrative Law and Director of the Centre for Social Science Research on the Environment (CeSaM). She finished her trial period as a lawyer in 2003.

Anne Christine Brusendorff holds a Master of Laws (University of Copenhagen, Denmark, and London School of Economics and Political Science, UK), and a PhD (University of Copenhagen, Denmark). She has dealt with the maritime and response fields within the Helsinki Commission (HELCOM) since 1998 and has been HELCOM executive secretary since 2003.

Hans Christian Bugge has been Professor of Environmental Law at the University of Oslo since 1998. He holds a doctorate in regional planning from the Université de Paris,

France, and is *dr. juris* of the University of Oslo, Norway. Before becoming an academic lawyer in 1991, he held various senior positions in Norway's Ministry of the Environment and its Pollution Control Authority. He has also worked with development issues, *inter alia*, as deputy minister for development cooperation.

Theofanis Christoforou has been with the European Commission Legal Service since 1984, where he is now a legal adviser. He holds law degrees from the Universities of Thessaloniki (Greece), College of Europe (Bruges, Belgium), University College London (UK) and Harvard Law School (US). He has worked in the areas of law, science and economics. He has participated in the Uruguay Round trade negotiations as a legal adviser to the European Commission. He has acted as counsel in more than 150 cases before the Court of Justice and the Court of First Instance of the European communities on a variety of issues of community law and international law. He has also handled several cases before the General Agreement on Tariffs and Trade (GATT) 47 and the World Trade Organization (WTO) dispute settlement panels and the appellate body (AB). He has published a number of articles on issues of international trade law, genetically modified organisms (GMOs), competition law, the precautionary principle and risk assessment. Currently, his main area of academic interest and research is the interface of science, law, economics and adjudication.

Nicolas de Sadeleer has been the recipient of one of the first EU Marie Curie chairs, which was established at the law faculty of the University of Oslo, Norway, from 2004 to 2005. He has taught law in several universities in Belgium, France, Peru, Thailand and Norway, and has worked as a consultant for several national and international authorities. Nicolas de Sadeleer's areas of research and teaching include European Community (EC) and international environmental law; health and consumer law; free movement of goods; and Belgian environmental law – subjects on which he publishes and speaks extensively. Among other publications, he is the author of *Environmental Principles* (Oxford University Press, 2002) and *Droit International et Communautaire de la Biodiversité* (Dalloz, 2004).

Peter Ehlers is President of the Federal Maritime and Hydrographic Agency of Germany, Professor at Hamburg University, Law Faculty, Germany, former HELCOM chair (1984–1986 and 2000–2002) and Chairman of the Maritime Committee (1987–1997).

Ole Kristian Fauchald was awarded the degree of *dr. juris* for the thesis *Environmental taxes and trade discrimination*, published by Kluwer International in 1998. Thereafter, he worked as an adviser to the Ministry of Environment for two years, before returning to the Faculty of Law at the University of Oslo as Associate Professor.

Tore Henriksen is an Associate Professor at the Faculty of Law of the University of Tromsø, Norway, and became *dr. juris* in 2001. His main research interests are the law of the sea and international environmental law.

Erkki Hollo has been Professor of Law (real estate and environmental law), Faculty of Law, at the University of Helsinki, Finland, since 1997, and was Professor of Economic

Law at the Helsinki University of Technology from 1977 to 1993. He was also Justice of the Supreme Administrative Court for the periods of 1983 to 1986 and 1993 to 1997. He is the Chairman of the Finnish Environmental Law Association (1980–), President of the Comité Européen de Droit Rural (2005–), member of the World Conservation Union (IUCN) Law Commission (1989–), and member of the Academy of Sciences in Finland and Latvia. He has published 20 books and 200 articles, mostly on environmental and property law.

Aðalheiður Jóhannsdóttir is an Associate Professor at the Faculty of Law, University of Iceland, Reykjavík, Iceland. Her main field of research and teaching is international environmental law, EC environmental law and Icelandic environmental law. Currently she is working on a doctoral thesis in international environmental law that covers issues relating to the international legal order and the protection of biodiversity.

Jussi Kauppila, LLM, is a researcher at the Finnish Environment Institute (SYKE), based in Helsinki, Finland. Since 1998, Jussi Kauppila has worked in drafting, implementing and researching different fields of environmental law. His current work includes the regulation of GMOs, as well as the analysis and future revision of Finnish waste legislation.

Tapani Kohonen, PhD, graduated in limnology in 1985 from the University of Helsinki, Finland. Having worked as a researcher from 1970 to 1985, he has subsequently worked at the Finnish Ministry of the Environment, and since 1991 has been Counsellor for International Affairs. He acted as Chairman of HELCOM Technological Committee for six years before being elected Executive Secretary of the Helsinki Commission for a three-year period, as of August 1996.

Gabriel Michanek, LLD, is Professor in Environmental and Natural Resources Law in the Division of Law, Luleå University of Technology, Sweden. He has been engaged in research and education in environmental law since 1980. He was involved in the development of environmental legislation in the Baltic States between 1997 and 2000. He has worked as a judge in the Environmental Court of Appeal and as an expert in several state commissions for the development of environmental legislation in Sweden.

Anne Ingeborg Myhr is currently employed as a senior scientist at the Norwegian Institute of Gene Ecology in Tromsø, Norway. She has an MSc in biotechnology from Norges Teknisk-Naturvitenskapelige Universitet (NTNU), Trondheim, and a PhD from the University of Tromsø. The title of her PhD thesis was *Precaution, Context and Sustainability: A Study of How Ethical Values May Be Involved in Risk Governance of GMOs*. Myhr's current research engagements include the use of DNA vaccines, an interdisciplinary project, elaboration of philosophical perspectives on GMOs, and capacity-building in risk assessment and management of GMO use and release in the developing world.

Annika Nilsson, LLD, is Associate Professor in Environmental Law at the Law Faculty, Lund University, Sweden. Her fields of research include, *inter alia*, Swedish and EU chemicals law, the principle of substitution and the precautionary principle, integrated product policy, and administrative aspects on environmental law.

Hanna Paulomäki graduated in ecology from the University of Helsinki, Finland. She has been working with nature protection and sustainable development issues since 1996 and in the field of international environment policy since 2000. Since 2005, she has been working as a scientific assistant at the Helsinki Commission.

Minna Pyhälä has degrees in marine biology, as well as in environment and development. She has been working with nature conservation and sustainable development issues since 1994 and in the field of international environment policy since 2003. She has been working at the Helsinki Commission since 2004.

Gerd Winter is a Professor of Public Law and the Sociology of Law at the University of Bremen, Germany. He is Director of the Research Unit for European Environmental Law (FEU). His current focus of research is on the institutional dimensions of global environmental change. His recent publications include *Multilevel Governance of Global Environmental Change* (ed) (Cambridge University Press, 2006) and *Die Umweltverantwortung Multinationaler Unternehmen* (ed) (Nomos Verlag, 2005).

Table of Legislation

INTERNATIONAL AGREEMENTS AND OTHER INSTRUMENTS

EUROPEAN COMMUNITY (EC) LEGAL INSTRUMENTS

EC Treaty

EC soft law instruments

EC law (fisheries)

EC law (environmental protection)

EC law (chemicals)

EC law (food safety)

EC law (genetically modified organisms)

DOMESTIC STATUTES AND RELATED INSTRUMENTS

Denmark

Iceland

Table of Cases

WORLD TRADE ORGANIZATION (WTO) DISPUTE SETTLEMENT BODY

EUROPEAN FREE TRADE ASSOCIATION (EFTA) COURT

EUROPEAN COMMUNITY COURTS

European Court of Justice

Tribunal of first instance

DANISH CASE LAW

Danish court judgements

Appeal Board cases

FINNISH CASE LAW

Decision of the Finnish Supreme Administrative Court (*Korkein hallinto-oikeus*, KHO)

Decisions by the Finnish Board for Gene Technology (*Geenitekniikan lautakunta*)

ICELANDIC CASE LAW

Supreme Court Cases

NORWEGIAN CASE LAW

SWEDISH CASE LAW

Decision by the Swedish Government

Decision by the National Environmental Licensing Board (*Koncessionsnämnden för miljöskydd*)

Decisions by the Swedish Board for Agriculture (*Jordbruksverket*)

US CASE LAW

List of Figures and Tables

FIGURES

TABLES

List of Acronyms and Abbreviations

AB	Appellate Body
AIS	Automatic Information System
BAT	best available technology
BEP	best environmental practice
BSE	bovine spongiform encephalopathy
BSPA	Baltic Sea Protected Area
CAA	Clean Air Act
CBA	cost-benefit analysis
CBD	Convention on Biological Diversity
CeSaM	Centre for Social Science Research on the Environment
CFC	chlorofluorocarbon
CFI	Court of First Instance of the European Community
CFP	Common Fisheries Policy
CMR	carcinogen, mutagen, reproductible
CO_2	carbon dioxide
CoP	Conference of the Parties
CRA	Congressional Review Act
DDT	dichlorodiphenyltrichloroethane
DEHP	di-octyl phthalate
DNA	deoxyribonucleic acid
EC	European Community
ECDIS	Electronic Chart Display and Information Systems
ECE	United Nations Economic Commission for Europe
ECHR	European Convention of Human Rights
ECJ	European Court of Justice
EEA	European Economic Area
EEA Agreement	Agreement on the European Economic Area
EEC	European Economic Community
EEZ	exclusive economic zone
EFSA	European Food Safety Authority
EFTA	European Free Trade Association

EIA	environmental impact assessment
EPA	Environmental Protection Act (Finnish)
ESA	EFTA Surveillance Authority
EPA	Environmental Protection Agency (US)
EU	European Union
FAO	Food and Agriculture Organization (UN)
FCCC	Framework Convention on Climate Change
FDA	Food and Drug Administration (US)
FEU	Research Unit for European Environmental Law
g	gram
GATT	General Agreement on Tariffs and Trade
GE	genetic engineering
GHG	greenhouse gas
GM	genetically modified
GMO	genetically modified organism
HCFC	hydrochlorofluorocarbon
HELCOM	Helsinki Commission
H_0	null hypothesis
IARC	International Agency for Research on Cancer
ICES	International Council for the Exploration of the Sea
IGO	Intergovernmental Organization
IMO	International Maritime Organization
IPPC	Integrated Pollution Prevention and Control Directive
IUCN	World Conservation Union
kg	kilogram
LRATP	Convention on Long-Range Transboundary Air Pollution
MARPOL	International Convention for the Prevention of Pollution from Ships
m	metre
mg	milligram
MIT	Massachusetts Institute of Technology
MMO	genetically modified micro-organism
NAFO	North-West Atlantic Fisheries Organization
NEAFC	North-East Atlantic Fisheries Commission
NELN	Nordic Environmental Law Network
NEPA	National Environmental Policy Act (US)
NGO	non-governmental organization
NTNU	Norges Teknisk-Naturvitenskapelige Universitet
OECD	Organisation for Economic Co-operation and Development
OMB	Office of Management and Budget (US)
OSHA	Occupational Safety and Health Administration (US)
OSHAct	Occupational Safety and Health Act
OSPAR	Convention for the Protection of the Marine Environment of the North-East Atlantic
PA	precautionary approach
PAH	polycyclic aromatic hydrocarbon
PBT	persistent, bioaccumulative and toxic

PCB	polychlorinated biphenyl
PCP	pentachlorophenol
PCT	polychlorinated terphenyl
POP	persistent organic pollutant
PP	precautionary principle
ppm	part per million
PRA	Paperwork Reduction Act
R&D	research and development
REACH	Registration, Evaluation and Authorization of Chemicals
RFA	Regulatory Flexibility Act
SAC	Special Area of Conservation
SCAN	Scientific Committee for Animal Nutrition
SEA	socio-economic analysis
SME	small- and medium-sized enterprise
SPA	Special Protection Area
SPS Agreement	Agreement on the Application of Sanitary and Phytosanitary Measures
STECF	Scientific, Technical and Economic Committee for Fisheries (EC)
SYKE	Finnish Environment Institute
TAC	total allowable catch
TBT Agreement	Technical Barriers to Trade Agreement
TBT	tributylin
TSCA	Toxics Substances Control Act (US)
UCS	Union of Concerned Scientists
UK	United Kingdom
UN	United Nations
UNCED	United Nations Conference on Environment and Development
UNCLOS	United Nations Convention on the Law of the Sea
UNECE	United Nations Economic Commission for Europe
UNEP	United Nations Environment Programme
US	United States
vPvB	very persistent, very bioaccumulative
VUB	Vrije Universiteit Brussels
W&H	Walker and Harremöes framework
WHO	World Health Organization
WTO	World Trade Organization

Introduction

CHAPTER 1

Origin, Status and Effects of the Precautionary Principle

Nicolas de Sadeleer

PERSPECTIVES ON THE PRECAUTIONARY PRINCIPLE

Although fairly recent in the history of environmental law, no other environmental principle has produced as much controversy as the principle of precaution. Indeed much ink has been spilled in a wide variety of books, journals and other publications over the status and the legal effects of the precautionary principle.

A brief discussion of the principle is warranted to make clear the baseline against which the different authors contributing to this volume have been addressing their topics.

In a nutshell, precaution epitomizes a paradigmatic shift. Whereas under a preventive approach a decision-maker intervenes provided that the threats to the environment are tangible, pursuant to the precautionary principle, authorities are prepared to tackle risks for which there is no definitive proof that the damage will materialize. In other words, precaution means that the absence of scientific certainty as to the existence or the extent of a risk should henceforth no longer delay the adoption of preventative measures to protect the environment.

Disputes have arisen as to whether precaution should be labelled as a 'principle' or merely as an 'approach'. As a matter of course, this debate reflects different perceptions as to the suitable regulatory response to avoid environmental and health damages amid uncertainties. Proponents of an 'approach' take the view that precaution is not legally binding, whereas a legal principle is clearly embedded within the legal system. For my part, I consider this as semantic squabble. Indeed, from a legal point of view, the question is whether precaution could become a principle of customary law in international law, on the one hand, and a general principle of environmental law at the national level, on the other. The answer to that question depends upon whether a number of criteria set out by courts and scholars alike are fulfilled.

The significance of precaution lies in its challenge to conventional science. As a matter of fact, the rise of new technologies has caused a new generation of risk to emerge: chlorofluorocarbons (CFCs), persistent organic pollutants (POPs), genetically modified organisms (GMOs), hormone-disrupting chemicals, electromagnetic fields, etc. Presenting unique challenges to the ability of science to anticipate and prevent harm, these post-industrial risks are fundamentally different from other risks. First, their impacts are much wider and diffuse. Second, they are permeated with uncertainty. Insufficient experience makes it impossible to determine their probability with accuracy. It is also difficult to determine the damage they may provoke, in terms of localization, and of latency between the first exposure and the actual impact of damage, frequency, duration, nature and scale. Uncertainty may impinge upon any one of these factors or all of these factors. As a result, uncertainty is the linchpin around which the principle is organized.

Its significance also lies in its challenge to traditional legal systems, many of which are permeated by the need for certainty. The operator's civil liability can be incurred provided that the victim is able to shed light on the link of causation between the operator's behaviour and the ensuing damage. A World Trade Organization (WTO) member is able to enact a food safety measure, provided that its regulatory choice is based upon clear scientific evidence resulting from a risk assessment. This presupposes continuous recourse to scientific expertise, with experts being able to provide flawless data to both courts and decision-makers. However, at first glance precaution provides for the possibility to act while uncertainties have not yet been cleared.

Discussions about the status and the functions of the principle have greatly intensified with respect to WTO trade issues. Indeed, much of the recent debate has focused on the question of whether the principle fosters protectionism in justifying arbitrary standards that could not be met by developing countries and, as a result, jeopardizes innovation. In addition, vigorous debate ensued as to the extent to which WTO members could be relieved of the requirement to furnish proof when confronted with a significant risk.

However, little thought has been dedicated so far to the implementation of the precautionary principle in a wide array of environmental areas. Indeed, this book highlights that the principle is of uttermost relevance to a spate of issues – ranging from fisheries, the discharge of chemicals and nature conservation to marine pollution – where the free movement of goods is not directly at stake. Therefore, it is the purpose of this book to explore, through various analyses of regulatory settings, some of the key issues arising in applying precaution to risk assessment as well as to risk management.

Although scientific uncertainties vary widely from one sector to another, every lawyer has to answer questions that are essentially similar. Does the adoption of a precautionary measure require a minimum set of indications showing that the suspected risk is well founded, or are public authorities relieved of all requirements to furnish proof when confronted with a severe risk? Is there an obligation for scientists to disclose the uncertainties? Do the scientists need to carry out in any case a risk assessment, and according to which methodology? Is it possible to draw the line between uncertainty and ignorance? Must the decision-maker aver a serious, significant, irreversible or collective risk? As for its implementation, should action be limited exclusively to moratoria, or are control and surveillance measures sufficient? And if this is possible, for how long should the precautionary measures last?

It is the aim of this book to provide insights as to how the principle – or the approach – can be fleshed out into different environmental policies in giving emphasis to the complex relationship between the scientific research carried out by risk assessors and the duty for risk managers to decide how safe is safe enough. In addition, the book deals extensively with the status and the scope of the principle in some international instruments, such as the Convention for the Protection of the Marine Environment of the North-East Atlantic (OSPAR), the Helsinki Commission (HELCOM), the 1995 Fish Stock Agreement, European Community law and the legal order of the five Nordic countries.

Given that the present volume is the outcome of more than two years' collaboration between Nicolas de Sadeleer's European Union (EU) Marie Curie Chair on Risks and Precaution established at the law faculty of Oslo and the Nordic Environmental Law Network, as well as various universities in the Nordic countries, the extent to which the principle can be effective from an environmental perspective is chiefly assessed from a regional perspective. In particular, the following analyses chiefly encompass the five Nordic countries (Norway, Sweden, Denmark, Finland and Iceland). Although Norway and Iceland are not EC member states, their environmental legislation is, to a great extent, permeated by EC secondary law. Accordingly, it would have been difficult to deal with the legal systems of these five countries without paying heed to the developments of EC law. Indeed, it is nowadays nearly impossible to draw a clear line between EC law and national legal orders in as much as the national environmental protection statutes are, to a great extent, permeated by EC secondary law. As a result, besides several chapters dealing exclusively with EC law, most of the authors have been giving emphasis to specific EC obligations in their respective fields.

As a matter of fact, this book has been long in the making. Thanks to the support of the EC Marie Curie Chair, numerous meetings and seminars were held in the course of the years 2004 to 2005 in different university departments and administrations across these countries with a view to discussing the implementation of the precautionary principle. In addition, most of the contributors to this volume convened at an international conference on Ecological Risks and Precaution in the Nordic Countries that was held in Oslo at the end of May 2005. As a result, most of the chapters of this volume arise from this conference, which was organized under the auspices of the EU Marie Curie Chair. Lastly, Chapter 2 of this book was undertaken with the support of the EU Marie Curie Chair in Oslo on Risks and Precaution, as well as the Interuniversity Attraction Pole 'The Loyalties of Knowledge' at the Vrije Universiteit Brussels (VUB) in Brussels. In addition, the Interuniversity Attraction Pole gave the editor the opportunity to edit the book over the course of 2006. In this respect, the editor is very grateful to Professor Hans Christian Bugge (University of Oslo) for being so supportive to the project overall and to Professor Serge Gutwirth (VUB) for his continuous encouragement to delve into the strenuous relationship between law and science.

STRUCTURE OF THE BOOK

This volume is divided into four main parts.

It begins with an in-depth analysis of the status and the functions of the principle in the EC legal order in the light of a spate of judgements dealing with issues as diverse as nature protection, hazardous chemicals, food safety and waste management. In contrast to most of the Nordic legal orders, the principle of precaution is enshrined in the EC Treaty, as well as in a number of provisions of directives and regulations binding the member states. Given the importance of EC environmental law, the three Nordic EC member states, as well as the two European Free Trade Association (EFTA) members, are being called upon to take into account the precautionary principle in their decision-making process. Thanks to EC law and the European Court of Justice's (ECJ's) case law, one can expect further developments in this field.

With the aim of shedding light on the extent to which the precautionary principle is already enshrined in national legislations, Part II gathers five national reports covering the whole Nordic region.

Given that the principle of precaution has already been encapsulated in 1992 in the OSPAR and the HELCOM conventions, Part III explores the manner in which it is being concretely fleshed out into ecological conservation measures. The issue of fisheries is dealt with in a specific chapter.

The ultimate avatar of the Promethean myth – biotechnology – has been the favoured field for implementing the principle. The lingering uncertainties have led the EC, as well as several national law-makers, to adopt specific regimes intended to cope with the potential health and ecological dangers stemming from that technology. In contrast to water pollution, the risks are characterized by their novelty. Part IV explores the manner in which the principle is being fleshed out in EC, Norwegian, Swedish, Danish and Finnish law.

The failure of EC chemicals policy to reduce health and environmental risks has been related to a general preference for a certainty-seeking regulatory style in which formal science-based and standardized risk assessments have been singled out as the predominant tool for decision-making. However, data are often incomplete and results may be unclear and even contradictory. As a result, it is difficult to provide with accuracy evidence as to the extent of the risk. Most of the Nordic countries have been rather dissatisfied with the internal market approach supported so far by the EC institutions. Much more emphasis has been given hitherto in Northern Europe to the need to substitute hazardous chemicals with less hazardous substances. Needless to say, the precautionary principle has been at the core of the debate that accompanies the Registration, Evaluation and Authorization of Chemicals (REACH) reform. To a great extent, regulatory experiences in the Nordic countries with respect to chemicals could foster a new approach based on precaution and substitution alike. Part V gathers several contributions assessing the manner in which these principles could reconcile the chemicals policy with sustainable development.

By combining 18 analyses of different, albeit intertwined, regulatory frameworks in which precaution has been applied either expressly or implicitly, the book should make a contribution to the ongoing debate over the relevance of a new risk approach in the field of environmental protection.

PART I

European Community Law

Introduction: The Precautionary Principle in European Union Law

Nicolas de Sadeleer

Emphasizing the status and role of the precautionary principle at the European Union (EU) level is relevant for the following reasons. First, three of the five Nordic countries are European Community (EC) member states and are therefore obliged to apply the principle when it is explicitly or implicitly stated in secondary law, whereas the two other states (Norway and Iceland) are parties to the European Economic Area (EEA) Agreement, which encompasses most of the internal market obligations and large sectors of the EC environmental legislation. Secondly, Nordic states have played a key role in developing the principle, particularly within chemical and fishery policies (see Chapters 11, 17, 19 and 20). It comes as no surprise that the principle has been endorsed implicitly or explicitly by different national administrations in the Nordic countries with a view to enhancing a higher level of environmental and health protection than that which is required at Community level. As will be further discussed below, the recourse to the principle has become the linchpin of safeguard clauses invoked by Danish and Swedish authorities in order to depart from EC harmonized standards.

This chapter attempts to set the scene to explain how European courts interpret the precautionary principle. In particular, it is the aim of the chapter to illustrate the Janus face of the principle: on the one hand, the interpretation endorsed by the European courts could restrict the room for manoeuvre of Denmark, Finland and Sweden when they wish to depart from EU harmonized standards; on the other, the principle could also bolster new reforms within various environmental sectors.

CHAPTER 2

The Precautionary Principle in European Community Health and Environmental Law: Sword or Shield for the Nordic Countries?

Nicolas de Sadeleer

INTRODUCTION

This chapter attempts to set the scene for this book on the rise of the precautionary principle in the environmental legislation of the Nordic countries, chiefly by explaining the status of the principle in European Community (EC) law and the manner in which it might influence further developments in those countries.[1] Hence, this chapter will serve as a baseline against which other authors may discuss the way in which the precautionary principle has been substantiated in different Nordic environmental legal systems or applied by various administrations in those countries. Space limitations prevent us from discussing the status of the principle in international law except briefly to touch on the obligations flowing from the World Trade Organization (WTO) legal order, which are particularly pertinent for sanitary and phytosanitary measures.

By and large, this chapter aims to illustrate the two sides of the principle: the interpretation endorsed by the European courts could restrict the room for manoeuvre of Denmark, Finland and Sweden when they wish to depart from European Union (EU) harmonized standards; but it could also support new reforms within various environmental sectors.

Known at the start of the 1990s by only a few specialists in environmental law, the precautionary principle has been able to establish itself as a new general principle of community law within the space of a decade.[2] This chapter will not reopen discussion on the meaning of this principle other than to recall its function as the expression of a philosophy of anticipated action not requiring that the entire corpus of scientific proof be collated in order for a public authority to be able to adopt a preventive measure. Enshrined in paragraph 2 of Article 174 of the EC Treaty – a provision declaring the principles underpinning Community action in the field of environmental protection – it has, however, not been defined by the EC Treaty framers, even though there are various definitions in international environmental law. The academic literature has, thus, considered first whether it is a restricted sectoral principle, applicable only to environmental policy, or a more general principle of Community law and, second, whether its application is limited to Community institutions only.[3] It has also addressed the question as to whether the principle could also be invoked by the member states to justify technical measures hindering the free movement of goods. As far as the manner of application is concerned, various questions remain unanswered. Must one aver a serious, significant, irreversible or collective risk? Does the adoption of a measure require a minimum set of indications showing that the suspected risk is well founded, or are public authorities relieved of all requirements to furnish proof when confronted with an important risk? As for its implementation, should action be limited exclusively to moratoria, or are control and surveillance measures sufficient? And if this is possible, for how long should these measures apply? Praised by some, disparaged by others, the principle is, indeed, no stranger to controversies.[4] Consequently, it is not the purpose of this chapter to outline, even in broad terms, the irresistible rise of the precautionary principle within EC law and to summarize the controversies swirling around this process.[5]

What deserves attention is how Community case law has not only managed to extend the scope of application of the precautionary principle to all policies involving scientific uncertainty, but has also introduced extremely useful clarifications on the application of the principle, particularly in the domain of public health.

As a matter of fact, one needs to draw a line between, on the one hand, the health and food safety cases, where scientific knowledge is far more advanced than it is in the environmental sector, and, on the other, genuine environmental cases (such as waste management and nature conservation), where the uncertainties are far more important given the difficulty of predicting the reactions of ecosystems to ecological risks (e.g. climate change). In addition, the stricter approach endorsed by the European courts with respect to the health and food safety cases can be explained by the fact that those cases chiefly deal with the placing on the market of products – genetically modified organisms (GMOs), food additives and medicinal products – where a fundamental principle of the EC Treaty, the free movement of goods, is at stake. In sharp contrast to this, the environmental cases so far decided by the European Court of Justice (ECJ) deal mostly with the interpretation of provisions of several environmental directives, rather than with the functioning of the internal market.

To begin with, we will discuss the status of the principle in the EC constitutional order. In the second section, the focus will be placed on the manner in which the principle is used by the ECJ to solve environmental cases. After this discussion, the focus will shift to recent Court of First Instance (CFI)[6] and ECJ[7] judgments dealing with health protection issues, which have clarified both the status of the principle and its manner of application. In this respect, it is worthy of note that the CFI judgments draw, to a large extent, upon the case law of the ECJ, which, conversely, endorses most of the CFI's observations. In any case, those cases give rise to a number of questions.

STATUS OF THE PRECAUTIONARY PRINCIPLE UNDER EUROPEAN COMMUNITY (EC) LAW

Status of the precautionary principle under the EC treaty

The precautionary principle has only latterly gained respectability under Community law. Although it had been enshrined as a general principle of international environmental policy at the 1992 United Nations Conference on Environment and Development (UNCED) at Rio de Janeiro, its introduction into the EC legal order had to await the adoption of the Maastricht Treaty, with its elevation to the same status as the other principles of environmental law laid down in Article 174(2), a provision obliging institutions to base their environmental policies on principles drawn from public international law.

Let us turn to two fundamental observations with regard to this provision.

First, Article 174(2) is drafted in such a way that the institutions are obliged to apply precaution when carrying out action in the environment field. The use of the indicative rather than the conditional confirms that such provision is binding: 'Community policy on the environment ... shall be based on the precautionary principle'. However, in contrast to rules of determinate content, the precautionary principle set out in the Article 174(2) always allows for the possibility of accommodation. In other words, the EC institutions may depart from it under particular circumstances.

Second, Article 174(2) does not provide a definition either of the principle, or of the closely linked principles encapsulated in that provision. The lack of definition could be justified on the grounds that the implementation of these principles across a wide range of policies is rather contextual.

To fill this gap, the European Commission produced a communication in February 2000 seeking to inform all interested parties of the manner in which the Commission applies or intends to apply the principle when taking decisions relating to the containment of risk.[8] The communication describes precaution as a risk management tool that is part of a risk analysis framework. While the communication is typically a soft-law instrument, it is not devoid, however, of any legal consequences. Indeed, applying the principle of equal treatment, the EC judiciary can ascertain whether an EC measure is consistent with the guidelines that the institutions have laid down for themselves by adopting such a communication.[9]

The hopes placed in that principle are just beginning to find concrete expression, although this development appears more advanced in the field of public health than in that of the environment.[10] Its main appearance in environmental matters is in regulations concerning dangerous substances, food safety and GMOs, particularly their effects on people and the environment.[11]

Clarifications brought by the case law of the European Court of Justice (ECJ) and the Court of First Instance (CFI)

The jurisprudential definition of the precautionary principle runs as follows: 'where there is uncertainty as to the existence or extent of risks to human health, protective measures may be taken without having to wait until the reality and seriousness of those risks become fully apparent'.[12]

Given this broad definition, the principle covers an array of environmental issues ranging from wildlife conservation measures to chemical management issues.

In addition, the field of health protection was immediately able to put the precautionary principle on a firm footing: on the one hand, the objectives of environmental policy also embrace those of the protection of health (Article 174(1)), while, on the other, all policies and actions undertaken by the European Community should ensure an increased level of protection of human health (Article 152). On the basis of these premises, the European Court of Justice extended, initially implicitly[13] and then subsequently explicitly,[14] the precautionary principle to the domain of public health.[15]

With regard to the broad scope of the principle, further guidance has been provided by the Court of First Instance. In the case *Artegodan*, the CFI confirmed that the precautionary principle's scope of application went wider than environmental policy insofar as it is intended to apply to all areas of Community action, with a view to ensuring an increased level of protection of health, the environment and consumer safety. According to the CFI, the extension of its field of application is justified by the requirement to pursue an increased level of consumer (Article 153), environmental (Article 174(2)) and health (Article 3, p) protection, as well as by the different integration clauses which the EC Treaty contains in the areas of environmental (Article 6) and health (Article 152(1)) protection.[16]

Due to its highly abstract nature and particularly broad scope of application, the precautionary principle could then be defined 'as a general principle of Community law requiring the competent authorities to take appropriate measures to prevent specific potential risks to public health, safety and the environment, by giving precedence to the requirements related to the protection of those interests over economic interests'.[17] Furthermore, the CFI laid particular emphasis upon the autonomous nature of the principle:

> Since the Community institutions are responsible, in all their spheres of activity, for the protection of public health, safety and the environment, the precautionary principle can be regarded as an autonomous principle stemming from the above mentioned Treaty provisions.[18]

Accordingly, the emphasis upon autonomy enhances the independent nature of that principle. Whereas the ECJ has so far been more careful in speculating about the nature of that principle,[19] the CFI has itself explicitly enshrined a new general principle of EC law. Its establishment, as such, thus opened up the possibility of the application of the principle in areas where EC law did not expressly provide for it. Moreover, such creativeness on the part of the CFI allowed for the derivation of a new general rule from a range of particular applications in the domains of health and the environment, which, in turn, allowed it to devise from this general principle new applications in other areas that had previously been marked by uncertainty. In other words, the principle can be applied in areas where no explicit reference is to be found.[20] Finally, the recognition of this status provides a supplementary argument to those international law writers who defend the position that precaution is already a principle of customary international law.[21]

The status of the precautionary principle in the member states legal orders

Member state actions may not, in principle, be reviewed on the basis of the Article 174(2) principles.[22] That case makes clear that the directing principles of the EC Treaty do not directly apply to national authorities; they are addressed to EC institutions. Nonetheless, this view is not shared by the EC institutions.[23] In addition, we believe that this interpretation is insufficiently nuanced. Indeed, a distinction must be drawn between areas covered by secondary law and those which are not. Furthermore, a distinction should also be drawn between principles that are explicit in EC secondary legislation and those that are implicit.

In areas that have not been harmonized, the precautionary principle enshrined in Article 174(2) EC cannot constrain national authorities and is accordingly devoid of direct effect. Nevertheless, in areas that have been harmonized, the EC Treaty's environmental principle as set out in Article 174(2) may apply both directly and indirectly to member states through secondary legislation.

First, the principle may apply in an autonomous manner to national authorities if the latter are obliged to apply EC regulations that recognize one or more of the principles contained in Article 174(2) EC as such.[24] By way of illustration, in Directive 2001/18/EC on the deliberate release of GMOs, the precautionary principle is explicitly mentioned in two articles. In this case, the principle embodied in secondary legislation requires national authorities to conduct risk assessments of GMO release notifications in the light of the precautionary principle. By the same token, the principle can underpin implicitly the whole regulatory framework contemplated by the EC law-maker. For instance, with respect to the assessment procedure laid down in the Habitats Directive 92/43/EEC, account must be taken of the principle of precaution referred to in Article 174(2) EC, although the principle is not mentioned in that directive (see Chapter 15).[25]

Although member states are under no obligation to apply the precautionary principle outside the context of Community law, nothing prevents them from invoking it to justify measures relative to the health and life of persons under Article 30 EC. In other words, if Community institutions have to consider the principle in risk management phase, member states are able to take precautionary measures in such domains as are relevant to their competence. As a general principle, the precautionary principle binds the member states in so far as they act within the scope of EU law.[26] As far as the free movement of goods is concerned, it must be pointed out that the precautionary principle has been used by the ECJ in order to delimit and to clarify the obligations imposed on member states, particularly when the latter invoke safeguard clauses enshrined in secondary law (e.g. the *Monsanto* case).

This argument also appears to find implicit confirmation in the jurisprudence of the court. Academic writing has already stressed that the *Sandoz*[27] case amounted to an application of the precautionary principle before it had even been developed.[28] Furthermore, the cases *Greenpeace France* and *Toolex* implicitly confirmed that recourse to the precautionary principle could put a stop to the free movement of GMOs and dangerous substances.[29]

Several advocates general already recognize the right of member states to invoke the precautionary principle in the context of measures taken on the basis of Article 30 EC. Accordingly, Advocate General Geelhoed has recognized that 'the precautionary principle can, within the context of the proportionality test, justify a level of zero tolerance',[30] while Advocate General J. Mischo finds that 'the greater the degree of scientific uncertainty, the wider the margin of appreciation of the member states with responsibility for the safeguarding of public health'.[31]

THE KEY ROLE OF THE PRECAUTIONARY PRINCIPLE ON THE INTERPRETATION OF ENVIRONMENTAL OBLIGATIONS

As a matter of fact, science is the lynchpin around which environmental law is organized.[32] Several factors explain why science is much more in evidence in environmental law than in other branches of the law. First, scientists detect, identify and set out the ecological problems to which the law must respond. Second, environmental crises are increasingly perceived through scientific descriptions of our physical world. As a result, risk assessments performed by scientists provide the cornerstone for much environmental legislation. Last but not least, science is often called upon to play a decisive role in judicial procedures.

Scientists thus play a decisive role in the conception and implementation of this legal discipline; all the regulations adopted in this field, without exception, are based on their calculations, computations or affirmations. Whether it is a question of setting a nuisance threshold, delimiting a protected area[33] or listing a species[34] for legal protection, decisions are based on scientific considerations. It is hardly surprising, then, that environmental law should be deeply marked by a heavy reliance on science. In fact, no area of public policy is comparably dependent upon science. Science has become both the basis and the justification for environmental decision-making: political decisions are legitimate because they are based on risk assessment performed by risk assessors who are legitimate because they apply sound science.[35]

Nevertheless, this marriage of law and reason is not entirely free of strife: legal rules are meant to provide predictability; yet, nature is unpredictable. While the jurist seeks certainty, the scientist points to the uncertainty inherent in ecological risk.

The precaution came to centre stage in the field of environment policy in response to the limitations of science in assessing complex and uncertain ecological risks. Indeed, environmental risks and, in particular, global risks confront assessors with serious difficulties: uncertainty is a persistent feature both of understanding the chain of causation as well as predicting the outcomes. Furthermore, the distance in time and space between sources and damages, the cumulative and synergistic effects, the unpredictable reactions of some ecosystems (potential resilience) and the large scale of impacts compound the methodological difficulties in assessing these risks.[36] There is a strong deficit in predictive capability. Moreover, damage to the environment is likely to be more controversial than damage to health. Whereas one usually agrees that activities endangering human health should be restricted or banned, people often disagree whether ecosystems, ecosystemic processes, species of plants and animals, or micro-organisms deserve any kind of protection.

Although unpredictable risks are rising, authorities tend to wait in the face of uncertainty and to react only to crisis events. They characteristically err towards belated and costly measures.

In this respect, precaution aims to bridge the gap between scientists working on the frontiers of scientific knowledge and decision-makers willing to act to determine how safe is safe enough. As a result, the precautionary principle has quickly developed into one of the foundations of the high level of environmental protection, an obligation laid down by the EC Treaty.[37] Needless to say, today, the majority of environmental directives and regulations follow a precautionary approach.

However, in contrast to the food safety regulations where the principle is expressly defined (see Part IV), few environmental directives and regulations specifically mention it in their operative provisions. As a result, the question arises as to whether the member states' authorities could eschew the principle on the grounds that it is not enshrined in secondary law? As discussed earlier in 'The status of the precautionary principle in the member states legal orders', where precaution is not explicitly set out in the operative provisions or in the recitals of a legal statute's preamble (directive or regulation), it may, nevertheless, directly apply to member states insofar as Article 10 EC obliges the member states to 'take all appropriate measures … to ensure fulfillment of the obligations arising out of this Treaty or resulting from action taken by the institutions of the Community' and to 'facilitate the achievement of the Community's tasks', as well as 'abstain from any measure which could jeopardize the attainment of the objectives' of the EC Treaty. Read in the light of the precautionary principle of Article 174, Article 10 EC imposes on national authorities wide-ranging obligations of environmental protection, preservation, conservation, prevention and precaution.[38] The cases commented in this second section are, indeed, testament to the binding effect of the principle with regard to member states' action.

Indeed, the ECJ's case law is testament to the extent to which the precautionary principle can play a key role in tilting the balance towards greater environmental protection.[39]

Restrictions brought to basic rights (such as property and economic activities) with a view to protecting the environment can be justified provided that, on the one hand, those restrictions correspond to objectives of general interest and, on the other, they do not constitute an intolerable interference impairing the very substance of the rights guaranteed.[40]

With respect to the first condition, it is sufficient to observe that the conservation of biodiversity,[41] waste management[42] and water protection,[43] and prevention of climate change[44] have been recognized by the ECJ as pursuing an objective of general interest restricting basic rights.[45]

With regard to the second condition, the precautionary principle enables the judiciary to endorse a broad interpretation of an array of environmental obligations, ranging from waste management to wildlife conservation.[46] Relying explicitly or implicitly upon the precautionary principle, the ECJ departs from a literal interpretation of obligations laid down in secondary law. As a result, measures impairing fundamental rights might be justified in the light of the principle.

As we will see in the *Greenpeace GM Bt Maize* case, the principle of precaution implies that the EC directives relating to GMOs be interpreted in such a way that gives full weight to environmental protection requirements.[47]

A further example is the differentiation between waste and product, which has been the subject of much heated academic debate, as well as litigation in EC law. Pursuant to Article 174(2) EC, European environmental policy aims at a high level of protection and must be based, in particular, on the precautionary principle and the principle that preventive action should be taken.[48] It follows that the concept of waste cannot be interpreted restrictively.

The precautionary principle also appears in various wildlife conservation cases, although it is not necessarily explicitly expressed as such.

For instance, the judgment *Armand Mondiet* of 24 November 1993 provides a further illustration of the role that the precautionary principle can play in decisions aimed at protecting cetaceans taken against a background of scientific uncertainty.[49] In this case, a ship owner challenged EC Regulation 345/92 forbidding tangle nets of over 2.5km on the grounds that no scientific data justified this measure and that it did not conform to the only information available, although the regulation provided that conservation measures should be drawn up 'in view of the information that was available'.[50] The ECJ took the view that in the exercise of its powers, the Council of Ministers could not be forced to follow particular scientific opinions.[51] It follows that the EC institutions did not make any manifest error of appraisal by banning certain tangle nets despite the uncertainties.

Another illustrative example is a judgment concerning wild birds, *Association Pour la Protection des Animaux Sauvages et Préfet de Maine-et-Loire et Préfet de La Loire-Atlantique.* The court favoured a determination of the end of the hunting season in a manner that guaranteed the optimal level of protection for avifauna.[52] It judged that in the absence of 'scientific and technical data relevant to each individual case' – that is, in cases of uncertainty – member states should adopt a single date for ending the season, equivalent to 'that fixed for the species which is the earliest to migrate', and not 'the maximum period of migratory activity'. This means that so long as a degree of uncertainty remains concerning the timing of pre-mating migrations of migratory birds, the strictest method of determining the close of hunting should override methods attempting to accommodate hunting interests on the basis of scientific approximation.

Another case in point is *Bluhme*, where the ECJ ruled that a Danish wildlife measure prohibiting the import of any species of bee other than the endemic sub-species *Apis mellifera mellifera* into a Baltic island was justified under Article 30 EC, notwithstanding the lack of conclusive evidence establishing both the nature of the sub-species and its risk of extinction.[53]

Recently, the ECJ handed down a landmark case assessing the validity of the Dutch environmental impact assessment (EIA) on fishing activities taking place within bird protection areas. In order for the project to be authorized, Article 6(3) of the Habitats Directive 92/43/EC provides for a specific environmental impact assessment procedure of plans or projects 'likely' to affect a conservation site.[54] According to the court, since the impact study regime covers plans and projects 'likely' to affect a site, the wording of this provision implies that the conductor of the study must be able to identify, according to the precautionary principle, even those damages that are still uncertain.[55] In addition, the Habitats Directive's authorization regime requires that the competent authority ensure that the project at stake will not adversely affect the integrity of the site concerned. Accordingly, the authorization can only be passed where the assessment demonstrates the absence of risks for the integrity of the site. 'Where doubt remains as to the absence of adverse effect on the integrity of the site', the directive requires, in line with the precautionary principle, the competent authority to refrain from issuing the authorization.[56] Although it is likely to restrict economic and property rights, this author-ization criterion 'integrates the precautionary principle'.[57] Conversely, a less stringent criterion would not be as effective in ensuring the fulfilment of the conservation objec-tives set forth by the EC law-maker.[58] In accordance with the logic of the precautionary principle, authorities can, if need be, order additional investigations in order to remove the uncertainty.[59] Of course, one should be aware that the strict interpretation endorsed by the ECJ is a consequence of the manner in which the authorization regime of projects endangering threatened habitats has been formulated by the law-maker.[60]

THE PRECAUTIONARY PRINCIPLE IN THE FIELD OF HEALTH PROTECTION

Why has an environmental principle been so much at the forefront in the field of health protection? The answer is straightforward: in a large number of cases, the principle has been invoked either to support a preventative health or consumer safety measure, or to contest the merits of such a measure. So far, the discussion in Europe has focused on the extent to which the principle can be applied in that field. It is the aim of this section to explore some of the key issues arising in the case law on this matter.

It must also be kept in mind that the principle is not only enshrined in Regulation No 178/2002 laying down the general principles and requirements of food law, but it is also defined as applying:

> ... in specific circumstances where, following an assessment of available information, the possibility of harmful effects on health is identified but scientific uncertainty persists, provisional risk management measures necessary to ensure the high level of health protection chosen in the Community may be adopted, pending further scientific infor-mation for a more comprehensive risk assessment.

The role of the precautionary principle in risk analysis: Status quo

As will be seen, the precautionary principle is located within the broader context of risk analysis, which comprises a two-step process: risk assessment and risk management.[61] The point here is not to delve into the highly complex world of risk analysis. It is merely to emphasize some of the key issues arising in the discussion of implementing a precau-tionary measure. Therefore, a brief discussion of the concepts of risk assessment and risk management is warranted to make clear the baseline against which the precautionary principle has to be applied with regard to measures likely to hamper the free movement of goods.[62]

First, the probability of the occurrence of harm is determined using a *risk assessment* procedure, in which experts examine both hazard and exposure – generally by mathematical modelling – in order to calculate an acceptable or tolerable level of contamination or exposure.[63] This systematic process involves a four-step approach: hazard identification (does a substance give rise to an adverse effect such as cancer, birth defects, etc.?); dose-response assessment (how potent a carcinogen is it?); exposure assessment (which groups of people are exposed to the substance, what is the environmental vehicle of exposure – air, water, soil – and for how long, and at what levels?); and risk characterization (what is the likelihood that any particular exposed person will develop cancer?).

However, the risk is not just then a question for experts. It takes on a distinct individual meaning when situated within its political, social and economic context. Accordingly, once the risk assessment procedure has been completed, a *risk management* decision must be taken by politicians, taking into account both legislative requirements and the economic, political and normative dimensions of the problem. Risk management, in contrast to risk assessment, is the public process of deciding how safe is safe enough. Indeed, 'societal, economic, traditional, ethical and environmental factors, as well the feasibility of controls' might appear as factors legitimizing the regulation of a specific risk.[64]

The first two stages are essential since they aim, on the one hand, to ensure as rigorous as possible a scientific basis for managing the risk (risk assessment) and, on the other, to recognize a margin of autonomy for the body authorized *in fine* to make a decision on the risk (risk management).[65] The distinction between the phases of assessment and management thus satisfies a dual requirement: on the one hand, the need to base a political decision on scientific facts and, on the other, the need to maintain the autonomy of politics vis-à-vis the results of scientific assessments.[66]

However, it is not easy to trace the boundary between the scientific domain and the political approach to risk management since there is no natural boundary between the two spheres that inevitably become intertwined at different stages in the decision-making process.[67] In reality, as will be seen, assessment and management overlap in a permanent reciprocal interplay (see the section on 'The relationship between risk assessment and risk management in the light of the precautionary principle'). Accordingly, the assessment of a risk often results from a managerial decision; conversely, new assessments are made following management decisions. As a result, this separation is by no means watertight.

Furthermore, it should be stressed at the outset that a number of public institutions consider the precautionary principle merely a risk management tool that has nothing to do with risk assessment.[68] By way of illustration, the European Commission communication of February 2000 describes precaution as a risk management took.[69] Similarly, the precautionary principle is seen by the ECJ as constituting 'an integral part of the decision-making processes leading the adoption of any measure for the protection of human health'.[70] This chapter does not endorse such an interpretation. From a legal point of view, nothing prevents the risk assessment stage from being carried out in accordance with the obligations stemming from the precautionary principle.[71] Indeed, in order to deal effectively with uncertainty, ambiguity and ignorance, assessors should apply precaution at an early stage.[72]

Risk thresholds

The degree of uncertainty required for application of the precautionary principle

While the precautionary principle does require that decision-makers adopt a risk-averse stance, must it accordingly oblige them to adopt preventive measures whenever a risk is suspected? Given the wording of international law definitions, it is beyond doubt that the principle covers serious risks, significant risks, as well as the risk of irreversible damage. Conversely, the principle does not encompass certain risks,[73] such as the effects of excessive alcohol consumption on human health.[74] But does it apply to speculative risks? The ECJ's and CFI's, as well as the European Free Trade Association (EFTA) Court's, reply to this is that a preventative measure cannot properly be based on a purely hypothetical consideration of the risk, founded on mere conjecture that has not been scientifically verified.[75] It follows that there must exist a threshold of scientific plausibility. Simply put, basic scientific knowledge is therefore necessary. In this way, the European courts exclude from the scope of application of the principle such risks qualified as residual – that is, speculative risks founded upon purely speculative factors and without a basis in science. The result, according to the CFI, was that 'the precautionary principle can therefore only apply in situations in which there is a risk, notably to human health, which, although it is not founded on mere hypotheses that have not been scientifically confirmed, has not yet been fully demonstrated'.[76]

In this way the European courts aligned themselves with the findings of several decisions handed down by the WTO Appellate Body, a court which has ruled against the precautionary principle's application to hypothetical risks.[77]

As to the assessment of suspected risks, the CFI highlighted its twofold task whose components are complementary:[78]

1   determining what level of risk is deemed to be unacceptable;
2   conducting a scientific assessment of the risk.

This calls for a closer analysis of those two obligations.

Setting the level of protection

As far as the first obligation is concerned, the determination of a level of risk that would be unacceptable from the perspective of the protection of human health depends upon the competent public authority's understanding of the specific circumstances of each particular case. On this matter, the CFI has, in fact, held that:

> ... *it is for the Community institutions to determine the level of protection which they deem appropriate for society. It is by reference to that level of protection that they must then, while dealing with the first component of the risk assessment, determine the level of the risk – i.e. the critical probability threshold for adverse effects on human health and for the seriousness of those effects – which in their judgment is no longer acceptable for society and above which it is necessary, in the interests of protecting human health, to take preventive measures in spite of any existing scientific uncertainty. Therefore,*

> *determining the level of risk deemed unacceptable involves the Community institutions in defining the political objectives to be pursued under the powers conferred on them by the Treaty.*[79]

It follows that the decision to invoke the principle will depend 'as a general rule on the level of protection chosen by the competent authority'.[80] In that respect, it should be highlighted that in the absence of harmonization and to the extent that uncertainties continue to exist in the current state of scientific research, 'it is for the member states to decide on their intended level of protection of human health and life'.[81] Accordingly, under Agreement on the Application of Sanitary and Phytosanitary Measures (SPS) case law, any quantifiable risk, no matter how small, may serve as a basis for sanitary measures. As a result, risk assessors could be called upon by decision-makers to assess the risks according to very stringent regulatory goals.

The CFI's reasoning is not devoid of legal consequences. In practice, this means that the fact of the decision-maker paying little heed to the level of protection would limit any subsequent recourse to the principle. Conversely, giving at an early stage the protection of health precedence over economic considerations would enhance the principle.

From a more ancillary point of view, one should acknowledge that experts cannot assess risks without knowing the legal requirements regarding the safety levels, which should serve as a baseline against which the assessments will be carried out. Of importance is the choice and the framing of the uncertainties do be dealt with: should the assessors delve into 'absolute risks' or every residual risk, or should they restrict themselves to comparing the risk entailed by the proposed technology with conventional risks?[82] Given the importance of correctly framing the hypothesis on the outcomes of the scientific assessment, this is typically an issue to be decided at the outset by the policy-makers and not by technical experts.[83] Indeed, if the frame becomes too narrow, salient questions may be excluded from further research.

What is more, the level of protection has to be determined on a case-by-case basis. Nonetheless, as far as EC law is concerned, there are no general regulatory guidelines for deciding whether a risk is acceptable or not.[84]

Risk assessment as a prerequisite for taking preventive action

Of course, risk can only be taken seriously if appropriate methodological tools are available. In this case the verification of the serious nature of a hypothesis should be undertaken using a specific technique that is recognized as a means of risk assessment. With regard to this obligation, the EC courts clearly stress the need to perform risk assessments while addressing uncertainties.

By way of example, in *Monsanto Agricoltura Italia*, the ECJ took that view that:

> ... *the risk assessment available to the national authorities provides specific evidence which, without precluding scientific uncertainty, makes it possible [to] reasonably ... conclude on the basis of the most reliable scientific evidence available and the most recent results of international research that the implementation of those measures is necessary in order to avoid novel foods which pose potential risks to human health being offered on the market.*[85]

It follows that those measures can be adopted only íf the member state has first carried out a risk assessment which is as complete as possible given the particular circumstances of the individual case'.[86]

To cite another example, in its judgment in *Commission* v *Denmark*, the ECJ again stressed the need to carry out 'a detailed assessment of the risk',[87] which, as a matter of fact:

> ... *presupposes, in the first place, the identification of the potentially negative conse-quences for health of the proposed addition of nutrients, and, secondly, a comprehensive assessment of the risk to health based on the most reliable scientific data available and the most recent results of international research.*[88]

By the same token, in the judgments *Pfizer Animal Health* v *Council* and *Alpharma* v *Council*, the CFI endorsed a similar approach, taking full account of the need to perform a scien-tific risk assessment – that is, 'a scientific process consisting [of] the identification and characterization of a hazard, the assessment of exposure to the hazard and the character-ization of the risk' as a prerequisite for the taking of preventive action.[89] Furthermore, the object of the risk assessment is 'to appraise the degree of probability of harmful effect on human health'.[90]

In this respect, both the ECJ and the CFI follow the jurisprudence of the EFTA Court, which had also found that the conducting of an assessment of risk was indispensable for the adoption of precautionary measures.[91] This calls for a thorough analysis of the scien-tific issues dealt with during the assessment process.

Issues dealing with risk assessments

Which risk assessment are we talking about?

Today, risk assessment is widely applied in international law in the field of 'food-borne' or 'pest- or disease-related' risks,[92] technical barriers to trade[93] and GMOs.[94] As far as EC law is concerned, risk assessment requirements are found in the areas of worker health and safety,[95] food safety,[96] pesticides,[97] environmental protection[98] and authorization schemes for dangerous substances,[99] GMOs,[100] pesticides[101] and biocides.[102] In a related vein, its attraction is reflected in political statements such as the communication of the EC Commission on the precautionary principle, which emphasizes that any approach based on the precautionary principle should start with a scientific evaluation as complete as possible.[103]

By placing emphasis upon the need to carry out a risk assessment, regardless of whether the empowering EC legal instrument contains any explicit reference to such an obligation, the EC courts construe the relevant Community principles relating to deci-sion-making in the face of uncertainty in line with the case law of the WTO Appellate Body on the interpretation of the SPS Agreement.[104]

As a result, some commentators have argued on the basis of *Pfizer* and *Alpharma* that the carrying out of a risk assessment had become a condition *sine qua non* for the imple-mentation of precautionary measures that could not be adopted unless experts had been trying to demonstrate with appropriate methods the likelihood that damage would otherwise be caused.[105]

With regard to the need to perform a risk assessment, the ECJ's and CFI's case law throws up more questions than it resolves. The following issues emerge as being of particular importance not only for EC institutions, but also for member states' scientific agencies. Indeed, by narrowly defining the scientific basis for health or environmental decision-making in terms of quantitative assessment, the risk assessment methodology required at the EC level can limit the ability of national authorities to take precautionary measures. Of particular importance in this respect is the Appellate Body's case law on implementing the WTO SPS Agreement.

Is a risk assessment required for precautionary decisions consistent with legal obligations that do not allow for a risk assessment procedure, as is the case for environmental protection acts?

In contrast to chemical and food safety legal instruments, the majority of the environmental directives do not provide for the need to carry out a risk assessment to classify hazardous waste, ban specific chemicals or protect endangered species.[106] In fact, Article 174(2) – the provision of the EC Treaty upon which those legal statutes are based – does not contain any such condition.[107] Simply put, the obligations and the safety thresholds laid down in the land filling directive, the waste incineration directive, the ozone layer protection directive and the chlorofluorocarbon (CFC) regulations were not based upon specific risk assessments conducted in accordance to the methodology described above. All of this is not to say that no scientific approach has been endorsed by the EC Commission while drafting those proposals. Indeed, each act has been based upon broad research into the existence and extent of potential environmental damage. Therefore, the answer to that first question is that the obligation to carry out a risk assessment with the intention of implementing a precautionary measure is only required in those areas where recourse to this procedure is expressly required by the act. It is hard to envisage any other result. In fact, an interpretation that, in the absence of express provision in the regulation or the directive, forced a public authority to carry out a risk assessment would be *contra legem*. Furthermore, if the EC law-maker were to decide, in the future, to request a risk assessment for any measure that restricted the presence of hazardous substances, even where such a measure fell under the headings of environmental, social and consumer policy, this could constitute a major political challenge for the EC institutions.[108]

What type of assessment is required?

What is its content and its methodology? From the outset, it must be stressed that there is no recognized method of risk assessment either in international law or in the EC legal order. Indeed, the substantive meaning of risk assessment is still to be clarified. For instance, as far as EC law is concerned, the risk assessment required by Regulation (EEC) No 1488/94 – laying down the principles for the assessment of risks to man and the environment of existing substances, comprising four stages (hazard identification, dose-response assessment, exposure assessment and risk characterization) – is not particularly relevant for the content of the risk assessment based on Annex II of the Directive 2001/18/EC on GMOs or the scientific methods used in fisheries to ascertain the total permissible catches.

As far as WTO law is concerned, it should be noted that the Appellate Body's case law offers some leeway with regard to the methodology of risk assessment dealing with sanitary and phytosanitary issues falling within the ambit of the SPS Agreement.[109] Since no specific methodology is prescribed, risk assessment can be conducted either quantitatively or qualitatively.[110] Furthermore, there is no requirement for a proper risk assessment to establish a 'minimum magnitude' or threshold level of degree of risk.[111] An SPS member's acceptable level of risk could even be set at 'zero risk'; hence, a risk assessment indicating a slight degree of risk can serve as a valid basis for state action.

Are the assessors required to assess the risks specifically or in the light of general studies?

The answer to that third question must be nuanced. In *Rheinheitsgebot*, the ECJ required that the German authorities come up with specific scientific evidence with regard to the risk entailed by additives in beer for German consumers.[112] In *Monsanto*, the ECJ ruled that precautionary measures presuppose, in particular, that the risk assessment available to the national authorities provides specific evidence, which, without precluding scientific uncertainty, makes it possible to reach a reasonable conclusion on the basis of the most reliable scientific evidence available and on the most recent results of international research that the implementation of those measures is necessary in order to avoid novel foods that pose potential risks to human health being offered on the market.[113] Last, but not least, a member state cannot systematically prohibit the marketing of a category of foodstuffs to which additives have been added without distinguishing the risks entailed by the use of each additive.[114] Looking again at the interpretation of the SPS Agreement made by the WTO Appellate Body, the EC institutions should specifically assess sanitary and phytosanitary risks falling within the ambit of the WTO SPS Agreement.[115]

Should the risk assessment reflect mainstream scientific opinion, including prevailing and dissenting views alike, or could it be based exclusively on a divergent opinion?

The problem goes even deeper with regard to dissenting opinions.

First, this raises the question as to whether there is a scientific majority or minority opinion. As a matter of course, drawing the line between scientists endorsing a majority thesis and others defending a minority point of view is not a scientific issue but a political one,[116] as has been seen by discussing the above cases. Bluntly speaking, science does not require a majority rule.

Second, as discussed above, whereas the EC law-maker and the CFI have both emphasized the principles of excellence, transparency and independence, they remain silent as to the role of dissenting scientific opinions.[117] Be that as it may, by requiring the active exercise of doubt, the precautionary principle invites decision-makers to open up the debate to marginal and dissenting opinions and to the conjectures and questions of a minority of the scientific community.[118] As a result, the appraisal of risks should therefore be conducted in an open fashion:

> ... only in this way can the framing assumptions adopted in the risk assessment and the treatment of associated uncertainties and trade-offs be tested and validated against the wider socio-political realities.[119]

Consequently, risk assessors cannot ignore the alarms sounded by a small group of experts until such time as the entire scientific community comes to support a previously minority opinion.[120] Inversely, decision-making should no longer be the prerogative of majority discourse alone, or the preserve of a scientific class close to the political elite. Expertise should therefore be employed in an open, transparent and pluralistic fashion. This argument is entirely consistent with WTO Appellate Body case law, which has held that risk assessment can set out both the prevailing view representing the mainstream of scientific opinion and the opinions of scientists who take a divergent view.[121]

Is it possible to address theoretical uncertainty?

The case law of the ECJ and CFI rejects the possibility of enacting a precautionary measure with a view to averting a 'hypothetical risk'. Hence, it would not be possible to enact a precautionary measure based upon a risk assessment dealing with theoretical uncertainty. By the same token, it should be pointed out that the interpretation of the SPS Agreement risk assessment obligations is rather strict in this respect. According to the WTO Appellate Body, the risk must be 'ascertainable' and not 'theoretical' since science can never provide absolute certainty that a given substance will never give rise to adverse health effects.[122]

A first issue arises for comment here. Since the linchpin of the precautionary measure is 'uncertainty', which is related both to the link of causation, as well as to the adverse effects, it is important to stress at the outset that a whole range of different types of uncertainty exists, ranging from lack of full evidence, lack of causal mechanisms, incorrect assumptions, extrapolation uncertainty, inconclusiveness, indeterminacy and ambiguity, all the way to complete ignorance.[123] This raises the question as to whether the courts should endorse a broad interpretation of the concept of 'theoretical uncertainty' encompassing issues such as ignorance, which is the source of inevitable surprises or unpredicted effects.[124]

In fact, the two concepts should be separated on the basis that ignorance mirrors a situation in which the possible outcomes are completely unknown or unknowable. In other words, they are not likely to be assessed and predicted. Furthermore, whereas additional research could reduce the level of uncertainty, it may also reveal new sources of ignorance; thus, in spite of further research, some issues may turn out to be fundamentally insoluble.[125]

At first sight, responding to ignorance may seem impossible. However, it must be borne in mind that ignorance is no less scientific than the probabilistic concept of risk and should not be eschewed by assessors. At least, the experts should point out the 'unknown unknowns'. The systematic search for blind spots could also be encouraged by law-makers.[126] In that respect, decision-makers have 'to accept the specificity of scientific discourse, which tends to keep questions open until something akin to a clear reputation of such hypothesis is established'.[127]

Finally, it is open to question whether the requirement to eschew hypothetical risk is not too stringent, particularly in relation to low probability risks.[128] Indeed, there may be situations in which political institutions wish to take steps to avert risks that have not been characterized as more than hypothetical.

Concluding remarks

One could therefore conclude under CFI and ECJ case law that the implementation of the precautionary principle obliges Community institutions or national authorities, where acting within the framework of a competence devolved by the European Community, to produce a risk assessment. Nonetheless, the courts have hitherto given little guidance as to how this analysis should be carried out.

Is the requirement to carry out a risk assessment suitable in order to assess unknown risks?

Particular attention has been hitherto drawn to the need for risk assessment. However, insufficient attention has been given to the public discussion taking place in the EU concerning the question as to whether risk assessments are well-tailored to address complex risks. Whatever reasons may exist for requiring risk assessment as a prerequisite for the taking of precautionary action, the process appears to be fraught with controversies. Paradoxically, while reliance on sound science is increasing at international and regional levels, sharp criticism of risk regulation is growing, particularly in the US;[129] indeed, the limitations of the risk assessment procedure have never been so clear.[130] Against this background, both lawmakers[131] and courts[132] are aware of the limitations of risk assessments.

First, risk assessments do not always provide scientific certainty concerning the causal link between exposure to an agent or a substance and adverse effects on health and the environment. This difficulty is compounded by the fact that all of the steps in risk analysis are becoming increasingly dependent upon the assumptions of risk assessors (about exposures and human behaviour), which may be explicit or implicit, with the attendant danger of bias caused by external factors (e.g. industrial or commercial interests).[133] Accordingly, the results of assessments carried out according to a single methodology may differ significantly from one another.[134]

Second, when the risk assessment procedure is overburdened by analytical requirements, it becomes a resource-intensive and time-consuming process too stringent to suit regulatory goals.[135] It can be so slow that it may lead to a process of ossification or 'paralysis by analysis'.[136]

Third, the scope of assessment may be too narrow, excluding certain disciplines and failing to achieve a holistic understanding of complex ecosystems (e.g. analysis may focus only on cancer, ignoring other potentially harmful effects).[137]

Fourth, the current risk assessment process has a negligible input from those dealing with risk management with regard to practical options for change or the validity and effectiveness of control measures. Nonetheless, experts cannot begin to assess something unless they have been instructed to do so.[138]

Fifth, subjective or ethical considerations are actually excluded and relegated to the decision-making process. Indeed, as a technical, analytical and objective exercise, risk assessment does not require any public involvement. Consequently, risk assessment functions as a more arcane procedure of a technocratic rather than democratic nature.[139]

Last, but not least, existing risk assessment methodologies are inherently biased in favour of avoiding over-inclusive regulatory measures for fear of imposing undue costs upon undertakings.[140]

Budgetary constraints, uncertainties and pressing deadlines call for faster, better and more representative assessment techniques that are meaningful for regulatory decision-making and more suited to cope with the numerous uncertainties affecting the process. This is particularly the case of chemicals where only a substantial paradigm shift will allow a start to be made to rectify an evaluation process fraught with difficulties.[141]

Scientific and political issues leading to the adoption of a precautionary measure

Incomplete, insufficient or inconclusive risk assessment studies leading to the adoption of precautionary measures

The European Courts' reasoning rests on a two-step approach. First, a risk assessment has to be carried out with the aim of reducing uncertainty (see the earlier section on 'Risk assessment as a prerequisite for taking preventive action'). Nonetheless, as indicated above, it may be impossible to carry out a full risk assessment because such investigations operate at the frontiers of scientific knowledge. As a matter of fact, scientists do not necessarily have an answer to everything. Their investigations do not always allow for an identification of the risks in a convincing manner. Indeed, in many cases, their assessments will demonstrate that there is a high degree of scientific and practical uncertainty in that regard.[142] In particular, in fields marked by uncertainty, they must even point to the limits of their knowledge or, where appropriate, to their ignorance. It is precisely at this stage that the precautionary principle comes into play.

Rather than rendering the principle nugatory, courts consider the need to take preventive measures with a view to protecting the environment and human health despite the uncertainties.

In the landmark case *National Farmers' Union,* the ECJ held that: 'Where there is uncertainty as to the existence or extent of risks to human health, the institutions may take protective measures without having to wait until the reality and seriousness of those risks become fully apparent.'[143] In subsequent cases, the ECJ and the CFI alike expressed the view that 'where it proves to be impossible to determine with certainty the existence or extent of the alleged risk because of the insufficiency, inconclusiveness or imprecision of the results of studies conducted, but the likelihood of real harm to public health persists should the risk materialize, the precautionary principle justifies the adoption of restrictive measures'.[144]

The rationale of these landmark judgments is the finding that scientific uncertainty constitutes the essence of the principle. As emphasized above, scientific uncertainty exists whenever there is no adequate theoretical or empirical basis for assigning probabilities to the occurrence or the extent of a risk (see the earlier section on 'Issues dealing with risk assessments').

It follows that a risk management measure could be decided despite the fact that the risk assessors were unable to determine the probability of the occurrence of the risk.[145] However, it is not entirely clear what the courts had in mind in referring to insufficiency, inconclusiveness and imprecision. This means that the factors triggering precautionary action are still open to debate.[146] At the very least, care should be taken to distinguish between these thresholds. The following examples are illustrative of the ways in which uncertainty pervades the risk assessment process:

- *Insufficiency:* for instance, the various scientific disciplines involved in assessing the risk are not sufficiently developed to explain the cause-and-effect relationship.
- *Inconclusiveness:* the realities of science dictate that the scientists, whatever the quality of their investigations, will never be able to eliminate some uncertainties; for instance, there may be too many unpredictable variables to enable the identification of the relative influences of each factor.
- *Imprecision:* this could be caused by the fact that the data to analyse the risks are not available or are out of date, and that there are information gaps, measurement errors, contradictions, indeterminacy and ambiguity.

Furthermore, the European courts clearly link insufficiency with uncertainty as a triggering factor of precautionary measures. In other words, insufficient results foster uncertainty. In that respect, attention should be drawn to the fact in interpreting Article 5(7) of the SPS Agreement, the WTO Appellate Body took the view that the application of the safeguard clause enshrined in that provision, which previously was deemed to reflect the precautionary principle,[147] 'is triggered not by the existence of scientific uncertainty, but rather by the insufficiency of scientific evidence'.[148] As a result, under the SPS Agreement, a precautionary principle could not be triggered by uncertainty but exclusively by insufficient results. It is difficult to follow this line of reasoning, particularly in the light of Articles 10(6) and 11(8) of the Cartagena Protocol on Biosafety, which link precaution and 'insufficient relevant scientific information and knowledge regarding the extent of the potential adverse effect'. By the same token, looking closely at the ECJ case law, insufficiency is triggering uncertainty. It would therefore appear that the Appellate Body's reasoning is mistaken.

As a matter of course, the courts offer no guidance on what should be the most reliable scientific evidence available that needs to be gathered. Thus, a particularly significant question arises for risk assessors and risk managers alike: how much information is needed in order to reach a decision? Thus far, some lessons can be drawn from the case law.

Ratione materiae, the following conditions have to be met:

- The risk management decision in the face of uncertainty precluding the realization of a full risk assessment study has to based 'on the most reliable scientific data available'[149] or on 'sufficiently reliable and cogent information' allowing the authority to understand the ramifications of the scientific question raised.[150]
- The decision must be based on 'solid and convincing evidence which, while not resolving the scientific uncertainty, may reasonably raise doubts as to the safety and/or efficacy of the ... product'.[151]
- There must be a detailed assessment of the risk.[152]
- The 'reliable scientific evidence' should rely upon recommendations made by international,[153] EC[154] or national scientific bodies.[155]

- The specificity of the risk must be ascertained in the light of geographical, ecological, nutritional or societal particularities.[156]

Ratione temporis, the following requirements have to be fulfilled:

- The risk must be backed up by the scientific data available at the time 'when the precautionary measure was taken'.[157]
- References to the latest research,[158] 'the most recent results of international research'[159] and new evidence[160] on the subject enhance the quality of the decision.[161]

Applying this array of criteria, the assessors should be able to reduce any lingering uncertainties and provide the risk managers with a sufficient scientific basis on which they can endorse their safety measures. Rather than formulating firmly established truths, their task is to formulate and transform the remaining uncertainties into functional estimates upon which decisions can be adopted. As a result, it could not be argued that precaution is anti-scientific. On the contrary, as has been stressed in the various judgments analysed, the assessors are called upon to investigate as thoroughly as possible and with an appropriate methodology those risks with which they are confronted. Indeed, applying precaution requires the application of the most rigorous science criteria with a view to characterizing uncertainties, filling gaps in knowledge and furthering research.

Conflicts between different schools of thought leading to the adoption of precautionary measures

Scientists usually do not acknowledge that their studies are inconsistent, incomplete, uncertain or insufficient. Indeed, the implementation of precautionary measures arises mostly within conflicting contexts.[162] Obviously, there is not a single scientific view on the existence and the extent of the suspected risk. Those controversies are exacerbated by the fact that some member states are increasingly distrustful of the findings or the Community's scientific committees and seek to adhere to the findings of their own national bodies to support national protective measures.[163] Accordingly, numerous cases ruled by the ECJ and CFI illustrate the tensions arising between different scientific bodies, or between a scientific advisory council and an EC institution.

Typical in this respect is the ban on virginiamycin, which was not based upon a single risk assessment study highlighting a specific risk to human health.[164] The EC institutions justified their ban invoking a Danish study on laboratory rats providing new evidence on the transfer of antibiotic resistance from animals to human beings, whereas the Scientific Committee for Animal Nutrition (SCAN) contended with the scientific results of that study.[165] The CFI took the view that the EC institutions were not bound to follow the committee's opinion as the EC institutions were sufficiently well informed to conclude that the Danish study on live rats could be considered as major fresh scientific evidence enabling the introduction of a precautionary measure.[166]

Another case in point is the court's judgment in *Commission v France*,[167] in which the ECJ condemned the French bovine spongiform encephalopathy (BSE) ban that had been unilaterally imposed. On the one hand, France argued that the commission had not taken into account the minority opinions within the *ad hoc* scientific committee, while, on the other, the commission contended that the French could rely only on the scientific opinion of their own national experts. Although the French authorities had founded their justification of the prohibition on imports of British beef on the precautionary principle, the ECJ, in a judgment of 13 December 2001, did not accept this argument. Finding against France, the court held that a member state could not invoke its own scientific expertise and ignore risk assessment that had been carried out by the commission in conformity with Community law.[168]

Although not referring to the principle, the *Toolex* judgment provides the most striking evidence of a precautionary approach to the resolution of a conflict between the commission and a member state failing to abide by EC harmonized standards.[169] This case arose from a challenge to the Swedish decision to ban the chemical substance trichloroethylene, which had been classified as a category 3 carcinogen under Directive 67/548/EEC on the classification of dangerous substances.[170] Although the Swedish ban was tantamount to a measure having an effect equivalent to a quantitative restriction within the meaning of Article 28 EC, the ECJ took the view that it was compatible with the EC Treaty insofar as it was necessary for the effective protection of the health and life of humans despite the scientific uncertainties surrounding the effects of exposure to the chemical.

Safeguard clauses leading to the adoption of precautionary measures

So far, the courts have pointed out that the various safeguard clauses contained in different directives and regulations – enabling member states to deal with exceptional situations by enacting provisional measures – give specific expression to the precautionary principle, and that the conditions governing recourse to these clauses established on the basis of Article 95(10) EC must therefore be interpreted in the light of that principle.[171]

The interpretation of a safeguard clause in the light of the precautionary principle allows for certain relaxation of the requirement to carry out a risk assessment that is as complete as possible (see the earlier section on 'Incomplete, insufficient or inconclusive risk assessment studies leading to the adoption of precautionary measures'). Therefore, scientific evidence accessible to national authorities could support, in the light of the precautionary principle, preventive measures at variance with EU harmonized standards.[172]

That said, it needs to be pointed out that the safeguard clause does not represent the most salient expression of that principle. Indeed, such clauses can be invoked by member states only provided that specific circumstances are met. In addition, they are provisional. Restricting the use of the precautionary principle to safeguard clauses would be tantamount to the emasculation of a principle purporting to address, at least in the environmental field, long-term risks.

The relationship between risk assessment and risk management in the light of the precautionary principle

Having thus outlined the limits of scientific analysis (see the earlier section on 'Incomplete, insufficient or inconclusive risk assessment studies leading to the adoption of precautionary measures'), we come to the political phase of risk analysis – namely, risk management, which involves setting the risk at an acceptable level. Nevertheless, this decision-making stage is not entirely separate from the scientific stage that is supposed to precede it.

Taking precaution seriously involves making judgments, which, though they must be informed as far as possible by scientific assessment, may go beyond it. Precaution is therefore testament to a new relationship with science where it is consulted less for the knowledge that it has to offer than for the doubts and concerns that it is in a position to raise.

Nonetheless, the precautionary principle implies neither less scientific assessment nor diminished political responsibility. The Community courts both reinforce and nuance the role played by scientists in decision-making. As seen above, the courts strengthen their importance by guaranteeing recent legislative developments through insisting on the requirement to carry out a systematic risk assessment. By contrast, it also loosens this linkage in two ways: on the one hand, by recognizing the limits of scientific expertise and, on the other, by obliging EC institutions, 'while dealing with the first component of the risk assessment', to clearly define the political objectives at issue. In other words, risk management presupposes that the authorities determine from the outset 'the level of protection which they deem appropriate for society'.[173] This requirement essentially amounts to a reinvigoration of political decision-making, with decision-makers no longer being able to seek refuge behind a façade of scientific pseudo-certitudes presented by their own experts. They are now forced to show their hand and face up to the consequences of their choices. It falls to them alone to set the level of protection and thereby assume political responsibility. Thus, the decision to act, or to refrain from doing so, now takes place within a political context: the determination of the acceptable level of protection (see the following section on 'Acceptable risk').

In addition, in the *Pfizer* case the CFI stressed that the authority must give particular consideration to:

> ... the severity of the impact on human health were the risk to occur, including the extent of possible adverse effects, the persistency or reversibility of those effects and the possibility of delayed effects, as well as of the more or less concrete perception of the risk based on available scientific knowledge.[174]

Likewise, the ECJ has also stressed in other cases that it could be appropriate to take into consideration the cumulative effect of the presence on the market of several sources, including both natural and artificial, of a particular nutrient and of the possible existence, in future, of additional sources that can reasonably be foreseen.[175] In this respect, the courts highlighted a particularly sensitive issue. As seen earlier, experts increasingly criticize imperfections in the risk assessments carried out both in Europe and the US. It follows that the authorities should request the risk assessors to emphasize in their studies the possibility of delayed adverse effects, along with the persistency, accumulation and reversibility of such adverse effects. In other words, they should encourage science to look at multi-causal pathways and complex interactions. Accordingly, this process will require a continuous dialogue between regulators and scientists.[176]

In this way, the CFI and the ECJ alike reject the notion of compartmentalization or demarcation that appears to follow from traditional methods of risk analysis.

Risk management

Thus far, the discussion has concentrated upon the extent to which risk assessors have to highlight uncertain risks with a view to providing decision-makers with the proper information. Indeed, risk is not just a matter for the experts. Various factors – *inter alia*, the institutional, social and economic contexts – play a decisive role in the determination of the threshold above which the risk is judged unacceptable, thus requiring isolation by means of appropriate regulatory measures.[177] Is the public ready to accept the risk? Is there any interest in catering for the public? How should the risk be distributed between the various strata of the population? The regulation of risk is a matter involving highly political choices. This means that additional obligations come into consideration in relation to risk management.

However, those choices are likely to be reviewed by the courts. This fourth section will be dedicated to the questions arising at the risk management level.[178] The discussion in this section will be structured in the following manner. It will start by considering the issue of the non-binding nature of scientific opinions (see 'Scientific opinions: A necessary but not sufficient condition for risk regulation'), moving on to address the issue of which risks are deemed to be unacceptable (see 'Acceptable risk'). Finally, it will address the question as to whether the precautionary principle is purely permissive or whether it might generate positive obligations for the competent authorities (see 'Permissive or compulsory?').

Scientific opinions: A necessary but not sufficient condition for risk regulation

Science is the cornerstone of precaution within the field of food safety and other health issues.[179] Accordingly, the scientific quality of the risk assessment that should precede the enactment of a precautionary measure must be enhanced by the fact that the competent public authority should entrust this task to scientific experts,[180] who, on completion of the scientific process, provide it with scientific advice.[181] This advice, in the interest both of consumers and industry, should be based on 'the principles of excellence, independence and transparency'.[182]

However, whereas experts have scientific legitimacy, they have neither democratic legitimacy nor political responsibilities.[183] Consequently, it is settled case law that the opinions of the scientific committees or the relevant agencies (such as the European Food Safety Agency) are non-binding.[184] EC institutions cannot therefore be criticized in cases concerning complex and sensitive public health issues for having taken the time necessary to address the relevant scientific issues and, in particular, for having referred such issues for a second examination by the competent scientific committee even though the act is silent on this point.[185] By the same token, the institutions 'may disregard the conclusions' drawn in the official scientific body of opinion, 'even though, in some places, it relies on certain aspects of the scientific analysis in the opinion'.[186] In other words, the institutions may also avail themselves of those parts of the scientific reasoning that they do not dispute.

However, EC institutions are subject to specific obligations. Although most of the scientific opinions do not bind the institutions, any unlawfulness of a requested opinion could be regarded as a breach of an essential procedural requirement, thereby rendering the institutions' decision unlawful. As a result, the courts may be called upon to review the formal legality of a scientific opinion, albeit restrictively (internal consistency, statement of reasons).[187] Furthermore, the CFI has held that the obligation to state comprehensively the reasons is particularly strict in the event of scientific uncertainty.[188]

It follows that when deciding to set aside a scientific opinion in order to upgrade the level of protection, the EC institutions 'must provide specific reasons for their findings by comparison with those made in the opinion, and its statement of reasons must explain why it is disregarding the latter'. In addition, as a matter of procedure, 'the statement of reasons must be of a scientific level at least commensurate with that of the opinion in question'.[189]

As far as the member states are concerned, while assessing the proportionality of a member state's measure providing for more stringent standards than the ones laid down under an EC directive, the commission must take into account the opinion of the EC scientific committee, which has called into question the validity of the EC standards.[190]

Acceptable risk

The courts have already stressed that the competent public authority had, when confronted by uncertainty, to undertake a balancing of its obligations and then decide either to wait until the results of more detailed scientific research became available, or to act on the strength of existing scientific knowledge. Where measures intended to protect human health are at issue, this balancing process depends upon the level of risk determined by the authority 'as being unacceptable for society' within the context of the particular circumstances of each individual case.[191] Since science is seen as a necessary but not sufficient condition for risk regulation, the political actors are allowed a significant degree of discretion in relation to the means of achieving safety objectives in the face of uncertainty. Moreover, in contrast to many international agreements requiring either significant or irreversible risk, EC directives (e.g. Directive 2001/18) and regulations (e.g. Regulation 178/2002) structured around the principle refer to a risk without such qualifying objectives. Accordingly, they offer a broader margin for manoeuvre to the institutions.

Nonetheless, their discretionary powers with regard to the type of preventive measure must be exercised in a manner that is consistent with a range of constraints stemming from EC law, some of which were outlined above (e.g. risk assessment and consultation of scientific bodies), and others which will be discussed below (for instance, proportionality).

Nevertheless, the question of the appropriate means for averting the manifestation of uncertain risks is an open-ended one. Indeed, the various judgments commented in this chapter do not address the issue of which measures are to be taken in the light of the precautionary principle.

It is settled case law that it is for the institution concerned to determine the level of protection that it considers appropriate for society, depending upon the circumstances of the particular case.[192] On the other hand, in the absence of harmonization and insofar as uncertainties continue to exist in the current state of scientific research, it is for the member states to decide on the desirable level of protection of human health and life.[193] This means that a risk management decision rests with each member state, which has a discretion in determining the level of risk it considers appropriate. Accordingly, the member state may invoke the precautionary principle.[194]

As a result, the precautionary principle gives rise to a number of disparate EC and national measures whose intensity and scope may vary from one extreme to another. At one end of the spectrum, the focus could be placed on soft measures, such as the provision of information to the operators and to the public concerning how products deemed to be at risk should be placed on the market and used. At the other end of the spectrum, precautionary measures may be absolute in character[195] if damage may be prevented from occurring by the adoption of preventive measures, including embargos,[196] bans, the destruction of hazardous products,[197] or a general zero-tolerance approach.[198]

The question we face here is whether, in the light of the principle of precaution, the most stringent measures are acceptable. In this respect, one might equally question the scope of paragraph 145 of the *Pfizer* judgment where the court judged that 'a "zero risk" does not exist, since it is not possible to prove scientifically that there is no current or future risk associated with the addition of antibiotics to feeding stuffs'.[199] Does this reasoning necessarily imply that any policy designed to eliminate risk is undesirable? Alternatively, is it possible to limit the scope of this interpretation to the single case of a product withdrawn from the market? The latter reading seems to be the more persuasive. Within this context one can appreciate the significance both of the recognition by the appellate body of the WTO that the level of protection adopted within a risk management framework could itself aim at a zero risk,[200] and of the EFTA Court's admission that a precautionary measure could, in exceptional circumstances, be directed at a zero-risk level.[201] In addition, according to the ECJ's established case law on the proportionality of national measures limiting the use of food additives, the determination of the extent to which member states intend to guarantee the protection of the health and life of persons is – in the absence of an exhaustive harmonization at Community level – at their own decision, although they must, of course, have given consideration to the requirements of the free movement of goods throughout the Community. The margin for manoeuvre reserved to the member states specifically allows them to set a very high level of protection where technical knowledge is not certain. This approach is encapsulated in the *Melkunie* judgment. The court accordingly found that zero tolerance towards the admissibility of pathogenic microorganisms in food waste was admissible, falling under the protection of human health under Article 30.[202] More recently, in *Walter Hahn*, the ECJ accepted that a member state could opt for a tolerance level equal to zero regarding the presence of listeriosis in fish, finding that 'as long as the provisional results of those scientific discussions have not been translated into Community law, member states have the right, by way of precaution, to set more stringent microbiological standards in order to protect human health and, in particular, the health of susceptible groups', whereas the CFI endorsed the same reasoning in its *Solvay Pharmaceuticals* judgment with regard to the prohibition of an additive in animal feeding stuffs.[203] By the same token, the zero-tolerance approach consisting of the prohibition of any contamination, even accidental, by unauthorized substances in feedstuffs is proportionate.[204] Last, but not least, the *Fedesa* case – recognized as one of the earliest instances of applying the precautionary principle – upheld the validity of measures based on a desire to eradicate consumer risk.[205] As convincingly argued by Christoforou, the pursuit of a zero risk does not, however, mean that one should seek to eliminate all risks; the aim is, by contrast, to limit their manifestation as far as possible.[206]

Against the background of the cases commented above, the debate on the acceptable level of protection must be more firmly rooted in each legal system's constitutional traditions. Although prevented from adopting a purely hypothetical approach to risk and orienting their decisions towards a level of 'zero risk',[207] EC institutions must still, however, respect their obligations under Articles 95(3), 152(1), 152(3), and 174(2) EC to ensure an increased level of protection of human health, consumer protection and the environment, which, in order to ensure compatibility with this provision, need not technically be the highest level possible.[208] Finally, it could be argued that the decision to eliminate every risk is an issue involving purely political responsibility and is, as such, one in relation to which judicial review should be highly deferential.

Permissive or compulsory?

Does this margin of appreciation mean that EC institutions could ignore the precautionary principle even where risks of serious and irreversible damage are suspected? In other words, is the recourse to the precautionary principle obligatory or facultative?

Initially, the ECJ held that 'the institutions may take protective measures without having to await' full certainty.[209]

The CFI, however, appeared to adopt a more categorical stance in the *Artegodan* case, holding that the precautionary principle constituted 'a general principle of Community law requiring the competent authorities to take appropriate measures'.[210] Against this background, the principle 'requires', pursuant to the rules applying to the reauthorization of a medicinal product, 'the suspension or the withdrawal of marketing authorization when new scientific evidence give rise to serious doubt as to the efficacy and the safety of the product'.[211] In *Pfizer*, the CFI observed that a public authority can, by reason of the precautionary principle, be *required* to act even before any adverse effects have become apparent.[212]

Last but by no means least, as will be seen, in the field of habitat protection, the principle requires that the administrative authorities refrain from giving their consent to a project that could negatively impact upon the conservation of a protected bird's habitat.[213]

One might wonder on a reading of these last cases whether the application of the precautionary principle has now become obligatory. It has been argued above that, as far as Community environmental policy is concerned, Article 174(2) obliges Community authorities to act in a manner informed by environmental principles (including the precautionary principle), without which one could not otherwise derive clear and precise obligations from this principle. The precautionary principle is, in fact, a norm of indeterminate content that offers public authorities some room for manoeuvre.[214] It is precisely this distinctive feature of principles – norms of indeterminate content allowing for a broader understanding – which proves to be all the more indispensable in the light of the heterogeneous nature of the factual situations that have to be regulated. In addition, the non-application of the precautionary principle always remains a possibility when, for example, the measure proves to be totally disproportionate to the pursued objective. Nonetheless, the principle obliges authorities (and it is at this level that it is binding) to take a position justifying their decisions. Being obliged to justify their legal statutes in the light of such a principle, the institutions will be able to reflect on the impact of their decisions. In this way the form sustains the substance.[215]

JUDICIAL REVIEW OF THE RISK MANAGEMENT PROCESS

Standard of review

In the majority of the disputes commented on so far, the contradicting interests of human environment protection and the free movement of goods have had to be weighed against one another.

It is important to note that the intensity of review exercised by EC courts varies extensively. One needs to draw a line between, on the one hand, the lawsuits brought by a private party against an EC measure and, on the other, the cases brought by the European Commission against member states. Whereas, in the former hypothesis, the CFI has to balance private freedoms (such as the right to property and the freedom to pursue a trade or business) vis-à-vis an EC public interest (the objective of a high level of health protection), in the latter cases, the ECJ has to weigh an EC public interest (free movement of goods) against a national public interest (the willingness to depart from EC harmonized standards).

As far as the member states' precautionary measures are concerned, the ECJ appears to apply more strictly the principle of precaution to the extent that those measures could jeopardize the functioning of the internal market.[216]

On the other hand, being fully aware of the difficulties of regulating either in controversial cases or where action is urgently needed, the Community courts rightly show themselves little inclined to penalize EC institutions for any mistakes that they may have committed in their desire to safeguard the general interest in cases where the institutions are required to undertake a scientific risk assessment and to evaluate highly complex scientific and technical facts.[217] Hence, the exercise of that discretion must be subject to a review limited to the question as to whether the institution committed a manifest error of appraisal or misused its powers.[218] In this respect, invoking the principle or the idea of precaution, the ECJ[219] and the CFI[220] have, on various occasions in the past, rejected lawsuits founded on manifest errors of appraisal committed by the institutions when taking decisions that were not fully justified in the light of prevailing scientific knowledge. The *Alliance for Natural Health* judgment offers a typical illustration of the approach endorsed by the ECJ with regard to the limitations entailed by the principle of precaution to the free movement of goods. The ECJ held that taking into account the precautionary principle, the authors of Directive 2002/46 on food supplements marketed as foodstuffs:

> ... could reasonably take the view that an appropriate way of reconciling the objective of the internal market, on the one hand, with that relating to the protection of human health, on the other, was for entitlement to free movement to be reserved for food supplements containing substances about which, at the time when the directive was adopted, the competent European scientific authorities had available adequate and appropriate scientific data capable of providing them with the basis for a favourable opinion.[221]

Indeed, the Community judiciary shows that it is not entitled to substitute its assessment of the facts for that of the Community institutions, upon which the European Treaty confers sole responsibility for that duty.[222]

This jurisprudence must be approved. Such freedom of action, nevertheless, seems, indeed, to be indispensable when the scientific proof collated by Community institutions does not dictate a ready-made solution. By acting in this way, the courts reinforce administrative discretion in the implementation of policy.

Testing the proportionality of the precautionary measure

The principle of precaution is intertwined with the principle of proportionality.[223] As a matter of fact, most of the important cases decided by the European courts with respect to precaution were brought by claimants averring that the contested regulation had been adopted in violation of the principle of proportionality insofar as the legal statute in question was manifestly inappropriate for realizing the pursued objective and that the institutions, which had a choice between various measures, had nonetheless not chosen the least restrictive one. While the function of the proportionality principle is well understood, its modes of application still give rise to conflicting opinions.[224]

Necessity test

This test requires a comparison between the various measures that are capable of achieving the desired result, and that the one which causes the least inconvenience should be retained. By way of illustration, the member state must demonstrate that the implementation of a precautionary measure is necessary in order to ensure that specific products (novel foods, food additives, enriched foodstuffs) do not present any danger for the consumer.[225] The *Pfizer* and *Alpharma* cases illustrate the central role that the necessity test occupies in determining the proportionality of a precautionary measure. The claimants had argued that the Community authorities should have waited, in line with the practice of Canadian and Australian authorities, for the scientific studies to show a sufficient likelihood of risk. As far as the violation of the necessity test was concerned, the court replied that:

> ... *the institutions cannot be criticized for having chosen to withdraw provisionally the authorization of virginiamycin as an additive in feeding stuffs in order to prevent the risk from becoming a reality, and, at the same time, to continue with the research that was already under way. Such an approach, moreover, was consonant with the precautionary principle, by reason of which a public authority can be required to act even before any adverse acts have become apparent.*[226]

Furthermore, the court was persuaded that the use of such antibiotics is not 'strictly necessary in animal husbandry and that there are alternative methods of animal husbandry even if they can lead to higher costs for farmers and, ultimately, consumers'.[227] Recalling that the proportionality principle, which forms part of the general principles of Community law, requires that the acts of the Community institutions do not go beyond the limits of that which is necessary for realizing the legitimate objectives pursued by the regulation at issue, the CFI confirmed that the regulation satisfied the necessity test.

Kemikaleinspektionen offers another interesting illustration of an approach favourable to precautionary action. The ECJ found that the Swedish regulation was appropriate and proportionate 'in that it offered increased protection for workers, whilst at the same time taking account of the undertakings' requirements in the matter of continuity'.[228]

Weighing up different interests: The proportionality test

After having confirmed the necessary character of the contested regulation, the courts still have to balance the 'pros and cons' of the decision to withdraw by weighing up the different interests in play. The culmination of the testing procedure – the proportionality test – *stricto sensu*, is supposed to allow the Community courts to compare the controversial decision with its objective effects – that is, with its effective consequences on the well-founded subjective frame of reference, consisting of the private interest of continuing to market a food additive. At this stage, the proportionality principle no longer requires balancing the advantages and disadvantages of the proposed measure compared with the other alternatives; rather, it requires a weighing-up of the respective importance of the objective pursued by the contested measure with the interests that are threatened by that measure.

With a few exceptions, the requirement to balance interests in a strict sense is the least well-established test in the court's jurisprudence.[229]

Averring a violation of the proportionality test, *stricto sensu*, Pfizer claimed that a withdrawal of a product's authorization could not be considered proportionate in the absence of a serious and identifiable risk and of proof that the source against which the action was to be undertaken constituted the most probable explanation for the risk which that action was intended to confront. Where these conditions are not fulfilled, the balance should tilt in favour of the holders of the marketing authorizations. Due to the great importance accorded to the protection of human health (see the following section 'Weighing the interests test and the pre-eminence of protecting public health over economic interests'), as contrasted with economic considerations,[230] the CFI nonetheless found that the measure at stake was not disproportionate. The CFI also added that restrictions could be placed on the free exercise of professional activities – itself one of the general principles of Community law – as long as these restrictions were effectively tailored to objectives of general interest pursued by the Community.[231]

Weighing the interests test and the pre-eminence of protecting public health over economic interests

Both the CFI and the ECJ have, on many occasions and in a wide variety of different settings, reiterated their view that health protection requirements should take precedence over economic interests.[232]

In line with the judgments of the ECJ, and the CFI in *Alpharma* and *Pfizer*, the latter court enshrined a new 'general principle' of Community law in *Artegodan*, by virtue of which the protection of public health 'must unquestionably take precedence over economic considerations'.[233] The CFI considered that such a principle requires, in the first instance, an exclusive focus on considerations relating to the protection of public health when considering whether to withdraw a medicine already placed on the market, and, second, a re-evaluation of the balance of benefits and risks presented by the medicine when new facts raise doubts over its efficacy or safety. Third, this new principle has an impact on the burden of proof placed on the decision-maker to withdraw the authorization to market a medicine, where such a decision is made with reference to the precautionary principle.[234]

The effect of the general principle is that the holder of an authorization to market a medicinal product, valid for five years, cannot invoke the principle of legal certainty and claim a specific protection of his interests for the duration of the validity of the authorization if the competent authority establishes *de jure*, with sufficient certainty, that the medicine no longer meets one of the criteria laid down in Directive 65/65/CEE, having regard to developments in scientific knowledge and new facts gathered through pharmacovigilance.[235]

Although the court's reasoning is convincing and sound, it also raises some questions.

Since the courts are silent on what is meant by its assertion 'by giving precedence to the requirements related to the protection of those interests over economic interests', one could wonder whether that principle must be strictly applied. Put simply, is that principle uncompromising? Given the fact that such a principle appears to be of extremely high value, the answer should probably be yes.

Nonetheless, the principle of giving precedence has to be balanced with the principle of proportionality. Interestingly enough, the CFI in *Artegodan* places on equal footing both the principle of giving precedence to health and the principles of proportionality and non-discrimination.[236] As a result, those various principles should guide the decision-maker in determining the appropriate level of protection. Similarly, in *Bellio F.lli Srl*, the ECJ took the view that even if the need to safeguard public health has been recognized as a primary concern, the principle of proportionality must be respected.[237]

There is a question as to whether this obligation to take the principle of proportionality into account is complied with when the necessity test and weighing of interests are subsequently carried out (see the earlier sections on 'Necessity test' and 'Weighing up different interests: The proportionality test'). Does it mean that equilibrium must still be found between the conflicting interests? Or does it mean that while weighing the interests, the decision-maker and the courts must both, ultimately, give precedence to requirements related to the protection of those interests over economic interests?

So far, the assertion that health interests have priority should not allow authorities to eschew economic concerns while assessing the necessity of the measure at issue (see the following section on 'Proportionality and countervailing risks').

Proportionality in the light of the duty of re-examination

The trend embedded within WTO and EC law requiring institutions to re-examine their precautionary measures in the light of new scientific information is particularly important in this respect.[238] Indeed, it is still possible for the authority to loosen the straightjacket of precaution when new elements show that the suspected risk does not constitute as important a risk as had initially been feared. In the BSE case, the ECJ found that the export ban was not disproportionate on the grounds, *inter alia*, that the measures were temporary pending the results of further scientific studies.[239] *Pfizer* provided further insights into assessing the proportionality of a measure likely to be re-examined. Where such restrictions, placed by way of the precautionary principle on the commercialization of a product, are not necessarily definitive, they thus appear all the more appropriate.[240] The withdrawal of the authorization for virginiamycin as a growth promoter thus constituted a provisional measure that was subject to the Community institutions' duty of re-examination.[241] Last, the ECJ held recently that by virtue of Regulation (EC) No 178/2002 on food safety, the Community legislature was entitled to adopt 'provisional risk management measures necessary to ensure a high level of health protection and may do so whilst awaiting further scientific information for a more comprehensive risk assessment'.[242]

Proportionality and countervailing risks

In the view of several US scholars, the elimination of one risk can mask the appearance of another.[243] Thus, curtailing a targeted risk could actually increase the occurrence of a countervailing risk. Often, however, the countervailing risks will be far more remote in time or place, or – significantly in our world of ultra-specialization – the new risks will be cognitively remote.[244] In this sense, *Pfizer* and *Alpharma* are cases in point. The claimants had highlighted the fact that the prohibition of using antibiotics as growth promoters would have significant negative effects on the environment, impacts that had not been taken into consideration by the Community authorities. The CFI replied that the contested regulation was founded:

> ... on a political choice, in respect of which the Community institutions were required to weigh up, on the one hand, maintaining, while awaiting further scientific studies, the authorization of a product which primarily enables the agricultural sector to be more profitable and, on the other, banning the product for public health reasons.[245]

Proportionality and cost-benefit analysis

As far as the third test is concerned, the CFI considered in *Pfizer* that a cost-benefit analysis (CBA) was a particular expression of the principle of proportionality in cases involving risk management.[246] The assessment of the economic ramifications of the decision to withdraw made by various national bodies under the terms of the regulation's procedure for adoption nonetheless satisfied this requirement of the principle of proportionality.[247] Such analysis should be carried out prior to adopting the preventive measure. It follows that EC institutions are left with a large degree of discretion relating to the means of assessing the economic costs entailed by implementing the relevant measure. In this respect, it should be pointed out that the different commitments of the EC institutions offer substantial leeway.

The court's requirement that the costs and benefits of a preventive measure be assessed gives rise to numerous questions. It should be apparent that, in contrast with US law, this requirement is rarely stipulated in Community legislation.[248] This obligation is, moreover, subject to lively criticism in American academic writing to the extent that it ignores so-called 'incommensurables' – that is, values which cannot be expressed in financial terms. In fact, while it is possible to calculate with precision the financial losses that result from the application of a precautionary measure, the financial benefits from protecting human health flowing from the application of the precautionary measure are more difficult to evaluate.[249] What price is to be put on human life?

Although it would appear useful for the public authorities to formulate prior to regulation an idea of the economic impact of their measures, the requirement that they undertake a detailed economic evaluation of the costs and benefits of the measure would also appear to be open to criticism. Applied to the letter, such a requirement would risk leading to a complete paralysis of normative action on risk management, as has happened in the US. The CFI's concession that the assessments carried out by the Danish and Swedish organs were satisfactory did not, in fact, appear to be applying the obligation derived from the proportionality principle in an excessively strict manner.

Nevertheless, the precautionary principle cannot legitimate a regulatory measure enacted on the grounds that the technology needs to be prohibited owing to the lack of technological needs In its judgment *Commission* v *Denmark,* the court condemned the Danish prohibition measure as disproportionate on the grounds that 'the criterion of the absence of the nutritional need of the population of a member state cannot, by itself, justify a total prohibition, on the basis of Article 30 EC, of the marketing of foodstuffs lawfully manufactured and/or marketed in other member states'.[250] Indeed:

> ... *the systematic prohibition under the Danish administrative practice on the marketing of enriched products which do not meet a nutritional need of the population does not enable Community law to be observed in regard to the identification and assessment of a real risk to public health, which requires a detailed assessment, case by case, of the effects which the addition of the minerals and vitamins in question could entail.*[251]

CONCLUSIONS

Precaution is testament to a new relationship with science where it is consulted less for the knowledge that it has to offer than for the doubts and concerns that it is in a position to raise. Confining scientific expertise to an ivory tower serves no purpose. On the contrary, the precautionary principle calls for bringing scientific expertise and the decision-making process closer to one another.

However, the precautionary principle did not take root in virgin soil: of necessity, it existed alongside other norms of the same type in the EC Treaty.

The principle first emerged in the environmental sphere and was later transposed into the area of public health, being enshrined in framework acts and applied widely by European courts. Needless to say, the two spheres, while related, are far from being similar. Interestingly enough, despite the fact that the principle is hitherto only included in the title on the protection of the environment, EC law-makers have been proclaiming it more widely in health protection acts (regulation on food law), rather than in environmental acts (e.g. the Registration, Evaluation and Authorization of Chemicals, or REACH, proposal does not encapsulate the principle).

It is worth making one further point here. While most of the authors have been focusing, in the wake of the WTO Appellate Body hormones case, on the recent case law relating to health protection, few have been dealing with the key role of the principle in the environmental sphere. Nonetheless, the differences between those two areas are striking. On the one hand, the principle has been construed by courts in the field of health protection (and, in particular, food safety) with a view to avoiding unduly restrictive practices. Indeed, the cases commented above mostly deal with measures regulating or prohibiting products (such as food additives, sun creams and chemicals) that have the aim of safeguarding public health. The European courts review those measures in an attempt to prevent EC or national authorities from hindering the free movement of goods. On the other hand, the courts endorse another approach while addressing the genuine environmental cases (e.g. wildlife protection and waste management). In this context, the principle of precaution supports broader interpretation of environmental obligations.

All in all, it is doubtful whether the lessons from the case law relating to health safety, particularly with respect to the obligation to carry out risk assessments, are really relevant in the resolution of all environmental cases.

NOTES

1   Research related to the issues dealt with in this chapter has also been funded by the Belgian Interuniversity Action Programme on 'Loyalties of Knowledge'. I am indebted to Professor Serge Gutwirth for his constant support.
2   For the genesis and impact of this principle on the Community legal order, see my previous works on this topic: de Sadeleer, N. (1999) *Les Principes du Pollueur-Payeur, de Prévention et de Précaution*, Collection Universités Francophones, Bruylant-A.U.F, Brussels; de Sadeleer, N. (2002) *Environmental Principles: From Political Slogans to Legal Rules*, Oxford University Press, Oxford.
3   For discussion on the precautionary principle at EU level, see Corcelle, G. (2001) 'La perspective communautaire du principe de précaution' *Revue du Marché commun*, vol 450, p447; Scott, J. and Vos, E. (2002) 'The juridification of uncertainty: Observations of the ambivalence of the precautionary principle within the EU and the WTO', in Joerges, C. and Dehousse, M. (eds) *Good Governance in Europe's Integrated Market*, Oxford University Press, Oxford, p25; Alemanno, A. (2001) 'Le principe de précaution en droit communautaire. Stratégie de gestion ou risque d'atteinte au marché intérieur', *Revue du droit de l'Union Européenne*, p917; Douma, W. T. (2002) *The Precautionary Principle: Its Application in International, European and Dutch Law*, PhD thesis, Groeningen University, The Netherlands.
4   Vigorous debate ensued – for instance, as to the extent to which the EU was more precautionary than the US. See, for example, Wiener, J. B. and Rogers, M. D. (2002) 'Comparing precaution in the United States and Europe', *Journal of Risk Research*, vol 5, no 4, pp320–321; Vogel, D. (2003) 'The politics of risk regulation in Europe and the United States', *Yearbook of European Environmental Law*, vol 3, pp31–42. See also the chapters of Kramer, L., Wiener, J. and Christoforou, T. on the roots of divergence between the US and the EU in Vig, N. and Faure M. (eds) (2004) *Green Giants?*, MIT, Boston, pp15–110.

5   For the genesis and impact of this principle on the Community legal order, see de Sadeleer, N. (2002) *Environmental Principles: From Political Slogans to Legal Rules*, Oxford University Press, Oxford.

6   Particular attention shall be paid to the decisions handed down on 11 September 2002 in the Cases T-70/99, *Alpharma* v *Council* and T-13/99 *Pfitzer Animal Health* v *Council* (Case T-13/99, *Pfizer Animal Health* v *Council* [2002] ECR II-3305), as well as the judgment of 26 November 2002 in the combined Case T-74/00, *Artegodan* v *Commission* (Joined Cases T-74/00, T-76/00, T-83/00, T-84/00, T-85/00, T-132/00, T-137/00 and T-141/00, *Artegodan GMbH* and *Others* v *Commission* [2002] II-ECR 4945). These cases have one point in common: each involved a challenge to the decision of a Community institution to withdraw medicines and food additives in the name of protection of health. For a commentary on the *Alpharma* and *Pfitzer* judgments, see Gonzalez Vaqué, L. (2002) 'El Principio de Precaución en la jurisprudencia comunitaria: La sentencia Virginiamicino' (Asunto T-13/99), *Revista de Derecho Comunitario Europea*, vol 13, pp925–942; Romero Melchior, S. (2003) 'La sentencia "Artegodan del Tribunal de Primera Instancia": El principio de precaución de nuevo en cuestió n', *Gaceta Jurídica de la Unión Europea*, vol 233, pp42–58; de Sadeleer, N. (2003) 'Le principe de précaution: Un nouveau principe général de droit communautaire', *Journal des Tribunaux de Droit Européen*, vol 99, pp129–134; MacMaolain, C. (2003) 'Using the precautionary principle to protect human health', *European Law Review*, vol 28, p723; Segnana, O. (2002) 'The precautionary principle: New developments in the case law of the Court of First Instance', *German Law Journal*, vol 3, no 10, pp11–12; Scott, J. (2004) 'The precautionary principle before the European courts', in Macrory, R. (ed) *Principles of European Environmental Law*, Europa Law Pub, Groeningen, pp 51–74; Ladeur, K.-H. (2003) 'The introduction of the precautionary principle into EU law: A Pyrrhic victory for environmental and public health law? Decision-making under conditions of complexity in multi-level political systems', *Common Market Law Review*, vol 40, no 6, p1455.

7   With regard to the various judgments handed down by the ECJ, it is in this context important to mention *Monsanto Agricoltura Italia*, ruled on 9 September 2003 (Case C-236/01), and *Commission* v *Denmark*, decided on 23 September 2003 (Case C-192/01). The first case relates to the qualification of a novel food and the prohibition of using certain food additives. For a commentary on the *Monsanto* judgment, see Dabrowska, P. (2004) 'Risk, precaution and the internal market: Who won the day in the recent Monsanto judgment?', *German Law Journal*, vol 2, pp1–10.

8   Communication from the Commission on the Precautionary Principle (COM (2000) 1), para 2.

9   Case T-13/99, *Pfizer*, para 119. However, the CFI did not review the conformity of the decision to ban virgianamicyn with the guidelines laid down in the communication of the European Commission on the grounds that the document was published after the measure at issue was adopted (para 122).

10 In contrast to other environmental acts where the principle is proclaimed exclusively in the preambles, the operative provisions of several acts dealing with GMOs encapsulate the principle (e.g. Directive 2001/18 on the deliberate release of GMOs). As to the recognition of the principle in the field of GMOs, see Christoforou, T. (2004) 'The regulation of GMOs in the EU: The interplay of science, law and politics', *Common Market Law Review*, vol 41, pp637–709.

11 This is particularly the case for food safety. See Schlacke, G. (1997) 'Foodstuffs law and the precautionary principle: Normative bases, secondary law and institutional tendencies' in Joerges, C., Ladeur, K.-H. and Vos, E. (eds) *Integrating Expertise into Regulatory Decision-Making*, Nomos, Baden-Baden, p169; Streinz, R. (1998) 'The precautionary principle in food law', *European Food Law Review*, vol 8, no 4, pp413–432; Gonzalez Vaqué, L., Ehring, L. and Jacquet, C. (1999) 'Le principe de précaution dans la législation communautaire et nationale relative à

la protection de la santé', *Review du Marché Unique et de l'Union Européenne*, vol 1, pp79–128. See, in particular, Regulation (EC) No 178/2002 laying down the general principles and requirements of food law, establishing the European Food Authority, and laying down procedures in matters of food (EC regulation on food law), which enshrines the precautionary principle in relation to its application in food law. Although the principle is regularly referred to in the recitals of the preambles of waste, water, air, wildlife, listed installations, environmental impact assessment, and chemicals directives and regulations, it is not mentioned in the operative provisions of those acts (e.g. recital 11 of the preamble of Directive 2000/60/EC Water Framework Directive).

12 Case C-157/96, *National Farmers' Union* (1998) ECR I-2211, para 63; Case C-180/96, *United Kingdom* v *Commission* (1998) ECR I-2265, para 99; and Case C-236/01, *Monsanto Agricoltura Italia*, para 111. See also Case T-13/99, *Pfizer*, para 139.

13 Although the principle is nowhere explicitly mentioned, the following judgments are thoroughly infused with the language of precaution: Case C-331/88, *Fedesa* (1990) ECR I-4023, para 9; Case C-180/96 R, *United Kingdom* v *Commission* (1996) ECR I-3903, para 73–78; Case T-76/96 R, *National Farmers' Union (NFU)* (1996) ECR II-815, paras 82–93, in particular para 89; Case C-352/98 P, *Bergaderm* (2000) ECR I-5291, para 53. See also Case T-177/02, *Malagutti-Vezinhet* v *Commission* (2004) ECR II-827, para 54.

14 See the various cases commented on below.

15 This view is shared by the EC institutions (Commission on the Precautionary Principle (COM (2000) 1), para 10; Council Resolution on the Precautionary Principle, 1).

16 Joined Cases T-74/00, T-76/00, T-83/00 to T-85/00, T-132/00, T-137/00 and T-141/00, *Artegodan*, para 183.

17 *Artegodan*, para 184. See also Case T-147/00, *Laboratoire Sévrier* v *Commission*, ECR II-85, para 52; Case T-392/02, *Solvay Pharmaceuticals*, para 121.

18 *Artegodan*, para 184.

19 While the ECJ has, in practice, endorsed a precautionary approach in the area of public health, it has abstained from referring explicitly to that principle, other than with regard to environmental protection case (e.g. nature conservation and waste management cases).

20 Scott, J. (2004) 'The precautionary principle before the European courts', in Macrory, R. (ed) *Principles of European Environmental Law*, Europa Law Pub, Groeningen, p54.

21 Trouwbost, A. (2001) *Evolution and Status of the Precautionary Principle in International Law*, Kluwer Law International, London.

22 In the *Peralta* case, the ECJ judged that former Article 130R 'confines itself to defining the general objectives of the Community in environmental matters. The responsibility for deciding upon the action to be taken is entrusted to the Council by Article 130S (new Article 174).' That case concerned a preliminary question relating to criminal offences. No EC secondary legislation concerning the environment was being directly considered since the Italian legislation transposed an international convention to which the EC was not party. In this case, the ECJ ruled that Article 130R did not contravene the Italian legislation being considered (Case C-379/92, *Peralta* [1994] ECR I-3453, para 58).

23 For example, Commission on the Precautionary Principle (COM (2000) 1), para 10. In its Resolution on the Precautionary Principle, the council takes the view that the principle applies both at the level of the EC institutions and at that of member states (Council Resolution on the Precautionary Principle, 1).

24 Dhondt, N. (2000) 'Environmental law principles and the case law of the Court of Justice', in Sheridan, M. and Lavrysen, L. (eds) *Environmental Law Principles*, Bruylant, Brussels, pp141–155.

25 In *Waddenzee*, the ECJ assessed the validity of a Dutch project in the light of the EC precautionary principle (Case C-127/02, *Waddenzee*). Remarkably enough, that judgment signifi-

cantly departs from earlier judgments of the Dutch Council of State, which refused to take into consideration the principle of precaution on the ground that it was not codified in the Dutch environmental legislation (12 May 2000, No E03.96.0068 AB 2000/395).

26 Scott, J. (2004) 'The precautionary principle before the European courts', in Macrory, R. (ed) *Principles of European Environmental Law*, Europa Law Pub, Groeningen, p54.
27 Case 174/82, *Sandoz* (1983) ECR 2445, para 18.
28 Opinion of the Advocate General Jean Mischo, para 82.
29 Case C-6/99, *Greenpeace France* v *Ministère des Affaires Etrangères* (2000) ECR I-5681; Case C-473/98, *Kemikalieinspektionen* v *Toolex Alpha AB* (2000) ECR I-1676 , paras 46 and 47.
30 Opinion of the Advocate General M.L.A. Geelhoed delivered on 13 December 2001, in Case C-121/00, *Walter Hahn*, para 51.
31 Opinion of the Advocate General Jean Mischo delivered on 12 December 2002, in Case C-6/99, *Greenpeace France* v *Ministère des Affaires Étrangères*, para 202.
32 Biondi, A. et al. (2003) *Scientific Evidence in European Environmental Rule-Making*, Kluwer Law International, The Hague, London and Boston.
33 Classifying protected areas under EC Birds and Habitats Directive is underpinned by scientific analysis of the ecological requirements of species and their habitats. See de Sadeleer, N. (2005) 'Habitats conservation in EC law: From nature sanctuaries to ecological networks', *Yearbook of European Environmental Law*, vol 5, pp215–252.
34 Where a member state wants to apply a higher standard of protection to a protected species that could hinder the free movement of goods, the assessment to be made of the proportionality of the prohibition of trade at issue 'cannot be performed ... without additional information, and that such an assessment requires a specific analysis on the basis of scientific studies and of the factual circumstances of the main proceedings'. Case C-510/99, *Xavier Tridon* (2001) ECR I-7777, para 58.
35 For instance, where a national authority of dispatch opposes the shipment of hazardous wastes on the grounds that its national waste recovery standards are higher than the standards of the importing member state, that authority must measure the risks 'not by the yardstick of general considerations, but on the basis of relevant scientific research' (Case C-277/02, *EU Wood Trading*, para 50).
36 Kasperson, J. X. and Kasperson, R. E. (eds) (2001) *Global Environmental Risk*, Earthscan, London.
37 Case C-127/02, *Waddenzee*, para 44.
38 Doyle, A. and Carney, T. (1999) 'Precaution and prevention: Giving effect to Article 130r without direct effect', *European Environmental Law Review*, vol 8, p44.
39 de Sadeleer, N. (2002) *Environmental Principles: From Political Slogans to Legal Rules*, Oxford University Press, Oxford, pp119–124.
40 Case C-293/97, *Standley* (1999) ECR I-2603, para 54.
41 Case C-67/97, *Bluhme* (1998) ECR I-8053, para 33.
42 Case C-302/86, *Commission* v *Denmark* (1989) ECR I-4607, para 9.
43 Case C-293/97, *Standley* (1998) ECR I-2603, para 54.
44 Case C-379/98, *Preussen Elektra* (2001) ECR I-2159, para 54.
45 That said, in some judgments, it is difficult to draw the line between the issue of the protection of health and ecological issues. See Case C-379/98, *Preussen Elektra*, para 54; Case C-293/97, *Standley*, para 56.
46 de Sadeleer, N. (2002) *Environmental Principles: From Political Slogans to Legal Rules*, Oxford University Press, Oxford, pp289–291.
47 Case C-6/99, *Greenpeace* v *France*.
48 Cases C-418/97 and C-419/97, *ARCO Chemie Nederland* (2000) ECR I-4512, para 39; Case C-9/00, *Palin Granit Oy* (2002) ECR I-3533, para 23; and Case C-1/03, *Paul Van de Walle*, para 45.
49 Case C-405/92, *Armand Mondiet* (1993) ECR I-6176.

50 Advocate General Gulmann concurred with the commission's argument that 'it is sometimes necessary to adopt measures as a precaution'. In order to conserve tuna stocks, for which insufficient scientific data existed, total allowable catch (TAC) had been based on that principle (Opinion of Advocate General M. Gulmann [1993] ECR I-6159, para 28).

51 Case C-405/92, *Armand Mondiet*, paras 31 to 36.

52 Case C-435/93, *Association pour la Protection des Animaux Sauvages et Préfet de Maine-et-Loire et Préfet de La Loire-Atlantique* (1994) ECR I-67, para 21.

53 Case C-67/97, *Bluhme*.

54 For a description of this procedure, see de Sadeleer, N. (2005) 'Habitats conservation in EC law: From nature sanctuaries to ecological networks', *Yearbook of European Environmental Law*, vol 5, pp215–252.

55 Case C-127/02, *Waddenzee*, para 44. See Chapter 15 in this volume.

56 Case C-127/02, *Waddenzee*, para 57.

57 Case C-127/02, *Waddenzee*, para 58.

58 Case C-127/02, *Waddenzee*, para 58.

59 See also the opinion of Advocate General Kokott in *Waddenzee*, paras 99–111.

60 See Verschuuren, J. (2005) 'Shellfish for fishermen or for birds? Article 6 Habitats Directive and the precautionary principle', *Journal of Environmental Law*, vol 17, pp265–283.

61 Albeit their importance from a sociological point of view, the issue of risk communication will not be addressed in this chapter, although it will emphasize the need to foster communication between risk assessors and risk managers.

62 On the topic of risk assessment and risk management, see Noiville, C. and de Sadeleer, N. (2001) 'La gestion des risques écologiques et sanitaires à l'épreuve des chiffres. Le droit entre enjeux scientifiques et politiques', *Revue du Droit de l'Union Européenne*, vol 2, pp389–449. On risk analysis in EC law, see Christoforou, T. (2002) 'Science, law and precaution in dispute resolution on health and environmental protection: What role for scientific experts?' in *Le Commerce International des OGM*, Paris, pp213–283.

63 US National Research Council (1983) *Risk Assessment in the Federal Government: Managing the Process*, US National Research Council, Washington, DC, p13.

64 For example, recital 19 of the preamble and Article 3(12) of Regulation (EC) Regulation No 78/2002 on food law emphasize 'other legitimate factors'. By the same token, Regulation (EC) 1829/2003 on GM food and feed provides that as risk assessments cannot provide all the information on which a risk management decision should be based, 'other legitimate factors relevant to the matter under consideration' may be taken into account (Article 6(6)). Likewise, the ECJ and the CFI have explicitly upheld the right to balance different factors in a number of cases (Case C-180/96 R, *United Kingdom* v *Commission* [1996] ECR I-3903, the judgment in that case (Case C-180/96 [1998] ECR I-2265); Case T-199/96, *Bergaderm and Goupil* v *Commission* [1998] ECR II-2805; Cases T-344 and T-345/00, *CEVA Santé Animale et Pharmacia Enterprises* v *Commission*, judgment of 26 February 2003, para 66). As far as WTO law is concerned, attention to 'other legitimate factors', such as taking into account the real use of the product, is deemed to be admissible (AB, *European Communities: Measures Affecting the Prohibition of Asbestos and Asbestos Products* (WT/ D135/AB/R) paras 162 and 174).

65 In this respect, following the example of the Cartagena Protocol on Biosafety (Articles 15 and 16), the EC Regulation (EC)178/2002 on food law distinguishes, in particular, between assessment that 'shall be based on the available scientific evidence and undertaken in an independent, objective and transparent manner' (Article 6(2)) and management that must bear in mind the risk evaluation, 'other factors legitimate to the matter under consideration' and the precautionary principle (Article 6(3)).

66 Opinion of the Advocate General M. Jean Mischo, delivered 12 December 2002 in Case C-192/01, *Commission* v *Denmark*, para 92.

67   This distinction was rejected by the Appellate Body of the WTO as not being inherent in the SPS Agreement (*EC Measures Concerning Meat and Meat Products (Hormones)* 16 January 1998 (WT/DS26/AB/R)). Indeed, SPS Article 5 encompasses both risk assessment (paras 1 and 2) and risk management issues (paras 4 to 6). For a critique of the premises underpinning the distinction between risk assessment and risk management, see de Sadeleer, N. (2002) *Environmental Principles: From Political Slogans to Legal Rules*, Oxford University Press, Oxford , pp184–186.

68   See, for instance, the positions defended by the EC Commission in its *Communication on the Precautionary Principle* and by the Scientific Steering Committee's Working Group on Harmonization of Risk Assessment Procedures in the Scientific Committees, advising the European Commission in the area of human and environmental health (*First Report on the Harmonization of Risk Assessment Procedures*, 2000).

69   Indeed, the communication highlights the commission's belief that precaution is chiefly a question of the political business of deciding how safe is safe: 'The precautionary principle is particularly relevant to the management of risk. The principle, which is essentially used by decision-makers in the management of risks, should not be confused with the element of caution that scientists apply in their assessment of scientific data' (summary, para 4).

70   Case C-236/01, *Monsanto,* para 133.

71   de Sadeleer, N. (2002) *Environmental Principles: From Political Slogans to Legal Rules*, Oxford University Press, Oxford, pp179–195.

72   van Swaneberg, P. and Stirling, A. (2003) 'Risk and precaution in the US and Europe', *Yearbook of European Environmental Law,* vol 3, p49.

73   de Sadeleer, N. (2002) *Environmental Principles: From Political Slogans to Legal Rules*, Oxford University Press, Oxford , pp158–159.

74   Although there may be uncertainty concerning the assessment of the impact of alcoholic beverage advertisements in Norway, 'such uncertainty does not arise in a domain which would allow for the invocation of the precautionary principle as developed in the case law' of the ECJ, CFI and EFTA Court (Case E-4/4, *Pedicel,* judgment of 25 February 2005).

75   Case T-13/99, *Pfizer,* para 143; see also case C-236/01, *Monsanto Agricoltura,* para 106; Case C-192/01, *Commission* v *Denmark,* para 49; Case C-41/02, *Commission* v *Netherlands,* para 52; Case T-392/02, *Solvay Pharmaceuticals,* para 129; Case E-3/00, *EFTA Surveillance Authority* v *Norway* (2000–2001) EFTA Ct Rep 73, para 29. In this last case, the Norwegian Food Control Authority rejected the application of a Danish company for authorization to sell 'fortified' cornflakes in Norway on the grounds that the addition of nutrients – which might entail allergy risks for some consumers – is only justified if there is an unmet nutritional need among the Norwegian population at large. According to the EFTA Court, a proper application of the precautionary principle presupposes, first, an identification of potentially negative health consequences arising from an additive and, second, a comprehensive evaluation of the risk to health based on the most recent scientific information (paras 16 and 21).

76   Case T-13/99, *Pfizer,* para 146.

77   *European Communities – DS 26 Measures Concerning Meat and Meat Products (Hormones),* Appellate Body, Doc WT/DS 26 and 48/AB/R (16 January 1998), para 186; *Australia – DS 21 Measures Concerning the Importation of Salmonids,* Appellate Body, Doc WT/DS18/AB/R (20 October 1998), para 129.

78   Case T-13/99, *Pfizer,* para 149.

79   Case T-13/99, *Pfizer,* para 151. On this point, see Case C-473/98, *Toolex* (2000) ECR I-5681, para 45.

80   Joined Cases T-74/00, T-76/00, T-83/00 to T-85/00, T-132/00, T-137/00 and T-141/00, *Artegodan,* para 186; Case T-392/02, *Solvay Pharmaceuticals,* para 125.

81   Case 174/82, *Sandoz* (1983) ECR 2445, para 16; Case C-192/01, *Commission* v *Denmark* (2003) ECR I-9693, para 42; and Case C-24/00, *Commission* v *France* (2004) ECR II-1277, para 49.

82   van Swaneberg, P. and Stirling, A. (2003) 'Risk and precaution in the US and Europe', *Yearbook of European Environmental Law*, vol 3, p52.
83   In the same vein, T. Christoforou takes the view that when science does not provide a definitive answer as to which data, models and assumptions should be used in the risk assessment, it is the task of the risk managers to provide risk assessors with guidance on the science policy to apply in such assessments. See Christoforou, T. (2002) 'The origins, content and role of the precautionary principle in EC law' in *Le Principe de Précaution: Aspects de Droit International et Communautaire*, Panthéon Assas, Paris, p212.
84   By contrast, in the US system, statutory formulations of the required level of safety are common and, in many cases, quantified.
85   Case C-236/01, *Monsanto Agricoltura Italia*, para 113.
86   Case C-236/01, *Monsanto Agricoltura Italia*, para 114. In particular, the court went one step further by not endorsing a literal interpretation of the safeguard clause laid down in the novel food regulation. Strictly speaking, that safeguard clause did not entail 'a risk assessment which is as complete as possible' of the risks at stake. Such requirement mirrors judicial activism where the court substitutes itself for the law-maker. In addition, with regard to scientific proof, the court appears to have been much more demanding in the *Monsanto Agricoltura Italia* case than in the previous *Greenpeace* case (Case C-6/99, *Greenpeace France* v *Ministère des Affaires Etrangères* [2000] ECR I-1676). Indeed, in the previous *Greenpeace* case, the court expressed the view that member states could enact precautionary measures in the light of the precautionary principle, relying on 'new informations' as to the extent of the risk to human health and the environment.
87   Case C-192/01, *Commission* v *Denmark*, para 47.
88   Case E-3/00, *EFTA Surveillance Authority* v *Norway*, para 30; Case C-236/01, *Monsanto Agricoltura Italia*, para 113; and Case C-192/01, *Commission* v *Denmark*, para 51.
89   Case T-13/99, *Pfizer*, paras 155–156.
90   Case C-192/01, *Commission* v *Denmark*, para 48.
91   Case E-3/00, *EFTA Surveillance Authority* v *Norway*.
92   WTO SPS Agreement, Article 5(1).
93   WTO TBT Agreement, Article 2(2).
94   Protocol on Biosafety, Article 10(1) and 15.
95   Directive 80/107/EEC on the protection of workers from the risk related to exposure to chemicals, physical and biological agents; Directive 89/391/EEC on the introduction of measures to encourage the improvements in the safety and health of workers at work; Directive 90/394/EEC on the protection of workers from the risks related to exposure to carcinogens at work.
96   Directive 89/107/EEC concerning food additives authorized for use in foodstuffs intended for human consumption, according to which the food additive must be subjected to appropriate testing and evaluation; Regulation 178/2002 of 28 January 2002 establishing the general principles of a general presumption against food legislation, instituting the European Food Safety Authority and fixing procedures relative to the safety of feeding stuffs (Articles 3.10 and 6.2).
97   According to Annex II(b) of the 1998 Rotterdam PIC Convention, regulatory action has to be taken 'as a consequence of a risk evaluation ... based on a review of scientific data'. See also Article 8(7) and Annex E of the 2001 Stockholm POPs Convention.
98   Directive 2000/60/EC establishing a framework for Community action in the field of water policy, Article 16(2).
99   See Chapter 20 in this volume.
100 Directive 2001/18/EC on the deliberate release of GMOs (Articles 2(8) and 4(1) and (2); Annexes II and III).

101 Directive 91/414/EEC concerning the placing of plant protection products on the market.
102 Directive 98/8/EC concerning the placing of biocides on the market.
103 One does find explicit references to risk assessment in the commission's communication of 2 February 2000 on the recourse to the precautionary principle.
104 Scott, J. (2004) 'The precautionary principle before the European courts', in Macrory, R. (ed) *Principles of European Environmental Law*, Europa Law Pub, Groeningen, p23.
105 Gonzalez Vaqué, L. (2002) 'El Principio de Precaución en la jurisprudencia comunitaria: La sentencia Virginiamicino' (Asunto T-13/99), *Revista de Derecho Comunitario Europea*, vol 13, p935.
106 On the contrary, risk assessment has become, by and large, an important component of US environmental law.
107 Among the conditions which EC environmental policy should take into account, Article 174(3) lists the criteria 'available scientific data'. As Krämer argues, there is 'any need to give scientific evidence that a specific measure would be effective... In particular, the precautionary/ prevention principle allows action without definitive scientific proof being available. This principle would lose much of its force if unequivocal data had to be produced before any measure could be taken.' See Krämer, L. (2003) *EC Environmental Law*, Thomson-Sweet and Maxwell, London, 5th edition, p27.
108 Environmental legal experts have the impression that risk assessment is frequently used to stop or slow down restrictions on the use of products or substances. See Krämer, L. (2000) 'Introduction into the EC Chemicals Regulation: Basic structures and performance' in Winter, G. (ed) *Risk Assessment and Risk Management of Toxic Chemicals*, Nomos, Baden Baden, p2023, and Krämer, L. (2003) *EC Environmental Law*, Thomson-Sweet and Maxwell, London, 5th edition, p22.
109 According to the WTO Appellate Body, there is no obligation to follow any particular methodology for conducting a risk assessment. In other words, members are not precluded from organizing their risk assessments along the lines of the disease or pest at issue. Furthermore, members are free to consider in their risk analysis multiple agents in relation to one disease. Appellate Body, *Japan: Measures Affecting the Importation of Apples*, WTO Doc WT/DS245/AB/R (23 November 2003), para 204.
110 Appellate Body, *EC – Hormones*, paras 184–186; *Australia – Salmon*, para 124.
111 While the panel required a risk assessment to establish a minimum magnitude of risk, the Appellate Body noted that imposition of such a quantitative requirement finds no basis in the SPS Agreement (Appellate Body, *EC – Hormones*, para 186). This was confirmed in a recent report of the panel (*European Communities – Measures Affecting the Prohibition of Asbestos and Asbestos Products* (WT/DS135), para 8.171) and the Appellate Body in the asbestos case (*European Communities – Measures Affecting the Prohibition of Asbestos and Asbestos Products*, WTO Doc WT/DS135/AB/R (12 March 2001), para 167) (hereinafter, Appellate Body, *EC-Asbestos*).
112 Case C-178/84, *Commission v Germany (Reinheitsgebot)* (1987) ECR 1227.
113 Case C-236/01, *Monsanto*, para 113.
114 Case C-192/01, *Commission v Denmark*, para 55.
115 In the *Hormones* case, the Appellate Body concluded that the risk assessment should have reviewed the carcinogenic potential, not of the relevant hormones in general, but of 'residues of those hormones found in meat derived from cattle to which the hormones had been administered for growth promotion purposes' (para 200). In *Japan: Measures Affecting the Importation of Apples*, the Appellate Body endorsed the same reasoning (para 199).
116 Ladeur, K.-H. (2003) 'The introduction of the precautionary principle into EU law: A Pyrrhic victory for environmental and public health law? Decision-making under conditions of complexity in multi-level political systems', *Common Market Law Review*, vol 40, no 6.

117   In particular, the CFI's case law stresses that the baseline against which the risks need to be assessed by the competent scientific body is 'the comparison between the most scientific representative scientific opinions with the scientific arguments' advanced by the undertakings'(Case T-27/98 *Nardone* v *Commission* [1999] ECR-SC I-A-267; ECR-SC II-1293, paras 30 and 88; *Artegodan*, para 200).

118   The European Commission has emphasized that 'even if scientific advice is supported only by a minority fraction for the scientific community, due account should be taken of their views, provided the credibility and reputation of this fraction are recognized'. See communication from the European Commission on the precautionary principle (COM (2000) 1), para 6.2.

119   Stirling, A. (1999) *On Science and Precaution in the Management of Technological Risk*, vol 1, EC Commission and IPTS, Seville, p7.

120   The importance of such a demand has been particularly apparent since the discussion on reducing CFC emissions into the stratosphere demonstrated that initial regulation had been delayed by certain scientific groups insisting on ever-greater certainty about the phenomenon of ozone layer destruction.

121   Appellate Body, *EC-Hormones*, para 194; *Asbestos*, para 178.

122   Appellate Body, *EC-Hormones*, para 186. In the *Australia-Salmon* case, the Appellate Body has stated that it will not be sufficient for governments to impose regulations simply on the basis of the 'theoretical' risk that underlies all scientific uncertainty (para 129). However, 'the scientific prudence displayed by the experts did not relate to the "theoretical uncertainty" that is inherent in the scientific method and which stems from the intrinsic limits of experiments, methodologies or instruments deployed by scientists to explain a given phenomenon' (*Japan: Measures Affecting the Importation of Apples*, para 241). However, the risk need not be 'ascertainable' in a scientific laboratory operating under strictly controlled conditions; actual potential for adverse effects on human health in the real world where people 'live, work and die' must also be taken into account. Appellate Body, *EC-Hormones*, para 187.

123   Christoforou, T. (2004) 'The regulation of GMOs in the EU: The interplay of science, law and politics', *Common Market Law Review*, vol 41, p703.

124   A study carried out by the European Environmental Agency has been highlighting the fact that the discovery of several risks completely ignored was the result of experiments conducted for other purposes (such as CFCs depleting the ozone layer and endocrine disruptors). They came as a surprise born of ignorance. See EEA (2001) *Late Lessons from Early Warnings: The Precautionary Principle 1896–2000*, Environmental Issues Report No 22, Copenhagen, pp169–170.

125   McGarvin, M. (2001) 'Science, precaution, facts and values', in O'Riordan, T., Cameron, J. and Jordan, A. (eds) *Reinterpreting the Precautionary Principle*, Cameron and May, London, p42; EEA (2001) *Late Lessons from Early Warnings: The Precautionary Principle 1896–2000*, Environmental Issues Report No 22, Copenhagen, pp169–170.

126   Of particular note in this respect is the requirement pursuant to Directive 2001/42/EC on assessing the effects of certain plans and programmes on the environment to carry out monitoring of the significant environmental effects of the implementation of plans and programmes in order, among other things, to identify unforeseen adverse effects and to be able to undertake appropriate remedial action (Article 10(1)).

127   Ladeur, K.-H. (2003) 'The introduction of the precautionary principle into EU law: A Pyrrhic victory for environmental and public health law? Decision-making under conditions of complexity in multi-level political systems', *Common Market Law Review*, vol 40, no 6, p12.

128   Scott, J. (2004) 'The precautionary principle before the European courts', in Macrory, R. (ed) *Principles of European Environmental Law*, Europa Law Pub, Groeningen, pp67–72; Peel, C. (2006) 'Precautionary only in name? Tensions between precaution and risk assessment in the

Australian GMO regulatory framework', in Fisher, E., Jones, J. and von Schomberg, R. (eds) *The Precautionary Principle and Public Policy Decision Making*, Elgar Press, London, p200.

129 See Applegate J. (ed) (2004) *Environmental Risk*, vol 2, Ashgate, Darthmouth.

130 Winter, G. (ed) (2000) *Risk Assessment and Risk Management of Toxic Chemicals*, Nomos, Baden Baden.

131 Typical in this respect is Regulation (EC) 1829/2003 on GM food and feed recognizing that, in some cases, scientific risk assessments cannot provide all information on which a risk management decision should be based (recital 32 of the preamble).

132 According to the ECJ, in many cases, 'the assessment of those factors will demonstrate that there is a high degree of scientific and practical uncertainty in that regard' (Case C-192/01, *Commission* v *Denmark*, para 51).

133 O'Brien, M. (2000) *Making Better Environmental Decisions*, MIT Press, Cambridge, Massachusetts, p27; UK Royal Commission on Environmental Pollution (2003) *XXIVth Report on Chemicals in Products*, TSO, Norwich, p8, para 1.21.

134 A quantitative risk assessment exercised performed by 11 different teams in the EC came up with 11 different results that differed by a million-fold. See Contini, S., Amendola, A. and Ziomas, I. (1991) *Benchmark Exercise on Major Hazard Analysis*, European Commission Joint Research Center, Ispra. By the same token, different models for assessing carcinogenicity can result in cancer predictions that differ by a factor of 100 or more when extrapolated to low doses. See Shapiro, M. (1990) 'Toxic substances policy', in Portney, O. (ed) *Public Policies for Environmental Protection*, Resources for the Futures, Washington, DC, p218. Given 'the uncertainty inherent in assessing the public health risks posed by the use of food additives', the ECJ acknowledges the possibility of conducting legitimately different risk assessments yielding to different scientific evidence (Case C-3/00, *Commission* v *Denmark*, para 63).

135 The current system of assessing chemicals is 'overloaded because of the difficulty of applying a cumbersome and expensive testing and assessment regime to the very large number of chemicals already on the market'. See UK Royal Commission on Environmental Pollution (2003) *XXIVth Report on Chemicals in Products*, TSO, Norwich, p9. The European Commission has estimated that 11 years of testing the approximately 30,000 existing chemical substances would result in total costs of above 2.1 billions Euros – a burden that should be shared by the private sector (*Strategy for a Future Chemicals Policy*, para 3.4).

136 In particular, this ossification process has affected the EC chemicals policy. See Chapters 17, 18 and 19 in Part V of this book.

137 The methods of assessment may appear too targeted, disregarding risks that are hardly quantifiable, with assessments also turning out to be ineffective on the grounds of their unwieldiness and cost. Generally speaking, experts restrict themselves to an analysis of the direct effects of products to the detriment of their indirect effects. Thus, the impacts of exposure to chemical substances are only studied in isolation, with no consideration being given to additional effects (such as the accumulation of various substances in human tissue) or those caused by synergy (that is, the combined effects of several toxic substances on an organism). Some of these limitations are becoming increasingly embarrassing in the context of the growing importance of new environmental problems. Carcinogenic, mutagenic or other substances that are toxic for reproduction (e.g. endocrinal interrupters) and persistent organic pollutants (e.g. lindane) are on the increase, and their interaction can cause various deleterious effects. The precautionary principle encourages a marked improvement in scientific awareness of the combined risks that substances and products can cause. The experts should accordingly broaden the scope of their inquiries to take in direct, indirect, immediate, diffuse and cumulative effects, as well as those resulting from synergy. On this point, see the Communication from the Commission on the Precautionary Principle (COM (2000) 1), para 6.3.1.

138 That issue has already been stressed by the CFI in the *Pfizer* case (para 149). See the section on 'The role of the precautionary principle in risk analysis: Status quo' (p18).
139 'Reliance on rigid risk assessment approaches that fail to incorporate public values is likely to be a key factor in the loss of public confidence in the process.' See UK Royal Commission on Environmental Pollution (2003) *XXIVth Report on Chemicals in Products*, TSO, Norwich, p11. See also de Sadeleer, N. (2002) *Environmental Principles: From Political Slogans to Legal Rules*, Oxford University Press, Oxford, p195.
140 Christoforou, T. (2004) 'The precautionary principle, risk assessment, and the comparative role of science in the European Community and the US legal systems', in Vig, N. and Faure, M. (eds) *Green Giants?*, Boston, MIT, p35.
141 UK Royal Commission on Environmental Pollution (2003) *XXIVth Report on Chemicals in Products*, TSO, Norwich, p10, para 1.33.
142 Case C-192/01, *Commission v Denmark*, para 51.
143 Case C-180/96, *United Kingdom v Commission* (1996) ECR I-3903, para 99.
144 Case C-192/01, *Commission v Denmark*, para 52; see also Case E-3/00, *EFTA v Norway*, para 31. Endorsing the same line of reasoning, the CFI considered in *Alpharma* and *Pfizer* that 'the impossibility of carry[ing] out a full scientific risk assessment does not prevent the competent public authority from taking preventative measures, at very short notice, if necessary, where such measures appear essential given the level of risk to human health which the authority has deemed unacceptable for society' (Case T-13/99, *Pfizer*, para 393).
145 This approach is entirely consistent with the WTO Appellate Body's judgment in the *Hormones* case, where it rejected the inclusion of the word 'probability' in the panel's interpretation of the definition of risk assessment, considering that it introduced a quantitative dimension of the notion of risk and therefore implied a 'higher degree or a threshold of potentiality or possibility', whereas the word 'potential' in paragraph 4 of Annex A of the agreement only relates to the possibility of an event occurring (paras 183 to 184).
146 According to the EC Commission, the following factors are deemed to be relevant to trigger a precautionary measure: 'the absence of proof of the existence of a cause–effect relationship, a quantifiable dose–response relationship or a quantitative evaluation of the probability of the emergence of adverse effects following exposure'. See European Commission, Communication from the Commission on the Precautionary Principle (COM (2000) 1), para 6.2.
147 *Hormones*, para 62.
148 *Japan: Measures Affecting the Importation of Apples*, para 184.
149 Case C-236/01, *Monsanto*, para 113; Case C-192/01, *Commission v Denmark*, para 51; Case T-13/99, *Pfizer*, paras 196 to 197. Under the Article 5(7) SPS safeguard clause, which mirrors precaution, the measure adopted provisionally must be based on the available pertinent information, including that from the relevant international organizations, as well as from SPS measures applied by other members.
150 Case T-13/99, *Pfizer*, paragraph 162.
151 Case T-74/00, *Artegodan* para 192.
152 Case C-192/01, *Commission v Denmark*, para 48; Case C-514/99, *Commission v France*, para 55; and Case C-41/02, *Commission v Netherlands*, para 48.
153 Case T-13/99, *Pfizer*, paras 300 to 310. In the case law on food additives, the ECJ has been stressing that member states should rely on the results of international scientific research and, in particular, on the work of the Community's Scientific Committee on Food. Another case in point is *Toolex*, where the ECJ highlighted that evidence has been gathered by the International Cancer Research Agency, set up by the WHO, of the risk of cancer from using the substance trichloroethylene. Likewise, national epidemiological studies are also relevant to substantiate the risk (Case C-473/98, *Kemikalieinspektionen*, para 43).

154 However, in the *Pfizer* and *Alpharma* cases, the CFI did not refer to the opinion provided by the EC scientific body.

155 With respect to the procedure provided under Article 95(4)EC allowing a member state to maintain its already existing national legislation departing from subsequent EC harmonization standards, the ECJ acknowledges that in order to justify national measures derogating from an EC rule, the member state may 'put forward the fact that its assessment of the risk to public health is different from that made by the Community legislature. In the light of the uncertainty inherent in assessing public health risks ... divergent assessments of those risks can legitimately be made without necessarily being based on new and different scientific evidence'. See Case C-3/00, *Commission* v *Denmark*, para 63. See Wennerås, P. (2003) 'Fog and acid rain drifting from Luxembourg over Article 95(4)', *European Environmental Law Review*, pp169–178. By the same token, in *Pfizer*, the CFI acknowledged that the EC institutions could pay heed to different member states' reports, rather than exclusively to the opinion of the appointed scientific body (para 308).

156 In *Reinheitsgebot*, the ECJ emphasized the importance of a country's eating habits to specific risk to human health. Case 178/84, *Commission* v *Germany* (*Reinheitsgebot*) (1987) ECR 1227. In the same line, in Case C-192/01, the ECJ took the view that 'the criterion of the nutritional need of the population of a member state could play a role in a detailed risk assessment' (para 54).

157 In *Pfizer*, the CFI concluded 'that a preventative measure may be taken only if the risk, although the reality and extent thereof have not been "fully" demonstrated by conclusive scientific evidence, appears nevertheless to be adequately backed up by the scientific data available at the time when the measure was taken' (para 145).

158 Case C-41/02, *Commission* v *Netherlands*, para 49; Case C-473/98, *Kemikalieinspektionen*, para 45. Likewise, authorities deciding the placing on the market of GMOs are called upon to update their findings in the light of the latest scientific research to be provided by independent scientific advice (Directive 2001/18/EC, Appendix II, B, indent 4).

159 Case C-236/01, *Monsanto*, para 113; Case C-192/01, *Commission* v *Denmark*, para 51; Cases C-154/04 and Case C-155/05, *Alliance for Natural Health*, 12 July 2005, not yet reported, para 53.

160 In *Artegodan*, the CFI stressed that the withdrawal of a marketing authorization of a medicinal product must, in principle, be regarded as justified only where a 'new potential risk' is substantiated by 'new ... medical data or information' (para 194). Although they were based on a consensus in the medical community, the changes brought to the appreciation of one of the scientific criterion as to how to classify the risks of a medicinal product did not fulfil that condition (para 211).

161 Of particular importance is the new evidence gathered by member states' authorities while assessing requests to depart from EC internal market rules in accordance with Article 95 (5) EC. Failure to deliver new scientific evidence that was not already considered at the time of the adoption of the relevant EC threshold is bound to lead to a rejection of the derogation request. See Scott, J. and Vos, E. (2002) 'The juridification of uncertainty: Observations of the ambivalence of the precautionary principle within the EU and the WTO', in Joerges, C. and Dehousse, M. (eds) *Good Governance in Europe's Integrated Market*, Oxford University Press, Oxford, p 256. On the contrary, a request for maintaining more stringent national measures pursuant to Article 95(4) EC does not require new scientific evidence (Case C-3/00, *Commission* v *Denmark*, para 62).

162 In that respect, see the line of reasoning of Advocate General Poiares Maduro in Case C-41/02, *Commission* v *Netherlands*, para 33. This is particularly the case in international law where the principle is invoked by claimants in cases dealing with marine pollution (*The Mox Plant* Case (*Ireland* v *United Kingdom*) Order of 3 December 2001 on Provisional Measures), dams (*Gabcikovo-Nagymaros* (*Hungary* v *Slovakia*), Judgment ICJ Rep [1997]) and fisheries

(*Southern Bluefin Tuna Cases* (*Australia* v *Japan; New Zealand* v *Japan*), Provisional measures, Order of 27 August 1999).

163 Scott, J. and Vos, E. (2002) 'The juridification of uncertainty: Observations of the ambivalence of the precautionary principle within the EU and the WTO', in Joerges, C. and Dehousse, M. (eds) *Good Governance in Europe's Integrated Market*, Oxford University Press, Oxford, p271.

164 Case T-13/99, *Pfizer*, paras 54–57.

165 In its opinion, the committee considered that the Danish study did not bring any new information to the subject.

166 Case T-13/99, *Pfizer*, para 298.

167 Case C-514/99, *Commission* v *France* (2000) ECR I-4705.

168 Case C-1/00, *Commission* v *France*, 13 December 2001, para 88.

169 Case C-473/98, *Toolex*, para 47.

170 Several scientists contended that classification owing to the hazards entailed by the use of the substance in question. Given that the EC committee was unable to reach agreement on an evaluation of that substance (Opinion of Advocate General Mischo, delivered on 21 March 2000, para 63), the Swedish government decided to ban the substance on the grounds that its use was endangering workers' health, and, consequently, endorsed a more stringent approach than the one contemplated at the EC level.

171 In a case concerning marketing approval for genetically modified maize, the ECJ took the view that the precautionary principle was already reflected in the of Directive 90/220/EEC on GMOs. One of the arguments made by the ECJ is that the precautionary principle was already reflected in the directive, *inter alia*, in the right of a member state to restrict provisionally or prohibit the use and/or sale on its territory of a GMO under the conditions set out in Article 16 (Case C-6/99, *Greenpeace France*, para 44). In line with the *Greenpeace France* judgment, the ECJ endorsed the view in *Monsanto* that 'the safeguard clause must be understood as giving specific expression to the precautionary principle' (Case C-236/01, *Monsanto*, para 110). For a discussion on the grounds of which a safeguard clause can be invoked by member state authorities, see de Sadeleer, N. (2003) 'Safeguard clauses under Article 95 of the EC Treaty', *Common Market Law Review*, vol 40, pp889–915.

172 In submitting a request with a view to maintaining more stringent product standards, a member state may base its application on its own assessment of the risk to public health (Case C-3/00, *Commission* v *Denmark*, paras 63 to 65).

173 As emphasized above, in the *Pfizer* judgment, the CFI placed emphasis upon the fact that it was 'for the Community institutions to determine the level of protection which they deem appropriate for society' (Case T-13/99, *Pfizer*, para 151). On this point, see also Case C-473/98, *Toolex*, para 45.

174 Case T-13/99, *Pfizer*, para 153.

175 Case C-192/01, *Commission* v *Denmark*, para 50; Case C-41/02, *Commission* v *Netherlands*, para 50; Case E-3/00, *EFTA* v *Norway*, para 29.

176 According to Bergkamp, 'where risk assessors cannot provide the desired information, or can provide only relatively uncertain or ambiguous information, they should make that clear'. See Bergkamp, L. (2003) *European Community Law for a New Economy*, Intersentia, Antwerp, p511.

177 By way of illustration, Regulation (EC) 1829/2003 on GM food and feed acknowledges the need to take into account other legitimate factors at the level of risk management.

178 According to the EC Commission, 'the reliance on the precautionary principle is no excuse for derogating from the general principles of risk management' (Section 6.3, para 2 of the *Communication on the Precautionary Principle*).

179 Reviewing the validity of Directive 92/41 modifying Directive 89/622/EEC concerning the labelling of tobacco products, the ECJ held that the recitals in the preamble set out clearly

the scientific reasons why a measure prohibiting the marketing of tobacco products for oral use had to be introduced (Case C-210/03, *Swedish Match AB*, 14 December 2004, para 65).

180 Indeed, the institutions are not empowered to entrust a purely advisory body with the duty to perform the risk assessment. Case T-13/99, *Pfizer*, para 289.

181 The ECJ's decision in *Monsanto* requires that the identification of a health risk posed by a novel food should normally be carried out by 'specialized scientific bodies' charged with assessing the risks inherent in novel food (Case C-236/01, *Monsanto*, paras 78 to 79 and 84). See also Case T-13/99, *Pfizer*, para 157.

182 Case T-13/99, *Pfizer*, para 159. Those principles were applied to the Scientific Committee for Animal Nutrition (SCAN) (para 209) and to the standing committee. Whereas SCAN abided by those principles, the standing committee was not considered by the CFI as an independent scientific body in the light of the principle of transparency (para 287). Last, it should be stressed that those principles are enshrined in the (EC) regulation on food law.

183 Case T-13/99, *Pfizer*, para 201.

184 Case C-405/92, *Armand Mondiet*, paras 31 to 32; Case C-120/97, *Upjohn* (1999) ECR-I-223, para 47.

185 Case C-151/98 P, *Pharos* v *Commission* (1999) ECR I-8157, para 26; Case C-352/98 P, *Bergaderm and Goupil* v *Commission* (2000) ECR I-5291, para 66. When the EC Commission finds itself facing a situation of continuing scientific uncertainty characterized by divergences between the scientific opinions adopted by the different consultative organs, it does not appear unreasonable for the commission to await the adoption of a re-evaluation of the risks at stake. In such a situation, the commission does not disregard in a clear and serious manner the limits of its discretion. Case C-198/03P, *Commission* v *CEVA Santé Animale SA*, judgment of 12 July 2005, not yet reported, paras 82 to 89.

186 Case T-13/99, *Pfizer*, para 200.

187 Case T-74/00, *Artegodan*, paras 199 to 200.

188 Case T-74/00, *Artegodan*, para 200.

189 Case T-13/99, *Pfizer*, para 199.

190 Case C-3/00, *Commission* v *Denmark*, paras 109 to 115.

191 Case T-13/99, *Pfizer*, para 161.

192 Case T-13/99, *Pfizer*, paras 151 and 153.

193 Case C-174/82, *ECR Sandoz* (1983) 2445, para 16; Case C-42/90, *Bellon* (1990) ECR I-4863, para 11; Case C-400/96, *Harpegnies* (1998) ECR I-5121, para 33; and Case C-192/01, *Commission* v *Denmark*, para 42. See also Case E-4/4, *Pedicel*.

194 Case C-286/02, *Bellio F.lli Srl* v *Prefetura di Treviso* (2004) ECR I- 3465, para 58.

195 For instance, the level of protection set in Regulation 178/2002 on food law is set as high as it can be – that is, no risk. See Christoforou, T. (2004) 'The regulation of GMOs in the EU: The interplay of science, law and politics', *Common Market Law Review*, vol 41, p663.

196 Case C-180/96, *United Kingdom* v *Commission* (1996) ECR I-3903, paras 73 to 78.

197 Case C-286/02, *Bellio F.lli Srl* v *Prefetura di Treviso*.

198 A zero-tolerance approach for pharmacological substances for which no maximum toxicological levels can be fixed is provided for under Regulation No 2377/90 laying down maximum residue limits of veterinary medicinal products in foodstuffs of animal origin. See the critics of Hanekamp, J. C. Frapporti, G. and Olieman, K. (2003) 'Chloramphenicol, food safety and precautionary thinking in Europe', *Environmental Liability*, vol 6, p209.

199 See also Case T-392/02, *Solvay Pharmaceuticals*, para 130. Along the same lines, the EC Commission emphasizes in its *Communication on the Precautionary Principle* that 'the measures envisaged ... must not aim at zero risk, something which rarely exists' (para 6.3.1).

200 *Hormones supra*, para 187.

201 EFTA Case E-3/00, para 23.

202 Case 97/83, *Melkunie* (1984) ECR 2367, para 15.
203 Case C-121/00, *Walter Hahn*, 24 October 2002, para 31; Case T-392/02, *Solvay Pharmaceuticals*, para 150. The CFI highlighted that the 'concept of zero tolerance does not refer to purely hypothetical risk and cannot therefore be compared to the concept of zero risk'.
204 Case C-286/02, *Bellio F.lli Srl*, para 61.
205 Case C-331/88, *Fedesa* (1990) ECR I-4023.
206 Christoforou, T. (2004) 'The regulation of GMOs in the EU: The interplay of science, law and politics', *Common Market Law Review*, vol 41, p227.
207 Case T-13/99, *Pfizer*, para 145.
208 On the reasonableness of the obligation to ensure a higher level of environmental protection, see the court's Case C-284/95, *Safety Hi-Tech* (1998) ECR I-4301, para 49.
209 *NFU*, para 99.
210 Case T-74/00, *Artegodan*, para 184; Case T-392/02, *Solvay Pharmaceuticals*, para 121.
211 Case T-392/02, *Solvay Pharmaceuticals*, para 192.
212 Case T-13/99, *Pfizer*, para 444.
213 Case C-127/02, *Waddenzee*.
214 de Sadeleer, N. (2002) *Environmental Principles: From Political Slogans to Legal Rules*, Oxford University Press, Oxford, pp 268–275.
215 de Sadeleer, N. (2002) *Environmental Principles: From Political Slogans to Legal Rules*, Oxford University Press, Oxford, pp319–326.
216 Douma, W. T. (2001) 'Comments on the *Commission's Communication on the Precautionary Principle*' in *The Role of Precaution in Chemicals Policy*, Vienna School of International Studies, Vienna, p107. See also the reasoning of Advocate General Poiares Maduro in his opinion delivered on 14 September 2004 in Case C-41/02, *Commission v Netherlands*, para 30. According to the Advocate General, 'the discretion that member states are allowed with regard to recourse to the precautionary principle is increasingly restricted the further they depart from scientific analysis and the more they rely on policy judgment', particularly in the cases of lack of data on account of the novelty of the product or the lack of resources in conducting scientific research (para 33). The ECJ did not address that issue.
217 Given its complexity and the need to seek additional information, the EC Commission did not breach, in a serious way, Community law while assessing the risks entailed by the use of progesterone in giving rise to liability on the part of the Community. Case C-198/03P, *Commission v CEVA Santé Animale SA*, judgment of 12 July 2005, not yet reported, para 93.
218 Case C-405/92, *Mondiet* (1993) ECR I-6176, para 32; *United Kingdom v Commission*, cited above, para 97; Case C-120/97, *Upjohn* (1999) ECR I-223, para 34; Case C-341/95, *Gianni Bettati v Safety Hi-Tech Srl* (1998) ECR I-4055, paras 34 and 35; Case T-13/99, *Pfizer*, para 169; Case T-74/00, *Artegodan*, para 201; Case T-392/02, *Solvay Pharmaceuticals*, para 126.
219 Case C-331/88, *Fedesa* (1990) ECR I-4023, para 9; Case C-180/96, *United Kingdom v Commission* (1996) ECR I-3903, paras 99 and 100; Case C-127/95, *Norbrook Laboratories Ltd* (1998) ECR I-1531. See also Case 174/82, *Sandoz* (1983) ECR 2445, para 17. By way of illustration, in its judgment *Commission v Denmark*, the ECJ endorsed a similar approach ruling that 'discretion relating to the protection of public health is particularly wide where it is shown that uncertainties continue to exist in the current state of scientific research as to certain substances, such as vitamins, which are not as a general rule harmful in themselves but may have special harmful effects' (Case C-192/01, *Commission v Denmark*, para 47).
220 Case T-199/96, *Laboratoires pharmaceutiques Bergaderm S. A.* (1998) ECR II-2805, paras 66 and 67. In *Pfizer Animal Health v Council* and *Alpharma v Council*, the CFI noted that 'the legislature has a discretionary power which corresponds to the political responsibilities given to it by Article 34 of the EC Treaty and Article 43 of the Treaty. Consequently, the legality of a measure adopted in that sphere can be affected only if the measure is manifestly inappropriate, regard

being had to the objective which the competent institution is seeking to pursue' (para 412). The court concluded that the adoption of the regulation in question did not constitute a manifestly inappropriate measure for the achievement of the pursued objective.

221   Cases C-154/04 and C-155/05, *Alliance for Natural Health*, 12 July 2005, not yet reported, para 68.

222   Case T-13/99, *Pfizer*, para 169.

223   By the same token, the polluter pays principle, which is also enshrined in Article 174(2) EC Treaty, reflects the principle of proportionality (Case C-293/97, *Standley*, para 52).

224   de Sadeleer, N. (2002) *Environmental Principles: From Political Slogans to Legal Rules*, Oxford University Press, Oxford, pp 291–301.

225   Case C-174/82, *Sandoz*, para 18; Case C-42/90, *Bellon* (1990) ECR I-4863, para 14; *Harpegnies*, cited above, para 34; Case C-236/01, *Monsanto Agricoltura Italia*, para 107. In the field of proprietary medicinal products, *Generics (UK) and Others* (1998) ECR I-7967, para 66.

226   Case T-13/99 *Pfizer*, para 444.

227   Case T-13/99 *Pfizer*, para 459.

228   Case C-473/98, *Toolex Alpha AB*, para 47. The ECJ rejected the EC Commission's argument, according to which the desired objective could have been achieved through the imposition of limit values on exposure to the chemical substance trichloroethylene.

229   A three-pronged approach has been contemplated in *Fedesa* (Case C-331/88, *Fedesa* [1990] ECR I-4023). While the tripartite test has received some support in the opinions of Advocate General W. Van Gerven, in practice the ECJ does not distinguish between the second and third tests. See Tridimas, T. (1999) 'Proportionality in Community law: Searching for the appropriate standard of scrutiny' in Ellis, E. (ed) *The Principle of Proportionality*, Hart, Oxford, p66; de Sadeleer, N. (1999) 'Le principe de proportionnalité: Cheval de Troie du marché intérieur?', *Law and European Affairs*, vol 3–4, p 379.

230   Case T-13/99, *Pfizer*, para 456.

231   Case T-13/99, *Pfizer*, para 457.

232   In several cases, the ECJ confirmed that economic considerations do not take priority over non-economic concerns and, in particular, health concerns: Case C-180/96 R, *United Kingdom* v *Commission*, (1996) ECR I-3903, para 93; Case C-183/95, *Affish* (1997) ECR I-4315, para 43; and Case C-473/98, *Toolex*, para 45.

233   Case T-74/00, *Artegodan*, para 173.

234   Case T-74/00, *Artegodan*, para 174. Later on, the CFI proclaims an even broader principle, the principle that the protection of public health, safety and the environment is to take precedence over economic interests (para 186).

235   Case T-74/00, *Artegodan*, para 177.

236   Case T-74/00, *Artegodan*, para 186.

237   Case C-286/02, *Bellio F.lli Srl*, para 60.

238   As far as EC law is concerned, see Regulation (EC) No 178/2002 laying down the general principles and requirements of food law, Article 7(2); EC Commission *Communication on the Precautionary Principle*, para 6.3.5. With regard to WTO law, see Article 5(7) of the SPS Agreement.

239   Case T-76/96, *NFU*.

240   Case T-13/99, *Pfizer*, para 460.

241   Case T-13/99, *Pfizer*, para 460.

242   Cases C-154/04 and C-155/05, *Alliance for Natural Health*, 12 July 2005, not yet reported, para 69.

243   See, in particular, the American literature: Graham J. and Wiener, J. (2005) *Risk v. Risk: Tradeoffs in Protecting Health and the Environment*, Harvard University Press, Cambridge.

244   Scott, J. (2004) 'The precautionary principle before the European courts', in Macrory, R. (ed) *Principles of European Environmental Law*, Europa Law Pub, Groeningen, p65.

245 Case T-13/99, *Pfizer*, para 468.

246 Case T-13/99, *Pfizer*, para 410.

247 Case T-13/99, *Pfizer*, para 469. The CFI points, for example, to the detailed analysis contained in the Swedish report of the economic effects of ceasing to use antibiotics for growth promotion in Sweden. That report was submitted to the council during the procedure leading to the adoption of the contested regulation.

248 See the Council Regulation (EEC) No 793/93 of 23 March 1993 on the evaluation and control of the risks of existing substances, obliging the national representative to 'submit an analysis of the advantages and drawbacks of the substance and of the availability of replacement substances' (Article 10(3)). On medicines, see the obligation on the risk-benefit ratio under the Directive 75/318/EEC of 20 May 1975 on the approximation of the laws of member states relating to analytical, pharmaco-toxicological and clinical standards and protocols with regard to the testing of proprietary medicinal products. Although the EC Commission requires an examination of the advantages and disadvantages of the precautionary measure, in its *Communication on the Precautionary Principle*, it is stressed that an economic analysis is needed 'where this is appropriate and possible' (para 6.3.4). In its 2002 Communication on Impact Assessment (COM (2002) 726), the EC Commission did not call expressly for CBA. According to the commission, an array of analytical methods can be used with a view to assessing impacts: 'The choice of method and the level of detail will vary with the nature of the problem and judgments about feasibility' (p15).

249 For an analysis of this subject, see Ackerman, F. and Heinzerling, L. (2004) *Priceless,* The New Press, New York and London; de Sadeleer, N. (2002) *Environmental Principles: From Political Slogans to Legal Rules*, Oxford University Press, Oxford, pp299; Contra Sunstein, C. R. (2002) *Risk and Reasons*, Cambridge University Press, Cambridge.

250 Case C-192/01, *Commission v Denmark*, para 54.

251 Case C-192/01, *Commission v Denmark*, para 56.

PART II

Comparative Analysis of the Status of the Precautionary Principle in the Nordic Countries

Introduction

Nicolas de Sadeleer

The Nordic countries consist of Denmark (including the Faroe Islands and Greenland), Finland (including Åland), Iceland, Norway and Sweden. As a matter of fact, similarities between these five countries are much more prominent than their differences.

First, since their historical developments have been very similar, their language – with the exception of Finnish – quite alike, their cultural links very close, their institutions rather similar, the Nordic countries have been cooperating extensively, particularly since 1952 through the Nordic Council and since 1971 through the Nordic Council of Ministers.

Second, the five Nordic countries are richly endowed with natural resources ranging from minerals, petroleum, hydroelectric power, fisheries and forest products to freshwaters. Given that most of the Arctic territories are sparsely populated and not industrialized, they harbour pristine ecosystems and, as a result, fascinating biodiversity. Unfortunately, environmental challenges faced by the Nordic countries are also rather similar. For instance, anthropomorphic climate change has had a clear impact on the Arctic flora and fauna: species of fish from further south are found further north, cod and plaice are decreasing in the North Sea, seabirds are being deeply affected by these changes, and plants are blossoming increasingly early.

Third, the Nordic countries are known to place environmental issues high on their political agendas. In other words, they have traditionally been seen as strong supporters of environmental and health policies. The 1974 Nordic Convention on the Protection of the Environment as well as the 2001 Nordic Strategy on Sustainable Development are testament to their willingness to integrate environmental concerns within an array of socio-economic sectors. An environmental consciousness has been central to the public acceptance of chemical control. Moreover, several Nordic countries have been pushing both at the international and at the European Union (EU) level for stronger environmental policies similar to their own. In particular, with respect to chemicals, they have played a key role in supporting a major reform of the EU chemicals policy.

Fourth, because they can be allocated neither to the Common law nor to the Romano-Germanic family, the legal systems of these five countries form a group apart from the other major legal families.

As a result, these countries differ dramatically in terms of government, culture, legal traditions and environmental concerns from other European nations. The question arises immediately as to whether, through innovative regulatory instruments, these five countries have been developing a more precautionary environmental policy than other member states of the EU. Of course, the difficulties in answering this question are compounded by the fact that most of the national environmental rules have not been harmonized thus far, and that the concept of precaution is likely to be subject to different interpretations.

Nonetheless, five national experts are trying to answer this question from a legal perspective. As will be seen, it would be quite a stretch to claim that precaution has always been at the forefront of the agenda of these countries.

CHAPTER 3

Denmark

Ellen Margrethe Basse

INTRODUCTION

The Danish administrative legal approach is based on a civil law tradition strongly focusing on fixed law and the traditional principles of public law. The implementation in Danish law of European environmental law can take the form of statutory rules, the preparatory words connected with the rules, court judgments and the administrative practice at national,[1] regional and local level. The general legal way of thinking in the Danish courts and administrative bodies – also in regard to environmental law – is based on the concept of modern law.[2]

Precaution is neither a part of customary law, nor is it a general principle of statutory rules.[3] The interest in the wordings of the legislators and the judgments of the Supreme Court – which is the prime interest in Danish legal reasoning – makes it very difficult to get the precautionary principle accepted as a legal principle. What characterizes Danish law with regard to precaution is best described as a precautionary approach in the framing of statutory rules and guidelines.[4]

In concrete cases there is typically a balance between whether a legal practice or an assessment should be based *solely* on traditional administrative law principles (especially the principle of legality, the official maxims and the proportionality principle), or if the obligations based on these principles have to be modified with reference to the precautionary principle. When balancing traditional protection of individual interests by applying public law principles and the protection of collective interests by applying environmental principles (e.g. the precautionary principle), the environmental principles hardly ever stand a chance.

THE PRACTICE OF THE DANISH LEGISLATOR

The Danish constitutional rights are all negative in character, meaning that they are rights that free the citizens from government intrusion, rather than rights to affirmative governmental assistance. The development of law and judicial practice in the environmental sector in Denmark is, therefore, not guided by environmental principles laid down in the constitution.

The statutory rules of the legislator are also without clear reference to the precautionary principle. As will be described below, the principle is only indirectly included and only in some – not all – of the environmental acts.

In Denmark, the central act aimed at preventing pollution is the Environmental Protection Act.[5] The precautionary principle is not mentioned in this act since the legislators, at its enactment in 1992, were much more interested in the principle of pollution abatement and the principle of cleaner technology than in the precautionary principle.[6] However, the act has been amended several times since. The Integrated Pollution Prevention and Control (IPPC) Directive rules, which are based on the precautionary principle,[7] have now been implemented as part of the approval scheme. The requirement for disclosure of possible consequences of environmental approvals covered by the IPPC Directive list is described in the statutory order on the approval system. This means that the precautionary principle will indirectly be guiding the decision-making process. The only environmental principles mentioned in the current act are the principle of rectification of damage at source, the principle of location and the principle on the use of best available technology (BAT), which are all explicitly laid down in sections 3 to 4. These principles form the underlying foundation of the administration of the act.[8] It appears from section 3(2)(i) of the act that when assessing the extent and nature of instruments to prevent and counter pollution, the authorities will put emphasis on the nature of the external surroundings and the effects that the pollution is likely to have on these. According to the preparatory work connected to this subsection, it may be seen as a codification of the precautionary principle. It is stated that:[9]

> *Today, the precautionary principle is already applied in the environmental area, primarily in connection with the establishment of threshold values for pollution with an impact on human health – for example, the air guidelines.*

> *It is now suggested to fix this practice by statutory rules. This means that now it will appear from the law text itself – with a wording to the effect that emphasis will be put on the possible impact on the surroundings – that when issuing rules and guidelines, the Ministry of the Environment may employ, for example, security factors when establishing threshold values or guidelines for pollution calculations in areas where there is not a sufficient basis of exact knowledge.*

> *The aim is not that an independent precautionary principle shall enter further into the decision of actual cases.*

It was thus not contemplated that the principle should be given a directing function in concrete administrative decision-making. The practice is described below.

The objectives of the Act on Environment Marine Protection are to prevent and reduce pollution and other negative impacts on nature and environment from activities on the sea. The act aims to implement several international conventions. The precautionary principle is not mentioned in the act. On the other hand, it enumerates other environmental principles. Section 3 establishes that the act will contribute to the protection of nature and the environment on a sustainable basis, emphasizing respect for the human conditions of life and the preservation of fauna and flora. The practice is described below.

In the very few situations covered by *the* Environmental Damage Act,[10] the tort system replaces fault-based liability with strict liability. The strict liability is triggered by specific hazardous industrial processes and facilities listed in an annex to the act. It includes provision for consideration of geographic proximity of the plants to the place where the damage occurred and other relevant considerations, such as the nature of the incident. The act does not have retroactive effect. This reflects the European common law tradition in which the tort of nuisance is historically deeply rooted in the protection of interests on land.

The Water Supply Act,[11] which regulates water consumption, and the Watercourse Act, which regulates landowners' possibilities of interfering with the physical shape and use, etc., of water,[12] are both old acts enacted and amended several times without any reference at all to the precautionary principle. The new Act on Environmental Goals and Objectives,[13] whose purpose it is to implement parts of the Water Framework Directive, the Ramsar Convention, the Wild Birds Directive and the Habitats Directive, does not contain any provisions on, or references in, the legislative material to the precautionary principle. Neither does the Act on Nature Protection[14] mention the precautionary principle. Still, biodiversity conservation and sustainable use of biological resources are characterized by the necessity of a precautionary approach.[15] In administrative practice, however, the precautionary principle will have no importance anyway. An exception to this stemming from a board decision will be briefly mentioned below.

The principle of substitution, which de Sadeleer underlines as a principle based on the same approach as the precautionary principle,[16] has been part of Danish law for many years.[17] Dating back to the 1980s, the substitution principle has been clearly stated in the Act on Chemical Products and Substances.[18] Since the amendment in 1989,[19] section 1 of the act has stressed that, in the administration, emphasis shall be put on preventing health hazards and environmental damage in the cycle of chemical substances and products. In the amendment to the act from May 2000, section 1 was extended; its objective was now to limit 'unnecessary environmental strain'. This extension was a necessary part of implementing the Biocide Directive. Problems of resistance in the target group of biocide products had to be avoided, and inefficient products should not be approved. Furthermore, the extension was essential in relation to implementing the rules on good plant protection practice and the integrated control laid down in the Plant Production Protection Directive. Section 30 of the act, which forms part of the chapter on limitation of the occurrence and use of chemical substances and on the composition of chemical products, provides that the minister of the environment may make decisions or lay down rules to limit or prohibit sale, import and use 'when it is found to be necessary in order to ensure that a chemical substance or product does not represent a health hazard or cause damage to the environment'.

The provision can be said to support a procedure based on the precautionary principle. Section 35(1) of the act further provides that national approval cannot be granted if the substance or product, based on available examinations or experiences, is supposed to constitute a particular health hazard or is particularly damaging to the environment. The principle has a directing function: section 35(2) of the act provides that the authorities may not issue approval of a pesticide 'if there are other agents or methods with the same field of use which are – or, based on examinations or experiences, are supposed to be – substantially less hazardously or significantly less damaging to the environment.

In section 35(4) it is, however, provided that plant protection chemicals must be approved pursuant to the principles established by the council. Likewise it appears from section 35(4) of the act that agents whose active ingredient or ingredients are listed in the Biocide Directive annexes shall be approved pursuant to the principles established by the European Parliament and the council in unison. This means that the substitution principle – taking into account the European Union (EU) harmonization requirements – may encourage the rejection of an application for approval of a pesticide, which is not based on using the less dangerous agent. In other words, the application of this environmental principle is limited by the harmonization requirements laid down in the EU rules on chemicals.

The precautionary principle may indirectly come to mark the gene technology area because it underlies the risk assessment requirement, which was introduced in the Act on Environment and Genetic Engineering[20] when it was amended in 2002.[21] The amendment was part of the implementation of the directive on the deliberate release into the environment of genetically modified organisms.[22] The directive states in Article 1 that the objective is in accordance with the precautionary principle. The precautionary principle is not directly mentioned in the Danish law text. The principle is mentioned in the preparatory work of the 2002 act. It is stated that the rules focus more on the precautionary principle than the former rules. The act reinforces the procedures for risk assessment in accordance with the directive. In June 2004, the Danish Parliament adopted a new Act on Growing, etc. of Genetically Modified Crops.[23] The new act establishes a legal framework for protecting non-genetically modified (GM)[24] crop-growing farmers against the spreading of GM crops – for example, through requirements of minimum distance. It also introduces a compensation scheme according to which non-GM crop-growing farmers can obtain compensation for losses suffered as a result of GM crops spreading. The authorities may then enter into the liability claim against the GM crop-growing farmer based on general liability rules. These rules ensure a precautionary approach.

The precautionary principle is a very important part of the Convention on Climate Change and the Kyoto Protocol. Denmark ratified the Kyoto Protocol on 16 May 2002. There is, however, no reference to the precautionary principle in the new Danish CO_2 Quota Act implementing the obligations laid down in the protocol and the Emissions Trading Directive.[25] The objective of the Act is to bring about a cost-effective reduction of carbon dioxide (CO_2) by means of a system of negotiable allowances.

THE PRACTICE OF THE
ADMINISTRATIVE AUTHORITIES

With reference to the distinction emphasized by de Sadeleer[26] concerning the establishment of general threshold values based on the precautionary principle, on the one hand, and the protection based on utilizing the precautionary principle in the concrete decision-making systems against concrete damage, on the other, it has to be stressed that the requirements of the Danish acts are normally only related to the former aspect.

Given the fact that most Danish environmental legislation is of an administrative nature, and that the statutory obligations are implemented by administrative authorities, it is necessary to focus on the administrative bodies, their employees and members of the appeal bodies, as well as their practice. The highest administrative level comprises members of government, including ministers.

Since use of a modern versus a post-modern regulatory style depends upon the political situation, it is relevant to state that the current liberal–conservative Danish government has a different attitude to environmental policy and legislation than had the former red–green government. The present government has a programme based on the ideas of liberalization, deregulation and decentralization affecting, *inter alia*, environmental law. It has signalled a major shift in the environmental policy towards greater use of market-based approaches. In its strategy for sustainable development *A Shared Future – Balanced Development*,[27] it is stated that the government wishes to explore how the use of market-oriented instruments can help to solve environmental problems in the most cost-effective manner for society. The change in policy was also explained in a report entitled *Making Markets Work for Environmental Policies: Achieving Cost-effective Solutions*.[28]

The special administrative appeal bodies – the Nature Protection Board of Appeal and the Environmental Protection Appeal Board – are very important bodies since they have the power to make final administrative decisions. Furthermore, these administrative authorities possess essential legal expertise to ensure a correct implementation of environmental principles. The practice established by the appeal bodies is therefore of special interest. The Ministry of the Environment has only a few lawyers among its employees. At the same time, a clear trend towards an increasing emphasis on the municipal level as the most important level for decision-making in concrete cases has emerged.

A precautionary approach in a given concrete case will typically entail that the applicant will be required to present documentation. This can, for example, be seen in the Environmental Board of Appeal's attitude towards a complaint from the addressee of an approval over certain conditions, which had been added by the Danish Environmental Protection Agency. The complaint concerned an approval pursuant to section 33(1) of the Act on Chemical Substances and Products and the Pesticide Statutory Order of a wood preservative. The board confirmed the strict documentation requirements laid down by the Environmental Protection Agency in its decision. The agency stated that the information presented by the applicant to the agency was not good enough. The board did not mention the precautionary principle even though it would have been in keeping with its argumentation.[29]

With respect to the practice based on the Environment Marine Act, the vulnerability of an international nature-protected sea area in the south-west Jutland coastal mudflats and the concrete risk that dumping of toxic harbour floor material represents to that area made the Environmental Board of Appeal put a restriction based on a precautionary approach on the dumping permit. The application in question came from the Coast Directorate and it concerned the dumping of floor material from the harbour of Esbjerg. The Board of Appeal did not mention the precautionary principle. It decided that the permit should be time limited due to the fact that the material was contaminated with heavy metals (such as copper) and anti-fouling materials (such as tributylin (TBT), polycyclic aromatic hydrocarbon (PAH) and Irgarol). Although the existing pollution called for more information than the Coast Directorate was able to present, the permission was granted and every decision made in 2001, 2002 and again in 2003[30] extended the permission for one year.

The Environmental Board of Appeal has also increased the information requirements in its assessment of applications for approval of sea lanes for high-speed ferries, which according to the application are planned to sail through international nature protection areas.[31] The board criticized the Danish Forest and Nature Agency because, as an approval authority, it had placed too much responsibility on the shipping company (the applicant) in terms of collecting data and suggesting an environmental impact assessment (EIA).[32] The board's information requirement was based on the demands for carrying out an EIA, not on an explicit utilization of the precautionary principle. So, the application of instruments based on the precautionary principle may indirectly have resulted in the Danish authorities' administrative procedures being partially based on precautionary principle conditions after all.[33]

With regard to the air emission of dangerous substances, the guidelines on air quality – filling out the Environmental Protection Act – are based on the precautionary principle. The Environmental Board of Appeal has had access to review whether there was an actual basis for deviating from these guidelines and the criteria in the guidelines elaborated by the Danish Environmental Protection Agency. In a case on environmental approval,[34] the board stated, regarding the conditions laid down as part of a licence to a cable company, that the classification of the substance di-octyl phthalate (DEHP) in main group 1 of the air guidelines, based on the toxicity of the substance, its long-term health effects and/or its unacceptable impact on the nature, had to be seen as motivated by the precautionary principle. The board stressed that the agency, as the reason for the classification of DEHP, had found that the available documentation makes it probable that long-term exposure to DEHP may cause serious, unacceptable, long-term impact on health and nature. Consequently, the agency has classified DEHP in main group 1 of the air guidelines. According to the board, such an assessment must have been made taking into consideration the precautionary principle, which appears – as described above – from the preparatory work to section 3(2) of the Environmental Protection Act. The board therefore remarked that such a principle, according to the legislative material, is relevant for the elaboration of the air guidelines. The board, however, is of the opinion that it may be called into question whether DEHP, with all probability, can be considered to be particularly dangerous to health or particularly damaging to the environment. On the available basis, the board will, however, not set aside the assessment of the agency since the lack of scientific documentation does not provide the certainty – which, in the board's opinion, is imperative – to change the classification made in the guidelines.

In administrative practice, the decision-maker, on the basis of the principle of proportionality, gives highest priority to the addressee's need of protection. This can, for example, be seen in a decision from 1996 where the Environmental Board of Appeal changed a general prohibition against the establishment of a disposal dump in a gravel pit to an enforcement notice setting the limits for the disposal. The enforcement notice thus replaced the prohibition notice, which had been issued by the lower administrative body with reference to the water supply interests in the area.[35] According to the board, the risk of a possible pollution in connection with a future depositing of waste materials could be limited by carefully ensuring that only non-polluted material was deposited in the remaining volume of the disposal dump. The motivation for changing the prohibition notice to an enforcement notice was, in other words, based on the principle of proportionality. The precautionary principle is not mentioned at all. The act has been changed to give a better protection of the water supply interests, and a board decision on such an issue would therefore not be the same today.

The most far-reaching enforcement decision based on the Environmental Protection Act with regard to including a precautionary approach is probably an old decision made by the Environmental Board of Appeal. In this case, the board reviewed an enforcement order issued against an environmentally approved heavily polluting enterprise.[36] The case concerned the restoration of a polluted estate, and the board agreed with the Danish Environmental Protection Agency that the criteria for cleaning up should basically be decided independently of the current use of the estate and that an enforcement notice, as a consequence, should be worked out in such a way that the site, after the clean-up, in principle, could be used for environmentally sensitive purposes (e.g. construction of family houses). The board put emphasis on the fact that, in general, earth pollution as such did constitute a permanent pollution risk as a result of the continued operation of the polluting company. Thus, the pollution of the estate would not have been averted before a complete clean-up had taken place. The board did not explicitly mention the precautionary principle. Instead, as part of its motivation for issuing an enforcement notice on a complete clean-up of the estate, the board mentioned the polluter pays principle, which is emphasized in the Environmental Protection Act section 4(4). This board's decision is seen as an isolated occurrence in so far as the board has never since imposed such an extensive clean-up obligation on an owner of a permitted activity.

In a complaints case concerning a permit granted by Ringkjøbing Amt pursuant to the Nature Protection Act to let the Forest and Nature Agency introduce beavers – which do not naturally live in Denmark – in two international nature protection areas (Flynder Å and Omme Å), a unanimous Nature Protection Board of Appeal[37] stated that the assessment should be based on the precautionary principle. The board wrote:

> *Previously, permission to introduce a large mammal in Denmark has not been granted pursuant to the Nature Protection Act. An important aim of introducing beavers is that the beaver – sometimes temporarily – will change the nature in which it is introduced and later spread to other areas. Regardless that beavers have previously been introduced in other countries and regardless of the existing literature describing the impact of introducing beavers, the board is of the opinion that it is uncertain exactly what impact on section 3 areas their introduction will have. It is estimated that the changes might be considerable in certain areas.*

> *Consequently, and in spite of the fact that the available material mostly indicates that the changes will take a nature-improving direction, the board does find that great caution should be exercised when introducing the first beavers.*
>
> *It is the board's opinion that, at the present stage, it is not sufficiently certain that the introduction of beavers will not have a negative impact on, for example, salmons in the Omme Å/Skjern Å creek system, in addition to which, attention is called to the fact that Skjern Å is a habitat for the special Skjern Å salmon population. Consequently, permission to introduce beavers in this area is changed to a rejection.*
>
> *Concerning the Flynder Å area where neither the special salmon strain nor any other red-listed species can be threatened by the introduction of beavers, the board does not have the same concerns. It is, however, the board's opinion that, based on the precautionary principle, it is necessary to tighten the conditions stipulated by the county.*

Thus, the board decision concerned the protection of a vulnerable area – an international nature protection area – against the risk of damage from introducing alien animals. The decision of the board, based on the precautionary principles, was, however, overruled by the High Western Court. The court stated that the board had failed to meet the obligations laid down in the Habitats Directive as implemented by the Danish Statutory Order on international nature-protected areas.[38]

Perhaps the Danish authorities are first and foremost interested in utilizing the precautionary principle when it comes to keeping existing national rules in force after EU harmonization. The Danish authorities did benefit from the principle in the European Court of Justice's judgment from 23 September 2003 on food safety – Case C-192/01, *Commission* v *Denmark*.[39]

THE LEGAL REASONING BY THE COURTS

All Danish courts are ordinary courts that include statutory rules, customary law and general legal principles, as well as judicial practice, in their reasoning. The Danish judges scrutinize the wordings of statutory rules and the legislator's remarks in order to identify the exact intentions of the legislator in making binding obligations by the framing of the rules. The judgments of the Danish courts are very short and without the extremely in-depth analysis known from the decisions of courts in common law jurisdictions. Furthermore, the analyses are shorter than seen in judgments made by other Scandinavian courts as the Danish judges prefer not to make long argumentations resulting in a precedent – and they certainly prefer not to make judgments of a participial nature. Most often, the dualistic approach to international law also keeps them away from taking the international and EU development of new principles into account.

The following definition of law made by Fred Rodell, professor of law at Yale University in 1939, is still a valid metaphor for the general opinion of the reasoning by Danish judges:

The law is the killy-loo bird of the sciences. The killy-loo, of course, was the bird that insisted on flying backwards because it didn't care where it was going but was mightily interested in where it had been.[40]

Some years ago I participated in a conference arranged by the Danish Parliament for the members of parliament. The conference theme was the quality of statutory rules made by the parliament. As part of the conference, all of the participants were divided into working groups. The group, which I was joining, presented a proposal on a clearer framing of the first part of the acts where the goals and the environmental principles are set out. We stressed the need for clearer descriptions of, for example, environmental goals and principles. Our proposal to the participants at the conference was very negatively received by the former president of the Supreme Court, who stood up and declared that the wording of the objectives in the acts would always be without any effect on the courts' judgments. This, he argued, was due to the fact that the judges never look at rules that only state the objectives of the acts – they are only interested in the clear legal writing in the precise rules stating rights and duties. In my opinion, this tells us a lot about the very traditional legal reasoning in the Danish courts.

As indicated above, the precautionary principle aims first and foremost to direct the political decision-making process. Therefore, the Danish judges do not accept the principle as part of the law. We have only one court case of relevance. It is the Easter High Court judgment from 1995[41] stating that the administrative body, when making the concrete permit to supply raw material based on the Raw Material Act, can endorse the coordination principle. The reason for this judgment is that section 3 of the act very clearly mentions coordination of the administration of the Raw Material Act with the Water Supply Act. Consequently, the regional county could include terms on protection of a water supply area.

Since protection of drinking water is of particularly high priority in Danish legislation, it is relevant to mention that the regulation of soil pollution is one of the highest priorities in Danish environmental law and policy. Among the environmental judgments on soil pollution are several cases on liability based on traditional principles of tort law that are founded on an approach far removed from the precautionary approach. In Denmark, negligence provides the basis for liability of, in most cases, environmental damage caused by soil pollution. It is also a vital aspect of determining the basis for the administrative enforcement orders as stated in several court judgments. Determining upon whom a duty to act lies and whether it could have been anticipated that the operator's actions/plants would give rise to the harm in question is based on a strong interpretation of foreseeability. Therefore, the structure of liability in Denmark has to be assessed as part of the evaluation of the importance of the precautionary principle. The precautionary principle is not mentioned in the judgments. Civil liability is only consistent with the precautionary principle as long as responsibility is based on a precautionary approach. Only a clear and foreseeable risk of incurring liability as a consequence of damage caused by pollution would persuade operators to take sufficient steps to prevent future incidents in line with this principle. The test of *culpa*, causation and foreseeability, as well as the burden of proof applied in the Danish liability cases, appears to be very rigorous in most of the judgments. In most cases, it does not allow room for the application of the precautionary approach.[42] The administrative authority, acting as a plaintiff, must show that the polluter who causes soil pollution has breached the duty of care[43] since foreseeability of harm is a vital part of the judgments. Based on the judgments, it is important to determine whether it could have been anticipated that the operator's action would give rise to the harm in question. An additional aspect of foreseeability concerns the extent to which the operator is expected to be aware of the general state of scientific knowledge regarding the likely long-term effects of his activities at the plants. This is surely a position that is not based on the precautionary approach.[44] There are few court cases based on a reversal of the burden of proof. The water contamination was found, for example, in a court judgment from 1989 to have been foreseeable by the operator. The contamination caused by the treatment of the hazardous waste material could have been foreseen by the operator since he had once before been brought to court on the same pollution problem and the recipient areas were very sensitive.[45]

As a consequence of the courts' judgments in the cases on soil pollution, parliament passed the Contaminated Soil Act in 1999.[46] Section 1(2)(ii) of the act declares that it aims especially to prevent health problems in connection with the use of contaminated areas. The precautionary principle is not mentioned. It is first and foremost the polluter pays principle and the protection of individual rights that are stressed in the act and the remarks of the legislator. In a book commenting on the act, Peter Pagh has stressed that it cannot be the duty of the ordinary house owner to observe the precautionary principle, and that to contemplate an application of the principle would be contrary to the priority of public efforts, which appears from the act.[47] This statement is based on the traditional public law approach – based on the principle of legality and the principle of proportionality.

CONCLUSIONS

All of the environmental principles are, in general, vague in the acts – and the precautionary principle is one of the missing principles.[48] The precautionary principle is, in fact, not mentioned at all in the wording of the acts. In Denmark the position of the precautionary principle depends upon the deeply rooted, historically conditioned attitudes about the nature of law. It is first and foremost the implementation of EU legislation that, balancing with the mentioned tradition, ensures some application of the precautionary approach in Denmark.

Nothing seems to change the actual regulatory style in relation to focusing primarily on the traditional modern regulatory style. The government and its supporting political parties want to use market-based instruments instead of environmental principles to ensure flexibility.

The traditional public law principles based on modern law regulatory style and the need to protect individuals against the use of public power are the most decisive principles in the decision-making systems. The principle of proportionality can, for example, be applied as a modification to the general rules and guidelines based on the precautionary principle. So, even in cases where the precautionary principle could be of relevance as part of the general guidelines, the authorities, in practice, focus on traditional public law principles instead – and reduce the directing function of the precautionary principle. A lack of interest in the precautionary principle with regard to concrete decision-making is very clear in the administrative practice. In some respects, the precautionary principle may, however, be a means of directing the balancing of interests in administrative cases where the decision-making is based on a wide discretionary power.

There are no court cases that include the precautionary principle. It is considered to be a political principle – and not a legal principle.

In the light of the precautionary principle, the liability approach and the often heavy evidential burden on the plaintiff used by the courts are inappropriate. The Act on Contaminated Soil, which was established to ensure a more precautionary approach than the approach used by the courts, is – as indicated above – not a very strong instrument in this respect.

NOTES

1   Including the judgments of the special appeal bodies.
2   Concerning modern law, see de Sadeleer, N. (2004) 'Environmental principles, modern and post-modern law', in Macrory, R. (ed) *Principles of European Environmental Law*, Europa Law Publishing, Groeningen, pp225f.
3   As stated by Winter, G. (2004) 'The legal nature of environmental principles in international, EC and German law', in Macrory, R. (ed) *Principles of European Environmental Law*, Europa Law Publishing, Groeningen, pp9ff.
4   de Sadeleer, N. (2002) *Environmental Principles: From Political Slogans to Legal Rules*, Oxford University Press, Oxford, p92.
5   Environmental Protection Act: The Consolidated Act No 753 of 25 August 2001 on environmental protection, as amended by Act No 475 of 7 June 2001, Act No 145 of 25 March 2002, Act No 260 of 8 May 2002, Act No 1151 of 17 December 2003, Act No 220 of 31 March 2004, Act No 314 of 5 May 2004, Act No 902 of 25 August 2004 and Act No 1373 of 20 December 2004 with later amendments.
6   *The Parliamentary Journal* (*Folketingstidende*) 1991–1992, second session, Annex A, column 1533.
7   Council Directive 96/61/EC of 24 September 1996 concerning integrated pollution prevention and control.
8   de Sadeleer, N. (2004) 'Environmental principles, modern and post-modern law', in Macrory, R. (ed) *Principles of European Environmental Law*, Europa Law Publishing, Groeningen, p234; and Winter, G. (2004) 'The legal nature of environmental principles in international, EC and German law', in Macrory, R. (ed) *Principles of European Environmental Law*, Europa Law Publishing, Groeningen, pp9ff.
9   *The Parliamentary Journal* (*Folketingstidende*) 1990–1991, second session, Annex B, column 978.
10 Act No 225 of 6 April 1994. Concerning this act, see Basse, E. M. (2003) *Environmental Law*, Kluwer International Law, Denmark, pp275f., and Wilde, M. (2002) *Civil Liability for Environmental Damage: A Comparative Analysis of Law and Policy in Europa and United States*, Kluwer International Law, Denmark, pp199ff., 211ff. and 235f.
11 Consolidated Act No 130 of 26 February 1999 on water supply, as later amended by Act No 355 of 2 June 1999, Act No 374 of 2 June 1999, Act No 1273 of 20 December 2000, Act No 466 of 7 June 2001, Act No 145 of 25 March 2002, Act No 1151 of 17 December 2003, Act No 435 of 9 June 2004 and Act No 1373 of 20 December 2004, with later amentments.
12 Consolidated Act No 882 of 18 August 2004 on water courses.

13 Act No 1150 of 17 December 2003 on environmental goals, etc. for bodies of water and international nature protection areas (Act on Environmental Goals and Objectives).

14 Consolidated Act No 884 of 18 November 2004 on nature protection, with later amentments.

15 Anker, H. T. and Basse, E. M. (2001) 'Rationality, environmental law and biodiversity', in Beckmann, S. C. and Kloppenborg Madsen, E. (eds) Aarhus University Press, Denmark, pp181ff.

16 de Sadeleer, N. (2002) *Environmental Principles: From Political Slogans to Legal Rules*, Oxford University Press, Oxford, p117.

17 It is now the consolidated Act No 21 of 16 January 1996, as later amended by Act No 424 of 10 June 1997, Act No 431 of 10 June 1997, Act No 231of 21 April 1999, Act No 256 of 12 April 2000, Act No 296 of 30 April 2003, Act No 441 of 10 June 2003, Act No 189 of 24 March 2004, Act No 315 of 5 May 2004 and Act No 1373 of 20 December 2004, with later amentments.

18 Act No 285 of 13 May 1987 on amendment of Act on Chemical Substances and Products. It has also been found in Swedish law. The role of the principle in Swedish law is, for example, treated in Nilsson, A. (1997) *Att byta ut skadliga kemikalier: Substitutionsprincipen – en miljörättslig analys* (*To Substitute Harmful Chemicals: The Substitution Principle – An Environmental Analysis*), Nerenius & Santerus Förlag, Stockholm. Peter Pagh has treated the importance of the principle in Danish law in Basse, E. M. (ed) (2002) *Miljøretten V. Risici, produkter og organismer* (Environmental Law V. Risks, Products and Organisms), Jurist – og Økonomforbundets Forlag, Copenhagen, pp81, 92ff., 111ff., 118, 151, 161, 180 and 183f.

19 Act No 341 of 24 May 1989 on the amendment of the Act on Chemical Substances and Products.

20 Act No 981 of 3 December 2002: Environment and Genetic Engineering Act.

21 Consolidated Act No 981 of 3 December 2002 on environmental and gene technology, as amended by Act No 436 of 9 June 2004, Act No 440 of 9 June 2004 and Act No 1373 of 20 December 2004, with later amentments.

22 Directive 2001/18/EC of 12 March 2001 on the deliberate release into the environment of genetically modified organisms.

23 Act No 436 of 9 June 2004 on growing, etc. of genetically modified crops.

24 GM is the acronym for genetically modified.

25 Act No 493 of 9 June 2004 on CO_2 allowance. The act was put into force by the Statutory Order No 550 of 17 June 2004 covering the emission of CO_2 from the period after 31 December 2004. Statutory Order No 829 of 3 August 2004 made Chapter 4 of the act come into force from 15 August 2004.

26 de Sadeleer, N. (2002) *Environmental Principles: From Political Slogans to Legal Rules*, Oxford University Press, Oxford.

27 The Danish government published it in August 2002.

28 Danish Government (2003) *Making Markets Work for Environmental Policies: Achieving Cost-effective Solutions*, Copenhagen.

29 The decision is published in (2004) *Decisions on Real Estate* (*Kendelser af Fast Ejendom*), Jurist – og Økonomforbundets Forlag, Copenhagen, pp438ff.

30 The decisions are published in (2003) *Decision on Real Estate* (*Kendelser om Fast Ejendom*), Jurist – og Økonomforbundets Forlag, Copenhagen, p417; (2002) *Decisions on Real Estate* (*Kendelser om Fast Ejendom*), Jurist – og Økonomforbundets Forlag, Copenhagen, pp442ff.; and (2001) *Decisions on Real Estate* (*Kendelser om Fast Ejendom*), Jurist – og Økonomforbundets Forlag, Copenhagen, p422. The decisions are also printed in (2002) Environmental Decisions and Judgments (*Miljøretlige Afgørelser og Domme*), Christians Ejlers' Forlag, Copenhagen, p713; and (2003) Environmental Decisions and Judgments (*Miljøretlige Afgørelser Domme*), Christians Ejlers' Forlag, Copenhagen, p678.

31   The decision is printed in (2003) Decisions on Real Estate (*Kendelser om Fast Ejendom*), Jurist –
     og Økonomforbundets Forlag, Copenhagen, pp429ff.; and (2003) Environmental Decisions
     and Judgments (*Miljøretlige Afgørelser Domme*), Christians Ejlers' Forlag, Copenhagen, pp694ff.

32   The precautionary principle, which is behind the EIA directive, has first and foremost been
     implemented as a part of the Planning Act (Consolidated Act No 883 of 18 August 2004 on
     planning).

33   Pagh, P. (2003) 'Forsigtighedsprincippet – fra luftighed til hard law' ('The precautionary
     principle – from soft law to hard law'), *The Weekly Judicial Legal Journal* (*Ugeskrift for Retsv'sen*),
     pp153–161.

34   The decision is printed in (1993) Decisions on Real Estates (*Kendelser om Fast Ejendom*), Jurist
     – og Økonomforbundets Forlag, Copenhagen, pp284ff.

35   The decision is published in (1996) Decisions on Real Estates (*Kendelser om Fast Ejendom*),
     Jurist – og Økonomforbundets Forlag, Copenhagen, pp266ff.

36   The decision is printed in (1993) Decisions on Real Estates (*Kendelser om Fast Ejendom*), Jurist
     – og Økonomforbundets Forlag, Copenhagen, pp293ff. See also Pagh, P. (2003)
     'Forsigtighedsprincippet – fra luftighed til hard law' ('The precautionary principle – from
     soft law to hard law'), *The Weekly Judicial Legal Journal* (*Ugeskrift for Retsv'sen*), p96.

37   The decision is published in (2000) Decisions on Real Estate (*Kendelser om Fast Ejendom*),
     Jurist – og Økonomforbundets Forlag, Copenhagen, p109.

38   Western High Court judgment of 13 November 2003, published in *The Weekly Law Legal
     Journal (UfR)* (2004), pp622ff. with reference to the Statutory Order No 782 of 1 November
     1998. See also Pagh, P. (2003) 'Forsigtighedsprincippet – fra luftighed til hard law' ('The
     precautionary principle – from soft law to hard law'), *The Weekly Judicial Legal Journal* (*Ugeskrift
     for Retsv'sen*), p96.

39   See also Scott, J. (2004) 'The precautionary principle before the European courts', in
     Macrory, R. (ed) *Principles of European Environmental Law*, Europa Law Publishing,
     Groeningen, p55.

40   See Bodenheimer, E., Oakley, J. B. and Love, J. C. (2004) *An Introduction to the Anglo-American
     Legal System: Readings and Cases*, fourth edition, Thomson West, Eagan, MN, p3, with refer-
     ence to the article of Fred Rodell, 'Woe Unto You, Lawyers', p23.

41   The judgment is published in *The Weekly Judicial Legal Journal (UfR)* (1995), p925.

42   Concerning the precautionary principles as part of the liability rules, see Wilde, M. (2002)
     *Civil Liability for Environmental Damage: A Comparative Analysis of Law and Policy in Europa and
     United States*, Kluwer International Law, Denmark, pp177f., 229, 241.

43   *The Weekly Judicial Legal Journal* (1995) pp505ff. (the *Purhus* case).

44   Wilde, M. (2002) *Civil Liability for Environmental Damage: A Comparative Analysis of Law and
     Policy in Europa and United States*, Kluwer International Law, Denmark, pp200f.

45   *The Weekly Judicial Legal Journal* (1989) pp353ff. (the *Vasby Grus* case).

46   Act No 370 of 2 June 1999 on contaminated soil, as amended by Act No 1109 of 29 December
     1999, Act No 447 of 31 May 2000, Act No 145 of 25 March 2002, Act No 355 of 19 May 2004 and
     Act No 1373 of 20 December 2004, with later amendments.

47   Pagh, P. (2000) *Jordforureningsloven med kommentarer* (*The Contaminated Soil Act with Comments*),
     Thomsons Forlag, Copenhagen, pp71f.

48   See also Pagh, P. (2004) 'Implementation and application of environmental principles in
     Danish law', in Macrory, R. (ed) *Principles of European Environmental Law*, Europa Law
     Publishing, Groeningen, pp95ff.

CHAPTER 4

Finland

Erkki Hollo

METHODOLOGICAL BACKGROUND

The explicit use of the precautionary concept is rather limited in Finnish law. One reason for this is that the concept has been referred to mostly in political contexts, whereas legal texts focus on the concept of prevention. The position of theory has limited its approach mainly to models originating from European Community (EC) law and, comparatively, from some national systems. However, the distinction between precaution and prevention seems to refer to concepts of certainty and proof and also to the appearance of risks in specific activities. Precaution is addressed as an objective whenever an activity may imply risks that cannot yet be foreseen or which are scientifically documented as manageable.

Precaution refers to activities or operations that include transport, waste management and so on. The Finnish concept of 'operation' is, in many legal contexts, not explicitly defined. This has the consequence that individuals may also be bound by the rule of precaution as well as by prevention. We may assign scales for analysis, one based on the study of impacts, the other on the estimation of certainty. When, for example, a well-known and, as such, 'safe' chemical is used in a factory, it may be estimated to have probable and identifiable impacts. In this case, prevention usually requires that necessary measures are taken to protect human health and, as far as required, the environment. The technology to be used in such circumstances may, of course, develop and the requirements of prevention may reach the level of best or, whenever appropriate, best available technology (BAT). The requirement of BAT may, to some extent, be characterized as 'luxury' in the sense that it is modified by the economic and also technical situation in the country concerned or on the market, in general.

SCALES OF IMPACT AND KNOWLEDGE

First on the scale, we start with a situation where the impacts are not 'safe', but, instead, pose a danger or a threat to health and the environment if the situation is not managed and properly secured. One can, however, assume that the situation as such is under control. Preventive measures are imposed on operators by specific security systems and controls, and society must ensure that measures are taken to protect human beings and natural resources in case of accident or disaster. During this stage, the concept of precaution does not necessarily bring any content of its own compared to the duty of prevention because the impacts of the substances are scientifically known and the technical requirements set on equipment are apt to be settled.

Next on the scale we enter, on the impact side, the zone of 'risks'. A risk is something that may imply an emission, a biological process, an incidental set of events and more. So both the source of the risk, as well as its effects, may lie in the grey zone if, on the other scale, the probability of a risk has passed the area of certainty towards uncertainty. The two ends of a risk – namely, its origin and its consequences – are not necessarily at the same level when we look at certainty or probability. It is feasible to introduce a new chemical or biotechnological product and to build up a system of prevention for keeping the substance in a contained procedure.

If the chemical behaviour of the substance under specific conditions is not foreseeable, the introduction may imply an unmanageable risk. This does not say anything about the consequences should such a risk materialize. Due to this lack of knowledge, security measures must be secure enough to work under unexpected natural conditions (e.g. an airplane crash on a laboratory that conducts research on genetically modified organisms). The substance itself may involve a direct security risk in the sense that it may make the security system collapse (explosion, infiltration, etc.) and then escape into the environment, also implying risks in relation to future consequences.

From a theoretical viewpoint, it has not clearly been explained which elements in the security or maintenance systems are manageable under preventive measures and which imply uncertainties in the control system. Therefore, it seems that sometimes legislators and practitioners work with the tool of prevention when they, in fact, should apply precaution. This could be the case with the limited use of pesticides and fertilizers.

On the scale of consequences, risks take on a different intensity. A chemical may, for instance, be scientifically analysed; but it may have limited unforeseeable effects under specific conditions of climate or geography. Thus, the precaution for the substance may differ from one country to another. But, typically, risks in the area of consequences usually imply precaution whenever knowledge is unsatisfactory or there is ignorance about consequences. One can make a distinction between known, but not sufficiently researched, consequences and situations where there is no knowledge at all about the existence of a risk. When comparing situations of uncertainty and ignorance, the distinction may appear to be rather vague: knowledge of the fact that there is no scientific proof may be described as a situation of uncertainty. A situation of ignorance could be identified when a new chemical or biological substance or feature is invented, involving applications of a category denoting inexperience. In such a case, there may not even be a basis for estimating the range of uncertainties.

If the activity in question involves, first, either undocumented, but probable or uncertain, risks or, second, the consequences have been based on ignorance – for instance, due to the novelty of the substance – precaution requires the 'zero-risk rule' to be applied.

SUMMARY OF SITUATIONS OF PRECAUTION

In summarizing the correspondence between the effects of an activity and the level of proof or knowledge, the following relations are seen to be relevant in defining precautionary measures:

- *Activity involving state of knowledge: prevention:*
  - (direct) impacts: known and probable;
  - danger (of impacts): known but to be eliminated.
- *Activity involving state of knowledge: precaution:*
  - risk: not (well) known, to be managed;
  - severe or unmanageable risk: precautionary measure.

FINNISH LEGISLATION

Semantically, Finnish legislation is not clear regarding application of the precautionary approach.[1] In Finnish, the term 'precaution' is translated as '*varautuminen*'; but legislation and political practice often refer to 'care' or 'caution' ('*varovaisuus*'). One reason for this seems to be that 'precaution' has originally been adopted from Swedish terminology that does not make a distinction between 'caution' and 'precaution' ('*försiktighet*'). Since Article 174 EC has adopted the concept of 'precaution', this translation into Finnish is based on the former wording. In addition to this unclear terminology, the definitions of the Finnish concepts 'caution' and 'precaution' are unsatisfactory. They are sometimes mixed in a confusing manner, and even prevention may be covered by the definition. For this reason, one could not say, generally, at what stage precaution may enter as a legal duty. On the other hand, we are dealing just with duty of care.

In legal literature, the precautionary principle is defined as a method of imposing duties of awareness and risk management whenever there is a scientifically undocumented but probable risk.[2] The prevention principle has been largely applied since the 1960s, especially in water protection law, and the practice adopted may have, in some specific cases, also covered probable but uncertain proved risks (of pollution).[3] For this reason, Finnish law has already been, before the adoption of European Community (EC) environmental law in 1994, apt to open legal paths for setting caution or precaution as a duty of the operator. According to Chapter 2, section 3 of the Water Act, a general duty of care and prevention is prescribed. An assessment of environmental impacts on water and water quality is required in all water and environmental permit matters. Often the operator has been obligated to enter research before a permit could be granted or an emission permitted. It seems, however, that, mostly, the risks supposed to be settled were imminent or, to some extent, probable. So, it was not a case of uncertainty of chemical or technical properties, but rather of the range or degree of impacts.

The legal basis for such a discretionary power of the licensing authorities, in this case the water courts, to require risk assessment was again based on linguistic formulations. The law is based on a general prohibition to pollute waters or to emit polluting substances, unless there is a permit (Chapter 1, section 19, amended 2000). The permit again can only be granted if pollution is properly taken care of. Since the Finnish language does not make a distinction between the present and future tense, the same term applies for real (that is, foreseeable) and potential (that is, eventual) impacts whenever the impacts may constitute 'pollution'. This has, at a rather early stage, enabled the authorities to require assessment of risk factors in the chain of pollution and to prescribe care or caution in cases of uncertainty.

The same has correspondingly been the case for air pollution when the Clean Air Act was enacted (67/25 January 1982). The health legislation (Currently Health Act 763/19 August 1994) also tends to react to dangers and risks that involve uncertainty. It is, however, unclear what degree of probability of risk would be required to enable a permit authority to impose additional obligations on the operator. It seems that though legal formulations opened the door in that direction, no remarkable steps of courage can be assigned before entering the current system in 2000.[4]

SUBSTANTIAL REGULATORY SYSTEM

Basic statements

The Finnish system can be assumed to have adopted the following statements in the regulatory system concerning precautionary measures:

- The emphasis of legal control lies in the prevention of predictable impacts and risks.
- There is a general duty of operators to identify risks.
- Legislation fails to define precaution in relation to probability of unknown risks.
- Generally unknown risks are, however, relevant for:
  - permitting hazardous activities; and
  - monitoring of eventual risks in relation to health and the environment (GMOs, chemicals, etc.).
- Failure of the operator to identify risks may lead to strict liability for damage.

CONTEXTS OF USE

Precautionary measures – often vaguely covered by the concept of prevention – may be found in the following legal contexts of Finnish environmental law. In the general legislation on pollution control (prevention) of the Environmental Protection Act (EPA, 86/4 February 2000), the precautionary principle has a certain strategic function. More detailed provisions appear in the specific legislation on chemicals, biotechnology, waste and some other related substances. For a more political background to the principle, one may refer to the constitutional provision on environmental basic rights in section 20 of the constitution (2000). According to this provision, nature and its biodiversity, the environment and national heritage are the responsibility of everyone. The wording does not express how the basis for the responsibility has to be defined. However, pieces of modern environmental legislation in preparatory works often refer to this ruling. It is obvious that Finnish law does not recognize an explicit or general rule of precaution. Instead, in particular contexts the precautionary principle has been addressed either directly or more as a political or programmatic concept. As mentioned earlier, a definition does not exist that distinguishes between prevention and precaution.

In section 4 of the Environmental Protection Act (EPA), environmental principles are listed as applicable for the strategies of the act. One of those principles is defined as follows:

> ... *(2) the proper care and caution shall be taken to prevent pollution as entailed by the nature of the activity, and the probability of the pollution, risk of accident and opportunities to prevent accidents and limit their effects shall be taken into account (principle of caution and care).*

The term 'caution' is also, in the Finnish original, equal to caution, not precaution. However, in the preparatory works of the bill,[5] the explanation of the term refers to the English term 'precautionary principle':

> *The principle of caution means that uncertainties appearing in the decision-making situation shall be taken into account. Pollution shall as far as possible be prevented already before a certain proof is presented on the causal link between specific operations and environmental damages.*

This formulation is not part of the legal act and does not say anything about the degree of required scientific knowledge or how the authorities are supposed to decide in cases of ignorance or situations of unavailable proof. In my opinion, the principle does not reach the level of precaution as it appears, for example, in Article 174 EC.

Another weakness of the ruling is that the principle is not directly applicable in permit matters. According to the bill, the principle shall be taken into account when administrative general rules are enacted. According to the EPA, the state government has the power to enact specific additional rules to be taken into consideration by permit authorities and, eventually directly, by operators and owners of installations. There is no reason to assume that these administrative rules would efficiently strengthen the role of precaution compared to the duty of care and prevention, to which every operator is committed. But, as mentioned earlier, environmental authorities have adopted a practice where a permit can be conditioned by different types of obligations to investigate or assess uncertain impacts and to adapt the activity to the results. As far as the EPA is concerned, no explicit precautionary practice or a duty to take precautionary measures seems yet to exist.

Section 8 of the EPA provides for a general prohibition to pollute groundwater; correspondingly, section 7a expresses a prohibition to pollute the soil. These provisions are interesting from a precautionary point of view because the prohibitions may include not only real polluting activities, but also a risk of pollution. The concept of pollution in the system of the EPA generally covers mere risk factors; but the definition (section 3) does not define the legal position of unknown or uncertain emissions or impacts. It appears that some kind of probability or likeliness of acute risk of pollution is required, at least as far as the use of administrative sanctions would apply.

In Finnish law, the permit system recognizes risk assessment as a regular tool for preventive measures. Since this is the case, precaution would not necessarily, in practice, lead to a need for specific considerations. Permit rules are vague and flexible as far as further investigations are required. The precautionary principle would, it appears, have an independent function only when there are no remarkable impacts to consider under the prevention rule and when precaution would be the only argument (e.g. for the refusal of a permit). As far as this case is concerned, the precautionary principle does not seem to be applicable in Finnish environmental law.

ENVIRONMENTAL IMPACT ASSESSMENT

The Act on Environmental Impact Assessment (EIA Act 468/10 June 1994) implements the requirements of EC Directive 85/337/EEC. Risk assessment as such is an element of the environmental impact assessment because the concept of 'impact' relates to potential future direct and indirect effects (section 2 of the act). Effects must also be assessed, *inter alia*, in relation to health and biodiversity, which tend to be interests requiring precaution. Finnish legislation does not differ from the concepts of the EC directive, which again, on the basis of Article 174(2) EC, does not seem to exclude a precautionary approach from the environmental impact assessment. Since the environmental impact assessment deals with assessment and not decision-making, the exclusion of an assessment of rather hypothetical risks would not make sense either. It is then up to the integrated Integrated Pollution Prevention and Control Directive (IPPC) and other permit systems to estimate the need for precautionary measures.

The Finnish environmental impact assessment (EIA) legislation has one list of operations and installations (in between the two lists of the directive) for which an assessment is required. In addition to that, there is a case-by-case consideration within the competence of the Ministry of the Environment to prescribe the assessment of environmental impacts. This area of discretion covers the operations listed in the directive, which are not in the mandatory list of the act and corresponding decree. Here, in individual cases of consideration, precaution may have a role to play because criteria for prescribing environmental impact assessment on a case-by-case basis are related to the area of impacts and the affected population, to the amount and structure of impacts and also to the probability of impacts (Decree on EIA 268/5 March 1999, section 7). The last criterion of probability has not been further developed; but it seems that scientific uncertainty or ignorance could be relevant to the ministry. It emphasizes that the discretion is based on and limited by law, which prevents additional political viewpoints from being taken into account.

SPECIFIC ORDERS OF RISK MANAGEMENT

Precaution is typical for hazardous activities, which are also largely regulated by sectoral legislation. One typical category is the production and use of nuclear energy, which will not be further discussed in this chapter. Generally, these regulatory areas of hazardous activities, which are vital for modern societies, require non-tolerance of particular emissions, so the measures in question must be based on security requirements and the rule of prevention (radiation, pharmaceutical laboratories and more). As far as these and related economic activities are concerned, we find classifications of hazardous substances and wastes that (depending upon the situation) involve, first, a total prohibition of emissions and/or, second, the duty to perform risk assessments and to maintain technical safety. There are risks inherent in activities, and accidents may occur during transportation, field experiments and commonplace incidents, or due to human error.

From an environmental point of view, there are three areas that essentially require full risk assessment and precaution in case of scientific uncertainty because the control of emissions cannot be fully safeguarded. These sectors are particularly represented in the Chemicals Act (744/14 August 1989), the Gene Technology Act (377/17 March 1995) and the Waste Act (1072/3 December 1993). In the Finnish system, most activities covered by these acts also are regulated under the EPA (environmental permit) and the EIA acts. So, for instance, approval of a chemical according to the Chemicals Act does discount the need for an environmental permit. Generally, those sectoral laws are based on the principles of duty of care and precaution. Uncertainties that may imply harmful emissions to health or nature are not tolerable – especially as far as they can be pointed out in a risk assessment.

According to the Chemicals Act, while carrying out activities under the act (production, import and treatment), sufficient care and precaution shall be taken to prevent damage to health and environment, as far as the amount and hazardous nature of the chemical in question may require (section 15). Chemical legislation has been fully harmonized with EC law. The use of surrogates is another feature of regulation (section 16a): in order to prevent damage caused by chemicals, the operator shall, whenever it is reasonably possible, choose among the least risky available chemicals and methods.

The Gene Technology Act is based on the duty of care principle. The aim of the act is to promote the safe use and development of gene technology in accordance with the precautionary principle and in a way that is ethically acceptable. It also aims at protecting human and animal health and the environment when these might be affected by the contained use or deliberate release of genetically modified organisms (GMOs) into the environment (section 1). Risk assessment is a central duty of GMO operators. The operator who carries out the contained and deliberate use of GMOs has to make a risk assessment in order to obtain knowledge of the need for preventive measures. In this context, potential adverse effects on human and animal health and the environment must be assessed, as far as the effects may occur directly or indirectly through the transfer of GMOs.

The evaluation will be based on the newest scientific and technical knowledge concerning the adverse effects. While using genetically modified organisms, care and caution required by the organism or organisms in question will be observed (section 8a). It seems, considering the Finnish wording 'care and caution' ('*varovaisuus*'), that no 'real' precaution ('*varautuminen*') is required. This would mean that uncertainties will be assessed, but that uncertainty or ignorance do not prevent the activity if the preventive measures are estimated to be satisfactory. This is in line with the original objective of the legislation, which is to find a reasonable balance between economically favourable activities and the level of environmental protection.

The Waste Act aims at supporting sustainable development, and preventing and combating hazards and harm to health and the environment. Precaution as such is not formally a guiding principle of the act; instead, preventive measures are set in dimension with economical and technical conditions. The management of hazardous waste follows EC principles and rules. In this context, precaution may be required for the protection of health and the environment (see also EC Directive on Toxic and Dangerous Waste 91/689). It seems that the technical coverage of the regulation of waste disposal and treatment, especially concerning hazardous waste, has attained such a degree of guarantee mechanisms that there is no need or space for additional considerations on precaution. These considerations may, of course, become relevant as they emerge from other areas as chemical and biotechnological regulatory orders in connection with waste issues (e.g. the disposal of GMO-based waste).

LIABILITY AND PRECAUTION

Environmental liability may by defined in three contexts – namely, civil law, public law and criminal law liability. Precaution has a role in setting criteria for strict liability as it occurs in civil environmental law. Administrative and public law usually apply when damage has already occurred or is likely to occur. Mere neglect of precaution therefore seems to be irrelevant for categories of liability. Neglected security measures may, perhaps, under specific conditions, when a real risk can be proved, lead to administrative sanctions

Strict liability, as it appears in civil environmental law, may have a connection to the criteria of precautionary measures. In some legal systems, a person who on good grounds estimates that an operator is not following up necessary security or precautionary requirements may take, in order to protect himself from damage, preventive action and claim compensation for the costs from the operator. Such a provision exists in the Finnish Act on Environmental Damages (Act 737/19 August 1994, section 6). The criteria for evaluating what costs caused by preventive measures taken have been 'necessary' could be defined on the basis of the prevention and precautionary principles.[6] A neighbour could, for instance, expect that in the case of hazardous substances and gases, a proper risk management programme is developed and implemented for the operation. If this is not the case, the potential victim would be entitled to take measures of his or her own. Of course, in most systems, a permit authority estimates and prescribes in an administrative order the need and content of precautionary measures, which are supposed to satisfy the needs of eventual victims, as well. But in the Finnish system, strict civil liability is not limited to illegal activities or to professional activities. Therefore, it seems reasonable that civil precautionary claims, whenever justifiable, exceeding the level of protection set in permit conditions, should be taken up by the court. Until now, there is no court practice on this matter.

NOTES

1 English translations of Finnish law are not officially approved. Instead, they are published by either responsible ministries or law publishers. Here the versions are based on the website versions of Finlex (see www.finlex.fi).
2 See, for example, Ranta, J. (2000) *Varautumisperiaate ympäristöoikeudessa* (*Precautionary Principle in Environmental Law*), PhD thesis, University of Helsinki, which gives an overview of the concept's impact – especially the impact of the concepts 'precaution' and '*Vorsorge*' on EC law and foreign studies. Ranta's approach is to implement the precautionary principle as an example of environmental principles of law, not just as a political way of argumentation. On precaution in international trade of GMOs see also Utter, R. (2006) '*Muunnelmia varautumisesta*' (Variations of Precaution), in *Business Law Forum*, Helsinki, pp223–242.
3 Water Act 264/19 May 1961.
4 See, for example, the decision of the Supreme Administrative Court (SAC) Yearbook 1986 A II 88. A pharmaceutical company applied for the approval of an air notification according to the Clean Air Act. The court stated, on the basis of scientific expertise, that there was not satisfactory knowledge of the impacts of some chemicals on the neighbourhood. Additional specific obligation on prevention, caution and investigation were prescribed.
5 Government's Bill 84/1999 to the diet.
6 See, for example, Hollo, E. (2001) 'Environmental liability and the precautionary principle', in *Liber amicorum for Gunnar Schram*, Almenna Bókafélagið, Reykjavik, pp201–216.

CHAPTER 5

Iceland

Aðalheiður Jóhannsdóttir

INTRODUCTION

This book offers a welcome opportunity to continue researching the precautionary principle under Icelandic law. Although differently structured, the contribution of this chapter builds upon findings presented in the article 'Not business as usual: A study of the precautionary principle' written in 2000.[1] In this article, I did not find any explicit references to the precautionary principle in the environmental legislation,[2] nor did court decisions[3] indicate that the principle had been given any specific attention. The precautionary principle was, nevertheless, present in the Icelandic legal system. Examples occurred in several (administrative) regulations (decrees) implementing international commitments under the ozone regime,[4] as well as the identical European Community (EC) acts.[5] In addition, the principle was present in legislation[6] and regulations transposing EC directives on the use of genetically modified organisms (GMOs) and genetically modified micro-organisms (MMOs) into Icelandic law in line with the European Economic Area Agreement (EEA Agreement). Third, the precautionary principle (PP) was present in several regulations, either restricting or banning various hazardous and dangerous substances in line with the corresponding EC directives covering the subject matter and implemented through the EEA regime.[7] Based on these examples, I came to the conclusion that the precautionary principle had been unconsciously incorporated within the legal system.[8] Furthermore, in the application of individual provisions of the respective legislation and regulation, there was little or no room for balancing the PP's competing interests since they had already been balanced and the result (that is, bans, limitations, risk assessment and duty to submit information, etc.) was present in positive laws and regulations.[9]

Since all recent international environmental regimes, as well as the relevant EC legislation, in one way or another reflects some kind of a precautionary thinking, the importance of structuring national legislation in a particular manner was obvious. Therefore, I placed my emphasis on issues tied to the question of how the legislation should be structured in order to apply the principle, and on the necessity of developing criteria for the principle's application and operation within the legal system.

This chapter is meant to give an up-to-date overview on the same subject matter and the status of the principle under Icelandic law some six years later.

OUTLINE

Since this chapter is to serve as part of an overview of the situation within the Nordic states, the following discussion – with a few exceptions – is limited to the questions presented below. This provides an opportunity to compare the legal situation between states on issues such as the strength and legal status of this important principle of environmental law and one of the key principles in initiating sustainable development.

The key questions to be answered are as follows:

● Is the precautionary principle expressly or implicitly encapsulated in:
  – the Icelandic Constitution (see 'The constitution');
  – the general environmental or sectoral acts and regulations (see 'General and sectoral acts and regulations');
  – the administrative practice (see 'Administrative practice')?
● Do Icelandic courts refer to the principle while deciding on hard cases (see 'The practice of Icelandic courts')?
● To which extent has the principle been subject to an academic debate (see 'Academic debate')?
● Does the development in EC case law preclude the use of the principle in the Icelandic legal order or, on the contrary, foster its implementation (see 'Implemention of EC case law')?
● Does the development in European Free Trade Association (EFTA) case law preclude the use of the principle in the Icelandic legar order or, on the contrary, foster its implementation (see 'Implemention of EFTA court cases')
● Are there any obligations to perform risk assessment and cost-benefit analyses (see 'Risk assessments and cost-benefit analyses')?

Even though the precautionary principle can be applied in sectors other than the environmental one, I will limit the treatment to typical environmental legislation with one clear exemption: the Icelandic Foodstuffs Act No 93/1995 and EFTA Court Case E-3/00, or *the Kellogg's Case* (see 'The connection to EC law').

THE PRECAUTIONARY PRINCIPLE

Currently, the precautionary principle is being developed and worked on by legislators in many states, as well as being made part of international regimes and the secondary legislation of the EC. Concurrently, international courts have been adjudicating cases where the principle has been further elaborated upon. This development has led to diverse standard setting and several definitions of the principle, as de Sadeleer rightfully points out in his comprehensive overview of the principle's development under different legal systems and in diverse instruments.[10] Furthermore, problems related to particular concepts such as risk and damage, risk assessments and questions relating to the burden of proof are all of relevance.[11] I shall, however, not dwell on these problems since they have been covered by de Sadeleer.

Core elements

The precautionary principle consists of two basic, constantly competing, components. The former is the notion of risk and the likelihood of environmental degradation or damage (as well as health damage) and other irreversible consequences to materialize from a particular action or non-action within a reasonable time frame. The latter component ties to the economic consequences resulting from restrictions, particularly bans and official decisions, which control specific actions and activities. In the respective decision-making, usually these two basics have to be balanced against each other.[12]

As de Sadeleer stresses, it is absolutely necessary to comprehend the logic making up the precautionary principle and how it differs from the preventive principle's underlying rationale.[13] The objectives of both of these principles is to prevent and reduce environmental degradation and damage (including health damage). The preventive principle builds upon the proposition that if no preventive action or measures are undertaken, environmental damage will occur. What lies behind the proposition is certainty – that is, particular actions will cause environmental damage – and the certainty justifies the taking of preventive measures such as restricting, controlling and banning specific activities and substances, etc. On the other hand, the precautionary principle dictates that the precautionary action – which can be the same action as would be taken under the preventive principle – should be taken even though the environmental damage (or health damage) cannot be fully demonstrated or even fully proven. In other words, under the precautionary principle, it is the uncertainty that justifies taking the precautionary actions, and uncertainty as such should not be used to postpone taking the necessary precautionary measures.

As the precautionary principle has developed, increasing emphasis has been laid upon procedural instruments, such as risk assessment, in order to facilitate the evaluation of the risk or danger thought to be present. By relying upon these kinds of methods, the abstract decision-maker – a legislator or other competent decision-maker – should acquire better information before taking a decision that may have negative environmental impact.

The principle's application

The application of the precautionary principle must also be set in a particular 'legal system perspective' since, after all, no legal principle or rule exists or is capable of having any effect in a legal vacuum. First, rule of law states that the legal system's underlying principle builds on the premise that one is free to act unless particular actions have been restricted or banned by positive law.[14] In order to restrict this freedom, positive rules dictating and spelling out the restrictions, limitations, etc. must be present in the legal system. Second, the precautionary approach brings about several problems, such as the level of proof necessary to trigger its application. The traditional approach would be to lay the burden of proof on the claimant unless otherwise ordered by positive law. Third, the level of proof necessary is also a problematic issue since the notion of precaution builds on uncertainty, which should automatically lower the level. Individual legal systems – or, more correctly, individual law-makers – such as the Icelandic one, may have to respond to the issue in order to ensure legitimacy and to facilitate effective decision-making based upon the precautionary principle.

THE AGREEMENT ON THE EUROPEAN ECONOMIC AREA

The connection to EC law

Before proceeding, it is necessary to explain the link and the interaction between EC law and the Agreement on the European Economic Area (EEA Agreement). The agreement entered into force on 1 January 1994. The contracting parties are Iceland, Norway and Liechtenstein (EFTA states) and all member states of the European Union or a total of 28 EEA states. The EEA is first and foremost a free trade agreement, although other subjects fall under its scope: *inter alia*, the objective to promote environmental conservation on the basis of the principle of sustainable development, and the principles of preventive and of precautionary action (see the agreement's preamble). Apart from EC acts on classical nature conservation and the objective to conserve biodiversity, all relevant environmental EC legislation (secondary legislation) is therefore a part of the EEA. Article 73 of the EEA agreement provides the substantive requirements in the field of the environment; however, it does not include a reference to the precautionary principle.

Under the original text of the EEA, the relevant EC acts were directly referred to in the respective annexes of the agreement. After the agreement entered into force, new EC acts were made part of the EEA by decisions taken by the EEA joint committee. By these decisions, the relevant EC acts are inserted into the annexes depending upon the subject matter. Environmental issues are primarily found in two annexes: Annex XX on the environment and Annex II on technical regulations and standards, etc.

EEA law is not considered to have any direct effect in the Icelandic legal system. Under EEA's Article 7(a) and (b), the contracting parties are under the obligation to make the acts referred to or contained in the annexes a part of their legal order. Acts that correspond to an EC (EEC) regulation are, as such, to be made part of the internal legal order. Acts corresponding to a directive give the authorities of the contracting parties the choice of form and method of implementation.[15]

In line with EEA's Article 6, the provisions of the agreement and the acts made a part of the EEA Agreement are, in their implementation and application, to be interpreted in conformity with the relevant rulings of the European Court of Justice (ECJ) given prior to the date of signature of the agreement. Furthermore, in accordance with Article 3 of the ESA/Court Agreement,[16] both the EFTA surveillance authority and the EFTA court will pay due account to the principles laid down by the relevant rulings of the ECJ given after the date of signature of the EEA Agreement (including its protocols and annexes, as well as the acts referred to therein) that concern the interpretation of the agreement and the EC Treaty as far as they are identical in substance. For obvious reasons, the pertinent decisions of the ECJ are of relevance for the EEA Agreement and its application. As far as the precautionary principle is concerned, the ECJ has, *inter alia*, set the basic standard of proof (see Case C-157/96, *The Queen* v *Ministry of Agriculture, Fisheries and Food, and others*): the validity of Commission Decision 96/239/EC on emergency measures to protect against bovine spongiform encephalopathy (BSE or mad cow disease).[17]

The European Free Trade Association (EFTA) court

The EFTA court has also worked on the precautionary principle in relation to foodstuffs and has given important information on the principle's application.[18] In Case E-3/00, the *Kellogg's Case,* the question whether Norway had failed to fulfill its obligations under Article 11 of the EEA by applying Norwegian legislation prohibiting importation and marketing of cornflakes was addressed before the court. The cornflakes, which were lawfully manufactured and marketed in another EEA state, contained additional nutrients and vitamins – *inter alia*, iron. Norway argued that the prohibition could be justified under EEA's Article 13 on the basis of the precautionary principle.[19] In line with the ECJ's prior findings, the EFTA court stated that a contracting party could invoke the precautionary principle in order to prohibit importation as a means of attaining legitimate aims in protecting human health, and that it was within the discretion of the contracting party to decide the appropriate level of risk. The court furthermore stated that according to the precautionary principle, 'it is sufficient to show that there is relevant scientific uncertainty with regard to the risk in question';[20] however, a 'purely hypothetical or academic consideration will not suffice'.[21] The court finally emphasized that the principle of proportionality should be respected and the need to safeguard public health was to be balanced against the principle of free movement of goods.[22]

In order for Norway to fulfill EEA law, the court stated: 'authorization to market fortified cornflakes had been refused because of a lack of need, while Norway maintained as a matter of policy fortification of brown whey cheese with up to 10mg of iron per 100[g] of cheese to be freely sold in the country'.[23] Norway had not 'demonstrated that a comprehensive risk assessment had been carried out ... in response to Kellogg's submission of its application for authorization. A comprehensive risk assessment was only carried out in the course of the proceedings before the court.'[24]

The court finally concluded that due to certain procedural mistakes made by Norwegian authorities when preparing the decision to prohibit the importation of cornflakes, and since the Norwegian fortification policy as presented at that time did not fulfill the requirements of EEA law, Norway had at the relevant time failed to fulfill its obligations under Article 11 of the EEA.[25]

THE PRECAUTIONARY PRINCIPLE UNDER ICELANDIC LAW

The constitution

The Icelandic Constitution does not include any references to basic environmental principles similar to the Norwegian Constitution's Article 110(b) and Article 20 of the

Finnish Constitution.[26] Consequently, when environmental interests compete with interests enjoying explicit constitutional protection, one can, from the outset, expect the latter to prevail. This is particularly apparent if it is necessary to restrict property rights and the right to conduct economic activities.[27] On the other hand, the constitution encompasses all traditional human rights principles in line with the European Convention of Human Rights (ECHR). Furthermore, the text of the ECHR along with, *inter alia*, the ECHR's Protocol 1, have been made part of Icelandic law (see Act No 62/1994 of the ECHR).

To the best of my knowledge, no case has yet been brought before the Supreme Court of Iceland or any other Icelandic court, for that matter, where it has explicitly been argued that particular decisions of public authorities or the operation of specific polluting activities have given rise to considering a breach of the constitution's Article 71 – equaling ECHR's Article 8 – on the protection of privacy, of one's home, etc.

The legislation's character

Icelandic environmental legislation is, in all major respects, of a preventive nature, to a large extent reflecting recent international regimes on environmental issues, as well as the bulk of EC acts through the EEA regime. The legislation is not synchronized, and is found in several acts that are not all under the auspices of the Ministry for the Environment. This fact diminishes possibilities for integrating environmental objectives. Another drawback is the fact that most of the recent environmental principles, such as the precautionary principle, have not explicitly been spelled out in the legislation.

I have found one explicit example of the precautionary principle in the legislation's texts. It links to decision-making on the basis of the Foodstuffs Act No 93/1995. Under Article 28, the minister for the environment can enact precautionary and preventive measures relating to foodstuffs that may cause severe damage to human health. The act does not, however, give any specification on the quality of the information, which should otherwise lay the foundation for such a decision, the use of risk assessment procedures or the acceptable level of proof. Case E-3/00 should, nevertheless, provide the basic criteria in this respect as far as the free movement of goods under the EEA regime is concerned.

General and sectoral acts and regulations

Principal environmental acts

For clarification, the key environmental legislation having the objective to conserve, manage and control natural resources and their utilization will now be listed and briefly described. General comments will be made as to whether or not the legislation explicitly or implicitly reflects the precautionary principle or any risk assessment procedure laying the foundations for decision-making.[28]

Physical planning, land use and buildings

The Physical Planning and Building Act No 73/1997 has, *inter alia*, the objective to promote sustainable and rational land use, nature conservation and the conservation of the cultural heritage, all in order to avoid environmental damage and over-utilization of natural resources. The practical tools to reach the objectives are, first and foremost, different kinds of physical planning; the obligation to attain a developing consent for all projects having considerable impact on the environment; the duty to prepare an environmental impact assessment (EIA) for particular projects and operations; and, finally, the obligation to obtain a building permit before buildings are constructed. No explicit precautionary thinking is present in the act or in the practice of the Administrative Physical Planning and Building Complaint Committee.[29]

Environmental impact assessments

Act No 106/2000 on Environmental Impact Assessment mirrors the key EC directives on the subjects, and all are part of the EEA.[30] The precautionary principle, as such, is not mentioned in the act. However, the very purpose of an EIA and the EIA procedure is to demonstrate expected environmental effects of proposed activities and to highlight uncertainties. This is in line with the act's Article 9, paragraph 2, since the developer should propose the necessary monitoring mechanisms, especially when the environmental impacts from certain operations are uncertain. Article 9 does not, however, explicitly mention uncertainty in this respect; but this is clear from the preparatory documents.[31] Authorities preparing and taking the final decision must, furthermore, take the outcome of the EIA procedure into consideration while preparing the decision. Lastly, if the authority decides not to follow the outcome of the EIA, its reasoning for that decision must be made public.[32]

Nature conservation

Apart from a general reference to sustainable development in Article 1 of Act No 44/1999 on Nature Conservation, no recent environmental principle is explicitly mentioned in its text and no trace of any precautionary thinking is explicitly apparent as a tool for the decision-maker based upon its provisions. Act No 44/1999 applies to classical nature conservation issues, such as the establishment of nature reserves and protected areas, as well as the possibility of protecting particular organisms. The act also encompasses specific rules on the importation of alien organisms other than GMOs, particular animals for agricultural purposes, pets, ocean mammals and harvest. The minister for the environment is responsible for the respective decision-making, which apparently does not reflect any precautionary approach. The Nature Conservation Act also contains several general rules on the conservation of different kinds of wetlands, and rules on the extraction of material and planning within such areas on land and in the net laying area (115m out from the low-water line). Extraction in these areas is subject to permits issued by the respective municipalities under the Physical Planning and Building Act, and the Environmental Agency has the role of voicing its opinion on proposed extraction sites that are, depending upon their size, subject to an EIA.

Wild land-based species and birds

With a few exemptions, all wild land-based animals and birds are either subject to complete protection and hunting restrictions, or are managed by time frame schemes in line with the Protection and Hunting of Wild Species Act No 64/1994.[33] First, the act's provisions do not include references to any of the recent environmental principles, such as the precautionary principle. Second, the decision-making provisions have no explicit ties to risk assessment procedures. However, in the application of individual provisions, one can trace that the decision-making – for example, decisions to increase protection of a species or to ban hunting – is based upon the precautionary principle. The ptarmigan stock management offers an excellent example. Due to considerable fluctuation in the stock's size for which reasons are not fully known or agreed upon by scientists, the Minister for the Environment first banned ptarmigan hunting for several seasons and has now shortened the traditional hunting season in order to reduce the risk factors or even stock collapse.

Salmon and trout

There is a long tradition of managing and conserving salmon and trout in Icelandic freshwaters as well as offshore. Under the Salmon and Trout Act No 76/1970,[34] utilization is subject to certain fishing seasons and control, and is monitored by official research authorities. All offshore salmon and trout fishing[35] is prohibited. Based upon scientific information, several provisions of the act allow the competent authorities to restrict or ban fishing or particular fishing methods in order to prevent over-exploitation and stock decline. However, there is no visible link to the precautionary principle or to the use of risk assessments present in the individual provisions of the act. Even so, it would not be just to draw the conclusion that some kind of a precaution is not exercised in the decision-making. Finally, decisions related to salmon fish farming build upon the outcome of an EIA procedure that the decision-maker must take into consideration before granting a permit. If the EIA is not followed, the reasons must be made public.

Genetically modified organisms

Act No 18/1996 on Genetically Modified Organisms reflects the precautionary approach of EC directives on MMOs and GMOs that are part of the EEA's Annex XX. Even though individual provisions of the acts do not mention the precautionary principle in so many words, the duty to prepare a risk assessment and risk evaluation on the potential harmfulness of individual GMOs is present.[36] Furthermore, a licence to conduct activities involving GMOs can be withdrawn by the Environmental Agency if the risk increases, the categorization of GMOs changes, new information indicates that the risk has not been properly evaluated, or if new techniques make it possible to limit risk factors even further. One provision of Act No 18/1996 is of specific interest – namely, its Article 19, paragraph 2, under which the Minister for the Environment can ban or limit the placing of particular GMOs or products containing GMOs on the Icelandic market if they are thought to damage human health or the environment. Such a decision must be based upon scientific information provided by the

Environmental Agency and an opinion provided by the Consulting Committee on GMOs.[37] Particular drawbacks in applying the precautionary principle could, however, be present. The procedure would also be subject to the principles of the Public Administration Act No 37/1993. The act's basic principles would normally not allow for much uncertainty in the decision-making, at least if the decision would restrict importation. Finally, in line with the principle of proportionality, the measure having the least effects on the applicant's interests should normally be the one chosen by the authorities unless a clear provision stipulates otherwise.

Fisheries management

The Fisheries Management Act No 116/2000 has the objective of promoting the conservation of fish stocks and their efficient utilization, and thus of ensuring stable employment and settlement. The act's text does not refer to the precautionary principle in relation to the decision-making, nor is a transparent decision-making process present. This does not mean that the precautionary approach is absent when the Marine Research Institute evaluates the available data and prepares its formal recommendations, or when the minister takes the final decision. On the basis of recommendations from the Marine Research Institute, each exploitable fish stock is managed by decisions enacted by the minister for fisheries where the total allowable catch (TAC) is set for each fish stock.[38]

High seas fishing

Act No 151/1996 on Fishing outside the Icelandic Jurisdiction (high seas fishing) was enacted by the *Althing* (the central legislative assembly) in order for Iceland to fulfill the basic obligations under the Straddling Fish Stocks Agreement. The act's text does not mention the precautionary principle in so many words, which is, on the other hand, explicitly stipulated in the agreement's Article 5 and further worked on in its Article 6.[39] However, pursuant to the act's Article 7, the Minister for Fisheries has the power to enact administrative regulations in order to manage and control the high seas fisheries of Icelandic fishing vessels and sets the TAC, *inter alia*, to fulfill international obligations. The decisions are taken on the bases of recommendations of the Marine Research Institute in line with Act No 116/2006.

Pollution control and operating licences

Act No 7/1998 on Hygiene and Pollution Control is the principle legislation on pollution prevention and control from land-based sources and provides the legal bases necessary for the incorporation of all major EC acts on pollution prevention and control that Iceland is bound by through the EEA Agreement and its Annex XX. Among these EC acts is the Integrated Pollution Prevention and Control Directive (IPPC directive), which is basically incorporated within the Icelandic legal system with Regulation No 785/1999 on Operating Licences for Polluting Activities and Regulation No 786/1999 on Pollution Control. All large stationary operations likely to pollute the environment are subject to licensing procedure and official control. They are, furthermore, subject to best available technology (BAT) requirements and an EIA procedure in line with Act No 106/2000 on Environmental Impact Assessment.

Even though Act No 7/1998 implements all of the relevant EC directives on pollution control and most of the basic requirements of the Convention for the Protection of the Marine Environment of the North-East Atlantic (OSPAR), individual provisions unfortunately do not explicitly mention any recent environmental principle, such as the precautionary principle. It would, however, be incorrect to state that the precautionary approach is not present in this sector of the environmental legislation. This is due to the fact that many of the substantive requirements reflecting the principle are present in administrative regulations that incorporate the EC commitments through the EEA regime. On the other hand, the shortage of direct references to the precautionary principle in the act's substantial provisions, particularly in provisions on the decision-making procedures, leaves the procedure subject to the principles of the Public Administration Act No 37/1993.

Coastal areas and the sea

Recently, a new Act No 33/2004 on Protective Measures against Pollution of the Sea and Coastlines came into force. Its main objective is to protect the sea and coastal areas from land- and sea-based pollution. The act does not explicitly refer to the precautionary principle or connect the precautionary approach and risk assessments to its provisions. Nonetheless, its substantive provisions incorporating all of the basic international commitments have the objective of protecting the sea from pollution, *inter alia*, the OSPAR's as well as the International Maritime Organization's (IMO's) standards. Moreover, the BAT is a standard requirement for particular land-based operations. Therefore, presumably some kind of a precautionary principle lies in the substantive provisions of Act No 33/2004. Apart from the above, all major land-based operations likely to cause pollution on coastal areas and the sea are subject to an EIA and an operation licensing under the Pollution Control Act No 7/1998, reflecting the IPPC directive mentioned above.

Toxic and hazardous substances

Finally, Act No 52/1988 on Toxic and Dangerous Substances is mentioned.[40] The act applies to the manufacturing, importation, storage, usage and disposal of certain toxic and dangerous substances that are also subject to licensing, registration and official control. The act's inherent provisions do not explicitly mention any recent environmental principle, such as the precautionary principle or the principle of substitution; the decision-making provisions do not allow for much uncertainty and are subject to the basic principles of the Public Administration Act No 37/1993. However, this legislation provides the legal framework for the incorporation of part of the EEA's Annex II within the Icelandic legal system. Furthermore, the ozone regime is implemented by issuing regulations on the basis of the act. Therefore, the precautionary principle is present as far as obligations based upon the principle are reflected in the substantive provisions of regulations issued under the legal framework of Act No 52/1988.

Risk assessments and cost-benefit analyses

As mentioned earlier, the obligation to use risk assessment is explicitly present in Act No 18/1996 on GMOs and in regulations on the issue. Another example of a positive duty to perform a risk assessment can also be traced. Under Act No 49/1997 on Measures Against Avalanches and Landslides and the corresponding Regulation No 505/2002 on Danger Assessment for Avalanches and Landslides, Categorization and Utilization of Dangerous Areas and Provisional Assessment, municipalities in areas that have tradition-ally suffered from avalanches and landslides are under the obligation to assess the danger of such events. The assessments are prepared by the Meteorological Agency and are based upon information from several official institutes. All activities and develop-ment areas must be planned in line with the outcome of such assessments.

More classical examples are found in Regulation No 263/1998 on Risk Assessment in Industry. The regulation incorporates the Post-Seveso Directive[41] that is a part of the EEA Agreement. Under the regulation, operators of the industrial activities falling under its scope have the obligation to submit information on the operations and the substances involved in particular industrial processes, as well as the duty to prepare a risk assessment.

As far as formal cost-benefit analyses are concerned, I am not aware of such obligations explicitly spelled out in the enviornmental legislation. In practice, however, such assess-ments are carried out when all major operations and installations are prepared.

Administrative practice

Examples of administrative practice explicitly based upon the precautionary principle are available. A few are found in decisions relating to the EIA procedure and the quality of the EIA report. One of them concerns sediment dredging for diatomite extraction in Lake Mývatn (Lake Mývatn is a Ramsar site)[42] in north-eastern Iceland. Diatomite dredging began in the late 1960s and negative developments of the lake's ecosystem have already materialized, although scientists cannot fully explain the causal connections between the dredging and individual changes in the lake's ecosystem or predict precisely what to expect in the future. However, all leading scientists issued warnings as early as the beginning of the 1980s. In the Lake Mývatn EIA proceedings of 1999 to 2000, one of the principal concerns was how adverse environmental impacts could be expected by opening two new areas (area 1 and 2) for sediment dredging for diatomite in the lake. Leading scientists were in agreement on the point that adverse impact could be expected – and some of them pointed out that negative impact on the lake's ecosystem had already occurred – if the dredging was expanded and that there was a need for further research on both the biodiversity of the area and the on lake's ecological functions and the dependent wetland avifauna. They recommended that the extraction sites should not be enlarged and that all diatomite extraction from the lake should cease within a certain time frame. On the other hand, the Diatomite Extraction Company claimed, *inter alia*, that they were fulfilling the precautionary principle by abandoning dredging areas that had been used since the extraction began in the late 1960s. The company furthermore argued that dredging in new areas did not require any other approach and should not be subject to any other conditions than those for the old extraction site, opened during the late 1960s, and that should unacceptable environmental effects materialize, it would be possible to cease the extraction before any long-term damage would occur.

In the Central Planning Agency's final conclusion on the EIA for the sediment dredging from the lake, the precautionary principle was highlighted.[43] The agency stated that the Icelandic government was bound to follow the precautionary principle, and scientific uncertainty should not be used as a basis to allow certain activities. The agency furthermore referred to the Ramsar's term of 'wise use' without taking a clear stand on the meaning of the term. On the basis of general reference to the precautionary principle, however, after carefully scrutinizing the available information and data provided by the scientific community and the Diatomite Extraction Company, the agency concluded that the available information on proposed extraction in area 1 was not sufficient to determine the expected environmental effects. However, the agency decided that the environmental effects expected for extraction in area 2 were not deemed adverse.[44]

This decision on the EIA was appealed within the administrative system, and it was the minister for the environment who had the final say in the case (that is, as far as the EIA was concerned). The claimants argued, *inter alia*, that the agency had used scientific uncertainty to promote sediment dredging for diatomite extraction and that it had been in the interest of the Diatomite Extraction Company not to provide more information. The minister's verdict, which was basically the same as the agency's, stated, *inter alia*, that the precautionary principle had been followed since the EIA procedure had provided the necessary information and assessments.[45]

Administrative practices where the precautionary principle has been implicitly relied upon are probably present. At the time of writing, I have not found any clear examples.

The practice of Icelandic courts

Today I am only aware of one court case where the final decision could be understood as reflecting the precautionary principle, even though the principle is not mentioned in so many words. In Supreme Court Case No 456/1996, on Laká in Suður-Þingeyjarsýslu (Laxá is a river and a part of the Mývant Ramsar site), the court based its final decision on information provided by a scientific report where it was stated that the release of Atlantic salmon (*salmo salar*) into the upper part of the Laxá river could endanger the biotic community of the part and, in particular, the Icelandic population of the Barrow's goldeneye (*Bucephala Islandica*), and reaffirmed the decision of the Nature Conservation Agency to ban the release. In addition, the principle has also recently been directly referred to in court proceedings. In Supreme Court Case No 20/2005, or *Reyðarál* (Reyðarál is an aluminium smelter currently under construction), the precautionary principle is not mentioned, although the applicant had repeatedly referred to the principle before the lower court while arguing that a new EIA had been necessary for Reyðarál. The Reyðarál aluminium smelter's installation was considerably different from the one that was first planned and which had been assessed in an EIA procedure. The applicant, furthermore, argued that by not preparing a new EIA, this constituted a clear breach of the principle since the operation of the smelter was likely to cause considerable environmental effects and damage. Even though the lower court came to the conclusion that a new EIA was necessary, the deciding judge did not refer to the precautionary principle in his argumentation, but based the judgment on the fact that there were fundamental differences between the old and the new installations, and that even though the manufacturing capacity of the new one was lesser, a new EIA should be conducted in line with law. The Supreme Court reached the same decision but on the basis that the operating licence for the first planned smelter had not been issued when it was decided to use the old EIA for the new installation. Therefore, a positive requirement in Act No 106/2000 had not been fulfilled and a new EIA was needed for the new aluminium smelter.

Academic debate

Academic debate on the precautionary principle in a legal context and on problems relating to its incorporation within the legal system has unfortunately been slim. The only published article on the principle that I am aware of and having as an objective to analyse the legal situation under Icelandic law is the one mentioned at the start of this chapter. This is not due to non-interest in the principle, its function or how it should be developed in the law or applied. On the contrary, the most likely explanation is the lack of individuals having the necessary time and resources to be able to conduct environmental law research.

Implementation of EC case law

Due to the EEA Agreement, there are no particular obstacles in the Icelandic legal order that preclude the use of the precautionary principle – that is, the substance as such – as it has developed under EC law. In order to fully incorporate the principle, however, some general principles of the legal system (*inter alia*, principles relating to the burden of proof) may have to be altered in order for the precautionary principle to work properly in environmental decision-making. In line with the EEA's basic obligations and functions,[46] EC case law should influence the development and application of Icelandic environmental law that has its origins in the EEA and that is subject to incorporation within the legal system under the agreement's Article 7. These influences are, however, not always unequivocal in the field of environmental law or in its practice.

Implementation of EFTA court cases

Since the EFTA states can be brought before the EFTA court on issues relating to questions of whether or not they have fulfilled the EEA obligations, the EFTA court's decisions obviously have a decisive effect on how the relevant national legislation is structured, interpreted and applied. Even though the EFTA court has not covered many issues relating to the EEA's environmental legislation, its findings in Case E-3/00, the *Kellogg's Case,* are of inportance, at least as far as the free movement of goods and the envionrment are concerned.

CONCLUSIONS

The conclusions that can be drawn from this chapter are as follows. Even though explicit references to the precautionary principle are hardly visible in the legislation, the principle is undoubtedly part of the Icelandic legal system and administrative practice in the field of environmental legislation. This is particularly obvious when legislation transposing EC acts through the EEA regime into the legal system is analysed. Furthermore, in the practice of individual decision-makers and in some of the EIA proceedings, the precautionary principle is, to a certain extent, present. Finally, Icelandic courts recognize the principle even though clear cases when a judgment has explicitly been build upon the principle are still not available.

There are, however, particular issues present in the legal system that diminish the possibilities for applying the precautionary principle. The first relates to the fact that the constitution has not yet been adjusted to reprioritization of values and lacks all references to environmental goals and principles. Second, the legislator is yet to insert the bulk of all environmental principles, including the precautionary principle, into the respective legal texts. Third, due to unchanged principles on the burden of proof and the fact that if no specific administrative procedure is decided upon, the principles of the Administration Act apply, they do not allow for much uncertainty in decision-making and they should be proportional. Fourth, apart from two clear examples, transparent use of risk assessments and cost-benefit analysis in environmental decision-making is hardly evident in the legislation.

Compared with my findings in 2000, the results of this chapter's analysis suggest that they are, to a large extent, identical: that is, the precautionary principle is clearly present in the Icelandic legal system and has been explicitly applied in environmental decision-making. The legislation, however, must be further elaborated upon in order to make the principle work better within the legal system.

NOTES

1   Jóhannsdóttir, A. (2002) 'Not business as usual: A study of the precautionary principle', in *Afmælisrit til heiðurs Gunnari G. Schram sjötugum*, Almenna bókafélagið, Reykjavic, pp1–25.
2   I relied upon the following definition:

   The core is the understanding that precautionary measures must be taken – alternatively, that certain conduct and projects must be avoided – when there is reason to assume that the substance/ energy/project concerned may create adverse environmental interferences, even if there is no conclusive evidence of a causal relationship between cause and alleged effects.

   Ebbesson, J. (1996) *Compatibility of International and National Environmental Law,* Iustus Förlag, Uppsala, pp119–120.
3   It should be pointed out that environmental litigation is rather undeveloped under Icelandic law, and cases brought before courts are few. However, ministers' rulings and rulings of specific bodies established by law have built upon the precautionary principle.
4   Vienna Convention for the Protection of the Ozone Layer, 26 ILM 1529; Montreal Protocol on Substances that Deplete the Ozone Layer, 26 ILM 1550; and subsequent protocols.

5   The first regulation dates back to the year 1989. Currently, regulation No 586/2002 on Ozone Depleting Substance, with amendments, is in force.

6   See further Act No 18/1996 on Genetically Modified Organisms and several administrative regulations transposing the basic obligations of Directive 90/219/EEC, OJ L 117, 8 May 1990, p1, and Directive 90/220/EEC, OJ L 117, 8 May 1990, p15, with amendments, into the Icelandic legal system.

7   See Jóhannsdóttir, A. (2002) 'Not business as usual: A study of the precautionary principle', in *Afmælisrit til heiðurs Gunnari G. Schram sjötugum*, Almenna bókafélagið, Reykjavic, pp23–25.

8   The preparatory work accompanying the acts very seldom comments on the precautionary principle or explains how the principle is to be applied.

9   See Jóhannsdóttir, A. (2002) 'Not business as usual: A study of the precautionary principle', in *Afmælisrit til heiðurs Gunnari G. Schram sjötugum*, Almenna bókafélagið, Reykjavic, especially pp23–25.

10 See de Sadeleer, N. (2002) 'The precautionary principle', in *Environmental Principles: From Political Slogans to Legal Rules*, Oxford University Press, Oxford, pp91–149.

11 See de Sadeleer, N. (2002) 'The precautionary principle', in *Environmental Principles: From Political Slogans to Legal Rules*, Oxford University Press, Oxford, pp91–223.

12 Ebbesson, J. (1996) *Compatibility of International and National Environmental Law*, Iustus Förlag, Uppsala, pp119–120.

13 See de Sadeleer, N. (2002) 'The precautionary principle', in *Environmental Principles: From Political Slogans to Legal Rules*, Oxford University Press, Oxford, p91.

14 Exemptions from the general rule may be found by referring to public order and similar fundamentals.

15 See also Protocol 35 to the EEA Agreement; Case E-1/01, *Hörður Einarsson v the Icelandic State*, paras 51 to 52; *Report of the EFTA Court*, 2002, pp1–43; Björgvinsson, D, Þ. (2001) 'Bein réttaráhrif og forgangsáhrif EES-réttar', in *Líndæla Sigurður Líndal sjötugur*, Hið íslenska bókmenntafélag, Reykjavík, pp71–94.

16 Agreement between the EFTA States on the Establishment of a Surveillance Authority and a Court of Justice from 2 May 1992.

17 C-157/96, *The Queen v Ministry of Agriculture, Fisheries and Food, and Others* (1998) ECR I-2211, particularly paras 31 to 34 and 40.

18 Case E-3/00, *EFTA Surveillance Authority v Norway* (2000–2001), *Report of the EFTA Court*, pp73–86.

19 The Norwegian legislation only allowed fortification in the case of nutritional need in the Norwegian population. Norway argued the case, *inter alia*, with reference to the notion of risk (that is, fortified products would, in general, create a risk for public health and it was not decisive whether or not the fortification of the cornflakes in question created such a risk to public health). Norway, furthermore, referred to the present state of scientific research and that 'the fortification in question might be a health hazard when eaten in uncontrollable and unforeseen amounts' (Case E-3/00, *EFTA Surveillance Authority v Norway* (2000–2001), *Report of the EFTA Court*, para 5). Moreover, reference was made to the risks associated with excessive intake of iron for particular parts of the population. Since the mineral, iron, was thought to carry higher risks than the vitamins added, Norway limited the risk evaluation to that substance. Lastly, Norway argued that application of the 'precautionary attitude' (Case E-3/00, *EFTA Surveillance Authority v Norway* (2000–2001), *Report of the EFTA Court*, para 7) was reasonable since the causal relation between iron level in the body and certain diseases was not known. Case E-3/00, *EFTA Surveillance Authority v Norway* (2000–2001), *Report of the EFTA Court*, paras 1 to 3 and 5 to 7.

20 Case E-3/00, *EFTA Surveillance Authority v Norway* (2000–2001), *Report of the EFTA Court*, para 25.

21 Case E-3/00, *EFTA Surveillance Authority* v *Norway* (2000–2001), *Report of the EFTA* Court, para 29.

22 Case E-3/00, *EFTA Surveillance Authority* v *Norway* (2000–2001), *Report of the EFTA* Court, paras 23 to 25 and 27 to 29.

23 Case E-3/00, *EFTA Surveillance Authority* v *Norway* (2000–2001), *Report of the EFTA* Court, para 41.

24 Case E-3/00, *EFTA Surveillance Authority* v *Norway* (2000–2001), *Report of the EFTA* Court, para 42.

25 Case E-3/00, *EFTA Surveillance Authority* v *Norway* (2000–2001), *Report of the EFTA* Court, paras 35 to 39.

26 The Constitution is, however, under revisions and one of the leading environmental non-governmental organizations (NGOs) has proposed an amendment: a provision containing references to some of the recent environmental principles.

27 See as an example Supreme Court Case No 15/2000 from 13 April 2000, *Stjörnugrís hf. v. íslenska ríkið.* The case concerned the question of whether or not an intensive rearing of pigs (2.999 pigs) should be subject to an EIA; however, the Icelandic legislation had not been adjusted to reflect recent amendments in EC law.

28 The coverage to follow is not meant to give an exhaustive overview of Iceland's legislation relating to the management and conservation of the environment and natural resources, and is only meant to serve this chapter and its objectives.

29 The role of the committee is to review the decisions of the municipalities, *inter alia*, relating to the above mentioned consents and the implementation of the physical planning. See also Gunnarsdóttir, S. M. (2004) 'Aðild að málum sem varða umhverfið: Háskóli Íslands', unpublished.

30 Directive 85/337/EEC OJ L 175, 5 July 1985, p40, with amendments in Directive 97/11/EC OJ L 73, 14 March 1997, p5, and Directive 03/35/EC OJ L 156, 25 June 2003, p17. The last one has not yet been made a part of the EEA.

31 See further recent changes that were made on Act No 106/2000: see Act No 74/2005; Alþt. 2004–2005 A-deild, þskj. 241, and þskj. 1387 and 1388, and also Jóhannsdóttir, A. (2006) 'Er-at maðr svá góðr at galli né fylgi: Umfjöllun um breytingar á málsmeðferð mats á umhverfisáhrifum', *Guðrúnarbók. Afmælisrit til heiðurs Guðrúnu Erlendsdóttur 3 maí 2006*, Hið íslenska bókmenntafélag, pp1–19.

32 Jóhannsdóttir, A. (2006) 'Er-at maðr svá góðr at galli né fylgi: Umfjöllun um breytingar á málsmeðferð mats á umhverfisáhrifum', *Guðrúnarbók. Afmælisrit til heiðurs Guðrúnu Erlendsdóttur 3 maí 2006*, Hið íslenska bókmenntafélag, pp1–19.

33 Many of the act's provisions concern hunting rights, hunting methods and weapons, requirements that hunters have to fulfill, and other issues relating to the hunting of the wild animals subject to the legislation.

34 Act No 76/1970 is private ownership-based legislation – that is, most of its provisions have as a direct objective to protect the fishing rights of the landowners where salmon and trout lakes and rivers are situated and the quality and the quantity of the catch.

35 Offshore trout fishing beond the net layers area.

36 At the time of writing, Directive 01/18/EC on the deliberate release into the environment of genetically modified organisms and Repealing Council Directive 90/220/EEC have not been made part of the EEA or Icelandic legislation.

37 See Act No 18/1996 on Genetically Modified Organisms, Article 7; and Article 4 of Regulation No 275/2002 on the Contained Use of Genetically Modified Organisms and, finally, Article 9 of Regulation No 276/2002 on the Contained Use of Genetically Modified Organisms, other than Micro-organisms.

38 This is done by issuing a regulation for each fish stock for a designated period or season.

39 The precautionary principle is, on the other hand, mentioned in the preparatory documents accompanying Act No 151/1996, AlÞt. 1996, A-deild, Þskj.

40 The legislation that is originally from the 1960s is currently under revision and will be considerably changed.

41 Directive 96/82/EC on the Control of Major Accident Hazards Involving Dangerous Substances, OJ L 10, 14 January 1997, p13.

42 The sites are established under the Convention on Wetlands of International Importance, especially as Waterfowl Habitat, 1976 UNTS 246, usually referred to as the Ramsar Convention.

43 The Second Environmental Assessment and Decision of the Central Planning Agency, from 7 July 2000. To avoid misunderstanding, the final decisions and the licence for diatomite mining in Lake Mývant fall under the Minister of Industry, who is to take into account the outcome of the EIA procedure before issuing the licence. New mining areas in Lake Mývant were, however, never opened. The factory was shut down since its operation was no longer considered economically feasible and all diatomite dredging has now been brought to an end.

44 The Second Environmental Assessment and Decision of the Central Planning Agency, from 7 July 2000, in particular pp23–25 and 34 ff.

45 Verdict of the Minister for the Environment from 1 November 2000, p39 ff.

46 See, in particular, EEA's Article 6 and also Article 3 of the Agreement between the EFTA States on the Establishment of a Surveillance Authority and a Court of Justice.

CHAPTER 6

Norway

Hans Christian Bugge

INTRODUCTION

This chapter discusses the content and role of the precautionary principle in Norway's environmental policy and law. It will first deal briefly with the principle as a general *political* principle before presenting a theoretical model for analysing its possible *legal* content and role. Then we shall look at the principle in relation to the legal framework and application in some areas of environmental policy where the principle seems to play a role.

Until now, the legal discussion of the precautionary principle has been limited in Norway.[1] One reason for this may be the fact that there have been very few court cases in which the principle has been invoked, and – until now – not a single case before the Supreme Court. A leading theorist in Norwegian environmental law, Inge Lorange Backer,[2] describes the principle as closely related to the principle of prevention, primarily addressing legislators, but also public administration when applying the relevant acts.[3] In his view, the principle is not a very precise principle or concept in Norwegian law or policy. He links the principle primarily to situations of uncertainty; but he also discusses it as a more general principle of prevention, a principle for ensuring a safety margin in environmental policy, a principle of '*in dubio pro natura*' and – implicitly – a principle for 'reversing the burden of proof'.

In international texts and discussions, the expression varies between the 'precautionary *principle*' (Convention for the Protection of the Marine Environment of the North-East Atlantic (OSPAR) Article 2(a) and European Community (EC) Treaty Article 174), the 'precautionary *approach*' (Rio Declaration principle 15) and 'precautionary *measures*' (Framework Convention on Climate Change (FCCC) Article 3.3). One understanding is that the wording precautionary *approach* implies a weaker and less precise obligation than the precautionary *principle*. It is a matter of debate whether there is a basis for such a distinction. In my view, it is hard to see the difference in real content between OSPAR Article 2(a), principle 15 of the Rio Declaration and Article 3.3 of the FCCC. In Norwegian translations and debates, no systematic distinctions seem to be made between these various wordings. Here, we will treat them all under the wording 'the precautionary principle'.

In the Norwegian debate, no clear distinction is made between the precautionary principle as applied to risk *assessment* and risk *management*. It is, however, often underlined that the principle also implies *procedural* requirements: an assessment of environmental characteristics and possible effects of an activity or a product – including an assessment of the inherent risks, uncertainties and knowledge gaps. Hence, the rules on environmental impact assessment (EIA) in Norwegian law – which, to a large extent, correspond to the EC directives[4] – may be seen as one aspect of the precautionary principle as a legal principle. However, the precautionary principle is not mentioned in these rules and there are no precise legal requirements as to how thorough an assessment has to be in situations of scientific uncertainties. The EIA system is not limited to situations of uncertainty and therefore has a different field of application from the precautionary principle. The EIA rules will not be discussed further in this chapter.

It should be recalled that the principle may play a role in two different ways. It may justify active measures to address an existing problem, such as measures to reduce carbon dioxide (CO_2) emissions to avoid climate change. It may also give grounds for non-action in order to avoid possible new risks. In a Norwegian context, for example, the principle is used as an argument for avoiding exploration and exploitation of petroleum resources in certain vulnerable sea areas on the continental shelf. This distinction is not applied in the following text.

The uncertainty of the possible risk may refer to several elements: the nature and possible effects of the substance or product in question, how nature reacts to the exposure and the level of a safe tolerance limit ('how safe is safe'), and the probability of a certain event, such as an accidental leakage, to occur, etc. The sum of uncertainties has to be taken into account.

The precautionary principle challenges the principle of economic efficiency based on cost-benefit analyses, and it is criticized by many economists. The principle may be defined as a principle that sets aside economic efficiency by requiring measures that are not cost-effective, or which applies to situations where a cost-benefit analysis is impossible due to lack of certain knowledge. Theoretically, however, the precautionary principle may be applied within the framework of economic efficiency by putting a higher cost estimate on the potential and possible harm due to its uncertainty and higher cost of obtaining full information than the level that would be justified by present knowledge.

It is important to be aware that the development of the principle within the context of *international trade law* has given it a Janus-like face. Originally, the principle was meant as both a justification and an obligation for the state to take measures to protect the environment in case of a risk of serious or irreversible damage, even if the scientific basis for the measures is uncertain. However, in the context of international trade law, the legal problem is related to the use of the principle as an argument and basis for national measures to protect public health and the environment that may restrict international trade. Here, an equally important legal task has been to *delimit* the possibility for a state to invoke the principle by establishing strict conditions and criteria. Furthermore, in these cases, the burden to prove that the conditions are fulfilled and precautionary measures are justified falls on the state that has invoked it. This is the opposite position of the 'reversal of the burden of proof', which is seen as a consequence of the precautionary principle and which puts the burden of proof on the party who claims that his activity is safe.

It must be underlined that the conditions and criteria for applying the precautionary principle within international trade law are not fully relevant for the interpretation and implementation of the principle as a principle of environmental policy and law outside the sphere of international trade. There is, however, a danger from an environmental point of view that the trade-related conditions and criteria are also invoked outside international trade cases in order to limit the possibility of the authorities to carry out a strict environmental policy. I take this opportunity to warn against such a development.

THE PRECAUTIONARY PRINCIPLE AS A GENERAL PRINCIPLE OF NORWAY'S ENVIRONMENTAL POLICY

It is fair to maintain that Norwegian environmental policy has been based on a precautionary approach, in a wide sense of that concept, for more than three decades. A Ministry of the Environment was established in 1972. Important environmental legislation was adopted during the 1970s and early 1980s on the basis of a *principle of prevention*. New acts on hazardous products, pollution control and wildlife management introduced systems of general prohibition and control of activities that may be harmful to the environment.

The explicit precautionary principle in a stricter sense first appeared on the Norwegian scene at the United Nations Economic Commission for Europe (ECE) Ministerial Conference in Bergen in May 1990. As conference chair, Norway promoted the adoption of the Bergen Declaration on Sustainable Development in the ECE region, with its paragraph 7 on the precautionary principle: 'Where there are threats of serious and irreversible damage, lack of full scientific certainty should not be used as a reason for postponing measures to prevent environmental degradation.'

Similar formulations of the principle were adopted at subsequent conferences, including as principle 15 of the Rio Declaration.[5] This definition is dominant in official governmental documents. The further discussion of this chapter is based on this definition, thus limiting it to a principle for assessing and managing situations of uncertainty.

In 1997 the government presented a major White Paper to the *Stortinget* entitled *Environmental Policy for a Sustainable Development*.[6] Here the government states that the objectives of Norway's environmental policy will be based on two major principles: to respect nature's 'critical loads' and the precautionary principle. It says that:

> ... *if there is a risk of serious or irreversible damage, the lack of full scientific evidence shall not be used as a reason for damaging nature or for postponing measures of environmental policy. Possible negative effects must be given significant weight when laying down objectives [of environmental policy].*[7]

Since then, every governmental White Paper on environmental policy has stated that the 'critical load' approach and the precautionary principle are fundamental in Norway's environmental policy.[8] And the political platform of our present government, which was presented after the general election in the autumn of 2005, declares that the government will 'build its environmental policy on the principle of sustainable development, the precautionary principle and solidarity with future generations'.[9] The issue to be discussed in the following text is whether this is only 'lip service' to a good idea, or whether the principle is, *in fact*, applied in Norwegian environmental policy and law.

An immediate impression is that the principle is seen as a principle of environmental policy only, and environmental policy understood in a limited sense. A quick look at the policy in some of the economic sectors that are root causes of hazards and damage to the environment indicates that the role of the precautionary principle is very limited there. For example, it is difficult to see any influence of the principle in such policy areas as transport, agriculture, tourism, general land-use policy and planning, and coastal zone management, not to mention general economic policy that continues to be oriented towards maximum economic growth and a strong increase in private consumption. It is not even guiding Norway's climate policy.

The first target of Norwegian climate policy, established in 1990, was to reduce the emission of greenhouse gases (GHGs) to the 1989 level of 34 million tonnes by the year 2000, and some measures such as a CO_2 tax on the offshore petroleum industry were introduced. In 1995, however, this target was tacitly abandoned as unrealistic. Since then, the political debate on climate policy has mainly been about choice of instruments, with very limited effect on emissions. The Kyoto Protocol allows Norway to increase its average emission by 1 per cent compared to its 1990 level. The emissions have steadily continued to increase and are, at present, at more than 55 million tonnes, more than 10 per cent above the 1990 level.[10] It is difficult to see any sign of the precautionary principle in this (lack of) climate policy. Norway must make extensive use of the flexible mechanisms in order to fulfil its Kyoto obligation.

TURNING TO LAW: SOME GENERAL REFLECTIONS AND A SIMPLE ANALYTICAL MODEL

The concept 'legal principle' is not precise in Norwegian legal theory and raises questions of legal meaning without a clear answer. It is used and understood in several different ways. Some authors are generally sceptical about the concept of legal principles and want to restrict both the concept and the use of legal principles.[11] Others argue that principles are important to develop the law and that they play an increasing role in the development of Norwegian law.[12] It is anyway certain – maybe obvious – that the term 'principle' in itself does not say much about the legal meaning. Each 'principle' must be studied on the basis of the relevant sources to clarify its legal content and role.

At the outset, it is clear that the precautionary principle has some importance in Norwegian law. The numerous political statements about the principle as a fundament of Norway's environmental policy are themselves legally relevant. This is underpinned by the many international recommendations and treaties that lay down the principle, to which Norway is a party.

But when asking about its legal importance and role more precisely, clear answers are difficult to give. It is fair to state that the principle certainly plays a role as *a factor of interpretation* of the law. It may be used as an argument for an interpretation of the law that permits or even obliges the authority to take measures of risk assessment and risk management in accordance with the principle. But it has not the same strength as an argument in all fields of law and regardless of the type of case in question. A nuanced approach is required.

Another possible role of the principle relates to the *application* of the law within the framework of appreciation inherent in the various legal rules. The principle may have a legal importance by either *permitting* precautionary measures in case of uncertainty (what could be called 'the precautionary principle in a weak sense'), or *requiring* precautionary measures in case of uncertainty (what could be called 'the precautionary principle in a strong sense'). The possible rights and obligations in the application of acts depend, of course, partly upon the interpretation of the rule in question. There is a close link between interpretation and application of the act.

Parts of the following discussion are based on a simple *theoretical model*. I will make a distinction between the two possible roles of the principle and then apply these to three stages in the decision-making.

On the one hand, the principle may influence the interpretation and application in such a way that it implies *a right* for the public authority to apply precaution in case of uncertainty; in other words, the authority *may* apply precaution, but is not legally obliged to do so. On the other hand, the principle may mean *a duty* for the authority; the law *shall* be applied in accordance with the precautionary principle.

The question of whether there is a right or a duty may be looked into at three stages in the decision-making process:

1 the *assessment* of the risk and uncertainties (information-gathering);
2 the *evaluation* of costs and benefits – including possible risks and uncertainties;
3 the *decision on the outcome* of the case.

So, the *first* question is whether there is a right or a duty for the authority to ensure that the risks are thoroughly assessed and – consequently – the level of uncertainty illuminated. The *second* is whether the public authority has a right or a duty to take the uncertainty of possible effects into consideration in the sense that it is a relevant argument against the action or product in question. The *third* relates to the final decision: whether the authority has a right or duty to prevent or prohibit the action or product when there is uncertainty as to possible effects. These questions are now addressed in relation to the development and adoption of new laws, and the implementation of existing laws.

The precautionary principle: The role of the courts

When discussing the rights and obligations of the authorities related to the precautionary principle, the possible role of the courts is important. May – and will – the courts review decisions made by the legislator and the executive with regard to their application or non-application of the principle? From an environmental perspective, the courts may play both a positive and negative role. They may apply the principle to ensure an 'environmentally friendly' solution to a case. They may also censor the use of the principle by the authorities.

From a theoretical point of view, some will maintain that the very meaning of a principle being a principle of law implies that it ultimately may, and will, be upheld by the courts. However, this point of view is not at the base of this discussion. In my view, the principle has a legal nature to the extent that the legislator, or the executive authorities who apply the law, find it necessary to take the principle into account when making decisions. The question of court review of such decisions, and the possible consequences of legal flaws in legislative and executive decision-making, raises in itself several complex questions. It is not possible – at least not within the framework of this chapter – to discuss and draw conclusions about the final outcome of a court case where a party claims that the authority has either failed to apply the precautionary principle and thereby violated the law, or – to the contrary – has applied the principle unlawfully by prohibiting an activity without a sufficient legal basis. This will primarily depend upon the text of the relevant rule and its normal interpretation. But it also depends upon the general rules in Norwegian law concerning court review – an issue that cannot be treated in this chapter.

Here it should be kept in mind that the precautionary principle may be invoked in various ways in a court case. It may be used as a factor of *interpretation of a legal text.* In Norwegian law, the courts may always review the authority's understanding of the law. It may also be used when *assessing the facts* of the case if they are uncertain: what is the current situation? What are the relevant risks? What are possible scenarios for further development? The issue of court review of an authority's appreciation of facts is not entirely straightforward.

As mentioned, the principle has so far hardly been used by Norwegian courts, except in a couple of cases. However, this does not mean that the courts will not find the principle legally relevant if it is invoked. Our Supreme Court is quite sensitive to environmental arguments and concerns. For example, it recently laid down strict penalties for environmental crimes on the basis of preventive considerations. And a fair guess is that the court will refer to the precautionary principle and apply it as a general *guideline for legal interpretation* when it is relevant to the case. On the other hand, the court will most probably be very hesitant to censor the application of the principle by the legislator or the executive. However, I hesitate to indicate how far – or how strictly – the principle will be understood and applied by the courts. Neither the legal *content* of the principle nor the legal *weight* that it should be given are clear enough at this stage. What follows is simply an attempt to analyse and explore the issue further.

As a (possible) principle of Norwegian law, the precautionary principle is framed by, and has to be weighed against, other legal principles and rules. According to Norwegian public administrative law, a decision by a public authority has to be unbiased, and it must not be 'clearly unreasonable' or 'arbitrary'.[13] Hence, the application of the precautionary principle requires a thorough assessment of the possible risks and probabilities in each case. There have to be reliable indications that an unacceptable hazard may occur. It is difficult to define the lower threshold precisely; we lack relevant legal sources for drawing the line. If the possible hazards are serious or irreversible, the threshold should be low. In this respect, the courts will most certainly accept a wide margin of appreciation for the authority. But it is not possible to apply the principle if there is purely a theoretical possibility of harm. The principle must also be applied in a consistent way to avoid unfounded differences between otherwise similar cases.

THE ROLE AND IMPORTANCE OF
THE PRECAUTIONARY PRINCIPLE
FOR THE LEGISLATOR

The issue to be looked into here is whether the precautionary principle is of legal importance for the legislator – the Norwegian parliament, *Stortinget* – in some way or another.
We will take a look at constitutional rules and international obligations as a framework
for the legislator.

The precautionary principle in light of constitutional rules

For the legislator, possible obligations and limitations follow from constitutional rules
and international agreements to which Norway is a party. Theoretically, both constitutional rules and international agreements may oblige the legislator to take active steps to
prevent possible but uncertain environmental hazards. On the other hand, they may also
limit its freedom of action in this regard.

As the general rule, the Norwegian constitution – *Grunnloven* – does not *prevent* the
legislator – *Stortinget* – from basing new legislation on the precautionary principle. No
doubt, the necessary legislation *may* be adopted in order to clarify possible risks and
uncertainties, and to avoid environmental hazards even in case of uncertainty. New acts
may either lay down stricter obligations on existing activities or prohibit new activities.
Theoretically, the constitutional rules that restrict retroactive legislation (*Grunnloven*,
Article 97) and protect the right to property (mainly *Grunnloven*, Article 105) may, ultimately, set limits in this area as in any other area of legislation. But the principle itself
may influence the interpretation and application of these rules in an 'environmentally
friendly' way. This view may be based both on the consistent and explicit political
support for the principle in the *Stortinget* and the fact that Norway has accepted applying
the precautionary principle as party to numerous international recommendations and
treaties that lay down the principle.

In this context, the environmental article of *Grunnloven*, Article 110(b), is relevant. It
was adopted in 1992, and its first paragraph states:

> *Every person has a right to an environment that is conducive to health, and to natural
> surroundings whose productivity and diversity are preserved. Natural resources should
> be managed on the basis of comprehensive and long-term considerations whereby this
> right will be safeguarded for future generations as well.*

By underlining the needs to safeguard nature for future generations, it implicitly lays
down the principle of sustainable development. It is also argued by some that it contains
the precautionary principle, in spite of the fact that it neither explicitly nor implicitly
expresses the principle in its stricter meaning. The basis for this view is simply the
general observation that precautionary measures will be necessary to ensure the protection of nature and the welfare of future generations, in accordance with the principle of
sustainable development.

Whether the legislator is *obliged* to apply the precautionary principle when issuing new legislation is a different matter. The third paragraph of Article 110(b) says that the state authorities 'shall issue further provisions' in order to implement the principles laid down in the first (and second) paragraph of the article. This means an obligation for the legislator and the executive authorities to issue the necessary rules to protect the environment. However, it is up to the authorities to make the necessary trade-offs between environmental concerns and other objectives and tasks of society. It is my view that the duty of the legislator includes an obligation to ensure that environmental risks connected to new activities and products – including the inherent uncertainties – are properly assessed, made known and taken into consideration. However, the article is not sufficiently clear to create an obligation for the legislator to lay down as binding law the precautionary principle in its strict sense. In other words, *Grunnloven*, Article 110(b) gives support to the view that the legislator has a legal right to do it. Whether it implies a clear legal duty is, however, debatable.

Norway's international obligations in relation to the precautionary principle

Norway's environmental policy is framed by the fact that we are party to the most important international environmental treaties. Norway has ratified, *inter alia*, the UN ECE Convention on Long-Range Transboundary Air Pollution (LRTAP), with its most recent Gothenburg Protocol, the OSPAR Convention, the Framework Convention on Climate Change and the Kyoto Protocol, the Convention on Biological Diversity, the Stockholm Convention on Persistent Organic Pollutants, and the European Economic Area (EEA) Agreement. They all explicitly lay down the precautionary principle either in the preamble or in the operational article. As a party to these conventions and agreements, we are, of course, obliged to implement the precautionary principle in the way and to the extent this is required by the relevant treaties and protocols.

Norway applies the dualistic approach to international law. International rules do not become national law by ratification only; they have to be transformed into national law by the necessary legislative procedure. In case of possible conflict between international and national law, national law has priority. However, a 'principle of presumption' applies. Internal Norwegian law is 'presumed' to be in accordance with international law and will be interpreted accordingly at least in cases where there are several possible interpretations of the Norwegian legal text, and this text was part of Norwegian law before the international treaty was ratified.[14] It is a fair view that Norwegian law – as the main rule – shall be interpreted and implemented in accordance with our international obligations, including treaty obligations.

The European Economic Area (EEA) Agreement[15]

The Agreement on the European Economic Area (EEA) deserves some special remarks. The agreement makes Norway[16] a party to the European Union (EU) internal market without being an EU member. Broadly speaking, all EC treaty rules, as well as secondary legislation related to the four freedoms, apply to Norway.[17] Hence, the EEA Agreement forms a very important framework for Norway's environmental policy and law, both by its positive obligations and by the limitations inherent in its rules to protect free trade.

The EEA agreement was negotiated from 1990 until 1992, before the precautionary principle was part of Article 174 EC. This explains why the principle is not included in the operational part of the EEA Agreement, Article 73, which otherwise corresponds to former Article 130 A EC. Nevertheless, it seems fair to say that the principle today applies to the policy areas covered by the EEA agreement in much the same way as the principle applies to EC policy through Article 174 EC. One reason for this is that the principle is laid down in the preamble of the agreement. Its section 9 states that the contracting parties 'are determined to protect, conserve and improve the quality of the environment … in particular, on the basis of the principle of sustainable development, the precautionary principle and the principle of prevention'. It is the general view that the preamble is relevant for the interpretation of the treaty. Even more important, legal homogeneity within EEA as a whole is an important objective of the agreement.

The EEA Agreement is an 'ordinary' international treaty without entailing supranational authority. For EC secondary legislation to become Norwegian law, it has always to be formally adopted by the relevant Norwegian authority. In reality, the differences from the EU system are small. EC regulations are usually incorporated *verbatim* into Norwegian law. Directives are implemented by Norway in much the same way as by EU member states. The above-mentioned principle of presumption applies in case of conflict. If possible, Norwegian law will be interpreted in accordance with the requirements of EEA law.[18] Furthermore, the Norwegian EEA Act[19] states in its Article 2 that national laws that implement EEA rules have priority in case of conflict with other rules on the same issue. Regulations that implement EEA rules have priority in case of conflict with other regulations and subsequent laws. As a consequence, all EC regulations and directives that explicitly or implicitly build on or lay down the precautionary principle apply to Norway in the same way as to the EU member states.

This also means that the understanding and interpretation of the precautionary principle *in the context of trade law* follows that of EU law. In particular, the interpretation and application of the principle by the EC court guides the decisions by the EFTA court in similar cases. The EFTA court adjudicates in cases where it is maintained that an EFTA member state violates the EEA Agreement. Cases may be raised in much the same ways as cases before the EC courts, including through requests from national courts for advisory opinions. It follows from EEA Agreement Article 6 that the EFTA court will interpret and apply the rules of the EEA Agreement, including 'secondary legislation',[20] in accordance with the decisions taken by the EC court in similar cases. As mentioned, homogeneity within EEA as a whole is a fundamental objective.

The precautionary principle has been invoked and discussed in two cases before the EFTA court,[21] both related to food regulations. In these cases, the EC court's interpretation of the precautionary principle in a trade context played a decisive role. In the most recent case,[22] the Norwegian ban on alcohol advertising was challenged by the owner of a Norwegian wine journal as being in violation of Article 11 of the EEA Agreement, which corresponds to EC Treaty Article 28. The court discussed, *inter alia*, the precautionary principle as an argument to justify the ban. The court referred to the main EC court decisions where the precautionary principle has been invoked and discussed.[23] In accordance with these decisions and the criteria they lay down, the court stated that the precautionary principle can only justify national trade restrictions when 'the best available scientific knowledge is so insufficient, inadequate or unclear that it is impossible to decide with certainty the risks or hazards which may arise'.[24]

THE PRECAUTIONARY PRINCIPLE IN THE INTERPRETATION AND APPLICATION OF THE LAW: FOUR EXAMPLES

This section takes a look at four areas of environmental policy where the precautionary principle is particularly relevant: most thoroughly with regard to the control of chemicals and the protection of biodiversity, briefly with regard to genetically modified organisms (GMOs) and the protection of the Svalbard environment. The key questions are whether the principle may be applied and whether – in some cases – it must be applied.

Control of toxic chemicals

Control of emissions of chemicals into the environment has been a priority area for Norway's environmental policy for many years. In this field, it is fair to say that the precautionary principle clearly influences policy. In my view, it also has clear legal relevance. However, the development in this field is, to a large extent, marked by international recommendations and agreements – notably, recommendations from the North Sea conferences and pursuant to the OSPAR convention for emissions into freshwater and marine areas, the LRTAP convention with its protocols for emissions into the air and diffuse pollution, and the relevant EC directives on the marketing and control of chemicals, etc. Generally speaking, the Norwegian legislation in this field is harmonized with EC law with the obligations and limitations that this entails.[25]

The expressed general objective of Norway's chemical policy is that 'the emission and use of chemicals shall not have hazardous effects on health or on nature's ability to produce and reproduce'. Concentrations in the environment of the most dangerous substances will be reduced to their natural levels ('*bakgrunnsnivået*') and to about zero for man-made combinations.[26] For the most dangerous substances, the goal is 'zero emission': to eliminate emissions 'within a generation' by 2020. A specific plan of action has been adopted with defined targets to be reached for specific substances within 2005 or within 2010. The precautionary principle is clearly the decisive argument for this policy. The main legal basis for the policy on chemicals is the 1976 Product Control Act[27] and the 1981 Pollution Control Act.[28]

The objective of the Product Control Act is to prevent hazards to health and the environment from products.[29] It is the main legal instrument for controlling the use of chemicals and other hazardous products. It provides the government with a wide, discretionary authority to issue regulations and decisions to that effect. It is a normal interpretation, in my view, that measures may be taken even if the risk is uncertain – provided that there is reason for concern and that the risk exceeds a certain minimum level. This is underpinned by several articles in the act itself. For example, Article 3 lays down a general obligation of care for 'any person who produces, imports, trades, uses or in other ways deals with products that *may* have hazardous effects on health or the environment'. The issue of risk and uncertainty is inherent here. And Article 3(a) lays down the *principle of substitution*. The organization performing an activity using chemicals that *may* have hazardous effects has a duty to look for alternative and less risky substances and to use such substances if it does not entail unreasonable extra costs.

As a consequence, the authority has a *duty to assess risks and uncertainties* and to take this into consideration when making decisions pursuant to the act. Undoubtedly, the authority may, *inter alia*, prohibit the further marketing not only of products that clearly constitute 'an unacceptable risk',[30] but also when there are indications of this but no certain knowledge. For the most toxic and persistent chemicals, the act clearly implies a duty to strictly control emission even if there is uncertainty as to the precise effects. Here we are, in my view, very close to *a legal obligation* to apply the precautionary principle in the strong sense. There must be clearly documented and important reasons not to apply it. In addition to the purpose and whole system of the act, this conclusion is underpinned by the fact that *Stortinget* explicitly and repeatedly has based our chemicals policy on the precautionary principle.

Our 1981 Pollution Control Act applies to pollution from stationary sources and waste management. It lays down a general prohibition even to create a *risk* of pollution without a permit, and 'pollution' is defined as discharges that *may* create harm or nuisance. So, in fact, the act lays down a double safety margin. The problem of uncertainty regarding the causes and effects of pollution was discussed in the preparatory works and the parliamentary bill on the act. Undoubtedly, the authority has a *duty to assess* the risk of pollution and what the consequences will be when deciding on a regulation or an application for a pollution permit. It also has a *duty to consider* risks and uncertainties when making decisions. As to the final decision, it is in my view clear that an application for a pollution permit *may* be refused or strictly conditioned on the basis of a *possibility* of harm only, provided that the decision is based on a broad evaluation of the different positive and negative effects of the activity in question. This stems from the act's general prohibition to create a risk of pollution.

However, as a general rule, the pollution authorities are not *legally obliged* to base their final decisions on the precautionary principle. The key articles of the act require that different objectives and values – economic as well as environmental – are considered.[31] In other words, the authorities will make a broad evaluation of costs and benefits. It is clear that the objective of economic efficiency is inherent in the main principles and rules of the act besides the environmental goals, as in much of Norway's legislation on the use of natural resources. Hence, the pollution authorities may set aside even a considerable risk of environmental harm in favour of strong economic and social benefits. In the case of toxic and persistent chemicals, it may be argued that the final decision *must* be based on the precautionary principle in order to make its application consistent with that of the Product Control Act. But with the text of the act, it is difficult to find a clear legal basis for this view.

The EU Integrated Pollution Prevention and Control (IPPC) Directive[32] should be mentioned in this connection. The directive has been implemented in Norwegian law by a regulation pursuant to the Pollution Control Act.[33] The principle of best available technology (BAT) shall be applied in pollution permits for activities that are covered by the directive. When defining BAT in individual cases, the authorities will 'bear in mind' the precautionary principle, as well as the costs and benefits of the activity. Although the formulation is not very strong, it contributes to tilting the decision towards a safety margin in case of uncertainty. And it is clear that this regulatory condition for pollution permits is not regarded as being in conflict with the principle of a broad appreciation that is laid down in the act itself.

It is not disputed in Norwegian law that the person who wants to start an activity or market a product, and applies for a permit pursuant to these acts, has the 'burden of proof': he must prove that the activity or product does not entail an unacceptable risk. Lack of certain knowledge on this point is the applicant's problem, not that of the authority. This rule applies generally in Norwegian public administrative law, at least with regard to protection of health, safety, the environment and similar public objectives,[34] and it is underpinned by the precautionary principle.

An important part of the policy on chemicals relates to emissions from the *offshore petroleum industry*. Some years ago, it became evident that the marine pollution from oil and chemicals from the petroleum industry had reached clearly unacceptable levels and continued to increase. In the 1997 White Paper on *Environmental Policy for a Sustainable Development*,[35] the government launched the policy of 'zero discharge' from the offshore industry of oil and chemicals that may be hazardous to the marine environment. This objective is explicitly based on the precautionary principle, combined with the proposal to introduce the principle of substitution into Norwegian law. The 'zero discharge policy' has since been maintained and made more precise.[36] The objective should be reached by the end of 2005. In a recent report,[37] Norway's Pollution Control Authority stated that it, in fact, will be achieved to a very large extent. The report underlines the precautionary principle and the principle of substitution as the bases for this policy. The precautionary principle has also been written into the relevant regulation pursuant to the Petroleum Industry Act.[38]

Protection of biological diversity

This is another area of priority in Norway's environmental policy, and an area in which the precautionary principle is highly relevant since extinction of species is irreversible. What is the status of the principle as a political and legal principle in this field?

An important policy document is the 2001 government's White Paper entitled *Biological Diversity: Sector Responsibility and Coordination*.[39] It describes the current situation and challenges, and draws up main objectives, principles and strategies for the biodiversity policy. The document underlines that there are serious threats to Norway's biodiversity and that biodiversity loss is caused by numerous types of societal activities. Almost all areas of policy are relevant for biodiversity. The White Paper describes the influence of the different sectors, and the responsibilities and planned activities of each ministry.[40] It presents a very broad policy agenda and sketches a new, coherent and coordinated policy called 'knowledge-based management'.

The main objectives of the biodiversity policy are the conservation of living stocks of all known organisms and the identification of hitherto unknown species.[41] The precautionary principle is highlighted as the very basis for this policy, in combination with – and closely linked to – the 'ecosystem approach'. It is stated that if there are indications of possible serious or irreversible environmental harm, the lack of scientific certainty must not prevent the necessary steps to avoid possible effects. The precautionary principle will apply in all sectors. The ecosystem approach means a policy 'based on scientific as well as traditional and local knowledge in order to protect the functions of the ecosystem and [to ensure] that the activities in society do not exceed critical loads'. *Stortinget* supported these objectives and principles. Later White Papers have confirmed the commitment to the precautionary principle as a basis for the protection of biodiversity.

One may question whether these declarations are followed up in 'real life'. There have been several positive developments in nature protection policy, such as a significant increase of protected areas. On the other hand, the precautionary principle does not appear very clearly (to say the least) in economic and social sectors that are root causes of biodiversity degradation, such as land-use planning, transport, tourism, agriculture, watercourse management and fisheries, including fish farming.

Within *forestry* – one of the most important sectors for biodiversity protection – increased sensitivity to environmental problems and the development of more environmentally friendly forestry methods are leading to improvements. The purpose of the new Forestry Act[42] is 'a sustainable management of the country's forest resources', and it formally puts the protection of biological diversity on an equal footing with the industrial objectives. However, the precautionary principle is not expressed in the act and – significantly – it is not made reference to in the parliamentary bill on the act.

We now look into two other areas of biological diversity policy and law that are particularly sensitive and controversial in Norway: the protection of wildlife (predators, in particular) and wild salmon.

The key act for the protection of wild animals is the 1981 Wildlife Act.[43] Its explicit objective is to protect our biodiversity (Article 1), and it lays down a general principle of protection of all wild animal species. It is prohibited to kill, hurt, catch or harm wild animals, except in accordance with special regulations and permits pursuant to the act, such as hunting regulations. Permits to kill predators, in particular, may be issued in certain situations pursuant to a special regulation.[44] A general condition for such permits is that it does not 'threaten the survival of the stock'. There is no explicit mention of the precautionary principle in the act, in the preparatory works to the act or in the regulation. The question is whether the act's protection principle must be interpreted as including a precautionary principle, as well.

What seems clear is that the authorities *may* apply the act very strictly, and on the basis of precaution in case of scientific uncertainty. The principle of protection is, in itself, the legal basis for this. Even a small risk of endangering the stocks, and uncertainty about the possible effects of killing individual animals, may justify the prohibition of any killing. So it is clear that the authorities have *the right* to apply the precautionary principle in the management of predators and also the right to consider precaution.

Whether the authorities have *a duty* to apply precaution in case of uncertainty about possible effects may seem somewhat more doubtful. There is no clear, explicit basis for such a view. However, the protection principle implies that there must be vital stocks of each species. So the act must be applied in such a way that it removes *any risk* of extinction. This clearly points in the direction of the precautionary principle when interpreting and applying the principle of protection. The clear and repeated references to the precautionary principle in political documents on biodiversity protection amount to a legal duty for the administration to apply the principle.

A hot topic in this field of environmental law in Norway is the policy on predators, particularly wolves. It is controversial because the animals kill sheep and domesticated reindeer in the open grazing land, which is common in Norwegian mountains. Sheep farmers and owners of reindeer herds are strong voices against the protection of these species. The stock of wolves in Norway is limited and vulnerable due to inbreeding. According to some experts, it is clearly threatened by extinction. Nevertheless, on several occasions over the last few years, the government has decided to kill a limited number of wolves in order to keep the stock at a low level, thus accommodating the wish of the farming community. According to many experts, this violates the precautionary principle. It is in relation to this issue that the precautionary principle has been invoked and applied in a couple of local court cases.[45]

Stortinget has laid down certain guidelines as a compromise solution. Environmentalists maintain that this policy violates, or at least challenges, the precautionary principle as a general principle for the protection of biodiversity. However, it seems as if *Stortinget* sees this policy as being in accordance with the precautionary principle. Since the declared policy is still to keep vital stocks, the precautionary principle must govern relevant decisions.

The second case is the protection of *wild salmon stocks*. The Norwegian fjords and rivers are very important spawning and breeding areas for wild salmon. Norwegian salmon amounts to one fourth of the total stock of Atlantic salmon, with great genetic varieties: altogether 525 distinct stocks, each belonging to its 'own' river and – apparently – genetically different from the others. Fifty stocks have already become extinct, and one third of the remaining 525 stocks are regarded as threatened. Of these, 50 stocks are particularly important since they constitute around three-quarters of the total salmon resource.[46] There are several reasons for the decline in salmon stocks: harvesting, pollution of rivers, hydroelectric power development and other developments in the rivers, fish diseases and – last but not least – 'genetic pollution' caused by escaped salmon from the extensive salmon farming that takes place along the Norwegian coast and in the fjords.

In 2003, *Stortinget* designated 37 'national salmon rivers' and 21 'national salmon fjords' to protect the salmon stocks in these rivers and fjords. The main legal consequences are prohibitions of, or restrictions on, activities that may have negative effects on the wild salmon stock. The most important is the prohibition to establish new fish farms in the fjords and to move existing fish farms away from the most important vulnerable fjord areas within 2011. This is quite controversial as fish farming is an expanding and increasingly important industry along the Norwegian coast.

The establishment of salmon rivers and fjords has been strongly opposed by the fish farming industry. They have argued that 'the present knowledge is too weak to take measures which have so important consequences for the further development of the fish farming industry',[47] thus turning the precautionary principle on its head. On the other hand, the strong view of the environmental authorities and organizations has been that the measures are far from sufficient to protect the salmon stocks. If the precautionary principle was to be applied fully, far more extensive and much stricter measures must be taken. It is noteworthy – but hardly accidental – that there is no explicit reference to the precautionary principle in the main political documents on this particular matter.

Taking into account that the protection of the genetic variety of wild salmon probably is the most important task for Norway in the field of global biodiversity protection, this shows its limitations as a principle of Norwegian environmental policy.

In 2005, a new Aquaculture Act[48] replaced earlier acts on fish farming and sea grazing. A permit is necessary for all types of aquaculture. The act and the preparatory works put much emphasis on the environmental aspects, although the serious risk that it entails for wild salmon stocks is rather superficially treated in the bill. The act states explicitly that aquaculture has to be carried out in 'an environmentally secure way', and the ministry may issue the necessary regulations and decisions to this end (Article 10). Significantly, there is no mention of the precautionary principle in the text of the act or in the parliamentary bill. But it is stated (Article 11) that the authorities may require that the operator carries out necessary environmental assessments and monitoring. By environmental assessments is meant 'assessment to clarify, *inter alia*, the risk of pollution and ecological effects, including on biodiversity'.[49]

From these examples it can be concluded that the precautionary principle has legal importance in the field of biodiversity protection. The problem is that the principle is not really part of the policy of sectors that are at the cause – directly or indirectly – of the biodiversity loss. We witness this in the parliamentary bills on two new acts of great importance for biodiversity protection – namely, the Forestry Act and the Aquaculture Act. The precautionary principle is not mentioned in either of them. This illustrates the lack of consistency, and the limitations, of the principle as a general principle in both Norwegian policy and law.

Genetically modified organisms

The next example is our 1993 GMO Act.[50] The precautionary principle is not expressed explicitly in this act, either. But the act lays down a prohibition to release a GMO into the environment 'if there is a risk of negative effects on health or the environment'. Here, the authority is clearly *obliged* to apply the precautionary principle in a strict sense.[51] Whether the risk is manifest or there is a lack of certain knowledge about the possible risks, the wording obliges the authority to refuse an application for deliberate release. There is ample reference to the precautionary principle in the preparatory works to the act. It is somewhat doubtful whether the strict wording will be understood quite literally. But it is true that our GMO policy has so far been very strict (see Chapter 13 for further discussion).

The protection of the Svalbard environment

In 2001, Norway got its first act that explicitly states the precautionary principle – namely, the Environmental Act for Svalbard.[52] Svalbard is the vast, mostly ice-covered, islands in the Arctic (more generally known as Spitzbergen), whose nature is splendid but marginal and therefore extremely vulnerable. Its Article 7 is entitled 'the precautionary principle'. It states that if there is uncertainty as to the environmental effects of a planned activity, 'the authority shall be executed in a manner designed to avoid possible damage to the environment'. The wording is not quite clear and it deviates slightly from the international definitions of the principle. It provides not only a guideline but must be understood as a binding norm for the authorities as far as the wording goes. Apparently, it has been applied in a recent case, when a Norwegian company wanted to search for gold on one of the islands. The Ministry of the Environment turned down the application with reference to article 7.[53]

CONCLUSIONS

It is clear from this analysis that the precautionary principle plays a role in Norway's environmental policy and law that is not insignificant. It is equally clear that its political appearance and importance is variable and inconsistent. It is barely expressed in the legislation, and there has so far been no Supreme Court case where the principle has been invoked. It is a fundamental principle in the country's 'environmental policy'; but it is hardly reflected in the policy and law of important social and economic sectors that are the root causes of environmental degradation. This fact limits its legal importance as well.

It has legal importance as a principle of interpretation of legal texts, and a principle which – as a minimum – always requires an assessment of risks and uncertainties in the environmental field, and which must be taken into consideration in decision-making. In some areas of environmental law, the principle means a duty for the authorities to avoid serious or irreversible risks. Toxic and persistent chemicals, endangered species and the introduction of GMOs into the environment are the cases in point. We witness a development of the principle, although slow, from a legally relevant but still optional principle, to a legally compulsory principle, and gradually into new areas. It remains to be seen whether this development will continue and whether the principle one day will have enough precision and strength as a principle of law to set clear limits in wider areas of Norway's law.

NOTES

1   A major analysis of the topic carried out in the early 1990s by research fellow Halfdan Mellbye at the Faculty of Law, University of Bergen, Norway, has not been published. A short article by the same author is Halfdan Mellbye, H. (2000) 'Gjennomføringen av føre var-prinsippet i norsk rett' ('The implementation of the precautionary principle in Norwegian law'), in Ulfstein, G. (ed) *Forholdet mellom internasjonal og nasjonal miljørett* (*The Relationship between International and National Environmental Law*), Institutt for offentlig retts skriftserie no 5, Norway.

2   Backer is *dr. juris* and a former professor at the Faculty of Law, University of Oslo, with environmental law as one of his main subjects. He now serves as director general of the legal department of the Ministry of Justice.

3   Backer, I. L. (2002) *Innføring i naturressurs- og miljørett* (*Introduction to Natural Resources and Environmental Law*), utg, Oslo, in particular pp62–66.

4   Directives 85/337/EEC and 2001/42/EC.

5   The Norwegian government was not entirely satisfied with the final formulation of principle 15, which states that the precautionary approach will be applied by states only 'according to their capabilities'. This is expressed in the White Paper to *Stortinget* on the results of the Rio conference (St.meld. no 13 (1992–1993)).

6   St.meld. no 58 (1996–1997) *Miljøvernpolitikk for en bærekraftig utvikling.*

7   St.meld. no 58 (1996–1997) *Miljøvernpolitikk for en bærekraftig utvikling,* p13.

8   Every second year the government presents a White Paper on *The Government's Environmental Policy and the State of the Environment.* The last is St.meld. no 21 (2004–2005) from March 2005. Here it is stated that 'we must respect critical loads and apply the precautionary principle when there is a risk of serious environmental effects'.

9   'Politisk plattform for en flertallsregjering', October 2005, p5.

10   Since 2005, Norway has had a system of emission trading comparable to that of the EU, for a trial period of 2005 to 2007, Act No 99 of 17 December 2004 on climate quotas. However, the real impact of this system on CO_2 emissions is quite small.

11   One example from public administrative law is Eckhoff, T. and Smith, E. (2003) *Forvaltningsrett,* seventh edition, Universitetsforlaget, Oslo, pp30–31.

12   See, for public administrative law, Graver, H. P. (2002) *Alminnelig forvaltningsrett,* second edition, Universitetsforlaget, Oslo, pp32–39, and for environmental law, Backer, I. L. (2002) *Innføring i naturressurs- og miljørett,* fourth edition, Gyldendal Akademisk, Oslo, pp49–74.

13   This criterion is different from – and stricter than – a general principle of proportionality, which is not (yet) regarded as a general principle of Norwegian administrative law in the sense that the courts may try the proportionality of a decision. However, the courts have a duty to try possible 'misuse of authority' – '*détournement du pouvoir*' – and a decision is illegal if it is 'biased', 'clearly unreasonable' or 'arbitrary'.

14   There is some discussion between Norwegian theorists on the scope of the presumption principle, particularly whether it applies to international customary law only, or also to treaty law to which Norway is a party. In my view, there are good reasons to apply it to situations where the state of Norway has accepted an obligation by ratifying a treaty. There is also some uncertainty as to the strength of the presumption principle if the legislator intentionally adopts a rule that conflicts with the international rule.

15   See also Chapter 5 on Icelandic law in this volume.

16   Together with Iceland and Liechtenstein.

17   Nature conservation rules are not included in the agreement.

18   On the relationship between EEA law and Norwegian law, see Sejersted, F, Arnesen, F., Rognstad, O.-A., Foyn, S. and Kolstad, O. (2004) *EØS-rett,* second edition, Universitetsforlaget, Olso, Chapter 14.

19   Act No 109 of 27 November 1992.

20   Formally, there is no such thing as 'secondary legislation' in the EEA context. When 'EEA relevant' regulations and directives, decided by the EC, are formally adopted by the EEA committee, the EEA Agreement itself is amended accordingly.

21   Case E-3/00 concerning prohibition by the Norwegian government of additional nutrients and vitamins in Kellogg's cornflakes (see Chapter 5 in this volume) and Case E-4/4.

22   Case E-4/4.

23   Cases C-236/01 *Monsanto,* C-286/02 *Bellio F.lli Srl,* Case T-13/99 *Pfizer* and T-70/99 *Alpharma.*

24   In this particular case, the conditions were not fulfilled, the court argued, since the health risk of alcohol consumption is not uncertain. However, the court found the ban justified under EEA Agreement Article 13, which corresponds to Article 30 of the EC Treaty.

25   The relevant EC law is treated in other chapters of this book and will not be presented here. See, in particular, Chapter 2 of this volume. I discuss the issue in relation to national legislation only.

26 St.meld. no 21 (2004–2005) p67 (unofficial translation). For the corresponding 'zero-emission' policy of Sweden, see Chapter 16 on Sweden in this volume.
27 Act No 79 of 11 June 1976 on product control.
28 Act No 6 of 13 March 1981 on pollution control and waste.
29 Article 1.
30 Article 6(a).
31 Article 11; see also Article 2(a).
32 EC Directive 96/61 EC.
33 Regulation No 931 of 1 July 2004, Chapter 36.
34 See Graver, H. P. (2000) 'Bevisbyrde og beviskrav i forvaltningsretten' ('Burden of proof and proof requirements in public administrative law'), *Tidsskrift for Rettsvitenskap*, vol 4–5, p465.
35 St.meld. no 58 (1996–1997).
36 See, for example, the White Paper on the protection of the marine environment: St.meld. no. 12 (2000–2001) *Rent og rikt hav*.
37 Letter from Norway's Pollution Control Authority to the Ministry of the Environment dated 30 November 2005.
38 Act No 72 of 29 November 1996 on petroleum.
39 St.meld. no 42 (2000–2001) *Biologisk mangfold. Sektoransvar og samordning.*
40 The ministries of child and family; fisheries; defence; justice; education and research; municipal and regional affairs; culture; agriculture; the environment; trade and industry; oil and energy; transport; social services and health; and foreign affairs.
41 In the 2005 White Paper on the government's environmental policy and the state of the environment (St.meld. no 21 (2004–2005)), the objective is defined more precisely as stopping the loss of biodiversity by 2010.
42 Act No 31 of 27 May 2005 on Forestry.
43 Act No 38 of 29 May 1981 on Wildlife.
44 Regulation No 242 of 18 March 2005.
45 The precautionary principle was applied as an important factor in interpreting the Wildlife Act in a local court case concerning the killing of wolves some years ago. The judge found that the general principle of protection of the act must be interpreted and applied in accordance with the precautionary principle. He argued that the precautionary principle must be understood and applied as a principle that is meant to prevent the risk of a reduction of species, and found the killing of two wolves as violating the act and the principle. *Rettens Gang* (RG) (2000) p1025.
46 Information given in the 2002 White Paper on national salmon rivers and salmon fjords: St.prp. no 79 (2001–2002).
47 St.prp. no 79 (2001–2002) p33.
48 Act No 79 of 17 June 2005 on aquaculture.
49 Ot.prp. (parliamentary bill) no 61 (2004–2005) p65.
50 Act No 38 of 2 April 1993 on the production and use of genetically modified organisms.
51 Article 10(2). However, this strict rule does not apply if the GMO in question already has been approved in another EEA member state: Article 10(6).
52 Act No 79 of 15 June 2001.
53 Oral information from the ministry.

CHAPTER 7

Sweden

Gabriel Michanek

INTRODUCTION

The *precautionary principle* in Sweden is included in Chapter 2, section 3 of the 1998 Environmental Code.[1] It includes a general obligation to take precautions in order to 'prevent, hinder or combat damage or detriment to human health or the environment'. Such precautions shall be taken 'as soon as there is cause to assume that an activity or measure may cause damage or detriment to human health or the environment'.

The principle was codified in Sweden when the Environmental Code was adopted in 1998. However, it would be wrong to say that the 1998 principle is a new phenomenon in Swedish environmental law. Sweden already adopted a *precautionary approach*[2] in 1941 when the 1918 Water Act was amended to include a permit control of industrial waste water. The precautionary approach was further clarified and expanded after 1969. The historical background is described initially in this chapter. It is essential for the understanding of today's precautionary principle in the Environmental Code.

After a short overview of the code's most important components, which should be useful for non-Swedish readers, the precautionary principle is analysed in more detail. The *scope* of the principle is discussed. Since the Environmental Code aims not only at protection against pollution and similar nuisances, but also at nature conservation and rational management of natural resources and energy, what role does the precautionary principle play in this wider context?

Two crucial issues relate to evidence. First, the code is clear on the point that when it is uncertain if pollution (or other nuisance) may cause damage to health or the environment, it is, in principle, not the environmental authority (guarding public interests) or the neighbour (whose personal health or private property is threatened) who must prove the existence of a future damage in order to achieve protective measures or prohibitions. By contrast, the operator has to prove that damage will not occur in order to be spared from such restrictions. This issue – the operator's *burden of proof* – will be elaborated upon more closely. Second, an important question is also at what *standard of evidence* are requirements to take precautions triggered? This question will also be discussed, although a clear answer is not evident.

When discussing the application, in practice, of the precautionary principle, it is necessary to address some elements in the Swedish legislation that may be described as *contra productive* to the principle, especially provisions indicating that environmental interests shall be weighed against costs for the operator and other opposite interests (in some cases, opposite environmental interests), but also possible conflicts between the precautionary principle and the general legal principles of legality and legal certainty.

In this chapter, I have consulted legal texts and preparatory works.[3] Case law is meagre; but I have selected some verdicts that illuminate the application of the principle in connection with control of chemicals in big industrial installations.

A PRECAUTIONARY APPROACH

The birth of a precautionary approach in 1941

Swedish industry developed rapidly during the beginning of the 20th century without significant interference from environmental authorities requiring a reduction of pollutants, although, since 1880, there had been some legal support for such requirements.[4] The enforcement was occasional and often conducted when the damage was already a fact. Water quality in several lakes and sea bays had degraded substantially, and the Swedish Parliament decided, in 1941, to amend the 1918 Water Act in a way that should be regarded as a precautionary approach.

The 1941 amendment introduced a concession system for discharges of industrial wastewater.[5] It was as a principle rule generally prohibited to discharge such wastewater when the pollution caused 'detriment of any significance'. However, the operator had the right to apply for a licence at the Water Court,[6] which could exempt from the general prohibition. The operator was then obliged to prevent the pollution by taking 'reasonable' precautions.[7] So a precautionary approach was introduced in the sense that no new industrial discharges of any significance were allowed without a prior licence and reasonable precautions. It was generally assumed that such discharges caused danger to the health or the environment.

Environmental Protection Act 1969: Expanded and clarified precautionary approach

Although principally important, the 1941 amendment did not sufficiently improve the water quality near industrial installations. The Water Courts were criticized for imposing too lenient requirements. Besides, the scope of the legal control introduced in 1941 was too narrow. It included only water pollution emanating from discharges from certain kinds of installations, not from other forms of land use. Even more importantly, other forms of nuisances, especially air pollution, were excluded from an efficient legal control.[8] It was time for a new legal revision, resulting in the adoption in 1969 of the Environmental Protection Act.

The act was a cornerstone in Swedish environmental legal history. It applied to almost all kinds of pollution and other nuisances (noise, heat, smell, changes in landscape, etc., but not, for example, radiation). Thus, in 1969 Sweden introduced integrated pollution prevention control. The number of activities for which a licence was required increased significantly. The responsibility for licensing was transferred from the Water Courts to a new National Environmental Licensing Board (*Koncessionsnämnden för miljöskydd*) and (with regard to smaller installations) to the regional boards.

The act applied to so-called 'environmentally hazardous activities'. The term 'hazardous' was deliberately chosen to indicate that a risk of damage or other detriment was sufficient for the act to apply and to trigger constraints on the activity. This important approach was further explained by the minister in the Government Bill:

> *Damages can be counteracted … by taking into account the risk when considering if and under what conditions an activity may be conducted. It is in my opinion necessary that the authorities applying the legislation take into account the danger for the health interest and other public aspects that may be connected with still unknown or insufficiently explored pollutants. I consider it to be natural that* the uncertainty related to the danger of a substance shall not strike against the public but instead on the person [who] emits the substance into the air or the water. *This principle is of the greatest practical importance. It means that one does not have to wait to intervene until damages have occurred. It means also that a person who wants to discharge an insufficiently known substance, provided there is a well-founded reason to assume that the substance is dangerous, must be able to show that there is no risk for a detriment [this author's emphasis].*[9]

So, the Environmental Protection Act provided environmental authorities with the power to act in situations of uncertainty. The risk of damage or detriment was normally sufficient to trigger requirements on precautions (alternative locations, purification techniques, limitation of production, etc.), but also, occasionally, to prohibit the activity as such. The activity was, as a principle rule, prohibited (there were exemptions) if it was '*likely to cause* significant damage or detriment to human health or the environment' (this author's italics).[10]

However, there was an initial threshold. Loose speculations on possible impacts were not sufficient to trigger requirements. As pointed out in the preparatory works, there should be a 'well-founded reason to assume' that a substance is dangerous.[11] The risk had to be 'noteworthy'.[12] Thus, there was an initial task for environmental authorities, neighbours or environmental organizations to deliver at least some scientific material indicating a noteworthy risk. After passing this threshold, the burden on proof shifted to the operator (polluter).

While the law was essentially clear on the issue of burden of proof, it was blurry with regard to the question of how far-reaching the operator's assessment had to be in order to be released from the requirements on precautionary measures or prohibitions. There was no legally determined standard of evidence to apply. Preparatory works and case law did not provide any guidance with regard to this often crucial issue. It is reasonable to assume that the standard varied depending upon the circumstances in each case. *Westerlund* points out certain circumstances as probably relevant: the extent and the degree of complexity of the feared effect; the cost of investigating the environmental effects and appropriate precautions; the fact that the activity was either new or already existing; and the costs of combating the effect (if existing and not insignificant).[13]

Placing the burden of proof on the operator was important, in practice, and far-reaching requirements were sometimes imposed despite the uncertainty of the effects. There were several cases when the entire application was turned down because of insufficient assessment by the operator. However, the necessity of considering risks was confronted by another cornerstone in the Environmental Protection Act: balancing environmental interests against the operator's costs, as well as supply of jobs and other public benefits. In other words, although risks were deemed to be considerable (and even if severe environmental damage might occur), environmental requirements had to stand back if they were outbalanced by opposite interests.

An illustrative example is a permit case from the mid 1970s related to the metal industry, Rönnskärsverken, built in 1930 in the town of Skellefteå in northern Sweden, along a bay adjacent to the Baltic Sea.

The discharges into the Baltic and the air included many different substances, several of them typically very dangerous, such as cadmium, lead and mercury. The amount of certain pollutants was huge, in some cases more than 50 per cent of the total amount discharged in Sweden into air or water. Rönnskärsverken was, without competition, the single most polluting industry in Sweden.

Despite the great complex of discharges, and several years of monitoring, no severe impacts on the marine ecosystem in the surroundings of the industry were registered. Nevertheless, the National Environmental Licensing Board quoted the above-mentioned formulations in the preparatory works relating to risks and pointed out the operator's burden on proof. The board concluded, with regard to the situation at Rönnskärsverken, that even if far-reaching precautions were required, the pollution was '*likely to cause* significant damage or detriment to human health or the environment' (this author's italics). The activity thereby fulfilled the criteria for prohibition stipulated in the principle rule in section 6 in the Environmental Protection Act. However, section 6 also included an exemption if strong opposite public interest was deemed to be more important than the risks for health or the environment. It was (and still is) the government that carries out the weighing of interests in these severe conflict cases. In the case of Rönnskärsverken, the environmental risks were regarded as less weighty than the impacts on trade and industry and employment in the whole of northern Sweden. Consequently, the government approved a continuation of the heavily polluting activity in 1975.[14] Far-reaching requirements to decrease emissions were imposed in the form of gradually strengthened permit conditions. Today the discharges have been significantly reduced.

Next step: A precautionary approach in the legal control of chemicals

It was generally recognized that the control of industrial installations according to the Environmental Protection Act significantly improved the quality of air and water in many areas. Nevertheless, there were alarming observations in Sweden of the far-reaching decline of certain species' populations to levels close to extinction – for example, the yellowhammer (*Emberiza citronella*), the kestrel (*Falco tinnunculus*) and the osprey (*Pandion haliaetus*), due to release of mercury (e.g. in planting seeds), and the white-tailed eagle (*Haliaeetus albicilla*), due to exposure to polychlorinated biphenyls (PCB) and dichlorodiphenyltrichloroethanes (DDT).[15] It became obvious that the environmental impacts resulting from the fast introduction of new chemicals into the market could not be prevented solely by permit control of single installations. It was necessary to legally address the chemicals and to prevent risks at the initial stage.

The 1973 Act on Products Hazardous to Health and the Environment was the first Swedish framework statute for a coordinated control of all chemicals. It was at this time an advanced legislation from an international perspective. The legislator was clearly inspired by the precautionary approach developed in the Environmental Protection Act. Environmental authorities should be able to intervene already when they had:

> ... good reason to suspect a risk for damage. If so, the producer must, to avoid prohibitions or restrictions, as far as possible with respect to present scientific position prove that the suspicion is unfounded. He will otherwise have to accept that the authorities act according to the assumption that the product is health and environmentally hazardous. Thus, the uncertainty ... concerning the hazard of a substance will not strike against the public, but instead the person who intends to market the product in question.[16]

The act included a general obligation to take precautions, not only for producers but for all persons handling a product – for example, importers, salespeople, private consumers, farmers and operators of factories and other installations. In other words, the act provided for legal control throughout the entire life cycle of the chemical.

According to the preparatory work, one important precaution was to avoid a chemical if the same objective could be achieved by making use of a less hazardous alternative chemical, provided the costs of substituting the chemicals were not unreasonable. This requirement was generally called 'the principle of substitution'. It was closely linked to the precautionary approach: the obligation to avoid a chemical was based upon an assessment and comparison of risks related to this and the alternative chemical.

The 1973 act was substituted in 1985 with the similar the Act on Chemical Products. This framework act inherited the same precautionary approach[17] and, after an amendment in 1990, included the principle of substitution in the legal text.[18]

The Swedish legislation on chemical control was probably one of the most progressive in Europe. DDT and PCB were banned early and restrictions on the use of cadmium were far-reaching.

Lack of a precautionary approach in many environmental acts

Besides the Environmental Protection Act and the two statutes on chemical control, a clear precautionary approach could not be traced in other statutes related to environmental protection and the management of natural resources. The 1964 Nature Conservancy Act did not explicitly advise how to act in a situation of uncertainty with regard to environmental impacts; neither did the 1983 Water Act (which applied to the construction of hydropower installations and other water operations), the 1991 Minerals Act and the 1987 Hunting Act, to take a few examples. In fact, not even the specific legislation related to nuclear safety and radiation control – for example, the 1988 Radiation Protection Act and the 1984 Nuclear Technology Activity Act – tackled this issue explicitly.

One obvious reason for this difference in approach to risk consideration was the inconsistency in the environmental legal system before the Environmental Code. The acts were scattered. New legislation and amendments to existing legislation were developed essentially within their own legal culture; the coordination with other environmental statutes was poor.

THE ENVIRONMENTAL CODE PRECAUTIONARY PRINCIPLE

The Environmental Code: Objectives and substantial environmental requirements

Legal coordination was obviously a prime purpose of the Environmental Code, adopted by parliament in 1998. Sixteen acts – for example, the Environmental Protection Act, the Chemical Products Act, the Nature Conservancy Act and the Water Act – were substituted by a legal framework, including 33 chapters. The overarching objective of the code is to promote 'sustainable development'. For that purpose, the code, according to the legal text, 'shall be applied' so that certain 'sub-objectives' are met, including not only the protection of health and the environment against pollution or other nuisances, but also the preservation of biodiversity against different kinds of impacts (e.g. drainage) and, not least important from the sustainability perspective, the reuse and recycling of raw materials and energy in order to establish and maintain natural cycles.[19]

As a first step to implementing the objectives, the code provides a set of substantial environmental requirements, classified in the legal text as 'general rules of consideration' ('*allmänna hänsynsregler*').[20] The chief provision – Chapter 3, section 2 – includes the precautionary principle (see below). It generally requires taking protective measures, complying with restrictions and taking any other precautions (including the use of best possible technology) that are necessary to prevent or hinder damage or detriment to human health or the environment.[21] Besides the general obligation, or rather as specifications of it, Chapter 2 includes the following requirements:[22]

- to 'possess the knowledge that is necessary in view of the nature and scope of the activity or measure to protect human health and the environment against damage or detriment';
- to select a suitable site, where it is possible to achieve the purpose 'with a minimum of damage or detriment to human health and the environment';
- to 'conserve raw materials and energy and reuse and recycle them wherever possible'; and
- to 'avoid using or selling chemical products or biotechnical organisms that may involve risks to human health or the environment if products or organisms that are less dangerous can be used instead' (the so-called 'product choice requirement', corresponding to the previous 'substitution principle').

As in the Environmental Protection Act, the main function of Chapter 2 is to mitigate environmental impacts and risks, with far-reaching requirements, if necessary, but not in the first place to prohibit activities. In fact, only very occasionally are activities prohibited, according to the so-called 'stop provisions'.[23]

The code includes a wide range of other environmental instruments that cannot be elaborated upon here – for example, provisions for managing land and water areas (essentially, national physical planning provisions); protection of species and areas; environmental impact assessments (EIAs); environmental quality standards; and specific chapters for permitting and controlling polluting activities and water operations, and the handling of chemicals, genetically modified organisms and waste.[24] A great number of regulations and by-laws are subordinated to the code.

The precautionary principle

The precautionary principle in Chapter 2, section 3, of the Environmental Code is formulated as follows:

> *Persons who pursue an activity or take a measure, or intend to do so, shall carry out protective measures, comply with restrictions and take any other precautions that are necessary in order to prevent, hinder or combat damage or detriment to human health or the environment as a result of the activity or measure. For the same reason, the best possible technology shall be used in connection with professional activities.*
>
> *Such precautions shall be taken as soon as there is* cause to assume *that an activity or measure can cause damage or detriment to human health or the environment [this author's emphasis].*

It is obvious that, in most respects, the precautionary principle adopted in the code inherited the precautionary approach developed in the preparatory works and case law related to the Environmental Protection Act, as described above. The Government Bill refers to this act and emphasizes, again, that the burden or proof is placed on the 'operator'. This particular issue will never be subject to a balancing of interests.[25] It is also notable that the operator, in order to avoid requirements, must generally show not only that risks do not exist, but also that the activity complies with the legal requirements in all respects. It is, for example, not the licensing or supervising environmental authority which has to show that a certain requirement is reasonable; instead, it is up to the operator to prove that the requirement is unreasonable:

> *In connection with the consideration of matters relating to permissibility, permits, approvals and exemptions and of conditions other than those relating to compensation, and in connection with supervision pursuant to this code, persons who pursue an activity or take a measure, or intend to do so, shall show that the obligations arising out of this chapter have been complied with. This shall also apply to persons who have pursued activities that may have caused damage or detriment to the environment.*[26]

The shifting of the burden of proof does not automatically entail an obligation on behalf of the operator to carry out a far-reaching assessment of the risks at stake. As mentioned previously, the code is unclear on the issue of how strong the evidence must be that the operator must put forward – *the standard of evidence* – in order to be released from the obligation to take precautionary measures. It was stated in the Government Bill that the operator's obligation must be reasonable. It can also be concluded from the bill that precautions are triggered at different standards of evidence, depending on the type of activity in question.[27] So, the required standard of evidence must be determined individually, case by case. More legal certainty (ability to foresee the required standard) would be promoted if the courts would identify different *typical* risk situations where a certain standard applies. There is no sign of such an attempt so far.

The formulation 'cause to assume' means, probably, that there is an initial threshold for the environmental authorities, or private persons or groups, representing different environmental interests. Presumably, as before the code, an operator can never be obliged to assess a risk that is based merely on loose speculations.

The *scope of the precautionary principle* is wide. It applies as soon as there is cause to assume that the measure or activity may counteract 'the objectives of the code',[28] which are all covered by the term 'environment' in the legal text of Chapter 2. As mentioned above, the objectives of the Environmental Code are not only to protect health and the environment against pollution, but also, for example, to preserve biodiversity. This is important since the Nature Conservancy Act (before the establishment of the code) did not include an explicit precautionary approach. Furthermore, precautionary measures may be imposed to reduce the *risk* of inefficient use of natural resources and energy. The code is in this respect more far-reaching than the previous Environmental Protection Act.

The scope is also wide from other perspectives. While the precautionary principle in the Rio Declaration applies to the risk of 'serious or irreversible damage', the Swedish principle already applies where there is cause to assume *any* form of damage or detriment to health or the environment. Furthermore, section 3 applies to all physical or legal persons who pursue an activity (with some continuity) or take a single measure that is not of 'negligible significance in the individual case'.[29] The principle does not exempt non-commercial activities.

There is, so far, no case according to the Environmental Code where the content of the precautionary principle has been analysed and specified. This is somewhat surprising: first, because the legal text now includes the principle explicitly; second, because uncertainty concerning impacts on the environment is a typical component of most cases; third, because the principle is now related to quite different objectives than just pollution prevention; and, fourth, because the issue of required evidence standard is a crucial, but at the same time very unclear, issue when applying the principle.

In addition, the statements by the European Court of Justice (ECJ) concerning some aspects of the principle, discussed by de Sadeleer in Chapter 2 of this book,[30] are not reflected in Swedish case law. The Swedish courts cannot ignore the rulings of the ECJ since they, according to Article 10 EC, shall apply Swedish legislation in conformity with European Community (EC) law.[31]

None of the, so far, rather few cases in the Supreme Court relating to the Environmental Code refer to the principle. The Environmental Court of Appeal (*Miljööverdomstolen*), whose decisions have a significant guiding function as long as the

Supreme Court is silent in the matter, has only very occasionally mentioned the principle. It is reflected in a few cases concerning permits to big installations (several paper mills and one chemical factory) where hundreds of different chemicals were used in the industrial processes. The court was not satisfied with the operator's argument that producers and importers are solely responsible for providing information on chemical products. The general obligation to possess knowledge (Chapter 2, section 2) applies to all activities where chemicals are handled. This standpoint is important: first, because the introduction of a new chemical into the market is normally not subject to a permit trial (only registration); and, second, because the ecosystems that are targeted for the emissions from the particular installation are specific.

The licences issued in these cases included a specific condition requiring the operator to investigate the risks related to chemicals used within the installation, in consultation with the supervising authority, for the purpose of substituting environmentally hazardous chemicals with less hazardous ones. This obligation was supplemented with a sanction:

> *It is, from the year 2006, prohibited to use in the production such chemical products for which there is lack of documented knowledge concerning the risk for detriments to the environment as a result of poor biodegradability, potential acute or chronic toxicity and bioaccumulation. The supervising authority may, in individual cases, decide upon exemption from the requirement on documented knowledge and upon prolongation of the period.*[32]

This permit condition was based upon three provisions in Chapter 2: the product choice requirement ('substitution principle'), the requirement to possess knowledge about the activity and its risks, and the precautionary principle.[33] The cases reflect an important connection between the provisions: already the risk for damage triggers an obligation to investigate the characteristics of chemicals. The provided knowledge will facilitate an exclusion of hazardous chemicals, in line with the product choice requirement. Consequently, if the operator, after a certain period of time, fails to provide information on the characteristics, no matter how hard he or she tries, the use of the product is prohibited. In other words, the remaining uncertainty strikes against the operator. This construction presupposes that there is, at least, 'cause to assume' that a chemical is hazardous.

One of the cases from the Environmental Court of Appeal was appealed to the Supreme Court, which in a verdict in May 2006 (Högsta domstolen, dom 19 May 2006 i mål T 2303–05) did not approve the sanction quoted above as it breached the principle of legal certainty. I will return to this issue.

We turn, finally, to the question of risk consideration when the so-called 'stop provisions' (rules relating to prohibitions) are applied. The precautionary principle in Chapter 2, section 3, is explicitly linked only to the obligation to take precautionary measures. Nevertheless, as previously stated in the Environmental Protection Act, the 'stop provision' in Chapter 2, section 9, prohibits an activity or measure if it is '*likely to cause* significant damage or detriment to human health or the environment, even if protective measures and other precautions are taken as required by this code' (this author's italics).[34] It is in this connection that the operator must prove that this risk does not exist.[35] However, as I will explain in the following text, risks can be accepted if they are outbalanced by opposite interests.

The precautionary principle and contra-productive elements in the law

To understand the significance of the precautionary principle in relation what actually is required in terms of risk management, the principle has to be placed within a wider legal context, including:

- weighing environmental interests against opposite private and public interests;
- the principles of legal certainty and legality; and
- competing environmental interests.

Weighing environmental risks against opposite interests

The Environmental Code demands weighing environmental interests against costs and other interests when deciding upon the obligation to take precautionary measures. There is a general obligation to take the best possible precautions ('best possible technique'), which is normally a far-reaching requirement, especially for new activities. This is the legal 'standard' normally applied. However, a lower requirement will apply provided that the operator can prove that the standard requirement is 'unreasonable' in the individual case.[36] This is where the weighing of interests comes in and the chief question is if the costs related to precautionary measures are proportional to the expected results from an environmental point of view. It is fair to say that it is rather unusual that the courts lower the requirements on precautionary measures below the standard 'best possible technique', let alone that different standards applies to new, compared to existing, activities within the same branch. If environmental quality standards may be exceeded, the standard requirement will always apply.

Weighing of interests is also an essential component of the 'stop provisions'. Although observing a risk of 'significant damage or detriment to human health or the environment', the measure or activity is still allowed if 'special reasons' are at hand. According to the Government Bill, it must be proved that the 'advantages ... from a public and private point of view clearly outweigh the damage'. The power to decide is here directly (without appeal) transferred from the court (or administrative authority) to the government – in other words, to the highest political level.

The 'stop provisions' also include a second test level, to be applied if the risks are deemed to be extraordinary. So, although the government may find that 'special reasons' are at hand, the 'activity or measure cannot be undertaken if it is *liable* to lead to significant deterioration of the living conditions of a large number of people or substantial detriment to the environment' (this author's italics). However, the government is again vested with the power to grant an exemption if the 'activity or measure is of particular importance for reasons of public interest', such as job opportunities.[37]

As we can see, the construction is basically the same as previously in the Environmental Protection Act. The code contains no absolute safeguard in Chapter 2 against even possible severe damages to the environment. There are several cases according to the

Environmental Protection Act where activities were approved by the government, although such risks were identified. They were accepted because the opposing public interests were considered heavier.[38]

In one respect, legal protection was strengthened in the code. The government may not allow an activity or a measure if it is '*likely* to be detrimental to the state of *public health*' (this author's italics).[39] No balancing of interests is allowed when such health risks are at hand. However, this absolute legal protection does not apply if only a few persons may become seriously ill or even die; the expression 'detrimental to the state of public health' refers to a situation where people in the neighbourhood 'more commonly may be damaged by pollution or similar nuisances'.[40]

To conclude, while precautionary measures often are set to achieve a high level of protection according to standard 'best possible technique', occasionally situations arise where there is a risk for severe damage to human health or the environment – especially in connection with permitting existing, often old, industrial installations. With the exception just mentioned, Chapter 2 does not include an environmental 'hard core' element, providing absolute protection of, for example, biodiversity.[41] Not even exceeded environmental quality standards guarantee such a protection in Sweden if the permit case concerns the question of increasing the emissions from existing installations.[42]

Legality and legal certainty

As already explained, the Swedish precautionary principle includes two connected ingredients:

1 the obligation to take precautions in cases where the risk of damage or detriment occurs; and
2 the burden of proof placed upon the person who operates a factory, uses a chemical product, cultivates genetically modified crops, etc. (the 'operator').

However, in the wider legal context, the general principles of legality and legal certainty must be taken into account. These principles aim to protect the operator against arbitrary intrusion by public authorities. More precisely, the operator should be able to foresee legal requirements, as well as possible reactions from authorities supported by the requirements (legal certainty). That interest is supported if the requirements are clear, precise and follow directly from the legal text (legality).

Obviously, there is a fundamental conflict between the precautionary principle and the principles of legal certainty with regard to managing uncertainties. While the precautionary principle is based on the idea that remaining uncertainties fall upon the operator, the principles of legal certainty and legality will not trigger requirements on precautions unless the environmental authority has provided full, or close to full, evidence that damage will occur.[43]

One example of cases that now and then reach the courts, and where the principle of legal certainty prevails, relates to the obligation to possess knowledge about the activity and its risks.[44] As indicated above, this obligation is linked to the precautionary principle. It is common in practice that authorities need to require precautions in order to counteract possible damages to the environment. Since they are not well informed about the specifics of the activity, they serve an order requiring the operator to suggest possible precautions. The courts generally reject such requirements as they are not precise enough to comply with the principle of legal certainty.[45]

The above-mentioned Supreme Court case (19 May 2006 in T 2303–05) is a clear example of how precaution loses out against legal certainty. The court assessed a permit condition for a industry, which 'prohibited to use in the production such chemical products for which there is lack of documented knowledge' of certain risks for the environment. The Court stressed first (without explicitly referring to the precautionary principle) that:

> *the condition has an important purpose, which is well in line with the objectives of the Environmental Code. An operator must obviously ensure that he possesses the necessary knowledge of such chemicals that may be dangerous to health or the environment when being used in the activity.*

The court nevertheless disapproved the permit condition as it did not comply with the principle of legal certainty. As criminal sanctions are applied when permit conditions are breached, the operator must be able to foresee when a condition is fulfilled or not. The expression 'documented knowledge' was too unclear according to the court. It rejected the case to the Environmental Court of Appeal, which now has to clarify the condition. This very difficult task has not yet been conducted (November 2006).

As in Finland and Denmark,[46] it has been observed in the Swedish legal research that the precautionary principle is sometimes set aside when in conflict with the principles of legal certainty and legality.[47] It is in this context important to observe that the principle of legality is protected by the Swedish Constitution and the European Convention of Human Rights.[48] Although the principle in these provisions explicitly relates to the application of criminal law, the principle is presumably strengthened generally. It is also likely that the constitutional protection of private property in Sweden, strengthened some years ago, indirectly improves the status of the principles of legality and legal certainty. Finally, many of the court judges are not educated in environmental law, which in most law educations in Sweden is not a compulsory course. Lack of insight into the precautionary principle in combination with a relatively profound knowledge of, and reliance on, the principles of legal certainty and legality could partly explain the rather conservative attitude in the choice between the contradicting principles, but also the fact that the precautionary principle is only very rarely mentioned by the courts.

Competing environmental interests

As already said, the Environmental Code aims to prevent not only the risk of pollution and other impacts, but also the efficient management of natural resources and energy (including recycling and making use of renewable resources). These *environmental objectives sometimes compete*. A good example of such conflicts are the legal trials of new wind power installations in Sweden, where aesthetic aspects, in particular, but also noise emissions and 'shadowing' of communities, sometimes hinder installation in areas where the wind conditions are optimal. These cases reflect a conflict between the 'classical' risk for local impacts (the neighbour law aspect) and the implementation of a national and global climate policy in favour of future generations (the sustainability aspect).[49]

The precautionary principle in the entire environmental legal system

As already explained, a precautionary approach was historically rooted in the legislation related to controlling pollution (except radiation) and chemicals, but not in legislation concerning, for example, nature conservation and the management of natural resources. This situation was significantly changed by the Environmental Code: the general rules of consideration in Chapter 2, including the precautionary principle in section 3, apply to all aspects of environmental protection and to the use of natural resources and energy.

Nevertheless, it is not clear that the precautionary applies in all situations that are covered by the code. The sectoral chapters include some specific substantial environmental requirements that are additional to the general rules of consideration (Chapter 2). For instance, a licence for a water activity (such as construction of a hydropower dam) can be issued only 'if the benefits with regard to public and private interests are greater than the costs and damage associated with them'.[50] Does this provision already include also risks of damage to the environment? If so, who has the burden of proof with regard to the existence of possible damages? This is not clarified in the legal text or in the preparatory works.

Furthermore, an essential task for the government and the environmental authorities is to issue regulations and by-laws based upon provisions in the sectoral chapters in order to implement the objectives of the code. There is no *explicit* obligation to comply with the precautionary principle in Chapter 2, section 3, when such regulations and by-laws are issued – for example, restrictions under Chapter 14 concerning the use of chemical products. The specific empowering provisions in the sectoral chapters refer to the principle.

It is possible that the precautionary principle is applied in practice, consciously or not, when the additional substantial requirements in the sectoral chapters are applied and when subordinated legislation is issued, especially in the fields of pollution and chemical control due to the traditional application of a precautionary approach there. With a legal systematic interpretation of the code, one may also argue that Chapter 2 constitutes the 'root' of requirements, clearly reflecting the objectives of the code in Chapter 1, and therefore must be applied throughout all 'implementation branches' (sectoral chapters and subordinated legislation) of the code tree. This argument is reasonable when 'branch provisions' concern precautionary measures; but it is more far-fetched with regard to rules formulated as prohibitions since the precautionary principle in Chapter 2, section 3, applies explicitly only to precautionary measures. Nevertheless, the environmental code has to be criticized for not providing a *clear* legal text indicating a general application of the precautionary principle throughout the entire system of provisions.

Furthermore, despite the coordination achieved by the code, there are still numerous other acts and regulations that are significant for the protection of human health or the environment. Some of those – for example, the 1971 Roads Act – specifically require that Chapter 2 of the Environmental Code is applied and, therefore, also the precautionary principle. However, there is also legislation that does not link the procedures to Chapter 2 of the code and, thus, exclude the application of the precautionary principle. The most important example is physical planning of land and water areas according to the 1987 Planning and Building Act.

The scope of the Swedish precautionary principle is connected to the member states' obligation to comply with EC law. A precautionary principle is sometimes reflected in a specific directive, which then has to be transposed in the member states. This is the case with the detailed obligations to carry out investigations before a deliberate release of genetically modified organisms is conducted.[51] However, member states should be obliged to implement the precautionary principle, also in situations where there is no specific directive, including the principle. Article 6 EC demands environmental protection requirements to be integrated within the implementation of Community policies. The precautionary principle is an essential component of these requirements, emphasized in Article 174(2) EC and observed in several ECJ decisions. Thus, it is also, from the EC law perspective, necessary to review the entire Swedish environmental legislation in order to ensure a full application of the precautionary principle.

CONCLUSIONS

The Swedish precautionary principle in Chapter 2, section 3, of the Environmental Code is clearly inherited from a preceding precautionary approach, established in the 1941 amendments of the Water Act, but more clearly expressed in the 1969 Environmental Protection Act.

The precautionary principle impinges on risk assessment and, subsequently, on risk management. A risk, based not merely on loose speculations, falls upon the operator, who has to assess the risk more closely in order to be able to prove to some – not clearly defined – degree of probability that a damage or detriment will not occur. If the operator fails, he or she is, in principle, obliged to take precautionary measures or, very occasionally, is denied initiating or operating the risky activity. However, risk management is to be seen as a *separate phase* of the legal consideration where weighing of interests shall be conducted. Costs for the operator, need for employment, demand for energy and similar interests may outweigh the risks and lead to environmentally insufficient precautions, or even to the acceptance of an activity causing considerable risk of serious damage to the environment. Furthermore, the principles of legal certainty and legality are sometimes applied in contravention of the precautionary principle.

The Swedish Supreme Court has not referred to the precautionary principle. The principle is mentioned in some judgments of the Environmental Court of Appeal, but there are no guiding arguments related to the essence of the principle. This leaves us with considerable uncertainty regarding several aspects of the principle, not least the crucial question of the standard of evidence.

One cannot say that the essence of the Environmental Code's precautionary principle differs significantly from the precautionary approach developed in the 1969 Environmental Protection Act, except in one interesting respect. The Swedish principle applies in relation to all different objectives in Chapter 1, section 1, of the Environmental

Code, including not only risk for pollution and similar nuisances, but also nature conservation and efficient management of natural resources and energy. This broad scope may be regarded as an advantage from an environmental point of view, but it complicates the decision-making when different environmental objectives compete.

Although the precautionary principle is relevant in many different situations, there are situations covered by the code where it is unclear if the principle applies or not. There is also legislation besides the Environmental Code that is not connected to any precautionary principle. As a result, the precautionary principle does not explicitly govern all decisions that are important from an environmental point of view. This situation is not acceptable from an EC law perspective. Thus, to comply with Article 6 EC, Sweden must closely review the legislation to ensure that the principle is applied not only in relation to the entire Environmental Code system, including subordinated regulations and by-laws, but also when environmental aspects are considered according to other legislation outside of the code family.

NOTES

1   Many thanks to Professor Nicolas de Sadeleer and Professor Staffan Westerlund, and also to Professor Bertil Bengtsson and several of my other colleagues at Luleå University of Technology, Division of Jurisprudence, Sweden, for providing me with useful comments on this chapter.

2   I use the term 'precautionary approach' for the period before 1998 since the expression 'precautionary principle' was not then used in the Swedish legal texts. This distinction in terminology between principle and approach does *not* indicate a distinction in the meaning of the two; compare de Sadeleer, N. (2002) *Environmental Principles: From Political Slogans to Legal Rules*, Oxford University Press, Oxford, p92.

3   Although clearly subordinated the legal text and, of course, not legally binding, preparatory works play a relatively important role as legal source in Sweden.

4   Regulation 1880 Concerning Landowners' Right to the Water on his Land, section 12. Concerning the development of legislation for pollution control before 1969, see Darpö, J. (1994) 'Vem har ansvaret, Rättsläget idag och förslag för framtiden', *Naturvårdsverket, rapport*, vol 4354, pp10–30.

5   There were also restrictions concerning sewage water, but they were not as far reaching.

6   Certain civil courts were appointed as Water Courts. Their verdicts could be appealed to one High Water Court, in Stockholm. The Supreme Court was the last instance.

7   1918 Water Act, Chapter 8, section 32. If there was risk of severe damage, only the government was empowered to issue a licence.

8   Health Protection Ordinances applied, but mainly for the control of sanitary detriments in towns.

9   Prop. 1969:28, *Miljöskyddslagen* (Government Bill, this author's translation), p210. See also SOU 1966:65, *Luftförorening, buller och andra immissioner* (state commission report preceding the Government Bill), p211.

10   Section 6. In SOU 1966:65, *Luftförorening, buller och andra immissioner*, p221, the so-called Emission Experts Commission 'underline[d] that it is sufficient to *fear for* a significant detriment: in other words, that a considerable *risk* for such a detriment exists' (italics in original).

11   Prop. 1969:28, *Miljöskyddslagen*, p210.

12   SOU 1966:65, *Luftförorening, buller och andra immissioner*, p221.
13   Westerlund, S. (1990) *Miljöskyddslagen. En analytisk lagkommentar*, Åmyra Förlag, p14.
14   Governmental decision 18 June 1975, No 167/75 and National Environmental Licensing Board (Koncessionsnämnden för miljöskydd) No 3/75.
15   The recovery of the yellowhammer has been successful, while some other species – for example, the kestrel – have not fully recovered.
16   Prop. 1973:17, *Med förslag till lag om hälso – och miljöfarliga varor* (Government Bill), p96.
17   Prop. 1984/1985:118, *Om kemikaliekontroll* (Government Bill), p40.
18   Section 5. The principle is analysed by Nilsson, A. (1997) *Att byta ut skadliga kemikalier. Substitutionsprincipen – en miljörättslig analys*, Nerenius & Santerus, Stockholm, pp127ff. See also Michanek, G. (1993) 'Substitutionsprincipen', *Miljörättslig tidskrift*, vol 2, p127.
19   Environmental Code, Chapter 1, section 1.
20   Environmental Code, Chapter 2.
21   Environmental Code, Chapter 2, section 3.
22   Environmental Code, Chapter 2, sections 2 and 4 to 6.
23   Environmental Code, Chapter 2, sections 9 and 10.
24   See Michanek, G. and Zetterberg, C. (2004) *Den svenska miljörätten*, Iustus, Uppsala, pp97–414.
25   Prop. 1997/1998:45 I, *Miljöbalk* (Government Bill, www.lagrummet.se), p210.
26   Environmental Code, Chapter 2, section 1.
27   Prop. 1997/1998:45, *Miljöbalk I* (Government Bill, www.lagrummet.se), p210.
28   Prop. 1997/1998:45 I, *Miljöbalk* (Government Bill, www.lagrummet.se), p210.
29   Compare Environmental Code, Chapter 2, section 1.
30   de Sadeleer, N. (2007) 'The Precautionary principle in European Community health and environmental law', in de Sadeleer, N. (ed) *Implementing the Precautionary Principle*, Earthscan, London.
31   See also the Government Bill related to the 1994 Act on the Swedish Accession to the European Union: Prop. 1994/95:19, *Sveriges medlemskap i Europeiska unionen* (Government Bill, www.lagrummet.se), p488.
32   Environmental Court of Appeal 30 June 2004 in case M 10499–02. See also, for example, Environmental Court of Appeal 12 May 2005 in case M 3225–04 and 30 March 2005 in case M 9408–03.
33   Environmental Code, Chapter 2, sections 2, 3 and 6.
34   Environmental Code, Chapter 2, section 9.
35   Compare Environmental Code, Chapter 2, section 1.
36   Environmental Code, Chapter 2, sections 3 and 7. These issues are developed in, for example, Westerlund, S. (1999) 'Delkommentarer till miljöbalken', *Miljörättslig tidskrift*, vol 2–3, pp343–395; Bengtsson, B. (2001) *Miljöbalkens återverkningar*, Norstedts, Stockholm; Michanek, G. (2002) 'Att väga säkert och vikten av att säkra', in Basse, E. M., Hollo, E. and Michanek, G. (eds) *Fågelperspektiv på rättsordningen, Vänbok till Staffan Westerlund*, Iustus, Uppsala, pp69–91; and Michanek, G. and Zetterberg, C. (2004) *Den svenska miljörätten*, Iustus, Uppsala, pp134–137.
37   Environmental Code, Chapter 2, section 10.
38   One example – the case of Rönnskärsverken – is mentioned earlier in the section on 'Environmental Protection Act 1969: Expanded and clarified precautionary approach'.
39   Environmental Code, Chapter 2, section 10.
40   Prop. 1997/1998:45 II, *Miljöbalk* (Government Bill, www.lagrummet.se), p28.
41   Compare de Sadeleer, N. (2002) *Environmental Principles: From Political Slogans to Legal Rules*, Oxford University Press, Oxford, p372.

42 Chapter 16, section 5, prevents further pollution if there is risk of exceeding environmental quality standards in an area; but the section applies only to 'new' activities.
43 Nilsson, A. (1997) *Att byta ut skadliga kemikalier. Substitutionsprincipen – en miljörättslig analys*, Nerenius & Santerus, Stockholm, p419.
44 Environmental Code, Chapter 2, section 3.
45 See, for example, Environmental Court of Appeal 12 November 2004 in cases M 2824–04 and M 8011–03.
46 See Chapters 3 and 4 in Part II.
47 Nilsson, A. (2002a) *Rättssäkerhet och miljöhänsyn: en diskussion belyst av JO:s praxis i miljöärenden*, Santérus, Stockholm.
48 Constitution (*Regeringsformen*), Chapter 1, section 10. See also the 1994 Act on the European Convention on Human Rights, Chapter 1, section 1. The convention is incorporated through a specific Swedish act and is therefore applied as Swedish law.
49 Söderholm, P., Ek, K. and Pettersson, M. (2007) 'Wind power development in Sweden: Global policies and local obstacles', *Renewable and Sustainable Energy Reviews* vol 11, pp365–400; and Nilsson, A. (2002b) 'Man skall vara försiktig', in Basse, E. M., Hollo, E. and Michanek, G. (eds) *Fågelperspektiv på rättsordningen, Vänbok till Staffan Westerlund*, Iustus, Uppsala, p420.
50 Environmental Code, Chapter 11, section 6.
51 The Swedish Regulation 2002 on Release into the Environment of Genetically Modified Organisms, sections 6 to 7 and Annex 1. See also the Swedish Board of Fisheries Regulation 2004 on Genetically Modified Water Organisms. Compare Directive 2001/18/EC of the European Parliament and of the Council of 12 March 2001 on the deliberate release into the environment of genetically modified organisms. The precautionary principle is included in the preamble.

CHAPTER 8

Legal Status of Precaution in the Nordic Countries: A Comparative Analysis

Nicolas de Sadeleer

Given that the precautionary principle has been enshrined in several international environmental agreements concluded by the five Nordic states, one would imagine that the lawmakers in these countries would have proclaimed the principle in an array of statutes. So far only the Swedish 1998 *Mijobalk* and the Finnish 2000 Environmental Protection Act encapsulate the principle in provisions whose scope is rather broad. As a result, codification of environmental law appears to be the favoured vehicle for the rationalization of that branch of law, as well as for the recognition of the principle of precaution. Where the national lawmaker has not succeeded in codifying its environmental law, the recognition of the principle is patchy. For instance, the principle has been laid down in very specific statutes, such as the 1995 Icelandic Foodstuffs Act and the 2001 Norwegian Environmental Act for Svalbard.

The principle has been formulated rather broadly in the Swedish and Finnish environmental acts: operators are being called upon to take 'proper care and caution … to prevent pollution' (Finnish Environmental Protection Agency) or to 'take any other precautions that are necessary in order to prevent, hinder or combat damage or detriment to human health or the environment' (Swedish 1998 *Mijobalk*). The principle is not subject to the various thresholds with respect to the risk and the extent of the damage that underpin the definitions laid down in the provisions of most of the international environmental agreements. As a result, any type of risks falling within the ambit of these provisions could be subject to precaution.

In contrast, Norwegian, Icelandic and Danish environmental legislations do not embody the principle. In addition, the Norwegian and the Finnish constitutional duties to protect the environment are apparently too broadly framed to extract a principle of precaution. Nevertheless, being parties to several international agreements embracing the principle, these three states need to take it into account with respect to their international duties.

Throughout the Nordic region, furthermore, the principle has been embodied in a spate of political statements. As a result, in countries such as Norway and Denmark, precaution seems to have a political rather than a legal content.

However, it would be wrong to restrict the precautionary principle in the Nordic countries as a genuine political slogan. According to several authors, the principle underpins an array of statutes dealing with risks characterized by the difficulty of identifying the link of causation. Indeed, the different national experts have been placing emphasis upon the extent to which the genetically modified organisms (GMOs) regulations mirror a precautionary approach. Likewise, the Nordic countries have embraced an important element of the precautionary principle through recognition of the substitution principle, according to which the mere existence of an alternative substance that appears to be less dangerous than the hazardous substance in question is sufficient basis for a prohibition.

In sharp contrast to the developments in European Community (EC) law, where courts have been playing an important role (see Chapter 2 in this volume), very few judgments handed down by national courts are based on the assumption that a precautionary principle or approach has been infringed. To make matters worse, the literal interpretation endorsed by some national courts (Denmark) preclude the recognition of precaution as a general principle of law. The omens are also not good with regard to the recognition by national courts of precaution as an overarching principle. When antagonistic principles enter into conflict, courts enjoy wide discretion in determining the respective weight of such principles. As a result, in many jurisdictions, precaution stands no chance of outweighing more traditional principles, such as proportionality, legality or legal certainty (Denmark and Finland). Attention should be drawn to the fact, however, that in Sweden the balancing of interests has been clearly framed by the law-maker (1998 *Miljobalk*). In spite of the willingness of the Swedish legislator to seek greater clarity with regard to the weighing of interests, the hard core of environmental protection could still be outweighed by 'reasons of public interest'.

Needless to say, the complex relationship between risk assessment and risk management that underpins the development within EC law (see Chapter 2 in this volume) has hitherto not given rise to conflicting opinions.

Whereas Denmark became an EC member state in 1973, Sweden and Finland joined the European Community in 1995. These three countries are known to have recently exerted influence in Brussels on the development of specific environmental EC legislation. As mentioned above, the situation of the two other Nordic countries is rather different. Nonetheless, given that they are parties to the European Economic Area Agreement (EEA), all EC regulations and directives that explicitly or implicitly encapsulate the precautionary principle apply to Norway and Iceland in the same way as they do to EC member states. Strangely enough, although the precautionary principle has been enshrined in various environmental EC directives, it has not yet been incorporated within the various national administrative practices.

All of this is not to say that precaution does not underpin the environmental administrative approach in the Nordic countries. Chapters in other sections of this book on chemicals, fisheries, nature protection and genetically modified organisms (GMOs) clearly highlight the key role of precaution in managing specific environmental risks.

Broadly speaking, the manner in which precaution is being applied appears to be more beneficial for the protection of health and the environment than the approach contemplated by the EC institutions. Indeed, whereas the principle has been developed chiefly within a trade context in EC law, its implementation within the environmental realm in the Nordic countries appears to be much more flexible. In particular, less emphasis has been given to the obligations to carry out a risk assessment that is as complete as possible and to cost-benefit analysis. By and large, the burden of proof with respect to the safety of the process or the product is placed on the operator.

PART III

The Precautionary Principle and the Law of the Sea – A Nordic Perspective

Introduction: Precaution, Prevention of Marine Pollution and Conservation of Marine Resources

Nicolas de Sadeleer

Given that the five Nordic countries are known to have ancient maritime traditions, the implementation of a precautionary approach with regard to both sea pollution and fisheries deserves attention.

The precautionary principle has been at the forefront in the field of marine pollution where an abundance of data on pollution yielded little understanding but much concern. The Convention for the Protection of the Marine Environment of the North-East Atlantic (OSPAR) and Helsinki Commission (HELCOM) recommendations, both of which incorporate the precautionary principle, are probably among the most stringent international agreements relating to the marine environment. Both agreements call upon the parties to take precautionary measures 'when there are reasonable grounds for concern' (OSPAR) or 'where there is reason to assume' (HELCOM) that the marine environment will be impaired. Minna Pyhälä, Anne Christine Brusendorff and Hanna Paulomäki, from the HELCOM Commission, and Peter Ehlers and Tapani Kohonen, former HELCOM chairmen, describe, in Chapter 9, how the principle has been gaining momentum within the HELCOM framework. In particular, these authors analyse the manner in which the principle has been fleshed out into more concrete obligations enshrined in a wide array of recommendations enacted by the Conference of the Parties. Given that the Baltic Sea is the only sea almost entirely within the European Union (EU), the precautionary model contemplated in HELCOM could impinge upon EU environmental policies.

By the same token, marine fisheries management is intrinsically uncertain. Uncertainties relate to individual stocks being harvested, other affected species, and the likely impacts of fishing on the ecosystem of which the species form part. Given the risk of over-fishing and the eventual collapse of fish stocks, an explicit precautionary approach encapsulated in international agreements and national legislations is strongly needed. Developments in this area were fostered by the entry into force of the 1995 United Nations Food and Agriculture Organization (FAO) Code of Conduct for Responsible Fisheries and the 1995 United Nations Agreement on Straddling Fish Stocks and Highly Migratory Fish Stocks. Indeed, the UN agreement was the first global fisheries agreement requiring a precautionary approach, which is to be applied to fisheries conservation, management and exploitation measures. In this respect, Tore Henriksen from the University of Tromsø, Norway, examines in Chapter 10 how a precautionary approach has been embraced by fisheries authorities in the Nordic region.

CHAPTER 9

The Precautionary Principle and the Helsinki Commission

Minna Pyhälä, Anne Christine Brusendorff, Hanna Paulomäki, Peter Ehlers and Tapani Kohonen

INTRODUCTION

For three decades, the Helsinki Commission (HELCOM), the governing body of the Helsinki Convention, has been working to protect the marine environment of the Baltic Sea. This work has been driven by the specific environmental, economic and social situation in the Baltic region and the special sensitivity of the Baltic Sea.

Since the 1970s, HELCOM has had a holistic approach to restoring and protecting the Baltic Sea marine environment, taking into account the whole ecosystem as well as economic, social, recreational and cultural aspects of the people living in the riparian countries. During its 30 years of existence, HELCOM has closely cooperated with the scientific community to collect and disseminate environmental data that is used to regularly produce comprehensive assessments on the pressures affecting the marine environment and their effects on the whole marine ecosystem. These assessments are the basis upon which decisions are made to take further actions to reduce the impacts of human activities on the environment.

HELCOM's main role is to act as scientific adviser and environmental policy-maker. In addition to taking regional measures imposed by other international organizations, HELCOM supplements these by developing recommendations[1] of its own according to the specific needs of the Baltic Sea. Furthermore, HELCOM works to ensure that commonly agreed upon environmental standards are fully implemented by all of its contracting parties throughout the Baltic Sea and its catchment area.

HELCOM's vision for the future is a healthy Baltic Sea environment with diverse biological components functioning in balance, resulting in a good ecological status and supporting a wide range of sustainable economic and social activities. In pursuing this objective and vision, the riparian countries have jointly pooled their efforts in HELCOM.

THE START OF THE HELSINKI COMMISSION (HELCOM): A PROGRESSIVE STEP

The Convention for the Protection of the Marine Environment of the Baltic Sea Area (Helsinki Convention) was signed in 1974 by the ministers of environment from the then seven Baltic Sea states. The convention was developed in an era of increased environmental awareness and as a reaction to concerns about the worsening state of the Baltic Sea marine environment. During the 1970s, there was a lack of jointly elaborated scientific evidence and no common understanding of the state of the Baltic marine environment or the gravity of the problems affecting it (that is, no evidence of the extent of damage or whether the worsening state was irreversible or not). Nevertheless, the unique and sensitive nature of the Baltic Sea, coupled with the fact that it is a valuable resource for the riparian countries, resulted in the Baltic coastal states acknowledging that the sustainability and well-being of the Baltic Sea depends upon coordinated efforts and joint regional environmental standards. This initiative was backed by the 1972 United Nations Conference on the Human Environment, which opted for regional cooperation in areas such as the Baltic, where for geographical and ecological reasons regional cooperation could be carried out for a natural entity.

Although the 1974 Convention does not mention the precautionary principle *per se*, viewed in the light of the circumstances that led to its adoption, it can be interpreted as a precautionary step towards eliminating pollution to the Baltic Sea and restoring its ecological balance. The 1974 Convention was *avant garde* in that it took an overall approach to marine environmental protection by addressing all sources of marine pollution, whether from sources based on land, at sea or in the air, as well as by addressing the need to establish cooperation for eliminating pollution and responding to pollution incidents at sea.

The 1974 Convention also reflected a precautionary attitude since it was a forerunner in many areas. For example, the 1974 Convention mentions the need to counteract the introduction of hazardous substances such as dichlorodiphenyltrichloroethanes (DDTs) and polychlorinated biphenyls (PCBs) two years before measures were taken to restrict and market the use of such substances at a European level (European Directive 76/769/EEC) and more than two decades before global level actions were taken to phase out persistent organic pollutants.[2] The 1974 Convention was also progressive in that it entirely prohibited dumping,[3] thus imposing significantly stricter standards than regional[4] and global[5] conventions, which only prohibited the dumping of certain 'black-listed' substances, while allowing dumping of other 'grey-listed' substances, providing that certain procedures are followed.

Furthermore, HELCOM was a predecessor in taking regional measures to prevent pollution from ships.[6] Precautionary measures have been taken through common actions, ensuring a strict application of instruments provided by international fora.[7] On top of this, a Baltic-specific mandatory waste delivery requirement was adopted in the late 1990s,[8] paving the way for similar measures taken under the European Union (EU) in 2000.[9]

The focus of HELCOM has from the very beginning been on the prevention of pollution from shipping and cooperation in responding to incidents at sea. While the many measures taken by HELCOM to address accident preparedness are in themselves only an example of good management in the case of a pollution incident, later measures taken to also improve the safety of navigation[10] invoke a precautionary approach.

MONITORING THE ENVIRONMENT

Realizing the importance of scientific data to foresee potential threats to the Baltic marine environment, and thus also to identify the need for preventive measures, HELCOM set up its monitoring and assessment programme in 1979,[11] shortly after the signing of the 1974 Convention. The HELCOM monitoring programme was set up to investigate the natural variability in the Baltic Sea marine environment, as well as to identify and quantify the impacts of human activities to the marine environment – that is, pollution loads. Furthermore, the monitoring programme assesses the changes in the environment following regulatory actions.

The monitoring of the state of, and trends in, the marine environment supports the application of the precautionary approach, particularly when it is designed to allow for the detection of emerging issues of concern; it therefore helps to identify the need for new policies that counteract threats to the environment. The establishment of a monitoring programme was, thus, not in itself a decision on how to further regulate activities, but rather helped to establish a precondition for such decisions.

It was not until 1981, upon the release of a report compiled by the International Council for the Exploration of the Sea (ICES) and entitled *Assessment of the Effects of Pollution on the Natural Resources of the Baltic Sea* that there was a jointly approved, common understanding of the state of the Baltic marine environment and the possible impacts of human activities on the marine environment. Not only did the assessment provide valuable information on the then current state of the sea, but it was meant to serve as a baseline assessment for future monitoring of trends by the Baltic Monitoring Programme. In addition, the assessment served as a tool for evaluating whether the established Baltic Monitoring Programme provided a suitable basis for considering the need for additional preventive measures.[12]

PROACTIVE MEASURES ADDRESSING
EARLY WARNINGS

The findings published in the ICES assessment reaffirmed early concerns about the deteriorating state of the Baltic Sea marine environment. The 1974 Convention identified several hazardous and noxious substances whose introduction to the marine environment needed to be counteracted, including PCBs and DDTs. The assessment stated that there were strong indications that PCB substances were primarily responsible for immunological and reproductive disorders in Baltic seals, and led to the adoption of supplementary recommendations to limit the use and discharges of PCBs[13] and DDTs,[14] as well as a moratorium on the hunting of seals[15] in 1982. Considering that it was not until 1985 that Bergman and Olsson[16] found conclusive evidence of a causal link between the reproductive impairment in seals in the Baltic Sea and PCBs, the HELCOM measures taken in 1982 can be viewed as an expression of the precautionary approach. To this day, seal hunting is still only allowed if it can be scientifically proven that it will not cause unacceptable harm to the seal populations – an example of the adoption of a more rigorous version of the precautionary principle, with the burden of proof reversed.[17,18]

The first HELCOM periodic assessment on the state of the Baltic marine environment, covering the years 1980 to 1985 was published in 1986. Amongst other issues, this assessment confirmed that ongoing eutrophication was a serious threat to the Baltic ecosystem and needed to be addressed urgently. Measures to reduce nutrient inputs from land-based sources[19] and from shipping[20] were already taken in the 1974 Convention; however, the affirmation of the significance of the impacts of eutrophication led to increased monitoring of nutrient discharges into water and of emissions to the air,[21] as well as further actions to reduce waterborne as well as airborne nutrient pollution from point sources, such as industries and municipalities,[22] diffuse sources such as agriculture[23] and shipping.[24]

In 1987, measures for reducing pollution from agricultural pesticides were adopted. While agriculture was recognized as the source of pollution with regard to pesticides, it was simultaneously recognized that knowledge about their effects in the marine environment of the Baltic Sea was limited.[25] Once again, the measures taken by HELCOM, despite clear scientific evidence indicating threat, reflect precautionary action.

A ministerial-level meeting was held in 1988, where in response to the HELCOM assessment findings on inputs of pollutants and their effects on the marine environment, the ministers of environment of the Baltic Sea states decided that the loads of pollutants (nutrients, as well as hazardous substances) to the Baltic Sea should be reduced by 50 per cent from 1987 levels by the year 1995. In requiring a 50 per cent reduction in pollutant discharges, the ministers of the Baltic Sea states broke free from the classical scientific approach according to which a specific threshold is set for each pollutant according to the impact of the ensuing damages. To some extent, such political commitments embrace the precautionary approach.

The decision to reduce pollution discharges was reaffirmed by a ministerial meeting in 1998, which decided that there was a need for contracting parties to develop more specific targets to reduce discharges from point and diffuse sources by 50 per cent. These decisions have been followed by the adoption of numerous recommendations that address pollution from various industries and municipalities, as well as agriculture and managed forestry. Since then, HELCOM assessments have shown that 50 per cent reduction targets are not sufficient to combat eutrophication, and current objectives are to reduce pollution loads to levels that allow for good ecological status.

THE PRECAUTIONARY PRINCIPLE GAINS FORMAL RECOGNITION

The 1988 ministerial meeting was also exceptional in that, for the first time in HELCOM history, the resulting ministerial declaration explicitly refers to the precautionary principle. Ministers declared:

> ... *being convinced that damage to the marine environment can be irreversible or reme-diable only in a long term perspective and at considerable expense and that therefore, Contracting Parties to the Convention must adopt a precautionary approach and not wait for the full and undisputed scientific proof of harmful effects before taking action to prevent and abate pollution.*

HELCOM was ahead of its time as it was not until the 1990s that the principle was expressly adopted at a wider scale in other areas of environmental law, being accorded universal recognition at the United Nations Conference on Environment and Development (UNCED) in Rio de Janeiro in 1992.

A revised Helsinki Convention was adopted in 1992 in order to take into account the further strengthening of the environmental awareness that had paved the way for interna-tional environmental law developments, as well as developments in the region's political environment. The 1992 Convention was signed by the ministers of environment of the nine Baltic Coastal states, as well as by the then Czech and Slovak Federal Republic, Norway and the European Economic Community (EEC), and entered into force in 2000.

In addition to expanding the mandate of HELCOM, the revised 1992 Helsinki Convention included new environmental principles, amongst others the precautionary principle. Article 3(2) of the 1992 Convention, which defines the fundamental princi-ples and obligations of the convention, states that:

> *The Contracting Parties shall apply the precautionary principle – that is, to take preventive measures when there is reason to assume that substances or energy intro-duced, directly or indirectly, into the marine environment may create hazards to human health, harm living resources and marine ecosystems, damage amenities or interfere with other legitimate uses of the sea even when there is no conclusive evidence of a causal relationship between inputs and their alleged effects.*

This broad definition of the principle, when compared to its use in the 1992 Rio Declaration on Environment and Development (principle 15),[26] can be viewed as setting a lower threshold for its application in the Baltic Sea region. The lower threshold for scientific information needed, as implied by the 1992 Convention, can also be illustrated by comparing the use of the precautionary principle in the 1992 Convention for the Protection of the Marine Environment of the North-East Atlantic (OSPAR).[27] Whereas the 1992 Helsinki Convention applies the principle when there is *reason to assume* hazard, OSPAR states that it should be used when there *are reasonable grounds for concern.*

Besides explicitly affirming the precautionary principle, the redefinition of pollution in the 1992 Convention also embraces precaution. Article 2(1) of the 1974 Helsinki

Convention defined pollution as the introduction of substances or energy into the marine environment *resulting in hazard*. This definition of pollution required a proven effect of pollution before any preventive measures could be taken. The 1992 Helsinki Convention changed the definition of pollution to the introduction of substances or energy that is *liable to create hazards*. This means that it is no longer the proven effect but the potential risk of a threat which is the decisive factor for when preventive measures should be taken. Such reasoning lay behind HELCOM's objective on hazardous substances, which was adopted in 1998.[28]

The introduction of Article 15 on nature conservation and biodiversity to the 1992 Convention,[29] as well as the adoption of subsequent recommendations,[30] can also be interpreted as a manifestation of the precautionary principle. Although the article and recommendations do not mention the principle as such, the mere intention to conserve habitats and biodiversity in the region can be viewed as precaution against threat. Furthermore, the emphasis on ensuring the sustainable use of natural resources can be viewed as a measure to apply precaution when utilizing marine resources, even though no specific evidence of threat has been determined. Among marine conventions, HELCOM was a forerunner in adopting such regional measures.[31]

The 1992 Convention also introduces the need for risk assessments by addressing environmental impact assessments (EIAs) in case of proposed activities likely to cause a significant adverse impact on the marine environment. This new Article 7 lends further support to the precautionary principle.

The EIA is a procedural requirement rather than a decision in itself – for instance, to grant a permit to carry out a certain activity. It does, however, require that a Baltic Coastal state at an early stage considers whether an activity is likely to cause adverse impacts. According to the 1992 Convention, international law or supra-national regulations determine the need of an EIA. However, there are certain instances where HELCOM requires an EIA to be carried out – namely, prior to permitting the construction of new installations likely to affect the Baltic Sea[32] or activities such as marine sediment prospecting and extraction.[33]

The precautionary principle is explicitly mentioned in Annex II of the 1992 Helsinki Convention on the criteria for the use of best environmental practice (BEP) and best available technology (BAT). Other references to BEP and BAT within HELCOM[34] also implicitly underscore the use of the precautionary principle: such measures are recommended despite conclusive proof of the threat of an activity.

The above measures and actions taken by HELCOM are examples that illustrate the dedication of the region to act with precaution when taking measures to avert potential negative impacts of human activities on the marine environment of the Baltic Sea. Having recognized the value and importance of precautionary measures, HELCOM is continuing to develop this approach to environmental protection.

PRECAUTION REGARDING POSSIBLE FUTURE THREATS

HELCOM has developed a holistic, ecosystem-based approach to addressing the protection of the Baltic Sea marine environment by monitoring the state of, and trends in, the marine environment and using its assessments as the basis for developing measures to combat pollution and address pressures from human activities. Despite many achievements in reducing pollution loads to the sea and minimizing the impacts of human activities, the unique nature of the Baltic means that it can often take decades for the positive results of measures to be observed at sea. Much work remains to be done and HELCOM continues to be dedicated to improving the state of the Baltic Sea marine environment.

In recent years, HELCOM has developed ecological objectives to clarify its goals and is currently in the process of identifying indictors that can help to determine whether measures taken are effectively reducing threats to, and improving the state of, the marine environment. In this process, HELCOM intends to apply the precautionary principle by setting ambitious targets for good ecological status. Furthermore, well-planned monitoring, together with the participation of a wide range of stakeholders who ensure openness and transparency in HELCOM work, are essential components in a system that allows for the prediction of potential future threats. In other words, the framework developed by HELCOM allows for the region to remain clued in to the state of the marine environment and anticipate possible hazards to the sensitive and unique Baltic Sea – fundamental instruments for continuing to act with precaution.

NOTES

1   HELCOM recommendations can be characterized as soft law in that they are not legally binding. However, the fact that the recommendations are adopted unanimously, and that countries are required to report on their national implementation, diminishes concerns about the lacking legal nature.
2   International actions to regulate and phase out persistent organic pollutants (POPs):
   - 1995: An international working group was convened by United Nations Environment Programme (UNEP) Governing Council to develop assessments for 12 POPs. This working group determined that the data were adequate for these 12 POPs to justify the elimination or reduction of emissions and even, in some cases, to halt production and use.
   - 1997: International Agency for Research on Cancer (IARC) published the monograph on the evaluations of carcinogenic risks to humans regarding polychlorinated dibenzo-para-dioxins and polychlorinated dibenzofurans.
   - 1998: United Nations Economic Commission for Europe (UNECE), consisting of European countries, Russia, Canada and the US, agreed on a protocol that bans the production and use of some POPs, and scheduled some others (DDT, heptachlor, hexachlorobenzene and PCBs) for elimination at a later stage.
   - 2001: The Stockholm Convention on Persistent Organic Pollutants agreed on targeting 12 POPs.

3   Article 9 of the 1974 Convention on Prevention of Dumping.

4   Convention for the Prevention of Marine Pollution by Dumping from Ships and Aircraft (Oslo Convention), signed in 1972.

5   Convention on the Prevention of Marine Pollution by Dumping of Wastes and Other Matter (London Convention), signed in 1972.

6   These measures mirrored the measures in the 1973 International Convention for the Prevention of Pollution from Ships (later modified by the Protocol of 1978, MARPOL 73/78).

7   The Baltic coastal states succeeded in gaining 'special area' status for the Baltic Sea under MARPOL 73/78 Annexes I, II and V, implying clear obligations for the Baltic Coastal States to provide ships with reception facilities in ports, where they could deliver the substances that they were not allowed to discharge into the Baltic. The Baltic Sea region has thus served as a path-breaking example for other regions that have also been given the 'special area' status. This also applies for the 'SOx emission control area status' under MARPOL 73/78 Annex VI.

8   HELCOM Recommendation 19/7 concerning amendments to Annex IV of the 1974 Convention states that before leaving port, ships shall discharge all ship-generated wastes that are not allowed to be discharged into the sea in the Baltic Sea area in accordance with MARPOL 73/78 and the Helsinki Convention to a port reception facility.

9   Directive 2000/59/EC of the European Parliament and of the Council of 27 November 2000 on port reception facilities for ship-generated waste and cargo residues.

10   HELCOM has taken measures to improve the safety of navigation by addressing routing, pilotage, navigation in winter conditions, paving the way for and accepting the use of Electronic Chart Display and Information Systems (ECDIS), and development of an Automatic Information System (AIS) that monitors maritime traffic on a real-time basis.

11   HELCOM began coordinated monitoring of physical, chemical and biological variables in open sea areas of the Baltic Sea in 1979. In 1992, upon adoption of the revised Helsinki Convention, monitoring was extended to include coastal areas as well, and a cooperative monitoring programme was established.

12   HELCOM Recommendation 2/8 on the implications of the document *Assessment of the Effects of Pollution on the Natural Resources of the Baltic Sea*, adopted on 18 February 1981. The assessment was published in HELCOM's *Baltic Sea Environment Proceedings Series* (BSEP 5A).

13   HELCOM Recommendation 3/1 regarding the limitation of the use of PCBs, adopted on 17 February 1982, whereby contracting parties were recommended to prohibit the introduction of new articles or equipment containing PCBs and to develop national regulations for reducing discharges from existing sources.

14   HELCOM Recommendation 3/2 regarding the elimination of discharges of DDT, adopted on 17 February 1982.

15   HELCOM Recommendation 3/3 concerning protection of seals in the Baltic Sea area was adopted on 17 February 1982, with the acknowledgement that according to the document *Assessment of the Effects of Pollution on the Natural Resources of the Baltic Sea* there are strong indications that PCB substances are primarily responsible for the serious decrease in the reproductive rate of seals in the Baltic Sea region.

16   Bergman A. and Olsson M. (1985) 'Pathology of Baltic grey seal and ringed seal females with special reference to adrenocortical hyperplasia: Is environmental pollution the cause of a widely distributed disease syndrome?', *Finnish Game Reports*, vol 44, pp47–62.

17   HELCOM Recommendation 3/3 concerning protection of seals in the Baltic Sea area, adopted on 17 February 1982, 'recommends that the governments of the contracting parties to the Helsinki Convention, through their national instruments, ban all hunting of grey seals and harbour seals and ban or strictly regulate hunting of ringed seals both in national and international waters *until the natural reproductive rate can be scientifically shown to be sufficient*

enough to safeguard the survival of these species in the Baltic Sea area' (emphasis added); likewise, HELCOM Recommendation 9/1 concerning protection of seals in the Baltic Sea area, adopted on 15 February 1988, recommends that 'through their national instruments ban all hunting of grey seals, ringed seals and harbour seals in the Baltic area. In order to safeguard the survival of these species, the ban shall be maintained *until a natural health condition and a normal reproductive rate can scientifically be shown'* (emphasis added).

18 Despite the ban, selective elimination of seals has taken place in areas with high seal concentrations. This has especially been the case where there have been conflicts between seals and fishermen, and has occurred upon prior approval by national authorities. While this implies that the burden of proof is upon the hunter/fisherman to demonstrate the damaging effect of a specific seal, it does not apply to the conservation status of the seal population as such.

19 Annex III of the 1974 Helsinki Convention identifies the most important land-based sources of nutrient pollution to be municipal sewage and industrial wastes.

20 Annex IV for the 1974 Helsinki Convention contains regulations concerning sewage discharges from ships.

21 HELCOM Recommendation 7/1 concerning monitoring of airborne pollution load, adopted on 11 February 1986, and HELCOM Recommendation 9/7 concerning the guidelines for the Baltic Monitoring Programme, adopted on 17 February 1988.

22 HELCOM Recommendation 6/7 concerning the treatment of municipal sewage and industrial wastewater, with special emphasis on the reduction of discharges of nutrients, adopted on 13 March 1985.

23 HELCOM Recommendation 7/2, adopted on 11 February 1986, was the first recommendation concerning measures aimed at reducing discharges from agriculture, and was subsequently followed by the adoption of additional measures.

24 HELCOM Recommendation 11/12 concerning reduction of air pollution from ships, adopted on 14 February 1990, recommends, among other things, to apply best available technology to reduce nitrogen oxides emissions.

25 HELCOM Recommendation 8/2, adopted on 25 February 1987, concerning measures to reduce pollution by pesticides from agriculture.

26 Principle 15 of the 1992 Rio Declaration on Environment and Development states: 'In order to protect the environment, the precautionary approach shall be widely applied by states according to their capabilities. Where there are threats of serious or irreversible damage, lack of full scientific certainty shall not be used as a reason for postponing cost-effective measures to prevent environmental degradation.'

27 The 1992 OSPAR Convention states: 'the contracting parties shall apply the precautionary principle, by virtue of which preventive measures are to be taken when there are reasonable grounds for concern that substances or energy introduced, directly or indirectly, into the marine environment may bring about hazards to human health, harm living resources and marine ecosystems, damage amenities or interfere with other legitimate uses of the sea, even when there is no conclusive evidence of a causal relationship between the inputs and the effects'.

28 HELCOM Recommendation 19/5: HELCOM objective with regard to hazardous substances, adopted on 26 March 1998. It was decided that HELCOM's objective is 'to prevent pollution by continuously reducing discharges, emissions and losses of hazardous substances, with the ultimate aim of concentrations in the environment near background values for naturally occurring substances and close to zero for man-made synthetic substances'. The objective involves the application of the precautionary principle with the selection criteria and priority-setting of substances considering findings and work undertaken in other fora and not being limited to hazards already observed in the Baltic. It was decided that in developing the mechanisms of selecting and prioritizing substances and groups of substances, the

growing international research effort, especially in the OSPAR Commission, European Union (EU) and Organisation for Economic Co-operation and Development (OECD), should be taken into account. Furthermore, HELCOM should keep the selection and prioritization mechanisms under review to ensure that they remain effective in identifying all aspects of hazard and risk that should give rise to reasonable grounds of concern about substances, taking account of developments in OSPAR, the Intergovernmental Forum on Chemical Safety and the UNECE Convention on Long-Range Transboundary Air Pollution (LRTAP) on Persistent Organic Pollutants.

29 Article 15 of the 1992 Convention states that: 'contracting parties shall take all appropriate measures to conserve natural habitats and biological diversity and to protect ecological processes. Furthermore, the article emphasizes that such measures shall be taken to ensure the sustainable use of natural resources in the Baltic Sea area.'

30 HELCOM Recommendation 15/5 concerning a system of coastal and marine Baltic Sea Protected Areas (BSPAs), adopted on 10 March 1994, and HELCOM Recommendation 21/4 concerning the protection of heavily endangered or immediately threatened marine and coastal biotopes in the Baltic Sea area, adopted on 20 March 2000.

31 See, for instance, Annex V to the OSPAR Convention on the Protection and Conservation of the Ecosystems and Biological Diversity of the Maritime Area, adopted in 1998.

32 HELCOM Recommendation 17/3 concerning information and consultation with regard to the construction of new installations affecting the Baltic Sea, adopted on 12 March 1996.

33 HELCOM Recommendation 19/1 concerning marine sediment extraction in the Baltic Sea area, adopted on 23 March 1998.

34 For example, HELCOM Recommendation 17/10 concerning basic principles for the realization of BAT and BEP in the food industry, adopted on 13 March 1996, and HELCOM Recommendation 25/2 on the reduction of emissions and discharges from industry by effective use of BAT, adopted on 2 March 2004.

CHAPTER 10

The Precautionary Approach and Fisheries: A Nordic Perspective

Tore Henriksen

INTRODUCTION

The precautionary approach (PA) was introduced to fisheries conservation and management following the 1992 United Nations Conference on Environment and Development (UNCED) in Rio de Janeiro. It has been included both in treaties and non-binding documents.

The most prominent of the treaties is the 1995 United Nations Fish Stocks Agreement, which entered into force in 2001 (Article 6).[1] All the Nordic states and the European Community (EC) are parties to the Fish Stocks Agreement.[2] Regional fisheries management organizations established in recent years are required to apply the precautionary approach in regulating high seas fisheries.[3] The Food and Agriculture Organization (FAO) of the UN adopted, in 1993, the non-binding Code of Conduct for Responsible Fisheries,[4] laying down several recommendations for all types of marine fisheries management, including the application of the precautionary approach.[5] The North Sea Conferences focused in 1997 on the integration of fisheries and environmental issues.[6] The precautionary approach was one of the principles that the ministers of the environment agreed should guide the states in the protection of the North Sea and in ensuring the sustainability of fish stocks.[7] It has been argued that the precautionary principle/approach has become a norm of customary international law (McIntyre and Mosedale, 1997, p235). At any rate, it is safe to conclude that the Nordic countries are legally and/or politically obligated to apply the precautionary approach in the conservation and management of marine living resources, both within their 200 miles exclusive economic zone (EEZ) and on the high seas.

The natural questions are *if* and *how* the Nordic countries have implemented the precautionary approach. In answering these questions, the focus will be on *three* main issues. The first is on the role of science in the application of the PA. States are required to adopt measures to conserve and manage living marine resources based on the best scientific evidence available.[8] The precautionary approach was introduced in acknowledgment of the inability of science to provide full certainty on the effects of human activity and natural variations on the environment and its components (Shelton, 1996, p211). The focus will be on how the PA has influenced the development and presentation of scientific advice and specifically the work of the International Council of the Exploration for the Sea (ICES), which provides the Nordic countries with scientific advice on the conservation and management of living marine resources in the North-East Atlantic. Second, the focus will be on the status of the precautionary approach in national legislation. Is it explicitly referred to in the basic rules or is it simply applied in conservation and management? By including the precautionary approach in the basic legislation, it will have a higher status and it will also be easier to verify its implementation. Third, the focus will be on the actual application of the approach in three (EC, Icelandic and Norwegian/Russian) fisheries.

THE PRECAUTIONARY APPROACH TO FISHERIES CONSERVATION AND MANAGEMENT

Before these questions can be addressed, we need to find a general understanding of the concept in fisheries management. The reference in this chapter will be the precautionary approach, as regulated in Articles 5(c) and 6 of the Fish Stocks Agreement. These provisions are applicable both to the high seas and to the areas under national jurisdiction: in practical terms, the EEZs of the coastal states (Article 3(1)). Even if they are more elaborate, the provisions on the PA correspond to a high degree with Article 7.5 of the Code of Conduct for Responsible Fisheries. The Fish Stocks Agreement and its precautionary approach provision are directly applicable to the conservation and management of fish stocks occurring both on the high seas and in areas under national jurisdiction (so-called straddling fish stocks and highly migratory fish stocks). Subsequently, the PA is not applicable to fish stocks confined within areas of the high seas or to areas within the jurisdiction of coastal states. But there is no reason why the precautionary approach should not be applied to these stocks. The code of conduct, which applies to all fisheries irrespective of jurisdiction, confirms such understanding (Article 1.3).

But first some comments on the need of precaution in fisheries conservation and management and the background of the provisions as may be found in the Fish Stocks Agreement.

A need of precaution in fisheries conservation and management

The role of science is to assess the effects of fisheries on the living marine resources and to advise on their proper utilization through conservation and management measures. But the scientific information provided is uncertain. There are several complex factors of uncertainty and, thus, possible causes of error (Hilborn and Peterman, 1996, pp78–81). These include:

- *Measurement uncertainty*: describes the lack of or/and inadequate data on catches taken and efforts in a fishery and lack of and/or inadequate data from scientific surveys. The extent of unreported catches from the fishery is one example contributing to such uncertainties.

- *Estimation uncertainty*: arises when the stock is estimated (e.g. the size of the stock) and other parameters are derived (such as recruitment) based on the abovementioned data.
- *Process uncertainty*: when there is inadequate and insufficient information and/or ignorance about the relationship between the different elements of the ecosystem and their interaction. Examples of such uncertainties are the uncertainties about the effects of the variations in environmental conditions, such as sea temperatures on the fish stocks, and uncertainty as to the level of predation of the stock by other species, such as sea birds and sea mammals.
- *Model uncertainty*: is the uncertainty as to whether the mathematical model used in the stock assessment is able to reflect the real dynamics of the stock and/or the relationship with other species of the ecosystem.
- *Decision and implementation uncertainty*: relates to the uncertainty as to whether the decisions are taken on the basis of scientific information and as to their implementation and compliance.

The last type of uncertainty reflects that the PA does not only relate to scientific information but to socio-economic factors as well.

When conclusions are drawn on the state of the stock, based on the uncertain scientific information, two main types of errors may be made: the stock may be *underestimated* or *overestimated*. If the stock is underestimated, the conservation measures adopted will be stricter than necessary. The consequence is lost opportunities of fishing, which can be described as socio-economic costs. If the stock is overestimated, the measures necessary to conserve the stock are not taken. The stock is subsequently at risk of being over-fished since there will be some time before the information on the harmful effects of fishing occurs and action to correct the mistakes may be taken. There is, thus, obviously a need to apply precaution in fisheries management.

Precautionary principle or precautionary approach?

The obligation of states to display precaution is expressed through different concepts (Hewison, 1996, p313). In some treaties such as the OSPAR Convention[9] and the 1992 Water Convention,[10] states are required to apply the 'precautionary principle', while the 'precautionary approach' is used in the Rio Declaration[11] and in several regional fisheries agreements.[12] This begs the question whether there is a factual legal distinction between them or whether it is only a matter of semantics. There have been relatively extensive discussions in academia on the use of the concepts and whether they reflect deeper political and legal differences.[13]

States have been concerned about the use of the concepts and have insisted on maintaining a distinction. European states were not successful in their attempts to include the concept of 'precautionary principle' in principle 15 of the Rio Declaration (Fullem, 1995, p507). One possible explanation why states are unwilling to use the precautionary principle may be a concern that, through practice, it may be developed towards stricter and more inflexible obligations.

The precautionary approach was introduced to the United Nations Conference on Straddling Fish Stocks and Highly Migratory Fish Stocks, convened between 1993 and 1995.[14] States were initially sceptical about including the precautionary approach in fisheries management, arguing that it was intended for preventing pollution.[15] The FAO, requested by the UN conference to prepare information on the precautionary approach to fisheries management, also made a point of distinguishing between the precautionary approach and the precautionary principle, arguing that the principle had developed a 'strong negative undertone' and that the precautionary approach had a 'more acceptable image' and was more readily applicable to fisheries management.[16] Both the Fish Stocks Agreement and the FAO Code of Conduct for Responsible Fisheries use the precautionary approach concept.

In trying to distinguish the principle from the approach, the 'principle' has been explained as identifying the relevant factors to be taken into account and added weight to the decision-making, while the 'approach' is intended to describe the attitude to be held by the decision-makers (Hey, 1992, p304). The approach thus seems to involve less stringent obligations. But since principles as legal norms are relatively open and flexible and do not direct any particular solution, this seems to be a question of semantics. The reluctance of states to commit themselves to the precautionary principle is still a relevant factor to consider when interpreting and applying the obligations under the precautionary approach.

THE FISH STOCKS AGREEMENT AND THE PRECAUTIONARY APPROACH

The precautionary approach is paradoxically listed as one of the general principles to be applied by states to ensure the achievement of long-term conservation and sustainable use of straddling and highly migratory fish stocks (Article 5(e)).

In contrast to other environmental treaties, the precautionary approach is developed through a separate provision (Article 6) and an annex (Annex II) to the agreement. This could facilitate an effective implementation of the approach. At the same time, such detailed regulations on the implementation could also restrict the development of the approach, which probably was also the intention.

The obligation to apply the precautionary approach is mainly procedural, stipulating how states will go about achieving the objectives of long-term conservation and sustainable use of fish stocks. They are, *inter alia*, required to set and use reference points and to monitor and undertake research of the stock and its environment. These are, to lesser degree, directives on substance. One example is the requirement to adopt measures to limit access to and catches in new and exploratory fisheries (Article 6(6)).

It is important to note that the objective of the PA encompasses more than conserving and managing the stocks targeted in the fisheries. The PA shall be applied to protect the living marine resources and to preserve the marine environment (Article 6(1)). States are subsequently required to take into account the effects on other species of the ecosystem when adopting conservation measures for the target stocks and could be obligated to establish measures specially directed at protecting other species or their habitats. The obligation is elaborated upon in several of the provisions of Article 6. States are further required to protect the biodiversity of the marine environment (Article 5(g)). These obligations thus seem to overlap each other and must be read and applied in conjunction. The application of the precautionary approach could be regarded as an integral part of an ecosystem approach to fisheries management.[17]

Definition

The obligation to apply the precautionary approach is defined as follows:

> *States shall be more cautious when information is uncertain, unreliable or inadequate. The absence of adequate scientific information shall not be used as a reason for postponing or failing to take conservation and management measures (Article 6(2)).*

The precautionary approach is applicable where available information is uncertain. It is not only scientific information about the stock in question that is relevant. States are also to take into account uncertainties relating to environmental and socio-economic conditions (Article 6(3)(c)). But what does the obligation to be 'more cautious' mean under such circumstances? It is a relative obligation: the level of caution exerted will correlate with the quality of the information available. It would also be logical to link the level of caution with the potential negative consequences of fishing activities on stocks, other species and their environment. But there is no such link as states are to exert more caution when information is uncertain. This suggests that the PA shall be applied under all circumstances in fisheries management. In this sense, the PA differs from the concept in other international instruments where it is to be applied when certain thresholds are reached, such as threat of serious or irreversible damage.

But, again, what does the obligation to be 'more cautious' mean in practical terms? It does not entail a clear obligation of action. This is logical since the obligation refers to different types of uncertainties and, consequently, risks. The obligation could, rather, be understood as directing states on what evaluations and assessments to undertake in the conservation and management of living marine resources. States are required to be conscious of the risks related to the different alternative decisions or to be risk adverse. They are obligated to implement 'improved techniques for dealing with risks and uncertainties' (Article 6(3)(a)). Since the objective of applying the PA is to protect living marine resources, there are limits as to what risks states may accept.

The last part of the definition requires states not to use lack of 'adequate scientific information' as an excuse for not taking or postponing conservation measures. This does not entail a clear obligation of action and can probably not be construed as reversing the burden of proof in the way that some have argued. But the obligation directs states to base their assessments on the information that is actually available and not on the desired information. In that sense, the burden is shifted from those advocating to those opposing conservation measures.[18]

Implementing the precautionary approach

More information before regulation

The precautionary approach is usually associated with taking regulatory measures in situations of scientific uncertainty to prevent environmental damage or to prevent fish stocks from being over-exploited.

Paradoxically, regulatory action is not necessarily the first required response of states when applying the precautionary approach. An important strategy and obligation for states is to carry out more research, to collect more and new types of scientific data, and to monitor the status of the stocks. Evidently, the purpose is to reduce the uncertainties and, consequently, the risks before adopting regulations. This is the case in the provisions on the preservation of the marine environment and regulating situations where there are concerns for the status of a stock (Article 6(3)(d) and 6(5)).

According to the first provision (Article 6(3)(d)), states are to develop data collection and research programmes to assess the impacts of fishing on other species and the environment, and subsequently to adopt plans necessary to protect these species and habitats of 'special concern'. The term 'necessary' is used as a qualification of when and what measures to take. This reflects the fact that the obligation to prevent negative effects on the environment of fishing activities is more flexible than those concerning the fish stocks targeted. The reason is probably that measures adopted to protect other species and their environment could imply restrictions on the target fish stocks. In the second provision (Article 6(5)) regulating situations where there are concerns for the stock (e.g. recruitment problems), states are to subject it to enhanced monitoring. The measures in force with regard to the stock will be revised in light of the new information available following the monitoring.

There is an exception to this approach of delaying measures in cases of new or exploratory fisheries where states are required to take measures as soon as possible (Article 6(6)). States shall both regulate access to and catches from the fishery. This is a departure from the traditional approach, which has been to delay conservation measures until there is adequate information to assess at what level the fish stock may be harvested sustainably. The consequences have been over-exploitation of stocks at an early stage before there was adequate scientific information and knowledge. It would also be difficult to reduce efforts since many fishing vessels have become dependent upon the fishery. By regulating the fishery from the outset, the purpose is to prevent early overcapacity and over-fishing. However, the initial measures are to be temporary, based on general biological knowledge and analogies from similar species. States may allow for a gradual development of the fishery as they acquire more scientific data on the stock and on the impact of the fisheries on the long-term sustainability of the stock. As a consequence of this, states will be obligated to establish measures to restrict access to, and exploitation of, fish stocks that have so far been unregulated.

As a result, no fisheries may remain unregulated. Implementing the precautionary approach involves a *de facto* end to the open access regimes in high seas fisheries and fisheries in areas under national jurisdiction. When the flag states shall regulate access to these fisheries by the use of licences, there is a clear presumption that high seas fisheries are prohibited unless explicitly permitted (Article 18(3)). An important consequence of the introduction of the precautionary approach is that the duty to undertake scientific research and to monitor the state of the fish stocks and the environment has become clearer and more extensive. In this sense, the burden of proof has been shifted.

Illustrative of the level of caution required is the inclusion of *emergency measures* in the precautionary approach (Article 6(7)). Such measures shall be taken where a natural phenomenon or fishing activities have significant negative adverse effects on the fish stocks. El Niño is an example of a natural phenomenon occurring in the Pacific, which results in a rise in sea surface temperature and a drastic decline in primary productivity, the latter of which adversely affects commercial fisheries in this region.[19] The introduction of reactive measures indicates that states are not required to apply a strict version of the PA in the sense that they are to prevent all possible risks of fishing from materializing. During the negotiations, states were concerned that the PA may lead to moratoriums or bans on fishing. Therefore, it is stressed that the emergency measures are to be temporary and based on the best scientific evidence available.

Long-term management plans

Perhaps the most important instrument in the implementation of the precautionary approach is the obligation to adopt and use *reference points* for each harvested fish stock (Article 6(3)(b) and 6(4)). A 'reference point' is a value derived through scientific analysis, expressed, for example, in terms of mortality rates or biomass of the spawning part of a stock (Annex II, para 1). Since they are to direct the management of a fish stock by maintaining a stock above a certain level of biomass, the reference points serve as quantitative conservation and management objectives.

Reference points are not new in fisheries management. The *maximum sustainable yield* (MSY) is used as an objective for conserving living marine resources in the 1982 United Nations Convention on the Law of the Sea (UNCLOS) Articles 61(3) and 119(1)(a) for the exclusive economic zone (EEZ) and the high sea, respectively. The MSY describes the highest point of the curve traced between the annual standard fishing effort applied by the fleets and the yield that should result if that effort were maintained until equilibrium is reached.[20]

There are two important new elements of the reference points introduced through the Fish Stocks Agreement. First, the *binding* effect of the reference points is more pronounced and, second, the reference points are identified as a tool in implementing the precautionary approach.

The legal obligation to maintain stocks at the reference point (MSY) in UNCLOS is watered down by the introduction of other relevant economic and environmental factors. In contrast, through the Fish Stocks Agreement, states are required to set reference points and to take measures to ensure that they are not exceeded, and if they are, to automatically take predetermined action to rebuild the stock (Article 6(3) and (4)). Obviously, the reference points have gained a clearer binding status, both a legal duty to set them and a legal obligation to maintain the stocks within these limits.

In effect, the obligation to maintain the stock within the reference points requires states to develop a *management plan* for each stock. Such plans will include the reference points, necessarily the targets/goals on which the ordinary measures are to be based on, and the measures to be taken if they are exceeded. An effect of giving the reference point a clearer function is to promote more *long-term* considerations in fisheries management. But the Fish Stocks Agreement still leaves some decisions to be taken by the states.[21] First, they will decide at what level the stock is to be maintained (the actual reference points), which also would be impractical to include in a treaty, and, second, they will decide on the time frame and measures to rebuild the stock. States are to implement measures automatically in order to rebuild the stock if reference points are exceeded. But they are not obliged to adopt a moratorium until the stock has reached the reference point. The state may, depending upon the status of the stock, decide to rebuild it over a longer period of time, permitting a continued fishery. But the general obligation to ensure long-term conservation and sustainable use of the stock will limit its discretion.

The reference points are also instruments in the application of the PA. States are to apply the guidelines in Annex II (*Guidelines for the Application of Precautionary Reference Points in Conservation and Management of Straddling Fish Stocks and Highly Migratory Fish Stocks*) in setting and using the reference points (Article 6(3)(b)). States are advised to use two types of *precautionary reference points*: limit reference points and target reference points (Annex II, para 2). They have been likened with traffic lights (Davies and Redgwell, 1996, pp261–262). The target reference point is parallel to the green light, while the limit reference point serves as the amber light. There is no parallel to the red light because the states are not required to stop fishing when the limit reference points are exceeded and may, as mentioned earlier, decide to rebuild the stock over time.

The limit reference points will correspond to levels where the stock is maintained within what is described as *safe biological limits* (Annex II, para 2). This type of reference point will be set based on historic data and scientific information on the stock.

However, due to the uncertainty relating to the stock assessments, the effects on other species in the ecosystem and on other factors relevant to management, the total allowable catches and other management measures are *not* to be based on the limit reference points. States shall develop strategies to ensure that the risk of exceeding the limit reference point is low (Annex II, para 5). The concept of *risk* is in this way introduced to fisheries management. Risk in this context can be described as the probability of exceeding the limit reference point. The MSY is recommended to be used as a minimum standard for limit reference points and not as an objective for conserving the stock, as in the UNCLOS (Annex II, para 7).

The risk is handled through the establishment and use of the target reference points, which indicate the limit of the acceptable risk and, thus, the management objectives (Annex II, paras 2 and 5). The target reference points will direct the states in the adoption of the regular conservation and management measures. The measures will be designed to maintain the stock at levels above the target reference points.

The target reference points will necessarily have to be fixed at a higher biomass and a lower mortality rate than the limit reference point. A margin of safety or error is introduced to prevent the negative effects of overestimating the stock. The size of the margin will depend upon the quality of the scientific information available and upon the risk that states are willing to take. The evaluation of risk is complex: not only will uncertainty concerning scientific information be included, but also uncertainties concerning societal factors. The higher the risk that states are willing to take, the smaller the margin and, consequently, the higher the fishing opportunities and *vice versa*.

THE PRECAUTIONARY APPROACH IN NORDIC FISHERIES MANAGEMENT

The Nordic countries, including Greenland and the Faroe Islands, are coastal states located around the traditionally rich fishing grounds of the North-East Atlantic and its adjacent seas (the Barents Sea, North Sea and Baltic Sea). But marine fisheries have different importance in the life and economy of these countries: from the 'smallest' Finland, with catches at roughly 100,000 tonnes annually, to Norway and Iceland, with marine catches well above 2 million tonnes.[22] Norway has been among the top ten producer countries. The economies of Iceland and the Faroe Islands are dominantly dependent upon marine fisheries.

Most of the North-East Atlantic is subjected to the 200 nautical miles fisheries jurisdiction of these states through their exclusive economic zones (UNCLOS Articles 56(1)(a) and 57). However, many of the fish stocks are shared between the coastal states – for example, in the North Sea and in the Barents Sea. The coastal states are obligated to cooperate on the conservation and management of these stocks (UNCLOS Article 63(1)). The PA will have to be implemented through the bilateral agreements made by the coastal states.

In the remaining pockets of the high seas (areas beyond 200 nautical miles), states, in principle, enjoy the freedom of fishing (UNCLOS Article 87(1)(e)). Since the late 1960s, states have cooperated through the North-East Atlantic Fisheries Commission (NEAFC),[23] a regional fisheries management organization, on the conservation and management of the fish stocks on the high seas of the North-East Atlantic.

Two other intergovernmental organizations (IGOs) play important roles in the fisheries management of the North-East Atlantic The first is the European Community (EC), of which Denmark, Sweden and Finland are members. The Faroe Islands and Greenland are part of Denmark but its membership of the EC does not extend to them. The EC has almost exclusive competence to regulate the marine fisheries in its waters (that is, the maritime zones of its member states) and the fishing activities of community vessels on the high seas through a Common Fisheries Policy (CFP).[24] The EC has exclusive competence to enter into agreements with third states on fisheries conservation and management issues – for example, agreements on shared fish stocks.[25] Consequently, the EC is the coastal state/state fishing on the high seas. The member states are responsible for implementing the measures established under the CFP.

The second IGO is the International Council for the Exploration of the Sea (ICES), with headquarters in Copenhagen, Denmark.[26] The task of the ICES is to promote and coordinate marine research in the North Atlantic.[27] The ICES provides the EC, its member states (e.g. Norway, Iceland and Russia) and regional fisheries organizations such as NEAFC with *scientific advice* on the conservation and management of the living marine resources. The advice is based on data and research provided by scientists from its member states. The advice is not legally binding and the impact of the organization on managing the living marine resources depends upon its standing among the actors and whether it is considered to provide impartial and unbiased advice (Stokke and Coffey, 2004, p119).

In the following sections, the focus will first be on the role of ICES in implementing the precautionary approach in the North-East Atlantic. Thereafter, the implementation of the approach by the EC, Iceland and Norway will be evaluated.

The precautionary approach in scientific advice

The ICES provides advice on over 135 separate fish and shellfish stocks.[28] The advice for each stock usually includes an estimate of historical trends in landings, spawning stock biomass, recruitment and fishing mortality rate, a description of the 'state of the stock', the likely development of the stock using different rates of fishing mortality, and a forecast of spawning stock biomass and catch.

The ICES has, since 1998, as one of the first regional scientific advisory bodies, integrated the precautionary approach within its advice.[29] Its advice is based on reference points for the individual stock against which the status of the stock is evaluated. These reference points are intended to introduce risk aversion to fisheries management. In 2004, the ecosystem approach was introduced in ICES advice.[30] This means that, in addition to advising on single stocks, the ICES will advise on mixed fisheries issues (that is, when there are fisheries for several stocks within the same geographical area and the effects of fishing on the other target fish stocks) and on the ecosystem impacts of fishing (e.g. the habitat impacts of dragged gear or by-catch of sea birds). As referred to above, there is a close link between the precautionary approach and the ecosystem approach.

The ICES has described these reference points as 'benchmarks that should be avoided' to ensure that the exploitation remains within safe biological limits. The organization operates with two sets of reference points: limit reference points (Blim and Flim) and precautionary reference points (Bpa and Fpa), each consisting of two reference points. The reference points are stated in terms of a fishing mortality rate (also known as F), which is the portion of the stock captured during each year and the total biomass of the spawning part of the stock (also known as B).

The limit reference point, Blim, identifies the minimum spawning biomass of the stock below which ICES considers there is a high risk of a serious decline of the stock and from where recovery would be slow. The corresponding Flim indicates the upper limit of the fishing mortality rate, which, if maintained at that level, will take the stock down to the biomass limit. The reference points are set on the basis of historical data on the stock and on basic assumptions concerning the relationship between the spawning stock and recruitment, and are chosen so that below the points, there is a high risk that recruitment will be impaired.

The biomass and fishing mortality rate may, according to the ICES, only be estimated with uncertainty. The organization has established precautionary reference points (Bpa and Fpa) or what the ICES describes as the 'operational reference points', which are intended to take into account the uncertainties and to ensure that the risk that the stock falls under the limit reference points is low. The Bpa will be set on a higher level and the Fpa on a lower level than the corresponding limit reference points, meaning that the ICES uses 'buffer zones'. The ICES stresses that the precautionary reference points are not fixed, but will vary with the level of uncertainty and the willingness to take risk.

The status of the stock will be assessed against these reference points, and the conclusions made will guide the ICES advice. Figure 10.1 illustrates the status of the stock in relation to the different reference points. If the biomass of the stock is estimated at levels below the Bpa (light grey and dark grey zones), the ICES considers the stock as being at 'risk of reduced reproductive capacity'. It will advise states to take action to reduce fishing mortality in order to increase the biomass to levels above the Bpa. The reduction

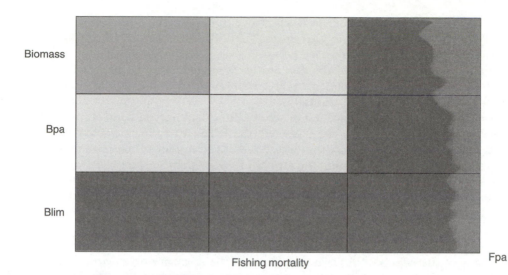

Figure 10.1 *Assessing the precautionary approach according to the International Council for the Exploration of the Sea (ICES)*
Source: St. meld. no 39 (2004–2005, p33)

may either be done by a large one-time reduction of the total allowable catch (TAC) or through a recovery plan if the level cannot be reached in a short period of time, and it also depends upon the status relating to the precautionary reference point (light or dark grey zone). If a recovery plan is adopted, a continued fishery will be allowed although at lower levels in order to allow the stock to be gradually rebuilt.

If the fishing mortality rate is estimated to be higher than Fpa, the ICES considers it at 'risk of being harvested unsustainably' and will recommend that the fishing mortality be reduced below this level (e.g. by adopting a lower TAC). But it may accept that the Fpa is temporarily exceeded when the biomass is higher than Bpa (upper light grey box) if states have mechanisms to prevent the stock from falling below Bpa.

These harvest control rules do not indicate what extra actions are recommended if the limit reference points are exceeded (dark grey zone). The real function of these reference points seems to be to identify and calculate the precautionary reference points. It is these reference points that set the limits for or identify the level of conservation of the stock. But ICES will obviously recommend more drastic actions to be taken in such situations, such as a moratorium on fishing.

The ICES has stressed that the precautionary reference points should not be used as targets for exploiting stock. Management measures should aim to keep the spawning biomass at higher levels than precautionary reference points and the fishing mortality rate below the reference points (within the mid grey zone). States are advised to set specific target reference points with this objective. The ICES considers setting these reference points the responsibility of the states since they include socio-economic considerations. By not using the precautionary reference points as objectives for exploiting stocks, the ICES argues that scientific advice would become more stable and fish stocks more sustainable. At these levels, the margin of error of the scientific advice will be low and less susceptible to alterations. There has also been concern voiced that the levels at which the limit reference points are set ('impaired recruitment') are less precautionary than envisaged by the Fish Stocks Agreement (Stokke and Coffey, 2004, pp120–121). As mentioned above, states are recommended to use MSY as a minimum standard for the limit reference points.

By outlining the actions to be taken by states (also called harvest control rules) when precautionary reference points are exceeded, the ICES, in reality, seeks to define the threshold for the conservation of fish stocks. It seems to consider socio-economic considerations only relevant when setting the target reference points, which are subjected to the biologically set precautionary reference points. As may be recalled from the earlier discussion on the precautionary approach, the definition of the buffer zone (target reference points of the Fish Stocks Agreement) is about identifying the level of acceptable risk. This decision is not a result of a scientifically unbiased process; rather, it concerns the risk that states are willing to take. Science may provide estimates of the probability of the effects of different decisions on the stock and its environment. But, ultimately, the decision is political and is affected by norms such as those provided for in international legal instruments. Socio-economic considerations will likely be part of the evaluation. The ICES has not surprisingly been criticized for not including socio-economic considerations in its application of the precautionary approach (Stokke and Coffey, 2004, p120).

The approach of the ICES raises questions on the relationship between, and the distribution of responsibility between, the scientists and management agencies. By setting these reference points, the ICES obviously aims to influence the management of the stocks. The organization defines biological benchmarks that the state may hardly ignore. But is it sound that scientific bodies have such influence on what is a political decision; what risks should the stocks be subjected to? Are they better qualified to decide on this than the management agencies? On the other hand, it is up to the governmental agencies to accept the use of the ICES reference points. These reference points will also provide the stocks with better protection against over-fishing.

There is a need to clarify the relationship between the scientists and the managers, and to increase the transparency and accessibility of the advice provided by the scientific bodies. The North-West Atlantic Fisheries Organization (NAFO), a regional fisheries management organization managing the fish stocks on the high seas in the North-West Atlantic has focused on these issues. In the 2004 framework[31] for the precautionary approach, the role of NAFO's Scientific Council is defined as determining the status of the stock, calculating limit reference points and safety margins, and conducting risk assessments. The political organ of NAFO, the Fisheries Commission, is responsible for specifying the management objectives and determining the target and limit reference points, as well as the management strategies.

The precautionary approach in the EC Common Fisheries Policy

In the beginning of the new millennium, the 1992 Common Fisheries Policy (CFP) was evaluated.[32] The conclusion was that there was a strong need to reform the CFP. Many of the fish stocks in EC waters were (and still are) considered to be over-exploited and outside what is described as safe biological limits. There was a warning that if the trend continued, stocks could collapse. Several (partly mixed) causes were identified, including the frequent adoption of annual catch limits in excess of the EU Commission proposals, overcapacity and poor enforcement. Gaps and weaknesses in scientific advice were also considered to contribute to the situation. In a communication to the Council and European Parliament on the application of the precautionary approach to the fisheries management, the EU Commission was more specific on the causes.[33] It argued that the annual negotiations in the Council on fisheries regulations had regularly resulted in the postponement of measures when there was scientific uncertainty regarding the need for more stringent measures. Such inaction could, over the years, according to the EU Commission, place the stock 'in an extremely vulnerable situation', which has lead to 'a *de facto* dilatory policy of stock management that has failed to safeguard or restore stocks'.[34] Both in the communication and in the evaluation of the CFP, it was recommended that the short-term approach to fisheries management be abandoned and a more long-term management of stocks adopted. The evaluation concluded with proposals introducing multi-annual management plans, which are compatible with the precautionary approach.[35] There was also a focus on the need to implement principles of the EC treaty, such as the integration principle and the precaution approach in the new policy.[36]

Some of the living marine resources of the EC waters also occur in the EEZs of neighbouring Norway, which is not a member of the EC and, subsequently, not included in the CFP. The cod and herring stocks of the North Sea are examples of fish stocks shared between the EC and Norway. A 1980 cooperation agreement on fisheries exists between the EC and Norway.[37] They hold annual negotiations on, *inter alia*, the conservation and management of these shared stocks, which usually result in an agreement on total allowable catches for the shared stocks and the allocation between the two parties.[38] The EC and Norway have also agreed on long-term management plans for several of the shared stocks, including the North Sea cod, haddock and herring.[39] The duty to apply the precautionary approach will apply both at the bilateral and state level.

In the following sections, the focus will first be on the introduction of the PA in EC legislation before assessing the use of the approach in the North Sea cod fishery.

Legislation

The legal framework of the EC's fisheries management is Regulation No 2371, adopted in December 2002 (hereafter the CFP regulation).[40] The CFP regulation was adopted as a result of the evaluation process and revised the pre-existing 1992 CFP regulation.

It is the Council that is the EC body competent and that is required to establish measures to regulate both access to (e.g. how many vessels may fish) and utilization (for instance, how the fisheries is to be performed and quantities to be caught) of the living marine resources and their allocation (Article 4(1) and Article 20).[41] In establishing the measures the Council shall, *inter alia*, take into account, the advice provided by the Scientific, Technical and Economic Committee for Fisheries (STECF) (Article 4(2)). STECF is established as an advisory body on biological, environmental, social and technical issues (Article 33(1)).[42]

The member states are required to implement and enforce the regulations adopted by the Council (CFP Regulation Article 23) and have limited rights under EC law, individually, to adopt measures for their maritime zones. They may adopt emergency measures in areas under their jurisdiction if 'there is evidence of a serious and unforeseen threat to the conservation of aquatic resources or ecosystem resulting from fishing activities' (Article 8(1)). They are also competent to adopt conservation measures within their 12 nautical miles (Article 9(1)). There are several requirements attached that restrict the right of individual member states to regulate the fisheries in their territorial sea or EEZ.

The objectives of the CFP regulation are complex and ambitious. It will ensure the exploitation of living resources that provide sustainable economic, environmental and social conditions (Article 2). It may be difficult to meet these partly conflicting objectives.

There are several references to the precautionary approach in the CFP regulation. However, there are no similar provisions as in the 1995 Fish Stocks Agreement that regulate the obligation to apply the approach.

From the *general objective*, it follows that the precautionary approach will be applied in taking measures to protect and conserve living marine resources in order to provide for their sustainable exploitation and to minimize the impact of fishing activities on marine ecosystems (Article 2). According to the preamble of the regulation, the precautionary approach is based on the same considerations as the precautionary principle of Article 174 EC (para 3). The precautionary principle will thus be relevant in the interpretation and application of the precautionary approach to fisheries management.

The precautionary approach is defined as follows:

> *The absence of adequate scientific information should not be used for postponing or failing to take management measures to conserve target species, associated or dependent species and non-target species and their environment (Article 3(i)).*

The definition is almost the same as that of Article 6(2) of the Fish Stocks Agreement, adding that the approach also aims at protecting the environment. The legal implications of the precautionary approach are not clear. The precautionary approach seems to point to types of considerations to be made by the Council in the decision-making process more than dictating the concrete actions to be taken. However, the provision/ definition must be read together with other provisions of the CFP regulation, which lay down the competences and obligations of the Council to regulate the fisheries. In this context, the precautionary approach implies that measures cannot be postponed merely because the scientific information available is considered inadequate. Subsequently, measures will be taken on the basis of the available information.

The Council may adopt several types of measures to regulate access to the fisheries and to ensure sustainable fish stocks (Article 4(2)). The measures include targets for sustainable exploitation of target stocks, as well as technical measures to reduce the impact of fisheries on non-target stocks and the environment (Article 4(2)(c) and (g)). The focus here will be on two of the measures: *recovery plans* and *management plans* (Article 4(a)(2) and 4(b)). These plans are to be 'drawn up on the basis of the precautionary approach' (Article 5(3) and Article 6(3)). The management plans and recovery plans are considered the most effective means of achieving sustainable exploitation because they foster long-term approaches (Preamble, para 6).

It is symptomatic that the provision on recovery plans is listed before management plans as the available measures (Article 5). This is probably because more stocks are in need of recovery plans than ordinary management plans. But the structure and content of these plans are much the same, although the conditions for the Council to adopt them are different. Therefore, the conditions for adopting recovery and management plans will be investigated and then the content of the plans will be elaborated upon.

The Council shall adopt *recovery plans* for fisheries exploiting stocks, which are 'outside safe biological limits' (Article 5(1)). *Management plans* shall be adopted for the stocks within safe biological limits, but 'as far as necessary' (Article 6(1)).

Since the concept of 'safe biological limits' is decisive for the adoption of both types of plans, it is important to explore its meaning. It is defined as 'indicators of the state of a stock … inside which … there is a low risk of transgressing certain limit reference points' (Article 3(l)). The definition is not very informative. 'Limit reference points' is defined as values of parameters such as biomass or fishing mortality rate to be avoided because they are related to stock collapse or impaired recruitment (Article 3(j)).

When reading these two definitions together, the decision as to whether a stock is within or outside 'safe biological limits' depends upon both the identification of the levels associated with its collapse and impaired recruitment, and the probability that the stock is at or below these levels (risk). With regard to the first-mentioned elements, these are biological parameters and obviously have to be identified through scientific procedures. It is natural to assume that this refers to the limit reference points proposed by the ICES for the stock in question. The ICES operates with a similar definition for limit reference points.[43] Such understanding is also supported by the requirement that recovery plans shall also be drawn up, taking into account 'limit reference points recommended by relevant scientific bodies' (Article 5(3)). The ICES may be such body. If the biomass is estimated at below the ICES limit reference point (Blim), the obligation of the Council to adopt a recovery plan for the stock is long overdue. The risk has materialized. The Council will be required to adopt a recovery plan for a stock at a much earlier stage when there is a high probability that the stock is below the limit reference point or high risk of 'transgressing certain limit reference points'. Then the stock would be outside safe biological limits. But at what level is a stock outside safe biological limits and when is the risk unacceptable? Although the general objectives of the CFP regulation will give some directions, the Council still has some discretion in deciding when the risk (probability that the stock is at a limit reference point or lower) has exceeded acceptable levels and is required to adopt a recovery plan. The relatively high and ambiguous threshold for adopting recovery plans could be questioned.

The Council does not have a strict obligation to adopt *management plans* for fish stocks. It shall adopt such plans 'as far as necessary' to maintain the stocks within safe biological limits (Article 6(1)). This condition probably relates both to the threshold for adopting such plans and to the content of the plans. The stocks, which are not subjected to management plans, will be regulated through traditional annual management measures, such as TACs and technical measures (Preamble, para 9). The multi-annual approach of management plans is considered to be more consistent with the objective of sustainable exploitation (Preamble, para 6). This will limit the discretion of the Council to decide whether to adopt such plans. The adoption and implementation of a management plan will require a substantial amount of scientific information, which will not be available for all stocks. It will especially be the case in new and exploratory fisheries, but also in many existing fisheries where there is little scientific information available. Although the management plans are not feasible for such fisheries, the precautionary approach is especially applicable in such situations. In contrast to the Fish Stocks Agreement, the CFP regulation does not include any special requirements for regulating such fisheries. The adoption of measures to prevent over-fishing of such stocks at an early stage may be inferred from the general obligation of the Council to regulate the fisheries and the special obligation to apply the precautionary approach.

The EC has agreed on management plans for several fish stocks shared with Norway and other coastal states in the region.[44] But these plans have yet to be incorporated within EC legislation. The Fisheries Commission has initiatives under way to move away from annual decisions towards establishing more management plans to ensure long-term sustainability of stocks and stable conditions for the fishing industry.[45]

There are several requirements during the design of the recovery and management plans, but not all of them will be addressed here. The recovery and the management plans adopted by the Council will include *conservation reference points* (Articles 5(2) and 6(2)). Furthermore, the plans will be developed on the basis of the precautionary approach, taking into account the *limit reference points* recommended by the relevant scientific bodies (Articles 5(3) and 6(3)). A plan thus includes a set of reference points that we recognize from both the Fish Stocks Agreement and the ICES's application of the precautionary approach. The limit reference points will probably be identical to those set by ICES for the stock.

The definition of conservation reference points indicates that they will be set at levels where the biological risk is acceptable or at 'a desired level of yield' (Article 3(k)). These are relative subjective considerations and do not give very specific instructions to the Council at which level to set the conservation reference points. However, the duty to set these reference points has to be read in conjunction with the reference to the precautionary approach (Articles 5(3) and 6(3)) and the general objective of maintaining the stock within safe biological limits (Articles 5(2) and 6(1)). The reference to the precautionary approach requires the Council to take into account the uncertainties relating to the status of the stock, the effects of fishing, etc. The conservation reference points should therefore be set at levels of mortality rates and biomass where the risk of exceeding the limit reference points is low. Although the fixing of conservation reference points will be a political decision, they are most likely set at the precautionary reference points of the ICES. That has been the case in management plans agreed between the EC and Norway.[46]

The legal effects of these two reference points are uncertain. As discussed earlier, if the stock exceeds the limit reference points, the Council will probably be obligated to adopt a recovery plan. The objective of such a plan will evidently be to rebuild the stock to levels above these limit reference points, while the objective of the management plans is to maintain the stock well above such levels (Articles 5(3) and 6(3)). The function of the conservation reference points is more ambiguous (Articles 5(2) and 6(2)). The understanding of this writer is that 'targets' set by the Council for the recovery or maintenance of the stock are to be assessed against these reference points. The targets are to be expressed, *inter alia*, in terms of population size, fishing mortality and/or stability of catches. The targets are independent and operational instruments in the conservation of the stock. It follows on from their explicit listing as one of the conservation and management measures available to the Council (Article 4(2)(c)). Since the conservation reference points indicate the safe biological limits of the stock, and the targets will quantify what is considered sustainable exploitation, these targets should be set at values not higher (fishing mortality rate) or lower (population size) than the conservation reference points. The targets resemble the target reference points proposed by the ICES; but for some reason the Council has refrained from using this term. The recovery and management plans may also include targets relating to other living marine resources and to the maintenance or improvement of the conservation status of the ecosystem, thus introducing an ecosystem approach (Articles 5(2) and 6(2)).

The Council has been the delegated power to adopt the conservation and management measures under the recovery and management plans (Articles 5(4) and 6(4)). These measures may include those generally available under the CFP regulation (Article 4), such as catch limits, effort limits and technical measures. The Council is obviously required to use its powers and to adopt measures under these plans, otherwise the plans would be rendered useless and it would act in contravention of the objectives of the plans and of the CFP regulation itself. But the Council appears to have some degree of discretion as to which measures to adopt and their design. However, the reference to the 'targets' as discussed earlier suggests that this measure is an obligatory element of every plan. The recovery plans will include limitations to fishing efforts unless proven unnecessary. In addition, the Council may set harvesting rules, which are defined as a set of predetermined biological parameters to govern the catch limits.

It is not clear from these provisions what function the reference points have in setting and formulating these measures. There is no explicit reference to them in the relevant provisions. The reference points appear to have more of an indirect effect on the actions to be taken under the plans. They are indicators of the objectives of the plans (recovery to, and maintenance within, safe biological limits), and as such they will direct the measures to be adopted. The targets for exploiting the stock, which should be set on the basis of the conservation reference points, will be influential in adopting the measures. The harvesting rules, which directly govern the setting of the catch limits, may be seen as quantification of these targets.

The recovery and management plans will be multi-annual and will indicate the expected time frame for reaching the established targets (Articles 5(3) and 6(3)). This means that neither the targets nor the conservation reference points are strict obligations. Under a recovery plan, the Council may decide to adopt measures to rebuild a stock over a longer period of time, allowing a fishery to continue instead of adopting a moratorium on fishing that would mean a faster recovery. The Council may also adopt measures under a management plan that allows for exceeding the targets/conservation reference points as long as it has set a time frame for reaching them.

The measures to be adopted under the recovery plans and the management plans are to be subjected to a *proportionality* test (Articles 5(4) and 6(4)). There is to be proportionality between the *measure*, on the one hand, and the *objectives, target and time frame*, on the other, where the status of the stock and economic impacts of measures are two of the relevant considerations.[47] This naturally lends support to the understanding of management and recovery plans as precluding absolute or strict requirements. But when conservation status and biological characteristics are relevant considerations in the evaluation, the conclusion may well be that the measures are not adequate to achieve the objectives and targets set for the stock and that stricter measures have to be established.

There is need for flexibility in fisheries management; but the management and recovery plans to be adopted seem to give the manager a very high degree of freedom. The function of the reference points is unclear and the Council is not required to adopt harvest control rules, which are directly related to maintaining the stocks within these limits. The question is whether the plans, in fact, will promote a proper recovery of, and long-term conservation of, stocks. It would be more consistent with the precautionary approach of the Fish Stocks Agreement if the reference points were given a clearer function and mandatory role, and measures were set to prevent them from being exceeded.

The recovery plan for North Sea cod

The Council has not yet adopted management plans. It has, however, adopted several recovery plans, *inter alia*, for the cod stocks in the North Sea, Skagerrak and the Eastern Channel.[48] The focus here will be on the 2004 recovery plan for the North Sea cod stock.[49]

The EC expects that the recovery of these stocks will take between five and ten years under the condition of the regulation (Preamble, para 4). The target level for the recovery of the North Sea cod stock is set at 150,000 tonnes, which corresponds to the ICES precautionary reference point (Bpa) (Article 3). This is consistent with the Fish Stocks Agreement, where states are advised to use the reference points as targets for stock recovery (Annex II, para 4). When this target has been reached for two consecutive years, the stock may be removed from the recovery plan and there will, instead, be a management plan for the stock (Article 4). Such decisions may only be taken on the advice of the ICES, which is to be confirmed by STECF, the scientific committee of the EC.

The measures to be taken under the recovery plan include both limits on effort and on catches (Articles 5 to 7[50] and Article 8[51]). The Fisheries Commission has adopted measures to reduce catches of juvenile fish and has set mesh size requirements.[52] In 2005, the Fisheries Commission also established a special monitoring programme to ensure that the measures were implemented.[53]

Although the stock is considered to be outside safe biological limits and is under a recovery plan, the Council may set a total allowable catch and thus permit a fishery for the stock (Article 5). A TAC may be set if the cod stock has been estimated by STECF, based on ICES reports, to be above 70,000 tonnes, which corresponds to the ICES limit reference point (Blim). Apparently, no fishery will be allowed if the biomass of the stock is estimated at below Blim. The recovery plan regulation further stipulates the procedures for setting the TAC when the stock is above these limits (Article 6). This includes harvesting rules, *inter alia*, to prevent too wide variations of the TACs from year to year. There is an opening for setting a TAC even when the stock is below Blim in so-called 'exceptional circumstances' (Article 7). The Council may adopt a TAC even if the quantity of the mature stock is not estimated to reach the minimum level at the end of the year. The provision does not define what the 'exceptional circumstances' are, suggesting that the threshold for deviating from the main rule is low.[54] The Fisheries Commission's original proposal also included detailed procedures for monitoring, inspection and surveillance, and establishment of temporarily closed areas, which is not included in the final text.[55]

The ICES estimated the spawning part of the stock in 2003 and 2004 to be at 43,000 tonnes, which is well below its Blim.[56] Consistent with the control-harvesting rule of the recovery plan, the ICES recommended the total allowable catch to be set at 0 for 2004 and 2005. However, the Council set a TAC for 2005 at 27,500 tonnes.[57] In its proposal for regulation, the Fisheries Commission referred to Article 7 as a basis for adopting the TAC. But it argued that the provision was not directly applicable since there were 'substantial uncertainties in the assessment' of some of the stocks under recovery plans.[58] The scientific uncertainties do not seem to have been interpreted in favour of the fish stock.[59] The Council adopted additional measures, such as reduced fishing efforts, to limit the negative effects of the fishing.[60] The STECF does not consider a recovery of the stock to levels corresponding to Bpa to be realistic in the short term.[61]

Both the recovery plan regulation and the 2005 measures reflect a rather weak application of the precautionary approach. The PA is defined as an obligation not to use lack of adequate scientific information as a reason for not taking conservation action.[62] By using scientific uncertainty as a reason for not adopting more stringent measures, the Council is at odds with the precautionary approach and thus subjects the stock to a high risk of collapse. The regulations do not seem to properly implement the 1999 long-term management plan agreed between Norway and the EC on this shared fish stock.

In the CFP regulation, a requirement of proportionality between the measures is to be taken under the recovery plan, taking into account, among other elements, the status of the stock and the economic impact of the measures (Article 5(4)). When the scientific advisory bodies agreed that the stock would probably not recover in the short term, the proportionality assessment seemed to have gone in favour of the fishing industry. The reason why more stringent measures, such as a moratorium on fishing, have not been established is that they would have negative effects on the fishing industry, especially since North Sea fisheries are mixed. A moratorium on cod fishing would also have meant more restrictions in the other fisheries. When adopting the measures for 2006, the Council agreed on a 15 per cent reduction in the total catches of 2005, referring to the uncertainty relating to the available data and the maximum of 15 per cent annual variation.[63] The European Community still accepts the living marine resources to be exposed to high risks of over-exploitation.

The precautionary approach in other Nordic countries

Legislation

Norway, Iceland and the Faroe Islands have yet to incorporate the precautionary approach within their fisheries management legislation.[64] The precautionary approach has been introduced to these countries on the advice provided by the ICES.

When Norway ratified the Fish Stocks Agreement in 1996, the legislation was considered to be consistent with its rights and obligation under the agreement.[65] The fisheries legislation was viewed as being adequate in implementing the precautionary approach in Norwegian fisheries management. In addition, through White Papers it is confirmed that fisheries conservation and management measures are to be based on, *inter alia*, the precautionary approach.[66] However, the relevant legislation has the character of an enabling act. It does not have any explicit reference to the precautionary approach. The Norwegian legislation is currently under revision. A committee of experts has presented a draft proposal for new legislation where, *inter alia*, different principles of fisheries management, including the precautionary approach and ecosystem approach, are introduced.[67] Living marine resources will be managed through the application of a precautionary approach consistent with international agreements and guidelines (Proposal Article 1–6(a)). The proposal does not include any further instructions on reference points or other concrete measures to implement the approach. The reference to international agreements and guidelines means that both the Fish Stocks Agreement and the FAO Code of Conduct are relevant sources of interpretation. However, other principles, such as the needs of coastal communities, may give input that is in conflict with the PA. For example, the committee of experts was not able to agree on a proposal for a provision, which would reverse the traditional approach to fisheries management, requiring a permit before opening a new fishery. The majority feared such provision could lead to unacceptable restrictions on commercial fishing. This reversal would be consistent with the precautionary approach, as referred to above. Since the precautionary approach is to be applied in a manner that is consistent with the international agreements, such a reversal could still be required.

In the following sections, the focus will be on two major Icelandic and Norwegian cod fisheries in relation to their application of the precautionary approach.

Icelandic cod stock

The cod fishery is the most important fishery in Iceland, with an annual TAC of around 200,000 tonnes and accounting for 40 per cent of the seafood export.[68] Since 1995, there has been a governmental 'catch rule', fixing the annual TAC at 25 per cent of the fishable biomass.[69] The TAC is automatically set after the annual stock assessment. The catch rule was amended in 2000, requiring that the TAC should not vary by more than 30,000 tonnes from one fishing year to the next. The Icelandic government considers the policy to be in conformity with the PA.[70] But according to the ICES, actual mortality was higher than the catch rule, both in 2004 and 2005, and higher than levels consistent with long-term yields.[71] This was caused by an underestimation of the mortality rate and because the catches (in an effort-regulated part of the fishery) were larger than estimated.

The ICES has described the harvest rule as being consistent with the precautionary approach, provided that the implementation errors are minimal.[72] It is precautionary in the sense that only a small part of the mature stock is fishable and there is little room for the managers to deviate from this. The policy has evidently not been precautionary enough and has not taken into account scientific and socio-economic uncertainties. There have been no established precautionary reference points for the stock, which would provide the government with clearer indicators of the state of the stock and identify the acceptable risk, enabling the state to take action at an earlier stage.

North-East Arctic cod

The North-East Arctic cod in the Barents Sea is shared between Norway and the Russian Federation.[73] The stock has been managed by Norway and the Russian Federation through the Joint Norwegian–Russian Fisheries Commission since the mid 1970s.[74]

During the nearly 30 years of the Joint Norwegian Fisheries Commission's existence, there have been several crises in the cod fishery where the stock has been over-fished. This over-exploitation has partly occurred because the TACs were occasionally set above the recommendations of the ICES, and partly because scientific advice was based on an overestimation of the stock. In recent years, there has been growing concern for the quantity of under-reported catches, estimated at 20 per cent in addition to official catches.[75]

In response to a crisis during the late 1990s, the Joint Norwegian–Russian Fisheries Commission recognized that there were uncertainties in stock assessments and agreed to rebuild the stock to a biomass of 500,000 tonnes and reduce fishing mortality.[76] But it was not until 2002 that the Fisheries Commission adopted a strategy for managing the cod stock aimed at increasing the yield of the stock and ensuring more stable TACs, which included harvest-control rules.[77] The annual total allowable catch for a three-year period beginning from 2004 is to be calculated based on the precautionary reference point for fishing mortality set by the ICES (Fpa). The TACs for the consecutive years are to be based on the Fpa and on updated information, but may not vary more than +/–10 per cent from the previous year. The strategy has been amended to include measures to be taken if the spawning stock falls below the precautionary reference point, which could mean a reduction in the TAC larger than the limit of 10 per cent.[78]

In its regular assessment of the stock, the ICES considers the strategy to be consistent with the PA.[79] The strategy includes precautionary reference points, rules on how to maintain the stock within these limits, and measures to be taken if they are exceeded – all prescribed by the PA provisions of the Fish Stocks Agreement. A balance must be maintained between the need of the fishing industry to be predictable and the need to conserve stock, otherwise known as risk management.

The ICES also seems to be dominant in defining the precautionary level and the risk that the stock is to be subjected to. Perhaps it is the best solution, from an environmental point of view. However, a better solution that is more consistent with the precautionary approach would be if Norway and Russia could agree on a strategy where the objective is to maintain the stock at a higher level and to adopt target reference points, taking into account economic objectives. However, as long as there is overcapacity in the fishery, the states are likely to use the reference points set by ICES as targets. They will not set targets at lower levels, which would mean fewer fishing opportunities.

CONCLUSIONS

This chapter confirms that the precautionary approach, as regulated in international instruments, has been introduced to Nordic fisheries. It is also safe to conclude that it has not yet been fully implemented.

The ICES (the scientific advisory body) appears to have come furthest in implementing the PA by developing new concepts and by including uncertainty and risk in its advice. This has undoubtedly been decisive for the actions taken by the coastal states in recent years. The language applied by the ICES when providing advice based on the PA suggests that it has attempted to define the important objectives of conserving and managing fish stocks. This is natural; but it may also be problematic: it blurs the distinction between the responsibility of the ICES and the states to implement the precautionary approach. It also confuses the objectives of states in conserving and managing fish stocks and their environment. By defining the roles and responsibilities of the different actors (that is, the ICES and the states) in applying the precautionary approach, the decision-making process would become more transparent. It would also ensure that the PA is more effectively implemented.

Only the EC has explicitly incorporated the duty to apply the precautionary approach within its legislation. The introduction of the PA and other principles into fisheries legislation is important because the discretion of the state is restricted. But the assessment of the practice – although limited – suggests that there is not necessarily any link between legislation and the application of the PA. The cod fisheries of Norway and Iceland seem to be managed more in line with the PA than is the EC fishery. It is important to note that this PA is a relatively modified version of the PA found in the Fish Stocks Agreement and the FAO Code of Conduct.

The focus of the states has primarily been on developing management plans and recovery plans in ongoing fisheries, with relatively good scientific information, and on establishing reference points and harvest control rules, with less focus on the fisheries with a high degree of scientific uncertainty. In spite of the introduction of the precautionary approach, states are still reluctant to address situations where there is a high degree of uncertainty. The focus must gradually be turned in this direction to prevent history from repeating itself. Measures must be taken at an early stage to prevent fish stocks from being over-fished. The most effective way of implementing the PA is probably to reduce the overcapacity in most Nordic fisheries. Overcapacity is the most important reason why states are unwilling to take action when there is inadequate scientific information. Measures that mean less fishing opportunities require stronger reasoning/argumentation. The duty to display caution when information is uncertain has not yet been accepted as adequate reasoning.

NOTES

All internet references were accessed in January 2006.

1   The full title of the Fish Stocks Agreement is Agreement for the Implementation of the Provisions of the United Nations Convention on the Law of the Sea of 10 December 1982 relating to the Conservation and Management of Straddling Fish Stocks and Highly Migratory Fish Stocks.
2   An overview of state parties to the Fish Stocks Agreement may be downloaded from www.un.org/Depts/los/convention_agreements/ convention_overview_fish_stocks.htm.

3   For example, 2000 Convention on the Conservation and Management of Highly Migratory Fish Stocks in the Western and Central Pacific Ocean, Article 6, and the 2001 Convention on the Conservation and Management of Fishery Resources in the South-East Atlantic Ocean, Article 7.

4   Code of Conduct for Responsible Fisheries, Articles 6.5 and 7.5.

5   The FAO has developed technical guidelines to assist states in implementing the code of conduct. There are special guidelines on the Precautionary Approach to Capture Fisheries and Species Introduction, 1996, available at www.fao.org/fi/default.asp

6   Intermediate Ministerial Meeting on the Integration of Fisheries and Environmental Issues, Bergen, 13–14 March 1997, Statement of Conclusions from the Intermediate Ministerial Meeting on the Integration of Fisheries and Environmental Issues, available at www.odin.dep.no/md/nsc/Intermediate_meeting/023021–990005/dok-bn.html.

7   Intermediate Ministerial Meeting on the Integration of Fisheries and Environmental Issues, Bergen, 13–14 March 1997, Statement of Conclusions from the Intermediate Ministerial Meeting on the Integration of Fisheries and Environmental Issues, paras 2.3, 4.3 and 20.

8   United Nations Convention on the Law of the Sea, Articles 61(2) and 119(1)(a).

9   The Convention for the Protection of the Marine Environment of the North-East Atlantic, Article 2(2)(a).

10 Convention on the Protection and Use of Transboundary Watercourses and International Lakes, Article 2(5)(a).

11 Rio Declaration on the Environment and Development, principle 15.

12 See, for example, 2000 Convention on the Conservation and Management of Highly Migratory Fish Stocks in the Western and Central Pacific Ocean, Article 6, and the 2001 Convention on the Conservation and Management of Fishery Resources in the South-East Atlantic Ocean, Article 7.

13 This discussion is referred to in Peel, J. (2004) 'Precaution: A matter of principle, approach or process?', *Melbourne Journal of International Law*, vol 5, pp483–501.

14 *A Guide to the Issues Before the Conference*, prepared by the chairman, 'Issues to be addressed', para I(f) A/Conf.164/10. The papers of the conference are available at www.un.org/Depts/los/fish_stocks_conference/fish_stocks_conference.htm or in Levy, J.-P. and Schram, G. (1996) *United Nations Conference on Straddling Fish Stocks and Highly Migratory Fish Stocks: Selected Documents*, Martinus Nijhoff Publishers, The Hague.

15 *Earth Negotiation Bulletin* (1993) 'Precautionary principle', vol 7, no 5, available at www.iisd.ca/linkages/vol07/0705004e.html, and Hewison, G. (1996) 'The precautionary approach to fisheries management: An environmental perspective', *The International Journal of Marine and Coastal Law*, vol 11, p310.

16 A/Conf.164/INF/8 The Precautionary Approach to Fisheries with Reference to Straddling Fish Stocks and Highly Migratory Fish Stocks. See *A Guide to the Issues Before the Conference*, prepared by the chairman, 'Issues to be addressed', para I(f) A/Conf.164/10. The papers of the conference are available at www.un.org/Depts/los/fish_stocks_conference/fish_stocks_ conference.htm or in Levy, J.-P. and Schram, G. (1996) *United Nations Conference on Straddling Fish Stocks and Highly Migratory Fish Stocks: Selected Documents*, Martinus Nijhoff Publishers, The Hague.

17 The Conference of the Parties (CoP) under the Convention on Biodiversity adopted the Djakarta Mandate on Marine and Coastal Biodiversity in 1995 as a programme of action for implementing the convention. The programme was reviewed by the CoP in 2004, where the precautionary approach is identified as one of the basic principles in implementing the convention, Decision VII/5, Annex I Elaborate Programme of Work on Marine and Coastal Biodiversity, available at www.biodiv.org/programmes/areas/marine/defalt.asp.

18 Likewise, Freestone, D. (1999) 'Implementing precaution cautiously: The precautionary approach in the Straddling and Highly Migratory Fish Stocks Agreement', in Hey, E. (ed) *Developments in International Fisheries Law*, Kluwer Law International, The Hague, p317.

19 See further information on the web pages of the National Oceanic and Atmospheric Administration, www.pmel.noaa.gov/tao/elnino/el-nino-story.html.

20 A/Conf.164/INF/9 Reference Points for Fisheries Management: Their Potential Application to Straddling and Highly Migratory Resources, para 27. See also *A Guide to the Issues Before the Conference*, prepared by the chairman, 'Issues to be addressed', para I(f) A/Conf.164/10. The papers of the conference are available at www.un.org/Depts/los/ fish_stocks_conference/fish_stocks_conference.htm or in Levy, J.-P. and Schram, G. (1996) *United Nations Conference on Straddling Fish Stocks and Highly Migratory Fish Stocks: Selected Documents*, Martinus Nijhoff Publishers, The Hague.

21 Freestone, D. (1999) 'Implementing precaution cautiously: The precautionary approach in the Straddling and Highly Migratory Fish Stocks Agreement', in Hey, E. (ed) *Developments in International Fisheries Law*, Kluwer Law International, The Hague, p321.

22 The figures are downloaded from FAOSTAT, available at www.faostat.fao.org/faostat/ collections?subset=fisheries.

23 NEAFC is established through the 1980 Convention on Future Multilateral Cooperation in North-East Atlantic Fisheries, Article 3, which entered into force in 1982. NEAFC has seven member states, including Denmark (with respect to the Faroe Islands and Greenland), the EC, Estonia, Iceland, Norway, Poland and the Russian Federation. NEAFC is competent to adopt conservation and management measures for fish stocks on the high seas in the region: Articles 5 and 7. The organization may also adopt control measures for the area: Article 8. NEAFC has adopted conservation measures for several stocks. See the NEAFC website at www.neafc.org.

24 This competence is derived from Article 37 of the Treaty Establishing the European Community.

25 See more on this issue in Churchill, R. (1999) 'The EC and its role in some issues of international fisheries law', in Hey, E. (ed) *Developments in International Fisheries Law*, Kluwer Law International, The Hague, pp533–574.

26 The ICES operates under the Convention for the International Council for the Exploration of the Sea. But the organization was founded in 1902. The ICES has 19 member countries, including Denmark, Finland, Iceland, Norway, Russia and Sweden. See the ICES website at www.ices.dk.

27 ICES Convention Article 1(a).

28 For further information, see www.ices.dk/advice/fishstocks.asp.

29 *Report of the ICES Advisory Committee on Fishery Management and Advisory Committee on Ecosystems* (2004) vol 1, no 2, December. The guidelines are found in item 1.4, pp1–4–1–6, available at www.ices.dk/products/icesadvice/Book1Part1.pdf.

30 *Report of the ICES Advisory Committee on Fishery Management and Advisory Committee on Ecosystems* (2004) vol 1, no 2, December, item 1.3.

31 'Report of the Fisheries Commission Meeting, 26 Annual Meeting, 13–17 September 2004, Dartmouth, item 12', in *Meeting Proceedings of the General Council and the Fisheries Commission, September 2004–August 2005*, p97.

32 *Green Paper: The Future of the Common Fisheries Policy*, vol I, COM (2001) 135, available at www.europa.eu.int/eur-lex/lex/LexUriServ/site/en/com/2001/com2001_0135en01.pdf.

33 *Communication from the Commission to the Council and the European Parliament: Application of the Precautionary Principle and Multi-annual Arrangements for Setting TACs*, COM (2000) 803 final, available at www.europa.eu.int/eur-lex/lex/LexUriServ/site/en/com/2000/com2000_ 0803en01.pdf.

34 *Communication from the Commission to the Council and the European Parliament: Application of the Precautionary Principle and Multi-annual Arrangements for Setting TACs*, COM (2000) 803 final, p3, available at www.europa.eu.int/eur-lex/lex/LexUriServ/site/en/com/2000/com2000_ 0803en01.pdf.

35 *Green Paper: The Future of the Common Fisheries Policy*, vol I, COM (2001) 135, item 5.1, pp21–23.
36 The principles are found in Article 174(2) and Article 6 EC.
37 Agreement on Fisheries between the European Economic Community and the Kingdom of Norway.
38 For example, Agreed Record of Conclusion of Fisheries Consultations between the European Community and Norway for 2006, available at www.odin.dep.no/filarkiv/266244/Kvoteavtale_Norge_-_EU_2006.pdf.
39 Agreed Record of Conclusion of Fisheries Consultations between the European Community and Norway for 2006, available at www.odin.dep.no/filarkiv/266244/Kvoteavtale_Norge_-_EU_2006.pdf, Annex I, II and IV.
40 Council Regulation (EC) No 2371/2002.
41 The Commission is competent to adopt temporary emergency measures when there is evidence of a serious threat caused by fisheries to the conservation of marine living resources and there is need of immediate action (Article 7(1)).
42 See the STECF website at www.stecf.jrc.cec.eu.int/.
43 See Sub-chapter 4.1, 'The precautionary approach in scientific advice', and *Report of the ICES Advisory Committee on Fishery Management and Advisory Committee on Ecosystems* (2004) vol 1, no 2, December.
44 For example, Annex II: Arrangement on the Long-term Management of the Mackerel Stock to the Agreed Records of Conclusions of Fisheries Consultations between the Faroe Islands, the European Community and Norway on the Management of the Mackerel Stock in the North-East Atlantic for 2006, 26 October 2005, available at www.odin.dep.no/filarkiv/262170/Avtale_trepart_-_makrell_2006.pdf, and Annexes I to IV on the long-term management plans for cod, haddock, saithe and North Sea herring to the Agreed Record of Conclusions of Fisheries Consultations between the European Community and Norway for 2005, 26 November 2004, available at www.odin.dep.no/filarkiv/228576/Bilateral_arrangement_for_2005.pdf.
45 Proposal for a Council regulation fixing for 2005 the fishing opportunities and associated conditions for certain fish stocks and groups of fish stocks, applicable in Community waters and, for Community vessels, in waters where catch limits are required, COM (2004) 785 final, p2.
46 For example, Annex II: Arrangement on the Long-term Management of the Mackerel Stock to the Agreed Records of Conclusions of Fisheries Consultations between the Faroe Islands, the European Community and Norway on the Management of the Mackerel Stock in the North-East Atlantic for 2006, 26 October 2005, available at www.odin.dep.no/filarkiv/262170/Avtale_trepart_-_makrell_2006.pdf, and Annexes I to IV on the long-term management plans for cod, haddock, saithe and North Sea herring to the Agreed Record of Conclusions of Fisheries Consultations between the European Community and Norway for 2005, 26 November 2004, available at www.odin.dep.no/filarkiv/228576/Bilateral_arrangement_for_2005.pdf.
47 There is an additional requirement of proportionality in recovery plans concerning effort limits, which are only to be set if necessary to achieve the objective of the plan.
48 Recovery plan for northern hake (Regulation 811/2004) and southern hake and Norwegian lobsters (Regulation 811/2004); others are under way, *inter alia*, for sole and Baltic cod.
49 Council Regulation (EC) No 423/2004. In 1999, Norway and the EC agreed on a long-term management plan for the shared cod stock, which is under revision. See Annex II: Arrangement on the Long-term Management of the Mackerel Stock to the Agreed Records of Conclusions of Fisheries Consultations between the Faroe Islands, the European Community and Norway on the Management of the Mackerel Stock in the North-East Atlantic for 2006, 26 October 2005, available at www.odin.dep.no/filarkiv/262170/Avtale_trepart_-_makrell_2006.pdf, and Annexes I to IV on the long-term management plans for cod, haddock, saithe and North Sea herring to the Agreed Record of Conclusions of Fisheries

Consultations between the European Community and Norway for 2005, 26 November 2004, available at www.odin.dep.no/filarkiv/228576/Bilateral_arrangement_for_2005.pdf.

50 The TAC for 2005 is found in Annex IB of Council Regulation 27/2005, available at www.europa.eu.int/eur-lex/lex/LexUriServ/site/en/oj/2005/l_012/l_01220050114en00010151.pdf

51 Effort limits for 2005 are found in Article 12 and Annex IVa of Council Regulation 27/2005.

52 Commission Regulation (EC) No 2056/2001.

53 Commission Decision of 2 June 2005 (2005/429/EC).

54 The Commission's proposal did not include such an exemption, but opened for fishery below the minimum level of biomass, though within a fixed mortality rate and, thus, more stringent than in the final text: COM (2002) 773, Final amended proposal for a Council regulation establishing measures for the recovery of cod and hake stocks, Article 5, available at www.europa.eu.int/eur-lex/lex/LexUriServ/site/en/com/ 2002/com2002_0773en01.pdf.

55 COM (2002) 773, Final amended proposal for a Council regulation establishing measures for the recovery of cod and hake stocks, Article 5, available at www.europa.eu.int/eur-lex/lex/LexUriServ/site/en/com/ 2002/com2002_0773en01.pdf.

56 *Report of the ICES Advisory Committee on Fishery Management and Advisory Committee on Ecosystems* (2004) vol 1, no 2, item 4.4.1.a, pp2–200, available at www.ices.dk/products/icesadvice/Book2Part%201.pdf (December 2005).

57 The TAC for 2005 is found in Annex IB of Council Regulation 27/2005, available at www.europa.eu.int/eur-lex/lex/LexUriServ/site/en/oj/2005/l_012/l_01220050114en00010151.pdf.

58 COM (2002) 773, Final amended proposal for a Council regulation establishing measures for the recovery of cod and hake stocks, Article 5, available at www.europa.eu.int/eur-lex/lex/LexUriServ/site/en/com/ 2002/com2002_0773en01.pdf, pp2–3.

59 The ICES advice seems to be corroborated, to some degree, by the STECF, but also points to uncertainties in the estimates of the fishing mortality in Review of Scientific Advice for 2005, SEC (2005) 266, item 2.12, available at www.eu.int/comm/fisheries/doc_et_publ/factsheets/legal_texts/docscom/en/sec_2005_266_en.pdf.

60 Council Regulation 27/2005, Article 12 and Annex IVa, available at www.europa.eu.int/eur-lex/lex/LexUriServ/site/en/oj/2005/l_012/l_01220050114en00010151.pdf.

61 Review of Scientific Advice for 2005, SEC (2005) 266, item 2.12, p25, available at www.eu.int/comm/fisheries/doc_et_publ/factsheets/legal_texts/docscom/en/sec_2005_266_en.pdf.

62 Council Regulation 2371/2002 Article 3 (i).

63 Fisheries Council of December 2005 – Results, available at www.eu.int/comm/fisheries/news_corner/autres/info_council201205_en.htm.

64 Sea Water Act of 3 June 1983, No 40, Norway (an unofficial translation is available at www.ub.uio.no/ujur/ulovdata/lov-19830603–040-eng.pdf), Fisheries Management Act, 15 May 1990, No 38, Iceland (an unofficial translation is available at http://eng.sjavarutveg-sraduneyti.is/laws/) and Act on Commercial Fisheries, 10 March 1994, No 28, Faroe Islands (available at www.logir.fo/menu/00012855.htm).

65 St.prp. no 37 (1995–1996), which is the proposal to the Norwegian Parliament for consent to ratify the Fish Stocks Agreement.

66 St.meld. no 51 (1997–1998) and St.meld. no 49 (2004–2005).

67 NOU 2005: 10 *Lov om forvaltning av viltlevende marine ressurser* (Act on the Management of Living Marine Resources, author's translation), only available in Norwegian at www.odin.dep.no/fkd/norsk/dok/andre_dok/nou/ 047001–020002/dok-bn.html.

68 Information from the Icelandic Ministry of Fisheries, available at www.fisheries.is/stocks/cod.htm.

69 Information from the Icelandic Ministry of Fisheries, available at www.fisheries.is/managem/legisl.htm.
70 Information from the Icelandic Ministry of Fisheries, available at www.fisheries.is/managem/legisl.htm.
71 *Report of the ICES Advisory Committee on Fisheries Management and Advisory Committee on Ecosystems* (2004) vol 1, no 2, item 4.2.1.b, available at www.ices.dk/products/icesadvice/Book2Part%201.pdf, and *Report of the ICES Advisory Committee on Fisheries Management and Advisory Committee on Ecosystems* (2005) vol 2, May 2005, item 1.4.2, available at www.ices.dk/committe/acfm/comwork/report/2005/may/cod-iceg.pdf.
72 *Report of the ICES Advisory Committee on Fisheries Management and Advisory Committee on Ecosystems*, (2005) vol 2, May 2005, item 1.4.2, available at www.ices.dk/committe/acfm/comwork/report/2005/may/cod-iceg.pdf.
73 More information on the stock may be found at the Norwegian Institute of Marine Research website at www.imr.no/english/__data/page/4003/Marine_Resources_2004.pdf.
74 The Commission is established under the Agreement of 11 April 1975 on Cooperation in the Fisheries Sector (*Avtale om samarbeid i fiskerisektoren*) and its functions are developed in the Agreement of 15 October 1976 on Mutual Fisheries Relations (*Avtale om gjensidige fiskeriforbindelser*), following the establishment of Norwegian and Russian (Soviet) EEZs.
75 *Report of the ICES Advisory Committee on Fisheries Management and Advisory Committee on Ecosystems* (2005) vol 3, May, item 1.5.1, available at www.ices.dk/committe/acfm/comwork/report/2005/may/cod-arct.pdf.
76 See, for example, the *Report of the 29th Session of the Joint Norwegian–Russian Fisheries Commission*, November 2000, available in Norwegian at www.odin.dep.no/odinarkiv/norsk/fid/2001/annet/008041–990032/dok-bn.html.
77 'Fundamental principles and criteria for long-term and sustainable management of living marine resources of the Barents Sea and Norwegian Sea' ('*Grunnleggende prinsipper og kriterier for langsiktig, b'rekraftig forvaltning av levende marine ressurser i Barentshavet og Norskehavet*'), available in Norwegian at www.odin.dep.no/odinarkiv/norsk/fid/2002/pressem/008041–070143/dok-bn.html.
78 *Report of the 33rd Session of the Joint Norwegian–Russian Fisheries Commission*, item 5.1, available in Norwegian at www.odin.dep.no/filarkiv/225563/Protokoll_33._sesjon.pdf.
79 *Report of the ICES Advisory Committee on Fisheries Management and Advisory Committee on Ecosystems* (2005) vol 3, May, item 1.5.1, available at www.ices.dk/committe/acfm/comwork/report/2005/may/cod-arct.pdf.

REFERENCES

Churchill, R. (1999) 'The EC and its role in some issues of international fisheries law', in Hey, E. (ed) *Developments in International Fisheries Law*, Kluwer Law International, The Hague
Davies, P. and Redgwell, C. (1996) 'The international legal regulation of straddling fish stocks', *British Yearbook of International Law*, vol 67, pp199–274
Freestone, D. (1999) 'Implementing precaution cautiously: The precautionary approach in the Straddling and Highly Migratory Fish Stocks Agreement', in Hey, E. (ed) *Developments in International Fisheries Law*, Kluwer Law International, The Hague
Fullem, G. (1995) 'The precautionary principle: Environmental protection in the face of scientific uncertainty', *Willamette Law Review*, vol 31, pp495–522
Hewison, G. (1996) 'The precautionary approach to fisheries management: An environmental perspective', *The International Journal of Marine and Coastal Law*, vol 11, pp301–332

Hey, E. (1992) 'The precautionary concept in environmental policy and law: Institutionalizing caution', *Georgetown International Environmental Law Review*, vol 4, pp303–318

Hilborn, R. and Peterman, R. M. (1996)'The development of scientific advice with incomplete information in the context of the precautionary approach', in *Precautionary Approach to Fisheries, Part 2: Scientific Papers*, FAO Fisheries Technical Paper (no 350/2), FAO, Rome, pp77–101

Levy, J.-P. and Schram, G. (1996) *United Nations Conference on Straddling Fish Stocks and Highly Migratory Fish Stocks: Selected Documents*, Martinus Nijhoff Publishers, The Hague

McIntyre, O. and Mosedale T., (1997) 'The precautionary principle as a norm of customary international law', *Journal of Environmental Law*, vol 9, pp221–241

Peel, J. (2004) 'Precaution: A matter of principle, approach or process?' *Melbourne Journal of International Law*, vol 5, pp483–501

Shelton, D. (1996) 'The impact of scientific uncertainty on environmental law and policy in the United States', in Freestone, D. and Hey, E. (eds) *The Precautionary Principle and International Law: The Challenge of Implementation*, Kluwer Law International, The Hague

Stokke, O. S. and Coffey, C. (2004) 'Precaution, ICES and the Common Fisheries Policy: A study of regime interplay', *Marine Policy*, vol 28, pp117–126

St.meld. no 39 (2004–2005) 'Om dei fiskeriavtalane Noreg har inngått med andre land for 2005 og fisket etter avtalane I 2003 og 2004', White Paper on the fisheries agreement Norway has entered into with other states in 2005 and the fisheries according to the 2003 and 2004 agreements

PART IV

Precaution, Genetically Modified Organisms and Biodiversity

Introduction

Nicolas de Sadeleer

The ultimate avatar of the Promethean myth – biotechnology – has been favoured by the agro-industry in order to improve the quality of some agricultural products. However, biodiversity is already facing serious threats stemming from agricultural productivity. Attempts to conserve biodiversity must grapple with a wide range of uncertainties, as well as ignorance. The difficulties are compounded by the lack of sufficient data, as well as the complexity to model the functioning of ecosystems. Indeed, there are still major gaps in understanding how ecosystems and species interact and react against new threats. In some cases, uncertainties cannot be reduced by gathering more accurate data; in other words, uncertainty is intractable. By and large, information upon which a reliable assessment of the likely impacts on ecosystems could be conducted will probably be insufficient.

The extent to which genetically modified organisms (GMOs) pose a risk of adverse effects to the environment, as well as to human health, remains hitherto controversial. Moreover, these controversies have so far been exacerbated by the relative novelty of gene technology, coupled with the lack of data available regarding the potential health and environmental impacts.

Risk issues entailed by placing GMOs on the market and their spread in the environment have so far received considerable attention in both European Community (EC) and Nordic countries. In this respect, newer regulatory instruments, such as Directive 2001/18/EC, give greater emphasis to better risk assessments, with a view to reducing uncertainties. Encapsulated in this directive, precaution is, indeed, at the heart of the EC regulatory framework.

Given the reluctance of Europeans to accept the benefits of gene technology, precaution has gathered momentum from a societal point of view. Thanks to the importance of the public debate on this topic, risk assessment cannot fully be separated from considerations of risk management. Accordingly, the regulatory approach contemplated at EC, as well as at national, levels entails social choices about what level of risk the community views as tolerable. As a result, expertise and decision-making are intertwined rather than separated.

In Chapter 11, Anne Ingeborg Myhr describes the various types of uncertainties one encounters when assessing potential risks stemming from gene technology.

Chapter 12 describes the EC regulatory background, made up of a cluster of somewhat arcane directives and regulations. In particular, Theofanis Christoforou prompts the question: does the high level of environmental and health protection, achieved through EC procedures, preclude member states from endorsing more stringent policies towards marketed GMOs?

From a regional perspective, Ole Kristian Fauchald (Chapter 13) and Jussi Kauppila (Chapter 14) describe the manner in which uncertainties are being taken into account in three Nordic countries.

Last, but by no means least, Helle Tegner Anker (Chapter 15) offers a critical analysis of the Danish and the European Union (EU) natural habitats conservation regime, where experts and regulators alike have to deal with uncertainties with regard to, among other things, the impact of an array of socio-economic activities on protected ecosystems. In the same way as in the field of GMOs, precaution is at the core of the impact assessment procedure of the EC habitats directive.

CHAPTER 11

Uncertainty and Precaution: Challenges and Implications for Science and the Policy of Genetically Modified Organisms

Anne Ingeborg Myhr

INTRODUCTION

Use of the precautionary principle in connection with scientific uncertainty in risk assessment and management is, at present, controversial. With regard to genetic engineering (GE), the precautionary principle plays an important role in genetically modified organism (GMO) regulation, such as the Cartagena Protocol, an international agreement on transboundary movement of GMOs, and in other regulations – for example, the Norwegian Gene Technology Act of 1993 and the European Union (EU) Directive 2001/18/EC. This chapter does not focus on the legal practice related to the precautionary principle, but instead argues that the implementation of the precautionary principle may have implications for scientific practice. Application of the precautionary principle requires that indications of adverse impacts are documented in some way, and that risk-associated research is initiated. Hence, implementation of the precautionary principle involves emphasizing the importance of the scientists' responsibility with regard to identifying and acknowledging uncertainty. Precautionary-motivated science needs to be built on a basic research agenda; it involves broadening the scientific focus, reflexivity and interdisciplinary approaches.

USE OF GENETIC ENGINEERING (GE) AND RELEASE OF GENETICALLY MODIFIED ORGANISMS (GMOs)

Genetic engineering is a very broad term that covers various ways of modifying the genomes of living organisms. Genetic engineering involves the insertion of synthetic genetic material or the transfer of genetic material from one organism to another, within the same species or between species. Genetic engineering promises better human and/or animal health, food improvement and environmental protection. For instance, the introduction of genetically modified crops holds promise for higher yields of food, with less use of chemicals (James, 2004). In addition to crop plants, many different GMOs have been developed, including viruses, bacteria, fungi, insects, trees and animals, for basic research purposes or are under development for applied purposes. On the other hand, the environmental release of GMOs, and the use of medicine or food ingredients from genetically modified (GM) sources, raises concerns about potential undesirable health and environmental impacts.

Scientific uncertainty regarding GE use and GMO release

Several reports have been written on science-based concerns related to the use and release of GMOs (see, for instance, NOU, 2000; Expert Panel of the Royal Society of Canada, 2001; ESA, 2004; NRC, 2004). The uncertainties described in these reports can be placed in two categories – epistemological and methodological uncertainty:

1 Epistemological uncertainty is related to the imperfection of the current scientific understanding with regard to the proposed benefits and the potential adverse effects of an activity. This may be due to the novelty of the activity, where the epistemic uncertainty may be reduced by doing more research and empirical effort, or to variability or complexity inherent in the system under consideration, which may be irreducible since it originates in the inherent randomness of ecological systems, and social, economic and cultural dynamics.
2 Methodological uncertainty is related to the choice of methods and models used to investigate the consequences of GMO use and release. Methodological uncertainty results from not fully understanding the interactions among variables and the relevance of models used to predict the behaviour of multivariable systems.

Epistemological uncertainty regarding GMO use and release

Several aspects of epistemological uncertainty with regard to the potential health and environmental risks of GMO use and release are presented in the following sections.

Health risks

Current genetic modification methods do not provide precise information about the location and number of inserts, and the transgene(s) may introduce new properties to the GMO. In addition, secondary effects of the introduction of the transgene(s) may arise from the expression products of the new genetic material(s), or the insertion(s) may cause pleiotropic effects, which divert the gene expression patterns of the recipient organisms. Changes within the GMO or its product may have unexpected effects on protein production and metabolic activities – for instance:

- *Toxic or allergic responses*: the expression of a constituent (not previously present in the plant), or the enhanced expression of an existing protein or another constituent, may have unforeseen effects. At present, the proteins introduced into GMOs are evaluated for their physiochemical properties, sequence homology (with known allergens) and, occasionally, their allergenic activity. Spök et al (2005) have recently published a paper where they argue that the current methods used in the risk assessment of GMOs do not predict or exclude allergenicity. Accordingly, they argue that there is a need to improve methods by comparing the non-GMO with the whole GMO regarding their potential to elicit allergic reactions. The allergenic risk posed by GMOs is of concern both after consumption and regarding the inhalation of pollen and dust.

- *Nutritional changes*: the insertion of transgene(s) that encode new protein(s) or other constituents may cause a change in the levels and activities of inherent enzymes, nutrients and metabolites (Kuiper and Kleter, 2003).
- *Antibiotic resistance*: the use of antibiotic-resistance genes, such as markers for the selection of GM plants, entails potential for the transfer of genes to bacteria already present in the alimentary tract of the consumer, which may result in increasing numbers of antibiotic-resistant bacteria. GMOs with antibiotic-resistant genes have been considered unwelcome in Norway since 1997, and some of them will be abandoned in Europe after 2008.
- *Gene-silencing phenomenas*: the genetic insertion may not only affect the target properties, but also the stability of expression. Instability of expression, such as gene silencing of the inserted transgene (that is, the inserted transgenes are not expressed at all), may happen after the initial transformation of the organism. Gene silencing of the inserted transgene has been experienced, for instance, when more than one transgene has been inserted (Qin et al, 2003).

Environmental risks

The main potential environmental risks associated with GMO use and release are (see also Figure 11.1):

- *Changed use:* introduction of insect-resistant and herbicide-tolerant crops often involves a change in agricultural practice. For instance, the use of insect-resistant (*Bt*) crops may cause the development of pesticide-resistant insects, and cross-pollination of wild relatives by herbicide-tolerant plants may cause the development of herbicide-tolerant weeds (Benbrook, 2005). These events may result in an extensive use of chemicals and thus limit options for conventional and organic farmers.
- *Displacement:* even if the GMO has been extensively studied before its introduction, a change may occur in the interactions with, and responses to, the environment. New interactions between the GMO and the ecological systems may also transpire. Key issues may be the behaviour of the GMO in the area of release and in the surrounding areas, especially regarding reproduction, dispersal and survival over time and space. Different climatic and environmental conditions may affect the persistence and dispersal properties of the GMO.
- *Non-target effects:* research has indicated that the longevity and reproduction of beneficial predatory insects have been affected by the consumption of caterpillars fed on Bt-maize (Hilbeck et al, 1998). It has been reported that the larvae of monarch

butterflies have been harmed by pollen from Bt-maize under laboratory conditions (Losey et al, 1999). However, whether there are any effects on lacewings, monarch butterflies or other non-target organisms under real-life agricultural conditions is disputed, and contradictory results have been reported (Poza et al, 2005).

• *Gene flow:* gene flow to non-GMO relatives used in agriculture and to wild relatives may occur through cross-pollination or horizontal gene transfer (Ellstrand, 2001; Nielsen and Townsend, 2004). It is crucial to improve understanding of gene flow mechanisms and how agricultural and environmental conditions influence the frequency of gene transfer.

Methodological uncertainty regarding GMO use and release

Methodological uncertainty is related to the choice of methods and models used to investigate the consequences of GMO use and release. In the process of performing risk assessment and management, the different scientific disciplines disagree about the choice of methods and models to be used. For instance, agricultural biotechnologists refer to the practice of conventional plant breeding, while ecologists refer to the consequences of introducing exotic species in order to make up for the lack of anticipatory knowledge. Furthermore, methodological uncertainty results from not fully understanding the interactions among variables and the models used to predict the behaviour of multivariable systems. For instance, the potential for gene flows to agricultural and natural environments is a new worry for regulators and scientists, involving economic and legal concerns regarding how to ensure co-existence, as well as environmental concerns regarding potential adverse effects on biodiversity. Therefore, it is crucial that methods for detection and monitoring are initiated with the purpose of following up the performed risk assessment, of mapping the actual health and environmental effects, and

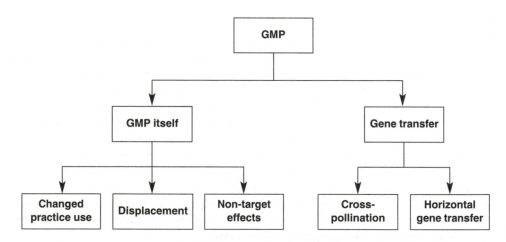

Figure 11.1   *Potential ecological effects regarding genetically modified organism (GMO) use and release*

Source: adapted from Myhr and Traavik (2003a)

of identifying unforeseen adverse effects. Long-term monitoring provides baselines against which to compare future changes, as well as input data to improve regulation systems (Cranor, 2003).

UNCERTAINTY IN IMPLEMENTING THE PRECAUTIONARY PRINCIPLE IN GMO REGULATION

Uncertainty and the significance of evidence in assessing risk

With the aim of discussing risks and uncertainty in connection with genetic engineering use and GMO release, the first step is for scientists to become conscious of the role that they play in producing information and the subsequent political use of this knowledge (Myhr and Traavik, 2003a). The prime responsibility of scientists has been to strive for increased knowledge in an unbiased and reliable manner. The responsibility of scientists has been well reflected in the traditional methods of pursuing and communicating scientific discoveries, and by exposing the results to objective scrutiny by the scientific community. More recently, it has been argued that scientists also have obligations towards the environment and society that is not limited to research conduct, but implies taking into consideration the social and ethical implications of research as a whole (Stirling, 1999). However, the impact of this on scientific practice is still disputed. For instance, with regard to the communication of uncertainty and complexity in scientific studies, there are two threads: present results with as little interpretation as possible, or interpret results in order to influence their policy use. For instance, environmental scientists have an extended ethical responsibility since they are deliverers of ideas for environmental management and policy (Buhl-Mortensen and Welin, 2000). This leads us to the difficulties of hypothesis testing and the threshold for evidence. Scientists make assumptions, choices and inferences in their research, based on professional judgement and standard practices, which if not known by the public or policy-makers may make scientific results appear to be more certain than is warranted. For instance, in observational studies of complex and poorly understood systems, errors in the independent variables, errors arising from choosing the wrong model to analyse and interpret data, and biases arising from the research methodology may occur (Kriebel et al, 2001). Experimental reports with a handful of replicates and low statistical significance could fail to expose the risk associated with a particular activity. Under the assumption 'safe until proven otherwise', the regulator may not boost the rigour of testing, and statistically weak indications of harm may be considered insignificant and, hence, remain unreported.

Statistical testing: False positives versus false negatives

In the practice of statistical testing, researchers often formulate a so-called null hypothesis (H_0). The H_0 is usually stated in terms of 'no adverse effect'. If the outcome of a statistical test warrants the rejection of the H_0, the scientist will normally accept the alternative hypothesis H_1 – there is an adverse effect. Hypothesis testing operates on the basis of limiting false positives (which erroneously predict an adverse effect when there is, in fact, none) to ensure that the observed result supports the H_0. Hence, errors of false positives occur when one rejects a true H_0. In contrast, a false negative is made by not rejecting a false H_0 – that is, there is an ecological adverse effect and the H_0 is wrong (see Table 11.1).

In traditional scientific practice, one ought to have complete and supportive information before claiming a cause–effect relationship. Consequently, the statistical significance of the result must be strong enough to allow only a small probability (p) that the result is due to chance or has been based on speculation. By convention, in a false positive setting, the probability of this error being made is determined by the significance level of α – often at 5 per cent. Hence, if there is less than 95 per cent confidence that there is an effect, H_0 is not rejected. In such situations, scientists are prone to assume that the evidence is not strong enough to reject the H_0, that there is no effect due to limitations of the experimental design or test, or that the data variables are too similar to detect an effect. Such practice implies postponing action in order to prevent harm until a product or an activity is proven harmful, or until plausible connection of effects can be established (Lemons et al, 1997; Buhl-Mortensen and Welin, 1998). However, when making decisions about accepting a scientific hypothesis (or not), one also needs to take into account both the empirical evidence and the seriousness of the two possible types of mistakes: accepting an incorrect hypothesis and rejecting a correct one. Hence, in risk-related research, standards and burden of proof have to be differentiated from those used in fields where high certainty and high consensus exist among scientists. In this context, the power of studies to detect relevant risk becomes important. Statistical power refers to the probability of correctly rejecting H_0 – that is, statistically detecting an effect if it exists. According to Lövei and Arpaia (2005), power analysis is rarely considered in laboratory tests of the impact of GM plants on arthropod natural enemies. Hence, they argue, in future studies of non-target effects, power analysis needs to be employed since this may help in research planning (giving indications of sample size and duration of project) and may clarify the interpretation of results.

The report *Late Lessons from Early Warnings: The Precautionary Principle, 1896–2000* (EEA, 2001), describes, in 14 cases, that not taking precaution may have human, ecological and economic costs, and stresses the need to learn from past failures in order to heed

Table 11.1 *Type I and type II errors in ecological studies*

Reality — Test results	H_0 is true	H_0 is false
The investigation does not show adverse effects	Correct (1–α)	Type II error False negative (β)
The investigation shows adverse effects	Type I error False positive (α)	Correct Statistical power (1–β)

Note: null hypothesis H_0 = there are no adverse effects.

early scientific evidence of risks. This means that risk to society and the environment may be increased because a bias towards avoiding false positives discourages risk-associated research and communication of early warnings. Accordingly, given the asymmetry in the consequences of avoiding false positives versus false negatives, application of the precautionary principle would entail a research agenda that identifies potential threats to health and the environment before they become real.

Systematization of uncertainty to enhance the quality of (and to direct further) research

The notion that uncertainty is only a statistical concept or represents insufficient data may leave out many important aspects of uncertainty when performing risk assessment (Wynne, 1992; Giampietro, 2002). For instance, uncertainty with regard to GMO release and use can be presented at different levels:

- *Uncertainties that refer to situations where we do not know or cannot estimate the probability of the hazard, but the hazards to consider are known.* This may be due to the novelty of the activity, or to the variability or complexity involved. For instance, the frequency of horizontal gene transfer from GMOs to non-GMOs may be influenced by agricultural and environmental conditions, which may differ from the estimates gained under laboratory experiments (Nielsen and Townsend, 2004).
- *Ignorance that represents situations where the kind of hazard to measure is unknown (that is, completely unexpected hazards may emerge).* This has historically been experienced with, for instance, BSE, dioxins and pesticides (EEA, 2001). With regard to GMOs, for instance, unprecedented and unintended non-target effects may emerge. Non-target effects include the influence on and interactions with all organisms in the environment, and may be direct or indirect. Direct effects concern eco-toxic effects on other organisms – for instance, adverse effects on insects, such as larval feeding on insect-resistant plants (Losey et al, 1999; Obrycki et al, 2001), or effects on soil organisms (Saxena and Stotzky, 2000). Indirect effects concern effects on consumer health, contamination of wild gene pools or alterations in ecological relationships.

Employment of model-based decision support – as, for instance, the Walker and Harremöes (W&H) framework (Walker et al, 2003) – may help to identify the types and levels of uncertainty involved. The W&H framework has been developed by an international group of scientists with the purpose of providing a state-of-the-art conceptual basis for the systematic evaluation of uncertainty in environmental decision-making. One of the main goals of the W&H framework is to stimulate better communication between the various actors in identifying areas for further research and in decision processes. In this framework, uncertainty occurs in three dimensions:

1 location where the uncertainty manifests itself – for example, distinguish between context (ecological, technological, economic, social and political), expert judgement and considerations, and models (model structure, model implementation, data, outputs, etc.);

2 nature – degree of variability that can express whether uncertainty stems primarily from inherent system variability/complexity, or from lack of knowledge and information;
3 level – the severity of uncertainty that can be classified on a gradual scale, from 'knowing for certain' to 'complete ignorance'.

Krayer von Krauss et al (2004, 2005) have demonstrated and tested the W&H framework with the purpose of identifying scientists' and other stakeholders' judgements of uncertainty in the risk assessment of GM crops. In these studies, the focus was on the potential adverse effects on agriculture and cultivation processes of releasing herbicide-resistant oilseed crops. Krayer von Krauss et al (2004, 2005) interviewed seven experts in Canada and Denmark. To identify the experts' view on the uncertainty of location, the authors presented a diagram showing causal relationships and key parameters to the experts. With the purpose of identifying the level and nature of uncertainty, the experts had to quantify the level and describe the nature of uncertainty on the key parameters in the diagram. By asking the experts to identify the nature of uncertainty, it was possible to distinguish between uncertainty that may be reduced by doing more research, and ignorance that stems from system variability or complexity.

Approaches that define and systematize the uncertainty involved, such as the W&H framework, may help to use scientific knowledge more efficiently in directing further research and in guiding risk assessment and management processes.

DEALING WITH THE ECOLOGICAL UNPREDICTABILITY OF GE AND GMO RELEASE

Further research does not necessarily reduce uncertainty. Instead, it may often reveal unforeseen complexities and irreducible uncertainty. In Chapter 2 of this volume, de Sadeleer dealt with the legal implications of the unpredictability of risk when applying technology. This section focuses on the biological and ecological dimensions of unpredictability as a result of genetic engineering and GMO release.

Unpredictable effects related to GMO use and release may arise due to the interaction between the introduced transgenes(s) and the recipient genome, or due to unanticipated interactions between the GMO and the ecological system. Hence, one needs to be aware that there will always be an inevitable gap between limited experimental conditions and reality, where the consequences of an activity can never be fully predicted. This is because uncertainties regarding the behaviour of complex systems have nothing to do with a temporary insufficiency of knowledge; rather, it has everything to do with the objective structural properties of complex systems. The study of complex systems is about understanding the indirect effects and problems that are difficult to solve because the causes and effects are not obviously related (Gundersen and Crawford, 2002; Scheffer et al, 2002; Chu et al, 2003). Putting pressure on a complex system in one area can often have effects on another because the parts are interdependent. Under such circumstances, the normal scientific approach of trying to produce a best estimate or unequivocal answers will not be useful. There is, therefore, a need to supplement current methods with new approaches that facilitate an understanding of complex ecological issues. This makes it necessary to involve of a wide range of scientific disciplines, as well as independent scientific institutions, in gathering scientific knowledge. Involving scientific disciplines on a wide basis may:

- assist in exploring alternative means of problem solving, as well as alternative indicators that can be used in risk assessment;
- provide a diverse source of data and information, including information on uncertainties, which may be of relevance to risk assessment;
- assist in the evaluation and critical review of assumptions, methods, procedures and results.

This will ensure that both mainstream and minority opinions are considered, and will avoid the abuse of science by scientists biased in favour of a specific agenda. Hence, the different methods and models representing the varying disciplines may be seen as compatible providers of information and models for studying the problem or the system. With more diversity in the approach, more data will be generated and more responses will be available to understand complexity and changing conditions.

THE INFLUENCE OF NORMATIVE STANDARDS IN RISK ASSESSMENT AND RISK MANAGEMENT

Risk assessment and management strategies are developed within particular frameworks, including normative standards and preferences regarding our relationship to the natural environment and the protection/promotion of human health. For instance, EU Directive 2001/18/EC states that an environmental risk assessment needs to consider direct and indirect effects, and immediate and delayed effects, as well as potential cumulative and long-term effects due to interaction with other GMOs and the environment. Article 1 of the Cartagena Protocol specifies that the entire objective of the document is to protect and conserve biodiversity according to a precautionary approach. One of the purposes of the Norwegian Gene Technology Act is that use of GMOs will be in accordance with the principle of sustainable development (see Chapter 13 in this volume). The Norwegian authorities have used the concept of sustainability to deny marketing a herbicide-resistant species of oilseed rape (Myhr and Traavik, 2003b). The applicant was the Belgian firm Plant Genetic Systems. The oilseed rape was genetically modified to tolerate the herbicide gluphosinate. Before the Norwegian Biotechnology Advisory Board had evaluated the application, highly relevant scientific results were published: a GM herbicide-tolerant oilseed rape had transferred its transgene to a weedy relative (Mikkelsen et al, 1996). In response to this, the board advised against marketing, acknowledging that potential transfer of resistant genes to relatives may create weed problems and thereby increase herbicide use. The authorities considered that potential transfer of herbicide-resistant genes to wild relatives might create weed problems and therefore increase herbicide use – and, hence, would be incongruent with sustainability.

However, Plant Genetic Systems did not consider gene transfer to other organisms as a risk. Neither did the UK authorities, who approved the commercial release of the herbicide-tolerant plants. This case illustrates that normative standards may affect the scope of risk management relating to GMO use and release, as well as influence acceptability of risks with low probability.

CONCLUSIONS

This chapter has argued that there is a need to achieve wise management of uncertainties with regard to the potential adverse effects of genetic engineering and GMO release. This challenge has to be met through scientific conduct and approaches that aim to:

- Expose, contextualize and improve the framework and context of the methodological design of health and environmental studies to ensure the scientific and social robustness of knowledge generated through the project, and the imperative to initiate and communicate early warning research.
- Acknowledge the complexity of human and environmental systems.
- Realize that different normative conceptualization of frameworks affects the scope of research and the final outcome.

These points are crucial for implementing precaution in risk management and for providing scientific understanding – the basis for such management.

REFERENCES

Benbrook, C. (2005) *Harvest at Risk: Impacts of Roundup Ready Wheat in the Northern Great Plains*, Western Organization of Resource Councils, Billings, MN, www.worc.org/issues/Benbrook.html

Buhl-Mortensen L. and Welin S. (1998) 'The ethics of doing policy relevant science: The precautionary principle and the significance of non-significant results', *Science and Engineering Ethics*, vol 4, pp401–412

Chu, D., Strand, R. and Fjelland, R. (2003) 'Theories of complexity: Common denominators of complex systems', *Complexity*, vol 8, pp19–30

Cranor, C. (2003) 'How should society approach the real and potential risks posed by new technologies?', *Plant Physiology*, vol 133, pp3–9

EEA (European Environment Agency) (2001) *Late Lessons from Early Warnings: The Precautionary Principle, 1896–2000*, EEA, Copenhagen,www.reports.eea.eu.int/environmental_issue_report_2001_22/

Ellstrand, N. (2001) 'When transgenes wander, should we worry?', *Plant Physiology*, vol 125, pp1543–1545

ESA (Ecological Society of America) (2004) *Genetically Engineered Organisms and the Environment: Current Status and Recommendations*, ESA, Washington, DC, www.esa.org

Expert Panel of the Royal Society of Canada (2001) *Elements of Precaution: Recommendations for the Regulation of Food Biotechnology in Canada*, The Royal Society of Canada, Ottawa, www.rsc.ca

Giampietro, M. (2002) 'The precautionary principle and ecological hazards of genetically modified organisms', *Ambio*, vol 6, pp466–470

Gundersen, L. and Crawford, S. H. (2002) *Panarchy: Understanding Transformations in Human and Natural systems*, Island Press, Washington, DC

Hilbeck, A., Baumgartner, M., Fried, P. M. and Bigler, F. (1998) 'Effects of transgenic *Bacillus thuringiensis* corn-fed prey on mortality and development time of immature *Chrysoperla carnea*', *Environmental Entomology*, vol 27, pp480–487

James, C. (2004) *Preview: Global Status of Commercialized Biotech/GM Crops: 2004*, ISAAA Briefs no 32, ISAAA, Ithaca, NY

Krayer von Krauss, M., Casman, E. and Small, M. (2004) 'Elicitation of expert judgments of uncertainty in the risk assessment of herbicide tolerant oilseed crops', *Journal of Risk Analysis*, vol 24, pp1515–1527

Krayer von Krauss, M. P. and Janssen, P. H. M. (2005) 'Using the W&H integrated uncertainty analysis framework with non-initiated experts', *Water Science and Technology*, vol 52, no 6, pp145–152

Kriebel, D., Tickner, J., Epstein, P., Lemons, J., Levins, R., Loechler, E. L., Quinn, M., Rudel, R., Schettler, T. and Stoto, M. (2001) 'The precautionary principle in environmental science', *Environmental Health Perspectives*, vol 109, pp871–876

Kuiper, H. A., and Kleter, G. A. (2003) 'The scientific basis for risk assessment of regulation of genetically modified foods', *Trends in Food Science and Technology*, vol 14, pp277–293

Lemons, J., Shrader-Frechette, K. S. and Cranor, C. (1997) 'The precautionary principle: Scientific uncertainty and type I and type II errors', *Foundation of Science*, vol 2, pp207–236

Losey, J. E., Rayor, L. S. and Carter, M. E. (1999) 'Transgenic pollen harm monarch larvae', *Nature*, vol 399, p214

Lövei, G. L. and Arpaia, S. (2005) 'The impact of transgenic plants on natural enemies: A critical review of laboratory studies', *Entomological Experimentalis et Applicata*, vol 114, pp1–14

Mikkelsen, T. R., Andersen, B. and Jørgensen, R. B. (1996) 'The risk of crop transgene spread', *Nature*, vol 380, p31

Myhr, A. I. and Traavik, T. (2003a) 'Genetically modified crops: Precautionary science and conflicts of interests', *Journal of Agricultural and Environmental Ethics*, vol 16, pp227–247

Myhr, A. I. and Traavik, T. (2003b) 'Sustainable development and Norwegian genetic engineering regulation: Applications, impact and challenges', *Journal of Agricultural and Environmental Ethics*, vol 16, pp317–335

Nielsen, K. M. and Townsend, J. P. (2004) 'Monitoring and modelling horizontal gene transfer', *Nature Biotechnology*, vol 22, pp110–114

NOU 2000: 29 (2000) *GMO-mat, Helsemessige konsekvenser ved bruk av genmodifiserte næringsmiddel og næringsmiddelingredienser* (*GM Food: Health Impacts through the Use of GM Food and Food Additives*), Statens Forvaltningstjeneste, Oslo

NRC (National Research Council) (2004) *Biological Confinement of Genetically Engineered Organisms*, National Academic Press, Washington, DC

Obrycki, J. J., Losey, J. E., Taylor, O. R. and Hansen, L. C. (2001) 'Transgenic insecticidal corn: Beyond insecticidal toxicity to ecological complexity', *BioScience*, vol 51, pp353–360

Poza, M., Pons X., Farinós, G. P., López, F., Eizaguirre, M., Castañera, P. and Albajes, R. (2005) 'Impact of farm-scale Bt maize on abundance of predatory arthropods in Spain', *Crop Protection*, vol 24, pp677–684

Qin, H., Dong, Y. and von Arnim, A. G. (2003) 'Epigenetic interactions between *Arabidopsis* transgenes: Characterization in light of transgene integration sites', *Plant Molecular Biology*, vol 52, pp217–231

Saxena, D. and Stotzky, G. (2000) 'Insecticidal toxin from *Bacillus thuringiensis* is released from roots of transgenic Bt corn *in vitro* and *in situ*', *FEMS Microbiology Ecology*, vol 33, pp35–39

Scheffer, M., Carpenter, S. R., Foley, J. A., Folke, C. and Walke, B. (2002) 'Catastrophic shifts in ecosystems', *Nature*, vol 413, pp591–596

Spök, A., Gaugitsch, H., Laffer, S., Pauli, G., Saito, H., Sampson, H., Sibanda, E., Thomas, W., van Hage, M. and Valenta, R. (2005) 'Suggestions for the assessment of the allergenic potential of genetically modified organisms', *International Archives of Allergy and Immunology*, vol 137, pp167–180.

Stirling, A. (1999) 'On science and precaution on risk management of technological risk', Final Report of a project for the EC Forward Studies Unit under the auspices of the ESTO Network, SPRU, University of Sussex, www.sussex.ac.uk/Units/gec/gecko/r9e-prc-.htm

Walker, W. E., Harremoes, P., Rotmans, J., Sluijs, J. P., van der Asselt, M. B. A., van Janssen, P., Krayer von Krauss, M. P. (2003) 'Defining uncertainty: A conceptual basis for uncertainty management in model based decision support', *Journal of Integrated Assessment*, vol 4, pp5–17

Wynne, B. (1992) 'Uncertainty and environmental learning: Re-conceiving science and policy in the preventive paradigm', *Global Environmental Change*, vol 2, pp111–127

CHAPTER 12

Genetically Modified Organisms in European Union Law

Theofanis Christoforou[1]

INTRODUCTION

During the past decade, the application of modern biotechnology in agricultural production has sparked, in Europe, a public debate of unprecedented nature. Almost since the first commercial release in 1994 of a genetically modified tomato in the US market, the opposition to genetically modified organisms (GMOs) has spanned across nations, political ideologies, religious beliefs and activist organizations. This debate is still ongoing, with almost all segments of the society actively participating. It raises questions primarily about trust in science, transparency in risk governance and consumer choice.

In the early 1990s, the European Community (EC) legislator took the lead worldwide. It adopted a horizontal approach to regulation, harmonizing national provisions concerning GMOs and genetically modified (GM) micro-organisms, with the objective of ensuring free movement of goods in the internal market while aiming for a high level of health and environmental protection. However, the public debate and, in some cases, the civil unrest and even disobedience that followed, particularly during the years 1996 to 2001, rendered revision of the first Community legal framework necessary. Scientific and international legal developments soon followed and they further reinforced the need to update and complete the regulatory framework. To understand, therefore, the background of the Community's attitude to regulating GMOs and GM products, it is necessary to also take into account the political, socio-economic, scientific and broad ethical concerns that have shaped it.

This chapter is organized as follows. The following section on 'The regulatory framework' provides a brief analysis of four basic laws that regulate almost all aspects of production, import, marketing and export of GMOs and GM products in the EC. 'The co-existence of national community legislation in the area of assessing and marketing GMOs and GM products' then discusses the coexistence of Community and member state power in the regulation of GMOs and GM products by focusing on the pre-emptive effects on state power which the Community harmonization measures and their decentralized implementation and application can have. This latter issue is of particular importance for the Nordic countries (see, in particular, Chapters 13 and 14 in this volume).

THE REGULATORY FRAMEWORK

The objective of this section is not to provide a complete descriptive analysis of all of the existing legislation regulating the import, production, marketing, traceability, labelling and export of GMOs and GM products in the Community. Rather, its focus will be on those aspects of the legislation and implementing measures that are necessary to ensure discussion – namely, first, to undertake a broad overview of the attitudes of the Community institutions and of the member states in the decentralized system of managing marketing authorizations of GMOs and GM products in their territory; second, to shed some light on the complexities that the interface of science, law and policy in the area of risk regulation may generate and the implications that these complexities can have on the GMO approval process; and, third, to pave the way for the subsequent review of the legislation and any implementing measures with the relevant provisions of international law and, in particular, the World Trade Organization (WTO) agreements.

The aspects of the Community legislation that will be examined here are the object and scope of the legislation in question; the appropriate level of health and environmental protection that the legislation aims to achieve; the authorization procedure that it establishes; the degree of regulatory harmonization that it accomplishes; and, last but not least, the state of play about its implementation and application by the relevant Community institutions and member state authorities.

General

The Community legislation that regulates nearly all aspects of GMOs and GM products, whether for deliberate release as seeds or for experimental purposes into the environment, or for use in food or feed, is of either horizontal or sector-specific (vertical) nature. There are several acts of diverse nature and regulatory density, laying down a coherent legislative framework. Only a broad, comprehensive review of all of these acts is likely to reveal the common thread that ties them closely together. In this section, however, only the basic four pieces of the horizontal EC legislation will be examined, although occasional reference to some other (sector-specific) legislation will also be made, when necessary for the purposes of the analysis. These four acts of Community law are:

1 Directive 2001/18/EC on the deliberate release of GMOs into the environment;[2]
2 Regulation (EC) 258/97 on novel food and food ingredients;[3]
3 Regulation (EC) 1829/2003 on GM food and feed;[4]
4 Regulation (EC) 1830/2003 on the traceability and labelling of GMOs and GM products.[5]

The 2000 Cartagena Protocol on Biosafety to the Convention on Biological Diversity,[6] although equally important, will not be discussed.

Deliberate release of genetically modified organisms (GMOs) into the environment: Directive 2001/18/EC

General

The cornerstone of the initial regulatory framework was Directive 90/220/EEC, under which the commercial release of 18 GMOs, in total, has been authorized in the Community, mostly by a European Commission decision following a qualified majority vote in the regulatory committee.[7]

Around 1996, however, several questions concerning certain scientific aspects of GMOs and GM products, for which an application has been made, were raised by a number of member states concerning, in particular, potential adverse effects on health and the environment. Moreover, member states considered that the regulatory framework was inadequate, particularly with regard to the principles for risk assessment, labelling, and mandatory post-market traceability and monitoring.[8] For those reasons, several member states started to raise objections to placing new GMOs on the market, invoking the safeguard clauses provided for in Article 16 of Directive 90/220.

Around 1997 to 1998, it was becoming all too clear that Directive 90/220 ought to be revised immediately in order to adapt it to the rapid developments on the scientific and regulatory fronts, and to the international legal framework. Consequently, in 1998, the European Commission submitted a proposal to the Council and the European Parliament to replace Directive 90/220, taking account of the above scientific and regulatory developments.

Directive 2001/18 entered into force on 14 April 2001. It repealed, as of 17 October 2002, Council Directive 90/220/EEC.[9] It is the central piece of Community legislation in the area of GMOs regulation.

Object and scope

Part B of the directive deals with the deliberate release into the environment of GMOs for experimental (that is, field trial) purposes, which are, in principle, limited in the territory of an individual member state, and Part C deals with the placing of products on the Community market that consist of or contain GMOs.

Recitals 5 and 7 and Article 1 of the directive clarify its dual objective: first, to protect human health and the environment from the deliberate release of GMOs; and, second, to approximate the laws of the member states on the deliberate release of GMOs and to ensure the safe development of industrial products utilizing GMOs. But the directive also has other more specific objectives. It introduces a mandatory post-marketing monitoring system of GMOs and traceability at all stages of their placing on the market.[10] It also establishes an advanced system for the direct information and consultation of the general public in the authorization procedure.[11] Another objective is to inform the consumers by means of appropriate labelling that a product placed in the market 'contains genetically modified organisms' and of the name of the GMOs.[12]

It is also important to note that, by virtue of Council Directives 2002/53/EC[13] and 2002/55/EC,[14] the environmental risk assessment laid down in Directive 2001/18 is also made applicable to the inclusion, in a common catalogue, of varieties of agricultural plant species for certain seeds and plants, as well as to the marketing of such vegetable seeds.

The scope of the directive, therefore, is very broad. Importantly, however, the directive does not cover products derived from GMOs that are subjected to other manufacturing processes. They are covered by the novel food regulation and the regulation on GM food and feed, as is explained below.[15]

Authorization procedure

The directive lays down a system of prior notification and approval procedure, at the end of which the competent authority of a member state – that is, the one that has received the notification ('lead' member state) – may give or refuse to give, as appropriate, its consent for the deliberate release or the placing on the market of the GMOs, as these terms have been defined above, unless objections are raised in the process by the other member states or the European Commission. The directive establishes harmonized procedures and criteria that require a case-by-case evaluation of the risks to human health and the environment and a step-by-step introduction of evaluated GMOs into the environment.[16]

With regard to the placing of GMOs on the market, Article 13 of the directive provides that a company intending to market a GMO must first submit an application to the competent national authority of the member state where the product is to be first placed on the market. The same article, and Annexes II to IV of the directive, lay down the documentation and other particulars that the application must include – in particular, a full assessment of the GMO in question in terms of risks to human health and the environment.[17]

For experimental field trial releases, Article 6 lays down the information, evidence and other particulars that the notification should contain for a 'standard' authorization procedure, and Article 7 lays down the requirements for the so-called 'differentiated' procedure.[18] Only the competent authority of the member state where the notification was made (the lead authority) is responsible for granting the consent for the *standard* procedure for experimental releases. Conversely, under the *differentiated* procedure for experimental releases and the placing of GMOs on the market under Part C of the directive, all of the competent authorities of the member states may potentially be involved in evaluating the applications.

In addition, if the competent (lead) national authority gives a favourable opinion on the marketing of the GMO concerned, this member state informs the other member states via the European Commission. If there are no objections raised by another member state or the European Commission, the competent authority that carried out the original evaluation can grant the consent for placing the product on the market.[19] The product may then be placed on the market throughout the Community, in conformity with the conditions, if any, attached to that consent.[20] But if 'reasoned objections' are raised and maintained according to Articles 15, 17 and 20 of the directive, a decision has to be taken at Community level. According to Article 28 of the directive, the

European Commission first asks for the opinion of its relevant scientific committees on 'reasoned objections' that relate to possible adverse effects on human health and the environment. If the scientific opinion is favourable, the commission then proposes a draft decision to the relevant committee that, in accordance with Article 30 of the directive, is the relevant regulatory committee set up by Decision 1999/468/EC on comitology procedures.[21] If the regulatory committee gives a favourable opinion, the commission adopts the approval decision. If the opinion is not favourable or no opinion is given within the time limit, a draft decision is submitted to the Council of Ministers for adoption or rejection by qualified majority. If the council does not act within three months, the European Commission can adopt the decision.[22]

Appropriate level of protection

A discussion of the appropriate level of health and environmental protection and of the degree of harmonization achieved by the directive is relevant for the purpose of determining the extent of pre-emption operated by the directive in Community law. In other words, such a discussion is relevant for delineating the degree of residual subject-matter power that is left to the member states to take action in their territories in the field covered by the directive.[23] This subsection examines the issue of defining the appropriate level of protection in this area. The issue of the degree of harmonization achieved and the attendant member state pre-emption will be examined in 'The co-existence of national community legislation in the area of assessing and marketing GMOs and GM products'.

The level of risk a society considers acceptable for a specific product, substance, process or activity at a given moment in time is frequently called appropriate level of (health or environmental) protection.[24] Defining this level of protection is a function of many considerations and factors, such as the understanding that experts, regulators and lay people have of science and its role as a tool to identify, analyse and predict risk; the nature and extent of the risk (serious, irreversible, etc.); and the confidence of the general public in the capacity of the regulatory system to avoid, eliminate or reduce risk. It should be noted that although the acceptable level of risk can be defined both in qualitative and quantitative terms, in the Community it is practically never expressed in a precise quantitative manner, such as a 1 in 1 million risk of death from the use of a specific product. It is interesting to note that Community law uses the terms high *level* of health or environmental protection to be achieved,[25] not terms such as significant *risk* to be avoided, which is frequently the approach of other jurisdictions (such as of the US). However, there is no doubt that even a qualitative expression of the acceptable level of risk, such as significant or serious or irreversible risk, also includes or implies a chosen level of health or environmental protection.

The level of protection may (but does not always have to) be chosen in advance of adopting a specific measure or in an abstract manner in framework legislation, such as Directive 2001/18. But it may also be decided on a case-by-case basis at the time of taking a specific regulatory measure, in implementation of framework legislation. The Community regulatory system, like most other systems, adopts a mixed approach that entails defining the appropriate level of protection either in the primary or secondary legislation in a general manner (and through the choice of the procedure to be followed), or when adopting specific implementing measures on applications for the authorization of individual products or processes to be placed on the market.

A combined reading of several provisions of the directive indicates that its aim is to achieve 'a high level of safety for the general population and the environment'.[26] Recital 47 of its preamble explains that 'the competent authority should give its consent only after it has been satisfied that the release will be safe for human health and the environment'. It should be noted that the directive refers to 'the risk' or 'a risk', without qualifying adjectives such as 'serious' or 'irreversible'.[27] It is significant that the regulatory action is to be based on the precautionary principle, which, in this case, according to Article 4(1) of the directive, requires member states to ensure that 'all appropriate measures are taken to avoid adverse effects on human health and the environment which might arise from the deliberate release or the placing on the market of GMOs'. The use of the terms 'to avoid' and 'might arise' in this context imply that there is no tolerance of identified risk. The concept of risk in this context is also very wide and covers 'any direct or indirect, immediate, delayed or unforeseen effects on human health or the environment.'[28] It is important to note that the environmental risk assessment must also take account 'of potential long-term effects associated with the interaction with other organisms and the environment'.[29] In addition, Annex II to the Directive 2001/18 clarifies that the analysis should examine 'the cumulative long-term effects' relevant to the release and the placing on the market of the GMOs.

Therefore, the level of protection chosen in the directive is a level of no risk, and this explains the obligation placed on the applicant manufacturer to demonstrate the safety of the GMO that he wishes to place on the market. Because the regulatory decision is required to be based on the precautionary principle, and especially in light of the way that this principle is interpreted and applied in the Community,[30] the burden is on the applicant manufacturer to demonstrate, to the satisfaction of the competent authorities, the 'safety' or 'lack of harm' of the product. As the European Commission's communication on the precautionary principle has indicated, measures based on the precautionary principle may be adopted when there are 'reasonable grounds for concern' or when there are 'valid reasons to consider' that there may be a risk. This corresponds to a standard of proof comparable to proof beyond reasonable doubt, set in most Community legislation in the broad area of pre-marketing approval of substances or processes. The candidate products, substances or processes are deemed to be dangerous unless and until the interested manufacturer carries out the necessary scientific work and demonstrates 'adequately' or 'sufficiently' (not on the basis of balance of probabilities), the safety of his product – in other words, the manufacturer must satisfy the determined acceptable level of risk. Because the risk assessment has to be conducted on a case-by-case basis, the applicant manufacturer has to demonstrate safety for each individual product, not a class of products.

Novel food and novel food ingredients: Regulation (EC) 258/97

General

Regulation 258/97 on novel foods and food ingredients was, until very recently, another important piece of Community legislation. But Article 38 of Regulation 1829/2003 on

GM food and feed has now modified and substantially reduced its scope. Nevertheless, Regulation 258/97 is discussed here in some detail because several applications to authorize placing novel food and novel food ingredients on the market have been made while it has been in force, and because its scope and implementation have given rise to disputes within the Community and between the Community and third countries.

Object and scope of the regulation

Regulation 258/97, which entered into force on 15 May 1997, applies to the placing of novel foods and food ingredients on the Community market that have not hitherto been used for human consumption to a 'significant degree' – hence, the use of the adjective 'novel'.[31] However, what a 'significant' degree of consumption is of such a food or food ingredient is not defined.

Article 1(2) lays down six categories of novel food and food ingredients that fall within the scope of the regulation – that is, those which:

- contain or consist of GMOs as defined in Directive 2001/18;
- are produced from but do not contain GMOs;
- have a new or intentionally modified primary molecular structure;
- consist of or are isolated from micro-organisms, fungi or algae;
- consist of or are isolated from plants and from animals, except those obtained by traditional propagating or breeding and which have a history of safe food use;[32] and
- those to which has been applied a production process not currently used when this gives rise to significant changes in the composition or structure affecting their nutritional value, metabolism or level of undesirable substances.

The first two categories have now been removed from the scope of Regulation 258/97 by Regulation 1829/2003 on GM food and feed.[33] Of importance is also the fact that Article 2 of Regulation 258/97 excludes from its scope three categories of products covered by other specific Community legislation – that is: food additives,[34] flavourings[35] and extraction solvents,[36] provided that the safety level under the specific legislation 'corresponds to the safety level' of this regulation.[37]

It is also important to note that, by virtue of Council Directives 2002/53/EC[38] and 2002/55/EC,[39] certain *plant varieties* are accepted on the common catalogue of varieties of agricultural products or for the production or marketing of *vegetable seed* within the Community, only if the food or food ingredient derived from them meet the risk assessment requirements and have already been authorized pursuant to Regulation 258/97.

Recitals 1 and 2 of the preamble to the regulation clarify that it has two broad objectives: first, to harmonize the national laws in this area that hinder free movement of goods in the Community and, second, to protect public health. Thus, paragraph 1 of Article 3 provides that food and food ingredients 'must not present a danger for the consumer', and paragraph 2 requires that any placing on the market should be done in conformity with the procedures and the criteria laid down in the regulation. The regulation has, however, two more specific objectives: to avoid misleading and not to nutritionally disadvantage the consumers.[40] The means employed to achieve these two specific objectives are: first, a single safety assessment and harmonization of the authorization or notification procedure at Community level before placing them on the market; and, second, imposing appropriate labelling requirements.

Authorization procedure

The regulation establishes a dual system for placing novel foods and novel food ingredients on the Community market: *application* to obtain an authorization or a simple *notification* by the interested party.

The authorization procedure follows a structure similar to the one described above for Directive 2001/18. The applicant – that is, the person responsible for placing the novel food or food ingredient on the Community market – must submit a request to the competent authority of the member state in which the product is to be placed on the market for the first time, and must forward a copy of it to the European Commission. Articles 4(2) and 4(4) and Article 6 of the regulation lay down the information and data that the applicant has to submit to the competent authority with its request.[41]

The member state where the application is submitted will either carry out the initial assessment itself or request the commission to arrange for another member state to carry it out.[42] The member state where the initial request was made will inform the applicant that he may place the product on the market where no assessment additional to the initial one is required, and that no reasoned objection by any member state or the commission has been presented with regard to its application.[43] If the initial assessment report indicates that an assessment additional to the initial one is required or that a reasoned objection has been raise by a member state or the commission, the authorization decision will be taken at Community level by comitology procedure in accordance with Article 13 of the regulation.[44] The authorization decision must indicate, as appropriate, the conditions of use, the designation of the product and any specific labelling requirements.

Article 11 of the regulation, as modified by Article 62(1) of Regulation 178/2002, provides that the European Food Safety Authority (EFSA) shall be consulted for 'any matter falling within the scope of this regulation likely to have an effect on public health', including, presumably, any comment or reasoned objection that relates to public health made by a member state or the commission in accordance with this regulation. Conversely, for any comment or objection that does not relate to public health, but to issues such as the presentation or the labelling of the food or food ingredient or to ethical considerations,[45] the EFSA is not consulted. Such comments or objections are reported directly to the Standing Committee on the Food Chain and Animal Health and are decided in accordance with the applicable comitology procedure.

Regulation 258/97 has two specific regulatory features: the concept of substantial equivalence and the specific labelling requirements. They are examined briefly below since they are crucial in evaluating the regulation and its interaction with the other relevant provisions of Community law – in particular, the WTO agreements.[46]

Substantial equivalence

According to Article 3(4) of Regulation 258/97, a novel food or food ingredient that is substantially equivalent to an existing (conventional) counterpart can be placed on the market without having to follow the full evaluation and authorization procedures of the regulation, as these have been described above. The product may be put on the market by the applicant simply *notifying* the European Commission of his decision to do so, provided, of course, that the other conditions of the regulation are fulfilled.[47]

It is not Regulation 258/97 itself but the Commission's Recommendation 97/618 that attempts to clarify the content and the important regulatory implications flowing from the use of the concept of substantial equivalence. In essence, it means that if a novel food or food component is found to be (in part, or as a whole) substantially equivalent to an existing food or food component, it can be treated in the same manner as the existing (conventional) food with respect to safety, keeping in mind that the establishment of substantial equivalence is not a safety or nutritional assessment in itself, but an approach to compare a potential new food with its conventional counterpart. The regulation uses, therefore, the concept of substantial equivalence as a short cut to a full authorization procedure for certain types of novel foods or food ingredients without requiring a standard safety assessment.[48]

Substantial equivalence is decided either on the basis of 'scientific evidence available and generally recognized', or on the basis of an opinion delivered by one of the food assessment bodies of the member state that is responsible for preparing the initial assessment report referred to in Article 6(2) of the regulation. According to Article 3(4),[49] substantial equivalence for the purpose of marketing a novel product is decided by reference to the composition, nutritional value, metabolism, intended use and the level of undesirable substances contained in the novel food or food ingredients in question. However, as A. G. Alber has pointed out in his opinion in the *Monsanto* case,[50] the above criteria, relating essentially to the nutritional physiology of the products, are not in themselves adequate in demonstrating equivalence in terms of no risk to human health. In addition, there is considerable leeway in the interpretation of this concept and of those other concepts upon which it is based, such as 'generally recognized' scientific evidence. This has led to a considerable amount of criticism being levied against it and was viewed to be inherently anti-scientific because it was thought to provide an excuse for not requiring, *inter alia*, complete toxicological tests. The Court of Justice in the *Monsanto* case accepted that the mere presence in novel foods of residues of transgenic protein at certain levels does not preclude those foods from being considered substantially equivalent to existing foods; consequently, the court considered that Directive 90/220 is allowed to use the simplified procedure for the purpose of placing those novel foods on the market.[51] However, the court made it clear that since the protection of public health is a fundamental objective of Regulation 258/97, the concept of substantial equivalence cannot be interpreted in such a way that the simplified procedure (which according to the wording of the first subparagraph of Article 3(4) of the regulation is in the nature of a derogation) amounts to a relaxation of the safety requirements that must be met by novel foods.[52] This signifies that it is not possible to use the simplified procedure in the case where the existence of a risk of potentially dangerous effects on human health can be identified on the basis of the scientific knowledge available at the time of the initial assessment. The court also found that the precautionary principle should be taken into account.[53]

The court's decision in the *Monsanto* case also requires that the identification of a risk should normally be carried out 'by specialized scientific bodies charged with assessing the risks inherent in novel foods'.[54] It is also significant to note that the court ruled that unpredictable effects on human health, which the insertion of foreign genes may produce, if such effects were identifiable as a danger to human health according to available scientific evidence at the time of the initial examination by the competent body, would have to be subjected to a risk assessment and a finding of substantial equivalence would therefore be excluded.[55] The crucial question, therefore, is to decide whether the 'available scientific evidence' at the time of the initial evaluation by the national risk assessment authority indicates possible adverse effects. The judgement of the court on this point appears to be open to a broad interpretation, as any available scientific evidence – and not only that generated for the initial risk assessment – may be relied upon for such a finding.[56]

It should be noted, however, that from the regulatory point of view, the above uncertainty in the finding of substantial equivalence has now been considerably reduced in the area of GM food and feed by Article 38(2) of Regulation 1829/2003, which amended Article 3(4) of Regulation 258/97 and confined the application of the concept of substantial equivalence to only two categories of novel food or food ingredients – that is those consisting of or isolated from micro-organisms, fungi or algae;[57] and those consisting of or isolated from plants and food ingredients isolated from animals.[58] Furthermore, the possible use of the concept of substantial equivalence as a regulatory tool in the area of GM novel foods has been further reduced by the deletion of Article 9 of the regulation, so that now the full risk assessment requirements of Directive 2001/18 will be applicable.[59]

Labelling

According to Article 6(1) of the regulation, an application for authorization must contain an appropriate proposal for the presentation and labelling of the novel food or food ingredient. Article 8 of the regulation imposes, in addition to requirements from other Community legislation concerning labelling of foodstuffs,[60] specific labelling requirements 'in order to ensure that the final consumer is informed' of the characteristics or food property that render a novel food or food ingredient 'no longer equivalent' to an existing food or food ingredient, such as the composition, nutritional value or nutritional effects and intended use of food. Consequently, when a novel food or food ingredient is found to be 'no longer equivalent',[61] the labelling must indicate 'the characteristics or properties modified, together with the method by which that characteristic or property was obtained'. It should be noted that the modified characteristics or properties of the novel food, as well as the process or production method used to obtain them, which must also be indicated on the label, play a central role in determining substantial equivalence.

Specific labelling is also required in two additional instances: first, when the novel food contains material that is not present in an existing equivalent foodstuff and that 'may have implications for the health of certain sections of the population'; and, second, when the presence of such material 'gives rise to ethical concerns'. These specific labelling obligations apply to all novel food and food ingredients, whether subject to the authorization or notification procedure, when they are found to be substantially equivalent.

Therefore, the specific labelling requirements of Regulation 258/97 play a dual role: first, to inform the consumer about *the presence* in the novel food or food ingredients of certain characteristics or properties, such as the presence of protein and/or DNA resulting from genetic modification, that may be important for the consumer to know or may have ethical concerns; and, second, to warn the consumers directly about possible health implications (e.g. allergenicity).

Appropriate level of protection

Like Directive 2001/18, it is evident from a combined reading of several provisions of Regulation 258/97 that it pursues a level of protection of 'no health risk'. Regulation 258/97 also pursues a 'no risk' policy of misleading the consumer, subject, of course, to the tolerance levels for an adventitious or technically unavoidable presence to be explained.[62] As the Court of Justice held in the *Monsanto* case, the objectives pursued by the regulation should enable the member states 'to avoid novel foods which pose potential risks to human health being offered on the market', and the level of protection implied is that only products that are 'without any danger for the consumer' should be authorized.[63] The safety of the novel food and food ingredients must be established by the applicant.[64] The applicant must also provide additional specific labelling to ensure that consumers are 'adequately' informed.[65]

Genetically modified food and feed: Regulation (EC) 1829/2003

General

Regulation 1829/2003 is the other central piece of Community legislation in the GMO area. Unlike Directive 2001/18, however, the adoption of Regulation 1829/2003 took, in total, just about two years, a remarkable achievement considering the scope and importance of its regulatory content.

Object and scope

Regulation 1829/2003 has two broad objectives: first, to ensure a high level of protection of human life and health, animal health and welfare, and environmental and consumer interests in relation to genetically modified food and feed; and, second, to ensure the effective functioning of the internal market. To achieve these objectives, the regulation provides for:

- Community procedures for the authorization and supervision of genetically modified food and feed; and
- specific provisions for the labelling of genetically modified food and feed.

The scope of the regulation is also quite broad. Recital 11 of the preamble to the regulation and Articles 3 and 4(4) explain the scope of the regulation. An authorization under the regulation may be granted either to a GMO to be used as a source material for the production of food or feed, and in products for food and/or feed use that contain, consist of or are produced from it, or to foods or feed produced from a GMO. Thus, where a GMO used in the production of food and/or feed has been authorized under this regulation, foods and/or feed containing, consisting of or produced from that GMO will not need an authorization under this regulation, but will be subject to the requirements referred to in the authorization granted with regard to the GMO in question. Furthermore, foods covered by an authorization granted under this regulation will be exempted from the requirements of Regulation 258/97 concerning novel foods and novel food ingredients.[66] In addition, recital 16 of the preamble to the regulation explains that it covers food and feed produced 'from' a GMO, but not food and feed produced 'with' a GMO. The determining criterion is whether material derived from the genetically modified source is present in the food or feed.

The scope of the regulation also extends to certain other food and feed products – that is, additives, flavourings, animal nutrition and additives in feeding stuffs for the purpose of safety assessment.[67]

Authorization procedure

The regulation establishes an advance system of prior notification and approval procedure that is the same for GM food and feed. While the application to obtain the authorization is submitted to the national competent authority of a member state, in the end, the authorization is granted by the European Commission and it is valid for ten (renewable) years throughout the Community.[68] Thus, the regulation lays down clear rules for the assessment and authorization of GMOs and GM food; but responsibilities are shared between member states and the Community. The regulation establishes a 'one door, one key' procedure for the scientific assessment and authorization of GMOs and GM food and feed, resulting in a centralized, clear and transparent Community procedure, where an operator is able to file a single application. Therefore, compared to the authorization procedure of Directive 2001/18 and of Regulation 258/97, the procedure under this regulation is far more streamlined and less cumbersome than before for the applicants.

Articles 5 for food and 17 for feed of Regulation 1829/2003 lay down the information, data and other particulars that the applicant has to submit in order to obtain the authorization.[69] The data should demonstrate that the food or feed does not have adverse effects on human health or animal health or the environment, does not mislead the consumer, and does not differ from the food that it is intended to replace to such an extent that its normal consumption would be nutritionally disadvantageous for the consumer.[70] The applicant must also provide, *inter alia*, the following: a designation of the food or feed and its specification, including the transformation event(s) used;[71] a detailed description of the method of production and manufacturing of the product; a proposal for labelling or evidence that the characteristics of the food or feed are not different from those of its conventional counterparts; a reasoned statement that the food or feed does not give rise to ethical or religious concerns; and methods for detection, sampling and identification of the transformation event (including, when applicable, food or feed produced *from* the GMO food or feed).[72]

The assessment of the application – including, where necessary, a risk assessment – is carried out by the EFSA, if possible within six months; but it *may* ask the food assessment body of a member state to carry out the safety assessment or the environmental risk assessment.[73] The EFSA submits its opinion to the European Commission, the member states and the applicant, and renders it public, subject to observing the confidentiality requirements. The commission should prepare, within three months of receiving the opinion of the EFSA, a draft decision to be taken under the relevant comitology procedure.[74] The commission is entitled to 'take into account' the opinion of the EFSA, any 'other relevant provisions of Community law' and, most importantly, 'other legitimate factors relevant to the matter under consideration'.[75] Recital 32 of the preamble to Regulation 1829/2003 explains the significance of the phrase 'other legitimate factors relevant to the matter under consideration' as follows:

> *It is recognized that, in some cases, scientific risk assessment alone cannot provide all the information on which a risk management decision should be based, and that other legitimate factors relevant to the matter under consideration may be taken into account.*

Other legitimate factors, therefore, are broader factors which, although not directly related to the toxicological properties of the products in question, are relevant in the risk assessment and risk management decision-making. In this regard, it should be noted that Recital 19 to Regulation 178/2002 included as legitimate factors societal, economic, traditional, ethical and environmental factors and the feasibility of controls.

Of course, where the European Commission's draft is not in accordance with the opinion of the EFSA, the commission is required to provide 'an explanation for the differences'. Thus, it is clear that the risk assessment proposed in the opinion of the EFSA, to the extent that it has direct risk management implications, is not as such binding on the commission,[76] which is (with the Council) the responsible risk management authority within the constraints of the relevant comitology procedure.

An authorization may be modified, suspended or revoked on the basis of a prior opinion of the EFSA by a European Commission decision in accordance with the applicable comitology procedure (regulatory committee).[77] Any safeguard measures concerning products already authorized that are 'likely to constitute a serious risk to human health, animal health or the environment' shall be taken in accordance with the emergencies procedure laid down in Articles 53 and 54 of Regulation 178/2002.[78]

Labelling

The provisions on labelling are a very important component of Regulation 1829/2003 and have been the subject of considerable discussion in the Council and European Parliament and with several trade partners of the Community. Labelling is required for foods that are delivered to the final consumer or mass caterers in the Community, and that contain or consist of GMOs or are produced from or contain ingredients produced from GMOs.[79] The objective of labelling is threefold: to inform consumers and livestock farmers in order to enable them to make an informed choice; to warn certain sections of the population of possible health implications; and to identify the characteristics or property that may give rise to ethical or religious concerns.[80]

The regulation lays down different labelling requirements that must be applied irrespective of the detectability of DNA or protein resulting from the genetic modification in the final product. In this respect, the labelling requirements of this regulation go one significant step further than those of Regulation 258/97 on novel foods and food ingredients.

The process or production method of the GM food or feed is now a relevant factor that can alone justify labelling, whether for the purpose of informing the consumers in order to enable them to exercise their choice in the market place, to warn them of any possible health effects, or when it is associated with ethical or religious concerns.

However, no labelling is required for foods or feed that contain material in a proportion no higher than 0.9 per cent of the individual food ingredients (or of each feed) that it contains, provided, of course, that the responsible operator can demonstrate that the presence of such GM material is adventitious or technically unavoidable, and on condition that the operator has taken the appropriate steps to avoid their presence.[81]

Appropriate level of protection

According to Article 1(a), the regulation provides the basis for ensuring 'a high level of protection of human life and health, animal health and welfare, environment and consumer interests' in relation to GM food and feed. The remaining provisions of the regulation have, therefore, to be read in light of the above overall objectives. In addition, pursuant to Article 1, they have to be interpreted 'in accordance' with the general principles laid down in Regulation 178/2002 on food law, amongst which is the precautionary principle.

Thus, when granting an authorization, Articles 4(1) for food and 16(1) for feed clarify how high the level of protection is to be placed that the regulation aims to achieve: the GM food and feed 'must not have adverse effects' on human health, animal health or the environment. The EFSA, when conducting the risk assessment, must apply the environmental safety requirements of Directive 2001/18 in order to ensure that, in the case of GMOs or food containing or consisting of GMOs, 'all appropriate measures are taken to prevent' the adverse effects on human and animal health and the environment 'which might arise' from the deliberate release of GMOs.[82] Therefore, it follows from a combined reading of these provisions and the terminology used that there is *no level of risk* that is tolerable in the authorization procedure. Consequently, the level of protection set in the regulation is set as high as it can be – that is, *no risk* – when a risk has, of course, been identified in the risk assessment.

The inevitable consequence of this no risk standard in the authorization procedure is that emergency (safeguard) measures by the member states or the European Commission can be taken only when 'it is evident' that the authorized products 'are likely to constitute a serious risk' to human health, animal health or the environment.[83]

Article 47 of the regulation also lays down a transitional (three-year) measure for the adventitious or technically unavoidable presence of GM material in food or feed that is not higher than 0.5 per cent, but which has benefited from a favourable risk evaluation. Thus, this tolerance (threshold) level applies in food or feed that contain, consist of or are produced from GMOs, provided the operators are in a position to demonstrate that they have taken the appropriate steps to avoid the presence of such GM materials in the food or feed. Since this transitional tolerance level is limited to GMOs that have already received a favourable risk evaluation, it does not affect the no-risk level of protection, as explained above. It is an expression of the principle of reasonableness, and its introduction was only meant to facilitate the co-existence of various kinds of agricultural crops and intra-Community and international trade in such products.

The level of protection as applied to labelling, for the purpose of informing the consumers or for reasons of ethical concerns, is set equally high. Frequently, in the production of food, feed or seed, it is practically impossible to achieve products that are 100 per cent pure. Minute traces of GMOs in conventional food and feed could arise during cultivation, harvest, transport or processing. This is something that is not particular to GMOs. With this background, the regulation's objective is to ensure legal certainty and, hence, to establish certain thresholds of adventitious presence above which conventional food and feed have to be labelled as consisting of, or containing, or being produced from a GMO.

Thus, labelling is not required for adventitious presence, or for the presence of GMOs that is technically unavoidable up to a 0.9 per cent threshold for both food and feed.[84] This tolerance level, whose application is not provisional, is an expression of the principle of reasonableness rather than an attempt to lower the appropriate level of health or environmental protection.

It should be noted that Regulation 1829/2003 places clearly and squarely the burden on the applicant, who must be established in the Community, to demonstrate 'adequately and sufficiently' the safety of the GM food or feed that the applicant wishes to place on the market.[85]

Traceability and labelling of GMOs and GM product: Regulation (EC) 1830/2003

General

This regulation is a necessary complement to the two basic acts regulating GMOs and GM products in the Community. Although of horizontal nature, it is the instrument by which the objectives of Directive 2001/18 and of Regulation 1829/2003 can be achieved. It was proposed by the European Commission and was adopted by the Council and European Parliament at the same time as Regulation 1829/2003 on GM food and feed.

Object and scope

Paragraph 3 of the preamble and Article 1 of the regulation explain the specific objectives pursued by it:

- facilitate accurate labelling in order to give consumers the right of free and independent choice;
- monitor the effects on the environment, the ecosystems and human and animal health from harmful or hazardous GM products by enabling the adoption of appropriate measures, including, when necessary, the immediate withdrawal of products; and
- facilitate the smooth functioning of the internal market.

The preamble of the regulation also provides that its objectives have to be pursued in accordance with the precautionary principle.

The traceability and labelling requirements of the regulation apply to two categories of products:

1 products consisting of, or containing, GMOs' and
2 food and feed produced from GMOs.[86]

In both cases, the products must have been placed on the market in accordance with the other relevant Community legislation applicable to such GM food and feed.

The nature and scope of the traceability and labelling requirements

The transmission and holding of information that products contain or consist of GMOs, or are produced from GMOs, and of their unique identifiers (codes) at each stage of their placement on the market provide the basis for their appropriate traceability and labelling.[87] The information and codes may be used to access specific information on any specific GMO from the Community register and, thus, to facilitate identification, detection and monitoring in accordance with the provisions of Directive 2001/18/EC. The regulation thus facilitates a withdrawal from the market of food and feed that can be limited to a GMO, which, subsequent to its authorization, is found to pose a risk or its withdrawal is required for some other valid reason, thus respecting the principle of proportionality. The capacity, therefore, to take this kind of limited and targeted action should prove beneficial to farmers, traders and consumers when problems in specific cases arise.

The regulatory content and the structure of the regulation are simple. The traceability requirements consist of obliging operators, at the first stage of placing a product on the market, to ensure the transmission in writing (to the operator receiving the product):

● that it contains or consists of GMOs; and
● the unique identifier(s) assigned to those GMOs.[88]

The operators receiving that information are also obliged to ensure, at all the subsequent stages of placing that product on the market, that the information is transmitted in writing to the operators receiving the products. Similar traceability obligations apply when placing products produced *from* GMOs on the market. In such cases, the operators must transmit in writing to the operators receiving the product:

● an indication of each of the food ingredients that is produced *from* GMOs;
● an indication of each of the feed materials or additives that is produced *from* GMOs; and
● for both food and feed, if there is no list of ingredients, an indication that the product is produced *from* GMOs.

To ensure the transmission of such information and identifier(s), the operators are also obliged to have in place 'systems and procedures' to allow the holding of the information and the identification numbers for a period of five years from each transaction with regard to the operator by whom, and the operator to whom, the products have been marketed.[89] Thus, the objective is to ensure that throughout the whole chain of marketing of such GMO products, the information and the unique identifiers are passed from one stage on to the other and can thus be traced back at any moment in time.

The labelling requirements consist of placing on the operators the obligation to ensure that the following words appear on or in connection with the display of certain products: 'this product contains genetically modified organisms' or 'this product contains genetically modified (name of organism(s))'. The products that should bear this kind of labelling are:

- pre-packaged products consisting of or containing GMOs; and
- *non-pre*-packaged products sold to the final consumers.[90]

However, neither of the above traceability nor the labelling requirements apply to traces of GMOs found in products in a proportion no higher than the tolerance threshold of 0.9 per cent, or lower thresholds, established pursuant to Articles 21(2) and 21(3) of Directive 2001/18, or in other specific Community legislation, as amended by Article 7 of Regulation 1830/2003, provided that they are adventitious or technically unavoidable,[91] or to traces of materials consisting or containing GMOs in products, intended for direct use as food or feed or for processing, in a proportion no higher than the threshold established for those GM materials of 0.9 per cent or 0.5 per cent, in accordance with Articles 12, 24 and 47 of Regulation 1829/2003, provided that the traces of GMOs are adventitious or technically unavoidable.[92] Transmission and storage of information will reduce the need for sampling and testing of products. To facilitate a coordinated approach for inspection and control by the member states, the European Commission is developing a system for assigning unique identifiers to GMOs and a technical guidance on sampling and testing methods prior to the application of Regulation 1830/2003.[93]

Appropriate level of protection

Regulation 1830/2003 provides effective means of tracking the movement of GM products through the production and distribution chains. Traceability is designed to facilitate the monitoring of any effects of GMOs on the environment and to verify the accuracy of labelling claims. It may additionally enable products to be withdrawn from the market, in a targeted and proportionate way, if any unexpected adverse effects were to arise. Labelling of all foods produced from GMOs, irrespective of whether there is DNA or protein of GM origin in the final product, can also ensure the right of consumers to make a free choice in the marketplace.

Therefore, the level of protection this Regulation aims to achieve is directly and inextricably linked to the level of protection pursued by Directive 2001/18 and Regulation 1829/2003, the implementation of which it is clearly designed to facilitate. Thus, Article 1 of the Regulation explains that, while seeking to ensure the smooth functioning of the internal market, it also recognizes that the withdrawal of authorized GM products, which in appropriate cases may be total, is an appropriate risk management measure in the event that they are proven to be hazardous.

THE CO-EXISTENCE OF NATIONAL COMMUNITY LEGISLATION IN THE AREA OF ASSESSING AND MARKETING GMOS AND GM PRODUCTS

There are a number of other provisions of Community law, in addition to the four basic legislative acts discussed in the previous section, that relate to other aspects of GMOs and GM products in the Community. Moreover, their number and regulatory impact are growing constantly. This section discusses only the effects that the previously analysed legislative acts can have on the power of member states to regulate the same area in their territory. The analysis here is based essentially on the pre-emptive effect of harmonization measures on member state power by distinguishing, in particular, between the decentralized application of Community law and the residual state power in this area of risk regulation. The objective here is to identify some of the reasons that have been influencing the regulatory behaviour of the member states so far, and which, in turn, may have had some impact on the attitude of the Community institutions in the evaluation and authorization processes.

The degree of harmonization achieved by the Community legislation on GMOs and GM products and the scope of pre-emption on member state power

General

The rules applicable in Community law to selecting the appropriate legal basis allow the Community courts to subject the legal act, and any possible implementing measures, to a judicial review in order to decide whether the act is within the competence of the Community or the relevant Community institution, or within the power of the member states, and whether the correct procedure and voting majority have been followed.[94] The legal basis, therefore, together with the content of the legal act and the extent of its harmonization and regulatory effect, normally determine the division of powers between the Community and its member states in the area of GMO regulation. The discussion here will focus on Directive 2001/18; but the analysis will be equally applicable to Regulation 258/97 and Regulation 1830/2003 since they are all based on Article 95 EC, have a similar structure and achieve a degree of harmonization that is equivalent. Some specific references to Regulation 1829/2003 on GM food and feed will be made separately as this regulation is based on a wider list of treaty articles.[95]

Degree of harmonization and scope of pre-emption

As a general rule and in accordance with the EC Treaty principles of specific attribution of powers, the power that the Community enjoys under Article 95 EC is *a priori* not exclusive. The power it has is shared with the member states; but it has the potential to become exclusive when the specific field or activity is completely (or exhaustively) harmonized by the Community measure in question.[96] This is the so-called principle of pre-emption of national power because of occupation of the field. The more comprehensive the Community legislation is, the less power is left to the member states to take action in the same field. It is important, therefore, to examine, first, the terms of Directive 2001/18 in order to determine the degree of harmonization that it has achieved.[97]

It is very important to stress from the outset that Directive 2001/18, in view of its wording and regulatory content, can be considered to have achieved a level of harmonization that is nearly complete (or exhaustive) with regard to its specific objectives, as they have been explained above. Indeed, Article 1(1) provides that GMOs may only be deliberately released or placed on the market in conformity with Parts B or C of the directive. The notification and authorization procedures provide for a decision to be ultimately taken, granting or rejecting the application at Community level.[98] In addition, Article 22 provides that member states may not restrict or impede the placing on the market of GMOs that comply with the requirements of the directive.

The preliminary conclusion, therefore, is that the text of the Directive 2001/18 has achieved complete harmonization and that its provisions do not allow member states to take national action on grounds other than those laid down and under the conditions specified therein. However, before concluding on this point, it is important to examine in more detail what are the grounds and conditions specified in the directive under which member states may take implementing action. They essentially relate to the adoption of national safeguard measures and to the processing of applications for granting a marketing authorization of GMOs and GM products submitted to the national authorities.

Thus, Article 23 of Directive 2001/18 allows member states to take national safeguard measures and provisionally restrict or prohibit the use and/or sale of a GMO in their territory when they have 'detailed grounds' for considering that a GMO, which has received a consent, 'constitutes a risk to human health or the environment'.[99] The existence of a safeguard provision in the directive does not, however, signify that the degree of harmonization achieved is incomplete. In principle, the member states, when acting on the basis of the safeguard provision, will be acting within the harmonized confines of that provision.

With regard to marketing authorizations, several other provisions in the directive allow the member states to 'make comments' or raise 'reasoned objections' during the evaluation and authorization procedure.[100] But the directive does not define what the meaning of these terms or their scope is. It appears, however, from the text of Article 18(1) of Directive 2001/18, read in conjunction with Article 28(1), that these 'comments' or 'objections', when they relate to risk on human health or the environment, must be submitted first to the relevant scientific committee advising the European Commission. Its opinion is then taken into account in the authorization procedure, in accordance with the relevant comitology procedure. It also appears, from an *a contrario* interpretation of the text in Article 18(1) of the directive, that 'comments' or 'objections' of other nature and scope may be raised by the member states, which are not necessarily of a nature relating strictly to human or environmental risk. Such other 'comments' or 'objections' are decided by applying the relevant comitology procedure, in accordance with Article 30(2) of the directive.

The first point to underline, therefore, with regard to the application of safeguard measures as well as to the resolution of objections raised by the member states in the authorization process, is that the system laid down by Directive 2001/18 requires that any kind of difference or objection, in the appreciation of the scientific information among the member states and between one or more of the member states and the European Commission, regarding risks to human health or to the environment, should be submitted to the relevant scientific committees advising the Commission. But it is equally important to stress that the mechanism for the resolution of eventual different or diverging scientific opinions between the various national scientific committees and those advising the Commission in this area does *not* necessarily require a unique, harmonized scientific outcome in all cases because the scientific opinion of the EFSA in this area has no formal overriding effect on the opinions of the corresponding national scientific committees.

Indeed, Articles 28 to 30 of Council Regulation 178/2002, which are now applicable in case of divergent scientific opinions in the area of GMOs evaluation, oblige any national and/or European Commission bodies and committees, whose scientific views on a specific substance or product diverge, to cooperate 'with a view to either resolving the divergence or preparing a joint document clarifying the contentious scientific issues and identifying the relevant uncertainties in the data'. But the subsequent opinion of the relevant scientific committee of the EFSA, including the joint document referred to above, is only advisory for the European Commission and the Council.[101] The resolution of any remaining scientific differences in the scientific assessment of the GMOs and GM products between a member state and the European Commission (or another member state) will, therefore, have to be sought, ultimately, not at the risk assessment phase, but in the politically accountable risk management phase at Community level by applying the relevant comitology procedure.[102]

This analysis inevitably raises the question of whether the member states are entitled, in their risk management decision on specific applications for marketing authorization, to individually pursue a level of health or environmental protection higher than that contained in the European Commission's proposal or when having to decide on a Commission proposal in the Council. The answer to this question needs to be viewed first in the light of Article 95 EC, the legal basis of the Directive 2001/18, but also of Article 37 EC, which is one of the legal bases of Regulation 1829/2003 on GM food and feed.

The Amsterdam Treaty, which amended the text of Article 100(a) EC, entered into force on 1 May 1999. Interestingly, Article 95 EC allows the member states, under the conditions specified in paragraphs 4, 5 and 6 thereof, to choose a level of protection higher than that deemed appropriate in a Community harmonization measure, such as Directive 2001/18 in this case. But Article 95 EC now makes a distinction in the national measures according to whether the provisions notified are national provisions already in place *prior* to Community harmonization or *new* national provisions which a member state *now* seeks to introduce.[103] In the former case, under Article 95(4) EC, the maintenance of existing national provisions must be justified on grounds of the major needs referred to in Article 30 EC or relating to the protection of the environment or the working environment.

The introduction of *new* national provisions under Article 95(5) EC, however, must be based on new scientific evidence relating to the protection of the environment or the working environment on grounds of a problem specific to that member state, arising *after* the adoption of the Community harmonization measure.[104] Thus, not all the requirements referred to in Article 30 EC can be taken into account when examining new national measures, in the application of Directive 2001/18.[105] This is because the legal rules laid down by the Amsterdam Treaty amendments in Article 95 now differ from those that were laid down in the former Article 100(a) of the EC Treaty, on which Directive 90/220, the predecessor of Directive 2001/18, was based.

However, Directive 2001/18 repealed Directive 90/220 as from 17 October 2002. According to Article 35 of Directive 2001/18, notifications concerning placing GMOs on the market as, or in, products received pursuant to Directive 90/220, and in respect of which the procedures of that directive had not been completed by 17 October 2002, shall be subject to the provisions of Directive 2001/18.[106] These transitional provisions are important because some of the applications for placing GMOs on the market were submitted under Directive 90/220/EEC before the date of entry into force of the Amsterdam Treaty; but the evaluation or the final decision on the application for authorization for some of them was completed only after the Amsterdam Treaty's entry into force.[107] In addition, in some other cases, the evaluation of the application has still not been completed.[108]

As already explained, Regulation 1829/2003 on GM food and feed is not based only on Article 95 EC, but also on Articles 37 and 152(4)(b) of the EC Treaty. Therefore, the possibility for the member states to also invoke the grounds mentioned in Article 30 EC or other mandatory requirements is, at least with regard to this regulation, potentially open. As a rule, Article 30 EC allows the maintenance of national restrictions on the free movement of goods, justified, *inter alia*, on grounds of public morality, public policy, or the protection of the health and life of humans, animals or plants or the environment, which constitute mandatory requirements recognized by Community law. However, it is established case law that recourse to Article 30 by a member state is no longer possible where a Community legal act harmonized the measures necessary to achieve the *specific* objective, which would be furthered by the member states' reliance upon Article 30 (that is, the so-called 'harmonizing away' of the member states' powers).[109]

It is also important in this connection to recall that in the *Toolex* case,[110] which involved the notification, classification, packaging and labelling of dangerous substances, the Court of Justice held that the power of the member states to invoke the exceptions laid down in Article 30 EC and the other defences based on mandatory requirements was *not* pre-empted by the relevant Community legislation applicable at the time.[111] The decisive test, according to the European Court of Justice (ECJ),[112] was to identify whether the Community act provided for the harmonization of the measures necessary to achieve the *specific* objective that would be furthered if the member state were allowed to rely, in its national measure, upon Article 30 EC. On the other hand, as explained above, the mere adoption of the Community rules does not automatically pre-empt national power if they are not yet, or cannot be, implemented effectively.[113] Regulation 1829/2003 on GM food and feed should be interpreted in the light of the above principles and case law. It allows, in the adoption of the risk management measure, taking into account the opinion of the EFSA, as well as 'any relevant provisions of Community law and other legitimate factors relevant to the matter under consideration'.[114] To be sure, a risk management decision based on 'other legitimate factors' will normally be decided at Community level by the European Commission in the context of the relevant comitology procedure or, in some cases, by the Council.

To sum up, therefore, primary Community law provisions in the area of common agricultural policy or the general harmonization provisions of the Amsterdam Treaty are, in principle, capable of conferring power on the Community that is or may become, over time, exclusive if the competence conferred has been exercised and the regulatory content of the adopted measure is complete and implemented effectively.[115] This seems to be the case with the four legal acts in the area of GMOs and GM products discussed here. Of course, any persisting disputes in this area will ultimately be decided by the Community courts in the light of the breadth of harmonization achieved and the degree of pre-emption operated by Directive 2001/18 and other Community legislation in this area.

Shared responsibility in implementing Community legislation in the area of GMOs and GM products

The above is admittedly a standard, formal way of analysing the scope and breadth of the harmonization pursued by Directive 2001/18. Although the legal basis is undoubtedly important in determining the institutional and decision-making procedures to be followed for adopting the Directive, it alone does not say much about the concrete nature of the economic activities that are likely to be affected by the adoption of the legal act, or of the attitude that the Community institutions and the member states are likely to adopt when actually implementing and applying it.

Another less formalistic and more sophisticated analysis would look closer into the structure (both horizontal and vertical) and the national regulatory discretion (both general and specific) that the directive can accommodate in the specific field.[116] This exercise must also be examined in the broader context of risk regulation in the Community. Such an analysis will not be properly understood if the specific nature of the Community's quasi-federal structure, in general, and risk governance, in particular, is not taken into account.

Directive 2001/18, like its predecessor Directive 90/220, established a regulatory system for the authorization of GMOs for deliberate release into the environment or for placing GMOs on the market whose structure is not very common in Community law. The authorization system that characterizes Directive 2001/18 is a *decentralized* system that consists of two phases – the national and the Community – the smooth functioning of which requires *close cooperation* between the national authorities and the European Commission.[117]

The application for a marketing authorization is submitted to a member state and the evaluation is, in principle, conducted and the authorization is granted by that member state. But the GMOs, once authorized to be placed on the market, may circulate in the territory of all the other member states. This result is achieved by means of an advanced, albeit quite complex, system in which all of the member states may potentially participate in the risk evaluation and risk management process and in the resolution of any dispute, whether of technical, scientific or regulatory nature, initially at national and, where necessary, Community level. This is the *new era* in the governance of risk regulation in the Community, which, according to Directive 2001/18, must, in addition, involve the direct consultation of the general public. The authorization procedure used in Regulation 1829/2003 on GM food and feed is still another more recent variant of this new approach because the marketing authorization can only be granted by the European Commission at Community level, even if the applications have to be submitted in the first place to the competent authorities of a member state. Therefore, to the extent that the Community legislative acts in this area have achieved complete harmonization, the member states still retain, in principle, implementing powers of administrative nature only in the *decentralized* enforcement system established by the Community measures.[118]

The issue of determining the breadth of harmonization and the pre-emptive effect on member state power seems to be much more broad and complex in the area of risk regulation, particularly under Directive 2001/18 and Regulation 1829/2003, than in other areas of Community law. This is because, as already explained, Article 95 allows member states to aim for a higher level of health or environmental protection and may adopt even new measures based on new scientific evidence relating to the protection of the environment or the working environment on grounds of a problem specific to that member state. Equally, Article 37 EC allows member states, in principle, to invoke the exceptions of Article 30 and other imperative reasons, as explained above. Moreover, the implementation of their responsibilities sometimes entails a certain margin of discretion for the member states, the exercising of which is not always possible to circumscribe neatly in advance. The broad point being made here, therefore, is that Community law in the area of GMO regulation has essentially given to the national risk assessment and risk management authorities, in the implementation of the rules, a role that sometimes is not simply 'executory' in nature. Instead, the design of their role is sometimes to involve them more actively and substantively in the *decentralized* implementation and application of the Community regulatory system. This is because the regulatory system in the area of GMOs touches upon supreme values, such as human health or the environment (and, more recently, animal health and welfare), which have traditionally been of immense importance in the governance of risk and the empowerment and legitimacy of politics at national and local level. The question that arises, therefore, is whether the traditional lenses of legal analysis are sufficient to capture the new dynamics that the regulation of GMOs has generated in our democratic system of risk governance. This issue is also intimately linked to the decision-making process, particularly the applicable comitology procedure, which is put in place to resolve different assessments and perceptions of risk and other ethical and legitimate factors between the member states and the Community institutions.

Conclusion on the division of powers and extent of pre-emption between the Community and its member states in the area of GMOs and GM products regulation

To sum up on this complex and quite delicate area of Community law, it seems possible, in theory at least, for the member states when adopting specific implementing measures to take into account broader concerns, pursuant to the specific grounds and the power that they have under Articles 37 and 95 EC, when these concerns are legitimate to the matter under consideration and necessary to achieve a level of protection in their territory that is higher than that pursued in the measure proposed by the Commission or the measure ultimately adopted by the Council. However, it is also true that the possibility of having recourse to such new national measures is, in reality, extremely limited in this area because of the very high level of protection of 'no risk' that is pursued by the Community legislation currently in place.

Furthermore, in areas where the level of harmonization under Directive 2001/18, Regulation 1829/2003 and Regulation 1830/2003 is not complete – for instance, with regard to the rules on ethical concerns or on the co-existence of conventional, organic and GM crops – the member states will continue to have the power to take national measures,[119] provided that the other conditions laid down in the EC Treaty are also respected.

CONCLUSIONS

Questions about the use of modern biotechnology in agriculture assume – in today's context of global markets – important socio-economic dimensions. The public's perception of risk, as well as theories about cultural, social and moral preferences all point to substantial differences in risk cognition and consumer reaction to risk between the member states and countries around the world. Different regulatory approaches about risk also reflect different national priorities about the economic importance of modern biotechnology, compared to other societal values and the ability of science to provide as clear answers as possible about potential harm from modern biotechnology.

The regulation of GMOs and GM products in the European Union has been shown to be a daunting task. Its complexity is further increased by the federal structure of risk governance applied in the Community's legal system. During the period of 1990 to 2003, the Community's policy on GMOs and GM products constantly evolved in an attempt to follow consumer reaction to possible harm from modern biotechnology and the rapid advances in scientific research. At the same time, it has also influenced, as much as tried to anticipate, international regulatory change.

Broadly speaking, the Community's policy in this area has been driven by three policy goals: first, to lay down a comprehensive, coherent, science-based and, at the same time, precautionary regulatory framework dealing with almost all aspects of placing GMOs and GM products on the market and their deliberate release into the environment; second, to respect free movement in the internal market while ensuring a very high level of health and environmental protection; and, third, to balance the interests of the biotechnology industry with those of the consumers, but above all to win the confidence of the latter in the Community regulatory process. With the recent adoption of Directive 2001/18 on the deliberate release of GMOs into the environment, and of Regulations 1829/2003 and 1830/2003 on GM food and feed and their traceability and labelling, respectively, the bones and most of the flesh of the Community's legislative framework are now in place.[120]

The success of its implementation and effective application, however, may very well depend upon a number of conditions, such as the ability of the responsible national and Community institutions to demonstrate to all stakeholders involved that excellence, independence and transparency are applied, especially in risk assessment, as well as in the risk management and communication phases, and that other legitimate factors that seem to be so dear to consumers today are properly taken into account in the authorization process.

NOTES

1 The author expresses his personal views only. This chapter is a substantially abridged and updated version of Christoforou, T. (2004) 'The regulation of GMOs in the EU: The interplay of science, law and politics', *Common Market Law Review*, vol 41, pp637–709. The author wishes to thank Professor Nicolas de Sadeleer for his precious help in the elaboration of this chapter.

2 Directive 2001/18/EC of the European Parliament and of the Council of 12 March 2001 on the deliberate release into the environment of genetically modified organisms, OJ L 106, 17 March 2001, p1, as last amended by Council Decision 2002/811/EC, OJ L 280, 18 October 2002, p27.

3 Regulation No 258/97 of the European Parliament and of the Council of 27 January 1997 concerning novel foods and novel food ingredients, OJ L 43, 14 February 1997, p1.

4 Regulation (EC) No 1829/2003 of the European Parliament and of the Council, of 22 September 2003 on genetically modified food and feed, OJ L No 268, 18 October 2003, p1.

5 Regulation (EC) No 1830/2003 of the European Parliament and of the Council of 22 September 2003, concerning the traceability and labelling of genetically modified organisms and the traceability of food and feed products produced from genetically modified organisms and amending Directive 2001/18/EC, OJ L No 268, 18 October 2003, p24.

6 The Cartagena Protocol on Biosafety was concluded, on behalf of the Community, by Council Decision 2002/628/EC, OJ L 201, 31 July 2002, p48, and its provisions were implemented mainly by Regulation (EC) No 1946/2003 of the European Parliament and of the Council of 15 July 2003, OJ L 287, 5 November 2003, p1.

7 Of those 18 products, only three were approved without objections being raised from the member states. For the other applications, where objections had been maintained, the European Commission followed the authorization procedures under Directive 90/220 and the comitology procedure (regulatory committee) provided therein.

8 More labelling provisions were subsequently introduced in 1996/1997 by a technical adaptation of Annex III to Directive 90/220/EEC.

9 Council Directive 90/220/EEC of 23 April 1990 on the deliberate release into the environment of genetically modified organisms, OJ No L 117, 8 May 1990, pp15–27.

10 Recitals 42 and 43, Articles 4(6), 19(3)(f) and 20, and Annex IV to Directive 2001/18.

11 Recital 46 and Article 24.

12 Recital 40, Article 13(2)(f), 19(3)(e), 21 and 26, and Annex IV (8).

13 Council Directive 2002/53/EC of 13 June 2002 on the common catalogue of varieties of agricultural plant species, OJ No L 193, 20 July 2002, p1. Articles 4 and 7(4)(a) and (b) of this directive provide that in case of the genetically modified varieties falling within its scope – that is, beet, fodder plant, cereal, potato and oil and fibre plant – there will be no deliberate release into the environment unless an environmental risk assessment has been carried out in accordance with Directive 2001/18. The variety shall be accepted 'only if all appropriate measures have been taken to avoid adverse effects on human health and the environment'. According to Article 16 of the directive, seed varieties accepted in accordance with its provisions would not be subject to any marketing restrictions in the Community.

14 Council Directive 2002/55/EC of 13 June 2002 on the marketing of vegetable seed, OJ No L 193, 20 July 2002, p33. This directive applies to the production (with a view to marketing) and to the marketing of vegetable seed within the Community. According to Articles 4(2) and 7(4) of the directive, the member states should not officially accept genetically modified varieties for certification, for verification as standard seed and for marketing unless an

environmental risk assessment has been carried out in accordance with Directive 2001/18. The variety shall be accepted 'only if all appropriate measures have been taken to avoid adverse effects on human health and the environment'. According to Article 16 of the directive, seed varieties accepted in accordance with its provisions would not be subject to any marketing restrictions in the Community.

15 The exceptions to its broad coverage are mentioned in Article 12 of Directive 2001/18, which places outside its scope products that are authorized by specific sectoral Community legislation on condition that requirements regarding risk assessment, risk management, labelling, monitoring, information to the public and safeguard clauses are 'at least equivalent' to that laid down in the directive.

16 See, for example, Recitals 18 and 24 of the preamble to Directive 2001/18.

17 Three supplementary Council decisions and one European Commission decision have been adopted to implement the directive, particularly with regard to the specific data and other requirements to be submitted in the notification procedure. They are Council Decision 2002/811/EC of 3 October 2002 supplementing Annex VII to the Directive, OJ L 280, 18 October 2002, p27; Council Decision 2002/812/EC of 3 October 2002 establishing the summary information format, L 280, 18 October 2002, p37; Council Decision 2002/813/EC of 3 October 2002 establishing the summary notification information format, OJ L 280, 18 October 2002, p62; and Commission Decision 2002/623/EC of 24 July 2002 establishing guidance notes supplementing Annex II to the Directive, OJ L 200, 30 July 2002, p22.

18 The difference between the two types of procedures is that the 'standard' is complemented by a 'differentiated' procedure in terms of the nature and extent of information to be supplied or the time periods to be respected in the evaluation and release of the GMOs for experimental purposes, which meet certain safety criteria where sufficient experience has been obtained from the releases of certain GMOs in certain ecosystems. See also Annex V to the directive. The evaluation of the GMOs in a differentiated procedure will be carried out under the 'simplified' procedure laid down by Commission Decision 94/730/EC, OJ L 292, 12 November 1994, p31.

19 Articles 15(1) and 15 (3) of Directive 2001/18.

20 Article 19 of Directive 2001/18.

21 OJ L 184, 17 July 1999, p23.

22 During the notification process, the public is also informed of, and has access to, publicly available data on the internet – for example, the summary notification format, the assessment reports of the competent authorities and the opinion of the scientific committees.

23 But this will also be important when examining the compatibility with the relevant provisions of the WTO agreements of the directive and any implementing measures taken by the Community institutions and/or the member states with regard to the applications for marketing authorizations submitted for specific products.

24 See, for example, Case T-13/99, *Pfizer* v *Council* (2002) ECR II-3305, para 151, and Case T-70/99, *Alpharma* v *Council* (2002) ECR II-3945, para 164. For an in-depth analysis of these two cases, see Chapter 2 in this volume.

25 For example, Articles 3(p), 95(3), 152(1), 153(1) and 174(2) of the EC Treaty.

26 For example, Articles 2(3), 4(1), 16(2) and 23(1) of Directive 2001/18.

27 For example, Article 13(2)(h) of Directive 2001/18.

28 For example, Article 13(2)(h) of Directive 2001/18, and Recital 43 of the preamble.

29 See Section A, Objectives of Council Decision 2002/811/EC of 3 October 2002 establishing guidance notes supplementing Annex VII to Directive 2001/18/EC of the European Parliament and of the Council on the deliberate release into the environment of genetically modified organisms and repealing Council Directive 90/220/EEC, OJ L 280, 18 October 2002, p27.

30 See European Commission, Communication on the Precautionary Principle, COM(2000) 1 final, 2 February 2000.

31 The terms 'foods' and 'food ingredients' are not defined in this Regulation, but in Article 2 of Regulation 178/2002 with regard to food (OJ No L 31, 1 February 2002, p1), and in Directive 2000/13 with regard to food ingredients (OJ No L 109, 6 March 2000, p29).

32 It should be noted that Section X of Part II of the European Commission's Recommendation 97/618/EC states, *inter alia*, that:

> *Documentation on previous use of the novel food source in the Community or the novel food source and/or the novel food in other parts of the world is important to establish a baseline for assessment. However, history of food use outside the Community is not of itself a guarantee that the novel food can be safely consumed in the Community.*

See Commission Recommendation 97/618/EC of 29 July 1997 concerning the scientific aspects and the presentation of information necessary to support applications for the placing on the market of novel foods and novel food ingredients and the preparation of initial assessment reports under Regulation (EC) No 258/97 of the European Parliament and of the Council, OJ No L253, 16 September 1997, pp1–36.

33 However, according to Article 1(2) of Regulation 258/97, new novel food or food ingredients may, where necessary, be added in the future to the scope of Regulation 258/97.

34 Council Directive 89/107/EEC of 21 December 1988 on the approximation of the laws of the member states concerning food additives authorized for use in foodstuffs intended for human consumption, OJ No L 40, 11 February 1989, p27, as last amended by Directive 94/34/EC, OJ No L 237, 10 September 1994, p1.

35 Council Directive 88/388/EEC of 22 June 1988 on the approximation of the laws of the member states relating to flavourings for use in foodstuffs and to source materials for their production, OJ No L 184, 15 July 1988, p61, as last amended by Directive 91/71/EEC, OJ No L 42, 15 February 1991, p25.

36 Council Directive 88/344/EEC of 13 June 1988 on the approximation of the laws of the member states on extraction solvents used in the production of foodstuffs and food ingredients, OJ No L 157, 24 June 1988, p28, as last amended by Directive 92/115/EEC, OJ No L 409, 31 December 1992, p31.

37 According to Article 2(3), the European Commission is charged with the task of ensuring the correspondence regarding the level of safety between the provisions of the different acts.

38 Council Directive 2002/53/EC of 13 June 2002 on the common catalogue of varieties of agricultural plant species, OJ No L 193, 20 July 2002, p1. Articles 4(5) and 7(5)(a) of this directive provide that genetically modified plant varieties falling within its scope – that is, beet, fodder plant, cereal, potato and oil and fibre plant – will not be accepted in the common catalogue unless the food or food ingredients derived from them meet the safety assessment requirements and have already been authorized pursuant to Regulation 258/97. According to Article 16 of the directive, seed varieties accepted in accordance with the provisions of this directive would not be subject to any marketing restrictions in the Community.

39 Council Directive 2002/55/EC of 13 June 2002 on the marketing of vegetable seed, OJ No L 193, 20 July 2002, p33. This directive applies to the production (with a view to marketing) and marketing of vegetable seed within the Community. According to Articles 4(3) and 7(5) of the directive, member states should not officially accept for certification, for verification as standard seed, and for marketing genetically modified varieties unless the food or food ingredients derived from them meet the safety assessment requirements and have already been authorized pursuant to Regulation 258/97. According to Article 16 of the directive, seed varieties accepted in accordance with the provisions of this directive would not be subject to any marketing restrictions in the Community.

40 The meaning of the term 'nutritionally disadvantageous' for consumers is not defined in the regulation; but presumably it means something other than dangerous or misleading for the consumer.

41 Pursuant to Article 4(4) of the regulation, the European Commission has, by Recommendation 97/618/EC of 29 July 1997, laid down the scientific aspects and the presentation of information necessary to support applications for the placing on the market of novel foods and novel food ingredients and the preparation of initial assessment reports, OJ L 253, 16 September 1997, p1.

42 Article 6(2) of Regulation 258/97.

43 Article 4(2) of Regulation 258/97.

44 Articles 6(3) and 6(4), 7 and 13, respectively, of Regulation 258/97.

45 Articles 6(4) and 8(1)(c) of Regulation 258/97.

46 It is important in relation to the concepts of 'like products' and the use of the so-called 'process and production method' in the regulation of products in international trade law.

47 Article 5 of Regulation 258/97. The European Commission is simply required to forward within 60 days to the member states a copy of the notification and, upon request, further details. There is no time limit within which objections, if any, may be raised by the commission or the member states. It should be noted that 13 of the novel food products approved so far under Regulation 258/97 concern processed foods and have all been notified as substantially equivalent. See European Commission, *Questions and Answers on the Regulation of GMOs in the EU*, MEMO/03/196, Brussels, 10 October 2003, *supra*.

48 Case C-236/01, *Monsanto Agricoltura Italia* (2003) ECR II-8105, paras 129 and 137.

49 As modified by Article 38(2) of Regulation 1829/2003 on GM food and feed.

50 See paras 63 to 73 of the Opinion of Advocate General Alber, of 13 March 2003, in Case C-236/01, *Monsanto, supra*.

51 See Case C-236/01, *Monsanto, supra*, para 84.

52 See Case C-236/01, *Monsanto, supra*, para 80.

53 See Case C-236/01, *Monsanto, supra*, para 133.

54 See Case C-236/01, *Monsanto, supra*, paras 78 to 79 and 84.

55 See Case C-236/01, *Monsanto, supra*, para 81.

56 This is particularly the case when national safeguard measures are adopted on the basis of Article 12 of the regulation since, in such cases, there is only a requirement to carry out as full a risk assessment as possible regarding the circumstances of the case in question, and to adopt a safeguard measure if the available evidence makes it possible to reasonably conclude that it may pose potential risks to human health. See the judgement of the Court of Justice in Case C-236/01, *Monsanto, supra*, paras 112 to 113.

57 Referred to in Article 1(2)(d) of the regulation.

58 Referred to in Article 1(2)(e) of the regulation.

59 Article 9 of the regulation is deleted by virtue of Article 38(1) of Regulation 1829/2003 on GM food and feed, and the risk assessment and labelling requirements for novel foods and food ingredients containing or consisting of a GMO are now regulated by the updated and stricter requirements of Regulation 1829/2003 and of Directive 2001/18.

60 See Directive 2000/13 of the European Parliament and of the Council of 20 May 2000 on the approximation of the laws of the member states relating to the labelling, presentation and advertising of foodstuffs, OJ L No 109, 6 May 2000, p29.

61 For the purpose of labelling, novel food or food ingredients shall be deemed, pursuant to Article 8 of Regulation 258/97, to be no longer equivalent 'if scientific assessment, based upon an appropriate analysis of existing data, can demonstrate that the characteristics assessed are different in comparison with a conventional food or food ingredient, having regard to the accepted limits of natural variations for such characteristics'. It should be noted

that it is not only the process or production method used but also the modified characteristics of the novel food that are used in determining substantial equivalence.

62 See Articles 3(1) and 12 of Regulation 258/97.

63 See Case C-236/01, *Monsanto, supra,* paras 113 and 133.

64 Recital 8 of the preamble to and Article 6(1) of Regulation 258/97.

65 Article 8 of Regulation 258/97.

66 Except where they fall under one or more of the categories referred to in Article 1(2)(a) of Regulation 258/97 regarding a characteristic that has not been considered for the purpose of the authorization granted under Regulation 1829/2003.

67 Thus, Recitals 12 to 15 of the preamble to Regulation 1829/2003 explain that food additives authorized under Directive 89/107/EEC (OJ L 40, 11 February 1989, p27, as amended by Directive 94/34/EC of the European Parliament and of the Council, OJ L 237, 10 September 1994, p1) fall under Regulation 1829/2003 if they contain, consist of or are produced from GMOs. Equally, *flavourings* for use in foodstuffs and to source materials falling under Directive 88/388/EEC (OJ L 184, 15 July 1988, p61, as amended by Commission Directive 91/71/EEC, OJ L 42, 15 February 1991, p25) that contain, consist of or are produced from GMOs should also fall within the scope of Regulation 1829/2003 for the safety assessment of the genetic modification. In addition, feed materials used in *animal nutrition* under Directive 82/471/EEC (OJ L 213, 21 July 1982, p8, as last amended by Directive 1999/20/EC, OJ L 80, 25 March 1999, p20) fall within the scope of Regulation 1829/2003 when they contain, consist of or are produced from GMOs using different technologies that may pose risk to human or animal health and the environment. Finally, *additives* in feeding stuffs to which the authorization procedure laid down in Directive 70/524/EEC applies (OJ L 270, 14 December 1970, p1, as last amended by Regulation (EC) No 1756/2002, OJ L 265, 3 October 2002, p1) also fall within the scope of Regulation 1829/2003 when they contain, consist of or are produced from GMOs.

68 Articles 5(2) and 7(5) for food and Articles 17(2) and 19(5) for feed of Regulation 1829/2003.

69 Where a product is likely to be used as both food and feed, a single application should be submitted and this should give rise to a single risk assessment and to a single European Commission authorization decision. See Article 27 of Regulation 1829/2003.

70 Article 5(3)(e) and Article 17(3)(e) of Regulation 1829/2003.

71 The term 'transformation event' denotes the event where a conventional organism is 'transformed' through the introduction of modified DNA sequences, resulting in the formation of a GMO.

72 As already explained, Regulation 1829/2003, unlike Regulation 258/97, no longer uses the concept of substantial equivalence as a short cut for authorization purposes.

73 Articles 6(3)(b) and (c) and 18(3)(b) and (c) of Regulation 1829/2003. The safety assessment will be carried out in accordance with Article 36 of Regulation 178/2002. The environmental risk assessment will be carried out pursuant to the relevant provisions of Directive 2001/18. However, when the application concerns GMOs to be used as *seeds* or other *plant-propagating material,* the EFSA *must* ask a national competent authority to carry out the environmental risk assessment.

74 See Articles 5 and 7 of Decision 1999/468/EC. See also Articles 7(3) and 19(3) of Regulation 1829/2003.

75 Articles 6(6) and 7(1) for food and Articles 18(6) and 19(1) for feed of Regulation 1829/2003.

76 The non-binding nature of the opinions of the scientific committees has been decided several times by the Court of Justice and Court of First Instance in other comparable areas of Community law. See, for example, Case C-120/97, *Upjohn* (1999) ECR I-223, para 47, and

Case C-405/92, *Armand Mondiet* (1993) ECR I-6133, paras 31 to 32 and 36 (both judgments hold the opinion that the scientific committee is not of a mandatory but of an advisory nature only); see also Case T-13/99, *Pfizer* (2002) ECR II-3305, paras 196 and 201 (which holds that the European Commission is not obliged to follow the opinion of the scientific committee because its opinion is of an advisory nature only, and that scientific legitimacy is not a sufficient basis for the exercise of public authority in the regulation of risk).

77   Articles 10 and 22 of Regulation 1829/2003. With regard to GM products currently authorized, Articles 8 and 20 of the regulation provide that they will remain eligible for marketing.

78   Article 34 of Regulation 1829/2003.

79   Article 12(1) of Regulation 1829/2003. It also applies to feed, as defined in Article 15(1) and in accordance with the provisions of Articles 24 to 25 of Regulation 1829/2003.

80   See, in particular, Recitals 20 to 22 of the preamble to the regulation.

81   Articles 12(2) and 12(3) for food and Articles 24(2) and 24(3) for feed of Regulation 1829/2003.

82   Articles 6(4) and 18(4) of Regulation 1829/2003.

83   Article 34 of Regulation 1829/2003. The use of the adjective 'serious' in relation to 'risk' is notable; this does not appear in the section of the regulation concerning the authorization phase. Since the emergency measures are posterior to authorization and must be adopted under the provisions of Articles 53 and 54 of Regulation 178/2002, interim protective measures can be adopted provisionally by the European Commission or a member state subject to their extension, amendment or abrogation by subsequent decision at Community level, in accordance with the applicable comitology procedure.

84   Articles 12(2) and 24(2) for food and feed, respectively, of Regulation 1829/2003. See, in particular, Recital 24 of the preamble to Regulation 1829/2003, which explains the rationale of this tolerance (threshold) level. Therefore, this 0.9 per cent tolerance level applies only to food and feed, which contains, consists of or is produced from GMOs that have already been authorized in the Community. It is obvious that the tolerance thresholds of 0.9 and 0.5 per cent cannot be cumulated because the first applies only to labelling, while the second applies only for the purpose of obtaining the marketing authorization. Before the adoption of Regulation 1829/2003, the tolerance level had been set at 1 per cent of the food ingredients by Commission Regulation 49/2000, which had amended Article 2(b) of Council Regulation 1139/98. But both of these latter regulations have now been repealed by Regulation 1829/2003 on GM food and feed.

85   See Articles 4(3), 5(3)(e), 8(6), 9(3) and 12(3) for food, and Articles 16(3), 17(3)(e), 20(6), 21(3) and 24(3) for feed of Regulation 1829/2003.

86   See Article 2 of Regulation 1830/2003, except with regard to medicinal products for human or veterinary use falling under Regulation 2309/93.

87   See Article 3(4) of Regulation 1830/2003. See also Commission Regulation (EC) No 65/2004 of 14 January 2004, establishing a system for the development and assignment of unique identifiers for genetically modified organisms, OJ L 10, 16 January 2004, p5.

88   Article 4(1) of Regulation 1830/2003.

89   Articles 4(4) and 5(2) of Regulation 1830/2003. However, pursuant to Article 6(1) of the regulation, operators are not obliged to hold this information and the identifiers when other Community legislation provides that this information and the lot numbers are clearly marked on the package – for example, in case of pre-packaged products.

90   Article 4(6) of Regulation 1830/2003.

91   Articles 4(7) and 7(2) of Regulation 1830/2003.

92   Article 4(8) of Regulation 1830/2003.

93   Articles 8 and 9 of Regulation 1830/2003.

94   Case C-300/89, *Commission* v *Council* (1991) ECR I-2867.

95 Regulation 1829/2003 is based on Articles 37, 95 and 152(4)(b) of the treaty. Equally, Regulation 187/2002 laying down the general principles and requirements of food law, to the extent that it is made applicable by reference to the acts discussed here, is also based on Articles 37, 95, 133 and 152(4)(b) of the EC Treaty.

96 See, for example, Case 218/85, *CERAFEL* v *Albert le Campion* (1986) ECR 3513, para 16; Case 255/86, *Commission* v *Belgium* (1988) ECR 693, para 10.

97 Since the placing of GMOs and GM products on the market also covers imports into the Community, the directive and the other regulations also regulate trade with third countries. In the external trade relations field, the principle of pre-emption operates through the so-called ERTA doctrine. See Case 22/70, *Commission* v *Council (ERTA)* (1971) ECR 263, paras 17 to 19 of the judgement. See also Opinion 2/91, *ILO Convention* (1993) ECR I-1061, and Opinion 1/94, *WTO Agreements* (1994) ECR I-5267.

98 See, for example, Case C-6/99, *Association Greenpeace France and Others* v *Ministère de l'Agriculture et de la Pêche and Others* (2000) ECR I-1651, paras 28 and 47 (which holds that a member state is obliged to issue its consent when no objection has been raised on an application or when an application to place a GMO on the market has received the favourable opinion at Community level). This case concerned the interpretation of Directive 90/220/EEC.

99 See, for example, Case C-236/01, *Monsanto, supra* (concerning an Italian safeguard measure taken under Article 12 of Regulation 258/97).

100 See, for example, Articles 7(4), 15, 17 and 20 of Directive 2001/18.

101 See, by analogy, C-120/97, *Upjohn* (1999) ECR I-223, para 47; and Case T-13/99, *Pfizer* v *Council, supra,* para 196.

102 See Articles 5 and 7 and Article 8 of Council Decision 1999/468/EC of 28 June 1999, laying down the procedures for the exercise of implementing powers conferred on the Commission, OJ No L 184, 17 July 1999, p23.

103 For a general discussion of national measures based on Article 95 of the EC Treaty, see de Sadeleer, N. (2003) 'Procedures for derogations from the principle of approximation of laws under Article 95', *Common Market Law Review,* vol 40, pp889–915.

104 With regard to the ban on the use of GMOs in the region of Upper Austria on the grounds that they constitute a specific risk to regional biodiversity and small-scale farming, see Cases C-492/03 and T-235/04, *Austria* v *Commission,* and T-366/03, *Land Oberösterreich* v *Commission,* paras 64 to 69, where the Court of First Instance of the European Community (CFI) rejected Austria's claim because it did not succeed in demonstrating the specificity of the risk at issue.

105 See Case C-512/99, *Germany* v *Commission* (2003) ECR I-845, paras 40 to 41.

106 This transitional provision reflects established case law according to which new rules apply immediately to the future effects of a situation that arose under the old rules. Indeed, as long as no final decision – through either approval or rejection – was taken under Directive 90/220 for the pending applications, no new legal situation affecting these applications can be said to have been established in the meantime; hence, they have been correctly submitted to the new legal regime established by Directive 2001/18. See, for example, Case C-1/00, *Commission* v *France* (2001) ECR I-9989, paras 45 to 46.

107 Article 35(2) of Directive 2001/18 provided to notifiers of pending applications during a period up to 17 January 2003 to supplement and update them in accordance with the new requirements of the directive.

108 The continued handling of the pending applications is commonly referred to as *de facto moratorium* in the authorization of GMOs in the Community. This characterization, however, does not seem to be appropriate. Some of the legal issues raised by the continued handling of the applications for some GMOs and GM products are discussed in Christoforou, T. (2004) 'The regulation of GMOs in the EU: The interplay of science, law and politics', *Common Market Law Review,* vol 41, pp689–695.

109 See, in particular, Case C-1/96, *The Queen* v *Minister of Agriculture, Fisheries and Food, ex parte Compassion in World Farming Ltd* (1998) ECR I-1251, para 47; Case C-5/94, *The Queen* v *MAFF ex parte Hedley Lomas* (1996) ECR I-2553, para 18.

110 Case C-473/98, *Kemikalieinspektionen* v *Toolex Alpha AB* (2000) ECR I-5681. See also the developments in Chapters 2 and 16 of this volume.

111 See Case C-473/98, *Toolex, supra,* paras 34 to 49.

112 See Case C-473/98, *Toolex,* paras 25 to 33, and Case C-1/96, *The Queen* v *Minister of Agriculture, Fisheries and Food, ex parte Compassion in World Farming Ltd,* paras 47 and 64 to 69.

113 See, for example, Case C-1/00, *Commission* v *France, supra,* paras 115 and 124.

114 See Article 7(1) of the proposal.

115 See, for example, Case C-1/00, *Commission* v *France, supra,* para 124, and the Opinion of Advocate General Mischo of 20 September 2001, paras 133 and 168 to 169.

116 For an analysis of the European Commission's proposals in the area of GMOs and GM food and feed, see Scott, J. (2003) 'European regulation of GMOs and the WTO', *Columbia Journal of European Law,* vol 9, pp213–239.

117 See, for example, Case C-6/99, *Association Greenpeace France, supra,* para 33, where the Court of Justice qualified as 'close cooperation' the involvement of both the European Commission and the competent national authority in the authorization procedure under Directive 90/220/EC. See also para 132 of the judgement of the court in Case C-236/01, *Monsanto, supra,* with regard to the authorization procedure under Regulation 258/97.

118 See Case C-6/99, *Association Greenpeace France, supra,* para 54.

119 See, for example, Article 43(2) of Regulation 1829/2003 on GM food and feed, amending Article 26(a) of Directive 2001/18 by introducing measures to avoid the unintended presence of GMOs (the so-called 'co-existence' problem). See also Commission Recommendation 2003/556 of 23 July 2003.

120 Some member states, however, seem to require the adoption at Community level of binding rules on the co-existence of GM crops with conventional and organic farming, and specific rules on strict liability for environmental damage. So far, the harmonization achieved is incomplete. See Commission Recommendation 2003/556/EC, *supra.*

CHAPTER 13

Genetically Modified Organisms and Precaution in Norwegian Law

Ole Kristian Fauchald

INTRODUCTION

The precautionary principle has, together with requirements concerning sustainable development and usefulness to society, been a core element in the regulation of deliberate release of genetically modified organisms (GMOs) in Norway. The Norwegian legislation on GMOs was adopted in 1993 (the Act relating to the Production and Use of Genetically Modified Organisms, Act No 38 of 1993, hereafter the GMO Act) and has essentially remained unchanged since it was adopted. However, the link established in 1992 between Norway and the European Union (EU) through the Agreement on the European Economic Area (EEA Agreement) means that, to a large extent, the framework within which the legislation has been applied has been dominated by issues concerning the relationship between the criteria set out in the GMO Act and the legislation adopted by the EU.

Despite the close relationship between Norway and the EU through the EEA Agreement, which, *inter alia*, means that Norway is part of the internal market for trade in goods, Norwegian authorities have so far pursued a policy on marketing GMOs that differs significantly from that of the EU. Given the fact that Norway is depending upon the political will of the EU in order to continue its cooperation with the EU through the EEA Agreement, which gives Norway, Iceland and Liechtenstein a unique possibility of participating in political processes within the EU, it is remarkable that Norway has been willing to deviate from the policy of the EU on such a politically important issue as the marketing of GMOs. This indicates the extent to which Norwegian politicians have considered GMOs to be a major political issue.

This chapter will not address all aspects of GMOs. It will focus on the deliberate release of GMOs into the environment. In addition to the use of GMOs for agricultural or aquacultural purposes, it will cover the use of living GMOs for food and feed. Issues concerning the use of GMOs in processed food or feed, contained use of GMOs and transborder movement of GMOs from Norway to other countries will not be specifically addressed.[1]

The following sections will first address the international legal framework within which Norwegian authorities are making decisions concerning the marketing and labelling of GMOs. An overview of the status for GMOs in Norway then follows, as well as the framework for decision-making. The latter part of this chapter will address the way in which the precautionary principle has been, and may be, applied in individual cases.

THE INTERNATIONAL FRAMEWORK FOR NORWEGIAN LEGISLATION

Norway is party to a number of treaties of relevance to decisions concerning the release of GMOs. First, there are environmental treaties – in particular, the Cartagena Protocol on Biosafety (2001; hereafter the Cartagena Protocol) and the Aarhus Convention on Access to Information, Public Participation in Decision-Making and Access to Justice in Environmental Matters (1998; hereafter the Aarhus Convention). While the Cartagena Protocol is primarily of relevance to decisions concerning the export of GMOs, it is also of relevance as a justification of domestic policies in view of obligations under international trade law. In particular, the Cartagena Protocol is of relevance to the use of the precautionary principle when making decisions on marketing and labelling GMOs, and when determining the burden of providing information and evidence concerning the impacts of GMOs on human, animal or plant health and the environment.

The Aarhus Convention is primarily of relevance when setting out rules concerning the decision-making procedure to be applied when determining whether to allow the marketing of GMOs. In particular, the Aarhus Convention is relevant for public access to information on the properties of GMOs and their effects on health and the environment, and for participation in decision-making and access to justice in cases concerning decisions on the deliberate release of GMOs.[2] In relation to Norway, the Aarhus Convention has been important in establishing separate procedures for the impact assessment of GMOs.

Except from the points noted above, the above-mentioned treaties have been insignificant for the design and application of the Norwegian legislation on GMOs. Their main role has so far been to justify the maintenance of current GMO regulation in light of challenges that it may face under international trade law. Against this background, there will not be any separate analysis of the relationship between the Norwegian regulation of GMOs and the above treaties in this chapter.

Second, there are treaties that aim at reducing trade barriers. This is particularly the case for the following treaties under the Agreement Establishing the World Trade Organization (WTO): the General Agreement on Tariffs and Trade (GATT), the Agreement on Technical Barriers to Trade (TBT Agreement) and the Agreement on the Application of Sanitary and Phytosanitary Measures (hereafter the SPS Agreement). These agreements set out rules that have the potential to be of great significance to the design and application of measures to prevent negative health and environmental effects from the release of GMOs. Nevertheless, they were not considered when Norwegian authorities designed the basic system for regulating GMOs. One did not point to any potential problem in relation to the GATT, and the system was designed before the TBT and SPS Agreements were adopted. Moreover, the relationship to the GMO legislation was not considered when Norway subsequently ratified the WTO Agreement in 1994.[3] Finally, in relation to the application of the legislation in individual cases, issues concerning the relationship to the trade agreements have not been part of the formal justification for the decisions taken, and do not seem to have been a main concern in relation to the design and application of relevant measures.[4] Against this background, I do not intend to carry out any independent analysis of the WTO rules in this chapter.

Third, there are international regimes that aim at international harmonization of measures related to the contained use and deliberate release of GMOs. Such regimes can be found in the form of international standards under international institutions, such as under the 1991 International Plant Protection Convention in the form of obligations to base measures on international standards, such as in the SPS Agreement, and in the form of rules setting out a more or less closely defined framework for decision-making, such as in the legislation adopted by the EU. Since the first two forms of regimes have had limited effect on the design and use of Norwegian regulation, these regimes will not be addressed in this chapter.

With regard to the international framework in the area of GMOs, it is the legislation of the EU that has had a significant impact on Norwegian measures. The EU legislation of primary interest in the context of this chapter is Directive 90/220/EC on the deliberate release into the environment of genetically modified organisms (hereafter the 90/220 Directive), which has subsequently been replaced by Directive 2001/18/EEC on the deliberate release into the environment of genetically modified organisms (hereafter the 2001/18 Directive). Norway has actively participated in the preparation of the 2001/18 Directive; but this directive has not yet been included in the EEA Agreement.[5] The 90/220 Directive, which is still the only instrument on GMOs applicable under the EEA Agreement, has, in general, not been significant for the design of the GMO Act; but it has played an essential role in the way in which the act has been applied through adoption of regulations and through decisions in individual cases. Moreover, Norwegian participation in the development of Directive 2001/18 and other new secondary legislation on GMOs in the EU has been of importance to the design of Norwegian policy in this area. For these reasons, and also because the way in which the 90/220 Directive has been applied in Norway differs from the way in which the directive has been applied in the EU, this directive will be an essential part of the analysis in this chapter. Directive 2001/18 will be referred to wherever it may be of relevance.

STATUS FOR GENETICALLY MODIFIED ORGANISMS IN NORWAY

There is some biotechnological research in Norway, and some of this research aims at producing GMOs that may, at a later stage, be subject to deliberate release. Examples often cited are the production of a genetically modified winter-flowering begonia (*juleglede*), tobacco and aspen (*osp*).[6] However, so far none of this research has resulted in the application for deliberate release of any product based on GMOs, and Norwegian biotechnological industry is, in general, insignificant.

So far, only one application for the deliberate release of genetically modified tobacco and three applications for the deliberate release of carnation have been approved by Norwegian authorities. Norway is requested to make decisions concerning the marketing of all GMOs for which there are applications for marketing within the EU.[7] A number of these applications are under consideration in the Norwegian decision-making bodies. Norway has refused marketing of eight GMOs that have been accepted by the EU – namely, two applications for marketing of vaccines, five applications for plants and one application for micro-organisms.[8]

In the following, it will be of interest to analyse why Norway has rejected applications for marketing these products and the role that the precautionary principle has played in this context in light of the fact that Norway has allowed other GMOs to be marketed. Moreover, the status of the application processes for those GMOs that have not yet been subject to any decision also needs to be addressed in order to identify the role of the precautionary principle for the procedures followed during the application process. But before addressing these issues, we need to take a closer look at the general conceptual and regulatory framework for the decision-making procedure.

GENERAL CONCEPTUAL FRAMEWORK

It may be useful to distinguish between three general approaches that are essential to the design of decision-making procedures. One approach, which is generally regarded as the approach to be used unless there are specific and convincing arguments for other approaches, is to take decisions on the basis of cost-benefit analyses. According to this approach, the task of decision-makers is to identify relevant costs and benefits of alternative decisions, and to make the decision that gives the highest net benefit. This is generally the approach to be chosen where decision-makers have a broad margin of appreciation.

A second approach, which is most common where decision-makers' margin of appreciation is significantly limited through legislation, is to base the decision on cost-effectiveness. Here, the legislator has limited the options available and the factors that can be taken into account when making the decision, and a main task for decision-makers is to design the decision in such a way that the costs of the decision are kept to a minimum. There is no clear distinction between decision-making based on cost-benefit analyses and on cost-effectiveness. Both approaches may be of relevance in the context of a given decision.

A third approach is to base decisions on precaution. Such an approach is of relevance in cases where the available information on the effects of decisions is such that it is not possible to make a decision based on a cost-benefit analysis. Such cases occur primarily where there is uncertainty related to the costs of the decision. Hence, there is a fundamental difference between decisions based on a cost-benefit analysis and decisions based on a precautionary approach, as a cost-benefit approach will, by definition, not be available in cases where a precautionary approach is called for. Nevertheless, a decision-maker will, in many cases, be expected to take into account cost-effectiveness when designing decisions based on a precautionary approach.[9]

It can be argued that a cost-benefit analysis should be replaced by a proportionality test in cases where the precautionary principle is applicable.[10] In the opinion of this author, such a proportionality test would, in practice, be the same as an approach based on cost-effectiveness. Hence, a proportionality test should be regarded as a possible supplement to a precautionary approach in cases where several options are available to the decision-maker, but not as an element of, or a substitute for, a precautionary approach.

GENERAL LEGISLATIVE FRAMEWORK

It can be argued that the environmental clause in Section 110(b) of the Norwegian Constitution[11] is a general starting point for the application of the precautionary principle in the Norwegian legal system in the sense that it implicitly presupposes its existence. However, the provision neither explicitly refers to the principle, nor addresses issues concerning decision-making in cases of uncertainty. There is, thus, no reason to emphasize Section 110(b) when addressing the use of the precautionary principle in relation to GMOs.

Decisions concerning deliberate release of GMOs in Norway are regulated in Section 10 of the GMO Act (Act No. 38 of 1993):

1 *Deliberate release of genetically modified organisms may only occur subject to approval by the [Government]... A product may not be approved for placing on the market until it has been satisfactorily tested in natural environments that will be affected by the intended use ...*

2 *Deliberate release of genetically modified organisms may only be approved when there is no risk of harmful effects on health or the environment. Moreover, when deciding whether or not to grant the application, significant emphasis shall be placed on whether the deliberate release represents a benefit to the community and a contribution to sustainable development ...*

6 *Approval is not required for the placing on the market of a product that is approved for placing on the market in another EEA country pursuant to the rules laid down in Annex XX, Entry 25, of the EEA Agreement (Council Directive 90/220/EEC). The authorities responsible under the present Act, however, may still prohibit or limit such placing on the market if, in their opinion, it involves a risk to health or the environment or if the placing on the market is otherwise in conflict with the* purpose *of this Act [emphasis added].*

Since almost all GMOs for which approval is sought in Norway have been approved for placing on the market in a member of the EU, Section 10(6) is by far the most important provision in practice. According to Section 1 of the act, its purpose:

... is to ensure that the production and use of genetically modified organisms ... takes place in an ethically and socially justifiable way, in accordance with the principle of sustainable development and without detrimental effects on health and the environment.

One difference between Section 10(2) and Section 1 is that the latter does not refer to the criterion 'benefit to the community'. However, it can be asked whether this difference is of any practical importance. An assessment of usefulness to society would necessarily be included in an evaluation of the extent to which a GMO contributes to sustainable development. The main difference is, thus, whether benefit to the society should be regarded as an individual requirement or whether it should be regarded as part of an overall evaluation of relevant factors.

When analysing the criteria listed in the legislation, we may distinguish between those criteria that generally can be regarded as part of a cost-benefit analysis and those that point in the direction of a precautionary approach. In general, we may place benefit to the society and contribution to sustainable development as part of a cost-benefit analysis. The requirement with respect to benefit to the society means that there must be a net benefit to the society from the release of the GMOs. The requirement that release of GMOs contribute to sustainable development means that there must be net benefits both to present and future generations, and that release of GMOs must contribute to equitable sharing of benefits between those living today.

The requirement that there be no risk of harmful effects to health or the environment is a criterion that is closely related to a precautionary approach. We should, however, note the difference between cases where an applicant submits the application to Norwegian authorities and where there is a strict requirement concerning risks to health and the environment (see Section 10(2)), and cases where the applicant submits the application to a country of the EU and where Norwegian authorities have a far broader margin of appreciation when determining whether a certain risk to health or the environment is acceptable since the authorities 'may' simply still prohibit GMOs if they pose a risk to health or the environment (see Section 10(6)). This difference between the two provisions indicates that one may face situations where an applicant may argue that application of different standards represents discriminatory treatment in violation of Article 11 of the EEA Agreement.[12]

The focus in the following sections will be on how a precautionary approach is reflected in the decision-making procedures and practice of Norwegian administrative authorities,[13] with a main emphasis on how the issue of health and environmental effects has been addressed. But before addressing these issues, it is of interest to take a closer look at how the Norwegian legislation is linked to the EU's decision-making system.

NORWAY, THE AGREEMENT ON THE EUROPEAN ECONOMIC AREA AND THE EUROPEAN UNION

As noted above, for the time being, the directive in force for Norway under the EEA Agreement is the 90/220 Directive.[14] There are two main issues that need to be solved in the context of updating the EEA Agreement with the new secondary legislation in this area, particularly the 2001/18 Directive – namely, the modalities for the decision-making procedures and whether the European Free Trade Association (EFTA) states will be allowed adaptations to the text of the legislation.

Regarding the first issue, the question is whether a decision made by one party to the EEA Agreement (that is, the EU, Norway, Iceland or Liechtenstein) on allowing the release of GMOs shall be binding for all parties to the EEA Agreement, or whether there shall be an opening for a separate decision-making procedure for each party to the EEA Agreement. Following the logic of the establishment of an internal market, there is little room for accepting that each party to the agreement will have the right to maintain separate decision-making procedures for products. However, for some products that are regarded as sensitive due to their potential harmful effects, a need for separate decision-making by national authorities has been acknowledged. Such separate decision-making can either be carried out in the form of invoking narrow and provisional exceptions under the secondary legislation ('safeguard measures'), such as in the case of Directive 90/220 and Directive 2001/18, or in the form of opening for separate decision-making in each country, such as under Directive 98/8/EC concerning the placing of biocidal products on the market.

Since the secondary legislation on GMOs has opted for the use of safeguard measures, a question that remains is whether the EU can accept a decision allowing the marketing of a GMO by an EFTA state as binding for the whole of the EU. In the case of biocidal products under Directive 98/8/EC, the final decisions are made by the EU, and these final decisions will also be binding for the EFTA states unless they can invoke the safeguards clause.[15] A similar approach has been adopted in relation to other sensitive products, such as medicines. Against this background, it seems unrealistic to expect the EU to accept separate decision-making in the EFTA countries that may be given legal effects for the EU. Hence, the only realistic outcome seems to be that the EU makes decisions that are also binding for the EFTA states, unless the EFTA states can invoke the safeguards clause.

This leads us to the second issue – namely, the need for adaptations to the text of Directive 2001/18. Under Directive 90/220, the EFTA countries enjoy the following adaptation to Article 16:

> ... (b) Article 16 shall be replaced by the following:
>
> 1   *Where a Contracting Party has justifiable reasons to consider that a product which has been properly notified and has received written consent under this Directive constitutes a risk to human health or the environment, it may restrict or prohibit the use and/or sale of that product on its territory. It shall immediately inform the other Contracting Parties through the EEA Joint Committee of such action and give reasons for its decision.*
>
> 2   *If a Contracting Party so requires, consultations on the appropriateness of the measures taken shall take place in the EEA Joint Committee. Part VII of the Agreement shall apply.*

Moreover, the EFTA countries have been given an additional opportunity to apply their domestic legislation through inclusion of the following clause:

> ... (c) The Contracting Parties agree that the Directive only covers aspects relating to the potential risks to humans, plants, animals and the environment. The EFTA States

> *therefore reserve the right to apply their national legislation in this area in relation to other concerns than health and environment, in so far as it is compatible with this Agreement.*

Of these two elements, it is the adaptation to Article 16 of the 90/220 Directive (see (b) above) that is of primary relevance to the precautionary principle. As indicated earlier, the possibility of refusing release of GMOs on the basis of the criteria 'benefit to society' and 'contribution to sustainable development' are primarily part of a cost-benefit analysis.

If we compare the wording of the adaptation to Article 16 of the 90/220 Directive with the safeguard clause under Article 23 of the 2001/18 Directive,[16] we can conclude that the following main differences exist:

- Article 23 has detailed and strict conditions for invoking the safeguard clause while the adaptation text merely requires 'justifiable reasons'.
- Article 23 provides for a detailed procedure with strict deadlines for dealing with cases where a country has made use of the safeguard clause, while the adaptation text merely indicates that 'consultations on the appropriateness of the measures taken shall take place in the EEA Joint Committee', and refers to Part VII of the EEA Agreement, which contains procedural rules in Article 113 and indicates a possibility of taking measures to remedy 'imbalance' caused by safeguard measures in Article 114.
- Article 23 opens only for provisional exemptions that may be overturned by decisions by EU institutions, while the adaptation text indicates that the safeguard measure will be permanent unless it is voluntarily given up by the country that adopted it.

This shows that EFTA countries currently enjoy a broad margin of appreciation when determining the extent to which a precautionary approach should be taken in relation to deliberate release of GMOs. The question that is getting increasingly urgent is to what extent EFTA states will have to accept restrictions on this flexibility when including the 2001/18 Directive in the EEA Agreement. According to Article 102 of the EEA Agreement, there is an obligation to:

> *...take a decision concerning an amendment of an Annex to this Agreement as closely as possible to the adoption by the Community of the corresponding new Community legislation with a view to permitting a simultaneous application of the latter as well as of the amendments of the Annexes to the Agreement.*

Hence, there is an increasing pressure on the EFTA states to accept the new secondary legislation from the EU concerning GMOs. Moreover, if no decision on accepting the legislation is taken within a reasonable time, the affected part of the relevant Annex to the EEA Agreement 'is regarded as provisionally suspended, subject to a decision to the contrary by the EEA Joint Committee' (see Article 102(5)). Hence, the EFTA countries risk being excluded from cooperation with the EU on the regulation of GMOs, particularly participation in expert committees, if they cannot agree to make the 2001/18

Directive part of the EEA Agreement in the near future. This shows that three alternative outcomes are possible in relation to the 2001/18 Directive:

1   EFTA states may accept to make the directive part of the EEA Agreement without adaptations, an alternative that, to a large extent, will block their opportunity of following a more precautionary approach than the EU in the future.
2   EFTA states may achieve adaptations to the text of the safeguard clause of the directive and, thus, maintain a certain freedom to pursue a precautionary approach depending upon the wording of the adaptation text.
3   EFTA states may refuse to allow the directive into the EEA Agreement and, thus, face possible retaliation from the EU in the form of suspending their participation in developing EU policy in the field of GMOs.[17]

The outcome of the political process is highly uncertain. However, it can be mentioned that the current Norwegian government has expressed a willingness to refuse to make new EU legislation in the area of the internal market part of the EEA Agreement.[18]

MEASURES TO REDUCE UNCERTAINTY

Several measures that aim at, or may have the effect of, reducing uncertainty have been taken by Norway in the context of GMOs. This section addresses four such measures and discusses some specific issues of particular interest in the context of the precautionary principle. The first measure is the requirement that an environmental and health impact assessment be carried out by the party applying for a permit to release the GMO. A separate regulation on impact assessments has been adopted in accordance with Section 11 of the GMO Act.[19] According to Section 2–4 of the regulation, the authorities dealing with the application have full freedom to ask for supplementary information and to put the application on hold until such additional information has been supplied if they find that the information provided is not sufficient to make a decision. Sections 4–1 to 4–5 contain detailed rules on the content of the impact assessment. The impact assessment procedure gives the authorities a broad margin of appreciation and a broad opportunity to make use of a precautionary approach, particularly by postponing decisions until they have received such information that they deem necessary to determine the extent of risk to the environment or human health. Moreover, it should be noted that the burden of providing the information and carrying out the research rests with the applicant. This approach is in line with the polluter pays principle and the approach provided for under Article 15 of the Cartagena Protocol; but it may be at odds with the rules of the WTO, which indicate that the burden of demonstrating the need for trade-restricting measures rests with the state (see e.g. Article 2(2) of the SPS Agreement). It should also be noted that Norwegian authorities have made extensive use of this opportunity to ask for additional information, and that, in practice, such requests frequently resulted in applications being put on hold for an indefinite period of time. Whether this is due to the requests for additional information being too burdensome, or to applicants not being particularly interested in placing their products on the Norwegian market, is hard to determine.[20] Most likely the current situation is due to a combination of the two.

The second measure used to reduce uncertainty is public hearings. According to Section 13 of the GMO Act, all cases concerning deliberate release of GMOs shall be subject to a public hearing. The public shall have access to relevant information and they shall have a real opportunity to present their opinions and comments. In this way, public hearings may serve to generate additional information concerning the potential consequences of releasing the GMO and, thus, to reduce uncertainty. On the other hand, a public hearing may contribute to discovering new potential effects from releasing the GMO and, thus, be a generator for awareness concerning uncertainty in new areas. Such new awareness may become a basis for precautionary action.

A third measure used to reduce uncertainty is the establishment of a Biotechnology Advisory Board (*Bioteknologinemnda*). This board, which is an independent advisory institution appointed by the government, was established in 1991 and it has subsequently been regulated in Section 26 of the GMO Act. The members of the board serve in their personal capacity, and they represent a broad range of knowledge and interests. They serve as an essential contributor in the public hearing process, partly through their own input to the hearings, and partly as an 'information clearing house' and active participant in the public debate. Their statements are multidisciplinary; most often unanimous; in general, focused on pointing out areas in need of further clarification; and, in some cases, recommending a specific result.[21] Hence, in addition to generating information that may reduce uncertainty, the board also serves as an important source for awareness concerning uncertainty in new areas. Their input in the decision-making process may thus be an essential element for precautionary action.

Finally, there are the rules on access to information. Such rules are set out partly in Section 12 of the GMO Act and partly in the Act concerning Access to Environmental Information (Act No 31 of 2003). In some cases, the private party may argue that the information in question represents a business secret and thus must be kept confidential. However, such arguments are not available in all cases. According to Section 12 of the GMO Act, information regarding, *inter alia*, the purpose of using the GMO, the place in which it shall be used, methods and plans for surveillance, and assessment of potential effects of releasing the GMO shall be public regardless of whether they may be considered business secrets. Moreover, according to Section 11 of the Environmental Information Act, the burden of proof rests, to a large extent, with the private party invoking a confidentiality clause. In addition, this act gives the public access not only to environmental information held by public authorities, but also to such information directly from undertakings (see Chapter 4 of the act). Against this background, it can be concluded that the rules on access to information ensure a flow of information between interested parties and, thus, contribute to the process of reducing uncertainty. Moreover, the increased access to information may also contribute to awareness concerning uncertainties in new areas and, thus, contribute to establishing a basis for precautionary action.

Against this background, we may conclude that there are at least four main measures that may contribute to reducing uncertainty and the need for precautionary measures. On the other hand, it has also been indicated that these measures may contribute to awareness concerning uncertainties in new areas and, thus, may increase the likelihood that precautionary action will be taken.

LEVEL OF PROTECTION

In this section, it may be useful to distinguish between defining a level of protection and the taking of measures to achieve the level of protection. While the acceptable level of protection is generally considered to be mainly a political issue, measures taken to attain the prescribed level of protection ('risk management') are considered a more technical issue for which a precautionary approach may be appropriate in order to ensure that the chosen level of risk is achieved. However, this distinction is not always clear cut. One general decision may, in some instances, constitute a definition of a level of protection as well as the measure to achieve that level of protection. This will, for example, be the case when the measure is a complete prohibition of the production of a substance. Here, the measure shows that the level of protection is set at 'zero risk' tolerated. Hence, there is no need to define a level of protection. Moreover, it should be recognized that, in most cases, countries do not, in practice, first explicitly define a level of acceptable protection and, subsequently, proceed to design the measures needed to achieve that level.

Against this background, the distinction between level of protection and the measures taken to achieve the level of protection may be criticized for being too theoretical. Nevertheless, the distinction is of importance for analytical purposes; it has been introduced as a basic distinction in the SPS Agreement (see in particular, Article 5), and there may possibly be a development in the direction of increasingly designing relevant decision-making procedures according to the distinction. The main reasons why one has not, in a more systematic way, defined levels of protection prior to adopting measures seem to be that, to a large extent, such issues depend upon cultural and social traditions, such as differences in risk perception, and that there is a basic lack of knowledge about risks.

If we take a look at the Norwegian GMO Act, we can observe that there is no independent statement defining, in general, the acceptable level of protection. On the other hand, it can be argued that there is no need to define the acceptable level of protection separately as long as the conditions for allowing marketing of GMOs set out in the law indicate that there shall be 'zero risk' (see the phrase 'may only be approved when there is no risk of detrimental effects on health or the environment' in Section 10(2) of the GMO Act). However, the wording of Section 10(6), as well as statements in the preparatory works, in administrative decisions and in subsequent documents from relevant institutions, indicate that Section 10(2) cannot be read so strictly as to require a 'zero-risk' approach.[22] This is particularly so in cases where decisions are made on the basis of Section 10(6) of the act since this provision does not oblige the authorities to prohibit deliberate release of GMOs if they will have harmful environmental or health effects.

In the case of antibiotics resistance, there is an absolute prohibition against allowing deliberate release. In this case, there have been clear statements by both the Norwegian Parliament and the government that there shall be a 'zero-risk' approach.[23] This has been expressly reflected in legislation only in relation to GMOs used for food.[24] Nevertheless, it has, in practice, been strictly adhered to in other cases concerning deliberate release of GMOs.[25]

As to the relationship between level of protection and the precautionary principle, some will argue that one may apply the precautionary principle both when defining the level of protection and when determining the measures to be taken to achieve the level of protection. This understanding of the precautionary principle is based on a broad definition of the principle being applicable in the context of highly political decisions. Others will argue in favour of a more narrow understanding of the precautionary principle. The narrow understanding of the principle will relate it more closely to the process of risk assessment and subsequent decisions concerning measures to be applied in individual cases. This understanding of the principle is based on a more technical and administrative approach.

If we take a broad approach to the precautionary principle, we may conclude that the Norwegian policy when setting a zero-risk approach in relation to antibiotics resistance is based on a precautionary approach. However, since Norway has not defined an appropriate level of protection in other contexts, we will have to discuss the precautionary principle on the basis of the actual measures taken in cases of deliberate release of GMOs.

BURDEN OF PROOF

According to Section 10(2) of the GMO Act, the starting point is that the party applying for release of a GMO has the responsibility of demonstrating that the conditions for releasing the GMO are fulfilled. However, the act does not clearly allocate the burden of proof in cases where the GMO in question has been allowed to be released within the EU (see Section 10(6) of the GMO Act). According to this provision, one could argue that since the act states that the authorities 'may' prohibit the marketing of GMOs, it must be up to the authorities to demonstrate that the GMOs pose unacceptable risks or do not constitute a sufficient benefit to the society or contribution to sustainable development. Such an approach would also be in line with the adaptation text to Article 16 of the 90/220 Directive, which states that:

> *Where a Contracting Party has justifiable reasons to consider that a product which has been properly notified and has received written consent under this Directive constitutes a risk to human health or the environment, it may restrict or prohibit the use and/or sale of that product on its territory.*

On the other hand, it can be argued that the GMO Act contains additional conditions that do not fall within the scope of the decision-making procedure of the EU and that, at least in relation to these conditions, there must be an obligation for the applicant to provide relevant information to demonstrate that the conditions are fulfilled. Such an approach would be in accordance with the following text related to incorporation of the 90/220 Directive into the EEA Agreement:

> *The Contracting Parties agree that the Directive only covers aspects relating to the potential risks to humans, plants, animals and the environment. The EFTA States therefore reserve the right to apply their national legislation in this area in relation to other concerns than health and environment, in so far as it is compatible with this Agreement.*

Hence, according to this provision, Norway clearly has the freedom to place the burden of proof on the applicant, at least in relation to information necessary to demonstrate benefits to the society and contribution to sustainable development. There is an important overlap between information concerning health and environmental effects and information to demonstrate net benefit to society and contribution to sustainable development.

In addition, it can be argued that Norway, at least in the past, has adopted a stricter level of protection than the EU in relation to genes coding for antibiotics resistance, and thus that applicants should carry the burden of proving that releasing the GMOs will not violate the level of protection in Norway. One question that arises is whether Norway is allowed under the EEA Agreement to maintain a higher level of protection in relation to antibiotics resistance or other potential risks. The wording of the adaptation text indicates that there is some freedom for Norway to set a level of protection that is stricter than that adopted by the EU as long as there are 'justifiable reasons to consider that … such GMOs constitute a risk to human health or the environment'. If we assume that Norway can bring forward such reasons, it seems justifiable for Norwegian authorities to place the burden of proof that the GMO in question does not constitute such a risk on the applicant.

Finally, we are left with the question whether Norway is allowed to place the burden of proof on the applicant in cases where Norway has not defined a higher level of protection than the EU. As a starting point, one could argue that pursuant to the wording of the adaptation text, Norway should not be allowed to place the burden of proof on the applicant in these cases. On the other hand, Norway could, in practice, argue in most cases that a decision would have to be based on an overall assessment of the potential benefits, on the one hand, and risks of harmful effects of a GMO, on the other, and that as long as the applicant has not provided sufficient information concerning potential harms, the GMO cannot be approved. Such an approach has been widely applied by Norwegian authorities when considering individual applications. In a number of cases, the authorities have made requests for further documentation, and when the information provided has failed to convince the authorities that potential harms are insignificant or limited, the authorities have, in general, denied permissions to release the GMOs.

Placing the burden of proof on the applicant can generally be regarded as a precautionary measure. However, it can also easily be misused in the form of a measure that unreasonably distorts international trade. This discussion shows that Norway under the EEA rules has at least some freedom to take a precautionary approach when allocating the burden of proof. Moreover, there seems to be a limit to the extent to which such an approach can be used; but it is quite unclear where this limit shall be drawn. Finally, it is evident that Norway will not be able to continue the precautionary approach if the 2001/18 Directive is included in the EEA Agreement without an adaptation text similar to the current text. However, the need for an adaptation text will depend upon the extent to which a precautionary approach will be followed, in practice, under the 2001/18 Directive.[26]

One long-term problem of placing the burden of proof on the applicant is that research on the effects of GMOs will, to a large extent, be left to those having an interest in ensuring that the GMOs gain access to markets on as favourable terms as possible. Hence, there is a need for authorities to secure a certain amount of independent

research into the effects of GMOs in order to be able to check the quality of the information provided by applicants.

RISK ASSESSMENT

Issues discussed above, such as burden of proof and measures taken to reduce uncertainty, can be regarded as elements of the risk assessment process. In particular, the rules
on impact assessment are at the core of the risk assessment process in the context of
deliberate release of GMOs. These rules serve to indicate which risks must be assessed,
including which potential harmful effects to take into account.

The rules on impact assessment do not restrict the authorities' possibilities of
requesting information should they consider it necessary in order to show that the GMO
is sufficiently safe. In Section 4–2 of the regulation on impact assessment,[27] there is only
a non-exhaustive and illustrative list of information that must be presented with respect
to effects on health and the environment. According to Sections 4–4 and 4–5 of the regulation, the applicant has also a duty to present information on possible health or environmental effects from measures to be taken to avoid or remedy harmful effects of the
GMO, and from non-conventional or erroneous use of the GMO. All of these rules give
the authorities broad discretion when defining the scope and quality of information to
be presented in individual cases.

In many of the cases where a product has been approved for release within the EU,
Norwegian authorities have not been satisfied with the information that had been
presented by the applicant to the EU and have requested additional information. Such
requests must be understood in light of the requirement of Section 10(1) of the GMO
Act that a 'product may not be approved for placing on the market until it has been satisfactorily tested in natural environments that will be affected by the intended use'. A main
reason why some of the applications were rejected by Norway was that the applicant
failed to provide the additional information requested. In their overall assessment,
Norwegian authorities concluded that due to uncertainty regarding the harmful effects,
they could not allow release of the GMOs.

In other cases, the authorities stated that they considered the risks posed by the presence of genes coding for antibiotics resistance differently from the EU. The difference in
opinion between Norway and the EU was mainly related to the likelihood that such
genes could be transferred to other organisms.

The margin of discretion enjoyed by Norwegian authorities under the GMO Act and
related regulations means that they have been free to ask the applicant to make an assessment that is of specific relevance to the Norwegian environment, that possible indirect
and long-term effects of releasing the GMO be assessed, and even that possible effects
outside of Norway be considered. Moreover, Norwegian authorities have broad discretion when determining the quality of the information to be presented, and they thus
have an extensive possibility of taking a precautionary approach in the context of the risk
assessment procedure. Practice demonstrates that they have made use of this possibility.

So far, international standards have not been of importance in the context of this part
of the decision-making procedure. Once such standards are developed and must be used

as a basis for the decision-making procedure (see Articles 3.1 of the SPS Agreement and 2.4 of the TBT Agreement), Norway may have to reassess its policy of giving broad discretionary power to public authorities.

RISK MANAGEMENT

The measures taken to manage risks must be related to the defined or implied level of protection. A risk management measure is precautionary if it ensures achievement of a level of protection by a certain safety margin. If the level of protection is zero risk, the only available measure is prohibiting release of the GMOs. This will not in itself be a precautionary measure in such cases. However, there remains the problem of unlawful release of GMOs. A prohibition against release of a GMO may thus turn out to be insufficient in practice if it is not followed by a sufficiently strong control regime. It can thus be argued that even in cases where the level of protection is zero risk, and this has been followed up by a total prohibition of release of GMOs, there is room for precautionary measures when designing the control regime.[28]

Where the level of protection has not been clearly defined or where it indicates that some risk is acceptable, there is more room for taking precautionary measures. Precautionary measures may, in such cases, be both prohibitions against release of GMOs and to allow GMOs to be released provided that certain strict conditions are complied with. Such measures may be regarded as a precautionary measure depending upon the facts of the case and that they ensure that the level of protection is achieved by a safety margin. Given the lack of clear definition of the acceptable level of risk in the Norwegian GMO Act, most cases fall in this category.

Earlier, we have seen that Norwegian legislation and the EEA Agreement give Norwegian authorities a broad possibility of denying release of GMOs. Norwegian authorities thus have an extensive opportunity to pursue a precautionary approach in the context of risk management measures.

The next issue is which opportunities Norwegian authorities have when they want to take precautionary measures in cases where they permit the release of GMOs. Here, the question is which conditions they may set out in the permit. Section 15 of the GMO Act sets no limit on the conditions that may be used. It merely lists examples of possible conditions, including:

> ... *the best technical procedure and other means of production from the point of view of health and the environment, a duty to take out insurance or provide security for liability ... or measures for preventing and limiting possible detrimental effects.*

Moreover, Section 15 indicates that the approval may be time limited, and according to Section 5–1 of the regulation on impact assessment, the authorities may set as a condition that the applicant reports on the results of the release and undertakes additional examinations of the effects of release at a later stage. It can be observed that all of these conditions may apply to the applicant, and thus that the applicant may be regarded as responsible for fulfilment of the conditions.

There is no general restriction in the 90/220 Directive on the conditions that may be set when approving release of a GMO.[29] However, when the EU has accepted release of the GMO on certain conditions, Article 16 of the directive restricts the possibility of including additional conditions. The same is the case under Article 23 of the 2001/18 Directive. But, as has been noted above, Norwegian authorities enjoy broad discretion under the adaptation text of Article 16. Hence, Norwegian authorities have the option of taking a precautionary approach in the context of setting conditions for approval to release GMOs. This discretion may be substantially limited in cases where GMOs have been approved by the EU if the adaptation text of Article 16 is discontinued when the 2001/18 Directive is included in the EEA Agreement.

RESPONSIBILITY AND LIABILITY

Any person who intentionally or negligently contravenes the provisions of the GMO Act or the conditions set out in permits under the act may be liable to imprisonment for up to one year, and four years if there are especially aggravating circumstances (see Section 25 of the GMO Act). Hence, a person who sells or uses a GMO in violation of conditions set in the decision allowing the marketing of the GMO may be subjected to penal sanctions as a consequence of the violation.[30] There is also the possibility of imposing a coercive fine in accordance with Section 24 of the GMO Act.

There are separate rules on compensation in cases of damages in Section 23 of the GMO Act. There is strict liability – that is, the liability to pay compensation regardless of fault. Such liability may occur if the release causes 'damage, inconvenience or loss'. There is thus a low threshold for liability. One may as well become liable in cases where one has complied with all conditions set out in the approval. However, in these cases it can be argued that a higher threshold for liability should apply, requiring that the harmful effects were 'unreasonable or unnecessary' (see Section 56 of the Pollution Control Act – Act No 6 of 1981).

Section 23 of the GMO Act indicates that one may become liable for a broad range of both pecuniary and non-pecuniary losses. This is, in particular, indicated by the use of the word 'inconvenience' (*ulempe*). It should be recalled that a duty to take out insurance or provide security may be set as a condition for the approval (see Section 15 of the GMO Act). Finally, the liability would apply to any 'person responsible for an activity pursuant to' the GMO Act. This must be read as including any person carrying out activities relating to the production and use of GMOs.

Against this background, we can conclude that the rules on responsibility and liability reinforce the precautionary approach of the GMO Act in the sense that they give applicants strong incentives to minimize harmful and even inconvenient effects from GMOs. It can thus be argued that these rules, as such, constitute precautionary measures.

CONCLUSIONS

As a first impression, the Norwegian GMO Act seems to instruct public authorities to adopt a very restrictive practice in relation to approval of GMOs (see Section 10(2)). However, when examining the act in more detail, we see that in practical terms it is not particularly strict, and that it allows public authorities a broad margin of discretion in relation to both the decision-making process and the content of decisions (see Section 10(6)). The extent to which a precautionary approach is pursued by Norway is thus, to a large extent, dependent upon the political priorities of the government.

Norwegian authorities have broad opportunities to adopt a precautionary approach in relation to GMOs under the current rules of the EEA Agreement. The authorities have made active use of these opportunities and adopted a more precautionary approach than the EU in several cases. This approach has partly consisted in setting a higher level of protection than does the EU – that is, in the case of genes coding for antibiotics resistance – and partly in adopting a strict approach to the burden of proof, assessment of risks and risk management measures. The precautionary approach has been closely related to an overall assessment of whether the GMOs constitute benefits to the society and contribute to sustainable development.

The rules on GMOs under the EEA Agreement will most likely be updated in the near future, and it is unlikely that Norwegian authorities will be able to maintain the degree of discretion that they currently enjoy. Moreover, the authorities have so far not explicitly addressed the issue of compatibility of their GMO measures with international trade law. These factors indicate that Norwegian authorities are under heavy pressure to change their policy on GMOs. It is currently impossible to predict the speed with which, the areas in which, or the extent to which Norwegian policy will change as these are, in essence, political questions. However, this chapter may serve to clarify the legal framework within which such political decisions will have to be taken.

NOTES

1   This distinction is basic in the sense that the former group of GMOs has the ability to reproduce (unless they have been made infertile), while the latter group has no such ability. However, this distinction is generally not reflected in the rules that have been adopted in Norway to regulate the use of and trade in GMOs (see, *inter alia*, Section 9(f) of the GMO Act).

2   See, in particular, Decision I/4 adopting Guidelines on Access to Information, Public Participation and Access to Justice with respect to Genetically Modified Organisms (MP.PP/2002/7) and Decision II/1 on Genetically Modified Organisms of the Meeting of the Parties to the Aarhus Convention. The latter decision introduced more specific rules on GMOs into the convention.

3   See *Stortingsproposisjon* No 65 (1993–1994) proposition from the government concerning ratification of the Agreement Establishing the World Trade Organization, in particular pp105–106, 110.

4   Those decisions where Norwegian authorities have refused approval of GMOs that have been approved in the EU can be found at www.odin.dep.no/md/norsk/tema/biomangfold/

aktuelt/022031–990074/dok-bn.html (in Norwegian, accessed on 8 December 2005). For more details, see Haugseth, E. L. (2001) *Utsetting av genmodifiserte organismer,* Institutt for offentlig retts skriftserie, Oslo, No 2/2001, Chapter 5, and Plahte, J. (2002) 'Regulering og forvaltning av ustetting av genmodifiserte organismer i Norge 1993–2000', *Retf'rd*, no 96, pp76–92.

5   Directives and other secondary legislation adopted by the EU are included in the EEA Agreement through references in the annexes to the agreement. Directive 90/220 has been included through a reference in Section IV of Annex XX to the agreement para 25. The annexes can be accessed at http://secretariat.efta.int/Web/EuropeanEconomicArea/ EEAAgreement/annexes (accessed on 8 December 2005).

6   See Plahte, J. (2002) 'Regulering og forvaltning av ustetting av genmodifiserte organismer i Norge 1993–2000', *Retf'rd*, no 96, pp 84–87.

7   The reasons why Norway has to make decisions in relation to these applications are partly that many of the applications are for marketing in the whole area covered by the EEA Agreement, and partly that the EEA Agreement makes Norway part of the internal market of the EU. Hence, a product that is allowed to be marketed in the EU can be marketed in Norway unless a decision to the contrary has been made. For an overview of the status of applications for release of GMOs in Norway, see www.dirnat.no/archive/attachments/02/80/GMOli042.pdf (in Norwegian, accessed on 8 December 2005).

8   See http://odin.dep.no/md/norsk/tema/biomangfold/aktuelt/022031–990074/dok-bn.html (in Norwegian, accessed on 8 December 2005).

9   In the reference to the precautionary approach in Principle 15 of the Rio Declaration, it is stated that: 'Where there are threats of serious or irreversible damage, lack of full scientific certainty shall not be used as a reason for postponing *cost-effective* measures to prevent environmental degradation' (emphasis added).

10 On the issue of the precautionary principle, cost-benefit analysis and proportionality, see Chapter 2 in this volume .

11 The wording of the relevant part of Section 110(b) of the Norwegian Constitution runs as follows:

Every person has a right to an environment that is conducive to health and to natural surroundings whose productivity and diversity are preserved. Natural resources should be made use of on the basis of comprehensive long-term considerations whereby this right will be safeguarded for future generations as well.

12 Article 11 of the EEA Agreement corresponds to Article 28 of the Treaty Establishing the European Community.

13 No case concerning GMOs has so far been brought before a Norwegian court.

14 See Section IV of Annex XX to the agreement, para 25. The annexes can be accessed at http://secretariat.efta.int/Web/EuropeanEconomicArea/EEAAgreement/annexes (accessed on 8 December 2005).

15 See Forskrift No 1848 of 18 December 2003, om godkjenning av biocider og biocidprodukter (biocidforskriften).

16 Article 23 of the 2001/18 Directive states that:

Where a Member State, as a result of new or additional information made available since the date of the consent and affecting the environmental risk assessment or reassessment of existing information on the basis of new or additional scientific knowledge, has detailed grounds for considering that a GMO as or in a product which has been properly notified and has received written consent under this Directive constitutes a risk to human health or the environment...

17 For a discussion of possible consequences of not making a Directive part of the EEA Agreement, see Eriksen, T. A. (2003) Norges muligheter til å reservere seg mot nytt EØS-

regelverk – direktivene om tilsetningsstoffer i n'ringsmidler, IUSEF No 41, Senter for Europarett, Oslo.

18 See Politisk plattform for en flertallsregjering, adopted at Soria Moria on 13 October 2005 (the Soria Moria Declaration), p8, which states that: 'If other means do not succeed, the government will consider making use of its right of reservation under the EEA Agreement if essential Norwegian interests are threatened as a consequence of EU legislation to be considered included in the EEA Agreement' (translation by the author).

19 Forskrift No 816 of 20 August 1993, om konsekvensutredning etter genteknologiloven.

20 On these issues, see also Chapter 12 in this volume.

21 The statements of the Biotechnology Advisory Board can be accessed at www.bion.no/uttalelser.shtml (in Norwegian only, accessed on 8 December 2005). An example of a statement containing a dissenting opinion can be found in the statement dated 24 February 2005.

22 See Haugseth, E. L. (2001) Utsetting av genmodifiserte organismer, Institutt for offentlig retts skriftserie, Oslo, no 2/2001, particularly pp44–51. See also Chapter 12 in this volume, in which Theofanis Christoforou concludes that the level of protection provided for under the 2001/18 Directive is a 'level of no risk'. He bases this conclusion on an analysis of several provisions and preambular statements in the directive, and not on an explicit political statement identifying the acceptable level of risk.

23 See in particular Innst. S. No 272 (1996–1997) 'Innstilling fra næringskomiteen om matkvalitet og forbrukertrygghet og framlegg fra stortingsrepresentant Erik Solheim på vegne av Senterpartiet, Sosialistisk Venstreparti og Kristelig Folkeparti om å be Regjeringen forby produksjon, import og omsetting av alle genmanipulerte produkter som inneholder gener som koder for antibiotikaresistens og å arbeide for internasjonale forbud på dette området'.

24 Forskrift No 257 of 4 March 2000, om forbud mot visse genmodifiserte n'ringsmidler og n'ringsmiddelingredienser.

25 The content of genes coding for resistance to antibiotics was the main reason for not allowing the release of GMOs in at least six cases. In one case, the authorities stated that permission to market the product may be given provided that the gene coding for antibiotics resistance is removed. Norwegian authorities have allowed use of such genes in one case that did not concern deliberate release. See See Plahte, J. (2002) 'Regulering og forvaltning av ustetting av genmodifiserte organismer i Norge 1993–2000', Retf'rd, no 96, pp89–90.

26 The 2001/18/EC Directive does, as a starting point, place the burden of proof on the applicant, and it can be argued that it provides for a zero-risk level of protection (see Chapter 12 in this volume). However, there is a margin of discretion under the directive, and there is clearly a possibility that a GMO that may be regarded as acceptable by the EU or its member states under the directive may subsequently be regarded as unacceptable by Norwegian authorities.

27 Forskrift No 816 of 20 August 1993, om konsekvensutredning etter genteknologiloven.

28 The cases concerning GMOs containing genes coding for antibiotics resistance are clear examples. It has not been possible to carry out any examination of the Norwegian control regime for the purpose of this chapter. The Norwegian Food Safety Authority (Mattilsynet) has the main responsibility for control issues.

29 There is no restriction on the use of conditions in Directive 2001/18 (see, in particular, Article 19.3(c)).

30 In this context, it is remarkable that decisions to allow release of GMOs are made in the form of individual decisions that are not subject to the procedural requirements that apply to general regulations, including requirements concerning publishing. On the other hand, decisions to deny release of GMOs are made in the form of both individual decisions and general regulations.

CHAPTER 14

Genetically Modified Organisms and Precaution in Finnish and Swedish Law

Jussi Kauppila

INTRODUCTION

The legal core of the precautionary principle is that it allows or requires protective measures in the absence of scientific certainty. The principle reverses the burden of proof to the operator – or at least lessens the burden of proof on the authority.[1] Moreover, it is argued that fundamental scientific uncertainty should open decision-making for arguments that go beyond technical expertise on risks. The claim for a more reflexive risk management has been strong with regard to new technologies, such as gene technology.[2] Thus, a precautionary regulatory approach involves a qualitative reform of how we understand risks. For example, complex socio-economic effects of individual technological innovations could then have relevance in deciding about when the use of genetically modified organisms (GMOs) is legal or illegal.[3]

This chapter explores how precaution is implemented in the Swedish and Finnish laws on contained use and deliberate release of GMOs.[4] It makes a distinction between precaution as a legal principle and precaution as a regulatory approach, the latter referring to statutory rules inflicting precaution. The chapter comprises three major sections. 'Mechanisms for precaution' discusses the different legal mechanisms for precaution in the context of GMOs. In 'Finnish law' and 'Swedish law', an analysis is provided of Finnish and Swedish law on GMOs. Finally, this chapter concludes with some comparative remarks on the key mechanisms through which precaution is implemented within the two legal orders.[5] The foundational European Union (EU) law is analysed in Chapter 12 of this book.

MECHANISMS FOR PRECAUTION

Rules and principles

Following Dworkin's theory, rules and principles are the alternative legal forms for any regulatory idea – policies being left outside the legal order. Dworkin finds a qualitative

distinction between rules and principles with respect to how they function in legal decision-making. Rules have an 'all or nothing' content; they are either applied fully or not
at all. Therefore, simultaneous application of two or more contradicting rules is
excluded. Contrary to rules, principles are 'more or less' optimizing norms, which are
balanced against other applicable principles. When it comes to the role of principles in
legal decision-making, they can either be directly applied as norms in their own right or
used as interpretative tools in applying rules.[6]

Many regulatory ideas are first developed as principles within customary law or soft
law. The key environmental law principles have developed from soft law to legally
binding principles.[7] Legislators then strengthen the same regulatory ideas through statutory law. As a consequence, we end up with two separate mechanisms through which the
ideas are implemented: statutory rules that were originally inspired by principles, and
principles that may still be used as guidance when interpreting the rules. Thus, for
instance, a general rule laying a duty on the operators to monitor the long-term effects of
GMO field trials can be seen as an application of the precautionary principle.
Furthermore, when this general rule is applied case by case, the precautionary principle
can be used as an interpretative tool.

Status and weight of principles

In legal systems based on statutory law – and particularly in Nordic countries – principles
have been considered as permissible sources of law, something which decision-makers
may take into account if no better tools are available.[8] Only the most stabilized principles
of administrative and criminal law make an exception in this respect. The somewhat
controversial status of principles is due to the strong status of legality and the fact that
statutory law is dominated by rules.[9] However, the recent influence of European and international law has softened the strict rule positivism and strengthened the status of principles even in the Nordic countries. Environmental law provides a fruitful ground for
principles because statutory law is still sometimes open textured, leaving room for discretion to those who apply the law. This room is – at least in part – filled by principles.[10]

The normative weight of principles depends upon three main factors. First, each principle has – in Dworkin's words – a certain amount of institutional support. For instance,
the precautionary principle may be explicitly mentioned in statutes of national law,
either as a general objective or as an operational provision. In addition, the principle
may have been used, either explicitly or implicitly, in judicial and administrative practice
by national decision-making bodies. Furthermore, depending upon the field of application, the precautionary principle gains more or less support in European and international law. This support should be taken into account even in the national legal order.
European Community (EC) law is particularly understood as an integral part of national
legal orders.

Second, when the precautionary principle is applied, it is balanced against other principles that are applicable in the same situation. The general principles of administrative
law, such as the principle of proportionality, are of particular importance. Even constitutional rights, such as freedom of entrepreneurship or the principle of legality, counterbalance precaution. The amount and weight of countering forces vary from case to case.

On the other hand, the constitutional right to the environment may strengthen precaution. Third, and finally, since environmental law decision-making is a process of reciprocal interplay between facts and norms, the balancing of principles is inevitably tied to the facts of each situation. Thus, the normative weight of principles is in constant change depending upon both facts and other applicable norms in each situation.[11]

The legal framework for precaution in the regulation of GMOs

The precautionary principle – just as any other substantial norm – must be linked to power conferring and procedural norms in order to provide the mechanisms through which the principle is applied. In the regulation on GMOs, such a basic legal framework is the authorization procedure defined in the Directives 90/219/EEC and 2001/18/EC. In a regulatory system based on authorization (permit, licence and allowance), there are three main phases in which precaution can be modified into the detailed rights and duties of the operators:

1   The authorization procedure starts when the operator makes a notification/application for a permit to the competent permit authority. The application/notification shall contain all information that is necessary for the permit consideration. When GMOs are used, the application/notification shall always include a separate risk assessment made by the operator. Within the discipline of risk analysis, risk assessment is understood as an exercise through which facts are provided for the risk management, which, in turn, is the normatively guided decision-making phase. However, risk assessment does not only provide facts for risk management, but involves a great deal of norms and interpretation as well. Thus, precaution can be applied in numerous small decisions within different phases of risk assessment: in collecting data, in recognizing potential harmful effects, or in making predictions about the nature and probability of the harm. All together, small differences in risk assessment rules and practices can lead to decisively different legal interpretations about the acceptable risk. Most importantly, after the notification/application for a permit has been made, the competent authority is usually empowered to require the operator to fulfil the risk assessment in order to reduce the uncertainties related to the effects of the activity. This power is – at least indirectly – a mechanism to apply precaution. From the operator's point of view, a decision according to which the competent permit authority requires the operator to complement the risk assessment has little practical difference to a decision according to which the application is rejected. Both decisions can be based on uncertainty about the effects of the use of GMOs. Moreover, both decisions mean that the use of GMOs cannot be carried out.[12]
2   When the competent authority makes a judgement that no more facts about the effects of the use of GMOs are required or available, it is time for the actual permit consideration – that is time to consider whether the notification/application is accepted or rejected. The permit consideration is guided by the so-called 'permit thresholds', the ultimate substantial norms describing which activities should be allowed and which should not. In other words, the permit thresholds define the 'level of protection' or – speaking in terms of risk management – the 'acceptable risk'.

Within the context of permit consideration, the competent authority has the power to set permit conditions. Permit conditions are detailed duties that an operator must carry out when using GMOs – for instance, duties to take specific safety measures in order to restrict any uncontrolled spreading of the GMOs, or duties to monitor the long-term effects of the use. Thus, permit consideration – including the setting of permit conditions – is the most important mechanism through which the precautionary principle can be applied.

3 Even after the permit has been issued, the authorities have legal means to limit the use of GMOs if this is to cause illegal adverse effects. Generally speaking, the legislator is usually very accurate in defining under which premises the competent authority may modify, nullify or otherwise restrict the use of a valid permit. These provisions provide the third key mechanism of applying precaution with respect to the use of GMOs.

In the following analysis of Swedish and Finnish law on GMOs, this division of the authorization procedure into three phases will be used to study how precaution may be implemented. Within this framework, the focus will be on the provisions that are relevant in defining the so-called acceptable risk.

FINNISH LAW

Applicable legislation and competent authorities

The drafting of specialized GMO legislation in Finland was triggered by the process of joining the EC. The Gene Technology Act (377/1995) entered into force in September 1995. Before this, the use of GMOs was primarily regulated through occupational safety standards and legislation on pollution control. There was no explicit authorization requirement for the use of GMOs. If the use of GMOs became subject to authorization, this was due to other characteristics of the activity in question, not because of using GMOs.[13] The focus of the regulation was on the human health effects of using GMOs in the laboratory.

The Gene Technology Act (hereafter the GMO Act) has remained the key regulatory instrument on gene technology. The newly revised (10 September 2004/847) GMO Act is supplemented by the governmental ordinance on gene technology (1053/2005), as well as the ordinances by the Ministry of Social and Health Affairs on the deliberate release of GMOs (110/2005) and contained use of genetically modified micro-organisms (1053/2005).

The Board for Gene Technology is the competent authority in Finland, as referred to in Directive 90/219/EEC and Directive 2001/18/EC. Thus, the board issues permits for both contained uses and deliberate releases of GMOs. The board consists of a chairman, a vice chairman and five members who represent different ministries. The members of the board are science and technology experts in the field of gene technology. According to Section 5 of the GMO Act, the board shall even have ethical expertise. The permit applications are brought before the board by the main secretary, who shall also – according to Section 5f of the GMO Act – have scientific expertise in gene technology. The decisions by the board can be appealed to the Supreme Administrative Court.

Despite many attempts by the government to promote biotechnology in Finland, research activity on green gene technology has been limited.[14] Obviously, this means that the available administrative practice is also limited – the total number of applications made for field trials is around 20. The Board for Gene Technology has accepted every application. Only two appeals to the Supreme Administrative Court have been made. Both appeals concerned access to information, not the acceptability of the use of GMOs as such.[15] Operators have never appealed on the decisions made by the board. No applications for market approval of GMO products have ever been made to the competent authorities.

Precaution as a principle

The GMO Act was recently revised (847/2004) in order to implement Directive 2001/18/EC. One of the new elements of the GMO Act is the reference to the precautionary principle in Section 1, a provision that manifests the general regulatory objectives of the act. The GMO Act is the only national legislative act in which the precautionary principle is mentioned explicitly.[16] It is clear that full implementation of Directive 2001/18/EC is the reason for mentioning the precautionary principle.[17] Writing general policy objectives in legislation is a common regulatory technique. Clauses on policy objectives usually serve as guidance in drafting more detailed secondary legislation. When it comes to applying law, such clauses may, at best, serve as permissible sources of law in hard cases.

However, Chapter 3 of the GMO Act lays down even general duties of care. According to Section 8(a): 'prudence and precaution shall be acknowledged in all uses of gene technology'. Moreover, Section 9 states that 'operators shall gain all necessary knowledge on the characteristics and health and environmental effects of GMOs, as long as this knowledge can be gained reasonably'. The original purpose of the general duties of care was to ensure that operators will:

- characterize the GMOs subject to use;
- assess the possible risks;
- provide the required risk management measures; and
- monitor the effects from the activity.

After the detailed rules on risk assessment and monitoring have been introduced, the general duties of care seem to have little relevance. In fact, the general duties of care entail principles rather than rules since they 'more or less' define duties for the operators.

Moreover, even though the general duties of care are addressed to the operators, they are modified into detailed permit conditions when the board issues permits. For example, a permit condition for a field trial on non-flowering genetically modified (GM) potatoes prohibited cultivation of any kind for two seasons after the trial had been carried through. The prohibition was to make sure that the GMO material, which possibly remains in the field for some time even after the GM potatoes have been removed, will be inactivated.[18] This kind of measure is an application of the precautionary principle: there is uncertainty about how long the GMO material will stay active in the field and whether it will spread to new cultivated plants. Another recent permit condition, which concerns a field trial on non-flowering birch, sets a duty on the operator to monitor the site of the trial and to report the results to the Board for Gene Technology for three years after the trial has been shut down.[19] Such permit conditions – when the risk for adverse effects is hypothetical – reflect the precautionary idea, although they are applications of more general principles of care widely applied in environmental law.

It is difficult to pinpoint the role of the precautionary principle in regulating the use of gene technology in Finland. This is partly because there is very little administrative practice. Moreover, the board has a tradition of reasoning its decisions only by stating whether the use is safe or not.[20] Nevertheless, the precautionary principle enjoys sufficient institutional support from the relevant EC and international law.[21] This should be reflected in the decisions made by the board. Moreover, the right to a sound environment guaranteed by Section 20 in the Finnish Constitution (731/1999) should foster precaution. Constitutional rights are also 'more or less' kinds of balancing norms, influencing the interpretation of law in hard cases. Thus, despite the vague status in national statutory law, the precautionary principle should be used as an interpretative tool in applying the GMO Act. In this process of interpretation, general principles of administrative law counterbalance precaution.

Precaution as a regulatory approach

Risk assessment

According to Section 8 in the GMO Act, it is the duty of the operator to make a risk assessment and attach it to the application that is submitted to the Board for Gene Technology. The board may use several so-called expert authorities in judging whether the risk assessment is sufficient or not. After the expert authorities have given their opinions, the board has three options: first, the board may request additional information on some points of the application; second, the board may issue the permit; and, third, the permit may be rejected. It has to be stressed that through the revision of the GMO Act (847/2004), the environmental risk assessment was explicitly established as the sole basis for providing knowledge on facts for the consideration of the permits. In other words, the role of the technical exercise called risk assessment was strengthened when deciding about the permit.

The principles and methods of environmental risk assessment are regulated in detail by Ordinance 110/2005 of the Ministry of Social and Health Affairs. The ordinance transposes – practically word for word – Annex II of Directive 2001/18/EC. The rules for risk assessment regarding the deliberate release of GMOs are extremely detailed. Furthermore, the expert and supervisory authority has provided soft law guidance on ecological and biological research methods applicable for assessing the risks of genetically modified plants.[22] For the contained use of GMOs, the risk assessment rules are more general, although the new Ordinance 1053/2005 of the Ministry of Social and Health Affairs aims for more detailed regulation than the annulled Ordinance 492/2000.

While considering the permit for the use of GMOs, the Board for Gene Technology may apply Section 18.3 of the GMO Act and require the operator to complement the risk assessment. In effect, the procedure goes back to the risk assessment phase. As mentioned, this is a concrete mechanism to apply precaution – to decide that the burden of proof still rests on the operator. In practice, this has happened rather often through unofficial communication between the operators and the authorities.[23] However, requests for new information must be reasoned and not based purely on hypothetical assumptions. The principle of proportionality has a significant role to play here, particularly since the available knowledge on the potential effects of the operation may vary from statistical uncertainty to ignorance. The board may not oblige the operator to collect or analyse data if this would clearly be disproportionate, even though the duty for risk assessment covers 'delayed effects', as well as 'cumulated effects' when GMOs are deliberately released into the environment. Regardless of the fact legal boundaries clearly exist with regard to the scope and depth of the duty for risks assessment, it is difficult to see how, in practice, these boundaries would be greeted. The Board for Gene Technology has access to updated knowledge on risk assessment through the network of competent authorities within the EC and other international contacts. The knowledge that is provided through these networks set the basis for what can be required, case by case, from the risk assessment. However, the line between scientifically based assumptions about hypothetical effects and purely hypothetical assumptions is blurred. Nevertheless, it must be drawn.[24]

Permit consideration

In the GMO Act, the legal premises to permit the use of GMOs are defined in separate provisions for contained use, field trials and market approval of GMO seeds. All of the so-called permit thresholds are flexible in the sense that the difference between legal and illegal is defined using a relatively broad language. Nevertheless, some obvious differences can also be found. The threshold becomes more and more stringent as the activity develops step by step from simple use of GMOs in laboratory conditions to releasing GMOs into the natural environment.

Section 13 of the GMO Act classifies contained use of GMOs in four different categories based on the magnitude of risk caused by the use. According to Section 15, only categories 3 and 4 are subject to the permit procedure. The activities that belong to categories 1 and 2 are subject to notification – meaning that the operator may start the activity without any decision from the board. Category 1 activities can be initiated right after the notification has been made, whereas in category 2 uses, the operator must wait 45 days before starting the activity. The operator is responsible for classifying each use when making the notification. If there is uncertainty about the classification of the use, the higher classification – and, thus, stricter protection measures – shall be used. This rule in Section 13.3 of the GMO Act is at the core of precaution: in uncertainty, stricter protection measures are applied. In fact, the Board for Gene Technology has, in some cases, altered the classification made by the operator.[25] The permit threshold for contained use in categories 3 and 4 is defined in Section 16a of the GMO Act as follows: the board 'shall authorize contained use unless it causes, according to the risk assessment defined in Section 8, *harm* to human or animal health or the environment, taking into account all the proposed containment and safety measures'.[26]

Section 18 establishes a stricter threshold for field trials on GMOs: the board 'shall authorize the release unless it causes, according to the risk assessment defined in Section 8, danger to human or animal health or the environment'. In the Finnish regulatory tradition, 'harm' expresses a somewhat higher acceptable risk level than 'danger'.[27] Therefore, as a point of departure, field trials are subject to a stricter threshold than contained use of GMOs. With regard to the burden of proof, both Sections 16a and 18 take a neutral stand: it is not pointed out if it is the operator who has to prove that the use of GMOs will not cause any danger or harm, or whether the Board for Gene Technology (CA) has to show that danger or harm will occur. In other words, the quantity of required proof is defined in loose terms; but the burden of proof is not clearly allocated. However, it has to be stressed that in Section 8 of the GMO Act, the risk assessment is defined, unconditionally and unexceptionally, as a duty of the operator. This means that – as a point of departure – the burden of proof is always on the operator.

The permit threshold becomes even stricter when the placing of a GMO product on the market is considered. Following Section 21 of the GMO Act, 'authorization shall be issued *if the risk assessment proves* that the product will not cause danger to human or animal health or the environment'. Again, as with field trials, a danger of harm means that the application has to be turned down. Furthermore, in placing products on the market, the burden of proof is expressly on the operator: it is the operator's task to prove through risk assessment that danger will not be caused. There is no administrative practice on placing GMOs on the market in Finland.

Despite the explained quantitative differences with respect to the burden of proof placed on operators, each of the three permit thresholds in the GMO Act can be described as 'unconditional rules of requirement'.[28] This means that in considering whether the permit for using GMOs should be issued or rejected, the board may only give relevance to the potential effects on health and the environment. Other aspects, such as ethical acceptance or potential socio-economic effects from the particular GMO innovation subject to use, fall outside the Board for Gene Technology's discretion. There is no balancing against any other effects or interests. In other words, if the potential effects on health and the environment cross the probability and magnitude threshold, the permit cannot be issued; if they do not, the permit must be issued. The rather technocratic approach taken by the legislator has been put into practice by the board. Since 2000, not more than four applications on new field trials have been made. All trials have been accepted because 'no harm to health or the environment is expected to occur'.[29]

Modification and nullification of permits

The Board for Gene Technology has a variety of effective legal measures to apply precaution even after the use of GMOs has been permitted pursuant to Sections 19a and 22 of the GMO Act. Intervention by the board can be justified on changes in the activity itself, but also based on new knowledge of the activity's risks. The legal preconditions for bringing restrictions to a valid permit, but also the available means of intervention, differ slightly depending upon what kind of use is in question. After receiving new information on the risks of the activity, the board may:

- restrict contained use of a GMO (Section 22.2);
- prohibit any illegal activity if the restrictions above are not sufficient to attain the required safety level (Section 22);

● alter the conditions of the permit for a field trial (Section 19a);
● postpone a field trial (Section 19a);
● nullify the permit for a field trial (Section 19a).

Due to the close link to common market regulation, interventions on market approvals of GMO products are regulated separately in the GMO Act. Moreover, it is the national government that decides about interventions on valid market approvals of GMO products within the Finnish territory. In this process, the Board for Gene Technology and the supervisory authorities have only an informative and advisory role. It is worth noticing that the board is still the competent authority when the permit for releasing GMO products into the market is issued.

According to Section 24 in the GMO Act, any intervention on a valid market approval requires that there is a serious danger to human or animal health or the environment. In the case when the board or the supervisory authorities find new information that is relevant to the risk posed by the product, they will inform the national government. The national government may then:

● temporarily restrict the use and marketing of a GMO product;
● prohibit the use and marketing of a GMO product (Section 24).

A relevant legal difference, if compared to the measures that apply to contained use and field trials, is that the permit for market approvals cannot be nullified or modified as such. Restrictions or a prohibition are temporary measures that restrain the operator from using the permit. When restrictions are removed, the permit is as valid as ever. Nullification of a permit is a heavier measure in the sense that the operator has to apply for a new permit if he or she wants to continue with the use later on.

There are, of course, general legal restrictions in applying any of the above explained measures. First, the 'acceptable risk' is always, to some extent, higher when a valid permit is modified, nullified or restrictions to use the permit are set: the GMO Act requires *significant new risks* before intervention can take place (Sections 19a, 22 and 24). The requirement for significance stems from the general principle of administrative and environmental law; the operator has the right to trust that a decision taken by a public authority will not be revised in an unpredictable way.[30]

Second, the measures applied have to be necessary to reduce the risks of the activity. The necessity test stems from the general principle that administrative measures have to be appropriate. Moreover, the general principle or proportionality hinders authorities from taking measures that are disproportionate to risks that emerge on the basis of new information. Therefore, available measures have to be prioritized, starting from necessary modifications to the activity and with nullification as the last option.

SWEDISH LAW

Applicable legislation and competent authorities

In Sweden, contained use of GMOs was first regulated through the Occupational Safety Act (1977:1160), while deliberate releases were covered by the Plant Protection Act (1972:319). Authorization for contained use was required from 1979 and for environmental releases of plants from 1990.[31] The Gene Technology Act (1994:900) entered into force in 1994 – a year before Sweden joined the EU – covering contained use and deliberate release of GMOs. The legislative structure changed yet again in 1998: the Gene Technology Act was annulled as the Environmental Code (1998:808) entered into force.

The Environmental Code is a comprehensive legal framework covering regulation on nature protection and pollution control, as well as some harmful substances. The code is the key statute even in the regulation of gene technology. In addition to the generally applicable provisions of the code, its Chapter 13 is devoted to gene technology alone. To supplement the code, separate governmental ordinances on contained use (2000:271) and deliberate release of GMOs into the environment (2002:1086) have been enacted. Furthermore, the competent authorities are empowered to give more detailed administrative rules within their own fields of competence.[32]

The administrative competence on the use of gene technology is fragmented, depending partly upon the type of use and partly upon the host organism. The competent authority on using gene technology in animals, plants and feed is the Board of Agriculture (*Jordbruksverket*). The board has decided on a total of 114 field trials on GMO plants, which makes it the most important competent authority in applying legislation on gene technology. The National Board of Forestry (*Skogsstyrelsen*) governs the use of gene technology in forestry. The Swedish Chemicals Inspectorate (*Kemikalieinspektionen*) has competence when genetically modified micro-organisms are released into the environment. The Work Safety Authority, on the other hand, is the competent authority for contained use of GMOs other than plants, feed and trees. Thus, for example, the competent authority for a field trial on GM potato is the Board of Agriculture and contained use of a GMO micro-organism would fall under the Work Safety Authority's competence. The Gene Technology Advisory Board has the general duty of monitoring developments in the field of gene technology, overseeing ethical issues and giving advice on the use of gene technology. For instance, the Gene Technology Advisory Board gives an opinion each time that a permit for the use of GMOs is considered.[33]

The research activity within 'green gene' technology in Sweden in considerably higher than in Finland. The Swedish Board of Agriculture, which is the most important competent authority in this respect, has decided on more than 100 applications for field trials. One obvious explanation for the difference is the fact that the environmental conditions in southern Sweden – where most of the field trials are carried out – are suitable for testing innovations that have market potential on a larger European scale.

Precaution as a principle of statutory law

Section 3 in Chapter 2 of the Swedish Environmental Code defines the precautionary principle as follows:

> *Persons who pursue an activity or take a measure, or intend to do so, shall implement protective measures, comply with restrictions and take any other precautions that are necessary in order to prevent, hinder or combat damage or detriment to human health or the environment as a result of the activity or measure. For the same reason, the best possible technology shall be used in connection with professional activities. Such precautions shall be taken as soon as there is cause to assume that an activity or measure may cause damage or detriment to human health or the environment.*

The preparatory act of the Environmental Code makes it clear that the provision is equal to the precautionary principle developed in international law.[34] The precautionary principle is one of the so-called general rules of consideration defined in Chapter 2 of the code (see also Chapter 7). The general rules of consideration, which are applied to all activities covered by the code, have a twofold function. First, they address general duties to operators. Second, they are applied by the permit authorities in issuing permits.[35] Thus, in the Swedish legal order, precaution is defined as a general principle of statutory environmental law. Like the other general rules of consideration, Section 2.3 is a 'more or less' kind of optimizing norm, which is balanced against other general rules of consideration in issuing authorizations.

In addition to section 2.3 of the Environmental Code, the precautionary principle is referred to in one of the introductory provisions of Ordinance 2002:1086 on the deliberate release of GMOs. According to Section 1.3 of the ordinance:

> *... in applying this ordinance the administrative authorities shall, according to the precautionary principle, make sure that all necessary measures will be taken in order to prevent negative effects on human health or the environment when GMOs are deliberately released into the environment or placed on the market.*

Section 1.3 is not an operational provision, but rather a policy aim. Nevertheless, it reflects the strong status that the principle has in Directive 2001/18/EC and reinforces the institutional support and weight of the precautionary principle in this particular context. In the latest administrative practice, the Board of Agriculture has constantly referred to the precautionary principle as part of the general legal basis for permit consideration with regard to field trials. The precautionary principle was the key norm in rejecting a field trial even though it was not explicitly mentioned.[36]

The precautionary principle is counterbalanced by Section 2.7 of the Environmental Code: all general rules of consideration shall only be applicable where compliance cannot be deemed unreasonable. In considering what is unreasonable, particular importance will be attached to the benefits of protective measures and their costs.[37] In other words, measures should be cost efficient in relation to the risk posed by the activity. However, the cost-benefit analyses cannot be taken into account in applying the so-called stop rule in Section 2.9. The stop rule defines the effects on health and environment that cannot be caused by any activity. Another example, then, is that even in applying the stop rule, the different public interests of the activity are balanced against each other. This will be analysed more closely below.

Precaution as a regulatory approach

Risk assessment

According to Section 2.2 of the Environmental Code, all 'persons who pursue an activity or take a measure, or intend to do so, must possess the knowledge that is necessary in view of the nature and scope of the activity or measure to protect human health and the environment against damage or detriment'. The provision is a general duty for the operators to be actively aware about the effects of their activities. With regard to the use of GMOs, this general duty is specified by the duty to make an 'investigation of the damage to health and the environment that the organisms are liable to cause' before contained use or deliberate release of GMOs into the environment (Section 13.8). The provision even sets a qualitative requirement for risks assessments, which have to be carried out 'in accordance with scientific knowledge and proven experience'. The magnitude of the risk assessment is defined case by case, depending upon the character of the operation and the organism.[38] The methods of the risk assessment are specified in the ordinances on contained use (2000:271) and deliberate release of GMOs into the environment (2002:1086). The rules on risk assessment are much more detailed with regard to deliberate release of GMOs into the environment than to contained use of GMOs.

Ordinance 2000:271 on contained use of GMOs only requires that classification of the contained use is part of the risk assessment. The Swedish Work Environment Authority has published soft law guidelines for assessing the risks of contained use of GMOs.[39] For deliberate releases, the principles and methods of risk assessment are defined in Appendix 1 to Ordinance 2002:1086. The defined principles and methods follow the wording in Appendix II of Directive 2001/18/EC on ecological risk assessment. Therefore, this chapter does not to repeat them here, but rather refers to the directive.

After the competent authority has received the application and the risk assessment, it may require the operator to supplement the risk assessment or to provide further information on the activity. The information must be necessary with regard to the risk (Section 18 in 2000:271 and Section 2.8 in 2002:1086). Thus, for instance, the principle of proportionality restricts the competent authority from requiring new knowledge from the operator if the cost of gaining the knowledge is disproportionate in relation to its relevance regarding the risk assessment.

Authorization requirement

All field trials and market approvals of GMO products are subject to permit procedures referred to in the Environmental Code (Section 13.12). For contained use, however, both notification and permit procedures are applied depending upon the classification of the use. In the ordinance on contained use (2000:271), different uses are divided into three (F, L and R) classes. According to Sections 23 to 26 of the ordinance, a permit is always required for R uses, while F and L uses are subject to notification procedure only.

However, according to Section 20 of the ordinance, the competent authority may oblige the operator to apply for a permit even for notified F and L uses.

Permit threshold: Environmental aspects

The general rules of consideration in Chapter 2 of the Environmental Code set the legal basis for considering the environmental and health aspects of using GMOs. The so-called 'stop rule' (Section 2.9) is the general threshold for considering whether an activity should be permitted or not. In fact, the provision contains two stop rules that both have their own balancing logic. The difference between the two thresholds is the magnitude of the potential harm: the more serious the potential harm is, the more stringent is the applied stop rule.[40] First of all, activities may not be 'likely to cause significant damage or detriment to human health or the environment' unless in special circumstances (Section 2.9.1). These 'special circumstances' shall be considered by the competent authority. However, even if the existence of special circumstances could be argued for, activity 'must not be undertaken if it is liable to lead to a significant deterioration in the living conditions of a large number of people or substantial detriment to the environment' (Section 2.9.2).

Nevertheless, the national government can allow an exception even if the latter and more stringent threshold in Section 9 is met 'if an activity or measure is of particular importance for reasons of public interest' (Section 2.10). However, this exception from the stop rule applies only to environmental effects, not to human health effects. In its consideration, the government may only balance different public interests against each other. The operators' private interest should not be taken into account.[41]

In considering any of the thresholds described in Section 2.9, the operator has to show that 'the obligations arising out of this chapter have been complied with'. This provision is a direct implementation of the precautionary principle since it lays the burden of proof on the operator. The standard of proof varies from case to case. As a starting point, the standard of the required proof is particularly high with regard to the use of GMOs because the whole regulatory framework is based on the idea that the operators have to show that the use of GMOs is safe. However, according to Section 2.7, the standard of required proof should not be unreasonable: the competent authority may not, for example, claim for risk assessment data that is costly in relation to its relevance in the risk analysis.

The general rules of consideration are the same for both contained use and deliberate release of GMOs into the environment. The variance in the level of protection between contained use and deliberate releases comes from the ordinances on contained use (2000:271) and deliberate release of GMOs into the environment (2002:1086). Both of these secondary acts address even substantial norms despite their apparent focus on procedures. The so-called step-by-step rule, according to which the GMOs have to be used in a laboratory before being released into the environment, comes indirectly from the principle of ecological risk assessment in Ordinance 2002:1086.

Permit threshold: Ethical aspects

Chapter 13 of the Environmental Code is specifically dedicated to the use of gene technology. Special attention is paid to ethical concerns as an issue that should particularly be considered with regard to the use of gene technology (Section 13.1). In fact, a permit for the use of GMOs should only be granted if the activity is justifiable on ethical grounds (Section 13.10). This means that ethical acceptability is an independent legal premise for permit consideration – the activity could be turned down solely on the basis of being considered unethical. The requirement for ethical acceptability was already established in the GMO Act (1994:900). To differentiate from the scientific risk assessment, ethical aspects should refer to the societal effects of the innovation at stake, not to the risks to health or the environment from the release itself. Furthermore, ethical acceptability is about balancing different public interests. Private interests, such as the potential economic value of the innovation for the operator, should not be considered. For instance, arguments relating to future changes in the structure of agriculture could be relevant.[42]

How, then, have ethical aspects shaped the consideration of the Board of Agriculture with regard to field trials on GMO plants? For a long time, explicit analysis of ethical acceptability of field trials was avoided.In effect, ethical acceptability became parallel to environmental safety.[43] Suddenly, ethical aspects became part of the reasoning in 2004. In each decision taken by the Board of Agriculture, there is a separate heading in the reasoning part under which ethical aspects are considered. Thus, ethical aspects are now automatically part of the permit consideration with regard to field trials on GMOs.

Two observations from the reasoning by the Board of Agriculture can be made: first, without exception, the mentioned ethical aspects have been supportive of field trials and gene technology, in general; and, second, ethical reasoning has been of general character without any direct link to the specific activity that is under consideration. For instance, the competitiveness of Swedish research and technology, in general, is mentioned repeatedly in the reasoning for permits. Only exceptionally have the potential benefits from a particular innovation at stake been considered. This has happened when the link between the innovation at stake and future environmental benefits has been clearly established. For example, a potato resistant to pathogens was expected to decrease the use of chemicals in cultivation. This was considered to be an ethical aspect favouring the permit for a field trial.[44] The Board of Agriculture has also continuously stated that making assessments on the ethical acceptability of individual field trials is difficult. This is why the reasoning concerning ethical acceptability is inevitably somewhat flat. The Board of Agriculture, in fact, seems to repeat the same arguments in its permit decisions rather mechanically. Many of the recent decisions made have included exactly the same copy-pasted reasoning as follows:

> *When dealing with a long-term breeding activity in which collecting basic data and information is the first priority, the benefit to the public good from a specific field trial can be hard to predict. However, it will be imperative for the competitiveness of Swedish agriculture that plant breeding is carried out by taking into account Swedish environmental conditions. This can be ensured by keeping up expertise and development potential in Swedish plant breeding. Thus, when viewed in a broader context, even specific field trials may contribute to the public good.*[45]

Permit threshold: Combining environmental and ethical aspects

As explained above, the Environmental Code requires the use of GMOs to ensure safety to human health and to the environment, as well as to be ethically acceptable. In theory, environmental and ethical acceptability are independent legal thresholds. In the decisions of the Board of Agriculture, the two thresholds are also considered independently: environmental and ethical considerations are, at first, formulated as separate sections; in the end, environmental and ethical aspects are combined in the overall consideration on whether the field trial will be permitted or not.

The basic legal premise that sets a threshold for the environmental and health effects of using GMOs (Section 2.9.1) follows a balancing logic: if an activity is likely to cause significant harm, it may only be taken if other considerations outweigh the harm. This balancing involves a cost-benefit analysis in which even the operators' private interests are balanced against the risks to health and the environment. Some uses of GMOs, particularly release into the environment, may even become subject to the more stringent stop rule (Section 2.9.2). The investigation into health and environmental effects – that is, the risk assessment – is the factual basis for considering if the activity should be permitted according to the mentioned thresholds.

The legal premise for the ethical acceptability of using GMOs (Section 13.10) opens the permit consideration for arguments that go beyond environmental risk assessment and operators' private interests. The activity's negative and positive effects to society as a whole should both be considered. Thus, the threshold for which activities should be permitted and which are not is very flexible in the sense that different prescriptions and understandings of risk come forward. In fact, it is very difficult to think of an argument that would be legally irrelevant when a permit for the use of GMOs is considered.[46] Due to the very open definition of risk, the competent authorities have a wide margin for discretion. On the one hand, an activity that has the potential for adverse effects to the environment may be allowed if the positive societal effects outweigh the adverse effects. On the other hand, an application can be turned down solely based on the negative societal impacts following from the trial or from the future commercial applications of the innovation.

The Board of Agriculture has so far rejected two applications. One of the rejections concerned a field trial on oilseed rape that was modified to be resistant to mycosis. The Board of Agriculture concluded that – due to the poor characterization of the transgene in the laboratory phase – there was a risk that traits would spread to wild relatives in the environment. The reasoning was based on the step-by-step principle, which is really an application of the precautionary principle. Because the transgene was poorly characterized in the laboratory, there was uncertainty about the effects in the natural environment. This uncertainty was interpreted in favour of the environment. In fact, the Board of Agriculture came to this conclusion despite the fact that mycosis is a severe problem in the cultivation of oilseed rape. Moreover, it was explicitly admitted in the reasoning that the transgenic oilseed rape, which was subject to the permit application, had the potential to bring significant economic benefits to farming. However, even though the potential benefits where considered to be 'significant', uncertainty about the environmental effects outweighed the benefits in the overall consideration.[47] Amongst the different versions of the precautionary principle, Section 2.3 of the Environmental Code seems rather stringent: 'precautions shall be taken'. On the other hand, it makes clear that there has to be 'cause to assume' adverse effects before measures can be taken.

The Board of Agriculture has not made a single decision based on ethical or socio-economic aspects. In fact, the decision explained above proves that such a possibility is theoretical. Moreover, it appears that the decisions about field trials are, in practice, based solely on risks to health and the environment. The legal premise for ethical accept-ability does not, in practice, set any real threshold for the use of GMOs. In this respect, the 'law in action' seems to differ considerably from the 'law in books'.[48]

Modification and nullification of permits

The general provisions on the supervision of activities in Chapter 26 of the Environmental Code apply even to the use of gene technology. However, more special-ized rules about how authorities can modify valid authorizations for the use of GMOs are laid down in ordinances on contained use 2000:271 (Section 20) and deliberate release of GMOs into the environment 2002:1086 (Chapter 2, Sections 15 to 16, and Chapter 3, Sections 44 to 45).

If the operator changes the activity, or if there is a change in the environmental condi-tions in which the activity takes place, or if the supervisory authority receives new knowl-edge that is significant in relation to the risk to health or to the environment posed by the activity, the authority may:

- set further conditions for the use of GMOs;
- limit the time of contained use;
- postpone a field trial;
- temporarily limit the use or marketing of a GMO product in Sweden;
- prohibit a contained use or a field trial;
- set a temporary prohibition on the use and marketing of a GMO product in Sweden.

It is worth noticing here that the substantive legal basis for intervention narrows funda-mentally after the permit has been issued. While ethical and socio-economic aspects are relevant legal arguments in issuing the permit, a rebalancing of ethical or socio-economic aspects cannot be legally effective after the permit has been issued. The permit can be modified only if the risk to health or to the environment is considered to be increased.

Furthermore, even the acceptable risk to health and the environment is somewhat higher with regard to a valid permit than when the permit is first issued. The increased risk based on new knowledge has to be significant before authorities can intervene. The general rule of consideration in the Environmental Code (Section 2.7) is applicable even here: measures cannot be economically unreasonable with regard to the achieved reduction of risk. Moreover, the measures applied have to be necessary and propor-tionate, starting from appropriate restrictions to more comprehensive prohibitions.[49] As required by the Directive 2001/18/EC, national bans on the use and marketing of GMO products can only be temporary.

CONCLUSIONS

The precautionary principle is explicitly mentioned in the Finnish GMO Act, but only as a general policy objective. To the contrary, in the Swedish Environmental Code, the precautionary principle is a clearly defined operational provision – an obligatory source of law in every decision made by the competent authorities. However, provisions in national legislation alone tell little about the status of the precautionary principle in the legal order as a whole. In both jurisdictions, the precautionary principle gains strong institutional support from the relevant EC law.[50]

More importantly, the regulatory regime for GMOs is strictly precautionary: it imposes an authorization procedure and very detailed risk assessment duties on activities that have not been – at least not empirically – proven to cause adverse effects to health or the environment. Within this framework, we can find rules and principles which – either explicitly of implicitly – reflect precaution by turning the burden of proof to the operator. Section 2.1 in the Swedish Environmental Code lays the burden of proof on the operator with regard to all activities covered by the code. Finnish legislation, to the contrary, has no explicit rule on the burden of proof. However, in both jurisdictions the duty to make a risk assessment when GMOs are used is always on the operator. The scale and depth of the required risk assessment is significant, particularly with respect to the release of GMOs into the environment. In effect, the burden of proof is not easily shifted to the authority. In conclusion, the regulatory regime as a whole provides a 'system impulse' of extra precaution whenever the law is applied and interpreted. Due to this system impulse, counterbalancing principles, such as proportionality and legality, have less significance and weight in the GMO context than in other fields of environmental law.[51]

With regard to the Dworkinian dichotomy between rules and principles, it is essential to point out a logical difference between Finnish and Swedish legislation in how substantial norms are formulated. The difference is particularly clear between the so-called permit thresholds – that is, the provisions defining the substantial law limits for the use of GMOs. In Sections 16, 18 and 21 of the Finnish GMO Act, the permit thresholds are formulated as unconditional rules: if any of the defined adverse effects to health or the environment will be caused, the permit will be rejected; and, *vice versa*, if no adverse effects will follow, the permit shall be issued.[52] Meanwhile, the so-called 'stop rule' in Section 2.9 of the Swedish Environmental Code is a balancing norm – and, therefore, a principle rather than a rule. Moreover, the precautionary principle itself is one of the so-called general rules of consideration applied in permit consideration. The explained difference in norm formulations is relevant for the role that principles play in decision-making. The Finnish Board for Gene Technology applies 'all or nothing' rules. Principles such as precaution may only be used as interpretative tools. To the contrary, the Swedish permit authorities apply principles directly as norms in their own right, despite the fact that the provisions in Chapter 2 of the code are named as 'general *rules* on consideration'.

Finally, one more distinction between the two jurisdictions deserves attention. By looking at the substantial legal premises for the use of GMOs, we find that Finnish and Swedish legislations hold fundamentally different ideas about the risks of gene technology. Finnish legislation on gene technology is a continuation of the tradition of industrial pollution control, focusing exclusively on the potential effects to health and the environment from the use of GMOs.[53] The Swedish GMO legislation, on the contrary, was already disconnected from the industrial tradition when the Gene Technology Act (1994:900) was enacted. The Swedish legislation approaches individual uses of GMOs as comprehensive technological risks, not only as emissions.[54] However, the explained difference seems to be very much a difference between 'law in books', not between 'law in practice'. Scientific risk assessment dominates the application of law even in Sweden.

However, the explained difference in regulatory approaches may prove to be significant in the future. One of the key aims of Directive 2001/18/EC on the deliberate release of GMOs into the environment was to reinforce public participation. According to Article 9 of the directive, consultation with the public is compulsory whenever field trials on GMOs are considered. Both Finland and Sweden have implemented the requirement in their legislation.[55] However, it will be interesting to see how, and about what exactly, the public will be consulted in Finland, where the role of scientific expertise is strongly emphasized in the substantive law. It is, in fact, illegal to consider the permit based on other knowledge than what is gained through the risk assessment.[56] Swedish law – despite facing obvious challenges in turning the 'law in books' into 'law in action' – at least provides a bedrock for more comprehensive management of gene technology, in which uncertainty is so profoundly present. And, at the core, precaution is about managing uncertainty.

NOTES

1 See Fisher, E. (2001) 'Is the precautionary principle justifiable?', *Journal of Environmental Law*, vol 13, no 3, p318, as well as de Sadeleer, N. (2002) *Environmental Principles: From Political Slogans to Legal Rules*, Oxford University Press, Oxford, p222. For different interpretations, see, for example, Marr, S. and Schwemer, A. (2004) 'The precautionary principle in German environmental law', in *Yearbook of European Environmental Law*, vol 3, pp124–148, Oxford University Press, Oxford.

2 Among others, Bryan Wynne has sharply criticized the dominance of science and expert cultures in framing technological risks. See Wynne, B. (2002) 'Risk and environment as legitimatory discourses of technology: Reflexivity inside out?', *Current Sociology*, vol 50, no 3, pp459–477, as well as Wynne, B. (2001) 'Creating public alienation: Expert cultures of risk and ethics on GMOs', *Science as Culture*, vol 10, no 4, pp445–480. See even van Zwanenberg, P. and Stirling, A. (2004) 'Risk and precaution in the US and Europe: A response to Vogel', in *Yearbook of European Environmental Law*, vol 3, Oxford University Press, Oxford, p47.

3 See de Sadeleer, N. (2004) 'Environmental principles, modern and post-modern law' in Macrory, R. (ed) *Principles of European Environmental Law*, Europa Law Publishing, Groeningen, pp223–236. See even Christoforou, T. (2004) 'The regulation of genetically modified organisms in the European Union: The interplay of science, law and politics', *Common Market Law Review*, vol 41, p684, and even Somsen, H. (2006) 'Some reflections on EU biotechnology regulation', in Macrory, R. (ed) *Reflections on 30 Years of EU Environmental Law*, Europa Law Publishing, Groeningen, p342. Both Christoforou and Somsen acknowledge a broad understanding of risk as a feature of EU law on GMOs. The discussion on risk society was started by social scientists; see Beck, U. (1992) *Risk Society: Towards a New*

Modernity, Sage, London, as well as Giddens, A. (1990) *The Consequences of Modernity*, Polity Press, Cambridge.

4   Contained use takes place in laboratory conditions, whereas deliberate release involves contact with the natural environment. As a legal concept in Directive 2001/18/EC, deliberate release of GMOs into the environment comprises both the so-called field trials and placing GMO seeds on the market.

5   The aim of the study is to analyse some key features with respect to the role of the precautionary principle in the two jurisdictions. Such a brief study does not fulfil the scope and depth required from a truly comparative legal study.

6   Dworkin, R. (1977) *Taking Rights Seriously*, Harvard University Press, Cambridge, pp22–28. On environmental principles, in particular, see Doherty, M. G. (2004) 'Hard cases and environmental principles: An aid to interpretation?', in *Yearbook of European Environmental Law*, vol 3, pp57–78.

7   de Sadeleer has described and analysed this evolution accurately. See de Sadeleer, N. (2002) *Environmental Principles: From Political Slogans to Legal Rules*, Oxford University Press, Oxford, p222.

8   According to Aarnio, sources of law are either obligatory, weakly obligatory or permissible. Aarnio, A. (1989) *Laintulkinnan teoria*, WSOY, Juva.

9   In his book about principles in Finnish administrative law, Tähti makes an attack against unfounded use of loosely defined principles in administrative decision-making, claiming this is a violation of legality; see Tähti, A. (1995) *Periaatteet Suomen Hallinto-oikeudessa*, Lakimiesliiton Kustannus, Helsinki.

10 See de Sadeleer, N. (2002) *Environmental Principles: From Political Slogans to Legal Rules*, Oxford University Press, Oxford, pp289–291. See also Kuusiniemi, K., Ekroos, A., Kumpula, A. and Vihervuori, P. (2001) *Ympäristöoikeus*, WSOY, Juva, pp70–90. Even though environmental legislation still contains open-textured or 'flexible' provisions, there is a tendency for more detailed legislation. The desire for details is particularly strong in the EU – waste legislation, perhaps, being the best example in this respect.

11 See Alexy, R. (2000) 'On the structure of legal principles', *Ratio Juris*, vol 13, pp294–304. Particularly with regard to decision-making in environmental law, see Kuusiniemi, K., Ekroos, A., Kumpula, A. and Vihervuori, P. (2001) *Ympäristöoikeus*, WSOY, Juva, pp154–175, and even Zwanenberg, P. and Stirling, A. (2004) 'Risk and precaution in the US and Europe: A response to Vogel', in *Yearbook of European Environmental Law*, vol 3, Oxford University Press, Oxford, p78.

12 The strict dichotomy between risk assessment and management has been powerfully criticized. See, for instance, de Sadeleer, N. (2002) *Environmental Principles: From Political Slogans to Legal Rules*, Oxford University Press, Oxford, pp174–180, and even Zwanenberg, P. and Stirling, A. (2004) 'Risk and precaution in the US and Europe: A response to Vogel', in *Yearbook of European Environmental Law*, vol 3, Oxford University Press, Oxford, pp49–51.

13 See the Government Proposal for Gene Technology Act (HE 349/1994 vp), p6. For instance, gene technology innovations were used in some industrial processes.

14 Green gene technology refers to the use of gene technology in forestry and agriculture. These are the most relevant fields of gene technology with regard to protection of the environment. Respectively, red gene technology refers to medicine and white to industrial processes.

15 In KHO 1998:38, the court ruled that the applicant had access to some of the information about risk assessment, which the board had denied based on business secrecy. In KHO: 699/1/02 T, the court ruled that the exact location of a field trial was within the public right of access to information.

16 The Environmental Protection Act (86/2000), for instance, defines several other principles, such as the principle of prevention, the polluter pays principle and the principle of

prudence, but not the precautionary principle. Nor is there any other provision based on the precautionary idea.

17 The Government Proposal for Changing the Gene Technology Act (HE 42/2004) detailed motivations for Section 1.

18 The Decision by the Board for Gene Technology, 17 May 2001, Dnr 1/MB/01. A similar condition is in the decision by the Board for Gene Technology, 21 April 2004, Dnr 1/MB/04.

19 The Decision by the Board for Gene Technology, 10 May 2005, Dnr 1/MB/05.

20 See, for example, the decisions mentioned above.

21 See Ranta, J. (2001) Varautumisperiaate Ympäristöoikeudessa, Gummerus, Saarijärvi, pp22–24, who recognizes principle-based decision-making in environmental law as an option for rule-based decision-making.

22 *Suomen Ympäristö* 736/2004. Guidance is available at www.ymparisto.fi/download. asp?contentid=32070&lan=fi (accessed on 15 December 2005).

23 Based on interviews of civil servants in the board and at the Finnish Environment Institute (SYKE). SYKE is the expert authority with regard to risk assessments on the deliberate release of GMOs into the environment.

24 Based on interviews of civil servants in the board and at the Finnish Environment Institute (SYKE).

25 Based on interviews of civil servants in the board and at the Finnish Environment Institute (SYKE). Such decisions have even been made through unofficial communication between the operators and authorities.

26 The translation is by the author. There is no official English translation of the GMO Act available.

27 One example of this is the general groundwater pollution prohibition in Section 8 of the Environmental Protection Act (86/2000): all activities that may pollute the groundwater, and therefore cause harm, are prohibited. See also Kuusiniemi, K., Ekroos, A., Kumpula, A. and Vihervuori, P. (2001) *Ympäristöoikeus*, WSOY, Juva, pp1131–1132.

28 The term unconditional rules of requirement (*absoluta kravregler*) comes from Staffan Westerlund. The antonym to unconditional rules of requirement is the so-called balancing norm (*avvägningar*). See Westerlund, S. (2003) *Miljörättsliga Grundfrågår*, Åmyra Förlag, Uppsala, pp338–344, and also Westerlund, S. (2000) 'Sustainable balancing', in Kivivuori, A., Kuusiniemi, K. and Salila, J. (eds) *Juhlajulkaisu Erkki Johannes Hollo*, Lakimiesliiton Kustannus, Helsinki, pp405–423.

29 The Decision by the Board for Gene Technology, 17 May 2001, Dnr 1/MB/01. A similar condition is in the decision by the Board for Gene Technology, 21 April 2004, Dnr 1/MB/04. The Decision by the Board for Gene Technology, 10 May 2005, Dnr 1/MB/05.

30 Kuusiniemi, K., Ekroos, A., Kumpula, A. and Vihervuori, P. (2001) *Ympäristöoikeus*, WSOY, Juva, pp70–90.

31 Zetterberg, C. (1997) *Miljörättslig kontroll av genteknik*, Iustus Förlag, Uppsala, p89.

32 Most competent authorities have guidance on how the notifications or applications should be formulated, and on fees and changes of procedure, etc.

33 Ordinance (1994:902) on the Gene Technology Advisory Board.

34 The Government Proposal for Environmental Code (1997/98:45, del 1), pp208–209. See also Michanek, G. and Zetterberg, C. (2004) *Den svenska miljörätten*, Iustus Förlag, Uppsala, p119.

35 The Government Proposal for Environmental Code (1997/98:45, del 1), pp208–209. See also Michanek, G. and Zetterberg, C. (2004) *Den svenska miljörätten*, Iustus Förlag, Uppsala, p119.

36 For the decision, see the section on 'Permit threshold: Combining environmental and ethical aspects'.

37 See Michanek, G. and Zetterberg, C. (2004) *Den svenska miljörätten*, Iustus Förlag, Uppsala, pp134–135.
38 See Michanek, G. and Zetterberg, C. (2004) *Den svenska miljörätten*, Iustus Förlag, Uppsala, p294. See even Zetterberg, C. (1997) *Miljörättslig kontroll av genteknik*, Iustus Förlag, Uppsala, pp185–188.
39 See the Swedish Work Environment Authority's guidelines for risk assessment regarding contained use of GMOs at www.av.se/english/topics/gmm/ (accessed on 15 December 2005).
40 The Government Proposal for the Environmental Code (1997/98:45, del 1), pp237–239.
41 See Westerlund, S. (2000) 'Sustainable balancing', in Kivivuori, A., Kuusiniemi, K. and Salila, J. (eds) *Juhlajulkaisu Erkki Johannes Hollo*, Lakimiesliiton Kustannus, Helsinki, p414.
42 See Michanek, G. and Zetterberg, C. (2004) *Den svenska miljörätten*, Iustus Förlag, Uppsala, p293, as well as Zetterberg, C. (1997) *Miljörättslig kontroll av genteknik*, Iustus Förlag, Uppsala, pp158–160.
43 See the Decision by the Board of Agriculture, 22 May 2002, Dnr 22–1104/02.
44 Decision by the Board of Agriculture, 21 March 2005, Dnr 22–450/05.
45 The translation is by the author. See decisions by the Board of Agriculture, 17 March 2005/Dnr 22–7951/04, 25 March 2004/Dnr 22–6371/03, 16 April 2004/Dnr 22–6371/03 and 4 May 2005/Dnr 22–8095/04.
46 In the latest decisions, the reasoning of the Board of Agriculture has been relatively transparent in considering the different negative and positive effects of field trials. See, for example, Decisions 17 March 2005/Dnr 22–7951/04 and 24 March 2005/Dnr 22–8254/04.
47 The decision by the Board of Agriculture, 14 June 2000, Dnr 22–312/00.
48 For ethical considerations in practice, see also Karlsson, M. (2003) 'Ethics of sustainable development – a study of Swedish regulations for genetically modified organisms', *Journal of Agricultural Ethics,* vol 16, pp51–62.
49 The role of the principle of proportionality in environmental law has been under constant debate in Sweden. Some see that the status of the principle is too high, making effective protection of the environment difficult. See Michanek, G. and Zetterberg, C. (2004) *Den svenska miljörätten*, Iustus Förlag, Uppsala, pp45–46, and even Westerlund, S. (1996) 'Proportionalitetsprincipen – verklighet, missförstånd eller nydaning?', *Miljörättslig Tidskrift,* vol 2, pp248–284.
50 For the status on the precautionary principle in EC law, see, for example, Professor de Sadeleer's introduction to this book in Chapter 1. See also Scott, J. (2004) 'The precautionary principle before the European courts', in Macrory, R. (ed) *Principles of European Environmental Law,* Europa Law Publishing, Groeningen, pp49–72. On GMO legislation, specifically, see Chapter 12 in this book. For the influence of EU environmental law in applying national law in Finland, see Kuusiniemi, K., Ekroos, A., Kumpula, A. and Vihervuori, P. (2001) *Ympäristöoikeus*, WSOY, Juva, pp219–221, and, for Sweden, see Michanek, G. and Zetterberg, C. (2004) *Den svenska miljörätten*, Iustus Förlag, Uppsala, pp91–93.
51 Thus, my division between precaution as a principle and precaution as a regulatory approach is partly misleading. The principle gains implicit institutional support from the whole legal regime that is originally based on the precautionary idea. At least for the Swedish part, the significant weight of precaution in the GMO context can be traced back to administrative practice; see the section on 'Permit threshold: Combining environmental and ethical aspects'.
52 This regulatory technique has prevailed in the Finnish environmental law for some time.
53 See Salila, J. (1999) 'Biotekniikan ympäristövaikutusten oikeudellinen sääntely', in *Ympäristöoikeudellisia tutkielmia,* vol 1, Suomen ympäristöoikeudellinen seura, Helsinki,

pp163–295, and Hollo, E. (1998) 'Biotekniikka ja luonnon monimuotoisuus – funktionaalinen näkökulma biotekniikan sääntelyyn', *Lakimies*, vol 5, pp735–756.

54 Achen has studied the preparatory process of GMO legislations in Norway, Denmark and Sweden. Whereas in Denmark the legislation is based on a traditional distinction between ethics, politics and law, in Sweden (and particularly in Norway) the three spheres are intermingled. See Achen, T. (1997) *Den bioetiske udfordring – En retspolitiske studie af forholdet mellem etik, politik og ret i det lovforberedende arbejde vedrørende bio- och genteknologi i Danmark, Norge og Sverige*, University of Linköping, Sweden.

55 In Finland, Section 36b of the GMO Act states that the public shall be consulted without saying much about the methods of consulting. Complementary Swedish provision is found in Section 10 of Chapter 2 in the ordinance on the deliberate release of GMOs into the environment (2002:1086).

56 Kumpula (2004) argues – I think correctly – that the precautionary principle cannot be fully fleshed if procedural rights are not meaningfully implemented. This is particularly important with regard to complex technological risks. See Kumpula, A. (2004) Ympäristä oikeutena, Suomalainen Lakimiesyhdistys, Helsinki, pp240–252.

CHAPTER 15

The Precautionary Principle and Nature Conservation Law: EU and Danish Experiences

Helle Tegner Anker

INTRODUCTION

A precautionary approach in modern nature conservation law is a necessity. Modern nature conservation law serves the purpose of protecting species, nature types and ecosystems as part of the wider biosphere. This is reflected in, *inter alia*, the Convention on Biological Diversity (CBD) and in the European Union (EU) Directive 92/43 on the conservation of natural habitats and of wild fauna and flora (hereafter the Habitats Directive).[1] However, an immense lack of knowledge characterizes the existence and relationships of species, nature types and ecosystems. Thus, an often significant degree of uncertainty exists in relation to the impact of human activities on biodiversity. Accordingly, the precautionary principle is reflected in the preamble of the CBD by 'noting also that where there is a threat of significant reduction or loss of biological diversity, lack of full scientific certainty should not be used as a reason for postponing measures to avoid or minimize such a threat'. The question is, thus, how the precautionary principle shall be applied or operationalized as part of nature conservation law. As expressed by de Sadeleer (see Chapter 2 in this volume), there are two basic elements in the application of the precautionary principle – namely, risk assessment (that is, creating an informed decision-making context) and risk management (that is, balancing the interests involved in light of the acceptable level of risk).[2] Both aspects are important in relation to nature conservation law.

Traditional nature conservation law has, to some extent, focused on the protection or conservation of specified species or designated areas by limiting harmful activities – for example, through general prohibitions/restrictions or licensing requirements for specified activities. However, modern nature conservation law, when adopting an ecosystem perspective, cannot rely on the delimitation of species, areas or harmful activities.[3] A fundamental regulatory challenge is to catch all potentially harmful activities, taking into account the issue of cumulative effects. Thus, broad impact assessment requirements – perhaps supplemented with substantive decision criteria that limit the balancing of interests in decision-making – characterize modern nature conservation law as reflected in the Habitats Directive. The Habitats Directive Article 6(3) includes both aspects – that is, a wide-ranging impact assessment requirement and a substantive decision criterion. Article 6(3) requires all projects and plans likely to have a significant effect on a site to be subject to an assessment, and sets up the decision criterion that a project or plan may only be agreed upon if it will not adversely affect the integrity of the site. Similar requirements, although less explicit with regard to impact assessment, follow from the species protection provisions of the Habitats Directive and Directive 79/409 on the conservation of wild birds (hereafter the Birds Directive).[4] The substantive decision criteria regarding species protection – for example, Article 12's prohibition on the deterioration or destruction of breeding sites or resting places – quite clearly presupposes an assessment of the risk of such effects by any activity. Other wide-ranging impact assessment requirements can be found in EU Directive 85/337 on the assessment of the effects of certain public and private projects on the environment (hereafter the EIA Directive)[5] and EU Directive 2001/42 on the assessment of the effects of certain plans and programmes on the environment (hereafter the SEA Directive).[6] However, the EIA and SEA directives do not include substantive decision criteria, as in Habitats Directive Article 6(3). Where impact assessment requirements reflect one limb of the precautionary principle – that is, risk assessment – by ensuring scientifically informed decision-making, the substantive decision criteria reflect the other limb of the precautionary principle – that is, risk management. The application of the precautionary principle may vary depending upon the existence of substantive decision criteria. Substantive decision criteria may clearly reflect an absolute level of acceptable risk decisive to the balancing of interests. It appears that the more strict the substantive decision criteria, the more effect is given to the precautionary principle with regard to risk management. This seems to be clearly reflected in the rulings of the European Court of Justice (ECJ) – in particular, regarding Habitats Directive Article 6(3) – and also in the practice of the Danish administrative appeal boards. The existence of substantive decision criteria may, however, also affect the risk assessment – for example, by increasing demands for scientific accuracy or by reversing the burden of proof.

Although the precautionary principle may not be explicitly stated in nature conservation law, it may, depending in particular upon impact assessment requirements and substantive decision criteria, gain an important role in the application of modern nature conservation law. This chapter will explore the role of the precautionary principle as applied or operationalized by impact assessment requirements and substantive decision criteria in the Habitats Directive and the EIA Directive. Furthermore, Danish nature conservation law and the implementation of the EU Habitats Directive and the EIA Directive in relation to the assessment of, and decision regarding, new projects will be analysed – in particular, through studies of the practice of the Danish Nature Protection Appeal Board.

GENERAL STATUS OF THE PRECAUTIONARY PRINCIPLE IN EUROPEAN UNION AND DANISH CONSERVATION LAW

Exploring the status of the precautionary principle in EU and Danish nature conservation law is an excursion into the wilderness of indirect insinuations. It follows quite clearly from the European Community (EC) Treaty Article 174 that EU environmental law should be based on the precautionary principle (see Chapter 1 in this volume). Explicit references to the precautionary principle in the different pieces of legislation are, however, rare. Neither the Birds Directive nor the Habitats Directive nor the EIA Directive refers to the precautionary principle. In the preamble of the 1997 amendment to the EIA Directive, a reference, however, is made to the precautionary principle as stated in EC Treaty Article 130R (now 174). As mentioned earlier, the impact assessment requirements of the EIA Directive, as well as the Habitats Directive, even without explicit reference, clearly reflect the precautionary principle in providing for a scientific assessment of the *potential effects* of proposed projects or plans. Furthermore, the substantive decision criterion of the Habitats Directive limits the balancing of interests – that is, the risk management – by prescribing an absolute level of acceptable negative effects. The impact assessment requirements and the substantive decision criteria in the EIA Directive and the Habitats Directive will be analysed below in light of the rulings of the European Court of Justice.

Danish nature conservation law does not make any explicit reference to the precautionary principle. The primary pieces of legislation are the Nature Protection Act and, to some extent, the Planning Act.[7] The Planning Act provides for general protection of the countryside through a rural zone permit requirement. Furthermore, the EIA Directive has been implemented in the Danish Planning Act. The Nature Protection Act provides for, *inter alia*, a general protection of certain habitats and also for the individual nature conservation orders. The Habitats Directive has primarily been implemented through a statutory order on the delimitation and administration of international nature protection areas. The statutory order does not, however, clearly reflect the structure of Habitats Directive Article 6. During 2004, an amendment of the Nature Protection Act (and a new Forest Act) was adopted, providing new instruments to deal, in particular, with existing farming and forestry activities affecting Natura 2000 areas. The 2003 Act on Environmental Objectives obliges the authorities to draw up so-called Natura 2000 plans with the purpose of specifying the objective of favourable conservation status and of identifying the necessary measures to be taken to achieve the objectives or to avoid deterioration. The first Natura 2000 plans are expected to be adopted in 2009, parallel to the adoption of water district plans.

Although the precautionary principle may be difficult to retrieve in written rules, it can be expressed through the choice of regulatory instruments, emphasizing, for example, impact assessment or absolute levels of acceptable risk. Such instruments set up requirements for decision-making – that is, procedural requirements regarding the level of information, as well as substantive requirements regarding the balancing of interests. Through such instruments, the precautionary principle has gained increasing importance in the application of the law – for instance, as expressed by the ECJ, as well as by the Danish administrative appeal boards (the Nature Protection Board of Appeal and the Environmental Protection Board of Appeal). Thus, the precautionary principle is being developed within nature conservation law as a legally binding principle. It appears that the precautionary principle does not only have a permissive character – giving the authorities an opportunity to act; it also has an obliging character – imposing a duty upon the authorities to act.[8]

RISK ASSESSMENT AND RISK MANAGEMENT IN EU NATURE CONSERVATION LAW

In this section the analysis of EU nature conservation law is confined to the Habitats Directive. Apart from the Birds Directive, many other EU directives are important to nature conservation – for example, Directive 2000/60 establishing a framework for community action in the field of water policy (the Water Framework Directive) and other directives; however, they are not discussed in this chapter.[9] Furthermore, the scope of the study will be limited to habitat protection as opposed to species protection, and the focus will be on the regulation of new projects or activities as reflected in Habitats Directive Articles 6(3) and 6(4). In order to more precisely ascertain the dependence of the precautionary principle upon the specific requirements of the Habitats Directive, a comparison will be made with the assessment requirements of the EIA Directive.

The Habitats Directive: Article 6(3)

The Habitats Directive sets the goal of achieving a favourable conservation status for natural habitats and species of wild fauna and flora of European Community interest (see Article 2). *Favourable conservation status* is defined in Article 1, *litra* (e) for natural habitats and *litra* (i) for species as:

> ... *[the] conservation status of a natural habitat will be taken as favourable when:*

- its natural range and areas it covers within that range are stable or increasing; and
- the specific structure and functions which are necessary for its long-term maintenance exist and are likely to continue to exist for the foreseeable future; and
- the conservation status of its typical species is favourable as defined in (i).

> ... *[the] conservation status of a species will be taken as favourable when:*

- population dynamics data on the species concerned indicate that it is maintaining itself on a long-term basis as a viable component of its natural habitats; and
- the natural range of the species is neither being reduced nor is likely to be reduced for the foreseeable future; and
- there is, and will probably continue to be, a sufficiently large habitat to maintain its populations on a long-term basis.

As a distinct feature, the Habitats Directive thus employs an *ecosystem or resource perspective.*[10] Such a regulatory perspective reflects that the point of departure for regulating should be the (natural) resources or ecosystems as identified, rather than various activities such as construction, farming, forestry, fishing or hunting. The regulatory perspective may thus pose a regulatory challenge to legislation based on a more traditional activity perspective listing certain activities. A challenge is – in accordance with the precautionary principle – to catch all potentially harmful activities.

The ecosystem perspective is clearly reflected in Article 6(3):

> *Any plan or project not directly connected with or necessary to the management of the site but likely to have a significant effect thereon, either individually or in combination with other plans or projects, shall be subject to appropriate assessment of its implications for the site in view of the site's conservation objectives. In light of the conclusions of the assessment of the implications for the site and subject to the provisions of paragraph 4, the competent national authorities shall agree to the plan or project only after having ascertained that it will not adversely affect the integrity of the site concerned and, if appropriate, after having obtained the opinion of the general public.*

Article 6(3) thus requires an assessment of the implications of any plan or project likely to have a significant effect on the site either individually or in combination with other plans or projects. The only exemption to the assessment requirement applies to projects or plans directly connected with or necessary to the management of the site. Apart from the assessment requirement, Article 6(3) also provides a substantive decision criterion stipulating that the authorities can agree to the plan or project only after having ascertained that it will not adversely affect the integrity of the site concerned. Derogation from the substantive decision criterion can only be made in the absence of alternative solutions, on the basis of imperative reasons of overriding public interest, and by taking all necessary compensatory measures (see Article 6(4)).

Article 6(3) thus clearly reflects the two main elements of the precautionary principle: risk assessment and risk management. The application of Article 6(3) can be divided into four different steps:

1 definition of plans and projects;
2 screening of potential significant impact;
3 assessment; and
4 decision.[11]

The EU Commission has in its guidelines regarding Articles 6(3) and 6(4) identified the two stages – screening and appropriate assessment. This is followed by the requirements in Article 6(4) as the third stage (assessment of alternative solutions), and a fourth stage: assessment of compensatory measures.[12] According to the guidelines, the precautionary principle, in this respect, implies that there will be no significant effects on a Natura 2000 site (screening), or that there will be no adverse effects on the integrity of the site (assessment), or that there is an absence of alternatives or that there are compensatory measures.

The *definition of plans and projects* should, according to the European Commission and the European Court of Justice, be interpreted in a broad sense as also reflected in EIA

Directive Article 1(2), including construction works and other interventions in the natural surroundings and landscape.[13] This is in accordance with the precautionary principle, which aims to consider all potential effects independently of a (narrow) listing of activities. The ECJ in case C-127/02, *Waddenzee* stated that an activity such as mechanical cockle fishing was covered by the concept of a plan or project as set out in Article 6(3) (para 27). The ECJ, furthermore, declared that 'mechanical cockle fishing, which had been carried on for many years but for which a licence entailing a new assessment both of the possibility of carrying on that activity and of the site where it may be carried on falls within the concept of plan or project within the meaning of Article 6(3)'. This does not, however, mean that any renewal or review of an existing licence constitutes a distinct plan or project within the meaning of Article 6(3). The question is whether it is the establishment of a 'new' or amended project – for example, using new production methods or affecting new areas – or the fact that a new or reviewed permit is required that may trigger an assessment requirement. Normally, existing (harmful) activities shall be dealt with according to the general provision in Article 6(2). However, it appears from case C-127/02 that review procedures regarding existing activities are subject to Article 6(3) as far as they entail a new decision on whether to carry on the activity (see the following section 'Risk assessment according to the EIA Directive' on the similar distinction regarding the EIA Directive).

The assessment requirement in Article 6(3) can hardly be confined to projects (or plans) that are already subject to a permit procedure or the like. The decisive criterion is whether a project (or a plan) is likely to have a significant effect on a site – not whether a permit is required or not. Thus, member states must establish permit procedures or other relevant administrative procedures regarding projects or plans subject to an Article 6(3) assessment. According to de Sadeleer, a notification scheme or implicit authorization scheme will not satisfy the requirements of the Habitats Directive, and an express act authorizing the activity is necessary.[14] This does not, however, exclude a notification scheme aimed at identifying plans or projects with a potential significant impact – that is, for screening purposes. If, however, an assessment is deemed necessary, then a permit system must be put in place in order to either accept the plan or project (as modified) in accordance with Article 6(3), or to grant an exemption according to Article 6(4).

The second step regarding Article 6(3) is to determine whether a plan or a project is likely to have a significant effect and thus be subject to an assessment. The screening criteria 'likely to have significant effect' clearly reflects the precautionary principle since it is the probability and not the certainty of significant effects that will trigger the assessment requirement.[15] The ECJ in case C-127/02, *Waddenzee* specified that 'in the light, in particular, of the *precautionary principle* ... by reference to which the Habitats Directive must be interpreted ... *such a risk exists if it cannot be excluded on the basis of objective information* that the plan or project will have a significant effect on that site, either individually or in combination with other plans or projects' (para 44; emphasis added). This implies that in the case of uncertainty or doubt regarding the absence of significant effects, an assessment must be carried out. The significance criterion is closely linked to the conservation objectives established for the site. According to the ECJ in the *Waddenzee* case, a plan or a project that is *likely to undermine the conservation objectives* of the site concerned must necessarily be considered likely to have a significant effect (para 49). Although the ECJ advocates a strict interpretation, it seems to exclude certain minor effects not likely to undermine the conservation objectives. Significance does not follow from the mere potential effect on the conservation objectives, but from the likelihood of undermining the objectives in a short- or long-term perspective. The precautionary principle is, as mentioned above, clearly reflected by emphasizing the likelihood of effects. However, a threshold is established excluding insignificant effects. Nevertheless, a reversed burden of proof appears to exist since it must be demonstrated that no effects will be significant – that is, likely to undermine the site's conservation objectives. If any doubt exists as to the significance of likely effects, then an assessment must be carried out.

As reflected in Article 6(3), the screening of plans and projects must take into consideration the cumulative effects of other plans or projects. It is, however, not clearly defined what other plans or projects should be taken into consideration. The concept of cumulative effects has primarily been established to deal with several minor or negligible effects that may add up to a significant effect.[16] However, in view of the precautionary principle, a broad definition of other plans or projects must be presumed, including not only similar (minor) plans or projects. Planned but not yet realized projects may also be included. The European Commission even mentions projects that have not yet been proposed.[17] However, the proportionality principle may limit the extent to which other projects should be included. Furthermore, it is not quite clear how to deal with cumulative effects in a situation where the activity in question is insignificant, compared to the effects of other activities. The question is whether the pressure of other activities leads to the result that any additional effect will be significant, or whether a presumption can be made that the effect in itself should be at least measurable compared to other effects.

The third step with regard to Article 6(3) is carrying out an *assessment*. Article 6(3) does not establish more specific requirements in relation to the assessment. An assessment shall assess the implications for the site – for example, a Special Area of Conservation (SAC) designated according to the Habitats Directive or a Special Protection Area (SPA) designated according to the Birds Directive. The conservation objectives of the site – or the habitat types or species – are crucial to the assessment.[18] According to the ECJ in case C-127/02, *Waddenzee* 'all aspects … which *can*, either individually or in combination with other plans or projects, affect those objectives must be identified in the light of the *best scientific knowledge* in the field' (para 54; emphasis added). It is quite clear that a (risk) assessment is a scientific exercise based on objective information.

The conclusions of the assessment determine whether the activity can be authorized or not – that is, the fourth step in taking a decision. The substantive decision criterion embedded in Article 6(3) is that the activity shall only be agreed to if it *will not adversely affect the integrity of the site*. According to the ECJ in case C-127/02, *Waddenzee*, this stringent criterion incorporates the precautionary principle and makes it possible to prevent, effectively, adverse effects on the integrity of protected sites (para 58). The ECJ interpreted this obligation as meaning that the authorities shall have made certain that the activity will not adversely affect the integrity of the site – that is, 'that no reasonable scientific doubt remains as to the absence of such effects' (para 59). The burden of proof is thus reversed: the absence of likely harmful effects must be shown as opposed to showing likely harmful effects. The reversal of the burden of proof thus appears to be a consequence of the stringent substantive decision criterion and not a result of the assessment requirement. It appears that a significance criterion must also be adopted in relation to the substantive decision criterion since the plan or project would otherwise not be subject to an assessment. Consequently, adverse effects must be interpreted as effects that are likely to undermine the site's conservation objectives. However, it also appears from the ECJ ruling in case C-127/02, *Waddenzee* that a relatively low threshold must be expected: see 'no reasonable scientific doubt' regarding such effects.[19] Applying such a stringent scientifically based criterion or threshold in a risk management decision leaves very little room for balancing interests or even considering the proportionality principle. The criterion is absolute.

However, one possibility for exemption exists according to Article 6(4) where, in spite of a negative assessment, a plan or project can be authorized if certain criteria are met. These criteria are that no alternative solutions exist, that there are imperative reasons of overriding public interest, and that all compensatory measures are taken.

In case C-209/02, *Commission* v *Austria (Wörschacher Moos)* regarding the extension of a golf course in an SPA, it was not contested that the requirements of Article 6(4) were not fulfilled. The ECJ declared that Austria had violated Article 6(3) by authorizing the extension despite a negative assessment of its implications for the habitat of the corncrake (*Crex crex*).

The European Commission has, in a few cases regarding priority habitats or species, given an opinion according to Article 6(4). In the Swedish railway case (*Botniabanan*) the European Commission accepted the arguments of the Swedish government that no sustainable alternatives existed and that there was an overriding public interest. However, the commission did not accept the proposed compensatory measures as sufficient.[20]

Risk assessment according to the EIA Directive

The EIA Directive (and the SEA Directive) provides a horizontal assessment requirement for certain projects and plans. In this section, only the requirements of the EIA Directive regarding projects will be compared to requirements of the Habitats Directive Article 6(3). A distinct difference lies in the *ex-ante* delimitation of projects potentially subject to an assessment. Whereas the Habitats Directive employing an ecosystem approach applies to any projects (or plans) that may affect a site, the EIA Directive employs an activity approach by listing certain projects and groups of projects that may affect the environment. Although the EIA Directive in Article 2 indicates that all projects that may negatively affect the environment should be subject to an environmental impact assessment, the reference in Article 2 to Article 4 confines the application to the projects listed in Annex I and II. Annex I projects will always be subject to an environmental impact assessment, whereas Annex II projects may be subject to an environmental impact assessment either determined by thresholds established by the member state or by an individual screening of each project. The member states shall ensure that all Annex II projects that may adversely affect the environment are subject to an environmental impact assessment (see Article 2). The scope of the EIA Directive regarding projects is thus more limited than Habitats Directive Article 6(3). This means that an Article 6(3) assessment cannot be limited to projects subject to an environmental impact assessment according to the EIA Directive.[21]

Regarding the question of when a project is a 'new' project that requires an environmental impact assessment, the ECJ has, in the preliminary ruling case C-201/02, *Wells*, established that it would undermine the effectiveness of the directive to regard the adoption of decisions which, in circumstances such as those of the main proceeding, replace not only the terms but the very substance of a prior consent as mere modifications of an existing consent. Consequently, a decision determining new conditions was considered to constitute a new consent within the meaning of Article 2(1) of the EIA Directive (paras 46 to 47). The specific circumstances of the case should be noted, however: that the quarry, based on a 1947 permit, had been dormant during a longer period before operations recommenced in 1991. It should also be noted that the court apparently distinguished between modifications to existing permits (not subject to an EIA) and 'new' consents (subject to an EIA). Thus, the ruling in case C-201/02 does not imply that all review procedures of existing permits are considered to constitute a 'new' consent within the meaning of the EIA Directive. This appears to have been confirmed by the ECJ in case C-121/03, *Commission* v *Spain*, stressing that it is the creation or alteration of a project (pig farms) that may trigger an environmental impact assessment procedure. The court dismissed the claim of the European Commission that farms created before the entry into force of the 1997 Directive, but subject to authorization procedures after that date, had violated the requirements of the EIA Directive as amended by the 1997 Directive by not being subject to an environmental impact assessment when being authorized. Only to the extent that the farms, according to the original version of the EIA Directive, should have been subject to an environmental impact assessment at the time of establishment or amendment had the directive been violated (paras 93 to 97).

The determination of whether an Annex II project may have significant effects on the environment has been subject to several court cases. Regarding the possibility for the member states to establish thresholds, the ECJ has clearly stated that the member states cannot exclude, globally and definitively, one or more classes of projects from the assessment requirement.[22] The basic requirement is that all Annex II projects that may significantly affect the environment by virtue, *inter alia*, of their nature, size or location shall be subject to a requirement for development consent and an assessment with regard to their effects (see Article 2(1)). Regarding individual screening of Annex II projects, the criteria laid down in Annex III must be examined, including the issue of cumulative effects. The ECJ, however, appears to have been reluctant to examine whether these criteria – and the general significance criterion – have been met in specific cases. In the screening cases presented before the court, it has been established either that an appropriate screening has not taken place – for example, case C-87/02, *Lotto Zero* and case C-83/03, *Fossacesia* – or that sufficient proof has not been established by the European Commission that a screening has not taken place, as in case C-117/02, *Commission* v *Portugal*.

The latter case concerned the establishment of a holiday resort in a national park area later designated as an SAC according to the Habitats Directive. According to Portugal, a proper screening had been carried out before the consent was given, which found that significant effects would not occur since the area did not only include areas of high environmental value and the location was chosen precisely because of the degraded state of the vegetation. The European Commission had not fulfilled the requirement to prove that the obligations of the EIA Directive had not been complied with since it had not provided a minimum of proof of the effects that the project was likely to have on the environment. The European Commission could not merely point out that the information provided showed that the project in question was located in a highly sensitive area where the flora had already deteriorated, at the very least, without presenting specific evidence to demonstrate that the Portuguese authorities made a manifest error of assessment when they gave consent to the location of the project in an area specifically envisaged for projects of that type (para 87).

Although case C-117/02 primarily draws upon the failure of the European Commission to specify the potential significant effects in an attempt to address a failure of the member state, it appears that the ECJ does not, to the same extent as Habitats Directive Article 6(3), stress the need to reverse the burden of proof. The existence of potential significant effects must be established contrary to emphasizing the absence of such effects. A similar burden of proof is likely to apply to private litigants filing law suits before national courts. Thus, the precautionary principle appears to be less influential within the EIA Directive in the absence of substantive decision criteria. The procedural nature of the EIA Directive appears to prevail.

The scope of the EIA Directive with regard to the effects that should be examined is broader than that of Habitats Directive Article 6(3). The potential effects on a Natura 2000 site (SAC or SPA) are only one of many elements that may be included in an environmental impact assessment (see Article 3 and Annex IV). Annex IV essentially requires information regarding all relevant environmental effects. Certain additional requirements are established, including information on alternatives, mitigation measures, etc. Furthermore, certain procedural obligations must be met, including public consultation, which is not mandatory according to Habitats Directive Article 6(3).

If a project that falls within EIA Directive Annex I and II is to be subject to an assessment procedure according to Habitats Directive Article 6(3), the project should, at the same time, be subject to an environmental impact assessment procedure according to the EIA Directive. In such cases, an assessment should fulfil both the requirements of the Habitats Directive – that is, an in-depth scientific study of the effects on the site's conservation objectives – and the broader and more procedural requirements of the EIA Directive. However, certain projects (or plans) subject to an Article 6(3) assessment may fall outside the scope of Annex I or II of the EIA Directive. One such example could be golf courses that are not listed in Annex I or II, but clearly could have significant effects on a Natura 2000 site.[23] Similarly, certain EIA projects may have adverse effects but not significantly affect the conservation objectives of a Natura 2000 site and thus not be subject to an Article 6(3) assessment.

DANISH NATURE CONSERVATION LAW

Danish nature conservation law – and Danish environmental law, in general, do not refer to the precautionary principle as such (see Chapter 3 in this volume). The application of the precautionary principle in the administration of law can, in most cases, be traced to EU obligations or even rulings from the European Court of Justice. Danish nature conservation law has historically provided a relatively high level of protection of certain areas or habitats. The 2004 Nature Protection Act (*Naturbeskyttelsesloven*) dates back to its predecessor, the 1917 Nature Conservation Act (*Naturfredningsloven*), laying down the basis for the issue of individual nature conservation orders. It is estimated that approximately 4 per cent of the land area is subject to nature conservation orders. Since 1937, the general protection of, for example, coastal areas[24] and other habitats through a general prohibition to alter the state of the area has increased. The general protection of lakes, heaths, bogs, meadows, etc. now extends to approximately 10 per cent of the land area. However, exemptions may be granted from the general protection provisions of the Nature Protection Act. The Nature Protection Act does not, as such, specify any impact assessment requirement. However, a substantive decision criterion can be found in the prohibition to alter the state of, for example, habitats referred to in the act. As part of the implementation of the Habitats Directive, the statutory order on delimitation and administration of international nature protection areas sets up certain requirements (see the following section 'Implementing the Habitats Directive, Article 6(3)'). In 2004, the Danish government realized that the statutory order did not provide a sufficient means of implementing the Habitats Directive, particularly in relation to existing activities, such as farming and forestry. Specific amendments to the Nature Protection Act and a new Forest Act[25] were passed in order to provide new instruments for regulating, in particular, existing activities in order to achieve a favourable conservation status or to avoid deterioration. The authorities are obliged to seek an agreement with farmers, foresters and other landowners regarding land-use practices if necessary. If an agreement cannot be reached, the authorities shall issue an order or prohibition as necessary. However, according to the new rules, the loss incurred by such an order or prohibition must be compensated. Furthermore, a notification scheme has been set up in order to make a screening of new or amended land-use practices, otherwise not subject to any permit procedure (see the following section on 'Implementing the Habitats Directive, Article 6(3)').

Besides the Nature Protection Act, the Planning Act ensures a general protection of the countryside through the requirement of a rural zone permit for construction, subdivision and change in use of buildings or areas. The purpose of this requirement, which dates back to 1969, has been to protect the countryside against new and unplanned urban or industrial development. There is no reference to the precautionary principle in the Planning Act. The Planning Act, however, also implements the environmental impact assessment requirements[26] of the EIA Directive, whereas the SEA Directive has been implemented by a separate act.[27]

The administration of nature conservation law in Denmark has primarily relied upon the regional authorities – that is, the county councils. However, as of 1 January 2007, the county councils will be abolished and the administration of environmental law, in general, will be transferred to the local authorities (municipalities). This also applies to nature conservation law except in a few areas, such as coastal protection, which is considered a national (state) task of the Ministry for the Environment. There is generally a possibility of appealing decisions to the administrative appeal boards (see Chapter 3 in this volume). The Nature Protection Appeal Board is competent within the area of, for example, the Nature Protection Act and the Planning Act. The Nature Protection Appeal Board is composed of a chairman, qualified as a high court judge, two supreme court judges and a number of politicians, representing the political parties of the Parliamentary Finance Committee. The rulings of the administrative appeal boards can be appealed to the High Courts.

Implementing the Habitats Directive, Article 6(3)

The implementation of Article 6(3) of the Habitats Directive has been fraught with difficulties in Denmark. The difficulties primarily relate to a lack of appreciation of the ecosystem approach embedded in the Habitats Directive, as opposed to the more traditional activity approach. Thus, Article 6(3) has, to some extent, been limited to apply to certain listed activities. Furthermore, a certain reluctance to transform the wording of Article 6(3) directly into national legislation can be noted. Consequently, certain limitations exist regarding the scope of the Danish assessment requirement, and a clear and precise implementation can hardly be claimed to exist. As a consequence, the administrative appeal boards have, in a number of cases, been forced to apply Article 6(3) directly.

The primary piece of legislation for implementing the Habitats Directive is Statutory Order No 477 of 7 June 2003 on delimitation and administration of international nature protection areas (the statutory order on international nature protection areas).[28] A statutory order is legally binding, but it must have a basis in an act of law. The statutory order is issued according to several environmental acts, including the Planning Act and the Nature Protection Act. The order cuts horizontally across different environmental acts. International nature protection areas – that is, habitat areas (SACs), bird protection areas (SPAs) and Ramsar areas – are delimited according to the annexes of the statutory order. As of October 2005, a total number of 254 SACs covering approximately 11,000 square kilometres have been designated. About 30 per cent of the areas are terrestrial, covering 7.4 per cent of the total land area. The marine areas cover 7.5 per cent of the Danish marine area.

When it comes to implementing Habitats Directive Article 6, the statutory order is somewhat unclear. It includes an obligation not to give consent in a specified number of cases if the activity may deteriorate natural habitats and the habitats of species, or disturb, to a significant degree, the species for which the area has been designated (see the section on 'Danish nature conservation law'). This provision (incorrectly) relies upon the wording of Article 6(2) of the directive. There is no clear requirement to perform an impact assessment for such activities. However, it follows from Section 6(3) that a consent must be accompanied by a statement indicating that the project will not be detrimental to natural habitats and the habitats of species, or disturb to a significant degree the species for which the area has been designated. Thus, some sort of assessment regarding activities that may have a significant effect on the site is presumed. It is doubtful, however, whether this is a sufficiently precise implementation of Article 6(3). With regard to proposals for plans that may significantly affect an international nature protection area, there is a specific requirement to perform an impact assessment prior to the adoption of the plan (see Section 6(1)). If the plan will harm the integrity of the site, degrade natural habitats and the habitats of species, or disturb to a significant degree the species for which the area has been designated, the plan cannot be approved (see Section 6(2)). Thus, a more precise implementation of Article 6(3) appears only to have been established with regard to proposals for plans.

Apart from the unclear wording of the statutory order, particularly regarding Article 6(3), the listing of consent procedures in Section 4 of the statutory order quite clearly confines the application of Article 6(3) to activities or projects requiring a permit.

Furthermore, the listed consent procedures may fall short of including all relevant consent procedures. The consent procedures primarily relate to land-based activities, whereas sea-based activities are generally covered by sectoral legislation, in some cases including specific requirements regarding international nature protection areas.

There are examples of the Danish courts and the administrative appeal boards having applied the Habitats Directive Article 6(3) directly. One case concerned the introduction of beavers in two international nature protection areas.[29] As addressed by Basse in Chapter 3 of this volume, the Nature Protection Appeal Board had, in stressing the precautionary principle, only granted one of the two exemptions sought from the general habitat protection provisions of the Nature Protection Act. Such consent procedures are listed in the statutory order, and apparently an assessment had been carried out regarding the Skjern Å site hosting the protected Skjern Å salmon population. Due to the uncertainties regarding the effects on the Skjern Å salmon population, the appeal board refused to grant an exemption for that site. However, the appeal board did grant an exemption for the other site. This decision was brought before the Western High Court by the Danish Anglers Association, claiming that no assessment had been carried out regarding a nearby habitat (SAC) on the other site (Nissum Fjord). The Western High Court could not find any evidence that a sufficient assessment had been carried out regarding that site and thus overruled the exemption granted by the appeal board.[30] Subsequently, the appeal board has, on the basis of an assessment carried out by the relevant county council, concluded that the introduction of beavers would not damage natural habitats and the habitats of species, or disturb to a significant degree the species for which the area has been designated.[31] The Appeal Board thus reaffirmed the exemption granted in 2001.

In another appeal case, the Nature Protection Appeal Board has, with explicit reference to the ruling of the ECJ in case C-127/02, stressed the wording and the structure of Article 6(3).[32] In this case, the regional authorities (the county council) had granted exemptions from the general protection provisions of the Nature Protection Act for the establishment of a 300m sandy beach south of an existing maritime harbour and a path through the reeds in an area designated as an SAC, SPA and Ramsar site. The decision was appealed by the Danish Ornithological Organization to the Nature Protection Appeal Board. The appeal board referred to the direct effect of Article 6(3) as confirmed by the ECJ in C-127/02, *Waddenzee*. Consequently, the board, on the basis of the precautionary principle, stressed the Article 6(3) requirement to perform a screening of all projects and, if a significant effect could not be excluded, to make a more detailed assessment on the basis of the best scientific knowledge. According to the appeal board, the county council's decision that a significant effect could be excluded on the basis of objective information was not justified. Since a proper assessment had not been carried out, the board rejected the decision by the county council.

As part of the renewed implementation of the Habitats Directive in 2004, a *notification scheme* was set up in the Nature Protection Act and the Forest Act for certain listed modifications to existing activities that would normally not require a permit. The list includes, for example, clear-cutting, cultivation of permanent grasslands, cessation of grazing and significant changes in manure application. Such 'projects' shall be notified to the authorities, who will then decide whether an assessment of the project is necessary. However, the notification scheme only applies to listed 'projects' within the site. This is not in compliance with Article 6(3), which applies also to projects outside the site that may negatively affect the site. The reason for limiting the Danish notification scheme to projects taking place within the boundaries of a site was that a broader notification scheme would contradict the rule of law and legal certainty since it would be very difficult for individuals to predict whether a 'project' outside the site should be notified or not.[33] A general notification scheme could, at least in principle, solve this problem – but could, on the other hand, lead to overregulation. Another implementation problem is that the list of 'projects' may turn out to be incomplete – that is, it does not catch all activities that may constitute a 'project'. Furthermore, as mentioned in the section on 'Implementing the Habitats Directive, Article 6(3)', a notification scheme alone may not satisfy the requirements of the Habitats Directive. Yet, the notification scheme is only intended to provide for a screening of potential significant effects. Although no precise rules are set up, the scheme must be interpreted in accordance with the Habitats Directive. Accordingly, if significant effects cannot be excluded, an assessment shall be carried out in concordance with a permit procedure. The latter, however, does not follow from the Danish rules. On the contrary, the Danish system only provides for action if the assessment shows that the conservation objectives of the site will be undermined. In such cases, the activity should be prevented from taking place either through agreements or by imposing a prohibition order. As a consequence of the Danish rules, the latter will imply the payment of compensation to the landowner subject to a prohibition.

Implementation of the EIA Directive

The implementation rules adopted according to the Planning Act set up an environmental impact assessment (EIA) procedure for projects.[34] The EIA procedure is currently incorporated within the regional planning procedure. If an EIA is required – for example, Annex I projects or Annex II projects that may significantly affect the environment – the adoption of a regional planning guideline is required before the project can be initiated.[35] However, a regional planning guideline cannot in itself lay down binding conditions regarding the project. If no other permit – for example, an environmental licence – is required, a specific EIA permit is needed. This 'permit' system has created some confusion, particularly on how to regulate negative impacts resulting from a project. With regard to Annex I projects, the impact assessment requirement is, in the statutory order, confined to new projects or amendments equivalent to new projects. However, other amendments of Annex I projects should be subject to a screening (according to Annex II).

Annex II projects are subject to an individual screening regarding the potential effect on the environment. The decisive criterion is, as in the EIA Directive, whether the project (due to character, size or location) may have a significant impact on the environment. The screening criteria of Annex III of the directive are incorporated within the statutory order. A screening decision can be appealed to the Nature Protection Appeal Board.

In the practice of the Nature Protection Appeal Board, there appears to be no explicit reference to the precautionary principle – except for livestock projects potentially affecting an international nature protection area (see the following section on 'The case of livestock installations'). However in some cases, the appeal board has used the argument that significant effects could not be excluded and, thus, have required an environmental impact assessment.[36] However, this does not appear to be applied more generally, and examples of major projects not being subjected to an environmental impact assessment have also been recorded, such as the construction of a new opera house in Copenhagen.

When an environmental impact assessment is carried out, it must fulfil the requirements of Annex IV of the statutory order, drawing upon EIA Directive Annex IV. The Danish rules are slightly more explicit than the directive regarding the examination of alternatives, including the zero-action alternative and other alternatives than those examined by the developer. This means that the authorities have an obligation to examine reasonable alternatives proposed by, for example, the public during a public hearing. The Nature Protection Appeal Board has, however, demonstrated a certain reluctance regarding alleged failures to provide adequate and sufficient information in an EIA.

In a 2003 decision on the establishment of a biotechnology industry, the board did not consider the lack of an assessment on sewage water issues as a significant defect in the assessment.[37] The establishment of the biotech company would significantly increase the demands for the municipal sewage water plants (and potentially affect international nature protection areas). However, the board considered that such effects could be assessed at a later stage. In a decision on a new bypass road in the Wadden Sea area, the Nature Protection Appeal Board did not criticize the assessment's conclusion that the isolation of 80ha of marshland would not affect the integrity of the site (MAD 2004.797). Although the Article 6(3) criterion was apparently used, the precautionary principle did not seem to influence the decision. Certain compensatory measures had been taken; but the case was not dealt with as an exemption according to the Article 6(4) criteria.

The relationship between environmental impact assessment and Article 6(3) of the Habitats Directive has not directly been dealt with in Danish law apart from the specific procedures laid down in the Nature Protection Act. If a project is subject to a screening according to the EIA rules, then a screening according to the Habitats Article 6(3) is likely to be incorporated within the EIA screening procedure. This may imply a more explicit use of the precautionary principle regarding livestock installations (see the following section). If both an environmental impact assessment and an Article 6(3) assessment are required, normally the Article 6(3) assessment will be carried out as part of the broader environmental impact assessment procedure (see the following section on the *Esromgaard* case).

The case of livestock installations

In Denmark, intensive farming occupies approximately 60 per cent of the land area. Furthermore, Denmark has an intensive livestock production of a considerable size – in particular, pig production. The environmental consequences of farming, especially the effects of nutrients on the aquatic environment, has been subject to political and legislative initiatives since the mid 1980s. The result has been a quite strict general regulation of, for example, livestock density, manure storage and spreading, fertilizer book-keeping and nitrogen utilization norms. The entire country is designated as a nitrate-sensitive zone according the Nitrates Directive. The effects of livestock production and manure spreading on terrestrial habitats and protected areas have received increased attention since the late 1990s. The effects on terrestrial habitats are primarily related to ammonia depletion. Accordingly, certain general restrictions have been imposed in order to reduce ammonia volatilization from livestock installations and from manure spreading.

With regard to the Habitats Directive, the effects of farming on designated areas – aquatic as well as terrestrial – are extremely difficult to avoid. This is a general problem in almost all parts of Denmark since the 254 SACs are spread across the country. Furthermore, the diffuse character of nutrient pollution is difficult to handle in a decision-making context. Due to the somewhat confusing implementation of Habitats Directive Article 6(3), there is no reference to the establishment or amendment of livestock installations below the threshold for an environmental licence (Integrated Pollution Prevention and Control, or IPPC, permit) since there is no environmental permit procedure for projects falling below this threshold.[38] The 2004 notification scheme only applies to land-use practices, such as increased use of manure or fertilizers, but not to livestock installations as such.

However, the establishment, extension or amendment of livestock installations are all subject to the EIA rules either as Annex I projects (above a certain size limit) or as Annex II projects. It has been stated by the Nature Protection Appeal Board that a livestock project only falls outside the Annex II category of 'intensive livestock installations' if the environmental effects are, without doubt, insignificant.[39] This means that, in practice, all establishments, extensions or amendments – no matter how small – shall be subject to a screening procedure. Thus, the precautionary principle can be said to have influenced the delimitation of livestock projects subject to the EIA rules. However, a pre-screening or fast-track procedure has been established in order to deal with insignificant projects.

The situation regarding livestock installations is, thus, that – with certain variations – the establishment, extension or amendment of installations of up to 250 animal units[40] will not be subject to an environmental licence (IPPC), but subject an EIA screening. If an EIA is needed, an EIA permit is required.

The precautionary principle has clearly been reflected in a number of screening decisions by the Nature Protection Appeal Board, particularly regarding the effects on international nature protection areas. The Nature Protection Appeal Board has, in several cases, stated that, normally, the general environmental restrictions would be sufficient to deal with the negative effects of livestock installations unless the livestock installation may affect sensitive areas, indicating that an EIA is not required. In relation to international nature protection areas – that is, habitat, bird protection or Ramsar areas – the appeal board has explicitly applied a precautionary principle, stressing that uncertainty regarding the effects should lead to the requirement of a full environmental impact assessment.[41] Similarly, the appeal board has stressed that the cumulative effects should be afforded special attention concerning such areas. In areas where ecological thresholds (for example, in relation to ammonia) have already been transgressed, the appeal board appears to have adopted very strict standards. In one case, the appeal board required an environmental impact assessment of a project leading to an additional load of 0.08kg of nitrogen per hectare per year in a bog designated as an SAC.[42] The county council administration had not considered that such an additional load could constitute a significant effect. The Nature Protection Appeal Board did not refer to any explicit scientific arguments to support its decision. Thus, the decision taken by majority voting appeared to be more political than scientific since the board is political in its composition. The board has, in more recent cases, emphasized the Article 6(3) screening criteria 'that a significant effect cannot be excluded on the basis of objective information', and relied upon the scientific assessment provided by the county council. In one of the cases, an additional load of 0.01kg of nitrogen per hectare per year in a bog designated as an SAC was considered to be insignificant.[43] These rulings appear to reflect a precautionary approach in accordance with Habitats Directive Article 6(3).

If an environmental impact assessment is carried out, the assessment must comply with the above mentioned requirements. The Nature Protection Appeal Board has set up stricter requirements regarding an assessment, involving potential effects on international nature protection areas. This has been reflected in a case regarding the extension of a pig farm that could potentially affect the aquatic environment of Esrum Lake designated as an SAC (MAD 2001.768 – *Esromgaard* case). This case arose in 1996, and ten years later, it has still not come to an end. Following the decision of the Nature Protection Appeal Board, the case was returned to the county council. The county council has undertaken a new environmental impact assessment and is about to make a final decision in the case. The farmer presented a new proposal, which – due to modifications of existing farming practices – will not lead to any additional pollution. The calculations were, however, attached with some uncertainty, ranging from +/−15 per cent. The county council, therefore, with reference to the precautionary principle, declared that such an uncertainty is not acceptable. As a result, the farmer must demonstrate that after the expansion there will be a total reduction in pollution of 15 per cent. This appears to express a very strict application of the precautionary principle – perhaps even stricter than that applied by the ECJ in case C-127/02, *Waddenzee* of 'no reasonable scientific doubt' regarding the effects likely to undermine the site's conservation objectives.

In another case, the minister for the environment vetoed the adoption of regional planning guidelines for a livestock production that would cause an additional load of 110kg of nitrogen per year to the Waddenzee, compared to a total emission from all sources of 5000 to 10,000 tonnes of nitrogen per year – that is, an additional load of 0.0011 per cent, which, according to the regional authorities, would not be detectable. According to the minister, authorizing the project would, however, be in conflict with Habitat Directive Article 6.[44]

It follows from the foregoing that the possibilities of establishing or expanding livestock installations in Denmark are, in fact, quite limited, especially due to the potential effects on international nature protection areas. A quite strict interpretation of the precautionary principle appears to have been applied in these cases.

CONCLUSIONS

The application of the precautionary principle in nature conservation law is a necessity. The complex interrelation between human activities and the state of nature necessitates a thorough assessment of potential risks and a strict management of such risks, particularly when deciding upon new projects or plans. Risk assessment and risk management are two basic elements in the application of the precautionary principle (see Chapter 2 in this volume). In this chapter, the role of the precautionary principle as expressed by impact assessment requirements (risk assessment) and substantive decision criteria (risk management) in relation to new projects within EU and Danish nature conservation law has been explored.

Although explicit references to the precautionary principle may be difficult to retrieve in written nature conservation law, the principle can be expressed through the choice and application of regulatory instruments emphasizing, for example, impact assessment or substantive criteria regarding the absolute level of acceptable risk. Such instruments set up conditions for the decision-making (procedural) requirements regarding the level of information, as well as substantive requirements or limits regarding the balancing of interests. Through such instruments, the precautionary principle has gained an increasing importance in the application of law – for example, as expressed by the ECJ, as well as by the Danish administrative appeal boards.

The strength of the precautionary principle appears to depend rather strongly upon the extent to which both the risk assessment and the risk management aspects are reflected in the legislation. Environmental impact assessment requirements in accordance with the precautionary principle aim at ensuring an assessment of *potentially significant effects*. This includes a determination of significance on the basis of scientific information. However, assessment requirements that, like the EIA Directive, are limited to certain specified projects do not ensure that all potentially problematic projects are examined. The delimitation of projects – although broadly interpreted – may thus hamper the full application of the precautionary principle. In nature conservation law, the ecosystem perspective, which aims to catch all potentially harmful activities, has been expressed in the broader impact assessment requirement of Habitats Directive Article 6(3). This expands the application of the precautionary principle as expressed by the ECJ in case C-127/07, *Waddenzee*. The determination of potentially significant effects according to the ECJ presupposes a reversed burden of proof – that is, 'such a risk exists if it cannot be excluded on the basis of objective information that the plan or project will have a significant effect on that site'. A similar clear reversal of the burden of proof has not been established regarding the EIA Directive.

It is likely that the strength of the precautionary principle in relation to Habitats Directive Article 6(3) can be explained by the *substantive decision criterion* established in Article 6(3) – that is, it 'may not adversely affect the integrity of the site' – contrary to the mere procedural nature of the EIA Directive. The ECJ has interpreted the substantive decision criterion in light of the precautionary principle as implying 'that no reasonable scientific doubt remains as to the absence of such effects', again expressing a reversed burden of proof. The substantive decision criterion, as mentioned above, reflects the risk management aspect of the precautionary principle: the establishment of an absolute level of acceptable risk as the basis for balancing interests. Strict substantive decision criteria thus appear to reflect and imply a rigorous application of the precautionary principle as reflected in the Habitats Directive.

Furthermore, the strength of the precautionary principle – at least in a Danish context – may vary depending upon the political context – that is, how strong the political pressure or will is to apply stringent requirements. In Denmark, new or amended livestock installations are thus subject to a strict application of the precautionary principle regarding risk assessment and risk management. The application of the precautionary principle in Danish nature conservation law appears almost entirely to rely upon the more or less direct application of the Habitats Directive. There are no explicit references to the precautionary principle in nature conservation legislation. However, the precautionary principle has, to some extent, been applied by the administrative appeal boards – in particular, addressing the impact (risk) assessment requirements – and by risk management through the substantive decision criteria of the Habitats Directive. However, it appears that some variations exist depending upon the political context.

The role of the precautionary principle in nature conservation law has, in this chapter, been confined to discussing the *ex-ante* regulation of new (or amended) projects. However, nature conservation – and, in particular, the requirements of the Habitats Directive to ensure a favourable conservation status – necessitates a regulation of existing activities, as well as active management. The precautionary principle may also, in this respect, play an important role in determining the level of action that is needed to ensure a favourable conservation status.

NOTES

1   OJ 1992 L206/7.
2   For an in-depth analysis of the precautionary principle, see de Sadeleer, N. (2002) *Environmental Principles: From Political Slogans to Legal Rules*, Oxford University Press, Oxford.
3   On the inadequacy of more traditional approaches such as area designation, see Ebbesson, J. (2003) 'Lex Pernis Apivorus: An experiment of environmental law methodology', *Journal of Environmental Law*, vol 15, pp153–174.
4   OJ 1979 L103/1.
5   OJ 1985 L175/40, as amended by Directive 97/11, OJ 1997 L73/5 and Directive 2003/35, OJ 2003 L156/17.
6   OJ 2001 L197/30.
7   For an overall introduction to Danish environmental law, see Basse, E. M. (2004) *Environmental Law Denmark*, second edition, Kluwer Law International/DJØF Publishing, Copenhagen. More specifically on Danish nature protection law, see Anker, H. T. (2003) 'Danish nature conservation law in the Wadden Sea area', in Lambers, K. et al (2003) *Trilateral or European Protection of the Wadden Sea*, Sdu Utguivers, Den Haag, pp73–87, and Anker, H. T. (1999) 'Denmark', in Heyen, E. V. (1999) *Naturschutzrecht im Ostseeraum*, Nomos, Baden Baden, pp7–25.
8   On this distinction in an EU context, see Scott, J. (2004) 'The precautionary principle before the European Court of Justice', in Macrory, R. (ed) *Principles of European Environmental Law*, Europa Law Publishing, Groeningen, pp49–72.
9   For a general introduction to EU nature protection legislation in a comparative context, see Verschuuren, J. (2004) 'Effectiveness of nature protection legislation in the EU and the US: The Birds and Habitats Directives and the Endangered Species Act', *Yearbook of European Environmental Law*, vol 3, pp305–328.
10 On the ecosystem perspective, see Gipperth L. and Elmgren, R. (2005) 'Adaptive coastal planning and the European Union's Water Framework Directive – a Swedish perspective', *Ambio*, vol 34, pp157–162, and Gipperth, L. (2003) 'Miljökvalitet och förutsebarhet', in Björkman, U.

and Michanek, G. (eds) *Miljörätten i förandring*, IUSTUS Förlag, Uppsala. On a resource perspective based on New Zealand experiences, see Anker, H. T. (2002) 'Integrated resource management – lessons for Europe?', *European Environmental Law Review*, vol 11, pp199–209.

11 Pagh, P. (2005) 'Bestemmer ejeren eller den spidssnudede frø?', *Ugeskrift for Retsv'sen*, pp25–33.

12 European Commission (2001) *Assessment of Plans and Projects Significantly Affecting Natura 2000 Sites: Methodological Guidance on the Provisions of Article 6(3) and (4) of the Habitats Directive 92/43/EEC*, European Communities, Luxembourg

13 European Commission (2000) *Managing Natura 2000 Sites: The Provisions of the Habitats Directive 92/43/EC*, European Communities, Luxembourg, p33, and de Sadeleer, N. (2005) 'Habitats conservation in EC law', *Yearbook of European Environmental Law*, vol 5, p243.

14 de Sadeleer, N. (2005) 'Habitats conservation in EC law', *Yearbook of European Environmental Law*, vol 5, p244.

15 European Commission (2000) *Managing Natura 2000 Sites: The Provisions of the Habitats Directive 92/43/EC*, European Communities, Luxembourg, p34, and de Sadeleer, N. (2005) 'Habitats conservation in EC law', *Yearbook of European Environmental Law*, vol 5, p244.

16 For an example, see de Sadeleer, N. (2005) 'Habitats conservation in EC law', *Yearbook of European Environmental Law*, vol 5, p243.

17 European Commission (2000) *Managing Natura 2000 Sites: The Provisions of the Habitats Directive 92/43/EC*, European Communities, Luxembourg, p35.

18 See also European Commission (2000) *Managing Natura 2000 Sites: The Provisions of the Habitats Directive 92/43/EC*, European Communities, Luxembourg, p38, and European Commission (2001) *Assessment of Plans and Projects Significantly Affecting Natura 2000 sites: Methodological Guidance on the Provisions of Article 6(3) and (4) of the Habitats Directive 92/43/EEC*, European Communities, Luxembourg, pp28–30.

19 The WTO Appellate Body has also stressed that a risk must be ascertainable and not theoretical since science can never provide absolute certainty that a given substance will never give rise to adverse (health) effects; see de Sadeleer, N. (2002) *Environmental Principles: From Political Slogans to Legal Rules*, Oxford University Press, Oxford, pp105–108

20 Opinion of the commission C (2003) 1309, www.europa.eu.int/comm/environment/nature/nature_conservation/eu_nature_legislation/specific_articles/art6/index_en.htm.

21 See case C-143/02, *Commission* v *Italy*.

22 See case C-72/95, *Kraaijeveld*, and case C-392/96, *Commission* v *Ireland*.

23 See case C-209/02, *Commission* v *Austria (Wörschacher Moos)*.

24 The so-called beach or dune protection zone was, in 2004, extended from 100m to 300m with certain modifications.

25 Act No 454 of 9 June 2004, amending the Nature Protection Act, and Act No 453 of 9 June on Forests.

26 The Planning Act regulates land-based activities. Environmental impact assessment of sea-based activities is regulated through various pieces of sectoral legislation.

27 Act No 316 of 5 May 2004 on environmental assessment of plans and programmes.

28 The first statutory order on international nature protection areas was issued in 1994. The 1994 order was, in 1998, replaced by a new one, including the proposed Danish SACs.

29 The case of the Nature Protection Board of Appeal was published in *Kendelser om fast ejendom* (KFE) 2000.109.

30 The court ruling is published in *Ugeskrift for Retsv'sen* (UfR) 2004.622V.

31 Published in *Miljøretlige Afgørelser og Domme* (MAD) 2004.384.

32 Published in *Miljøretlige Afgørelser og Domme* (MAD) 2005.

33 L 146 (Proposal of 28 January 2004 on the amendment of the Nature protection Act, etc.), FT 2003/04 A.

34 Statutory Order No 1006 of 20 October 2005 on supplementary rules according to the Planning Act (replacing the former 1999 and 1994 statutory orders).
35 As from 1 January 2007, regional plans will no longer exist and the EIA requirement will be incorporated into the municipal planning procedure.
36 For example, MAD 2000.786, where the regional effects of a furniture warehouse could not be excluded.
37 MAD 2002.313. A complaint regarding this decision has been brought to attention of the EU Commission.
38 In 2005, the minister for the environment announced the preparation of a new Act on Livestock Installations that will introduce a significantly lower threshold than the IPPC Directive regarding environmental licences.
39 MAD 2003.769.
40 One animal unit equivalates 100kg of nitrogen.
41 *Naturklagenævnet Orienterer* (NKO) 330.
42 *Naturklagenævnet Orienterer* (NKO) 342.
43 Nature Protection Appeal Board case no 03–33/250–0102.
44 Ministry for the Environment (Miljøministeriet), May 2005.

PART V

The Precautionary Principle and Chemicals

Introduction

Nicolas de Sadeleer

Unlike waste management policy, the regulatory approach regarding the safety of chemicals has been underpinned by rather cumbersome, time-consuming and expensive scientific assessments. Despite the fact that the precautionary principle enables the adoption of risk reduction measures even where there is a suspicion of risk, chemical assessment procedures still call for absolute certainty. However, while risk assessments draw extensively on science, data is often incomplete and results may be unclear or contradictory (see the section on 'Is the requirement to carry out a risk assessment suitable in order to assess unknown risks?' in Chapter 2 of this volume). In fact, at every stage of the assessment process, risk assessors are confronted with incomplete information and knowledge gaps. When data is deficient or clear indications about impacts are lacking, risk assessment leaves room for uncertainty and error. Since it is difficult to establish causal links between exposure to chemicals and health or environmental effects, there is generally a significant degree of uncertainty in estimates of the probability and magnitude of effects associated with a chemical agent. As a result of limited knowledge, experts are not always able to provide conclusive evidence of a threat to human health and the environment.

From the outset, it should be stressed that the Nordic countries have been, for many years, at the forefront of developing new environmentally friendly technologies with a view to reducing the hazards from chemical substances. Indeed, there may be some reasons for concern. Given that the chemicals released from products and processes into the Baltic Sea are nearly always trapped in a large brackish ecosystem, wildlife has been severely affected by pollutants. Needless to say, there is still great uncertainty around the question of which substances have contributed to these effects. As a result, the chemicals policies in the Nordic countries are more developed (using different policy tools, such as ecological taxes, green procurement and subsidies) and restrictive (focusing on restricting chemicals risks and phase-outs of the most harmful substances) than the more general policies of the broader European Union (EU).

Given the economic importance of Swedish industries and the fact that the precautionary principle has been enshrined in Swedish statutes on chemicals for more than three decades, it was necessary to shed some light on the manner in which precaution has been fleshed out in Swedish law and policy. In this respect, Annika Nilsson, in Chapter 16, provides us with a critical analysis of the main features of her national regime. Although the Swedish legislation is increasingly permeated by European Community (EC) legislation and the principles underpinning the internal market, she highlights that precaution has developed somewhat differently in Sweden than in the EU.

The failure of EC chemicals policy to reduce health and environmental risks has been chiefly related to a general preference for a certainty-seeking regulatory style in which formal, science-based and standardized risk assessment has been singled out as the predominant tool for decision-making relating to chemicals. A major reform was launched at the end of 2003 with a view to replacing a cluster of directives and regulations by a new regulation, known as the Registration, Evaluation and Authorization of Chemicals (REACH). This proposal, which is still in the process of being adopted by the Council of Ministers and the European Parliament, has been characterized as one of the most debated pieces of legislation in European history. Given the potential impacts of REACH when it will enter into force in 2007, two authors explore key questions that arise regarding the impact of the forthcoming EC regulation upon national policies considered in Nordic countries.

As a matter of course, REACH has embraced an important element of the precautionary principle through recognition of the substitution principle, according to which the mere existence of an alternative substance that appears to be less dangerous than the substance in question is a sufficient basis for prohibition. Indeed, thinking of alternatives increases the likelihood of finding more appropriate solutions and of fostering research. Against this background, Gerd Winter, in Chapter 17, advocates that substitution should become a proactive tool in order to curtail uncertain risks.

So far, Nordic countries have been intent upon interpreting and implementing EC law on chemicals as minimum standards. In other words, several chemicals have been prohibited, although they have been placed on the market elsewhere. Accordingly, in Chapter 18, Nicolas de Sadeleer explores the extent to which REACH would lead to a complete harmonization of the legal regime dealing with existing chemical substances. Such harmonization would, to a great extent, curtail the right of Nordic countries to maintain or to adopt standards departing from EC internal market measures.

On the other side of the Atlantic, REACH has come in for considerable criticism from authorities and undertakings alike. It was therefore important to understand where the roots of the controversy lay. In this respect, in Chapter 19, Nicholas Ashford explores the factors that have been undermining the level of human and environmental protection in the US. In particular, he emphasizes that there has been a temptation to demand more detailed scientific and economic evaluation on a case-by-case basis of substances considered for regulation, which has been hindering any possibility of applying the precautionary principle in the US. The issue is, as a matter of course, of particular importance given the emphasis placed on developing economic assessment in the process of authorizing or restricting hazardous chemicals. It remains to be seen whether this factor will hinder the implementation of the future REACH regime.

CHAPTER 16

The Precautionary Principle in Swedish Chemicals Law and Policy

Annika Nilsson

INTRODUCTION

In this chapter, the precautionary principle is discussed from the perspective of Swedish chemicals law and policy.[1] As Nicholas de Sadeleer has explained in Chapter 1 of this anthology, the precautionary principle does not, in itself, have one single and specified 'true meaning' that is permanent. It must be defined and interpreted. The definitions and interpretations may vary on the grounds of values and preferences, and depending upon the contexts and circumstances in which the principle is to be applied. Swedish chemicals law and policy provides *one* possible approach to the precautionary principle.[2] In some respects, precautionary thinking has developed somewhat differently in Sweden than in the European Union (EU), in general, and in some of the member states. The Swedish understanding of the precautionary concept may focus more on its benefits for protecting health and the environment, and its potential for promoting sustainable development, than the general EU approach. However, such a claim must not be exaggerated. The differences are not always evident, either in law or in practice. Furthermore, Sweden is a member of the EU and is part of the global society, and is thus bound by international agreements – by will just as by law. Nevertheless, some differences are evident and important in the perspective of sustainable development.

This chapter aims to present some overall and general characteristics of Swedish law and policy with regard to chemicals, with the focus on the precautionary principle. The task given was to present Swedish *law* on the matter. But in the application of a precautionary approach to chemicals, the rather ambitious chemicals *policy* gives important legal guidelines and is a strengthening component in other respects. The efficiency in the combination of law and policy should not be ignored.

Since the aim is to present 'the Swedish model', it is more productive to discuss general characteristics of precaution in Swedish chemicals law and policy than to elaborate upon details and single provisions. Of course, specific regulations will be discussed when this contributes to the chapter; but in this context, the sum is more interesting than the individual parts.

DIFFERENT PERSPECTIVES ON CHEMICALS

It is well known that the wording of a problem has a very large influence on the solutions sought and chosen. An important dividing line between EU and Swedish chemicals law and policy may be that *the problem is differently worded and understood*. As an introduction to Swedish law and policy, it is appropriate to outline some general characteristics for the EU approach, one the one hand, and the Swedish approach, on the other, in order to elucidate some of the differences.

This depiction will be understood as a rough sketch and must not be taken literally. But it may promote an understanding of the inherent logic of the different perspectives and, thus, to promote an understanding of *why* the differences occur.

In *EU law*, chemicals are basically regulated within the spheres of the internal market (Article 95 of the EC Treaty) and free movement of goods (Article 28).[3] The overall objective, in these sectors of EU law and policy, is to promote the development of the internal market and trade between the member states. The general rule is that goods, chemicals included, *may be placed on the market and transferred* in and between the member states.

It is recognized that chemical substances, and products containing certain substances, may cause damage or detriment to human health or the environment because of their intrinsic properties. According to Article 95(3), the European Commission's proposals on health and environmental law will aim at a high level of protection. Nevertheless, the central question to consider is: are the goods dangerous enough to motivate restrictions on their admittance to the market? The question is worded, and answered, in general terms. The possible restrictions are of a general character, and once placed on the market the substance is, generally, allowed all over the EU.

Since the primary aim of Articles 95 and 28 is to promote the functioning and development of the internal market and to ensure free movement of goods, restrictions are considered exemptions from the main principles, when they are 'needed'. Restrictions should not be more restrictive than 'necessary'. This starting point influences the demand for, and the burden of, proof: yes, restrictions may be adopted, but there is a heavy burden to prove that the problem is serious enough to motivate a (general) moderation of the initial preference.

The question worded above may possibly be answered in the affirmative when it addresses a single substance for which data shows, with a high degree of certainty, that it is, indeed, very dangerous. However, the product will only be regarded as dangerous enough to motivate restrictions if the substance is very hazardous and its concentration in a final product is high or the risk of leakage or spread is considerable. With such an understanding of the problem, it is natural to *limit the risk assessment to the substance only as a substance*. The complex product is, in most cases, not problematic because of its chemical content as long as it is a functional product.[4] When the question is answered in the negative, the principles of the internal market and free movement of goods apply.

EC chemicals policy and law can be said to be *producer oriented* and *product oriented*. Products are, as a main rule, allowed on the market. The risk approach is based on a conception that most chemicals may be used safely within safe handling routines. It is supposed that risk may be adequately controlled by such handling routines. One starting point for such a conception must be that there is a level of 'acceptable risk' that is possible to identify and control. If you keep within this level, there is no need for further restrictions or for continuous risk reduction. Further demands are not required even when there *are* technically and economically adequate alternatives that are evidently preferable from a health and environmental perspective. Furthermore, risk assessment is, to a large extent, limited to single substances and how they are handled *as substances*. When they transform to air pollution or goods, they are no longer of interest for the chemicals policy. In this very limited sense it may, in many cases, be purposeful to talk about 'safe handling' and 'adequate control of the risk'. But the fact that all substances and goods that are let into the eco-cycle, as time goes, transform into waste and, further, into pollution to air, water or land, is not an insight that to a high degree characterizes either the current EU chemical legislation or the Registration, Evaluation and Authorization of Chemicals (REACH) proposal.

Swedish chemicals law has its base in the Environmental Code. The aim of the code is, according to its Chapter 1, Section 1, to promote sustainable development. The code will be applied so to ensure, *inter alia*, that human health and the environment are protected against damage and detriment, whether caused by pollutants or by other impacts. Thus, the problems with regard to chemicals are expressed in terms of the overall environmental objective. Of course, when it comes to explicit regulation, Swedish chemicals law is to a high degree influenced by and dependent upon EC law. In Swedish law, there is also a noticeable dividing line between the regulation of 'chemicals as goods' and other environmental issues. But the fundamental starting point is that chemicals shall not cause damage or detriment to human health or the environment.[5] The overall objective of Swedish chemicals law and policy is to *decrease or avoid exposure* of dangerous substances.[6] Thus, the question is: how can one reduce the damage and detriment caused by chemicals?

Of course, safe handling routines for hazardous substances are an important part of a policy aimed at reducing damage and detriment from chemicals. But there is an awareness in Sweden that this is not enough. The aim is primarily to minimize the use of dangerous substances and to substitute them with less dangerous ones. The principle of substitution, chemical-reducing techniques and other expressions of the principle of best available techniques with regard to chemicals are cornerstones of the strategy. General provisions regulate important issues, but are complemented by individually designed requirements.

One fundamental insight into the Swedish perception of the 'chemical' problem is that all substances brought into the eco-cycle, individually or as components in goods, will, in the longer perspective, spread throughout the biosphere. Another insight is that our knowledge of risks related to the spread of a vast amount of substances, with possible long-term cumulative and synergistic effects, is frequently more or less negligible. With this understanding of the problem, it is logical to apply a quite ambitious precautionary policy and, to some extent, a revised burden of proof to the benefit of those who ask for restrictions.

The Swedish manner of formulating the problem allows for a chemical policy that tackles the issue in a more general and overall way. The more complex question is: how can one reduce risk as far as possible without hindering activities? The focus has shifted compared to EU law. The main focus in Swedish chemicals law is that *the user*, as far as possible, shall be able to *achieve the intended result.* The general question may also be worded as follows: how may the desired *function* be achieved in a way that causes as little damage or detriment to human health and the environment as possible?

SETTING THE LEVEL OF PROTECTION

Definition of the task

As Nicholas de Sadeleer points out in Chapter 2 of this volume, an important task for the application of a precautionary approach is to decide which level of protection to uphold. Professor de Sadeleer discusses the issue in terms of 'what level of risk is unacceptable?' This way of formulating the objective may be understood as a negative definition: law and policy shall not intervene until the unacceptable level is passed.

In Sweden, this task has been differently approached. The desired level of protection is worded positively, both in policy and in law. Since chemicals law and policy in Sweden, as mentioned earlier, is part of environmental law and policy, it is necessary to bring all of these components into the discussion.

Setting the level in Swedish chemicals policy

A fundamental base for Swedish environmental policy comprises the 16 environmental objectives that address different aspects of environmental quality.[7] (The future development of environmental and chemicals policy is not known at the moment, due to recent changes in the Swedish Parliament and Government.) The objectives define the state of the environment that the environmental policy aims to achieve. The overall goal is that: 'Within one generation, the major environmental problems currently facing us shall be solved.'

Several of the environmental objectives – for example, the objectives of clean air, natural acidification only, zero eutrophication, good quality groundwater and a sustainable built environment – target issues closely related to chemicals.[8] In this context, the presentation is limited to the objective especially designated for the purpose: a non-toxic environment.

The environment must be free from man-made or extracted compounds and metals that represent a threat to human health or biological diversity.

The significance of the objective is further specified as follows:[9]

- The concentrations of substances that naturally occur in the environment are close to the background concentration and their impact on ecosystems is negligible.
- The levels of foreign substances in the environment are close to zero.
- The overall exposure in the working environment, the housing environment and the ecological environment to particularly dangerous substances is close to zero; with regard to other chemical substances, levels are not harmful to human health.
- Contaminated sites have been localized, investigated and, where necessary, remedied.

- All fish in Swedish seas and lakes are suitable for human consumption with regard to the presence of substances that do not occur naturally in fish.

In order to establish a tangible framework for progress towards these objectives, the Swedish Parliament has adopted a number of interim targets. These targets indicate the direction and timescale of the action to be taken. With regard to the environmental objective of a non-toxic environment, nine interim targets have been set.[10]

Interim targets 1 and 2 concerns *knowledge* of chemical substances' intrinsic properties with regard to health and environmental protection, and of dangerous substances in goods. The timetables are quite ambitious: by 2010, data will be available on the properties of all deliberately manufactured or extracted chemical substances handled on the market. By 2020, data will be available on the properties of the most important unintentionally produced and extracted chemical substances. By 2010, information on the content of dangerous substances will be provided for all goods. These information requirements will apply to both new and existing substances.

Interim target 3 aims to *phase out dangerous substances.* The timetables are different for respective substances or group of substances; but the longest time limit is 2010. Within that time frame, newly manufactured products will, as far as possible, be free from substances that are carcinogenic, mutagenic and toxic for reproduction, from organic substances that are persistent and bioaccumulating, and from mercury, cadmium and lead. Products already in use, containing such substances, shall be handled in such a way that the substances in question are not released into the environment.

Interim target 4 aims for the *continuous reduction of health and environmental risk from chemical substances.* Risks associated with manufacturing and use of chemical substances will be reduced continuously up to 2010, according to indicators and ratios established by the authorities concerned. Within the same time period, the occurrence and use of chemical substances that impede the recycling of materials shall decrease. This target applies to substances not covered by interim target 3.

According to *interim target 5, guiding standards for environmental quality* will be established by 2010 for at least 100 selected chemical substances not covered by interim target 3. The aim of this interim target is to define the meaning of the wordings 'close to background concentrations' and 'close to zero'.

Interim targets 6 and 7 concern *remediation of contaminated sites.* This is an important issue; but since it concerns chemicals more as 'pollutants', these targets are not further discussed here.

In late November 2005, parliament adopted *two new interim targets* related to *chemicals in food.* By 2010, action plans will be adopted that result in continuous decrease of the content of dioxins in food. By 2015, the exposure of people to cadmium in food and at work will be at such a level that it is safe from a long-term health perspective.

It must be emphasized that the environmental objectives are *political* objectives, not *legal* objectives. Nevertheless, they obviously have a large influence both on law and on policy. The government realizes that it will be difficult to achieve all the interim targets to a sufficient degree within the defined time frames. But a wide range of actors are working towards achieving the objectives, and a broad raft of policy instruments is to be used. The Ministry of Sustainable Development and the national authorities concerned, primarily the Chemicals Inspectorate and the National Environmental Protection Agency,[11] are actively involved in EU discussions and in the development of a global strategy for chemicals. Research on chemicals and environmental toxicology has been strengthened. A systematic database of knowledge with regard to unintentionally produced and extracted chemical substances is on the agenda. Education on chemicals legislation and risks, addressed to both industry and authorities, has been improved. Industry has been stimulated to demand, on a voluntary basis, further information on dangerous substances found within their suppliers' products and to continue to apply the substitution principle. The national authorities have strengthened their supervision with regard to existing legislation. The government has expressed that in order to improve EC chemicals policy and law some countries need to lead from the front, and that Sweden will act as such a forerunner, when appropriate with regard to the protection of health and the environment. The precautionary principle and principle of substitution will continue to be applied.

In addition, in order to promote environmental objectives, the government has presented a strategy for *non-toxic and resource-saving environmental life cycles*.[12] This strategy aims to ensure that what is extracted from nature will be used, reused and, finally, disposed of in a sustainable manner with a minimum of resources involved and without harm to nature. The National Environmental Protection Agency has identified the following strategic areas: non-toxic and resource-efficient production; non-toxic and resource-efficient consumption; and non-toxic and resource-saving treatment of waste. The Chemicals Inspectorate and the National Environmental Protection Agency have taken action to promote the implementation of these strategies.

Setting the level in Swedish chemicals law

Since Swedish chemicals legislation is integrated within the Environmental Code, the relevant provisions in the code also apply to chemicals. The overall ambition of the code is set in Chapter 1, Section 1, and is further specified in Chapter 2.

The purpose of the Environmental Code, according to Chapter 1, Section 1, is to promote sustainable development, which will ensure a healthy and sound environment for present and future generations. The code shall be applied in such a way as to ensure, *inter alia*, that human health and the environment are protected against damage and detriment. The environmental objective of *a non-toxic environment* may be regarded as the government's further specification of this generally worded objective, with regard to chemicals. It is, of course, not legally binding but must be regarded as a source of interpretation. In the absence of valid arguments showing another direction, and counteracting environmental objectives, the environmental objective of a *non-toxic environment* must be understood as a specification on how health and the environment may be protected according to the code.

It is appropriate to stress that the integration of chemicals law within environmental law in the Environmental Code is not a new characteristic for Swedish law. At least since the 1973 Act on Health and Environmentally Hazardous Goods,[13] and further developed in the 1985 Act on Chemical Products,[14] chemicals have been regarded as an environmental issue in Swedish chemicals legislation. As a complement, the 1969 Environmental Protection Act applied to 'environmentally hazardous activities' – a concept that includes the handling and use of chemicals, *inter alia*, in industry.

THE PRECAUTIONARY PRINCIPLE IN THE ENVIRONMENTAL CODE

The precautionary principle has been part of Swedish environmental policy and legislation for more than three decades. Since the principle's development and recent status in Swedish law are presented in Chapter 7 of this volume, only a short discussion on the issue is held here.

It has been discussed whether there is a difference between prevention and precaution. As Professor Hollo elucidated at the Marie Curie Conference on the Precautionary Principle in Oslo in May 2005, it is impossible to distinguish clearly between the two principles; instead, a sliding scale applies. People seldom act within the frames of either full certainty or total absence of knowledge. The Swedish approach, as described earlier, may be summarized as reducing risk, as far as is possible and reasonable. According to this approach, the more certain we are the more preventatively we act, and conversely; the more uncertainty involved the more precautious is the action. Of course, the presence of uncertainty influences the 'possible and reasonable assessment', but not the fact that action will be considered.

As is well recognized, the precautionary principle may be worded and understood in different ways. Sandin has identified four dimensions of the principle, which are quite elusive.[15] The *threat* dimension concerns the possible threat. The *uncertainty* dimension concerns the limits of knowledge. The *action* dimension concerns the response to the threat – that is, which action to consider. The *command* dimension concerns the level of determination in which the action is prescribed. Sandin has also shown how the specification and strength of the precautionary principle depend upon how the four components are worded. Vagueness or weakness in any of the dimensions will weaken the principle as a whole.[16]

Chapter 2 of the Environmental Code may be characterized as 'the core' of the code. The chapter's title is 'General rules of consideration', which may be somewhat misleading for a person who is unfamiliar with Swedish environmental law. The rules are not solely for 'consideration'. On the contrary, they are generally applicable orders for prevention and precaution. Chapter 2, Section 3, runs as follows:

> *Persons who pursue an activity or take a measure, or intend to do so, shall implement protective measures, comply with restrictions and take any other precautions that are necessary in order to prevent, hinder or combat damage or detriment to human health or the environment as a result of the activity or measure. For the same reason, the best available technology shall be used in connection with professional activities.*
>
> *Such precautions shall be taken as soon as there is cause to assume that an activity or measure may cause damage or detriment to human health or the environment.*

This provision prescribes a rather extensive precautionary standard, as analysed by the model presented by Sandin.[17]

The threat must not be 'severe or irreversible' to trigger the precautionary principle in the Environmental Code. The requirement to hinder, prevent or combat *damage and detriment* for human health and the environment applies to all measures and activities that are *not negligible* with regard to the aim of the code.[18] Thus, damage and detriment from handling chemicals, which is not negligible to the aim, shall be hindered and prevented.

According to uncertainty, measures shall be taken *as soon as there is cause to assume* damage or detriment to human health or the environment. As Michanek discusses in Chapter 7 of this volume, Swedish law does not provide guidance for determining the level of probability required. But the wording of the law indicates that the evidence does not have to be unambiguous or complete. The certainty for the assumption of a threat does not have to be larger than *passing the threshold.*

As is well known, it is common that risk assessments performed by different scientists, perhaps with different methods, often give different answers.[19] It is also well known that scientists, in general, are risk aversive with regard to incorrect claiming of causality. As has been intensively discussed lately, not least by several of the speakers at the Marie Curie Conference in Oslo, decision-makers ought to be more risk aversive against errors with regard to negligence of risk. The Swedish approach demonstrates a way of handling scientific information in political and legal decision-making; it allows for listening to the facts presented by the scientists, evaluating them as facts and then acting in accordance to what is appropriate from a legal or political point of view.

The wording of the command in the Environmental Code is expressed as 'action *shall* be taken'. The additional wording in the official English translation of the code of 'necessary' may lead to a restrictive interpretation, implying that measures shall be taken only to the extent that they are necessary. The value of the Swedish wording is closer to 'required': any precautions required to hinder damage and detriment shall be taken.

The code is not very precise on which kind of action to take. The wording 'protective measures, restrictions and any other precautions that are necessary' is intended to be just as wide as it is. A very wide range of actions may come into question.

The Environmental Code, nevertheless, does not prescribe that any threat, of whatever magnitude, shall be hindered by all means, with no regard to the certainty of its occurrence or to the costs of its hindrance. As discussed in Chapter 7 of this volume, the context for applying the precautionary principle is set by balancing different interests. The concept of best available technology (BAT) includes consideration of what is possible with regard to the operator's economical situation. The cost-benefit analysis, in accordance with Chapter 2, Section 7, of the code, hinders extensive demands for precaution. A measure is assessed to be unreasonable if the benefits from that measure do not outweigh its costs.

A general conclusion may be that a substantial threat will be prevented also when there is uncertainty of its occurrence and the measures are rather costly. If the evidence of the occurrence of the threat is more comprehensive, and/or preventive measures are easily and cheaply performed, measures are taken also to prevent less substantial threats.

PRECAUTIONARY ACTION IN SWEDISH CHEMICALS LAW AND POLICY

As stated earlier, the general rules of consideration in Chapter 2 of the Environmental Code also apply to the handling of chemicals. The rules of consideration are, for several activities and situations, further specified in ordinances and prescriptions. But in the absence of any specification of their significance, the rules are directly applicable to individual cases. The competent authority may interpret them in a trial for permit or in supervision, and prescribe detailed measures of precaution.

Further regulation that specifically addresses chemicals is found in Chapter 14 of the Environmental Code, which regulates 'chemical and biotechnical products'. The somewhat imprecise concept of 'chemical products' includes substances and preparations. The government may also prescribe that products that contain or are treated with chemical products are covered by provisions in, or prescriptions issued by, the code.

Chapter 14 is, to a large extent, built up as a framework law that gives legal ground for further regulation of different aspects on chemicals, such as classification of chemicals, notification of new substances, labelling and safety data sheets, and authorization of plant protection products and pesticides. Chapter 14 also provides legal ground for additional prescriptions with regard to matters referred to in Chapter 14 and in Chapter 2, or which are necessary for the implementation of EC legislation. The government or the competent authority may, if necessary for reasons of health and environmental protection, prohibit the handling, import or export of chemicals, and lay down special conditions for the handling.[20]

EC law on chemicals is implemented primarily through these provisions. It should be underlined that Swedish law on chemicals does not, except in a few cases, diverge from EC chemicals law. Sweden has, so far, invoked Article 95.4 of the EC Treaty to maintain more stringent national regulations concerning chemicals for food colourants,[21] creosote[22] and cadmium in fertilizers.[23] Since the focus of this chapter is on those elements of Swedish chemicals law that *do*, to some extent, deviate from EC law, issues that are harmonized by EC law on chemicals are not further discussed here.

Swedish law outlines a few general provisions that specifically concern hazardous substances and that are, to a certain extent, more restrictive than EC law and, hence, may be of interest here. The handling of polychlorinated biphenyls (PCBs) and polychlorinated terphenyls (PCTs), including sale and use, is generally prohibited. Exemption may be granted in individual cases if this is justified on specific grounds.[24] Cadmium is generally prohibited as a colorant for finishing and as a stabilizer, and, as mentioned above, is also restricted with regard to its content in fertilizers. The use and handling of trichloroethylene and two other chlorinated solvents are generally restricted and, to a large extent, prohibited. Mercury is generally prohibited for several types of uses. Lead in ammunition is subject to far-reaching restrictions.[25] In addition, according to these restrictions, an exemption may be granted if it is justified on specific grounds.

The Swedish prohibition on trichloroethylene was subject to a trial at the European Court of Justice (ECJ) in the *Toolex* case.[26] The ECJ's judgment shows that EC law does not necessarily hinder a national general prohibition, combined with the possibility of granting exemptions, even though it constitutes, in principle, a measure having an effect equivalent to a quantitative restriction within the meaning of Article 28 of the EC Treaty.[27] Such a prohibition may be accepted by the ECJ if it concerns matters that are not harmonized by secondary Community law, if it is based upon considerations for the protection of the health and life of humans or the protection of the environment, and if it is necessary, appropriate and proportional.

With regard to the scope of secondary law adopted on the grounds of Article 95, the ECJ stated, in the *Toolex* case, that Directive 76/769,[28] in itself, does no more than stipulate certain minimum requirements. Hence, the directive clearly presents no obstacle to the regulation by member states of the marketing of substances that do not fall within its scope.[29] The ECJ's judgment in the *Willi Burstein* case provides further guidance on the scope of that directive.[30] In this case, the court stated that the directives cited by Mr Burstein apply to products treated with the dangerous preparations or substances listed in Annex I to Directive 76/769 only if it is expressly so provided. Since Directive 76/769[31] does not apply to products treated with PCP, its salts and esters or with a preparation produced from that substance, the member states remain, in principle, free to fix limit values for such products independently.[32]

The conclusion drawn by the Swedish legislator and by Swedish lawyers is that EC law does not hinder national general regulations on matters that are not explicitly regulated in EC law if they pass the test with regard to Articles 28 and 30 EC and the *rule of reason* and do not conflict with other community law.

A national general regulation explicitly restricting specific substances such as the one questioned in the *Toolex* case may, as the court stated in its judgment,[33] in principle be regarded as constituting a measure having an effect equivalent to a quantitative restriction within the meaning of Article 28 EC. If so, it has to be justified under Article 30 or the *rule of reason*. But it is, first, worth noting that not every possible national restriction has been judged to have an equivalent effect. One example is the *Peralta* case,[34] where the ECJ, *inter alia*, held that the purpose of the legislation in question was not to regulate trade in goods, and that the restrictive effects that it might have on the free movement of goods were too uncertain and indirect for the obligation that it laid down to be regarded as hindering trade between member states. The court's conclusion was, therefore, that Article 28 (previously Article 30) does not preclude legislation such as the national legislation in question in the *Peralta* case.[35]

Second, it is worth noting that the internal market and free movement of goods are not the only objectives emphasized by the EC Treaty. A high level of protection and improvement of the quality of the environment shall be promoted. The ECJ has, several times, stipulated that protection of health and the environment is one of the most important community aims. Applying a generally worded national provision with the aim of health or environmental protection in an individual case may well be in line with promoting this Community aim and, thus, in principle, is justified by the EC Treaty. Indeed, ambitious promotion of any of the two aims must now and again give rise to conflicts, where the magnitude of the interests involved in a specific situation may be decisive.

In individual cases, it is important to balance different interests and to identify the objects for protection. The conclusion is, accordingly, that application in individual cases of generally formulated national provisions – genuinely aiming at protection of health and the environment – is consistent, to a considerable degree, with EC law.

This section, thus, now focuses primarily on the application of chemicals law in individual cases. A strategic aspect of the precautionary principle is how the gathering and spread of knowledge and information are handled by law and policy. In Swedish environmental and chemicals law, there are some additional provisions concerning this issue, compared to the requirements in EC law.

The burden of proof for compliance with the obligations prescribed in Chapter 2 of the Environmental Code is placed on the operator. In addition, the importance of knowledge is especially emphasized. Actors who pursue an activity or undertake a specific measure must possess the knowledge that is necessary to protect health and the environment. These provisions, in combination with the precautionary principle, have been used rather creatively in a number of judgments from the Environmental Court of Appeal, as discussed in Chapter 7 of this volume. Since the operator is obliged to possess sufficient knowledge, a condition of the licence for environmentally hazardous activity has prescribed that chemicals for which documented knowledge of risk is unavailable must not be used.[36] One of the judgments has been appealed by the operator to the Supreme Court that admitted the case.[37] The Supreme Court stated in a judgment on 19 May 2006 that such a condition may be acceptable in principle, but the wording of the condition in this case was not sufficient with regard to legal certainty. The case was remanded to the Environmental Court of Appeal.

According to Chapter 14 of the Environmental Code, the manufacturer or importer shall give a notification to the Chemicals Inspectorate concerning the chemical product if the volume produced or imported exceeds 100kg per year. The information is registered in the product register. Information required consists of the following: data for identifying the product and the producer; information on the product's function; whether it is intended for consumer use; whether it is a plant protection product; how it is classified; its components; and the percentage of each component that contributes to the classification. The data required is not at all comprehensive and should be easily accessible to the manufacturer or importer.[38]

It is important to note that the obligation to record import and use to the Chemicals Inspectorate, and registration in the product register, is completely different from notification of new substances according to current EC law and the registration obligation in the REACH proposal. The notification obligation in Chapter 14 requires only that specified information, easily available by the manufacturer, is handed over to the Chemicals Inspectorate. Furthermore, the notification is to be delivered the year after manufacture or import. These provisions give no grounds for ordering further information or any protective measures.

The aim of the product register is to provide the Chemicals Inspectorate with general information on the movement of chemicals in Sweden and the purpose for which they are used. The information may contribute to the design of efficient general supervisory activities. If the use of a certain dangerous substance is increased, the Chemicals Inspectorate obtains information on this and may react, if appropriate. The registration of function and intended use of chemicals also provides an overview of possible candidates for substitution.

The product register is not open to the public on the grounds of free access to public records, which otherwise generally applies to all information held by Swedish authorities. Information may be handed out to other authorities, researchers, organizations and the public; but a secrecy assessment is made before any information is handed out. No information is distributed on the content of single products.

Swedish law prescribes two types of permit obligations for handling chemicals. Operations that fall within the definition of environmentally hazardous activity require a licence in accordance with the general permit obligation for such activity if the type of operation is included in the annex to Ordinance 1998:899 on environmentally hazardous activity and health protection. In addition to industrial activities, waste management and other environmentally problematic installations, handling of large amounts of certain hazardous chemicals is a specific ground for the licence obligation to apply.

According to Chapter 14 of the Environmental Code, an authorization obligation is prescribed for the professional import of very toxic products from countries outside the EU; for the professional transfer of toxic products; for the private import of toxic products from countries outside the EU; and for private handling of toxic products. Note that professional *use* does not require authorization,[39] neither does import from the EU. Authorization is not required until the chemical is transferred within Sweden, or when the user is a private consumer. This authorization obligation may be regarded as a complement to the licence obligation: it aims to ensure that handling that is not subject to such a trial is performed by people who possess the necessary knowledge and that safe handling routines are followed.

The precautionary principle is, of course, also to be applied in the trial for licence or authorization. A large petroleum company applied for a licence to relocate large parts of its petroleum base. The Environmental Court of Appeal found that the suggested relocation would result in largely increased transports of petroleum close to the inner city of Stockholm. The Stockholm Fire Defence argued that every increase of petroleum transports would increase the risk of an accident and stated that the fire defence was not dimensioned for a large petroleum accident in the densely populated area. The Environmental Court of Appeal found that the permit could not be granted.[40]

Swedish chemicals law also gives legal grounds for issuing different conditions for the use of chemicals. Conditions may be prescribed in a permit or by the supervisory authority.

A condition concerning safe handling, commonly ordered in licences, may be worded as follows:

> *Chemical products and hazardous waste shall be stored in tight containers with a necessary embankment on secure ground and also, in other aspects, will be handled so that spills and losses are prevented. Fluid chemicals shall be stored within an embankment that contains the largest container and, additionally, 10 per cent of the volume of the other containers. When storing outdoors, the embankment shall be protected against precipitation or be dimensioned to store 100mm of rain.*[41]

Conditions may also be prescribed concerning a reduction in chemicals used in an individual case, or restrictions with regard to the area in which the handling may take place. In one case, the municipal Board of Environmental Protection had specified that the spread of manure was not allowed closer than 100m to houses or water reservoirs. The order was appealed and was dismissed by the Environmental Court of Appeal. Although the court did not object to the prescription, the reason for dismissal was that the Board of Environmental Protection had not given sufficient cause. The board had prescribed a far-reaching general restriction without presenting its considerations concerning the need for protecting the single houses and reservoirs concerned, and without considering the cost to the farmer.[42] Accordingly, if sufficiently justified, such an order would have been passed.

The principle of substitution is an important characteristic for the precautionary principle as it is understood in Swedish chemicals law and policy. According to Chapter 2, Section 4, of the Environmental Code:

> *Persons who pursue an activity or take a measure, or intend to do so, shall avoid using or selling chemical products or biotechnical organisms that may involve risks to human health or the environment if products or organisms that are assumed to be less dangerous can be used instead. The same requirement shall apply to goods that contain or are treated with a chemical product or a biotechnical organism.*

The principle of substitution was explicitly expressed in Swedish law in 1949 in an edict concerning labour health.[43] It was highlighted in the preparatory works for the Act on Health and Environmentally Hazardous Goods and the Act on Chemical Products.[44] The principle was introduced as an explicit legal provision in the Act on Chemical Products in 1991.[45] During the following years, a number of municipal supervisory authorities tried to apply it in cases concerning the handling of chemicals at local level. Most cases were appealed. The municipal supervisory authorities' decisions were repealed, on formal grounds.[46] Since the supervisory authorities have to consider the efficiency of their efforts, they soon chose other means of supervision.

In the 1998 Environmental Code, the principle of substitution received a prominent position. However, the ambiguity that appeared in previous attempts to apply the principle was not resolved. The preparatory works obviously do not intend to elucidate and clarify the principle of substitution and its application. The government has emphasized that it is not a rule of prohibition, but a rule of consideration and behaviour. On the other hand, it is clear that it provides grounds for conditions in licences and for supervisory prescriptions.[47]

Compared to previous law, the Environmental Code clarifies that the obligation of substitution applies not only to substances, but to all goods that contain or are treated with a chemical product. And it does not apply only to severely hazardous substances. Since the code aims to prevent and hinder any damage and detriment, the decisive issue is whether a chemical or a product that is less dangerous can be used instead. The intended function is not questioned by the principle of substitution; but there may be alternative ways of reaching it.

The legal provision of substitution is worded as a general obligation. Nevertheless, general prohibitions of specific substances are not issued on the grounds of this principle. Such prohibitions may conflict not only with EC law, but also with the inherent characteristics of the principle – a prohibition may not be grounded on the principle of substitution unless there is an alternative way of reaching the intended function. According to the ordinance questioned in the *Toolex* case, the general prohibition was complemented by the possibility of exemption, which was granted if no safer replacement product was available and provided that the applicant continued to seek alternative solutions that were less harmful. The judgment shows that a prudent application of the principle of substitution is accepted in EU law and has, accordingly, strengthened its position in Swedish law. However, the principle of substitution is applied mainly in individual cases and, to a large extent, voluntarily as a result of the operator's consideration (sometimes *obligation* to consider) of available information.

The following wording may be used for the application of the substitution principle in a licence:

> *The operator shall, in consultations with the supervisory authority, investigate the use of chemicals with the aim of substituting hazardous chemicals with less hazardous ones. Additionally, the operator, when introducing new chemicals, shall consult with the supervisory authority. The company shall contribute to the documentation when such is lacking.*[48]

However, a condition or a prescription on substitution must not be too extensive or vague. According to principles of legality and legal certainty, generally emphasized by the Environmental Court when supervisory orders are appealed, prescriptions must be precise and clear enough that the operator can understand the obligation and foresee how to comply with it. This issue has been discussed in a judgment by the Environmental Court of Appeal. The Environmental Court prescribed a condition that 'The operator shall during a probation period investigate, in accordance to the government's environmental objective "a non-toxic environment", the prerequisites and consequences of substitution of chemicals to less hazardous chemicals.' The Environmental Court of Appeal revoked this condition. The statement of reasoning is rather illustrative. The court stated that the use of chemicals shall be taken into consideration in the trial for licence for environmentally hazardous activity, and that there may be reason to regulate the use of chemicals in specific conditions. Accordingly, it is possible to decide on a probation investigation before establishing permanent conditions. But the principle of substitution aims at a continuing process where chemicals are substituted when less hazardous ones are developed or identified. The application of the principle presupposes that the person handling the chemicals recurrently will reconsider the choice of chemicals. The occurrence of this process would often be better ensured by efficient supervision, where the supervisory authority, of course, has to consider the provision of reasonableness in Chapter 2, Section 7, and what otherwise is regulated in the permit. A licence may be granted for a limited time, to ensure a new trial, if this is justified. It is also possible to prescribe a condition, if legal grounds are already established in the trial, that a certain chemical shall be substituted. But the condition that the Environmental Court has established in this case, claimed the Court of Appeal, is general in its wording and in its aims regarding hazardous chemicals. It is not connected to any specific chemical that may be used in the operation and where substitution may be possible. The connection to a possible, permanent condition is weak. The Court of Appeal agreed with a statement of the municipal Board of Environmental Protection, implying that the principle of substitution would be best provided for by a combination of supervision and constructive contribution from the company.[49]

The principle of substitution is not, generally, aimed at identifying 'the best' chemical. That would, in most cases, be an impossible issue. The principle merely aims at identifying 'less dangerous' chemicals. But according to Swedish law, prescriptions must be precise enough to comply with the principle of legal certainty. If a specific condition on substitution is demanded in an individual case, the substitute must be identified. Such a condition may be worded as follows:

> *In mobile diesel machines used within the operation site, only such fuel may be used that complies with the class 1 for diesel in Act 2001:1080 on motor fuels, or other requirements that the supervisory authority finds equivalent or better with regard to environmental protection.*[50]

Substitution is a means of preventing the use of chemicals that are more dangerous than necessary for the intended purpose. However, several chemicals are dangerous enough to motivate their reduction on the grounds of their intrinsic properties. As discussed earlier, Swedish chemicals law and policy includes a strategy for phasing out hazardous substances.

The Chemicals Inspectorate has, for several years, published an observation list, including chemicals that are assumed to be so hazardous that they should preferably be phased out from use. The list also includes chemicals that are not subject to formal restrictions by law, but are still assumed to be so hazardous that they are improper to use. The observation (OBS) list was recently replaced by a database, available on the internet and in English,[51] called PRIO. PRIO is a priority-setting guide intended to be used voluntarily by, *inter alia*, environmental managers, purchasers and product developers to identify the need for risk reduction and to find information on substances that have properties that are hazardous for health or the environment. Health inspectors, risk analysts and other persons who need such information may also find the database useful. The target groups are primarily Swedish actors. References are made to Swedish legislation and other Swedish considerations. But the database would likely be of considerable interest to actors from other countries.

The database provides information, but it is not legally binding. For example, the Environmental Court granted a licence for an environmentally hazardous activity, including a condition that 'new products must not be produced, or existing products modified, which would result in the use of chemicals included on the Chemicals Inspectorate's OBS list'. The Environmental Court of Appeal, to which the judgment was appealed, stated that, for several reasons, it is inappropriate to prescribe general restrictions in the use of chemicals grounded on the observation list. The condition was revised by an extended commission of investigation and after consultation with the supervisory authority with regard to the use of chemicals.[52]

The PRIO database is composed of two prioritization levels. The *phase-out* level contains the properties of greatest concern, such as carcinogenic chemicals, persistent, bioaccumulative and toxic (PBT), very persistent, very bioaccumulative (vPvB) and particularly hazardous metals. According to Swedish chemicals policy, those substances should be avoided. The *priority risk-reduction* level categorizes mutagenic and environmentally hazardous chemicals and the long-term effects and potential of PBT and vPvB. The use of substances with such properties should always be assessed with regard to the intended use and on the basis of the risk that may occur.

Some, but not all, of the substances in PRIO are subject to formal restrictions. The database does not provide any restrictions in addition to what otherwise follows from Swedish legislation. But PRIO may be used as an efficient tool in the overall application of the general rules of consideration when it comes to chemicals and the chemicals policy. It gives guidance to courts and supervisory authorities; but, first and foremost, it gives guidance to considerate operators who wish to develop their operations in a more sustainable direction.

CONCLUSIONS

Swedish chemicals law is, to a large extent, harmonized with EU chemicals law. But the different starting points in EU and Sweden, respectively, have lead to the development of different aims and wordings of the problems concerning chemicals, and different under-standings of the need for health and environmental protection.

Each model seems to be logical within its own system. The more narrow EU approach may be more appropriate from the perspective of a narrower understanding of the problem, and also with regard to the more general means available for regulation within the EU. The wider approach in Sweden is founded on a more general understanding of the problem, and also on the possibility of using means especially suited for the actual situation.

The differences when it comes to legal practices must not be exaggerated. But the approach held by Swedish law and policy must be said to take a few steps further towards sustainable development. Damage and detriment shall be hindered and prevented as far as possible with regard to environmental, technical and economical concern. The focus on the *use* and the *function* of chemicals ensures that the best possible substances and techniques available are used when handling chemicals. But it also ensures that the demands do not go so far (except in cases where severe detriment is probable) that the intended function is hindered.

If commonly applied, such a focus would ensure that the process of replacing dangerous chemicals with less harmful substances continues. Furthermore, the effects on technical development would be negligible since the intended function is not ques-tioned. Economic development in chemical industries *which cannot compete* in this process would, of course, be reduced. But such losses would be counterbalanced by economic development in companies that are competitive with regard to protecting health and the environment. Thus, environmentally sustainable development would be promoted without obstacles to overall technical or economic development.

NOTES

1 The author's research project on the Precautionary Principle in Swedish Environmental law is financed by *Riksbankens Jubileumsfond.*
2 The wording *one* is not a claim that it is homogenous in all situations, but that the overall policy may be summarized and concluded as a certain approach.

3   Of course, chemicals are also, in some respect, addressed in environmental law focusing on air or water pollution. But the aim of that legislation is to *reduce emissions*, not to regulate chemicals.

4   It is interesting to notice, however, that chemicals in products have become an important issue for EU *waste law*. The two directives of the European Parliament and of the Council, Directive 2000/53/EC on end-of life vehicles and Directive 2002/95/EC on the restriction of the use of certain hazardous substances in electrical and electronic equipment, adopted on the grounds of Article 175, restrict the use of certain hazardous substances in the products concerned as a strategy to reduce the amount of waste. This issue is further discussed in the 2003 report *An Integrated Product Policy in the EU*, Report 5338, Swedish National Environmental Protection Agency, Stockholm.

5   KEMI (Chemicals Inspectorate) (2004) *Information om Varors Innehåll av Farliga Kemiska Ämnen*, Report 6/04, KEMI, Sundbyberg, p1.

6   KEMI (Chemicals Inspectorate) (2004) *Information om Varors Innehåll av Farliga Kemiska Ämnen*, Report 6/04, KEMI, Sundbyberg, p1.

7   Fifteen of them were first presented in the Government's Bill 1997/98:145 *Svenska miljömål. Miljöpolitik för ett hållbart Sverige*, and adopted by parliament in 1999. They are further developed in Government's Bills 2000/01:130 *Svenska miljömål – Delmål och åtgärdsstrategier* and 2004/05:150 *Svenska miljömål – ett gemensamt uppdrag* (hereafter the Government's Bill 1997: 98:145, 2000/01:130 and 2004/05:150). The latter presented a 16th environmental objective that was adopted by parliament in autumn 2005.

8   For further information on the environmental objectives, see www.internat.naturvardsverket.se (information is also available in English).

9   The Government's Bills 2000/01:130, p58, and 2004/05:150, p53.

10 The Government's Bill 2004/05:150, Chapter 8.

11 Other important actors are the Building and Planning Board, with regard to the indoor chemicals environment, and the National Food Administration, with regards to chemicals in food.

12 Government's Bill 2002/03:117 *Ett samhälle med giftfria och resusrssnåla kretslopp*, and further developed in the Bill 2004/05:150.

13 Lagen (1973:329) *om hälso- och miljöfarliga varor*, Section 5.

14 Lagen (1985:426) *om kemiska produkter*, Section 5.

15 Sandin, P. (1999) 'Dimensions of the precautionary principle', *Human and Ecological Risk Assessment*, vol 5, no 5, pp889–907.

16 Sandin, P. (1999) 'Dimensions of the precautionary principle', *Human and Ecological Risk Assessment*, vol 5, no 5, pp889–907.

17 Sandin, P. (1999) 'Dimensions of the precautionary principle', *Human and Ecological Risk Assessment*, vol 5, no 5, pp889–907.

18 The Government's Bill 1997/98:45 *Miljöbalk* (hereafter the Government's Bill 1997/98:45), Part I, pp205.

19 An interesting example on this is the study performed in Rydén, C. (2002) *From Data to Decision: A Case Study of Controversies in Cancer Risk Assessment*, Karolinska University Press, Stockholm, where the author shows how 25 risk assessments concerning trichloroethylene gave different conclusions.

20 Further and more detailed provisions are found in Ordinance 1998:941 *om kemiska och biotekniska produkter* and in other governmental ordinances, and in prescriptions issued by the Chemicals Inspectorate and the National Environmental Protection Agency (the Building and Planning Board issue prescriptions that affect the indoor chemicals environment).

21 The European Commission's Decision 1999/5/EC on the national provisions notified by the Kingdom of Sweden concerning the use of certain colours and sweeteners in foodstuffs, OJEC L 003, 7 January 1999.

22   The European Commission's Decision 1999/834/EC on the national provisions notified by the Kingdom of Sweden concerning the limitation to the placing on the market and use of creosote, OJEC L 329, 22 December 1999.

23   The European Commission's Decision 2002/399/EC on the national provisions notified by the Kingdom of Sweden under Article 95(4) of the EC Treaty concerning the maximum admissible content of cadmium in fertilizers, OJEC L 138, 28 May 2002.

24   The Government's Ordinance 1985:837 om PCB m.m.

25   The Government's Ordinance 1998:944 om förbud m.m. i vissa fall i samband med hantering, införsel och utförsel av kemiska produkter.

26   Case C-473/98, Kemikalieinspektionen v Toolex Alpha AB (2000) ECR I-5681 (hereafter Toolex).

27   Case C-473/98, Toolex, para 35.

28   Council Directive 76/769/EEC on the approximation of the laws, regulations and administrative provisions of the member states relating to restrictions on the marketing and use of certain dangerous substances and preparations.

29   Case C-473/98, Toolex, para 30.

30   Case C-127/97, Willi Burstein v Freistaat Bayern (1998) ECR I-06005 (hereafter C-127/97, Willi Burstein).

31   As amended by Directive 91/173.

32   Case C-127/97, Willi Burstein, paras 30 to 31.

33   Case C-473/98, Toolex, para 35.

34   Case C-379/92, Criminal Proceedings against Matteo Peralta (1994) ECR I-3453 (hereafter C-379/92, Peralta).

35   Case C-379/92, Peralta, paras 24 to 25.

36   Environmental Court of Appeal, inter alia, 12 May 2005, M 3225–04. See also Chapter 7 in this volume.

37   Supreme Court, 28 November 2005, T 2303–05.

38   The two-paged formula for the notification is available at www.kemi.se/upload/Produktregistret/Docs/Hur_o_varfor/produktanmalan.pdf.

39   But the use may be of such a nature that the licence obligation for hazardous activity ensues.

40   Environmental Court of Appeal, 3 April 2003, M 6068–02.

41   Environmental Court of Appeal, 23 March 2005, M 9336–02.

42   Environmental Court of Appeal, 6 October 2005, M 7028–04. Similar discussion is found in the cases M 3534–04 and M 3538–04, which concerned the use of pesticides on railways.

43   Arbetarskyddskungörelse 1949 No 208.

44   The Government's Bills 1973:17 Med förslag till lag om hälso- och miljöfarliga varor, p96, and 1984/85:118 Om kemikaliekontroll, p21. The principle of substitution in these previous acts is analysed in Westerlund, S. (1985) Lag om kemiska produkter, Publica Juridik, Liber.

45   By SFS 1990:239. The principle is further elaborated in Michanek, G. (1993) 'Substitutionsprincipen', Miljörättslig tidskrift, vol 2, pp127–158.

46   Nilsson, A. (1997) Att byta ut skadliga kemikalier, Nerenius & Santérus Förlag, Stockholm.

47   Government's Bill 1997/98:45, p228. The principle of substitution in the Environmental Code has been discussed by Zetterberg, C. (2003) 'Kemikaliers vara eller icke vara', in Michanek, G. and Björkman, U. (eds) Miljörätten i förändring – en antologi, Rättsfondens skriftserie 36, IUSTUS, Uppsala, pp117–135; Bengtsson, B., Bjällås, U., Rubensson, S. and Strömberg, R. (2004) Miljöbalken. En kommentar, Nordstedts Juridik, Stockholm; and Michanek, G. and Zetterberg, C. (2004) Den svenska miljörätten, IUSTUS Förlag, Uppsala.

48   Environmental Court of Appeal, 19 October 2005, M 9030–04.

49   Environmental Court of Appeal, 15 March 2004, M 5528–03.

50   Environmental Court of Appeal, 27 January 2005, M 508–03.

51   See www.kemi.se.

52   Environmental Court of Appeal, 1 September 2003, M 4995–02.

CHAPTER 17

Risks, Costs and Alternatives in European Community Environmental Legislation: The Case of the Registration, Evaluation and Authorization of Chemicals (REACH)

Gerd Winter*

INTRODUCTION

Whenever the placing of dangerous products on the market is regulated, various consequences may emerge, including the following:

- A certain level of protection of human health and the environment will be reached.
- Consumers can no longer make use of the restricted product in order to satisfy their consumption goal.
- Alternative products or technologies possibly serving the same use will be developed or imported by the relevant industry.
- The profits thus far obtained from the production or importation of the restricted product collapse.
- The costs of developing or importing alternative products or technologies may be offset by the benefit drawn from sales of the same.

These consequences vary. In practice, due to an overestimation of the costs involved and an underestimation of the benefits of substitute products, authorities often abstain from a restriction, thus allowing environmental damage to persist. Conversely, when an overestimation of environmental risks occurs, authorities frequently restrict a product, thus hindering an essential use and causing unnecessary costs to industry.

Environmental product regulation in Europe has traditionally been based on criteria that focus on concerns for human health and the environment, but widely disregard the use value of restricted products, the profit drawn from their manufacture and sale, and the costs of placing substitute products on the market. In practice, however, as analyses of restriction procedures prove,[1] cost considerations do play a role and may even be decisive. This is legitimate where legal criteria provide the regulator with a discretionary margin, but less so in cases where the regulator is bound to take action.

The question is: should cost and other trans-environmental considerations be left to the discretion, and hidden in the practice, of regulators, or should they become part of the official set of criteria, thus inviting more structured reasoning. Contrary to this suggestion, the US cost-benefit analysis that was introduced as a legal requirement during the Reagan era allegedly impeded environmental protection (see Chapter 19 in this volume).[2] But I believe that this consequence is avoidable. A prudent consideration of trans-environmental concerns can avoid obstructive effects and, at the same time, prevent the contradiction of declared environmentalism and clandestine economics.

This chapter will present a concept of what trans-environmental criteria should be used in the risk assessment and risk management of toxic chemicals. Criteria to be taken into consideration include, besides the risk to human health and the environment, the loss of use value and the possibility of substitution, and the economic cost of restrictions as balanced against the return drawn from substitutes. The chapter will discuss whether such criteria are based in European Union (EU) constitutional principles, and how they are specified in the Proposal for a Regulation of the European Parliament and of the Council concerning the Registration, Evaluation and Authorization of Chemicals (REACH) that the European Commission submitted in 2003,[3] taking into consideration the European Parliament opinion on the same proposal adopted on 17 November 2005 and the draft common position of the Council as politically agreed on 13 December 2005.[4] The following questions will be posed:

● What basis do criteria for risk assessment and management have in EU primary (or 'constitutional') law?
● What logical framework is appropriate to structure the balancing of conflicting interests?
● What criteria will be established by the proposed REACH regulation?
● Should the criteria be the same when authorizing and restricting the placing of chemicals on the market?
● How can the risk assessment of chemicals be conducted in a precautionary way?
● How can considerations of substituting dangerous chemicals by less dangerous ones be entered into the assessment of regulatory options?
● How should regulatory costs be weighed against risk-reduction benefits?
● How can the concept be put in a practically manageable form?

THE CONSTITUTIONAL BACKGROUND

Constitutional law – EC or national, depending upon what authority has acted – may be invoked if an economically overprotective abstention from regulation is challenged for violation of health and environmental protection duties, or, inversely, if an environmentally overprotective restriction is accused of violating basic economic freedoms. Therefore, although the focus of this chapter is on analysing secondary European Community (EC) law, it also takes a brief look at the EC constitutional level.

The conventional checking of the constitutionality of EC secondary law proceeds according to three questions:

1 Does the regulation constitute an encroachment on economic freedom?
2 If so, is there justification by public interests (such as human health and the environment)?
3 If so, is the regulation proportionate to the public interest?[5]

However, this construction does not adequately reflect the fact that not only economic freedom, but also human health and the environment are – according to Article 174 EC – constitutionally protected. To protect these goods is not the legislator's political discretion, but its obligation. Thus, the Environmental Court of Justice (ECJ) has determined in the *Safety High Tech* case that Article 130r EEC (now 174 EC) 'sets a series of objectives, principles and criteria which the Community legislature must respect in implementing environmental policy'.[6] The doctrinal construction must indicate that environmental protection does not only legitimize governmental action should the legislator be politically willing to act, but that under certain conditions, action can be mandatory.[7] The German Federal Administrative Court has pronounced itself on this matter as follows:

> *In those cases where an encroachment on basic rights collides with the basic rights of third parties or other constitutional goods, the solution of such tension is to find a proportional balance of the conflicting constitutionally protected interests with an aim of optimization. The conflict between the basic right and other constitutionally protected goods must be solved by case-related balancing.*[8]

This means that the second and third questions must be modified. The following framework is proposed:

1 Does the regulation constitute an encroachment on economic freedom?
2 If so, is there justification by a public interest or even a legal mandate?
3 Is the regulation proportionate to the public interest? If the regulation is mandatory, is it optimal in view of both the economic freedom and the legal mandate?

The change from proportionality to optimality implies a slight readjustment of the weights of the balanced goods: the proportionality test starts from the perspective of basic freedoms and, thus, gives these priority. In contrast, the optimization test gives both goods – the basic freedom and the mandatory protection – equal weight.

In addition, cases are possible where, because of governmental inaction, a suit is filed in order to compel government to act. In that case, the questions to be posed are as follows:

1 Does the inaction encroach on a constitutional obligation to take a measure?
2 If so, would the envisaged measure encroach on an economic freedom?
3 If so, is the measure optimal in light of both the economic freedom and the legal mandate?

THE LOGIC OF WEIGHING CONFLICTING INTERESTS

The conventional concept of checking proportionality or optimality assumes a situation where two interests are in conflict with each other. However, political and administrative decisions often affect third or even more interests, which must be taken into consideration. In the realm of environmental product regulation, the third interest besides industry and human health/the environment is consumer welfare. In the case of dangerous products, those who benefit from the use of the product may be affected if the product is prohibited. For instance, heat-resistant asbestos may be missing in brakes and, thus, frustrate consumer needs if asbestos is prohibited.

The doctrinal concept of balancing two interests must therefore be open to multilateral consideration. This chapter proposes that a matrix should be used as a rationalizing tool (see Table 17.1). In this matrix, one dimension represents the environmental and social goods positively or negatively affected by a measure, and the other represents the alternative measures to be considered. Single or accumulated positive, negative and neutral symbols indicate the relative value of the goods and the intensity of their impacts. Of course, the variables and loadings of the matrix must be adjusted in accordance with the specific legislation and the individual case under consideration. An example is provided in Table 17.2 and further explained in the conclusions.

MATERIAL STANDARDS IN THE PROPOSED REACH REGULATION

Other than conventional legislation, the Regulation of REACH will not confine itself with laying down one-sided environmental protection criteria. Rather, it displays a quite ambitious set of criteria. As they are scattered over many different provisions in the proposed regulation itself and in its annexes (showing also some inconsistencies between criteria of authorization and of restrictions in placing chemicals on the market), they need some systematization and clarification. The rest of this chapter attempts to systematize and clarify them.

Table 17.1   *Matrix of balancing alternative measures*

	Interest A (e.g. economic freedom)	Interest B (e.g. consumption)	Interest C (e.g. environmental protection)
Option 1	+	−	++
Option 2	0	++	−
Option 3	++		+

Table 17.2 *Matrix of option assessment for regulating dangerous substances*

	Benefit for human health and the environment	Benefit for consumers	Benefit for producers
Option 1 (status quo)	− −	+	++
Option 2 (e.g. public warning) = > substance X remains	−	+	+
Option 3 (e.g. contamination limits in products) = > R&D of substitutes A and B	+	+	+
Option 4 (phasing-out ban of substance X) = > R&D of substitutes D and C	++	+	+

For the authorization of substances, the material standard is laid down in Article 57 of the proposed REACH regulation, which states:

2   An authorisation shall be granted if the **risk** to human health or the environment from the use of a substance arising from the intrinsic properties specified in Annex XIII is **adequately controlled** in accordance with Annex I, section 6, and as documented in the applicant's chemical safety report.

3   If an authorisation cannot be granted under paragraph 2, an authorisation may be granted if it is shown that *socio-economic benefits outweigh the risk to human health or the environment* arising from the use of the substance and if there are no suitable alternative substances or technologies. This decision shall be taken after consideration of all of the following elements:

(a) the risk posed by the uses of the substance;

(b) the socio-economic *benefits* arising from its use and the socio-economic implications of a refusal to authorise as demonstrated by the applicant or other interested parties;

(c) the analysis of the *alternatives* submitted by the applicant under Article 59(5) and any third party contributions submitted under Article 61(2);

(d) available information on the health or environmental *risks of any alternative* substances or technologies [emphasis added].

For restrictions of the manufacture, placing on the market or use of substances in preparations or articles, the material standards are contained in Article 65(1):

When there is an unacceptable risk *to human health[9] or the environment, arising from the manufacture, use or placing on the market of substances, which needs to be addressed on a Community-wide basis, Annex XVI shall be amended in accordance with the procedure referred to in Article 130(3) by adopting new restrictions, or amending current restrictions in Annex XVI, for the manufacture, use or placing on the market of substances on their own, in preparations or in articles, pursuant to the procedure set out in Articles 66 to 70 [emphasis added].[10]*

Article 66 regulating the procedure of preparing restriction measures refers to Annex XIV where the content of the dossier preparing the decision is specified. In doing so, Part C of Annex XIV implicitly expounds more material standards:

(a) Evidence that *implemented risk management measures* (including those identified in registrations under Articles 9 to 13) *are not sufficient* ...

(c) Identification of the available options for addressing the concerns identified in Part B. For restrictions, this includes evidence that *alternative substances and/or processes* have been considered in the preparation of the proposal.

(d) Identification of the administrative, legal or other tools by which the available options can be implemented.

(e) Justification for the option and implementation method selected. The options shall be evaluated using the following criteria:

i   *Effectiveness:* the action must be targeted to the effects or exposures that cause the risks identified and must be capable of reducing these risks to a level where the risk is adequately controlled within a reasonable period of time.

ii *Practicality:* the action must be implementable, enforceable and manageable. Priority should be given to those measures that can be implemented with the existing infrastructure.

iii *Monitorability:* [this involves] the ability to monitor the result of the implementation of the proposed action.

iv *A socio-economic assessment* may be made of the impact of the proposed action on the producers/importers and/or downstream users of the substance and on other parties. This assessment should follow Annex XV [emphasis added].

Annex XV contains guidance for the so-called socio-economic analysis (SEA), that applies both to authorizations and restrictions. The following elements may be included in a SEA:

• impact of a granted or refused authorization on the applicant(s) or, in the case of a proposed restriction, the *impact on industry* (e.g. manufacturers and importers); the impact on all other actors in the supply chain, downstream users and associated businesses in terms of commercial consequences, such as impact on investment, one-off and operating costs (e.g. compliance; transitional arrangements; changes to existing processes, reporting and monitoring systems; installation of new technology; etc.);[11]

• *impacts* of a granted or refused authorization or a proposed restriction *on consumers* – for example, product prices, changes in composition or quality or performance of products, availability of products, and consumer choice;[12]

- *social implications* of a granted or refused authorization or a proposed restriction – for example, job security and employment;
- availability, suitability and technical feasibility of *alternatives* and the economic consequences thereof, and information on the rates of, and potential for, technological change in the sector(s) concerned (in the case of an application for authorization, the social and/or economic impacts of using any available alternatives are identified in Article 59(5)(b));
- wider *implications on trade, competition and economic development* – in particular, small- and medium-sized enterprises (SMEs) – of a granted or refused authorization, or a proposed restriction (this may include consideration of local, regional, national or international aspects);
- in the case of a proposed restriction, proposals for *other regulatory or non-regulatory measures* that could meet the aim of the proposed restriction (this shall take account of existing legislation) – this should include an assessment of the costs linked to alternative risk management measures;
- in the case of a proposed restriction, the *social and economic benefits* of the proposed restriction – for example, worker health, environmental performance and the distribution of these benefits, such as, geographically or in population groups [emphasis added].

HARMONIZATION OF STANDARDS FOR AUTHORIZATIONS AND RESTRICTIONS ON PLACING CHEMICALS ON THE MARKET

It appears at first sight that the standards for authorizations and restrictions differ: for authorizations, a complex consideration of risks, socio-economic benefits, substitutability and costs is required, whereas for restrictions, the standard is simply whether the risk is unacceptable. However, the annexes to the proposed REACH regulation add some of the criteria missing in the provision on restrictions. This is, in particular, true with regard to the socio-economic analysis. Both substitutability and socio-economic analysis will explicitly be added should the draft Common Position of the Council be adopted.[13]

Authorizations and restrictions differ in one respect: an authorization procedure presupposes that the activity under scrutiny may not be undertaken *until* the authorization is given, whereas the restriction procedure is concerned with ongoing activities. This difference in the regulatory situation does not, however, justify a difference in material standards: risks should, in both cases, be weighed against costs in relation to a number of feasible alternatives. However, it does justify a difference in distributing the burden of proof between operator and regulator: in obtaining an authorization, the operator bears the burden of proving that his or her activity meets the legal standards, while in order to restrict an ongoing activity, the authorities must prove that the activity does not meet them. Authorization requirements presuppose that the activity is *prima facie* dangerous and should, therefore, not be admissible without the operator proving that it is safe. By contrast, powers of restriction presuppose that the activity is *prima facie* safe, but may be regulated after closer scrutiny. Hence, Article 57(1) of the proposed REACH regulation should be read to mean that the operator must prove that the risk is 'adequately controlled', while Article 65 should be understood to lay on the regulator the burden of proving that there is 'unacceptable risk'.

With the advent of socio-economic analysis, the question arises whether the allocation of the burden of proof known in relation to health and environmental risks should also apply to facts about socio-economic impact. The REACH proposal appears to follow this line with regard to restrictions because the consideration of socio-economic impact is contained in the formula for 'unacceptable risk' used in Article 65. The burden of proof therefore lies with the regulator. Strangely enough, the same appears to be true in cases of authorizations: Article 57, paragraph 3, of the proposed regulation, which allows for authorizations based on balancing costs and risks, is framed as an exception to paragraph 1, which strictly excludes an authorization if the risk is not adequately controlled. Exceptions to rules normally imply the shifting of the burden of proof. This would mean that while the operator must prove the adequacy of risk controls, the regulator must prove the exceptional situation that the costs outweigh the risks.

This solution disregards the rationale of submitting activities to authorizations. For this reason, the burden of proving costs should therefore be shifted to the operator. However, beyond this there is another reason for such shifting, which also covers restrictions: facts about regulatory costs are known to operators; but, in most instances, they are a black box for the regulator. Therefore, it must be the burden of the operator to submit and prove such facts should he or she claim that a restriction or refusal of an authorization causes excessive costs.

Legislation both on the European Community and the member state level often provides the authorities with the discretion to decide on authorizations and restrictions. It is noteworthy that the REACH proposal does not follow this line. Both authorizations and restrictions are obligatory if the conditions set out in the relevant provisions are given. The reason for this is that the balancing of interests, which is typical for discretionary powers, is structured in some detail by legislatory decision, thus not leaving much space for further administrative discretion.

PRECAUTION

The precautionary principle as commonly understood at Community level means that measures can, and sometimes must, be taken even if there is not yet proof, but rather a suspicion of dangerous effects. The measures should be provisional until better knowledge has been accumulated.[14] In addition, some member states such as Germany understand precaution to mean that measures should also be taken if the probability of an adverse effect is low, or if the adverse effect is not grave, or if the effect materializes in the distant future only, or if it occurs at a distant location. The term in German law, which embraces these situations of uncertainty, low probability, low severity, and long-term and long-range effect, is low risk.[15] Low risk is to be distinguished from cases of high risk or danger – that is, the scientifically based high probability of serious, imminent and nearby damage. The implication of this broader conception of precaution is that in situations of high risk (danger), measures of danger avoidance must be taken more or less irrespective of costs and the availability of substitutes, while in situations of low risk, measures of precaution can be taken after balancing other concerns, including regulatory costs.

The REACH proposal does not mention the precautionary principle, at least not explicitly. It does, however, use the term 'risk' to describe the situation that may trigger management measures.[16] Risk is commonly defined as the likelihood of a certain adverse effect, taking into account the level of certainty.[17] The term as commonly understood also covers situations of uncertainty and low probability of effect. Therefore, the use of the term 'risk' means that the regulator shall be empowered to take precautionary measures.

The quest for precaution in the REACH concept is reinforced by the fact that precaution was given EC constitutional status. According to Article 174(2) EC: 'Community policy … shall be based on the precautionary principle'. This was supported by the Court of First Instance in the *Pfizer* judgment.[18] In that case, the court examined Article 6(2) of Directive 70/524 on additives in feeding stuffs, which states that a substance may only be included in the list of food additives 'if … at the level permitted in feeding stuffs [the substance] does not endanger animal or human health'.[19] The Council had deleted a Pfizer substance from the list, claiming that this condition was no longer satisfied. Upon Pfizer's complaint, the court ruled that Article 6(2) could be read in terms of the precautionary principle, and accepted that the scientific basis of the Council decision was not secure.

In spite of this conclusion, it would be preferable for the sake of clarity if the proposed REACH regulation would explicitly make reference to the precautionary principle. This would be in line with more modern EC secondary law, such as the Integrated Pollution Prevention and Control (IPPC) Directive[20] and the Directive on the Release of Genetically Modified Organisms.[21] It would then be clear that risk management measures of dangerous substances (such as the refusal of authorization, a conditioned authorization and a marketing restriction) do not presuppose full scientific knowledge. It could even be framed to include the elements of the German definition – that is, non-severe or long-term or long-range effects.[22]

In the practice of risk assessment, it can occur that the state of knowledge is so undeveloped that no meaningful conclusion can be drawn on whether the substances pose a risk or not. In terms of rules of evidence, this is the situation of *non liquet*. The decision must, in such situations, be taken following the legislator's allocation of the burden of proof. Authorizations and restrictions differ in this respect. As noted earlier, an authorization could not be granted in such a situation because the operator bears the burden of proof. Inversely, the authorities could not issue a restriction if the substance is already placed on the market because it is they who bear the burden of proof in this case.[23]

The total risk of a substance depends upon both the substance's properties and the exposure to it of organisms and other end points. Such a twofold assessment is typical for product-related legislation, the idea being that a toxic substance *per se* may nevertheless be kept in containment, thus neutralizing the toxicity. The REACH proposal mirrors both aspects by making the authorization dependent upon whether the risk is 'adequately controlled'.[24] With this reference to exposure control, a more radical approach is rejected that would suppress the marketing of a substance based on a cluster of mere innate properties, such as toxicity, persistence, mobility and bioaccumulation, alleging that even if a substance may be controlled during its lifetime, it will, nevertheless, eventually enter the environment in the form of waste.

However, the term 'adequately controlled' is somewhat unclear. In particular, the baseline of expectable caution on the side of the user is not defined, other than in the biocides legislation, where reference is made to a user who observes the pertinent conditions of the authorization, taking into account the normal practice of use.[25] This means that a perfect user of biocides is not assumed, but rather one who has slightly negligent habits in daily life. Such a realistic standard should also apply in the chemicals area, at least when chemicals are used by end consumers.

In any case, even if a substance is not adequately controlled, Article 57 of the proposed regulation provides that it may, nevertheless, be placed on the market under certain circumstances. These are the already noted substitutability in light of the use value of the substance and the relative costs of different regulatory options, which shall now be discussed, in turn.

USE, VALUE AND ALTERNATIVES

General merits of testing alternatives

The fact that Article 57 and Annex XIV of the REACH proposal request producers and importers to consider the substitutability of a dangerous substance fits with a more general trend to open up environmental protection instruments for the testing of alternatives. Thinking of alternatives increases the likelihood of finding better solutions and may reduce the need for information: if an obviously less dangerous alternative can be found, the further investigation of the primary option can be disrupted and the intricate weighing of incommensurate risks and costs can largely be avoided.[26] The testing of alternatives originates from the US National Environmental Policy Act (NEPA)[27] and plays a major role in practical decision-making. The requirement was also introduced in the EC directives on environmental impact assessment (EIA),[28] as well as in the directives on occupational health,[29] on automobiles[30] and on electronic devices.[31] It could play a major role also in the area of chemicals control. For instance, in June 2003, the Ministerial Conference to the Convention for the Protection of the Marine Environment of the North-East Atlantic (OSPAR) asked the EC 'to promote the substitution of hazardous substances with safer alternatives, including promoting and facilitating the development of such alternatives where they do not currently exist'.[32]

Alternatives testing and risk-cost analysis

There is a need to clarify the relationship between the analysis of the substitutability of a substance and the costs of its restriction. The alternatives testing enquires whether a use benefit of a substance can be satisfied with a means that involves less environmental risks than the means under scrutiny. The risk-cost analysis enquires whether an environmental risk can be reduced with a means that involves less economic costs than the option under scrutiny. Both tests have a similar structure because they look for less intrusive means of reaching a certain goal. But the direction of enquiry is different. The alternatives testing asks: how many environmental resources shall be sacrificed for societal welfare goals? The risk-cost test, on the other hand, asks: how much societal welfare shall be sacrificed for the preservation of environmental resources?

One might argue that the difference in direction can be minimized by a more neutral framing of the questions. But there is, in fact, a difference if one either hinders society in reaching certain welfare goals or if one hinders the state in taking regulatory measures in light of the involved economic costs. In the first case, political and legal practice are less willing to conduct inquiries and to take action because they have to put societal welfare goals into question, a matter widely left for individuals to decide in liberal states. In the second case, political and legal practice is more at ease because it is widely accepted that state action should be kept to a minimum, and that it is a governmental task to collect information and take action in this regard.

Since the REACH proposal demands both of the tests, it is for the sake of clarity that the two operations should be kept separate. This means that if the risk assessment of a substance concludes that a risk is given and the denial of an authorization or a marketing restriction should be considered, two more tests apply: whether there are alternatives to serve the same goal, and whether the measure can be replaced by a less costly one. In more abstract terms, the alternatives and the risk-costs test require that the regulation is checked, first, in terms of the loss of use value and, second, in terms of the costs to industry.

Alternatives testing

As noted earlier, the REACH proposal prescribes alternatives testing both for authorizations and for restrictions. For authorizations, this is explicitly mentioned in Article 57, while for restrictions it must be extrapolated from the term 'unacceptable risk'. 'Unacceptable' is a risk where there are alternatives that serve the same use but involve less environmental risks. That this is a correct interpretation is evidenced by the already mentioned 'guidance' in Annex XV of the proposal.

With all its requirements put together, the alternatives testing proceeds as follows:

1   Identification of the use(s) of the substance under scrutiny.
2   Determination of the socio-economic benefit (or use value) of this substance.
3   Identification of alternative substances or technologies serving the same use(s).
4   (Rough) assessment of the risks of the alternatives.
5   Balance of benefits and risks of the primary substance and the alternatives.

Requiring an alternatives testing is a gain in rational decision-making because it structures the discretionary margin of government and thus makes the outcome more predictable. It is also to be welcomed that the alternatives considered not only examine other substances, but also other technologies. This broadens the possibility of reducing the use of dangerous substances. For instance, the authority, when considering suppressing a chemical cleanser that has environmentally harmful side effects, may take into account that the cleaning can be done equally well with hot water and a cleaning cloth.[33]

When identifying the use of an incriminated substance, one difficulty emerges. One substance often serves many different uses. For instance, a solvent may be used for paints, machines, cooling, cleaning and other uses at the same time. If alternatives testing is taken seriously, alternatives for all of the uses must be identified. However, there are probably only very rare cases where a use cannot also be served by other means. The analysis may also be simplified by concentrating on the core uses that the incriminated substance stands for.

Another concern is the mode in which, in the case of authorizations, the risk and the alternatives tests are linked in the REACH proposal: the link is such that the availability of substitutes shall only be considered if the risk is not adequately controlled.[34] If the risk is not adequately controlled, but the socio-economic benefit outweighs the environmental risk and no viable alternative is available, the authorization may, nevertheless, be given. In other words, if the result of the alternatives test is a negative one, an authorization may still result (provided that the socio-economic benefit prevails).[35]

This strips alternatives testing of some of its potential to rationalize the decision. Before it is conducted, the socio-economic benefit must be weighed against the environmental risk. This is very difficult to do because no common denominator exists. In particular, neither the benefits nor the risks can be expressed in monetary terms. Against this, if alternatives testing was applied as a first step, it could be said that if an alternative exists the authorization shall not be granted, notwithstanding whether the socio-economic benefit of the incriminated substance outweighs the risk or not. Only if no alternative is available will the difficult weighing of risk and benefit have to be made.

Moreover, the potentiality of alternatives testing could also be used in relation to those risks that appear to be adequately controllable. Assessing a risk as 'adequately controlled' often involves uncertainties. If alternatives are available, why should a risk not be prevented, even if there is still uncertainty about whether the risk is significant or controllable? Therefore, both with regard to authorizations and to restrictions, alternatives should be taken into account if the significance of the risk or its adequate controllability is uncertain, and if the risk is not adequately controllable.[36] Substitution would, in this way, become a proactive tool to prevent uncertain risks rather than only functioning as a 'negative' barrier against allowing uncontrollable but avoidable risks.

Be this as it may, one possible misunderstanding of the alternatives test must, in any case, be overcome. The availability of a substitute is at least, in practice, sometimes taken as a precondition of any regulatory action. For instance, the prohibition of chlorofluoro-carbons was only adopted when industry had developed a substitute. The same is true with asbestos, PCBs and other bans or restrictions of the recent past. In legal terms, however, substitutability is not a precondition of regulation. The testing of alternatives is, but not the actual availability of an alternative. If the adverse effect on human health or the environment is serious, the regulator is empowered and possibly also obliged to prohibit the substance even if no substitute is available. An understanding that disregards this would conflict with the constitutional protection of human health and the environment. It would be intolerable to sustain a serious risk for the only reason that no substitute is available to satisfy the relevant societal need. Article 57 of the proposal must be understood to mean precisely this: an uncontrolled risk that outweighs the socio-economic benefit must be prohibited even if no substitute is available. Of course, this does not exclude that a phasing-out scheme is built into the ban, allowing for time to develop alternatives.

RISK-COST ANALYSIS

Besides an analysis of the regulatory impact on the consumer, Annex XV of the REACH proposal also asks for a study of impacts on industry. The annex specifies what the proposed regulation says concerning authorizations in Article 57(3)(b) ('the socio-economic implications of a refusal to authorize') and concerning restrictions in Article 65, particularly regarding the notion of the unacceptability of the risk.

This requirement would be misunderstood if it were read to mean that regulatory costs to industry could lead to admitting uncontrolled risks. If, from the previous tests, it is concluded that a risk is significant and not adequately controlled, and that either substitutes are available or the use value outweighs the risk, then there is no way to authorize (or non-restrict) the substance for reasons of impact on industry. For instance, high-risk substances used for modest use values, such as decoration, cannot be authorized on the grounds that the relevant producers make good profits and provide jobs. To make profits and create job opportunities is perfectly legitimate even if the product is totally useless. Things are different, however, if the product poses a risk to human health and the environment. To endure such risks from a useless product for the only reason that the product provides profits and jobs would not only be politically unwise, but also a misbalance of constitutionally protected goods.

Risk-cost analysis is, however, not irrelevant in the regulatory calculus. Its proper role is not to contribute to the 'if at all' of the taking of measures, but rather to provide guidance for what kind of measure should be selected. It is concerned with what the risk methodologists call option assessment as opposed to risk assessment and evaluation.[37] If a risk is significant and not adequately controlled, measures must be taken. In most cases, however, several measures can be considered, ranging from a complete ban (or non-authorization) to conditioned restrictions and market information strategies, such as safety data sheets and public warnings. In order to evaluate the regulatory options besides effectiveness in light of the protection goal, the cost implications are a major criterion in identifying the best solution.

This kind of cost consideration envisaged here is a cost-effectiveness analysis rather than a full-blown cost-benefit (or cost-risk) study. The regulatory goal (that is, the control of the risk) should, in the normal case, be taken as authoritative for selecting appropriate measures, rather than being transposed into economic terms for balancing against economic costs, as a full benefit-cost analysis would require. This does not exclude the fact that small cuts in the level of protection are acceptable because not every regulatory option has exactly the same effectiveness. Only in the hardly realistic event that even the cheapest measure still involves exorbitant costs will it be reasonable to assess the economic benefit of reducing the risk and balancing it with the regulatory costs.[38]

When calculating the regulatory costs, it is important to note that the prohibition of a substance often releases creativity and effort to develop alternative substances, thereby opening competitive advantages for innovative producers. Occasionally, a radical prohibition can have much more productive effect than softer measures, which at first sight appear to spare industry. Such opportunities must be deducted from the immediate costs caused by the prohibition of the incriminated substance.

It may, nevertheless, occur that the new advantage accrues not to the initial producer, but to the competitors. This is not, however, a viable objection because nobody has a right to, or can legitimately demand, protection for a certain market share. It is true that a state and even the European Community sometimes takes a nationalistic approach and hesitates to prohibit substances, which can be substituted by products from external producers. Politically understandable as this is, such practice, however, touches upon limits set by the World Trade Organization's free trade requirements. Should, for instance, a contracting state prohibit the importation of less dangerous products for the simple reason that the domestic producers are not yet able to bring a similar product on the market, this would be a clear violation of Article XI of the General Agreement on Tariffs and Trade (GATT) and Article 2, para 2, of the Agreement on Technical Barriers to Trade (TBT).

CONCLUSIONS

In conclusion, a matrix outlining how to identify the regulation of dangerous substances is presented. In Table 17.2, the protected goods are listed in the horizontal dimension (the regulatory costs are considered as part of the yield – or loss – of the producer), while the instrumental options are placed in the vertical dimension, which also covers alternatives as a qualification of those options. The symbols in the cells represent two measurements combined: the intensity of positive or negative impact of an option on the protected good, and the relative weight of the protected good – (++) meaning effective service of a highly worthy good; (+) modest service of a modest good or modest satisfaction of a highly worthy good; (– –) effective disservice for a highly worthy good; and (–) modest disservice to a highly worthy good.

In our case, I have assumed the possible restriction of a persistent and toxic varnish (substance X) used for ship hulls. The options include the *status quo ante* (no action); a measure such as a public warning that will not effectively remove the substance from the market; the gradual phasing-out of the substance; and a strict ban of the substance. The protected goods to be considered include benefits for human health and the environment, for consumers and for producers.

Option 1 causes damage to human health and the environment, which is slightly offset by consumer and producer gains. Option 2 does not effectively abate health and environmental risks, and reduces, at the same time, the benefits for consumers and producers. Option 3, the fixing of contamination limit values, will lead to the development of substitutes, thus serving the needs of consumers and of human health and the environment, while the costs to producers will be offset by profits from the substitutes in the long run. Option 4 comes out best (in this scenario) because the gains for human health and the environment are more immediate and, thus, higher than in the other options. Under normal conditions substitutes will be developed. This would reflect the so-called Porter hypothesis, which claims that clear and strict regulation is often a better incentive for innovation than overzealous respect for cost effects.[39]

NOTES

* A previous version of this chapter was published in *RECIEL* (2006) vol 15, no 1, pp56–65.

1 Winter, G., Ginzky, H. and Hansjürgens, B. (1999) *Die Abwägung von Risiken und Kosten in der europäischen Chemikalienregulierun*, Erich Schmidt Verlag, Berlin, pp229–282.

2 Ashford, N. (2005) 'Implementing the precautionary principle: Incorporating science, technology, fairness and accountability in environmental, health and safety decisions', *International Journal of Risk Assessment and Management*, vol 5, no 2–4, pp112–123. See also Ashford in this volume.

3 Proposal for a Regulation of the European Parliament and of the Council concerning the Registration, Evaluation and Authorization of Chemicals (REACH), Com (2003) 644 (hereinafter REACH proposal).

4 Document No 15921/05. For the EP opinion see Document P6_TA (2005) 0434.

5 See Kingreen, T. (2002) in Callies, C. and Ruffert, M. (eds) *Kommentar zu EU-Vertrag und EG-Vertrag*, second edition, Luchterhand Verlag, Neuwied, Article 6, nos 64–66.

6 Case C-284/95, *Safety Hi-Tech* (1998) ECR I-4301, para 36.

7 Winter, G. (2004) 'The legal nature of environmental principles in international, EC and German law', in Macrory, R. (ed) *Principles of European Environmental Law*, Europa Law Publishing, Groeningen, pp19, 22–27; Köck, W. (2003) 'Das system Registration, Evaluation and Authorization of Chemicals (REACH)', in Rengeling, H.-W. (ed) *Umgestaltung des deutschen Chemikalienrechts durch europäische Chemikalienpolitik*, C. Heymanns Verlag, Köln, p47. In contrast, Krämer, L. (2003) *EC Environmental Law*, fifth edition, Sweet and Maxwell, London, p13, argues that the environmental principles only provide political guidance.

8 Judgment of 18 October 1990, Case 3 C 2.88, *Federal Administrative Court Reports* vol 87, pp37–45.

9 In the European Parliament Opinion of 17 November 2005, the following words are inserted after the word 'health': 'including that of vulnerable populations and citizens exposed early in life or continuously to mixtures of pollutants'. The insertion gives the precautionary approach more weight.

10 In the draft Council Common Position of 13 December 2005, the following sentence is added to the paragraph: 'For such decision the socio-economic consequences of the restriction, including the availability of alternatives, shall be considered.'

11 In the draft Council Common Position of 13 December 2005, the following words are added to the paragraph: 'taking account of the general market and technology development'.

12 In the draft Council Common Position of 13 December 2005, the following words are added to the paragraph: 'as well as impacts on human health and the environment as far as they affect consumers'.

13 See notes 10–12.

14 Communication of the Commission on the Application of the Precautionary Principle, 2 February 2000, Com (2000) 1.

15 Kloepfer, M. (2004) *Umweltrecht*, third edition, Verlag C. H. Beck, München, pp176 *et seq.*

16 Proposal for a Regulation of the European Parliament and of the Council concerning the Registration, Evaluation and Authorization of Chemicals (REACH), Com (2003) 644 (hereinafter REACH proposal), Article 57(2) and Article 65(1).

17 Banse, G. (1996) 'Herkunft und Anspruch der Risikoforschung', in Banse, G. (ed) *Risikoforschung zwischen Disziplinarität und Interdisziplinarität*, Sigma, Berlin, p8.

18 Case T-13/99, *Pfizer Animal Health* (2002) ECR II-3305.

19 See Council Directive 70/524/EEC of 23 November 1970 concerning additives in feeding-stuffs (1970) OJ L270 1, Article 6(2).

20   Council Directive 96/61/EC of 24 September 1996 concerning integrated pollution prevention and control (1996) OJ L257 26; Article 3 states 'any appropriate precautionary measures'.

21   Directive 2001/18/EC of the European Parliament and of the Council of 12 March 2001 on the deliberate release into the environment of genetically modified organisms and repealing Council Directive 90/220/EEC (2001) OJ L106 1; Article 4 states 'in accordance with the precautionary principle'.

22   Kloepfer (see note 15), pp176 *et seq.*

23   Appel, I. (2003) 'Besonders gefährliche Stoffe im europäischen Chemikalienrecht – Neuorientierung im Weißbuch zur Chemikalienpolitik', in *Das Europäische Weißbuch zur Chemikalienpolitik, Umwelt- und Technikrecht (UTR)*, vol 68, Erich Schmidt Verlag, Berlin, pp95, 118.

24   Proposal for a Regulation of the European Parliament and of the Council concerning the Registration, Evaluation and Authorization of Chemicals (REACH), Com (2003) 644, Article 57(2). For restrictions, exposure is – somewhat less systematically – mentioned in Annex XIV, Part C, (e) and (i).

25   Directive 98/8 on the placing on the market of biocides (1998) OJ L 128/1, Article 5.

26   See, for an elaboration of this argument, Winter, G. (1997) *Alternativen in der administrativen Entscheidungsbildung*, Nomos Verlag, Baden-Baden, pp12–19.

27   NEPA § 102 (1) (C), 42 U.S.C. §§ 4332.

28   Council Directive of 27 June 1985 on the assessment of the effects of certain public and private projects on the environment (1985) OJ L175/40.

29   Council Directive 89/391/EEC of 12 June 1989 on the introduction of measures to encourage improvements in the safety and health of workers at work (1989) OJ L183/1, and Council Directive 90/394/EEC of 28 June 1990 on the protection of workers from the risks related to exposure to carcinogens at work (sixth individual directive within the meaning of Article 16(1) of Directive 89/391/EEC) (1990) L196/1.

30   Directive 2000/53/EC of the European Parliament and of the Council of 18 September 2000 on end-of-life vehicles (2000) L269/34.

31   Directive 2002/95/EC of the European Parliament and of the Council of 27 January 2003 on the restriction of the use of certain hazardous substances in electrical and electronic equipment (2003) OJ L37/19.

32   See Bremen Statement of the Ministerial Meeting of the OSPAR Commission (Bremen, 25 June 2003), para 23(c), found at www.ospar.org/eng/html/md/Bremen_statement_2003.htm.

33   A similar test, including alternative technologies, applies to the authorization of pesticides. See, for an example, the Administrative Court of Braunschweig in an unpublished judgment of 29 April 1992 (6 A 6001/90), where the court found the risk of a pesticide unacceptable because instead of using the pesticide, the farmer could also have removed the weeds by mechanical means. For a more theoretical view, see Winter, G. (1992) 'Brauchen wir das? Von der Risikominderung zur Bedarfsprüfung', *Kritische Justiz*, vol 4, p395.

34   Article 57, paras 2 and 3.

35   No such stepwise order is foreseen for decisions on restrictions: see Annex XIV. The availability of substitutes is one among several points to consider.

36   Requiring that an analysis of alternatives must be submitted with the application for authorization the European Parliament has been a first step in this direction. However, this procedural requirement is not mirrored in the formulation of the substantive criterion for authorization. See European Parliament Opinion of 17 November 2005, Article 59, para 4 lit. db. The same requirement is also contained in the Political Agreement of the Council of 13 December 2005, Article 59, para 4 lit. da. In its recommendation for second reading of 13 October 2006 (A6–0352/2006) the EP has corrected this flaw by proposing that an authorization should *only* be granted if suitable alternatives do not exist, benefits outweigh

the risks and the risk is adequately controlled. This corresponds to what I am suggesting above.

37 See Risk Commission (2003) *Revision of Risk Analysis Procedures and Structures of Standard Setting in the Field of Environmental Health in the FRG*, Bundesamt für Strahlenschutz, München, www.bfs.de.

38 See Risk Commission (2003) *Revision of Risk Analysis Procedures and Structures of Standard Setting in the Field of Environmental Health in the FRG*, Bundesamt für Strahlenschutz, München, www.bfs.de. See also the proposals made by Winter, G., Ginzky, H. and Hansjürgens, B. (1999) *Die Abwägung von Risiken und Kosten in der europäischen Chemikalienregulierung*, Erich Schmidt Verlag, München, p418.

39 Porter, M. E. and van der Linde, C. (1990) 'The competitive advantage of nations', *Harvard Business Review*, pp73–93.

CHAPTER 18

The Impact of the Registration, Evaluation and Authorization of Chemicals (REACH) Regulation on the Regulatory Powers of the Nordic Countries

Nicolas de Sadeleer

INTRODUCTION

Chemical management policies are moving forward in the European Union (EU) as well as in its member states, spurred on by several factors, such as the lack of chemicals testing, the concern over the health and ecosystems impacts of chemicals, and, last but not least, long-term political commitments to environmental quality improvement and reduction of hazardous chemicals.

The Chemicals Policy Reform undertaken by the European Community (EC) institutions with the adoption on 29 October 2003 of the Registration, Evaluation and Authorization of Chemicals (REACH) proposal will certainly have wide ranging consequences, not only for the chemicals policy contemplated by the Nordic countries, but also for the chemical industry in these countries and for those industries using chemical substances. In this respect, the new EC policy may significantly impinge upon the free circulation of chemicals within the EU and between the EU and its trading partners.

All of the Northern European policies have a stronger focus on product-based risks than other EC countries.[1] Nordic government agencies also believe that they must develop policies to stimulate innovation in safer technologies and products. For instance, Danish and Swedish policies focus on aggressive phase-outs of the most harmful substances based on inherent hazards and lack of testing, while the Dutch approach is more conservative, with rapid screening, examination of use categories, and then specific restrictions and government–industry interaction to move towards safer substitutes. Put simply, Nordic countries are known to have achieved an advanced level of health safety as well as consumer and environmental protection in comparison with other European countries (see Chapter 16 in this volume).

However, Nordic countries may have to overcome several hurdles if they wish to maintain such a level of protection. Irrespective of the fact that these countries belong to the European

Economic Area (EEA) legal system (Norway and Iceland) or are EC member states (Sweden, Denmark and Finland), their national chemical policy measures may be deemed to constitute a means of unjustifiable discrimination or disguised restrictions to international trade, inconsistent with the free movement of goods provisions of the EC Treaty and the EEA.

The chapter's aim is to determine Nordic countries' room for manoeuvre within the confines of the EC rules and rules of EEA law (and the inclusion in Annex II of this agreement on the future REACH regulation).

STATE OF EUROPEAN COMMUNITY LAW ON CHEMICALS

The failure of the EC chemical cluster

Set up in the early days of the environmental debate, EC chemicals policy consists of a complex regulatory system made up of an intricate network of directives and regulations. While these instruments were primarily motivated by a desire to complete the internal market, they have recently begun to address environmental concerns.

The sixth amendment to Council Directive 67/548/EEC on the classification, packaging and labelling of dangerous substances, which established an EC-wide notification procedure for newly marketed substances (that is, substances placed on the market before 1981), was intended to increase knowledge of the effects of substances and thereby facilitate subsequent decision-making. Since 1982, producers and importers of new substances have been required to notify the competent national authority and to provide full information on any substance that is to be placed on the market. The 'notifier' may furnish the competent authority with a preliminary risk assessment. However, existing substances are exempt from notification. On the basis of the data provided by the manufacturer or the importer, the competent authority assesses the 'real and potential' risks to man and the environment posed by the notified substance, according to the provisions of European Commission Directive 93/67/EEC on the assessment of risks of dangerous substances to man and the environment. After the European Commission has provided this information to all other member states, the Community decides by way of a committee procedure whether and how to classify the new chemical substance.

From a precautionary point of view, the procedure is marred by a number of inadequacies.

From the outset, the emphasis has been clearly placed on the collection of scientific data and test results, while contextual issues pertaining to risk (such as familiarity, immediacy, latency, scope or novelty) are not included in the notification.

In addition, because the procedure applies only to new substances, which represent a very small percentage of substances on the market, the harmful effects of most chemicals on health and the environment have never been assessed. As a result, EC and EC member state authorities know surprisingly little about the risks presented by the most problematic chemicals. Of the more than 100,000 chemical substances in circulation, the classification of only 4500 existing and new substances has been agreed upon. For many of the rest, public authorities must rely on a provisional classification established by industry.

In order to fill the information gap relating to chemicals placed on the market before 1981, the EC law-maker adopted, in 1993, Council Regulation (EEC) No 793/93, which sets forth a system of evaluation and control of the risks posed by existing substances. According to the provisions laid down in this regulation, any Community importer or producer of an existing substance in quantities exceeding 1000 tonnes per year had to submit data on the eco-toxicity and environmental fate and pathways of that chemical to the European Commission. Member states were given responsibility for assessing the risks of specific substances on a list of priority substances requiring immediate attention because of their potential effects on man or the environment. A first priority list containing 42 substances (or substance groups) was published in the Annex to Commission Regulation (EC) No 1179/94. A second and third list followed in 1995 and 1997. These lists did not cover more than 0.1 per cent of existing chemicals.

Given that the risk assessments have been utterly laborious, the procedure under Regulation (EEC) No 793/93 did not yield proper results. To some extent, the emphasis placed on sound science has paralysed regulatory action. Accordingly, by 1999, only 19 of the prioritized existing substances had been assessed for risk. Different reasons explain this policy failure.

First, the majority of assessments have taken between 2.5 and 4.5 years to carry out. In particular, the obligation to assess the advantages and drawbacks of the substances and of the availability of replacement substances, which was a prerequisite to establishing a risk-reduction strategy, appeared to be a time-consuming exercise.

Second, despite the results of the few risk assessments performed, the Council has not been willing to place restrictions on the marketing and use of certain dangerous substances and preparations according to Council Directive 76/769/EEC. At present, there are restrictive measures for 41 substances or groups of substances, covering about 900 substances, in total. As a result, the risk reduction measures achieved by the EC chemicals policy appear relatively modest in the context of the human and financial resources required by the assessment procedures.

In short, owing to a huge backlog of datasets, this cluster of directives and regulations has been unable to cope with the increasing problems caused by hazardous chemicals.

REACH

The policy failure described above led the Council of Ministers to call for a substantial revision of the current policy in 1999. On 13 February, 2001, the European Commission adopted a White Paper setting out the strategy for a future Community Policy for Chemicals (COM (2001) 88 final). This has been followed by the adoption of the REACH regulation proposal by the European Commission on 29 October 2003. On 17 November 2005, the European Parliament adopted the text in first reading. The Council adopted a common position on 7 December 2005. REACH should be adopted, at the end of the co-decision procedure, perhaps in the course of 2007. So far, the proposal has created heated debate between the different stakeholders, institutions and member states. Whatever the outcomes of this lengthy regulatory process, one can expect that the future regulation will have a tremendous impact on national chemical policies.

The main objective of REACH is to ensure a high level of protection for human health and the environment in the light of the precautionary principle, while ensuring the efficient functioning of the internal market and stimulating innovation and competitiveness in the chemical industry. As a matter of course, the main drive of the White Paper is to resolve the so-called 'burden of the past'. The new system calls for the Registration, Evaluation, and Authorization of all Chemicals (REACH) marketed in the EU above 10 tonnes. The proposal includes, among others, the aims of:

- reducing the asymmetry between new chemicals and existing chemicals regulations;
- shifting the burden onto industry to test chemicals and assess risks;
- increased testing and information on chemicals;
- limitations on priority chemicals through an authorization process.

In addition, REACH calls for the replacement of various existing regulations on chemicals described above (Regulation (EEC) 793/93; Directive 76/769/EEC).

Needless to say, the precautionary and the substitution principles (the replacement of dangerous substances with less dangerous and suitable alternative substances), which underlie several provisions laid down in the proposal, have been at the core of the debates accompanying that reform. Endorsed by several Nordic countries (Norwegian Product Control Act 39, for instance), the principle of substitution is known to be an incentive to innovation. Nevertheless, the chemical industry fears that the recognition of such environmental principles could enhance a regulatory approach that is detrimental to their economic interests.

Weaknesses of the authorization and restriction procedures

As a matter of principle, REACH is likely to restrict, to a great extent, the abilities of the member states, as well as European Free Trade Association (EFTA) states, to enact their own safety standards.

At this stage, there are already good reasons for concern.

First, the European Commission's initial ambitions have been watered down (such as duty of care obligation and the content of the chemical safety report). Although the lawmaker is compelled to achieve a high level of environmental/health/consumer/worker protection pursuant to Article 95(3) of the EC, the European Parliament and the Council have been weighing various and even contradictory interests.

Second, the proposal leaves to the discretion of institutions whether a chemical substance should be assessed, subject to restrictions or banned. Moreover, decisions to be taken over persistant, bioaccumulative, toxic (PBT), very persistant, very bioaccumulative (vPB) and carcinogen, mutagen, reproductible (CMR) substances and endocrine disruptors are individual decisions that will not be taken immediately. Furthermore, REACH provides important derogations, notwithstanding the fact that those chemicals have been assessed to be of particular concern.

Third, the proposal leaves many issues undecided. These issues will have to be dealt with in EC Commission-led committees ('comitology' procedures), where Nordic states have little to say (Norway and Iceland do not vote; the other three Nordic countries cannot form a blocking minority on their own). Likewise, important issues have not been clarified, among which is the regulatory powers bestowed to the EC member states. Although REACH refers to the establishment of a 'central entity' – the Chemical Agency – it provides some room for a continued role for the member state authorities, both at the level of the assessment and at the level of licensing chemicals.

Fourth, it is not clear how the overlapping and convoluted web of obligations stemming, on the one hand, from REACH regulation and, on the other, from directives that will not be abolished (Cosmetic Product Directive, Pesticides 91/414/EEC Directive, Biocide 98/10/EC Directive and Occupational Health Directive) has been hitherto correctly addressed.

This section is primarily concerned with the issues of authorizations and restrictions (Titles VII and VIII). Since licensing and restricting chemicals at national and EC levels may impede the free movement of goods and, as a result, jeopardize the functioning of the internal market, there are grounds for believing that authorization (Title VII) and restriction (Title VIII) procedures will be at the core of divergent interpretations. Some institutions and member states would probably support a narrow interpretation of these provisions, while others would be keen to endorse a broader interpretation. In particular, EC member states, as well as EFTA states, should be aware that the scope of these procedures, the deadlines, the role given to national authorities, and the competences granted to the Chemical Agency and the EC Commission are of the utmost importance in terms of maintaining stricter standards at the national level.

In the following sub-sections, the relationship between Titles VII and VIII is first addressed. The focus is then placed on procedural rules that must be complied with in order to restrict the use or the marketing of substances. In addressing these procedural issues, some of the major deficiencies of the proposed regime are outlined.

Links between the authorization procedure (Title VII) and the restriction procedure (Title VIII)

The dividing line between authorization and restriction procedures is an extremely fine one. On the one hand, Annex XIII encompasses substances meeting the criteria laid down in Article 54 (such as PBTs and endocrine disruptors). On the other hand, pursuant to Article 65, any substance entailing 'an unacceptable risk to human health and or the environment' could, in principle, be listed under Annex XVI. Given that the terms 'unacceptable risk' are not defined, it could be argued that substances of very high concern meeting the criteria set out in Article 54 could also be restricted in accordance with the procedure laid down in Title VIII. The question arises immediately as to whether the same substance could be subject to two different procedures.

Seeking some legal certainty, the drafters of the proposal have been intent upon mitigating the risk that the two procedures could overlap. Indeed, Article 55(5) states that a substance already authorised under Title VII cannot be subject to new restrictions under Title VIII. Conversely, substances 'for which all uses have been restricted' under Title VIII cannot become subject to the procedure laid down in Title VII.

Given that the procedures and the regulatory outcomes of Title VII and Title VIII differ significantly, the inclusion of any chemical substance in one of the two lists is of utmost importance. On the one hand, substances falling within the scope of Title VII provisions have to be banned; on the other, substances subject to Title VII can still be placed on the market, although particular uses could be restricted.

Listing procedure of substances subject to authorizations (Title VII)

Insofar they are included in Annex XIII in accordance with the procedure laid down in Article 55, substances of 'very high concern' (Article 52) can be subject to the authorization procedure.

Based on the fact that an authorization can only be granted provided a number of conditions are fulfilled, the substances listed in Annex XIII are deemed to be prohibited (Article 53). Indeed, the principle is a prohibition of the most hazardous substances, and the exception is to allow their use through an authorization procedure. From a genuine legal point of view, the term 'prohibition' used in Title VII should be substituted for the term 'authorization'. That said, Title VII entails a reversal of the current approach where substances are marketed without restrictions and without prior authorization unless restrictions have been applied under Directive 76/769/EEC.

Needless to say, listing the substances belonging to the hazards categories set out in Article 54 (PBTs, vPvBs and endocrine disruptors) would be at the core of future debates. Undoubtedly, the Nordic countries would welcome an Annex XIII encompassing a great number of hazardous substances. Conversely, in case the EC Commission endorses a narrow approach in listing a small number of substances, several Nordic countries would probably take issue with the approach and depart from EC standards. For the time being, the listing procedure is far from perfect.

Scope of Annex XIII

Only the substances meeting the criteria laid down in Article 54 could be listed. Given that the authorization procedure laid down in REACH encompasses only class 1 and 2 substances, a carcinogen of class 3, such as trichloroethylene, which is banned in Sweden, cannot be selected with the objective of being included in Annex XIII (see the *Toolex* judgment on the banning of this substance in Sweden, as discussed below).

Problem of timetable and resources

It is well known that the selection of chemical substances can take several years before any regulatory action is decided upon.[2]

In this respect, Article 55(3) is rather unclear. When the selection process of the substances in accordance with the criteria laid down in Article 54 is complete, the Chemical Agency is compelled to submit a recommendation to the European Commission regarding the substances to be included in Annex XIII. However, the listing procedure is not straightforward. Given the complexities entailed by such a regulatory process, several lists will have to be adopted by the agency and, subsequently, by the European Commission. At the first stage, only the priority substances would be listed (two years after the entry into force of the regulation), whereas at subsequent stages, non-priority substances would have also to be included. To make matters worse, the European Commission's final adoption of the list is not subject to any deadline. As a result of the lack of clarity in selecting the priority substances, the agency and the

European Commission could become embroiled in a rather complex discussion on priorities and timetables. The question arises immediately as to when the listing process will come to an end. The proposal does not provide any answer to this crucial question.

Last, but not least, REACH states that the substances should be proposed to the European Commission according to the Chemical Agency's capacity to handle applications in the time allotted (Article 55(3)). In other words, the workload of the agency determines the regulatory agenda. Given that most of the agency's resources would probably be dedicated to the registration process, the listing of substances in Annex XIII may not be at the top of the political agenda. In addition, the agency will not be accountable in the event of regulatory failure. Put differently, if the agency is not endowed with the appropriate means to carry out its scientific and administrative tasks, no recommendation relating to listing could ever be submitted to the European Commission, which is the only authority empowered to regulate those substances.

From a legal point of view, such a condition is rather unorthodox. The obligation to seek a high level of environmental and health protection stemming from different provisions laid down in the EC Treaty cannot be diluted according to human and financial resources. On the contrary, the EC law-maker has first to set forth the regulatory objectives; later on, the law-maker has to determine the resources needed to reach those objectives.

Moreover, several questions arise regarding the listing process:

- Is the Chemical Agency's recommendation binding?
- Is the European Commission empowered to add new substances to the list because the Chemical Agency's recommendations are deemed to be unsatisfactory?
- Under which circumstances could the European Commission be empowered to add new substances to the list proposed by the Chemical Agency?
- Is the European Commission entitled to postpone forever the adoption of the priority list as well as the subsequent list?
- Does regulatory inaction on the part of the Chemical Agency and the European Commission authorize member states to maintain or to introduce measures impeding the free movement of goods (e.g. the Swedish ban on cadmium)?

It must be noted that the text of the proposal does not provide any guidance related to these issues.

Exemptions of particular uses or categories of uses

Article 55(2) provides that particular uses or categories of uses may be exempted from the listing in Annex XIII. Proposed by the Chemical Agency, these exemptions are adopted by the European Commission in accordance with the comitology procedure. Needless to say, these two institutions enjoy a wide margin of appreciation in determining the scope of the exemptions. Given that the substances listed in Annex XIII are deemed to be of 'very high concern', the regulation should at least set out strict criteria to determine the scope of these exemptions with the aim of seeking a high level of environmental protection.

Right of initiative

Pursuant to Article 66(2), member states have the right to submit a request before the Chemical Agency with a view to restricting the use of a chemical under Title VIII. The request can be rejected on the grounds that it is incomplete. If the request is deemed to be complete, the agency is compelled to submit it with two additional opinions (one on risk, the other on socio-economic aspects) to the European Commission. According to Article 69(1), the agency 'shall submit to the Commission' the two opinions. In other words, it is incumbent upon the agency to provide the European Commission with a list of the substances of 'very high concern'.

The right of member states to propose new substances to be added to the list and the obligation for the agency to instruct their proposals will allow national authorities to raise issues that would normally not be addressed by the agency. The European Commission has always had the possibility of rejecting a proposal submitted by a member state.

In contrast, these procedural requirements do not apply to member states' requests aimed at adding a chemical in Annex XIII. Indeed, pursuant to Article 56(3), member states are entitled to submit proposals to the Chemical Agency. However, the agency is not compelled to submit its requests to the European Commission on the grounds that, in light of Article 56(5), the agency '*may* include this substance in its recommendation'. It follows that the agency has a discretionary power to accept or refuse additional substances proposed by member states. In case the agency refuses to include the substance proposed by a member state in its recommendation, this issue cannot be dealt with by the European Commission.

In sum, the Chemical Agency and the European Commission are required to instruct member states' proposals for restrictions. In sharp contrast to this, there is no duty to instruct the member states' proposals aimed at adding additional substances to Annex XIII. It is difficult to understand the reasons justifying this difference of approach.

Granting of authorizations (Title VII)

Time limit for authorizing Annex XIII substances

According to recent EC legislative acts, such as Directive 98/8/EC on biocides and Directive 2001/18/EC on genetically modified organisms (GMOs), product authorizations are subject to a time limit (usually a maximum of ten years). In sharp contrast, REACH clearly departs from this regulatory trend: authorizations granted for the use of a substance of very high concern could be subject to 'a time-limited review whose duration will be determined on a case-by-case basis' (Article 57(6)). Considering the hazardous properties of the chemicals to be authorized, one can wonder whether such products should not be subject to a maximum time limit.

Weighing of interests for authorizing Annex XIII substances that are not adequately controlled

Although the risks are not 'adequately controlled', a chemical included in Annex XIII could be authorized 'if it is shown that socio-economic benefits outweigh the risk to human health or the environment arising from the use of the substance and if there are no suitable alternative substances or technologies' (Article 57(3)). Needless to say, vigorous debate has ensued regarding the scope of this derogation. Such derogation gives rise to critics on the grounds that substances subject to authorization are already deemed to be of high concern. For this reason, they shall be listed in Annex XIII after a convoluted scientific process (Article 57(2)). Assessment of the 'socio-economic benefits' may, at this final stage, take on a very subjective character. As a result, several member states could become increasingly unsatisfied with the weighing of interests and the subsequent granting of authorization.

Concluding remarks

In sum, a number of uncertainties about the future of the EC chemicals policy linger. After a closer look at the procedures laid down in the proposal, one can wonder whether REACH will improve the decision-making process pertaining to control and, if necessary, to reduction of health and environmental risks posed by certain classes of chemicals. Against this background, Nordic countries need to assess whether they should keep some room for manoeuvre in seeking higher standards of protection if the ones set forth by the future REACH regulation appear to be unsatisfactory.

Accordingly, the validity of more stringent national measures than the EC ones should therefore be assessed in the light of the obligations laid down in the EC Treaty and the EEA Agreement. However, some observers may see the adoption at the national level of more stringent measures than the international measures as masking a neo-protectionist policy. Therefore, such regulatory initiatives are likely to be reviewed by courts.

CHEMICAL REGULATORY MEASURES HAVING EQUIVALENT EFFECT TO QUANTITATIVE RESTRICTIONS UNDER ARTICLE 28 EC

This section begins with a brief commentary of the twofold approach underlying the functioning of the internal market. The focus then shifts to the negative harmonization process. Of particular salience is the question of whether Article 30 EC or Article 13 EEA could be invoked by state authorities in order to justify measures departing from EC standards. This section then goes on to examine the autonomy that states can continue to enjoy vis-à-vis the forthcoming REACH regulation.

The internal market: A Janus-faced strategy

In essence, the obligations related to the free movement of goods laid down by the EC Treaty and by EEA can be analysed as follows. Two institutional mechanisms have been promoted in order to ensure that divergent national policies will not jeopardize the unity of the internal market.

The first mechanism consists of preventing member states or the EFTA states from adopting measures that might jeopardize intra-Community trade by requiring strict compliance with Articles 28 and 29 EC or Articles 11 and 12 EEA, provisions which encapsulate the free movement of goods (negative harmonization). A national measure that is not consistent with free trade could be challenged before the ECJ, the EFTA Court or any national courts, and invalidated if found to be discriminatory or disproportionate.[3]

Known as positive harmonization, the second mechanism complements the first: directives and regulations are adopted with the purpose of avoiding market fragmentation through the application of diverging national rules. Against this background, the tensions that arise between free trade and environmental protection measures are generally resolved through harmonization of rules and practices. Nevertheless, this harmonization does not prevent EC member states from adopting stricter rules under specific circumstances (see the following section on 'Maintenance or introduction of national provisions departing from internal market harmonization measures').

The Nordic states' power to enact their own standards with regard to certain chemicals could thus differ depending upon whether or not:

- the subject matter has been completely harmonized by rules derived from the EC Treaty – in particular, product regulations and directives whose legal basis is Article 95 EC;
- these rules completely harmonize the subject matter;
- with respect to Iceland and Norway, these EC rules have been included in Annex II of the EEA Agreement.

As one might expect, member states enjoy more leeway when the subject matter has not been completely harmonized by the EC law-maker.

The following subsections examine the extent of the Nordic states' regulatory powers in the absence of harmonization rules (negative harmonization) and in the presence of harmonization rules (positive harmonization). This issue is illustrated in the light of the occasionally highly contrasted jurisprudence concerning the European Court of Justice's (ECJ's) interpretation of Article 28 EC.[4]

Negative harmonization

Under EC and EEA law, the free movement of goods is deemed to be one of the essential freedoms. Accordingly, pursuant to Articles 28 EC and 29 EC and Article 11 EEA, 'quantitative restrictions on imports and all measures having equivalent effect shall be prohibited'. Against this background, a national state measure prohibiting or restricting the use of a chemical that is authorized in the internal market could, in principle, be challenged before a national court or the EFTA Court and invalidated if found to be discriminatory or disproportionate.

However, national authorities can justify derogations relating to the health and the life of humans set out in Articles 30 EC and 13 EEA.[5] Nevertheless, the use of this clause must comply with several conditions.[6]

Absence of harmonization

First, in the light of the ECJ's case law, the national authorities are empowered to invoke Articles 30 EC and 13 EEA provided that the subject matter has not been completely harmonized by EC secondary law. In other words, for these two provisions to apply, there must be no EC measure occupying the field concerned.

Restrictive grounds for exceptions to the prohibition

Second, the use of Articles 30 EC and 13 EEA must be justified in the light of a non-economic reason (public morality and the protection of health and life of humans, animals or plants). Both provisions preclude arguments of a purely economic nature.[7] Put differently, only the existence of a risk to public health or plant and animal health may allow a member state to restrict the free movement of goods.[8]

Principles of non-discrimination and proportionality

Third, the prohibition or the restriction shall not constitute 'a means of arbitrary discrimination or a disguised restriction on trade between the contracting parties'. National rules or practices having, or likely to have, a restrictive effect on the importation of products are compatible with the EC Treaty or EEA provided that they are necessary for the effective protection of the health and life of humans. Put differently, a national rule or practice cannot therefore benefit from the derogation provided for in Articles 30 EC and 13 EEA by measures that are less restrictive of intra-Community trade.

No requirements concerning the length of the national measure and no specific authorization from the European Commission

In contrast to the safeguard clause embodied in Article 95(10) EC, EC member states as well as EFTA states invoking Articles 30 EC and 13 EEA clauses do not have to deal with exceptional situations of limited duration. Moreover, in contrast to Article 95(4) to 95(9) EC (see the following section on 'Maintenance or introduction of national provisions departing from internal market harmonization measures'), a member state is not required to seek European Commission approval for maintaining a measure that is equivalent to quantitative restriction.

In sum, the balance between free trade of chemical products and other interests (consumers, public health and the environment) may be interpreted as follows. Interests that could be impaired are deemed to be exceptions to the free movement of goods.

Nonetheless, several arguments can support a broader interpretation of Articles 30 EC and 13 EEA. First, the ECJ has been keen to support the view that health protection is an important value.[9] According to the court, 'health and life of humans rank foremost among the property or interests protected by Article 36 of the Treaty'.[10] Second, in accordance with the principle of integration enshrined in Article 6 EC and Article 73(2) EEA, environmental values should be placed on the same footing as internal market requirements. In endeavouring to encourage environmental and health protection, the preamble of the EEA indeed pays greater attention to those concerns than the EC Treaty. In my view, these commitments can shed new light on the conflict between free trade provisions laid down in the EEA Agreement and EFTA states' environmental and health protection.

Positive harmonization

Since 1967, harmonization of legislation in the field of chemicals has been the centre-piece of the EC internal market. Since the Amsterdam Treaty came into force, Article 95 has become the cornerstone of this policy. As a matter of principle, under EC law, the harmonization process under Article 95 prevents member states from adopting stricter rules than EC standards. Only in specific circumstances can Articles 95(4) and 95(5) allow member states to maintain or to introduce provisions relating to protection of the environment or the working environment after adoption of an EC-wide harmonization, provided that a number of conditions are fulfilled (see the following section on 'Maintenance or introduction of national provisions departing from internal market harmonization measures').

The situation is rather different under the EEA Agreement insofar as it is not the purpose of such an agreement to produce secondary law. Pursuant to Article 23 EEA:

> *Specific provisions and arrangements are laid down in: (a) Protocol 12 and Annex II in relation to technical regulations, standards, testing and certification... They shall apply to all products unless otherwise specified.*

At first glance, it appears that the regulations and the directives included in Annex II of the EEA Agreement leave few derogatory responsibilities to the EFTA states to the extent that those instruments are at the centrepiece of the internal market. As mentioned earlier, the core of the debate is whether or not REACH could entail a complete harmonization of the rules that apply to existing chemicals. One should remember that a complete harmonization curtails, irrespective of the legal basis chosen, the possibility for state authorities to adopt tighter standards. As a result, one has to distinguish, on the one hand, between the current situation where the ECJ has been keen to give member states some leeway (see the following subsection) and, on the other, the obligations stemming from REACH.

Partial harmonization under the actual chemical regime

It appears from recent ECJ case law that the actual directives and regulations concerning chemicals leave some room for manoeuvre to member states. For instance, in a landmark case handed down by the ECJ, Swedish authorities were allowed to ban the chemical trichloroethylene on the grounds that the use of this chemical was not regulated under Directive 76/769/EEC and Council Regulation (EEC) 793/93. Indeed, the ECJ supported a more restrictive reading of the basic instruments of the EU chemical policy in stressing that the EU legislation does not harmonize the conditions under which trichloroethylene was placed on the market. Accordingly, Sweden was free to enact measures directed at banning the use of this substance. The Swedish require-ments were justified on the grounds of the protection of human health under Article 30 EC and could be maintained.[11]

A closer look at the reasoning of the court is now provided.

Considering the rationale of Council Directive 67/548/EEC on the classification, packaging and labelling of dangerous substances and Council Regulation (EEC) No 793/93, the court stated:

> *The classification directive covers a very clearly defined field, namely the notification, classification, packaging and labeling of dangerous substances. As regards the use of such substances, the classification directive merely requires that their packaging bear safety recommendations designed to inform the general public of the particular care that should be taken when handling the substance in question. It does not harmonize the conditions under which dangerous substances may be marketed or used, which are the very matters that fall within the purview of national legislation, such as that in issue in the main proceedings.*

With regard to Council Regulation (EEC) No 793/93, the court found that it 'neither imposes obligations nor harmonizes rules on the use of substances in general or trichloroethylene, in particular'.[12]

The question of whether Council Directive 76/769/EEC allows member states to adopt tighter measures for chemicals was a more critical issue. One could contend with the fact that the purpose of this directive is to lay down minimum standards with the aim of restricting the use, manufacture or marketing of substances.

Nevertheless, the ECJ considered that this directive provides for minimal require-ments, thereby allowing member states to ban other chemicals that are not restricted under the directive:

> *Given that the marketing directive, in itself, does no more than state certain minimum requirements, as is plain from Article 2 thereof, mentioned in paragraph 7 of the present judgment, it clearly presents no obstacle to the regulation by the member states of the marketing of substances that do not fall within its scope, such as trichloroethylene.*[13]

The terms 'minimal standards' have to be interpreted in the sense that Council Directive 76/769/EEC lays down restrictions to the chemicals listed in Annex I.[14] Considering that trichloroethylene does not appear in the list of dangerous substances and preparations given in the annex, the ECJ reached the conclusion that the requirement laid down in Article 2 could not be applied.

As a result, the ECJ concluded that the two chemical directives and the regulation did not preclude the national authorities from adopting tighter standards than the ones laid down by the EC law-maker.

On the contrary, if the Swedish authorities were willing to apply tighter standards for a substance already listed in Annex I of Directive 76/769/EEC – for example, PCB – they would have to comply with the notification procedure pursuant to Articles 95(4) to 95(6) EC.

In addition, the court recognized in its judgment that the conditions imposed at the granting of a derogation are 'compatible with the substitution principle ... and which consists [of] the elimination or reduction of risks by means of replacing one dangerous substance with another less dangerous substance'.[15]

One has to conclude that at this stage the cluster of EC directives and regulations related to chemical management is not sufficiently developed to render any national prohibition or restriction on the production, the use and the marketing of a substance superfluous or disproportionate. Despite the state of harmonization of EU legislation on mainstream chemicals, there remains room for manoeuvre for the national authorities to regulate the use of existing chemicals. Provided that they are proportionate, the national measures are deemed to be valid (see the earlier section on 'Negative harmonization').

The extent of the harmonization achieved under REACH

The question arises as to whether REACH could preclude state authorities from pursuing a more stringent policy than the one achieved at EC level.

In the light of the *Toolex* case law, one may wonder whether the future REACH regulation would qualify as a 'comprehensive system' for chemicals management, thereby precluding a member state from enforcing more stringent measures with a view to increasing the level of environmental and health protection.

It is important to stress that the line between a comprehensive system leading to a full harmonization and a partial harmonization is a relatively fine one.

The ECJ has held that the following directives and regulations entailed a complete harmonization:

- Regulation 93/259/CE on the supervision and control of shipments of waste;[16]
- Directive 76/769/EEC relating to restrictions on the marketing and use of certain dangerous substances and preparations (the provisions of that directive does not entail a complete harmonization with regard to the substances not listed in its Annex I).[17]

Conversely, the following directives and regulations do not provide for a full harmonization:

- Article 5 of Directive 94/62/EC on packaging and waste packaging;[18]
- Regulation (EEC) No 793/93 on the evaluation and control of the risks of existing substances, which 'neither imposes obligations nor harmonizes rules on the use of hazardous substances';[19]
- Directive 67/548/EEC on the classification, packaging and labelling of dangerous substances, which 'does not harmonize the conditions under which dangerous substances may be marketed or used, which are the very matters that fall within the purview of national legislation'.[20]

Sometimes, the EC law-maker effected both exhaustive and minimum harmonization:

- Article 14 of Directive 79/409/EEC on bird protection.[21]

Furthermore, substances falling outside the ambit of a directive or a regulation can be freely regulated by a member state:

- Directive 76/769/EEC relating to restrictions on the marketing and use of certain dangerous substances and preparations, which 'clearly presents no obstacle to the regulation by the member states of the marketing of substances that do not fall within the scope' of its Annex I.[22]

Finally, member states are free to intervene whenever the harmonization provided for by the directive has not been completed in the sense that the annexes listing the substances whose use is authorized are still being compiled at Community level.[23]

Free movement of goods clauses (prohibiting member states from preventing the sale, use or possession of a product conforming to the directive), as well as safeguard clauses (permitting member states under certain circumstances to prohibit the marketing of products conforming to the directive) indicate the thoroughness of the harmonization process. However, the ECJ made clear in *Ratti* that a free movement of goods clause in the context of a directive seeking to eliminate differences in national rules that impede the internal market may have no independent value, and may simply complement the substantive provisions contained in the directive in question and be designed to ensure the free movement of the products in question.[24]

Arguments in favour of a complete harmonization

REACH has both a free movement of goods clause and a safeguard clause. Pursuant to Article 125, member states shall not prohibit, restrict or impede the free movement of a substance, on its own or in a preparation, which complies with the requirement laid down in the regulation. Nevertheless, they are allowed to invoke, in light of Article 126, a safeguard clause. Hence, ECJ case law holds that where an EC directive provides for the harmonization of measures designed to safeguard the protection of the health of animals and people and setting down EC procedures to ensure adherence, recourse to Article 30 EC is no longer justified; appropriate controls must be made and protective measures undertaken within the framework laid down by the harmonization directive.[25] Put in other words, the existence of a safeguard clause (Article 126) should impede the member states from invoking Article 30 EC in order to depart from the EC standards. At this stage, the consequences for EFTA states are rather unclear.

In addition, the authorization procedure appears to be a complete process due to the fact that it is not based on a case-by-case approach, but on a global risk assessment approach of all the substances meeting the criteria set out in Article 54. It should also be pointed out that state authorities have the possibility of addressing those issues with the Chemical Agency and the European Commission at different stages.

Furthermore, one could also argue that the regulation is chiefly aimed at ensuring the free movement of goods, thereby restricting the rights of member states to adopt tighter measures. This interpretation could be firmly buttressed by invoking various provisions:

- The regulation is based on Article 95.
- The main purpose of the regulation is 'to ensure the free circulation of such substances on the internal market' (Article 1(1)).
- The primary aim of the authorization procedure is to ensure the good functioning of the internal market (Article 52).

Against this background, the recent *Cindu Chemicals* judgment deserves particular attention. The ECJ took the view that Directive 76/769/EEC relating to restrictions on the marketing and use of certain dangerous substances and preparations 'amounts to a harmonization measure intended to eliminate obstacles to trade' within the internal market. As a result, the objective of that directive 'would not be attainable if the member states were free to widen the obligations provided for therein'.[26]

Last, in its statement on free movement of goods (Appendix IV to the *Council Political Agreement Common Guidelines*), the European Commission supports the viewpoint that 'REACH regulation completely harmonizes the conditions of manufacture, market placement and substance use that fall within its scope'. As a result, the regulation preempts national authorities to adopt more stringent measures, except through measures adopted within the framework of Articles 95(4) and 95(5) EC.

It follows that national authorities could be deprived of their right to regulate the substances that will be included in Annexes XIII (substances submitted to an authorization) and XVI (substances submitted to specific restrictions).

Arguments in favour of a partial harmonization

One also needs to consider the arguments that could support the opposite interpretation with the aim of enhancing the freedom of EC member states, as well as of EFTA states, to adopt tighter environmental and health standards.

With regard to the restriction procedure (Title VIII), the answer is straightforward. Members states are, indeed, empowered 'to maintain any existing and more stringent restrictions in relation to Annex XVI ... provided that those restrictions have been notified according to the Treaty' (Article 64(5)). It follows that member states could avail themselves of that right during a six-year period.

In terms of the authorization procedure (Title VII), the answer is perhaps more complicated. Attention should be drawn to the fact that the inclusion of priority chemicals in Annex XIII will not be complete for two years (Article 55(3)). In addition, the initial priority list will be followed by the adoption of complementary lists. Meanwhile, the question arises as to whether state authorities will be empowered to maintain their rights to ban a chemical not falling within the scope of Directive 76/769/EEC relating to restrictions on the marketing and use of certain dangerous substances as they are allowed so far in accordance with the *Toolex* case law.

This chapter argues that unless the listing of substances in Annex XIII is over, member states retain their rights provided that they comply with the rule of the EC Treaty or the EEA Agreement when exercising such a power. However, whenever the drafting of Annex XIII is definitive, Title VII will be deemed to function as a complete system, thereby leaving no further room for manoeuvre to state authorities. In other words, they will no longer be able to invoke Article 30 EC or Article 13 EEA.

Moreover, the question arises as to whether Annex XVI, which provides a supplementary mechanism comprising restrictions, is to be considered a complete system. In its *Toolex* judgment, the ECJ made clear that member states could restrict chemicals not yet listed under Annex I of Directive 76/769/EEC. It should be stressed that Annex I of Directive 76/769/EEC will be included in the future Annex XVI, although the mechanisms of inclusion are far from clear. The grounds for the ECJ's reasoning in *Toolex* was that Article 2 of Directive 76/769/EEC provides that 'Member states shall take all neces-sary measures to ensure that the dangerous substances and preparations listed in the annex may only be placed on the market or used subject to the conditions specified therein.' However, such provision is not provided for by REACH. According to Article 125 of REACH, member states shall not prohibit, restrict or impede the free movement of a substance, on its own or in a preparation, which complies with the requirement laid down in the regulation.

MAINTENANCE OR INTRODUCTION OF NATIONAL PROVISIONS DEPARTING FROM INTERNAL MARKET HARMONIZATION MEASURES

When REACH enters in force, Nordic countries intent upon maintaining more stringent existing standards or wanting to enact new standards regarding existing chemicals will have to overcome several procedural hurdles. Indeed, paragraphs 4 and 5 of Article 95 EC authorize the member states to implement, on condition of respect for certain condi-tions, more stringent measures than those provided for by a EC harmonizing norm, even though the directive or the regulation does not expressly recognize this right. The two paragraphs run as follows:

4 If, after the adoption by the Council or by the Commission of an harmonisation measure, a Member State deems it necessary to maintain national provisions on grounds of major needs referred to in Article 30, or relating to the protection of the environment or the working environment, it shall notify the Commission of these provisions, as well as the grounds for maintaining them.
5 Moreover, without prejudice to paragraph 4, if, after the adoption by the Council or by the Commission of a harmonisation measure, a Member State deems it necessary to introduce national provisions based on new scientific evidence relating to the protection of the environment or the working environment on grounds of a problem specific to that Member State arising after the adoption of the harmonisation measure, it shall notify the Commission of the envisaged provisions as well as the grounds for introducing them.

In contrast to Article 153(5) and Article 176 EC,[27] which establish the principle of minimum harmonization in areas relating to consumer and environmental protection, the conditions for implementation of paragraphs 4 and 5 of Article 95 are strictly circum-scribed *ratione materiae, personae et temporis*.[28] Due to the significance of the disputes which these derogation mechanisms have given rise to recently, a brief examination of the manner in which such mechanisms are implemented should be provided. This issue could, indeed, be of paramount importance in the coming years. In the past, the European Commission has been called upon to adjudicate on the admissibility of several requests related to national restrictions of chemicals such as pentachlorophenol (PCP), cadmium, creosote and tributylin (TBT).[29]

As explained below, the conditions applicable to the maintenance of national measures that predate an EC measure (paragraph 4) differ substantially from those that relate to the adoption, *a posteriori*, of a national measure (paragraph 5). Whether the national measure pre-exists REACH or post-dates the entry into force of the EC regulation determines the procedure to be applied.

Maintenance of existing national measures departing from internal market harmonization measures

The member state is obliged to notify the European Commission of its desire to maintain national measures due to 'major needs referred to in Article 30, or relating to the protection of the environment or the working environment'. Having said this, member states should encounter fewer difficulties in conserving protective measures than in adopting new ones because the latter can relate only to 'the protection of the environment or the working environment'.

The wording of the fourth paragraph calls for several observations.

At first, the invocation of concerns for public health, the environment or the working environment seems to preclude the possibility of having regard for considerations extraneous to the supposed hazard. Accordingly, the European Commission deemed that a national regime forbidding the use of sulphites in foods on the pretext that these substances did not 'perform a technical function … [or] correspond to a technical need which … [could not] be satisfied by other economically and technically usable methods' should not be pertinent to the purposes of public health. In this particular case, the national authorities bore the brunt of the burden of demonstrating the sanitary risk and could not simply point to the possibility of replacing such food additives with other substances.[30] Nevertheless, the ECJ judged that the technological need to use food additives was 'closely related to the assessment of what is necessary in order to protect public health. In the absence of a technological need justifying the use of an additive, there is no reason to incur the potential health risk resulting from authorization of the use of that additive.'[31]

As far as the wording of the new paragraph 4 is concerned, the condition of 'specificity' of risk – found in paragraph 5 – does not need to be satisfied in order for national measures to be maintained.

The fact that conditions relating to the maintenance of a more stringent rule have become less strict appears justified. In such cases, the national regime predates EC harmonization. The EC law-maker was aware of it, even if it did not consider it worth taking into consideration.[32] The introduction of a new measure could, on the other hand, constitute a more important danger undermining the internal market (see the following section).

Introduction of new national measures departing from internal market harmonization measures

Article 95(5) recognizes a right to adopt more stringent measures after the entry into force of the harmonizing norm. Nevertheless, the second derogation mechanism is subject to stricter conditions because 'the adoption of new national legislation is more likely to jeopardize harmonization. The Community institutions could not, by definition, have taken account of the national text when drawing up the harmonization measure.'[33]

Therefore, the reasons that can be given for invoking this second derogation mechanism appear to be less numerous than those that justify the maintenance of existing national norms. Only 'the protection of the environment' and that of 'working environment' can be invoked. This precludes the possibility of founding a derogation on a requirement, such as the Article 30 protection of human health.[34] There is, therefore, a fine line between the justifications embodied in paragraph 5 of Article 95 and those contained in Article 30 EC.

In addition, national measures should also satisfy three requirements: the risk that the measure is supposed to counter should be specific to the member state requesting the derogation; it should manifest itself after the adoption of the harmonization measure; and it should be supported by scientific proof. These conditions are clearly cumulative.[35] Each of them requires some clarification.

Specificity of the problem

First, the 'problem' or risk justifying the intervention of the member state should be 'specific' to the applicant state. It follows that member states are not allowed to invoke regulations of a general character.[36] In other words, particular demographic, geographic or epidemiological circumstances should render the problem particular to the state requesting the derogation.[37] By way of illustration, the geographic or social conditions of the interested state (e.g. population density, degree of industrialization, vulnerability of the groundwater and historic record of pollution) exacerbate the impact of particular problems. A contrario, the condition of risk specificity prohibits the adoption of national measures designed to solve a problem common to the whole of the European Community.

Date of the problem's emergence

The problem must arise after the 'adoption' – and not at the end of the implementation period – of the harmonization measure. This does not preclude the possibility of the risk already being present at the moment of drafting, or even adoption, of the EC harmonization measure and only later manifesting itself.

Scientific evidence

Finally, the right to introduce a national measure more stringent than the EC measure must be justified in the light of 'new scientific evidence'. To the extent that the draft of the EC harmonization measure proposed by the European Commission must already take into consideration, in accordance with Article 95(3), 'any new development based on scientific facts', the novel character of the scientific evidence has to be assessed in the light of those scientific discoveries that occurred after the adoption of the norm. This requirement must not, however, be subject to a literal interpretation since it is possible for scientific evidence already existing at the time of the adoption of the EC harmonization norm, but not entirely validated at that point, to justify the pursuit of a higher level of protection. In addition, nothing prevents new scientific evidence from being advanced by a minority of researchers (see Chapter 2 in this volume). The serious nature of the scientific evidence gathered by the member state matters more than the scientific consensus, which may even be clear.

On a semantic note, the English word 'evidence' – as opposed to 'proof' – does not necessarily imply that the cause of damage to the environment or to workers' health must be proved; 'evidence' can well consist of an indication of a possible link between the factor in question and the damage that occurs. As a result, member states requesting the derogation should only have to provide a minimum of data on the relation of cause and effect between the regulated activity and the suspected damage, rather than having to furnish irrefutable proof.

This last interpretation seems, in any case, justified, given the European Commission's obligation to take into account the precautionary principle when examining the serious nature of the scientific proof advanced by a member state. The commission has already applied this principle when it addresses requests for derogation.[38]

Account must also be taken of the fact that the ECJ is keen to adopt a lenient view regarding the nature of the risk assessment. The court, for instance, has recently accepted that:

> ... the applicant Member State may, in order to justify maintaining such derogating national provisions, put forward the fact that its assessment of the risk to public health is different from that made by the Community legislature in the harmonisation measure. In the light of the uncertainty inherent in assessing the public health risks posed by, inter alia, the use of food additives, divergent assessments of those risks can legitimately be made without necessarily being based on new or different scientific evidence.[39]

European Economic Area Agreement

Contrary to Articles 95(4) to 95(9) EC, the EEA Agreement does not provide for any derogation mechanism as laid down in Articles 95(4) to 95(9) EC.[40] Article 75 EEA states that the protective environmental measures referred to in Article 74 – which are included in Annex XX and not in Annex II – shall not prevent any contracting party from maintaining or introducing more stringent protective measures compatible with this agreement. Safeguard clauses and derogation mechanisms have to be included in *ad hoc* provisions of Annex II of the agreement through a negotiation process.

NOTES

1   Tickner, J. and Geiser, K. (2003) *New Directions in European Chemicals Policies,* Lowell Center for Sustainable Production, University of Massachusetts, Lowell, pp12–35.

2   Pallemaerts, M. (2003) *Toxics and Transnational Law*, Hart, Oxford, pp284–295.

3   On the scope of Articles 28 to 30 EC regarding environmental measures, see, among others, Temmink, H. (2000) 'From Danish bottles to Danish bees: The dynamics of free movement of goods and environmental protection – a case law analysis', *Yearbook of European Environmental Law*, vol 1, pp61–102; Van Calster, G. (2000) *International and EU Trade Law*, Cameron and May, London; Wiers, J. (2002) *Trade and Environment in the EC and the WTO*, Europa Law Publishing, Groeningen; Ziegler, A. R. (1996) *Trade and Environmental Law in the European Community*, Clarendon, Oxford.

4   ECJ case law is also relevant for Norway and Iceland. First, most of the EEA provisions relating to the free movement of goods are similar to the ones embodied in the EC Treaty. Second, Article 6 EEA states that:

> *Without prejudice to future developments of case law, the provisions of this Agreement, in so far as they are identical in substance to corresponding rules of the Treaty establishing the European Economic Community ... and to acts adopted in application of these two Treaties, shall, in their implementation and application, be interpreted in conformity with the relevant rulings of the Court of Justice of the European Communities given prior to the date of signature of this Agreement.*

5   According to EEA Article 13:

> *... the provisions of Articles 11 and 12 shall not preclude prohibitions or restrictions on imports, exports or goods in transit justified on grounds of ... the protection of health and life of humans, animals or plants ... Such prohibitions or restrictions shall not, however, constitute a means of arbitrary discrimination or a disguised restriction on trade between the Contracting Parties.*

6   Norberg, S., Hokborg, K., Johansson, M., Eliasson, D. and Dedichen, I. (1993) *EEA Law: A Commentary on the EEA Agreement*, Fritzes, Stockholm, pp347–351; Sejersted, F., Arnesen, F., Rognstad, O.-A., Foyn, S. and Kolstad, O. (1995) *EØS-rett*, Universitetgorlaget, Oslo, pp232–235.

7   We should refer to the case law of the ECJ. See, among others, Case C-120/95, *Decker* (1998) ECR I-1884, para 39.

8   However, Article 13 EEA makes no reference to the protection of the environment, whereas this issue is deemed to be a mandatory requirement in the sense of the *Cassis de Dijon* case law. As a result, environmental measures, *stricto sensu* (e.g. measures not related to wildlife conservation or public health, such as waste recycling requirements), are not covered by Article 13 EEA. In my view, this exclusion is not relevant for our topic since most of the chemical regulatory measures are aimed either at protecting wildlife or human life.

9   Case C-180/96, *United Kingdom* v *Commission* (1996) ECR I-3903, paras 90 and 100.

10 Case C-320/93, *Ortscheit* (1994) ECR I-5243, para 16.

11 Case C-473/98, *Kemikalieinspektionen and Toolex Alpha AB* (2000) ECR I-5681.

12 Case C-473/98, *Toolex*, para 31.

13 Case C-473/98, *Toolex*, para 31.

14 Heyvaert, V. (2001) 'Balancing trade and environment in the EU: Proportionality substituted?', *Journal of European Law*, vol 15, no 3, p397.

15 Case C-473/98, *Toolex*, para 47.

16 Case C-324/99, *DaimlerChrysler* (2001) ECR I-9897, para 33.

17 Case C-148/78, *Ratti* (1979) ECR I-1629, paras 25 to 27; Case 278/85, *Commission* v *Denmark* (1987) ECR 4069, para 22; Joined Cases C-281/03 and C-282/03, *Cindu Chemicals*, 15 September 2005, not yet reported, para 49.

18 Case C-463/01, *Commission* v *Germany*, 3 December 2004, paras 37 to 45.

19 Case C-473/98, *Toolex*, para 31.

20 Case C-473/98, *Toolex*, para 31.

21 Case 169/89, *Gourmetterie van den Burg* (1990) ECR I-2143, para 8.
22 Case C-473/98, *Toolex*, para 30. See also Case C-127/97, *Burstein* (1998) ECR I-6005, paras 22 to 23.
23 Case C-400/96, *Harpegnies* (1998) ECR I-5121; Case C-443/02, *Schreiber* (2004) ECR I-1629, para 20.
24 Case C-148/78, *Ratti*, para 13.
25 See, among others, Case 5/77, *Tedeschi* (1977) ECR 1555, para 35; Case 148/78, *Ratti* (1979) ECR 1629, para 36; Case 251/78, *Denkavit Futtermittel* (1979) ECR 3369, para 14; Case 190/87, *Moormann* (1988) ECR 4689, para 10; Case C-323/93, *Centre d'Insémination de la Crespelle* (1994) ECR I-5077, para 30; Case C-99/01, *Linhart*, 24 October 2002, para 18.
26 Joined Cases C-281/03 and C-282/03, *Cindu Chemicals*, 15 September 2005, not yet reported, paras 42 to 44.
27 Concerning the conditions for implementation of Article 176, see Case C-192/96, *Beside* (1998) ECR I-4029.61.
28 de Sadeleer, N. (2003) 'Safeguard clauses under Article 95 of the EC Treaty', *Common Market Law Review*, no 40, pp889–915.
29 See the list of decisions related to chemicals in Onida, M. (2006) 'The practical application of Articles 95(4) and 95(5)EC', in Pallemaerts, M. (ed) *EU and WTO Law: How Tight is the Legal Straitjacket for Environmental Product Regulation?*, VUB University Press, Brussels, pp92–93.
30 Decision 1999/830/EC relating to national provisions notified by Denmark relating to the use of sulphites, nitrates and nitrites in foodstuffs, para 20.
31 Case C-3/00, *Commission v Denmark* (2003) ECR I-2643, para 82.
32 Case C-512/99, *Germany v Commission*, para 41, and Case C-3/00, *Commission v Denmark* (2003) ECR I-2643, para 58.
33 Case C-512/99, *Germany v Commission*, para 41, and Case C-3/00, *Commission v Denmark* (2003) ECR I-2643, para 58.
34 See Case C-3/00, *Commission v Denmark* (2003) ECR I-2643, para 58. The European Commission, in particular, relied on this argument in rejecting the German prohibition of the commercialization of organostanic compounds (Decision 2001/570/EC of 13 July 2001, OJEC L 202/37, 27 July 2001, para 76). See also Decision 2000/509/EC made on 25 July 2000 on Belgian provisions (OJEC, L 205, 8 December 2000).
35 See Case C-512/99, *Germany v Commission*, para 41, and Case C-3/00, *Commission v Denmark* (2003) ECR I-2643, para 81.
36 See Cases T-366/03 and T-235/04, *Land Oberörsterreich*, judgment of 5 October 2005, not yet reported.
37 In its Decision 1999/830/EC, the European Commission considered whether the Danish population had a greater risk of allergy than other populations due to genetic disposition, diet and the natural environment (para 32). In its Decisions 2001/570/EC and 2000/509/EC on organostanic compounds, the European Commission refused to give consideration to the accumulation of the substance TBT in the ecosystems surrounding naval ports (Decision 2001/570/EC, para 74).
38 EC authorities have, accordingly, in four decisions handed down on 26 October 1999 relating to the prohibition of the use of a chemical agent (creosote), found that measures aimed at reducing the probability of prolonged exposure of the skin to this substance were justified in the light of the principle. See, for example, Decision 1999/835/EC, para 110; Decision 1999/833/EC, para 99; Decision 1999/834/EC, para 108; and Decision 1999/832/EC, para 104.
39 Case C-3/00, *Commission v Denmark* (2003) ECR I-2643, para 63.
40 Bugge, H. C. and Thrap-Meyer, R. (1995) *EØS Avtalen I Miljørettslig Perspektiv*, second edition, Universitetgorlaget, Oslo, pp91–96.

CHAPTER 19

The Legacy of the Precautionary Principle in US Law: The Rise of Cost-Benefit Analysis and Risk Assessment as Undermining Factors in Health, Safety and Environmental Protection

Nicholas A. Ashford

INTRODUCTION

Over the last 35 years since the first appearance of federal health, safety and environmental laws in the US, public health and the environment continue to be adversely affected by development,[1] and limits to industrial growth are now clearly visible in the examples of global climate disruption, changes in the reproductive health of all species, and shortages of petroleum, freshwater and natural resources. Furthermore, the kinds of risks of concern, and the nature of scientific uncertainty, are changing. These developments have sparked new interest in the concepts of precaution and prevention in many environmental and public policy arenas.

Advances in the understanding of the causes of disease and new damage mechanisms include endocrine disruption[2] and other low-dose effects of chemical exposures;[3] substances, such as nanoparticles, that can cross the blood–brain barrier; antibiotic, drug and pesticide resistance; climate disruption; and interactions between toxic chemicals, nutritional factors, infectious agents and genetics. Advances in scientific risk assessment include green chemistry, green engineering, predictive toxicology, structure activity relationships and rapid *in vitro* screens.[4] Advances in technological approaches include sustainable technology, products and system design.

With advances in science and technology have come changes in the kinds of uncertainty facing government agencies mandated to protect health, safety and the environment. These include classical uncertainty (expressed as probability distributions of dose–response relationships and obscured by the lack of sufficiently definitive information, contradictory evidence, or a deficiency in the knowledge of causal mechanisms and pathways), indeterminacy (where we know what we don't know), and ignorance (where we don't know what we don't know).[5] The general nature of uncertainty has shifted from classical uncertainty (which itself is now understood to be more complex than originally envisioned and is difficult to apply in many areas of concern), towards indeterminacy (as in the case of the extent of global warming) and ignorance (e.g. of possible risks to ecosystems from deliberately released genetically modified (GM) crops).

Partly because of changing science and partly because of inadequate governmental response, the trust in both government regulators and industry has declined, with a corresponding increased demand for the participation of the public, consumers, non-governmental organizations (NGOs) and citizens in decision-making related to protection of health, safety and the environment. This increased demand for participation has resulted in a more critical look at the bases for governmental decisions.

Government has approached the problems of risky technologies and products by constructing a two-step exercise: risk assessment followed by risk management.[6] Value judgments pervade both steps,[7] and the precautionary principle could be applied in choosing the data and models to inform risk assessment and also in deciding whether, to what extent and how to provide protection.[8]

This chapter argues that in the US, the governmental responses to these changes are wrong-headed and hide behind misguided formulaic methodologies of cost-benefit analyses and quantitative risk assessments ostensibly offered to provide more sensible and rational solutions[9] to guide approaches to health, safety and environmental problems, but in actuality motivated by desires to accommodate industrial and producer interests. Reflecting an increasingly anti-regulatory posture on the part of the federal government, the undemocratic use of these methodologies has seriously undermined health, safety and environmental protection in the US and (hopefully temporarily) rendered a precautionary approach to solving health and environmental problems to a historical relic. In the US, the undermining of protection is effectuated through:

- requiring regulations to be based on an increased level of scientific evidence or justification;
- allowing regulations to be delayed because of scientific uncertainty;
- allowing a *de minimis* risk to remain unprotected or requiring a 'significant risk' to be present before acting;[10] and
- requiring that the benefits of regulating exceed, or justify, the imposition of costs.[11]

These factors, of course, directly impact upon whether and to what extent the precautionary principle can be applied in the US.

The remainder of this chapter provides a brief history of the precautionary principle as developed in the US with comparisons to its evolution in Europe; a regulatory decision-making framework that agencies might follow, whether or not a precautionary approach is embraced; a brief account of the politics of the regulation of chemicals in the US; a capsule history of US chemical regulation and the use of the precautionary principle in US law; and suggestions for reclaiming health, safety and environmental protection through the creative use of the precautionary principle within the context of trade-off analysis: an alternative to cost-benefit analysis as a decision-making rationale that incorporates concerns for distributional effects (equity), accounts for technological change through the use of Technology Options Analysis, and otherwise avoids the biases of traditional cost-benefit analysis.[12] Contrary to the commonplace practice of both advocates and critics of the precautionary principle in placing risk assessment and the precautionary principle in conflict, this chapter argues that risk assessment has a sensible place in implementing the precautionary principle and that it is cost-benefit analysis, and the use of risk assessment there, that conflicts with the principle.

A BRIEF HISTORY OF THE PRECAUTIONARY PRINCIPLE

The precautionary principle has two distinct formulations:[13]

1   Where there are possibilities of large or irreversible serious effects, scientific uncertainty *should not prevent* protective actions from being taken.
2   Where there are possibilities of large or irreversible serious effects, *action should be taken*, even if there is considerable scientific uncertainty.

The first formulation in the international context appears prominently in the Brundtland formulation agreed to in the United Nations Conference on Environment and Development (UNCED) held in Rio de Janeiro in 1992, and recurs in many multilateral environmental agreements.[14] The second formulation appears in some multilateral agreements and in some European Union (EU) directives on environmental protection.[15]

In the US, a precautionary approach has been applied in various ways in decisions about health, safety and the environment for about 30 years, much longer than recent commentaries would have us believe, and earlier than the appearance of the precautionary principle in European law.[16] In interpreting congressional legislation, the US courts have argued that federal regulatory agencies are permitted, and sometimes required, to protect workers even when the evidence is 'on the frontiers of scientific knowledge' and to protect public health from emissions to air with 'an ample or adequate margin of safety' by 'erring on the side of caution'. One scholar seeks to make a distinction between a precautionary approach and the precautionary principle, asserting that 'with rare exceptions, US law balances precaution against other considerations, most importantly costs' and, hence, is better described as a preference, rather than a principle.[17] I find this distinction superficial, or at least unhelpful, if not often inaccurate; and when understood within the context of Roman/Napoleonic law-based European legal systems preferring 'codes' to court-based evolution of common law, this is a semantic rather than a real distinction.

In the US, in a series of industry challenges to regulations, courts acknowledged that even in the case where the scientific basis for a threat to health or the environment is not compelling, regulators have the discretion to 'err on the side of caution', often without laying down a specific requirement to do so, although the directive to do so is often found in the enabling legislation of various regulatory regimes. As we shall see in the section on 'The politics of regulating chemicals in the US', under *Chevron*,[18] court deference to agency policy judgments initially not only allowed, but encouraged, agencies to take a precautionary approach under a myriad of legislation, partly by relegating questions of the sufficiency of scientific evidence to the province of discretionary policy-making. In the early environmental decisions, rather than adopting stringent interpretations of statutory language requiring 'substantial evidence' in meeting the burden of proof for agencies to act, the courts adopted a deferential stance towards early environmental agency decisions, allowing them to relax the evidentiary showings in furtherance of protective public policy goals.

In the last decade or two, the precautionary inclinations of the American and Anglo-Saxon jurisprudential systems, as well as codified expressions of the precautionary principle in German law, for example, have found their way into multilateral environmental agreements and international law. Principle 15 of the Declaration of the 1992 UNCED (the Rio Declaration) states:

> *In order to protect the environment, the precautionary approach shall be widely used by States according to their capabilities. Where there are threats of serious and irreversible damage, lack of full scientific certainty shall not be used as a reason for postponing cost-effective measures to prevent environmental degradation.*

This is perhaps the best known, and often cited, statement of the precautionary principle. Note, especially, that the word 'approach' rather than 'principle' is used, and considerations of cost are certainly present in the phrases 'according to their capabilities' and 'cost-effective measures'. Nonetheless, it is acknowledged to be a principle – but one to be balanced in one way or another against other principles – no different than the situation in US law.[19] Curiously, this statement of the principle is expressed in the negative – uncertainty should not be used to delay protection – rather than a statement that protection should be embraced deliberatively even in the face of uncertainty (a subtle but important distinction), a formulation often more positively expressed in US case law.[20] The debate in Europe today is not whether the precautionary principle is a principle, but which formulation should be applied and whether it trumps other international law, particularly the manner in which risk assessment is addressed and is relevant to trade law involving the World Trade Organization (WTO).[21]

REGULATORY DECISION-MAKING FRAMEWORK

Whether taking a utilitarian approach that maximizes total welfare, ensuring that the costs and benefits are equal or commensurate, or seeking to protect certain beneficiaries with minimal considerations given to the costs of doing so in the face of scientific uncertainty, a regulatory agency responsible for protecting health, safety or the environment necessarily needs to answer *whether, where, when, how* and *to what extent* to intervene. Intervention could involve:

- notifying those (possibly) affected – for example, by warnings or labels;
- regulating exposure by limiting and controlling exposure or limiting production;
- eliminating production or use;
- treating those affected;
- compensating for harm.

Answering these questions, in turn, requires asking:

●   What are the criteria for deciding?
●   Who has the burden of persuasion?
●   What strength of evidence (burden of proof) triggers a requirement for what action?

This framework can be approached either through rational choice theory using cost-benefit analysis (see the following section on 'A capsule history of US chemical regulation and the use of the precautionary principle in US law') or by using a precautionary approach. Note that far from representing a binary approach (go, no go), the precautionary approach requires application at each juncture of decision-making – w*hether,* w*here, when, how,* and *to what extent* to intervene.[22]

THE POLITICS OF REGULATING CHEMICALS IN THE US[23]

The 1970s ushered in a period of intense environmental and workplace regulation. With the advent of the Reagan administration in 1980 and continuing more or less since then, the US beneficiaries have experienced a reversal of fortune in the decline of protection. In contrast, Europe began to take the lead in environmental health and safety regulation, 'trading places' with the US.[24] In the US, the decline of protection was effectuated through changes in:

●   legislation;
●   administrative practice by the executive branch through actions of the Office of Management and Budget (OMB);
●   direct congressional intervention;
●   agency policy/practices in standard-setting and subsequent judicial review by the appellate courts; and
●   extra-legal (i.e. political) activities compromising the government's duty to protect.

This section addresses the first three and the last of these developments, while the next section discusses key health, safety and environmental decisions made by the regulatory agencies. In contrast to the EU, over the last few decades, the executive branch of government exercised much more control and direction over the practice of risk assessment and cost-benefit analysis than its EU counterparts.

Congressional legislation

During the 1990s, the US Congress turned its attention to the impacts of agency rule-making on the regulated community, and enacted a series of laws designed to reduce those impacts. The genesis of these laws was the 1994 election, when the Republican party regained control of both houses of Congress for the first time in several years. Led by the then Speaker of the House Newt Gingrich, the Republicans brought with them an aggressive legislative agenda that they termed their 'Contract with America'. A chief plank in this agenda was 'regulatory reform,' which, broadly speaking, meant minimizing the costs and other burdens imposed by federal regulation on business and state and local government. A key goal of this reform movement was that all, or virtually all, federal regulation should be required to meet a cost-benefit criterion, which would have required a reduction in the stringency of those regulations whose costs were deemed not to be justified by the associated benefits. Although Congress came close to passing such sweeping legislation, it did not do so. However, Congress did enact two laws during this period that have had an impact on agency rule-making, especially in the areas of health, safety and the environment.

The first of these was the Unfunded Mandates Reform Act,[25] passed in 1995. This act requires that an agency prepare 'a qualitative and quantitative assessment of the anticipated costs and benefits' of any proposed 'major' rule (defined as a regulation whose aggregate impact is anticipated to be US$100 million or more in any given year), unless the preparation of such an assessment 'is otherwise prohibited by law.'[26] The statute also specifies, in some detail, the contents of the required cost-benefit assessment. Since many federal rules will exceed the US$100 million threshold, this law effectively imposes a cost-benefit 'overlay' on major federal regulation. It is important to note, however, that this law does not require an agency to abandon its particular statutory mandate in favour of balancing costs and benefits. That is, it does not impose cost benefit as a *substantive* decision-making criterion. Nonetheless, by requiring the agency to calculate the costs and benefits of major regulations, and to place this information into the administrative record, Congress clearly has elevated the importance of the cost-benefit criterion.

A year later, in 1996, Congress called for further review of agency decision-making with the passage of the Small Business Regulatory Enforcement Fairness Act.[27] A key aspect of this law was a series of amendments strengthening a 1980 statute known as the Regulatory Flexibility Act (RFA).[28] As amended, the RFA requires all agencies to publish a 'regulatory flexibility analysis' with any proposed or final rule likely to have a significant economic impact on a substantial number of small entities. The analysis published with a proposed rule is to include, among other things, 'a description of any significant alternatives to the proposed rule … which minimize any significant impact of the proposed rule on small entities'.[29] The analysis published with a final rule, in turn, is to include 'a description of the steps the agency has taken to minimize the significant economic impact on small entities', and a statement of the 'factual, policy, and legal reasons' why the approach taken in the final rule was selected instead of the other regulatory alternatives considered.[30]

The Unfunded Mandates Reform Act also imposes a substantive directive, albeit a 'soft' one, on major federal regulations. For any proposed regulation meeting the monetary threshold identified above, the agency must 'identify and consider a reasonable number of alternatives, and from those alternatives select the least costly, most cost-effective and least burdensome alternative that achieves the objectives of the rule'.[31] The agency can avoid this requirement, however, if it publishes 'an explanation of why the least costly, most cost-effective or least burdensome method of achieving the objectives of the rule was not adopted', or if the requirement is 'inconsistent with law'.[32] The focus of this latter exception would seem to be situations in which the agency's substantive mandate requires it to prefer a certain regulatory result even if it is not the cheapest effective alternative. In general, however, the directive to select the most cost effective of those alternatives that will fulfil an agency's mandate should not, in itself, require the agency to compromise its substantive mandate.

During the mid 1990s, Congress also considered, but did not pass, legislation that would have required agencies to perform a detailed risk assessment, according to specified criteria, before promulgating health, safety and environmental regulation. While it did not pass broad legislation of this nature, however, Congress did include risk assessment provisions in its 1996 amendments to the Safe Drinking Water Act, the statute under which the US Environmental Protection Agency (EPA) establishes health criteria for public drinking water supplies. Under these new provisions, risk assessments conducted under the act must be based on 'the best available peer-reviewed science and supporting studies conducted in accordance with sound and objective scientific practices', and on 'data collected by accepted methods or best available methods (if the reliability of the method and the nature of the decision justifies the use of the data)'.[33] Such a requirement can be expected to have an impact on the substance of environmental regulation.

During 2000, in the waning days of the Clinton administration, Congress enacted the Information (Data) Quality Act, which added a short rider to an appropriations bill. The law, which was supported and largely written by business groups, directs the Office of Management and Budget to 'issue guidelines ... that provide policy and procedural guidance to federal agencies for ensuring and maximizing the quality, objectivity, utility and integrity of information (including statistical information) disseminated by federal agencies'.[34] Because it establishes guidelines for the 'quality, objectivity, utility and integrity' of scientific data used by federal agencies, and because it also affords interested parties the right to challenge an agency's adherence to those guidelines, the law can be expected to have a significant effect on agency rule-making if it is vigorously enforced.[35] The OMB has since issued detailed guidelines for good guidance practices performing cost-benefit analysis[36] and cost-effective analysis.[37] The EPA has issued guidelines for carcinogenic risk assessment.[38] Together, these guidance documents influence the course and tenor of regulatory rule-making.

Unless there is a concomitant increase in agency resources, legislation that expands the responsibilities that an agency must fulfil before issuing its regulations – such as by requiring a cost-benefit analysis or a complicated risk assessment – will tend to reduce the number of regulations that the agency can promulgate because of the substantial burdens placed on regulatory agency resources. It also adds a chilling effect on agencies promulgating stringent regulations because of conservative constraints placed upon the actual undertaking of risk assessments.

Additional executive branch influence through the Office of Management and Budget

Administrative agencies sit within the executive branch. Accordingly, the executive also exercises considerable control over agency decision-making. Much of the executive's influence over the direction of an agency stems from the president's control of the appointment process. Most statutes that create an administrative agency also permit the president to appoint the agency's top decision-makers (the so-called political appointments), subject to the approval of the US Senate. The power to appoint includes the power to remove from office, along with all of the more subtle means of persuasion that lie between the two. The underlying theory, presumably, is that each new administration should be free, within the bounds of the applicable statutory mandates, to chart the direction of the agencies that operate within its purview. However, this approach often entails an inherent conflict because the direction favoured by the administration frequently differs from that favoured by Congress. This appears to be an accepted part of the political process.

The executive branch also wields considerable influence over the agencies through the budget process. Although final approval of the national budget rests with Congress, the budget is shaped, in large part, by the proposed budget submitted to Congress by the president. Even more directly than Congress, then, the executive branch can use its grip on the national purse strings to expand the size of those regulatory programmes that it favours and to contract the size of those it does not. Furthermore, since 1980, the president has used the Office of Management and Budget (OMB) to oversee an economic analysis of all proposed major regulations. This has had a significant effect on the regulatory initiatives proposed by the EPA, the Occupational Safety and Health Administration (OSHA) and the Food and Drug Administration (FDA).

President Reagan's 1981 Executive Order 12291 (the core substance of which remains in effect under a 1993 executive order issued by President Clinton) required the OMB to review significant new regulatory actions to ensure that the potential benefits to society outweigh the potential costs, with such benefits and costs to be quantified in monetary terms. In essence, this order imposed the cost-benefit criterion as a prerequisite to promulgation of federal regulations. The OMB has used the review authority granted by this order to delay the promulgation of several regulations. A precursor to this executive order was President Ford's 1974 Executive Order 11821, which required that all regulations issued by executive branch agencies should be accompanied by an inflationary impact statement, where 'inflationary' was defined by the Council on Wage and Price Stability as a situation in which the costs of the regulation exceeded the benefits. However, it did not require that the regulation should not be inflationary, but only that the inflationary impacts should be evaluated. Similarly, President Carter's Executive Order 12044 required federal agencies to analyse the economic consequences of significant regulations and their alternatives, though it imposed no cost-benefit requirement. Although President Clinton's 1993 executive order expressly revokes President Reagan's order,[39] it incorporates many of its basic concepts and retains the cost-benefit review as a key part of the OMB's role.

The Clinton order requires agencies to submit detailed information on anticipated costs and benefits for OMB review before they take any 'significant regulatory action', which is defined as an action that is likely to result in a rule that may have 'an annual effect on the economy of US$100 million or more', that may 'adversely affect in a material way the economy, a sector of the economy, productivity, competition, jobs, the environment, public health or safety, or state, local, or tribal governments or communities', or that may meet another of the criteria enumerated therein. The cost-and-benefit information submitted is to be quantified 'to the extent feasible'.[40] The OMB, in turn, is directed to 'provide meaningful guidance and oversight so that each agency's regulatory actions are consistent with applicable law, the president's priorities and the principles set forth in the executive order'.[41] The cost-benefit criterion is incorporated within the following Principle of Regulation stated in the order:

> *Each agency shall assess both the costs and benefits of the intended regulation and, recognizing that some costs and benefits are difficult to quantify, propose or adopt a regulation only upon a reasoned determination that the benefits of the intended regulation justify its costs.*[42]

The OMB has sought to impose the cost-benefit criterion on agency decision-making even when the underlying statute has required that the regulation be promulgated according to criteria other than cost-benefit balancing. It uses this criterion in its review of workplace health regulations proposed by the OSHA, for example, even though the Supreme Court has held that such regulations are to be set according to technological and economic feasibility, and not according to a weighing of costs and benefits.[43] This approach contravenes the executive order's directive that the OMB endeavour to ensure that agency regulation is 'consistent with applicable law'.

The philosophical tension between Congress and the president on the cost-benefit issue would appear to have been lessened by the former's embrace of the cost-benefit criterion in the Unfunded Mandates Reform Act of 1995. As discussed earlier, however, this law applies to a more limited class of 'major' regulations and does not require that the benefits of a regulation outweigh its costs.

The OMB has a limited, *congressionally delegated* authority to influence the content of agency regulations under the Paperwork Reduction Act (PRA).[44] The general purpose of the PRA is to reduce the public and private burdens incident to government data-gathering activities, and the act directs the OMB to oversee the work of other agencies in order to achieve this objective.

Direct congressional intervention in agency rules

A second key aspect of the Small Business Regulatory Enforcement Fairness Act discussed above was the creation of the Congressional Review Act (CRA).[45] As its name suggests, the CRA was designed to facilitate congressional review of agency rule-making. It requires that, before a final rule takes effect, the promulgating agency provides a report to Congress that includes, among other things, 'a complete copy of the cost-benefit analysis of the rule, if any', and the regulatory flexibility analyses prepared under the Regulatory Flexibility Act. If the regulation is a 'major' rule under the Unfunded Mandates Reform Act, it does not take effect until 60 days after this report has been submitted, unless the president determines that the rule should take effect immediately because one of four designated criteria has been satisfied.[46] This is intended to give the members of Congress time to review the regulation and, if they choose, to debate its merits. Moreover, Congress may (subject to a potential presidential veto) nullify any rule submitted under the CRA and prevent it from taking effect by passing a 'joint resolution of disapproval'.[47] Congress did exactly this when it repealed an OSHA standard on ergonomics in 2001.

Extra-legal activities compromising protection of health, safety and the environment

Aside from legislative and executive policy initiatives that have the effect of reducing protection of health, safety and the environment by imposing a cost-benefit calculus and formalistic risk assessment conventions upon regulatory agencies, two other areas of activity have seriously reversed earlier trends towards a precautionary approach: the political purging of agency science advisory boards and the selective removal of environmental scientists from study sections that review research grants by the agencies,[48] and the gradual replacement of members of the judiciary, at both the circuit court and Supreme Court level, with anti-regulatory ideologues.[49]

A CAPSULE HISTORY OF US CHEMICAL REGULATION AND THE USE OF THE PRECAUTIONARY PRINCIPLE IN US LAW

The history of the use of the precautionary approach in US law contrasts with that in the EU. Whereas in the EU, the precautionary principle appears first in food safety and then moves slowly to develop in environmental regulations and is yet to find full expression in the regulation of occupational health and safety, in the US, it begins strongly and emphatically in worker health and safety, then in the environment, and is weakly expressed in food safety law. In fact, interpretations of what constitutes sufficient scientific evidence and how precautionary agencies should be are given their strongest expression in occupational health and safety law,[50] which profoundly affects the development of these considerations in the environmental area.

The Occupational Safety and Health Act of 1970[51]

The Occupational Safety and Health Act (OSHAct) of 1970 specifically addresses the subject of toxic substances. It states, under Section 6(b)(5) of the act, that the secretary of labour, through the Occupational Safety and Health Administration (OSHA), in promulgating permanent standards dealing with toxic materials or harmful physical agents, shall set the standard that:

> ... *most adequately assures,* to the extent feasible, *on the basis of the* best available evidence *that no employee will suffer material impairment of health or functional capacity, even if such employee has a regular exposure to the hazard dealt with by such standard for the period of his working life [emphasis added].*[52]

Standards promulgated under this section of the act are reviewable by the circuit courts of appeal; the standard of judicial review is 'substantial evidence on the record as a whole'.[53]

The case *Industrial Union Department, AFL-CIO* v *Hodgson*,[54] promulgated a more stringent regulation for asbestos – at the time regarded as a lung toxin causing asbestosis, but not a carcinogen – and the industry challenged the standard, arguing that there was insufficient evidence to justify lowering the permissible exposure limit. In deferring to the agency's determination that a more protective level was needed, the DC Court of Appeals held that:

> *Some of the questions involved in the promulgation of these standards are on the frontiers of scientific knowledge, and consequently ... insufficient data is presently available to make a fully informed factual determination ... it rests, in the final analysis, on an essentially legislative policy judgment, rather than a factual determination, concerning the relative risks of under-protection as opposed to overprotection.*

One might regard this as an articulation of the permissive use of the precautionary principle.

In a subsequent case, *The Society of Plastics Industry, Inc* v *Occupational Safety and Health Administration*,[55] concerning an industry challenge to a very stringent OSHA standard of allowing no more than 1 part per million (ppm) exposure over an eight-hour period to the carcinogen vinyl chloride, the Second Circuit Court of Appeals reiterated the rationale in *Industrial Union* above, adding: 'Under the command of OSHA, it remains the duty of the secretary to act to protect the working man, and to act where existing methodology or research is deficient.' Here, applying a precautionary approach appears to be mandatory, rather than permissive, even under industry protests that achieving the standard was not technologically feasible.

These cases profoundly influenced the extent to which the Environmental Protection Agency regulated air pollutants under the 1970 Clean Air Act (amended in 1977 and 1990) and attempted to regulate toxic substances under the 1976 Toxic Substances Control Act.

After industry testing revealed formaldehyde to be an animal carcinogen in 1979, during the 1980s, under President Reagan, the OSHA initially did nothing to follow up on the prior Carter administration's intent to regulate it.[56] Regulatory agency decisions 'not to act', while technically reviewable by appellate courts, are notoriously difficult to counter. Ultimately, in 1992, 13 years after the animal study, the OSHA was forced to regulate formaldehyde, but chose to place the most minimal restrictions possible on allowable exposure, permitting lifetime risks of greater than 10^{-3} following the directives emanating from the Supreme Court benzene case discussed immediately below.

In a 1980 case involving the industry challenge to an OSHA regulation of the carcinogen benzene at 1 ppm over an eight-hour period, the appellate process reached the Supreme Court. In *Industrial Union Department* v *American Petroleum Institute*,[57] the Supreme Court added a requirement, with dubious legal justification, to the OSHAct that only 'significant risks' could be regulated under the toxic substances provision of the OSHAct. The court remanded the standard to OSHA to determine whether benzene exposure at 1 ppm was 'significant', offering guidance that 'significance' should lie somewhere between a lifetime risk of 10^{-3} (a clearly significant risk) and 10^{-9} (a clearly insignificant risk). The OSHA, under President Reagan, chose the 'bright line' at the least permissibly protective level of 10^{-3}. This heralded the end of the precautionary era in toxic substances regulation. Although President Clinton subsequently could have drawn the line differently, he did not change it.

The OSHA can also administratively and immediately establish 'temporary emergency standards' under the OSHAct; but much discretion is left to the OSHA to determine whether the requirements of a 'necessity to prevent grave danger' prevails in a particular case.[58] In addition, there is a provision in the OSHAct that authorizes the OSHA to go to a federal district court (a court of first instance) to restrain or halt an industrial operation in the case of imminent dangers.[59]

In addition to complying with specific standards, employers are also under a 'general duty' to provide workplaces and work free from 'recognized hazards likely to cause death or serious bodily harm'.[60] Again, defining what constitutes a 'recognized hazard' is left to the discretion of the OSHA.

Thus, what first appears as an emerging mandatory requirement to apply the precautionary principle for worker protection disappears after the benzene case into the abyss of agency discretion dominated by industry interests.

The 1970 Clean Air Act (CAA) (and amendments of 1977 and 1990)[61, 62]

The 1970 Clean Air Act (CAA) regulated both criteria pollutants (carbon monoxide, sulphur dioxide, nitrogen oxides, particulates, ozone and lead) under CAA Section 109,[63] and so-called hazardous pollutants under CAA Section 112.[64] Federal ambient air quality (concentration) standards were established for the former, and federal emission standards were to be established for the latter. The standard of judicial review in the DC Circuit Court of Appeals is 'arbitrary or capricious'. The ambient air quality standards were to be set by the EPA to protect public health 'with an adequate margin of safety' without consideration of economic costs; they were to be achieved through state-imposed emission levels in state permits on existing sources and through state-enforced federal emission limitations on new sources,[65] the latter taking economic burdens into account while permitting the standards to be 'technology forcing' in stringency.

The leading case interpreting standard-setting for criteria pollutants, *Lead Industries Association, Inc* v *Environmental Protection Agency*, addressed a new standard for airborne lead compound particulates.[66] There, the DC Circuit Court of Appeals agreed with the EPA that 'Congress directed the administrator to *err on the side of caution* in making the necessary decisions' (emphasis added). Furthermore, the court agreed with the EPA that:

- Congress made it abundantly clear that considerations of economic or technological feasibility are to be subordinated to the goal of protecting the public health by prohibiting any consideration of such factors.
- [I]t specified that the air quality standards must also protect individuals who are particularly sensitive to the effects of pollution.
- [I]t required that the standards be set at a level at which there is 'an absence of adverse effect' on these sensitive individuals.
- [I]t specifically directed the Administrator to allow an adequate margin of safety in setting primary air quality standards in order to provide some protection against effects that research has not yet uncovered.

It is hard to imagine a stronger endorsement of the precautionary principle. Note the absence of any specific reference to irreversibility of damage or persistence or biomagnification of the pollutant in the environment or the human body. But do note the specific concern for sensitive individuals, the explicit rejection of cost-benefit balancing, and the endorsement of action 'against effects that research has not yet uncovered'. But the precautionary approach was not long lived in the agency. Ronald Reagan won a two-term presidency in 1980 and 1984 and dramatically changed the landscape of US environmental regulation.

For hazardous air pollutants, the 1970 CAA similarly directed the EPA to set emission standards 'at the level which, in his judgment, provides an ample margin of safety to protect the public health'.[67] Departing from the rationale in *Lead Industries*, in an industry challenge to the EPA proposed emission standard for vinyl chloride, writing for a three-judge panel of the DC Circuit Court of Appeals, Judge Robert Bork in *Natural Resources Defense Council, Inc* v *Environmental Protection Agency*[68] opined:

> *We find that the congressional mandate to provide 'an ample margin of safety' 'to protect the public health' requires the Administrator to make an initial determination of what is 'safe … [T]he administrator's decision does not require a finding that 'safe' means 'risk free' or a finding that the determination is free from uncertainty. Instead, we find only that the Administrator's decision must be based upon an expert judgment with regard to the level of emission that will result in an 'acceptable' risk to health… This determination must be based solely upon the risk to health. The Administrator cannot under any circumstances consider cost and technological feasibility at this stage of the analysis …*
>
> *Congress, however, recognized in Section 112 that the determination of what is 'safe' will always be marked by scientific uncertainty and thus exhorted the administrator to set emission standards that will provide an 'ample margin' of safety. This language permits the administrator to take into account scientific uncertainty and to use expert discretion to determine what action should be taken in light of that uncertainty. Congress authorized and, indeed, required EPA to protect against dangers before their extent is conclusively ascertained. Under the 'ample margin of safety' directive, EPA's standards must protect against incompletely understood dangers to public health and the environment, in addition to well-known risks …*
>
> *We wish to reiterate the limited nature of our holding in this case because it is not the court's intention to bind the administrator to any specific method of determining what is 'safe' or what constitutes an 'ample margin'. We hold only that the administrator cannot consider cost and technological feasibility in determining what is 'safe'.*

Unable to shake the clear congressional intent in Section 112 to require standards to be set in the face of considerable scientific uncertainty and without regard to economic or technological feasibility, the three-judge panel of the DC Circuit invented a *de minimis* risk requirement to soften the blow. This case prompted Congress to amend Section 112 of the CAA in the 1990 CAA amendments to allow a technology-based approach to be used, directing the EPA to set technology-based emission standards (based on maximum achievable control technology) established on the level achievable by the 'average' performance of the top 12 per cent of the industry.[69] The EPA could establish more stringent emission standards for new sources.[70] Where technology-based standards were not practical, the EPA could resort to a health-based approach, protecting the public health with an ample margin of safety,[71] the original mandate of the 1970 CAA. Congress expressly provided that, ultimately, carcinogenic chemicals cannot present a risk greater than a 10^{-6} lifetime risk.[72]

In a later challenge to the EPA's revised standards for the criteria pollutants ozone and particulates, in *Environmental Protection Agency* v *American Trucking Associations, Inc,*[73] the Supreme Court reinforced the correctness of the lead case criteria, with concurring Justice Stephen Breyer echoing Judge Bork's rationale that protecting public health with an 'adequate margin of safety' does not mean a world that is 'free of all risk'.

Appellate court deference to the agencies as to what constitutes tolerable *de minimis* risks or significant risks that must be demonstrated in order to be regulated is a 'back door' pathway to reducing a precautionary approach by allowing risk assessments that do not clearly show calculable significant risks to justify non-action. Furthermore, by compromising the independence of agency science advisory boards and by eliminating research grants to scientists who do not think 'the right way', the federal government has greatly compromised the independence and integrity of science in the political process.[74]

The 1976 Toxic Substances Control Act (TSCA)[75]

Under the 1976 Toxics Substances Control Act (TSCA), the EPA must set standards for substances that present or will present 'unreasonable risks to health or the environment',[76] taking into account costs, effects on health and the environment, technological innovation and substitutes.[77] The EPA requires industry to test chemicals[78] if there is insufficient data and the substance 'may present unreasonable risks to health or the environment' *or* if there is a substantial quantity produced or exposure is deemed to be significant. If there may be a reasonable basis to conclude that a chemical presents (or will present) a 'significant' risk of cancer, mutation or birth defects, the EPA must either regulate or explain why it has chosen not too – that is, why the risk is not 'unreasonable'.[79] Upon challenge, any federal court of appeal can examine the standards to ensure that they are based on 'substantial evidence on the record as a whole' (the same standard of judicial review found in the OSHAct).[80] As with the OSHAct, the TSCA provides for emergency measures[81] and imminent hazards.[82] Under the TSCA, the EPA also requires industry to report 'significant adverse reactions' and information about their products' toxicity.[83]

Asbestos, the most notorious carcinogen known in the context of workplace, consumer and environmental exposure, did receive EPA attention during the 1980s. The EPA decided to ban the substance under the TSCA for many uses; but the standard was remanded to the agency for reconsideration by the Fifth Circuit Court of Appeals in *Corrosion Proof Fittings* v *EPA.*[84] As stated above, the TSCA requires the EPA to consider, along with the toxic effects on human health and the environment, 'the benefits of such substance[s] and mixture[s] and the *availability* of substitutes for such uses' (emphasis added). Because the EPA did not explore regulatory options other than a ban, and, more specifically, because the EPA did not evaluate the toxicity (and costs) of likely substitute products[85] in a search for 'least burdensome requirements', the court vacated the proposed standard and remanded it to the EPA for further proceedings. While, arguably, the court incorrectly interpreted the TSCA's requirements regarding mandating substitutes' toxicity (and cost) comparisons (the TSCA mentions only that the 'availability' of substitutes must be considered) and could have sought to establish regulation in another circuit court to give a more favourable result concerning what criteria need to be met in order to regulate, the EPA chose not to reinstate the asbestos ban, primarily because of the likely extensive burden on agency resources to perform extensive risk and economic assessments for substitutes. For all intents and purposes, the EPA regards the TSCA as a 'dead letter'.[86] The analytic burdens placed by the Fifth Circuit Court of Appeals effectively emasculated the TSCA regulation in the US.

RECLAIMING HEALTH, SAFETY AND ENVIRONMENTAL PROTECTION

The precautionary principle has been criticized as being both too vague and too arbitrary to form a basis for rational decision-making. The assumption underlying this criticism is that any scheme not based on cost-benefit analysis and risk assessment is both irrational and without secure foundation in either science or economics. This section contests that view and makes explicit the rational tenets of the precautionary principle within an analytical framework – trade-off analysis – which is as rigorous as uncertainties permit, and one that mirrors democratic values embodied in regulatory, compensatory and common law. It offers an approach to making decisions within an analytic framework, based on equity and justice, to replace the economic paradigm of utilitarian cost-benefit analysis. As will be seen, the strength of trade-off analysis is that it explicitly takes into account who bears the costs and who reaps the benefits.[87] This feature of trade-off analysis mirrors the increasing EU tendency to balance 'interests' rather than costs and benefits.[88]

The limits of cost-benefit analysis in addressing distributional concerns

During the past two decades, cost-benefit analysis has become the dominant method used by policy-makers to evaluate government intervention in the areas of health, safety and the environment. In theory, cost-benefit analysis of a policy option enumerates all possible consequences, both positive and negative; estimates the probability of each; estimates the benefit or loss to society should each occur, expressed in monetary terms; computes the expected social benefit or loss from each consequence by multiplying the amount of the associated benefit or loss by its probability of occurrence; and computes the net expected social benefit or loss associated with the government policy by summing over the various possible consequences.[89] The reference point for these calculations is the state of the economy in the absence of the government policy, termed the 'baseline'.

The mechanics of constructing a cost-benefit analysis can be seen with reference to Table 19.1, which presents a relatively disaggregated matrix of the various positive and negative consequences of a government policy for a variety of actors. The consequences are first separated into economic, health and safety, and environmental effects, and those affected are organized into policy-relevant groups of actors, such as producers, workers, consumers and 'others'. Initially, the consequences are represented in their natural units: economic effects are expressed in monetary units; health and safety effects are expressed in mortality and morbidity terms; and environmental effects are expressed in damage to ecosystems, etc. Economic analysis is used to evaluate monetary costs and benefits related to economic effects. Health and environmental risk assessments inform the entries in the last two columns of the matrix.

All of the consequences of a candidate policy (or regulation) are described fully in terms of the times during which they occur. What traditional cost-benefit analysis does is translate all of these consequences into 'equivalent' monetary units. This poses two problems. One is the difficulty, even arbitrariness, of placing a monetary value on human life, health and safety and a healthy environment. Another is that by translating all of these consequences into equivalent monetary units, discounting each to current value (since a US$/Euro invested now is expected to earn interest over time), and aggregating them into a single US$/Euro value intended to express the net social effect of the government policy, the effects on the economy from investing now in future health, safety and environmental benefits are weighted far more heavily than those benefits that occur in the future, including those to future generations.

As a decision-making tool, cost-benefit analysis offers several compelling advantages. It clarifies choices among alternatives by evaluating consequences systematically. It professes to foster an open and fair policy-making process by making explicit the estimates of costs and benefits and the assumptions upon which those estimates are based. And by expressing all gains and losses in monetary terms, cost-benefit analysis permits the total impact of a policy to be summarized in a single US$/Euro figure (cost-effectiveness analysis relies on a benefit-to-cost ratio, rather than a net benefit calculus, but otherwise shares the other weaknesses of a cost-benefit approach).

Table 19.1 *Matrix of policy consequences for different actors*

Group	Economic effects	Health/safety effects	Environmental effects
Producers	$C_\$$		
Workers	$C_\$$	$B_{H/S}$	
Consumers	$C_\$$	$B_{H/S}$	
Others	$C_\$$	$B_{H/S}$	$B_{Environment}$

This final step, however, may be stretching analytic techniques one step too far. An alternative approach, called trade-off analysis, begins in the same way as does cost-benefit analysis, but does not aggregate like effects into a single benefit or cost stream, and it stops short of assigning monetary values to non-monetary consequences. Instead, all effects are described in their natural units. The time period in which each effect is experienced is fully revealed; but future effects are not discounted to present value. All kinds of uncertainties are fully described: risk, probability distributions and indeterminacy. It is not possible to know what we don't know (ignorance), but confidence that we have fully described the world is a proxy for a belief that ignorance is not likely to be a problem. Trade-offs between worker health or environmental improvements and costs to producers and consumers are made apparent because the different cost and benefit elements are not aggregated.

Using trade-off analysis, politically accountable decision-makers could make policy choices in a transparent manner. Who bears the costs and who reaps the benefits from a policy option would not be hidden in a single aggregate US$/Euro figure. Decisions would be based on accountability rather than accounting. Note that while cost benefit is formulaic – that is, a single figure of merit is sought for a policy/regulation, such as the 'net benefit' or a 'benefit-to-cost ratio' – trade-off analysis seeks to 'bound the set of not clearly incorrect – that is, unfair – decisions'. This has important implications for policy choices. Under a cost-benefit framework, one can easily demand prioritization of risk-reduction options based on the ranking of net benefits or cost-benefit ratios – with choices representing violations of the ranking being allegedly inconsistent or irrational. However, where large uncertainties exist, and the distributions of risks and benefits are of concern, there is no uniquely correct prioritization scheme or metric demanding 'consistency'. Advances in risk assessment techniques and economic analysis that takes technological innovation into account through the deliberate undertaking of Technology Options Analysis (see below) can narrow the uncertainties, but can never provide a unique best answer. That process, ultimately, has to reflect political, social and value judgments – preferably informed by public participation/stakeholder processes and transparent for all to see. Taking care to include concerns for effects, their uncertainties and their distributional consequences – that is, exercising precaution – in order to make responsible, accountable decisions is possible using trade-off analysis, but not cost-benefit analysis.

Promoting rational technology choices

One important element often left out of the traditional cost-benefit matrix has been the consideration of technological alternatives.[90] Regulatory agencies have a mixed history in making information about cleaner and safer technologies available and promoting their adoption. Agencies could help to prevent pollution and accidents by helping firms to think about their technological options in a more formal and systematic fashion.

Options for technological change must be considered according to a variety of criteria, including economic, environmental, and health and safety factors. Identifying these options and comparing them against the technology in use is called Technology Options Analysis.[91] Unlike traditional technology assessment, Technology Options

Analysis does not require absolute quantification of all of the variables: one has only to demonstrate, in a *comparative* manner, that one technology is better or worse than another in performance, health, safety, ecological effects and so forth. It is likely to be less sensitive to initial assumptions than, for example, cost-benefit analysis, and would enable industry and government to identify more creative cost-effective solutions. Government might require industries to undertake Technology Options Analysis instead of traditional technology assessment focusing on technologies already existing within, or easily accessible to, the firm or industry. The latter would likely address only the technologies that industry puts forward; it may thus miss the opportunity of identifying and subsequently influencing the adoption or development of superior technological options.[92]

Once superior existing technologies – or technologies within easy reach – are identified, industries may be motivated to change their technology out of economic self-interest or in order to avoid future liability. On the other hand, government might either force the adoption or development of new technology, or provide technical or financial assistance. Requiring firms to change technology can itself be a risky venture. Adopting a technology new to a firm or industry introduces new uncertainties and financial risks. If this is done, policy should allow for error and accommodate industry for failures in *bona fide* attempts to develop new technologies – for example, by allowing more time or sharing the financial risk. Developing a new technology may often not be possible for the incumbent polluting or dangerous firm. New entrants displacing the dominant or prevailing technology may be required. To adopt environmental, health or safety requirements in this case takes considerable political courage; but the options of doing so should not be ignored.[93]

Whichever route government takes, the precautionary principle requires the investigation of technology options for developing and adopting cleaner and inherently safer (sustainable) technologies.

Which errors are worse?

Policy-makers must address both uncertainty about the nature and extent of health, safety or environmental risks, and about the performance of an alternative technology. First, they must choose whether to err on the side of caution or risk. With regard to the first type of uncertainty – scientific uncertainty – two mistakes can be made. A 'type I' error is committed if society regulates an activity that appears to be hazardous, but turns out later to be harmless (a 'false positive' in the parlance of experimental findings) and resources are needlessly expended. Another error, a 'type II' error is committed if society fails to regulate an activity because the evidence is not initially thought to be strong enough, but that finally turns out to be harmful (a 'false negative').[94]

A 'type III' error is said to occur when one provides an accurate (or precise) answer to the wrong problem.[95] Not taking into account opportunities to change technology restricts the decision-maker to 'static solutions' and thus gives rise to the further error of considering options within 'bounded rationality'.

Where uncertainty exists on the technology side, type I errors can be said to be committed when society mandates the development or adoption of a technology that turns out to be much more expensive or less able to reduce risks than anticipated, and when resources are needlessly or foolishly expended. Type II errors might be said to be committed when, because of insufficient commitment of resources or political will, a significant missed opportunity is created by which society fails to force or stimulate significant risk-reducing technology.[96] An important distinction between a cost-benefit approach and one based on precaution is that the former is 'risk neutral' in the balancing of costs and benefits with their attendant uncertainties, and the latter reflects 'risk averseness' for some kinds of errors.

Value judgments clearly affect decisions on whether to tolerate type I or type II errors with regard to *both* risk and technology choices. This is because the cost of being wrong in one instance may be vastly different from the cost of being wrong in another. For example, banning a chemical essential to a beneficial activity, such as the use of radio nuclides in medicine, has potentially more drastic consequences than banning a non-essential chemical for which there is a close, cost-comparable substitute. It may be perfectly appropriate to rely on 'most likely estimates' of risk in the first case and on 'worst-case analysis' in the second. A type II error on the technology choice side was committed in the case of the Montreal Protocol banning chlorofluorocarbons (CFCs) by creating a scheme through which DuPont and ICI, the producers of CFCs, were allowed to promote the use of their own substitute, hydrochlorofluorocarbons (HCFCs), rather than adopt a more stringent protocol that would have stimulated still better substitutes.

Evaluating errors and deciding which way to lean is not a precise science. However, making those evaluations and valuations explicit within a trade-off analysis that acknowledges distributional effects, accounts for uncertainties in risk assessments and considers opportunities for technological change will reveal the preferences upon which policies are based and may suggest priorities.

CONCLUSIONS

The application and discussion of the precautionary principle have focused on action to prevent or refrain from contributing to possible serious irreversible harm to health and the environment – whether on an individual basis or in terms of widespread environmental or health consequences. In particular, the precautionary principle has become embodied in regulations directed towards persistent and/or bioaccumulative toxic substances.[97] Lately, the principle has been applied to problems attended by indeterminacy and ignorance.

Here it is worth reviewing the fact that the nature of uncertainty in the problems that now concern health, safety and environmental regulators and advocates is changing. Formerly, concentrating on the magnitude of risks and their uncertainties – in a probabilistic sense – consumed the attention of the decision-maker. Since better science would be expected to yield a better basis for decisions, it could be argued that risk management decisions should await its arrival. Today, problems of indeterminacy and ignorance increasingly characterize the risks we face. It is no longer a question of waiting for the science to be developed. The limitations of 'knowing with greater accuracy' and 'not knowing what we don't know' attend – and will continue to attend in the foreseeable future – modern day risks and confound so-called rational approaches to dealing with these hazards. The social concern with genetically modified organisms (GMOs) or with bioterrorism are examples. The proponents of GMOs deride social attempts to exercise caution over risks we cannot estimate or imagine; but who is arguing that taking precaution against terrorism is 'irrational'? Ought we to expect 'consistency' in the management of highly uncertain (that is, indeterminable or unknowable), possibly catastrophic, risks? Clearly, a different theoretical framework is needed – one outside of deterministic rational choice theory.

I have argued elsewhere that the precautionary principle need not be restricted to cases of irreversibility or large uncertainty of effect.[98] If it is, as I contend, an alternative to cost-benefit analysis, it can be used wherever that approach gives an objectionable outcome. For example, it might also be applied to mitigate a harm that is ultimately reversible – if reversing the damage could be more costly than preventing it. And what of the cases in which there are no uncertainties – for example, when we know that future generations will be harmed? Cost-benefit analysis is biased against investing heavily in the present to prevent such future harm because of the use of discounting cost and benefit streams over time. And there are many situations in which we are aware of our ignorance: for example, we know that only a very small percentage of all chemicals in commerce have been tested for toxic effects.[99] In these cases, too, precaution is appropriate.

However, it is not the precautionary principle *per se* that is amenable to replacing cost-benefit analysis as a 'decision rule' for action. Nor does the precautionary principle replace risk assessment. Attempts to establish a threshold of harm above which the precautionary principle is triggered, for example, have been less than satisfactory.[100] Instead, a precautionary approach or principle is most useful in guiding the selection of policies, and aiding in the establishment of priorities, in an attempt to deliver justice and fairness within a more appropriate framework than cost-benefit analysis. Precaution rightly focuses on uncertainty and irreversibility as two important factors; but others must be considered as well, particularly technology alternatives. A complete list of the important elements must include:

- the *seriousness and irreversibility* of the harm addressed;
- the *societal distribution of possible costs and benefits* of policies and technologies;
- the *technological options* for preventing, arresting, reversing or mitigating possible harm – and the opportunity costs of selecting a given policy option;.
- *society's inclinations* regarding erring on the side of caution and erring on the side of laxity;
- the *nature of the uncertainty encountered*: classical uncertainty, indeterminacy or ignorance?

Nothing substitutes for a transparent and accessible decision-making framework in which the values and assumptions are clearly articulated and compared to alternative approaches. Trade-off analysis makes this possible, but also offers the opportunity to operationalize the precautionary principle by:

- *Minimizing uncertainty* through:
  - refinement of (comparative) risk analysis; and
  - undertaking (comparative) Technology Options Analysis.

- *Reflecting societal preferences for error avoidance* regarding:
  - risk avoidance (type I versus type II errors regarding requirements for the *reduction of risk*); and
  - cost avoidance (type I versus type II errors regarding requirements for *changes in technology*).
- *Changing the burden of proof* through:
  - consideration of creating a *sliding scale* for the burden of proof – that is, the strength of data/information needed to justify taking (or stopping) action, depending upon the hazard, extent of protection desired and action taken (notification, regulation, compensation, etc.); this means *linking causality to level of desired protection.*

Much of the discussion of the precautionary principle focuses on cause-and-effect relationships for which a high statistical confidence level (usually expressed as having a p value of ≤ 0.05 – that is, a small chance of the association being spurious or random) or a high strength of association is traditionally required in scientific publications. It should be remembered that the convention of requiring a p value no higher than 0.05 was an arbitrary historical choice. Critics of those wishing to invoke the precautionary principle by reducing the strength of causal proof would do well to remember this. In addition, other ways of knowing besides statistical correlations might be pursued.[101]

Other standards (burdens) of proof commonly invoked in public policy determinations include, in decreasing order of stringency, 'strict liability for harm' (in the area of compensation, the polluter pays principle is sometimes invoked in statutory language or by the courts in fashioning equitable relief to victims); 'clear and convincing evidence'; 'more probable than not' or 'preponderance of the evidence'; 'substantial cause or factor'; and 'contributing factor'. This sliding scale of evidentiary strength can be thought of as invoking the precautionary principle by expanding the 'allowable possible error' in factual determinations. An alternative to shifting the burden of proof that lessens the burden of proof required to trigger an intervention to prevent or mitigate harm to health, safety or the environment is to shift the *burden of persuasion* to another party.

Presumptions and shifts in the burden of persuasion

Part of the perceived fairness of the process involves the burden of persuasion – that is, the designation of which party has the burden of demonstrating or refuting a presumed fact. This is distinct from the burden or standard of proof – a term referring to the strength of the evidence (data and information) needed to justify taking action. Both terms are relevant in formulating the precautionary principle.

Much discussion has focused on cause-and-effect relationships between exposure/ other events and harmful effects for which a high statistical confidence level or strength of association is traditionally required. To escape the rigors of these requirements, some proponents of the precautionary principle argue that the burden of persuasion should be shifted to the proponents of a potentially harmful technology. Opponents argue against so radical a shift, pointing out that negatives are harder to prove.

Sometimes ignored by many commentators is the fact that burdens of persuasion often shift in the course of fact-finding. Thus, depending upon the nature of the intervention (notification, control, banning, treatment, compensation, etc.), even if it is necessary for the regulator or potential victim initially to prove a (potential) harm, that proof is sometimes not a very high burden. A presumed fact (though a rebuttable presumption) might even be established by statute on showing certain other factual elements, such as the very existence of harm. Then, the burden of persuasion shifts to the intended regulated industry or alleged (potential) wrong-doer to refute the presumed or initially established fact, often with a higher burden of proof. Legal injunctions against potentially harmful action are granted by the courts as equitable remedies. The commentators on the precautionary principle have often ignored a rich and important set of policy interventions or actions that are informed, but not dictated, by factual determinations. Regulatory agencies themselves – depending upon their statutory mandates – are not bound by traditional burdens of proof. Furthermore, reviewing courts usually give deference to factual findings by the agencies as long as they stay within the 'zone of reasonableness' defined by those mandates.

NOTES

1 This is not to say that some improvements have not also occurred; but the magnitude of problems in other areas has increased, and the nature of risks has also changed.
2 Colborn, T., Dumanowski, D. and Myers, J. P. (1996) *Our Stolen Future*, Dutton Press, New York.
3 Ashford, N. A. and Miller, C. (1998) *Chemical Exposures: Low Levels and High Stakes*, second edition, John Wiley Press, New York.
4 Hoefer, T., Gerner, I., Gundert-Remy, U., Liebsch, M., Schulte, A., Spielmann, H., Vogel, R. and Wettig, K. (2004) 'Animal testing and alternative approaches for the human health risk assessment under the proposed new European Chemicals Regulation', *Archives of Toxicology*, vol 78, pp549–564.
5 Wynne, B. (1992) 'Uncertainty and environmental learning', *Global Environmental Change*, vol 2, pp111–127.
6 National Academy of Sciences (1983) *Risk Assessment in the Federal Government: Managing the Process*, National Academy Press, Washington, DC.
7 Ashford, N. A. (1988) 'Science and values in the regulatory process', *Statistical Science*, vol 3, no 3, pp377–383.
8 See de Sadeleer, N. (2006) 'The precautionary principle in EC heath and environmental law: Sword or shield for the Nordic countries?' – Chapter 2 in this volume.
9 Indeed, the offered methodologies are based in so-called 'rational-choice' theory pioneered by the University of Chicago School of Law and Economics. See Ashford, N. and Caldart, C. (2007) 'Economics and the environment', in *Environmental Law, Policy, and Economics: Reclaiming the Environmental Agenda*, Cambridge, MIT Press, Chapter 3.
10 Rather than focusing on requiring minimum certainty before acting, agencies sometimes formulate their defence of no regulation by arguing that (conservative) risk assessments yield risks that are too small to justify action – that is, the risks are *de minimis*. See the discussion in the section on 'The politics of regulating chemicals in the US'. In the context of genetically modified foods, the then Food and Drug Administration (FDA) Commissioner David Kessler

stated that those foods were 'substantially equivalent' to foods produced by traditional production, thus glossing over small but possibly important differences vis-à-vis food safety. See Kessler, D. (1984) 'Food safety: Revising the statute', *Science*, vol 223, pp1034–1040.

11 There is the increasing tendency of the EU to balance 'conflicting interests' rather than costs and benefits. See Chapter 2 in this volume. This turns out to be a major feature of trade-off analysis rather than cost-benefit analysis, as discussed in the section on 'A capsule history of US chemical regulation and the use of the precautionary principle in US law'.

12 Ashford, N. A. (2005) 'Implementing the precautionary principle: Incorporating science, technology, fairness and accountability in environmental, health and safety decisions', *International Journal of Risk Assessment and Management*, vol 5, no 2/3/4, pp112–124. Based on an article written by Ashford, N. A. (2004) 'Incorporating science, technology, fairness, and accountability in environmental, health, and safety decisions', *International Journal of Occupational Medicine and Environmental Health*, vol 17, no 1, pp59–67, and reprinted in *Human and Ecological Risk Assessment*, vol 11, no 1, pp85–96.

13 For an extensive discussion of these two formulations, see Chapter 2 in this volume. See also de Sadeleer, N. (2002) *Environmental Principles: From Political Slogans to Legal Rules*, Oxford University Press, Oxford.

14 See Chapter 2 in this volume for an in-depth discussion.

15 See Chapter 2 in this volume for an in-depth discussion.

16 de Sadeleer, N. (2000) *Two Approaches of Precaution: A Comparative Review of EU and US Theory and Practice of the Precautionary Principle*, Centre d'Étude du Droit de l'Environment, Brussels. See also de Sadeleer, N. (2002) *Environmental Principles: From Political Slogans to Legal Rules*, Oxford University Press, Oxford, p139.

17 Applegate, J. S. (2000) 'The precautionary preference: An American perspective on the precautionary principle', *Human and Ecological Risk Assessment*, vol 6, no 3, pp413–443.

18 *Chevron, USA, v NRDC*, 467 US 837 (1984).

19 Attempts to distinguish 'approaches' from 'principles' by arguing that the approaches are flexible, whereas principles are not, fails a logical test. Principles in the law are not without their limits, and they are sometimes in direct conflict. For example, the freedom of speech can be said to be a fundamental principle of US law, but it is not absolute and may be compromised in favour of public safety: 'No one has the right to yell fire in a crowded theatre.'

20 See Hornstein, D. (1992) 'Reclaiming environmental law: A normative critique of comparative risk analysis', *Columbia Law Review*, vol 92, pp562–633.

21 See Chapter 2 in this volume; See also several papers by Majone, G. (2001) *The Precautionary Principle and Regulatory Impact Analysis*, Manuscript, described as an expanded version of a paper submitted at the International Seminar on Regulatory Impact Analysis organized by Progetto AIR, Rome, 15 June 2001; Majone, G. (2002) 'What price safety? The precautionary principle and its policy implications', *Journal of Common Market Studies*, vol 40, pp89–106; and Majone, G. and Everson, M. (2001) 'Institutional reform: Independent agencies, oversight, coordination and procedural control', in De Schutter, O., Lebessis, N. and Paterson, J. (eds) *Governance in the European Union*, Office for the Official Publications of the European Communities, Luxembourg, pp129–168.

22 In Chapter 2 in this volume, de Sadeleer emphasizes this point in observing that the precautionary principle applies to both risk assessment and risk management decisions and is not the province of risk management alone.

23 This section draws heavily on Ashford, N. and Caldart, C. (2007) 'Administrative law', in *Environmental Law, Policy and Economics: Reclaiming the Environmental Agenda*, MIT Press, Cambridge, MIT Press, Chapter 5.

24 See Vogel, D. (2003) 'The hare and the tortoise revisited: The new politics of consumer and environmental regulation in Europe', *British Journal of Political Science*, vol 33, pp557–580.

25   2 U.S.C. §§551–559, 701–706.
26   See 2 U.S.C. §1532.
27   Public Law 104–121, 26 March 1996.
28   5 U.S.C. §§601–612.
29   See 5 U.S.C. §603(c).
30   See 5 U.S.C. §603(a)(5).
31   See 2 U.S.C. §1535(a).
32   See 2 U.S.C. §1535(b).
33   See 42 U.S.C. §300g–1(b)(3)(A).
34   See Section 515 of the Treasury, Postal Service and General Government Appropriations Act for Fiscal Year 2001, enacted on 21 December 2000 as part of an omnibus spending bill. See Consolidated Appropriations FY 2001 of 2000, Pub, L. No 106–554, 114 Stat. 2763A–153 to 2763A–154.
35   See, generally, Revkin, A. L. (2002) 'Law revises standards for scientific study: Agencies face challenges on health and environment research', *The New York Times*, 21 March 2002, pA24.
36   See www.whitehouse.gov/omb/inforeg/.
37   See www.nap.edu/catalog/11534.html?send.
38   See www.pubs.acs.org/cen/news/83/i14/8314guidelines.html.
39   Executive Order 12866, 58 FR 51735 (30 September 1993).
40   See Executive Order 12866, Sections 3(f) and 6(a)(3)(B).
41   See Executive Order 12866, Section 6(b).
42   See Executive Order 12866, Section 1(b)(6).
43   See *American Textile Manufacturers Institute* v *Donovan*, 452 U.S. 490 (1981).
44   44 U.S.C. §3501–3520.
45   5 U.S.C. §§801–808.
46   See 5 U.S.C. §§801(a)(3) and 801(c).
47   See 5 U.S.C. §802.
48   See Steinbrook, R. (2003) 'Science, politics and federal advisory committees', *New England Journal of Medicine*, vol 350, no 14, pp1454–1460.
49   The effect is seen in the Supreme Court benzene decision, discussed in the following section on 'Congressional legislation', where more or less out of thin air, the court fashioned a 'significant risk' requirement for application of the OSHAct in clear contravention of the congressional mandate to the secretary of labour to set standards 'which more adequately [ensures], to the extent feasible, on the basis of the best available evidence, that *no employee* suffer material impairment of heath or functional capacity' (emphasis added), 29 U.S.C. §655(b)(5). But also see the discussion of the vinyl chloride decision of Judge Robert Bork, in the section on 'Additional executive branch influence through the Office of Management and Budget', who argued that the congressional mandate in Section 112 of the 1970 Clean Air Act to protect public health 'with an ample margin of safety' did not require the EPA to establish a level that was 'risk free'. Both a 'significant risk' (unacceptable risk) requirement and exclusion of '*de minimis* risks' (acceptable risks) from protection permitted and encouraged regulatory agencies, under conservative reviewing courts, to provide modest levels of protection under their statutes.
50   See Ashford, N. and Caldart, C. (1996) *Technology, Law and the Working Environment*, second edition, Island Press, Washington, DC.
51   29 U.S.C. §651–683.
52   29 U.S.C. §655(b)(5).
53   29 U.S.C §660.
54   499 F2d 467 (DC Cir. 1974).
55   509 F2d 1301 (2nd Cir 1975).

56 Ashford, N. A., Ryan, W. C. and Caldart, C. C. (1983) 'Law and science policy in federal regulation of formaldehyde', *Science*, vol 222, pp894–900, and Ashford, N. A, Ryan, W. C., and Caldart, C. C. (1983) 'A hard look at federal regulation of formaldehyde: A departure from reasoned decision-making', *Harvard Environmental Law Review*, vol 7, pp297–370. See also Rest, K. and Ashford, N. A. (1988) 'Regulation and technology options: The case of occupational exposure to formaldehyde', *Harvard Journal of Law and Technology*, vol 1, pp63–96.

57 448 U.S. 607 (1980).

58 Temporary emergency standards, which allow the OSHA to put into play immediate restrictions lasting six months without engaging in the long procedural process of promulgating permanent standards, might be compared to the 'safeguard principle' in EC environmental law, whereby EU member states reserve the right to address emergency situations without recourse to EC restrictions. Temporary emergency standards also implicitly incorporate the concept of proportionality through the requirement that these standards are 'necessary'. See Chapter 2 in this volume.

59 29 U.S.C. §662.

60 29 U.S.C. §654.

61 42 U.S.C. §7401–7671.

62 See Ashford, N. and Caldart, C. (2007) 'Limiting exposure to outdoor air contaminants: The Clean Air Act', in *Environmental Law, Policy, and Economics: Reclaiming the Environmental Agenda*, MIT Press, Cambridge, Chapter 7.

63 42 U.S.C. §7409.

64 42 U.S.C. §7412, otherwise known as Section 112 of the CAA.

65 42 U.S.C. §7411. A current controversy involves the EPA's relaxation of new source requirements for installing new pollution control equipment where there have been updates to coal-fired power plants. An additional concern is that the EPA now proposes to replace the mercury hazardous substance emission standard under Section 112 and to establish a cap and trade provision allowing mercury emissions from power plants (and other sources) be traded, thus creating 'hot spots'.

66 647 F.2d 1130 (DC Cir. 1980).

67 §7412(b)(1)(B).

68 824 F.2d 1146 (DC Cir. 1987).

69 §7412(d)(3).

70 §7412(d)(3).

71 §7412(d)(4).

72 §7412(f)(2).

73 531 U.S. 457 (2001).

74 On 18 February 2004, over 60 leading scientists – Nobel laureates, leading medical experts, former federal agency directors, and university chairs and presidents – following up on an initiative organized by the Union of Concerned Scientists (UCS), signed a statement voicing their concern over the misuse of science by the Bush administration. See the UCS website: www.ucsusa.org/scientific_integrity/.

75 15 U.S.C. §2601–2629.

76 15 U.S.C. §2605a.

77 15 U.S.C. §2605c.

78 15 U.S.C. §2603.

79 15 U.S.C. §2603f. As with OSHA reluctance to take action on formaldehyde, the EPA dragged its feet on formaldehyde, refusing to 'either act or explain' as required by this section of the TSCA. For a history of formaldehyde regulation, see Rest, K. and Ashford, N. A. (1988) 'Regulation and technology options: The case of occupational exposure to formaldehyde', *Harvard Journal of Law and Technology*, vol 1, pp63–96; and Ashford, N. and Caldart, C. (1996)

'The Toxics Substances Control Act', in *Technology, Law and the Working Environment*, revised edition, Island Press, Washington, DC, Chapter 4.

80   15 U.S.C. §2618.

81   15 U.S.C. §2605d.

82   15 U.S.C. §2606.

83   15 U.S.C. §2607.

84   947 F.2d 1201 (fifth Cir.1991).

85   Note the contrast with the result reached in the WTO panel's rejection of Canada's argument that France was obligated to assess likely substitutes for asbestos before it should be permitted to ban Canadian asbestos imports under Section XX of the General Agreement on Tariffs and Trade (GATT). Articles 8.218 to 8.223, *European Communities – Measures Affecting Asbestos and Asbestos-Containing Products*, Report of the Panel, WT/DS135/R, 12 March 2001 (00–3353).

86   There is a danger that REACH could suffer the same fate, with the result that regulation (authorization and restrictions) is not often vigorously pursued. Note, as discussed earlier, that comparative assessment of risks and costs are not nearly as burdensome as conducting separate risk and cost assessments. Whether using comparative assessment could circumvent the hurdle that the EPA needs to overcome to satisfy the requirements laid out in *Corrosion Proof Fittings* v *EPA* (note 84, *supra*) needs to be explored. Because the issue of alternatives needs to be considered in formulating regulations under the TSCA, this may well be possible. In contrast, because risk assessment seems to drive the REACH process, and because the consideration of alternatives seems to come in later, whether the use of comparative analysis in the context of REACH can circumvent the need for extensive risk analyses is unclear. See Koch, L. and Ashford, N. A. (2006) *Journal of Cleaner Production*, vol 14, no 1, pp31–46.

87   Criticisms of traditional cost benefit, of course, are not new. See Mishan, E. J. (1981) *Introduction to Normative Economics*, Oxford University Press, New York, and Fischhoff, B. (1977) 'Cost-benefit analysis and the art of motorcycle maintenance', *Policy Sciences*, vol 8, pp177–202.

88   See Chapter 2 in this volume.

89   Ashford, N. A. (1981) 'Alternatives to cost-benefit analysis in regulatory decisions', *Annals of the New York Academy of Sciences*, vol 363, pp129–137. See also Ashford, N. A. and Caldart, Charles C. (1996) 'Economic issues in occupational health and safety', in *Technology, Law and the Working Environment*, revised edition, Island Press, Washington, DC, Chapter 5.

90   Ashford, N. A. (1998) 'The importance of taking technological innovation into account in estimating the costs and benefits of worker health and safety regulation', in *Proceedings of the European Conference on Costs and Benefits of Occupational Health and Safety*, The Hague, Holland, 28–30 May 1997, pp69–78. See also O'Brien, M. (2000) *Making Better Environmental Decisions*, MIT Press, Cambridge.

91   Ashford, N. A. (2002) 'An innovation-based strategy for a sustainable environment', in Hemmelskamp, J., Rennings, K. and Leone, F. (eds) *Innovation-Oriented Environmental Regulation: Theoretical Approach and Empirical Analysis*, ZEW Economic Studies, Springer Verlag, Heidelberg and New York, pp67–107 (Proceedings of the International Conference of the European Commission Joint Research Centre, Potsdam, Germany, 27–29 May 1999).

92   This has direct relevance to the concerns for 'proportionality' in EU law. Assessing the 'necessity' of restrictive measures should ideally take into account not only the *regulatory* alternatives, but also the likely technological alternatives that could arise in the face of stringent regulatory options. Technology options analysis assists in the latter evaluation. Failure to fully investigate or plan for the stimulation of new technological solutions gives rise to 'technology' errors as important as the 'scientific' errors associated with inadequate, incorrect or incomplete risk assessments. See especially the discussion in the following section.

93 Ashford, N. A. (2002) 'Government and innovation in Europe And North America', in Sonnenfeld, D. and Mol, A. (eds) *American Behavioral Scientist: Special Issue on Ecological Modernization,* vol 45, no 9, pp1417–1434.

94 Ashford, N. A. (1988) 'Science and values in the regulatory process', in *Statistical Science,* vol 3, no 3, pp377–383.

95 Schwartz, S. and Carpenter K. (1999) 'The right answer for the wrong question: Consequences of type III error for public health research', *American Journal of Public Health,* vol 89, pp1175–1180.

96 One glaring error is committed when, under pressure from cost constraints, standards are not as stringent as health or environmental concerns might justify. Lax standards may not stimulate serious changes in technology, while stringent standards would. Stringent standards may actually be more economically beneficial for the society than lax standards, although there may be winners and losers within the industrial or product sectors. See the discussion of the Porter hypothesis and stimulating technological change through regulation in Ashford, N. A. (2002) 'Government and innovation in Europe And North America', in Sonnenfeld, D. and Mol, A. (eds) *American Behavioral Scientist: Special Issue on Ecological Modernization,* vol 45, no 9, pp1417–1434.

97 Aarhus Protocol on Persistent Organic Pollutants to LRTAP Convention, 1998.

98 Ashford, N. A. (2005) 'Implementing the precautionary principle: Incorporating science, technology, fairness and accountability in environmental, health and safety decisions', *International Journal of Risk Assessment and Management,* vol 5, no 2/3/4, pp112–124. Based on an article found in Ashford (2004), note 12, *supra.*

99 Indeed, the EU REACH Directive has been proposed to address these uncertainties, which could be resolved, in principle, if enough resources were devoted to researching toxicity. But see Koch, L. and Ashford, N. A. (2006) *Journal of Cleaner Production,* vol 14, no 1, pp31–46, for an argument that efforts to find safer technologies could be more cost effective and safer than reducing toxicological uncertainty.

100 See Chapter 2 in this volume.

101 Josephson, J. R. and Josephson, S. G. (1996) *Abductive Inference,* Cambridge University Press, Cambridge, UK.

Conclusion

CHAPTER 20

Lessons From International, EU and Nordic Legal Regimes

Nicolas de Sadeleer

Celebrated by some and disparaged by others, the precautionary principle is no stranger to controversy. Probably no other environmental principle has produced as much controversy as this principle does. Indeed, the debate on the advantages of the precautionary principle can be rather contentious, as in the European Union (EU), where undertakings regularly contend with it. In contrast, the principle has been subject to less criticism in Nordic countries. At the outset, the principle was proclaimed in 1989 at several Nordic Council conferences (Declaration of Nordic Parliamentary Conference and Declaration of the Nordic Council's International Conference on Pollution of the Seas). Moreover, the 1989 Bergen Ministerial Declaration on Sustainable Development in the United Nations Economic Commission For Europe (ECE) region, as well as the 1993 Declaration on Environment and Development in the Arctic, were testament to the willingness of the Nordic countries to buttress their sustainable development policies on precaution.

So far, there is still considerable confusion around the question of whether precaution could exert any influence on decision-making regulatory frameworks. Given that the precautionary principle is highly contextual, the debate must be, in our view, better anchored in facts. The purpose of this book was therefore to answer the question, through an array of legal analyses, of whether precaution could improve the decision-making process in face of uncertainty. To put this question into proper perspective, the implementation of the precautionary principle has been assessed in the five Nordic countries, as well as in other regulatory settings (the EU and the US) in a variety of ways, ranging from traditional environmental law (listed installations, waste management, nature protection and marine pollution) to product-related regulations (genetically modified organisms and chemicals), as well as the management of natural resources (fisheries). As a result, the studies presented in this volume reflect a rich array of perspectives on the manner in which precaution is influencing risk assessment and risk management alike.

Several observations may be drawn from these analyses regarding the legal effects of such a principle in international law, EU law, as well as in the five Nordic countries.

INTERNATIONAL LAW

In terms of international law, the precautionary principle has been successively established as a general principle of environmental policy in the Nordic region in various soft law documents (HELCOM 13/6). Abounding in declarations, resolutions and guidelines enacted in different international fora, it is, nonetheless, devoid of a binding effect on the grounds that these instruments themselves have no compulsory effects. Thus, despite their laudable intentions, soft law 'precautionary principles' do not take on the features that lead to the recognition of a normative principle.

This is not to say that when the precautionary principle is enshrined in a non-binding instrument, it is devoid of any functions. First, when endorsed in a soft law instrument, the principle assumes an interpretative value. Second, the non-binding principle can be used as a precursor to hard law; in other words, it may thus serve as forerunner of treaty law (see, in particular, the discussion on the 1995 United Nations Fish Stocks Agreement in Chapter 10). Third, the principle can also play a catalytic role in the customary international law-making process: it may act as a magnetic pole attracting and channelling state practice.

In the wake of the 1992 United Nations Declaration on Environment and Development, the precautionary principle has rapidly moved beyond the fields of marine and atmospheric pollution to encompass nearly all of the areas of international environmental law. Nordic countries have been ratifying most of the major agreements enshrining the principle, some of which are formulating precaution rather strictly – for example, the Convention for the Protection of the Marine Environment of the North-East Atlantic (OSPAR) and the Helsinki Commission (HELCOM).

One could be confused by the manner in which the principle has been formulated so far in these different international agreements. At a formal level, when a principle such as precaution is set out in a treaty or international agreement, it should have the normative value that attaches to that instrument. In national legal regimes where international treaties and conventions have a value superior to that of national law, recognition of the principle should then be imperative for the national law-maker. Nevertheless, one should be careful about the exact content of the agreement. In fact, the principle has been proclaimed in preambles (e.g. the Convention on Biological Diversity, or CBD) or in the operative provisions of conventions, either in the form of general obligations (e.g. OSPAR and HELCOM) or specific provisions (e.g. 1995 Fish Stocks Agreement). By way of illustration, precaution is encapsulated both as an objective and as an authorization to take a decision under the 2000 Cartagena Protocol on Biosafety.

Obviously, a distinction should be drawn between the principles found in the preambles of treaties and those elaborated upon in their operational parts. A principle can be normative provided that it is affirmed by an operative provision of an agreement. As discussed above, several international environment agreements in force in the Nordic region do contain provisions in which the precautionary principle is directly binding on state parties. For instance, the 1992 OSPAR Convention, as well as the 1995 Fish Stocks Agreement require that parties 'shall apply' the precautionary principle or the precautionary approach. In contrast, when the principle is merely mentioned in the preamble of the agreement, its role is simply to inform the more precise legal norms contained in the convention's operative provisions. In short, one must therefore consider, on a case-by-case basis, whether the terms used to describe the precautionary principle are sufficiently prescriptive in order to determine whether it could be considered to directly apply to states without, in turn, being laid down in implementing norms such as protocols.

Moreover, the diversity of formulations is disturbing. In the 1995 Fish Stocks Agreement, the principle is called an 'approach', whereas the 1992 OSPAR and HELCOM agreements refer to a 'principle'. Likewise, whereas HELCOM applies the principle when 'there is reason to assume' hazard, OSPAR states that it should be used when there are 'reasonable grounds for concern'. Nonetheless, it is fair to say that this diversity is testament to the contextual nature of the precautionary principle. Indeed, the way in which the principle applies in the field of biodiversity differs from the field of marine pollution.

In deciding to drastically reduce the discharge of pollutants into the Baltic Sea, HELCOM has implicitly embraced the precautionary principle. In so doing, HELCOM broke free from the sound science approach according to which a specific threshold must be set for each pollutant in relation to the impact of the ensuing damages (see Chapter 9). By the same token, North Sea conferences have served as a means for Northern European countries to advance a precautionary chemicals agenda.

While some environmental principles (for example, ensuring that activities within a state's jurisdiction or control do not cause damage to the environment of other states or of areas beyond national jurisdiction) have already obtained the status of a general principle of customary international law, the procedure appears to be a great deal more delicate in the case of the precautionary principle. Only the repeated use of state practice and consistent *opinio juris* are likely to transform precaution into a customary norm. Looking carefully at the state practice and the doctrinal debate in the Nordic countries, one is driven to the conclusion that the precautionary principle should be considered a principle of customary international law, at least from a regional perspective. Last, attention should be drawn to the fact that the various regional agreements analysed above are setting a lower threshold for the application of precaution, particularly with regard to the burden of proof (see Chapters 9 and 10).

EUROPEAN COMMUNITY LAW

Given that Nordic countries and the European Communities are parties to major international agreements providing propitious grounds for implementing a precautionary approach such as the 1995 United Nations Fish Stocks Agreement (see Chapter 10), it was salient in a book on Nordic countries to deal, by and large, with European Community (EC) legal issues. Moreover, most authors have been giving emphasis to the extent to which EC secondary law impinges upon various regulatory developments in the Nordic countries. To name just one example, Directive 2001/18 on genetically modified organisms has led the Finnish law-maker and the Swedish government to lay down the precautionary principle in their national regulations implementing that directive (see Chapter 14). Accordingly, in analysing the legal status of the precautionary principle in this part of Europe, one cannot avoid discussing the manner in which the principle has been dealt with in the EU legal order.

In much the same way than in international law, a large swath of EU policy programmes and political statements proclaim the precautionary principle. Given the non-binding nature of those instruments, the principle is deprived of any legal effect. In other words, whenever the principle is proclaimed in soft law, it does not constrain the EC institutions to act in a strictly determined manner.

So far, the precautionary principle has only been enshrined in the EC Treaty under Article 174(2) EC. No attempt has been made by the drafters of the European Constitution to broaden the scope of ambit of that provision. One further point may be worth making here. In sharp contrast to the various EU political statements, Article 174(2) EC is drafted in such a way that the EC institutions are called upon to apply precaution when carrying out action in the environmental field and, thanks to the integration clause of Article 6 EC, in areas such as consumer safety and public health. By the same token, national authorities are required to take the principle into account while applying the obligations stemming from EC secondary law (see, in particular, the use of precaution in the field of environmental impact assessment (EIA) regarding impacts on protected natural habitats, as discussed in Chapter 15).

That said, EC primary law, as well as secondary law do not provide a definition of the principle. The lack of definition could, perhaps, be justified on the grounds that the implementation of this principle across a wide range of EC policies is rather contextual. Nonetheless, given that the European courts have been asked to rule on the legality of a number of claims brought forward by claimants contending with an EC measure curtailing their economic rights (such as right to property, free movement of goods and right to operate an activity), or against member states enacting a measure hindering the free movement of goods, they have been eager to endorse a rather broad definition of the principle. That definition runs as follows:

> ... *where there is uncertainty as to the existence or extent of risks to human health, protective measures may be taken without having to wait until the reality and seriousness of those risks become fully apparent.*

Given its broad scope of application, the precautionary principle has been much at the forefront in the field of health protection, rather than in the field of environmental law (see Chapter 2). In addition, the EC law-maker has been placing more emphasis upon the principle in food safety statutes. For instance, the principle is enshrined in Regulation No 178/2002 laying down the general principles and requirements of food law, whereas few environmental directives and regulations specifically mention it in their operative provisions. For instance, neither the Integrated Pollution Prevention and Control (IPPC) Directive, the EIA Directive or the Habitats Directive refer to the principle as such.

Due to its highly abstract nature and particularly broad scope of application, the precautionary principle could then be defined as a general principle of Community law. So far, the Court of First Instance of the European Community (CFI) has been endorsing that interpretation. Whether the same interpretation will be endorsed by the European Court of Justice (ECJ) remains to be seen.

With respect to the case law of the EC jurisdictions, the use of the precautionary principle is likely to be subject to a number of criteria, among which is the need for authorities to carry out as complete a risk assessment as possible, although the impossibility of carrying out a full scientific risk assessment does not prevent them from taking preventative measures, where such measures appear necessary to avoid the occurrence of risks deemed to be unacceptable for society. In particular, it ought to be remembered that the precautionary principle should not be construed as an isolated legal requirement. On the contrary, it is merely a device among a broad package of regulatory requirements fostering good administration. Nonetheless, European courts have so far been deferential to the EC institutions' weighing of health interests and economic freedoms, provided that decision-makers abide by several procedural steps.

NORDIC COUNTRIES

Let us turn now to the approaches endorsed by the five Nordic countries. The above analyses provide useful reflections of the role of precaution in a part of the world known to pay heed to the quality of life of its citizens.

It is important from the outset to stress the difficulties of assessing the impact of the precautionary principle as interpreted by the European courts on the manner in which Nordic countries are contemplating the correct strategy with respect to intractable risks. One reason could be that only three of the five Nordic countries are EU member states. Furthermore, one has to bear in mind that two of these member states have joined the EU recently, in 1995. In addition, it is to be noted that there is truly no one Nordic environmental policy, but rather a series of different policies.

Several national authorities – for example, in Norway – have limited themselves to proclaiming the precautionary principle in policy documents. From a legal point of view, such a principle is, in that case, devoid of legal effect (see Chapter 6). In contrast to Norway and Denmark, the Swedish and the Finnish law-makers have been setting forth the precautionary principle in their environmental framework laws (see Chapters 4 and 7). In addition, both Finnish and Swedish definitions espouse a rather strong version of precaution that dictates what should be done by the operators, as well as by the authorities. For instance, in order to trigger the principle, the threat should not be severe or irreversible, a requirement which is often laid down in other legal instruments.

Nevertheless, the principle can also be enshrined in more specific statutes, as in the case of regulating GMOs (see Chapters 13 and 14) or the Environmental Act for Svalbard (see Chapter 6). Furthermore, it is fair to say that the express recognition of the precautionary principle has been ushering in new comprehensive regulatory regimes that deal with uncertainty, particularly in the field of chemicals (see Chapter 16).

Whenever the precautionary principle is encapsulated in a regulatory setting, its formulation differs from case to case. By way of illustration, although GMO regulations are laying down similar obligations on operators, precaution is set out as general policy objective under Finnish law, whereas it is defined as an operational provision under Swedish law (see Chapter 14). Such heterogeneity in formulating the principle is the result of the willingness to encompass a wide range of different decision-making frameworks, ranging from listed installations to nature protection. In addition, the manner in which the principle is implemented depends upon the contextual features of the decision-making setting.

However, the picture is not as idyllic as one might think. In contrast to chemicals and GMOs, the principle is proclaimed neither in binding provisions nor in soft law instruments in relation to forestry, although forests are still deemed to be a significant natural resource in Sweden, Finland and Norway. Although the recent Norwegian Forestry Act places biodiversity on an equal footing with production, it does not make reference to precaution. By the same token, although a precautionary approach has been introduced to the management of fisheries in the North-East Atlantic by the International Council for the Exploration of the Sea (ICES), Norway, Iceland and the Faroe Islands have yet to incorporate a precautionary approach within their fisheries management legislation (Chapter 10).

As a result, when considering the five national legal orders, a distinction must been drawn between principles embodied in soft law and hard law instruments. While the former are not binding, the latter could, in the future, play an important role in litigation.

This is not to say, of course, that precaution exerts no legal effects when it is not set out explicitly in binding statutory provisions. While Nordic environmental policies are not necessarily called 'precautionary' policies, they are certainly underscored by a strong and long-lasting anticipatory philosophy with regard to environmental risks. By according increasing importance to uncertainty, several regulatory settings have, indeed, brought the principle into play without expressly referring to it. In addition, attention should be drawn to the fact that the precautionary principle is closely linked to the substitution principle, according to which the mere existence of an alterative substance that appears to be less dangerous than the substance in question is sufficient basis for a restriction or a prohibition (see Chapters 16 and 17). Likewise, the shift of the burden of proof as to the safety of the technology enhances an implicit recourse to the precautionary principle (see Chapters 3, 4, 6, 7, 9 and 13 to 16).

Given that national administrations are endowed with a broad margin of appreciation, they do not have to overcome major hurdles in applying the precautionary principle (see Chapter 13). The principle could, indeed, be construed from provisions laying down general obligations. Various chapters clearly reflect the variety of ways in which the principle has been implemented in spite of a proper legal basis. For instance, although the principle may be difficult to retrieve in Danish written rules on nature protection, it can be deduced from an array of regulatory instruments (see Chapter 15). Likewise, although the principle is not directly applicable under the Finnish act on listed installations, authorities enforce it by requiring additional information on the risks (see Chapter 4). Last, decisions on licensing GMO products have been delayed until information about the potential threat could be forwarded to the authorities (see the Norwegian policy regarding GMOs in Chapter 13).

Moreover, in areas such as fisheries, GMOs and chemicals management, decision-makers in Nordic countries tend to take into account the lingering uncertainties in their decisions. The trend is, obviously, to rely upon other sources of information than genuine scientific expertise. In particular, the decisions on placing GMOs on the market tend to blend scientific issues and societal values (see Chapters 13 and 14). However, the extent to which the consideration given to uncertainty exerts an influence on the outcome of the decision is difficult to assess. Perhaps the success or failure to implement the principle depends upon the extent to which uncertainty is being taken into account by experts and decision-makers, rather than the outcome of the decisions.

In any case, the express or implicit recognition of the principle poses a number of challenges both to the experts and the decision-makers charged with implementing it. These challenges stem from, among other things, the variety of thresholds to which the principle is likely to be subject, the type of uncertainties that fall within the ambit of the principle, and the difficulty of weighing the conflicting environmental and socio-economic interests.

The distinction between risk assessment and risk management is not always clear cut. At a certain stage, the recourse to precaution entails a balance between scientific knowledge and societal values. Given that communities in Nordic countries are concerned with the protection of their natural resources, one could expect that the balance should tilt towards greater environmental protection. However, this is not always the case. As in EC law, the implementation of the principle faces hurdles, among which is the logic of most legal systems in striving to protect legal certainty (see, in particular, Chapters 3 and 4). The conclusion follows that there is a fundamental conflict between the precautionary principle and the principle of legal certainty (see Chapters 3, 4, 6 and 7). Furthermore, the principle of proportionality may impinge upon and even belittle the level of protection sought by national authorities (Chapter 2). Finally, the extensive use of cost-benefit analysis could hinder precaution (see, in particular, Chapters 2, 7, 16 and 19). Setting aside economic efficiency, the precautionary principle runs counter to the trend of exclusively adopting cost-effective measures (se Chapter 6). However, under Swedish environmental law, the 'stop rule' prevails over economic considerations in specific circumstances (see Chapters 7 and 14). In addition, nothing precludes the principle from being applied within the framework of economic efficiency by putting a higher cost estimate on the potential environmental harm (see Chapter 6).

Several authors have emphasized the importance of defining the acceptable level of protection (see, among others, Chapters 2 and 12 to 15), although few statutes precisely define that level. Some exceptions should, however, be mentioned. Several GMO statutes provide that a GMO may only be approved when its use entails no risk of detrimental effect to health and the environment (see Chapters 12 to 14). The public authorities can even apply a zero-risk policy, such as the Norwegian approach in relation to antibiotics resistance from GMOs and the discharge from offshore oil industry (see Chapters 6 and 13). By the same token, Norwegian and Swedish authorities are aiming at a zero emission target regarding the discharge of hazardous chemicals (see Chapters 6 and 16).

As an autonomous norm, the precautionary principle, as laid down in national legislation, may, indeed, yield concrete results mostly at the level of administrative jurisprudence. Indeed, the application of precaution in hard cases could be testament to the legitimacy of a new legal principle. However, in sharp contrast with case law in countries such as France, Belgium and The Netherlands, or the case law of the European courts (see Chapter 2), the courts in Nordic countries have not played a key role in developing the principle. However, the picture is perhaps more complex. For instance, the Swedish Board of Agriculture has constantly referred to the precautionary principle in adjudicating on the validity of GMO field trials (see Chapter 14), whereas the Danish Nature Protection Appeal Board has been paying scant heed to it (see Chapter 15).

It is worth making one final point. There has been an ongoing discussion in other EC member states on whether the Nordic economic and social model could be applied elsewhere. From a sustainable development perspective, one should also beg the question of whether the environmental anticipatory approach contemplated in these countries could also be exported. With respect to the restriction of hazardous substances and the discharge of pollutants, several Nordic countries are forging bold new paths in requiring higher safety thresholds. Therefore, the studies reviewed in this book show that there is much than can be learned from Nordic environmental policies.

Index